NEW
Historical & Genealogical Register

AND

ANTIQUARIAN JOURNAL,

PUBLISHED QUARTERLY, UNDER THE DIRECTION OF THE

New-England Historic, Genealogical Society.

FOR THE YEAR 1872.

VOLUME XXVI.

BOSTON:
PUBLISHED AT THE SOCIETY'S HOUSE, 18 SOMERSET STREET.
PRINTED BY DAVID CLAPP & SON.
1872.

Committee on Publication for 1872.

ALBERT HARRISON HOYT,
JOHN WARD DEAN,
WILLIAM HENRY WHITMORE,
WILLIAM SUMNER APPLETON,
WILLIAM BLANCHARD TOWNE.

Editor.

ALBERT HARRISON HOYT.

Facsimile Reprint

Published 1994 By

HERITAGE BOOKS, INC.
1540E Pointer Ridge Place, Bowie, Maryland 20716
(301) 390-7709

ISBN 0-7884-0126-2

GENERAL INDEX.

[Index of Names of Persons at the end of the Volume.]

- Notice -

The foxing, or discoloration with age, characteristic of old books, sometimes shows through to some extent in reprints such as this, especially when the foxing is very severe in the original book. We feel that the contents of this book warrant its reissue despite these blemishes, and hope you will agree and read it with pleasure.

Benj P. Richardson

NEW-ENGLAND
HISTORICAL AND GENEALOGICAL REGISTER
AND
ANTIQUARIAN JOURNAL.

VOL. XXVI. JANUARY, 1872. No. 1.

BENJAMIN PARKER RICHARDSON.

[Communicated by Rev. DORUS CLARKE, D.D.]

BENJAMIN PARKER RICHARDSON was born in Boston, at the corner of Pearl and High streets, April 23, 1802, and died in Boston, at 37 Boylston street, Nov. 17, 1870, aged sixty-eight years. On the paternal side he descended from Jeffrey Richardson, who was born in Yorkshire, Eng., in 1693, and emigrated to this country and died on Winter street, Boston, Sept. 29, 1775. On the maternal side he descended from Capt. Richard Brackett, who was born in Scotland, in 1610, and removed to America, and died in Braintry (Braintree), Mass., March 5, 1690–1. For the details of his descent from those venerable and venerated ancestors, the reader is referred to a volume entitled *Genealogical and Biographical Sketches of the Name and Family of Brackett and Richardson, by Jeffrey Richardson, Jr.*

His father, Jeffrey Richardson, was a witness of the Boston massacre, March 5, 1770. He possessed a large real estate in Boston, and owned the rope-walks, which extended from High street to Milk street, and which were destroyed by the Great Fire in 1794. In 1796, the town deeded to him "a tract of marsh land and flats at the bottom of the Common."

No incidents of a very remarkable character appear to have occurred in the early life of Mr. Benjamin P. Richardson. He was bred to business, and in 1826 he became a partner in the firm of J. Richardson & Brothers, iron merchants, who occupied the same store, No. 2 Central wharf, for the long period of 53 years. That firm conducted their business through that protracted term, and amid all the remarkable vicissitudes in commercial affairs which distinguished it, with the utmost harmony and with continued success.[1]

[1] It is worthy of note that the surviving partners, Messrs. Jeffrey and James B. Richardson, continue under the same firm at the same place. ED.

Mr. Richardson was remarkable for method and accuracy, and his private ledgers and letter books are models of beauty and correctness.[1] In the years 1822 and 1824, he made tours of observation through the Northern, Middle and Southern States, and scanned, with careful eyes, the state of the country and the condition of society in the regions through which he passed, and with ready pen entered his "random sketches" in a volume, filling 547 pages. He had letters of introduction to Thomas Jefferson and James Madison, who kindly received him and presented him to other distinguished gentlemen of that day.

Mr. Richardson collected a library, which was remarkably rich in works upon the early history of this country, in manuscripts, pamphlets, ballads and newspapers. Genealogy was with him a favorite study, or rather a recuperating pastime. Searching records, conversing with the aged, copying epitaphs, collecting antique relics, and pursuing, with indefatigable diligence, some clue which he had discovered, to find some connecting link in family records, which others had long sought for in vain, were his great delight.

In politics, Mr. Richardson was an ardent whig. He was a member of the house of representatives from Boston for five successive years; a member of the common council for six successive years; and a member of the school committee for seventeen successive years. He was also a member of the Water Board, and of various benevolent institutions.

In religion, he was an Episcopalian. He was a vestryman of Trinity Church, clerk of the Greene Foundation, and member for many years of the Massachusetts Board of Missions, besides sustaining many other important trusts in that denomination. A distinguishing feature of his life was inflexible honesty. His understanding was strong and accurate, and he had little tendency towards vacillation when his judgment was convinced that any given course was right. His bodily sufferings during his latter years consigned him to a long and weary seclusion from general society, but they sat, in stronger relief, the gentleness, the patience, and the submission which only the grace of God can administer in seasons of calamity. In health and prosperity a man may be resolute before the world, but in protracted suffering and in the chamber of death, nothing, as in the case of Mr. Richardson, but the supporting presence of the Angel of the Covenant can inspire true composure and peace into the soul.

Upon his demise, appropriate resolutions, offered by the Hon. Robert C. Winthrop, were adopted by the vestrymen and wardens of Trinity Church, expressive of the great loss they had sustained by the departure of their associate in office, and of their sympathetic condolence with the family in their bereavement.

[1] We are informed by his son that he commenced at the age of ten to keep an account of his expenses and to preserve his letters, which practice he continued during his life; and that his family have now his account books and letters from that age. Ed.

Nov. 27, 1828, Mr. Richardson was married to Rebecca, dau. of John Bridge, of Littleton, Mass., and they had four children:—

Rebecca Bridge, b. Oct. 28, 1829.

Sarah Cordelia, b. Jan. 30, 1832.

Benjamin Heber, b. Aug. 17, 1835, and

Edward Cyrenius, b. Feb. 29, 1840.

Mr. Richardson was admitted a resident member of the New-England Historic, Genealogical Society, Nov. 27, 1847.

[NOTE BY THE EDITOR.—We are permitted to add the following extract from a letter by the Rt. Rev. Manton Eastburn, D.D., Bishop of Massachusetts, who was an intimate friend of Mr. Richardson. It confirms the estimate of his character given in the preceding memoir.]

"I consider Mr. Richardson's example as having been most beneficial to others; and the remembrance of his uprightness makes me always think of him, now that he is gone, with the most unalloyed satisfaction. And this firmness of purpose, combined with a solid and vigorous understanding, is brought into strong relief by the gentleness, patience and submission with which he resigned himself to the will of God during the sufferings of his latter years. The strong man, consigned to a long and weary seclusion attended by constant bodily anguish, then became the little child. So that alike in his resolute life before the world, and in his quietness of spirit in the chamber of death, his character is one of great force."

EDWARD OXNARD.

[At our request, Edward S. Moseley, Esq., of Newburyport, has kindly prepared for the REGISTER the following brief sketch of his maternal ancestry, the Oxnards, and has appended interesting extracts from the extended diary kept by Edward Oxnard while in England.—ED. of *N. E. His. & Gen. Register.*]

THOMAS OXNARD, the progenitor, so far as is known, of the comparatively few families who bear that surname, at the present time, in the United States, came from the bishopric of Durham in England, and settled in Boston.

The precise date of his immigration has not been ascertained. The connection, however, which he formed with the family of Mr. Osborne on the 10th March, 1737, by his marriage at that time with his daughter Sarah, would seem to indicate either that he had been here sufficiently long, previous to his marriage, to have enabled him to establish his own reputation, or that he had left England with the prestige of a respectable position at home.

John Osborne, his father-in-law, was a native of Bristol, R. I., born in 1688, whose first wife was Sarah Woodbury of the same place. They subsequently removed to Boston, where she died in 1734. After her decease, Mr. Osborne was married three times: in 1745 to his third wife, Mrs. Hutchinson, the mother of Gov. Hutchinson. Two of his sons graduated at Harvard College:—John, in 1735; and Woodbury, whose name heads the list in the catalogue of that year, in 1739, both of whom, as well as Mrs. Oxnard, were children by his first wife. Mr. Osborne died in Boston in 1768.

Mr. Oxnard engaged successfully in commerce and the importation of merchandise. In 1740, he was one of the directors of what was known as The Silver Scheme, an association of merchants and others, composed of such men as Samuel Sewall, Edmund Quincy, Edward Hutchinson and James Bowdoin, who issued their notes in opposition to The Land Bank, or Manufactory Scheme, for the purpose of furnishing a circulating medium of which the merchants and traders were greatly in need. In 1746 his name appears, in company with those of other "prominent citizens," as a proprietor of real estate in Boston, attached to a memorial addressed to the freeholders and others assembled in town meeting.

To him belongs, what is now considered the honorable distinction of having been a subscriber to Prince's Chronology.

He was interested in the subject of free-masonry, and finally attained, in that fraternity, the high position of grand-master, which office he held at the time of his decease. The following notice of his appointment is copied from a Boston newspaper of that period:

"The Right Worshipful Thomas Oxnard having received a deputation, dated London, Sept. 23d, 1743, from the Rt. Hon. and most worshipful John, Lord Ward, Baron of Birmingham, in the county of Warwick, grand-master of Masons in England, appointing him provincial grand-master of Masons in the room of the right worshipful Grand-master Tomlinson, deceased: which being communicated, March 6, 1744, he was properly acknowledged, invested, installed and congratulated."

Mr. Oxnard's residence was on Tremont street, at some distance back from the road, the lot on which it stood extending from Winter to the next street running parallel with it on the north.

It is described in the inventory of his property on file in the probate office in Boston, the record of which has been recently examined, as "house and land fronting the common," and is appraised at what was then deemed the large amount of £1200.

At his decease, which took place June 26, 1754, he was buried under the old Trinity church. The following notice of his death and of the public services attending upon his funeral is extracted from the account published in one of the Boston newspapers of that time.

"A Grand Lodge was held in due form at Graten's in Roxbury, on June 26, 1754, but by reason of the death of the Right-worshipful Grand-Master Thomas Oxnard, this morning at 11 o'clock, the celebration was rather sorrowful than joyous. In honor of their right worshipful Grand Master, whose loss was sincerely lamented by all who had the pleasure and honor of his acquaintance, and more especially by the society over which he had for eleven years presided with dignity, they voted to attend his funeral in mourning with the honors of masonry and to invite the several lodges to assist on this mournful occasion."

"His corpse was attended to the grave by a numerous train of relatives, friends and acquaintances, and by the society of Free and Accepted Masons, dressed in black, clothed with white aprons and gloves, who walked before the procession, two and two.

"The grand-master's Jewel was carried on a tasseled black velvet cushion before the coffin. The deputy grand-master and other officers wore their Jewels pendant upon black ribbon.

"After the interment, the fraternity walked before the relations and returned with them to the mansion house of the deceased, where they took their leave. The whole attendance was conducted through a vast number of spectators, with great order and decency."

His widow, Mrs. Oxnard, in May, 1756, married Judge Samuel Watts of the Court of Common Pleas, and died in 1773. Her will was presented for probate before the Hon. Foster Hutchinson, Sept. 3d of that year; Sampson S. Blowers, H. C. 1763, afterwards the chief-justice of New Brunswick, to whom her son Edward in his diary makes frequent allusions, and with whom and whose family, while in England, he was on the most friendly relations, being one of the subscribing witnesses. The last item in it is as follows:

"I give to my servant Prince his freedom from the state of slavery and four pounds lawful money."

The children of Thomas and Sarah (Osborne) Oxnard were:

THOMAS, born in Boston in the year 1740. He removed to Falmouth after his father's decease, and in 1770 was appointed deputy-collector of that port, the only place in Maine for the collection of customs until the revolution. June 17, 1772, he married Martha Preble, the daughter of Brigadier Preble, of illustrious memory, and sister of the commodore. In 1774 there were but eight persons on the Neck in Falmouth who owned more shipping than he. After the burning of Falmouth by Mowatt, he left the country and was at length proscribed by the act of Massachusetts passed in 1778. Under the provisions of the absentee act of 1782, all his property was confiscated; previous to which, the same year, Martha Oxnard his wife was permitted, by a resolve of the general court, "to go to her husband at Penobscot with her two servant maids, and such part of her household goods as the selectmen of Falmouth should admit." In 1784 he was complained of for violating the law in returning from banishment, and on trial and conviction was committed to jail. The late Chief-Justice Parsons, then a practising lawyer in Newburyport, prepared a writ of *habeas corpus*, on the ground that the provisions of the treaty of peace were superior to and annulled all contradictory state laws.

On being relieved from molestation, he commenced business in Portland with his brother Edward. Although so warm an Episcopalian that he contemplated taking orders at this time, ultimately his religious views underwent so much change that he became a Unitarian. He died May 20, 1799. Capt. Preble, the historian of the Preble family, characterizes him as "a man of general intelligence, a constant reader, and of unimpeachable honor and virtue." His wife, who survived him twenty-five years, died Oct. 16, 1824. They had in all ten children, some of whom seem to have inherited the same traits of character exhibited by their renowned uncle, Commodore Preble—viz.:

Thomas, the eldest, during the war of 1812–15, commanded the True Blooded Yankee of 18 guns and 200 men, which, under his charge, became so destructive to British commerce, that a reward was offered by that government for her capture. He was endowed with undaunted courage, and neither the dangers of the seas, the menaces of a turbulent crew, nor the conflict with an enemy vastly his superior in force, could cause him for a moment to quail. He married Clarice (the sister of the late P. P. F. De Grand) of Marseilles, and was for many years the U. S. consul at that port, where he died June 16, 1840, interred at his especial desire with the American flag wrapped round him for a shroud. He left children, who survive, all born in France.

Edward, was lost in the privateer Dash, which foundered at sea in the war of 1812–15, leaving no descendants.

Ebenezer, died unmarried at Demerara, Oct. 22, 1800.

John, died at sea, unmarried, Dec. 20, 1802.

Martha, married her cousin Edward Oxnard. She died Jan. 30, 1860, leaving three sons and two daughters.

Mary, died unmarried, Jan. 7, 1796.

Henry, born Jan. 6, 1789; died Dec. 15, 1843, at his residence on Mt. Vernon street, Boston, leaving two sons and one daughter. An obituary notice of him in the *Boston Daily Advertiser* speaks of him "as combining with a vigorous constitution, daring enterprise, intelligence and rectitude of conduct. In all his vast and complicated mercantile transactions he had acquired such an exalted reputation for integrity, such a faithful adherence to all those high principles on which the institutions of society are founded and depend for their stability, as to have secured that public confidence and respect which are the most precious rewards, that man can hope to receive." For many years, he was the purchasing agent, in New Orleans, of the manufacturing corporations of Lowell.

Mehitable, married her cousin William Oxnard, and still survives. She has four sons and two daughters.

Enoch, was lost in the Dash in the war of 1812–15.

Stephen, was for many years the master of a merchant ship, and died in Portland, leaving one son and five daughters.

2. MARY, the second child of Thomas and Sarah (Osborne) Oxnard, was born in 1742. She married, May 22, 1765, Edward Watts, M.D., the son of Judge Watts, who had previously married her mother for his second wife, and being her mother's second husband. He died Jan. 9, 1799. She died, Jan. 19, 1812, and left descendants, one of whom, the Hon. Francis O. Watts, a grandson, died within a few years in Boston, universally lamented.

3. EDWARD OXNARD, the second son and third child of Thomas and Sarah (Osborne) Oxnard, was born in Boston on the 30th July, 1747. He entered Harvard College, and graduated there in 1767, his name standing the third in the list of graduates of that year, preceded only by those of Thomas Bernard, the son of Sir Francis and afterward himself a baronet, and Adam Winthrop. Since 1773 the names have been arranged alphabetically. As indicating the paucity of the family name on this side of the water, it may be stated, that it stands solitary and alone in the index of the Harvard graduates, and is not to be found therein, except as a middle name by his grandson, the Rev. William Oxnard Moseley, H. C. 1836, and his great grandson, W. O., Jr., 1869.

A cursory examination of the triennials of other colleges in New-England does not show a single graduate of that family name. At the time of his graduation, he united with his classmate Bernard in giving a ball to their mutual friends, the invitation to which, struck off from the copper plate used on that occasion, is here given,[1] showing that the "spreads" of the present day, as they are now termed, had their counter-part more than a hundred years ago.

[1] See the printed plate hereto annexed, for which we are indebted to the liberality of Mr. Moseley.—ED.

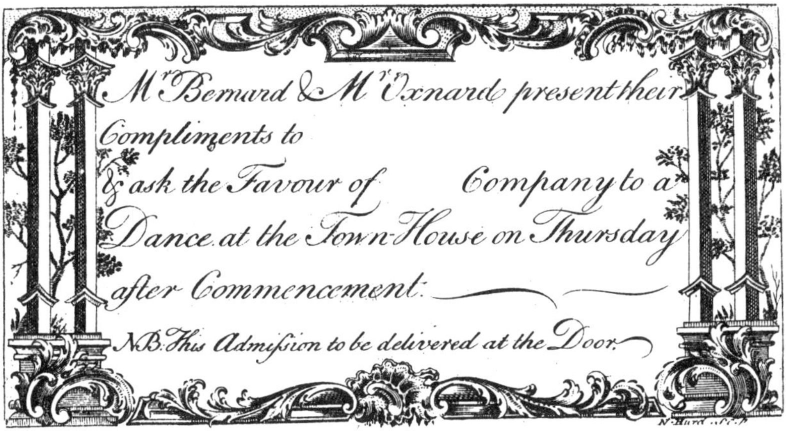
Mr Bernard & Mr Oxnard present their Compliments to

& ask the Favour of Company to a Dance at the Town-House on Thursday after Commencement.

N.B. This Admission to be delivered at the Door.

N. Hurd Scp

After leaving college, his elder brother having moved to Falmouth, Mr. Oxnard also engaged there in business with him. On the 11th Oct., 1774, he was married by the Rev. Dr. Haven, of Portsmouth, N. H., to Mary Fox, born Nov. 9, 1754, the daughter of Jabez Fox, H. C. 1727, who studied divinity, but whose health did not allow him to preach—who for the three years preceding his death in April, 1755, held the position of a member of the governor's council. He was the second son of John Fox, H. C. 1698, the minister of Woburn, who was the son of Jabez, H. C. 1665. At the time of the revolution, the Fox family were all whigs, and their sympathies and personal efforts given decidedly to its support. The ship "Fox," armed and fitted out principally by John Fox, the brother of Mrs. Oxnard, with 4 iron guns and no swords, but with scythes fitted into handles for boarding pikes, succeeded in capturing a letter-of-marque of 18 guns, with a very valuable cargo, which she took safely into Boston.

Notwithstanding the strong opposing feeling of the family into which he had married, it is not strange that Mr. Oxnard should have been influenced by considerations arising from his descent, political faith and religious belief, as a member at that time of the church of England, to remain loyal to the king and crown.

When therefore it became apparent that the sword was to be drawn, and the issue depended upon the success of either party in arms, he believed that his allegiance was due the mother country to which he was closely allied by hereditary ties; and under the impression that the rebellion, as he deemed it, ought and speedily would be crushed out by its overwhelming supremacy, he left America, arriving in England on the 17th August, 1775. Here his stay was unwillingly protracted until the 30th April, 1785, when he embarked for the U. S., by the way of Halifax.

The journal which he kept while in England, extracts from which are hereto appended, and to which this account of the family is but an introduction, shows, for the most part, the routine of his daily life, accounting for his employment almost every hour, and was evidently penned, either to remind him in after years of the little occurrences of the moment, or with the view of giving his friends a transcript of the events which befel him while an exile from his native land. Their publication in the REGISTER has been doubtless suggested, not from the literary talent they exhibit, or from any profound disquisition they contain, but because anything bearing on those times, whether socially or politically, has, at this day, an interest.

Mr. Oxnard was a member of the Adelphi Club in London, composed of about twenty-five loyalists, of which Gov. Hutchinson was one; and also of another society of a literary character. During his long absence, his time was principally spent in company with some of his fellow refugees, with whom he could mourn in sympathy over the cause of their exile. With Judge Sewall and his family, and Mr. Blowers, both in London and after his return to Halifax, where he became chief-justice, Mr. Oxnard was on intimate terms.

As with his brother Thomas, he was proscribed by name in the act passed by Massachusetts, in Sept., 1778. Unlike in character and in appearance to his brother, there was yet a remarkable uniformity in their action, and harmony in their respective opinions. Previous to the revolution they had been connected in business, and after Edward's return to the U. S. in 1786, they again united in it. At different times, they were both lay-readers in the episcopal church in Falmouth, and were doubtless influenced in their political action by their warm attachment to the church of England, leading to the sacrifice of property, country and kindred, yet ultimately both abandoned their previous opinions, owing in a great degree to the influence of the Rev. Dr. Freeman, of the King's Chapel in Boston, and became Unitarians. Edward died in Portland, July 2, 1803, as he was on the eve of moving into a large three-story house which he had built. His wife, Mary Fox, survived him in widowhood more than thirty years, dying in Portland, Aug. 22, 1835.

The children of Edward and Mary (Fox) Oxnard were:

1. Mary Ann, born Jan. 31, 1787; married June 17, 1810, the Hon. Ebenezer Moseley, of Newburyport. She died March 9, 1840, leaving issue, of whom two sons and two daughters are now living.

2. William, born Feb. 11, 1789; married his cousin Mehitable, and has children; died October, 1871, aged 82.

3. Edward, born July 13, 1791; married his cousin Martha, and has issue. The two brothers have always been interested together in commercial pursuits.

4. Lucy Jones, born June 9, 1793; married her cousin John Fox, Esq., of Portland, where he died within a few years, leaving three sons and one daughter who survive. One of the sons is the Hon. Edward Fox, who has held the position of judge of the supreme court in Maine, and now that of judge of the U. S. district court.

5. John, born March 26, 1795; married Catherine Stewart, and has children.

Newburyport, *Oct.* 26, 1871. M.

Extracts from the Journal of Edward Oxnard.

Aug 16—
1775. Made the English Coast called Plymouth.
Sept. 1st. This day took lodgings in Newgate Street, No 51, at 10–6 a week—for two rooms.
4— Engaged to dine with Alderman Brigham in company with Sir Thomas Trickling & Capt. Scott. By no means liked my company, as we differed in political sentiments. My cousin Gyfford called on me, and appeared to be very fond of seeing me.—A high Wilkite, I soon observed.
7— Received a card from Gov. Hutchinson to dine, could not, so waited on him in person to make my compliments. He appears low spirited; desired me to call again. Went with Mr. F. Green, Mr. Balch, Mr. Silsby, & Mr. Berry to see Sir Watkin William Wynns House in St. James Square. I think it extremely elegant.
10— This morning went to Mr. W * * s conventicle, stayed about two hours, came out by no means improved. the preacher was a mere boy, who made up his want of knowledge, by noise. from thence went to Newington Green to Mr Coxs to dinner. heard the great Dr. Price preach a funeral sermon, the text the last enemy, Death. The Dr. proved himself to be an ingenious and sensible divine.
12— This morning went with Mr. Curwen, Capt. Martin & Mr. Silsby to Chelsea; examined Battersea Bridge built wholly of wood—it looks very airy.
15— This morning at home, writing to America. dined with Mr. Newbrey—single dish. In the afternoon went with Mr. Watson to the Queens Arms to hear a disputation on predestination & election, which was poorly supported on either side—mere mechanicks, who thought themselves suffi-

ciently able to dispute on the most abstruse & intricate subjects. Mr. Berry spent the evening with me. had a good pot of porter together.

18th This morning went to the N. E. Coffee house.

Heard of two arrivals from America, but the letters have not come to hand. Dined at the Queen's Arms: then to the Carolina Coffee house to see Mr. Osgood from thence to Mr. Berry's, who carried me to the Robin Hood Society, which I find is visited by persons of better understanding, and situation in life than the Queen's Arms. The questions under discussion were whether Taxation promotes Industry, and whether it is equitable & right that Congress should confiscate the Estates of the Refugees in England: this last was determined to be unjust by a great majority.

The method of the Society is this: a president is appointed for a length of time, and he determines all disputes that arise. Every person, who is disposed has a right to dispute on the question, which is proposed the night before. The President begins asking the one at his left hand, and so goes on to his right. All are allowed to speak once to the question & then no longer than fifteen minutes. After every one has spoken that is inclined, the President sums up the arguments & delivers his opinion. After which, it is determined by a major vote of the Society.

20th This morning Mr. Head & Mr. Berry did me the honor of breakfasting with me, after which walked with Mr. Silsby towards the extreme south of the city. dined with Mr. Johnson, who is a counsellor at law, and is the Author of Chrysal or the adventures of a Guinea. As far as I am capable of judging, he is a sensible & agreeable man, well acquainted with the places to which he has travelled. In the evening went to the Haymarket to see Foote. The play was called the Commissary; the entertainment, cross questions. Their majesties were there. The King entered first, and the plaudit was universal: the Queen entered some time after. His majesty is a very good figure of a man. He seemed to be much dejected. Her majesty appears to be a small woman; her countenance carries such a sweetness, as attracts the esteem of all. She was dressed in white, with a diamond stomacher; a black cap with lustres of diamonds. A maid of honor stood behind her chair the whole time, as well as a Lord behind his majesty's. I observed the King & Queen conversed as familiarly together, as we in general do in public company. Two beefeaters stood on each side of their majesties the whole of the play. I take Foote to have been a good actor, but to have lost much of his humor and drollery by age.

I dislike much his entertainments, as they are pointed at particular persons, remarkable for some peculiarity.

9th Oct. Called this morning on Mr. Gray & Mr. Waldo. dined at Sheriff Hayley's in company with Mr. & Mrs. Amory, Mr. Harrison, Mr. Greene, Capt. Scott & Mr. Quincey. The dinner was the most elegant of any I have seen in England. Bacon & fowls, boiled & roast, roast hare, battered oysters &c; custards & cheese cakes, damson & gooseberry tarts—a fine pyramid of sweetmeats—wines of different kinds.

11th In the evening Mr. Quincey, Col. Pickman, Mr. Cabut & myself went to Covent Garden, but could not get in, the house being so exceedingly full, owing to their majesties being there. From thence went to Drury Lane, the play, "Win a wife & rule her." The pantomine, "Harlequin's Jacket," the scenery was beyond anything I have ever imagined & was shifted with the greatest dexterity. The house has been lately fitted up in a most elegant manner.

15th This morning went with Mr Cox to Islington to church. We gave some offence by taking possession of a pew. returned to Mr Cox' to dinner with Mr. Storey & family. In the afternoon we took a walk, as is too much the custom in this country on Sundays. See where the New River is carried over a field, so that one may walk underneath. I look upon this as great an undertaking as was ever performed.

From the source of this river to London, the distance is 44 miles. The projector ruined himself, but the present proprietors have made fortunes. a share that was bought for £100 when the owner died, which was about ten years ago, is now worth £3500. This River supplies a great part of London with the water to drink.

20.—. This morning Mr Silsby Berry & self rambled into the country, as far as Kensington Gravel pits.

In company with Mr. Berry went to Covent Garden Theatre to see the Tragedy of Cato played. The celebrated Mr. Sheridan performed the part of Cato to admiration. He justly merits the applause which his treatise on Elocution gives him, as an author. The Commonality take on themselves to determine the merits of a performance, and if it does not suit their taste, they express it by hissing; should that prove ineffectual, they pelt the actors with apples till they drive them from the stage or make some apology.

25.—. This morning was ushered in with the ringing of bells, it being the anniversary of the king's accession to the throne. Mr Sayer was sent to the Tower for attempting to seize the king's person. Five malefactors were executed at Tyburn, at which I attended & lost a good silk handkerchief by the pickpockets. The frequency of these executions appear to have no effect on the populace, for the number of criminals is by no means lessened by this mode of punishment. Drank tea & supped at Mr Lawrence'.

26.—. This morning went to St. James Park to see the king go in state to the parliament House. He rode in the State Coach, the elegance of which, it is beyond my power to describe—drawn by eight cream colored Horses, elegantly dressed with Blue ribbons. The number of people was fifty, if not sixty thousand, through whom the king passed with joyful acclamations. Spent the evening at the club.

Nov. 1st. This morning at home. Spent the evening with Mr. & Mrs. Geyer. Lost 7*s* at cards.

15.—. This morning very pleasant. visited Guildhall to see the tickets drawn in the Lottery, which is done much the same way as with us. There are two large wheels, and a blue coated boy stands at each, draws out a ticket, lifts his hand over his head & delivers it to another, who cuts it, and delivers it to one of the Commissioners, who declares the number. the process on the other side being the same, a commissioner declares it, blank or prize. Vast numbers daily attend in hopes of being the fortunate possessor of the £20,000 prize. Anxiety is strongly expressed on their countenances whenever the word "prize" is announced.

It is a great shame that so many lottery offices are permitted to be opened, being the means of injuring many, who gamble to a considerable amount to the great prejudice of their families. dined at the Queen' Arms by candle light, tho' but 3 o'clk. At this season of the year daylight in the city is very short, rendered so considerably by the narrowness of the streets, and the height of the houses. Drank tea at Mr Green' and treated very genteely. Mrs Green is a most amiable & humane woman. Meet here Mr Boylston, lately returned from his travels. He deals much in the marvellous.

[To be continued.]

WIGGLESWORTH'S ELEGY ON THE REV. BENJAMIN BUNKER, OF MALDEN.

[Communicated by JOHN WARD DEAN, A.M.]

THE following elegy, on the death of the Rev. Benjamin Bunker, written by the Rev. Michael Wigglesworth, is printed from the author's autograph copy, preserved among the EWER MANUSCRIPTS, vol. i. folio 8, in the library of the New-England Historic, Genealogical Society. It has twice been printed in newspapers. The first time, it was printed in the *Puritan Recorder*, Oct. 11, 1855, a religious paper of the Orthodox Congregationalist denomination, published in Boston. The copy was made by Dean Dudley, Esq., of Boston. A few years after, it was copied by Aaron Sargent, Esq., of Somerville, and printed in a Malden newspaper.

Upon the much lamented Death of that Precious
servant of Christ, M^{r}. Benjamin Buncker, pasto^{r}
of the Church at Maldon, who deceased
on the 3^{d} of ye 12th moneth 1669.

Mr Buncker's Character.

He was another Timothie
That from his very youth
With holy writt, acquainted was
And vers't ith' word of truth.
Who as he grew to riper yeers
He also grew in Grace;
And as he drew more neer his End,
He mended still his Pace.

He was a true Nathaniel,
Plain-hearted Israelite,
In whom appear'd sincerity
And not a guilefull sp'rite,
Serious in all he went about
Doing it with his Heart,
And not content to put off Christ
With the eternall part.

He was most sound and Orthodox,
A down-right honest Teacher,
And of soul-searching needfull Truths
A zealous, painfull Preacher.
And God his pious Labours hath
To many hearers blest,
As by themselves hath publiquely
Been owned & confest.

He hath in few yeers learned more,
And greater progress made
In Christianity, then some
That thrice the time have had.
A humble, broken-hearted man
Still vile in his own eyes
That from the feeling of his wants
Christ's Grace did highly prize.
Still thirsting to obtain more full;
Assurance of God's Love:
And striving to be liker Christ
And to the Saints above.
Although he was endu'ed with Gifts
And Graces more then many's;
Yet he himself esteemed still
More poor & vile then any.

In fruitless, empty, vain discourse,
He took no good content:
But when he talk't of Heav'nly things,
That seem'd his element.
There you might see his heart, & know
What was his greatest Pleasure,
To speak & hear concerning Christ
Who was his onely Treasure;

His constant self-denying frame,
To all true saints his love,
His meekness, sweetness, Innocence
And spirit of a Dove,
Let these be graven on our hearts
And never be forgot.
The name of precious saints shall live,
When wicked mens shall rot.

O Maldon, Maldon thou hast long
Enjoy'd a day of Grace;
Thou hast a precious man of God
Possessed in this place:
But for thy sin, thou art bereft
Of what thou did'st possess;
Oh let thy sins afflict thee more
Then do thy wants thee press.

Great strokes, Great Anger do proclaime,
  Great Anger, Greater sins.
We first provoke,[1] before the Lord [[1]offend.
  To punish us begins.
Good Lord awaken all our hearts
  By this most solemn stroke
To search for, find oute, and forsake
  Our sins that thee provoke

Awake, awake, secure hard hearts;
  Do you not hear the Bell
That for your Pastours Funerall
  Soundeth a dolefull Knell?
You that would never hear nor heed
  Th' instructions that he gave,
Me-thinks you should awake & learn
  One lesson at his Grave.

Repent, Repent, It's more then time
  The Harvest's well nigh past,
And Summer ended: but thy soul
  Not saved, first nor last.
The Belows they are burnt with fire,
  The Instruments are gone,
But still thy Lusts are unconsumed:
  Read then thy Portion;

If that the ffounder melts in vain
  (Thy lusts do not decay)
God will account thee worthless Dross
  Fit to be cast away.
Since words could not awaken us,
  God tries what blowes can do:
He strikes us on the head, & makes
  Us stagger to and fro.

Much more I might have said, but Time
  Will not the same permit.
Come let us put our mouths in Dust
  And down in Ashes sit.
The Lord hath giv'n us Gall to drink,
  And laid us in the Dust:
What shall we say? Behold we're vile,
  But thou, O Lord, art just.

If this, and such like awfull strokes
  Do not our hearts awaken,
Doubtless the Gospel will ere long
  Be wholly from us taken.
If we repent, return to God,
  Esteem his Gospel more
Improve it better: then the Lord
  Hath mercies yet in store

We append to the elegy the following lines by Mr. Wigglesworth, which we print from a copy in the autograph of the author preserved in the same volume, folio 9. These papers were presented to the above society by the late Miss Charlotte Ewer, who found them among the papers of her deceased brother, Charles Ewer, Esq., the first president of the society. The handwriting shows that these lines were written at an earlier period than the elegy.

1

When as the wayes of Jesus Christ
  Are counted too precise,
Not onely by some Babes or ffooles,
  But also by the wise:
When men grow weary of the yoke
  Of godly discipline,
And seek to burst those golden barres
  Which doe their lusts confine.

2

When some within, and some without.
  Kick down the Churches wall
Because the doore is found to be
  Too strait to let in all:
The best can then nought else expect
  But to be turned out,
Or to be trampled under foot
  By the unruly rout.

3

When as the ffoxes and wilde Boares
  Come in to dress the Vine,
The vinyard then is like to yield
  But very little wine,
When as the Sheep shall with the woolves
  For carnall ends comply,
If my Conjecture faile mee not
  They'l slaughter get thereby.

4

When Godly men cannot agree
  But differing mindes bewray
And by their fell dissensions
  Shall make themselves a prey.
Then O, New England is the time
  Of thy sad visitation,
And that is like to be the yeer
  Of God's fierce indignation.

5

When some shall strive to scrue the rest
  To their own apprehensions
In things where difference might be born,
  Then look for sad contentions
For those that conscientiously
  From others doe dissent
Against their consciences to act,
  Will never be content.

6

When of their Shepheards faithfulness
  The sheep suspitious grow
Or slight & undervalue them
  To who they reverence ow:
Or when the Shepheards force the sheep
  Where danger doth appeare,
Then both to Shepheards and to sheep
  Calamity is neere.

7

When Joshua and Zerubbabel
  Are thought for carnall ends
To favour the Samaritans
  By some of their best ffriends:
When such uncharitable thoughts
  Make many hearts to swell:
God grant them grace to act their part,
  Both warily and well.

GOV. BAREFOOTE'S WILL.

In The name of God Amen. I Walter Barefoote of Great Island in ye Prouince of New Hampshire in New England Esqr., being of sound perfect & disposing memory, tho weak in body, Do make & ordain this my present Last Will & Testament (reuoking all former Wills) in manner & form following. ffirst & principally, I commend my Soul into the hands of Almighty God, hoping through the Merits, Death & Passion of my Sauiuor Jesus Christ to haue full and free pardon & forgiueness of all my sins, & to inherit eternall life. And my Body I commit to the earth, to be decently buried at the discretion of my Executor hereafter named, And as to ye disposure of all such Temporall Estate as it hath pleased God to bestow upon me, I giue & dispose therof as followeth. ffirst I will that my Debts and ffuneral charges shall be paid and discharged. As to the disposing of all my Lands Tenements and Hereditaments, I the said Walter Barefoote do hereby deuise and bequeath to Thomas Wiggin my Brother in law and to my Sister Sarah his Wife, my House and Land with the appurtenances, situate and lying at Strawbery bank in Portsmouth in the said Prouince (now in ye possession of John Pickerin Senr.) And also my House and Land situate & lying at Greenland, containing about two hundred acres: And also my Lands lying & being at Merimack River, containing about thirteen hundred acres, To haue and to hold all the said Lands and p^rmisses to the said Thomas Wiggin and Sarah his Wife and her heirs for euer, they paying and discharging all my just Debts & Legacies by me hereafter giuen and bequeathed.

I deuise and bequeath to Joseph Clark son of John Clarke of Great Island aforesaid Mariner ffiue hundred acres of my Land in the Prouince of Maine, which I perchased of Cap^{tn} ffrancis Champernoon, adjoining to his Island, beginning at ye Stepstones & running to Brarboard harbour, To haue and to hold to the said Joseph Clark his heirs & assigns for euer, excepting forty acres by me disposed of. And I likewise deuise and bequeath to Thomas Wiggin aforesaid and Sarah his Wife ffiue hundred acres of my Land in ye said Prouince of Maine which I perchased of Colonell John Archdale, lying on backside of the said ffiue hundred acres, perchased of the said ffrancis Champernoon (as aforsaid) To haue and to hold to the said Thomas Wiggin and Sarah his Wife their heirs and assigns for euer.

I deuise and bequeath to my said Beloued Sister Sarah Wife of Thomas Wiggin aforesaid, all that my Land with the Sawmills & apurtenances lying and being at Lamprill river, formerly in the possession of Robert Wadleigh, To haue and to hold to her the said Sarah, During her natural life; and after her decease I deuise & bequeath the same to her Daughters Sarah and Susanna, To haue and to hold to them their heirs & assigns for euer, equally to be divided.

I deuise & bequeath to my Cousin Thomas Wiggin Son of the said Thomas Wiggin my Brother in law, all that my Land with the apurtenances lying & being at Lamprill riuer containing about Three hundred acres, which I purchased of William Hilton, Charles Hilton, & Samuel Hilton, And one hundred acres of marsh (or there about), the moiety or half part wherof I perchased of the said William Hilton, Charles Hilton, & Samuel Hilton, and the other moiety or half part I purchased of Robert Mason,

Eq^{r}: as by the Deeds of Sale may more fully appear, To haue and to hold to him the said Thomas Wiggin Junr: his heirs and assigns for euer.

I deuise and bequeath to Edward Hilton Son of Edward Hilton of Exeter in the said Prouince, the Debt due and owing to me from ye aforesaid Edward Hilton, his father, being Nine pounds, together with ye Bill by which it is due.

I deuise and bequeath to John Clark aforesaid, all that my Land lying and being at Saco in ye Prouince of Maine aforesaid, To haue and to hold to him his heirs & assigns for euer.

I deuise & bequeath to Joseph Clark son of the said John Clark, all that my Dwelling house (with the apurtenances) and Land containing half an acre, situate & lying on Great Island aforesaid, near the House of John Clark aforesaid, To haue and to hold to him ye sd Joseph Clarke his heirs & assigns for euer, but I will that Elizabeth Clarke his Mother shall haue the use of the said house and p^{r}mises during her natural life.

I deuise and bequeath to the other Children of the said John Clarke viz: Love, Isaac, & Jacob, all that my Land containing about seven acres, lying & being on Great Island aforesaid: and also one acre of Land adjoining to the said Land, and to John Lewis his House and Land, & which I formerly perchased of him; To haue and to hold to them their heirs & assigns for euer, to be equally deuided between them. I deuise and bequeath all that my Land at Spruce Creek in the said Prouince of Maine, containing about one thousand acres, which I formerly purchased of Doct^{r} Henery Greenland, I deuise it to him ye said Henery Greenland, To haue and to hold to him his heirs & assigns for ever.

I giue and bequeath to John Tufton Esqr: ten pounds to be paid him in current pay:

I giue and bequeath to Richard Chamberlain Esqr: Ten pounds in current pay.

I giue and bequeath to Robert Tufton & Catherine his Wife one hundred pounds in current pay.

I giue and bequeath to Joseph Rain ffiue pounds in current pay.

I giue and bequeath to John Lee (my Cousin) ffifty pounds in current pay.

I giue and bequeath to my beloued sister Sarah before named my Great Bible.

I giue and bequeath to Elizabeth Clarke aforesaid my two Chests which are at my House aforesaid, together wth all that is therein contained except the Writings, and so many yards of Dowlas as will make half a dozen Shirts, which quantity of Dowlas I do hereby giue & bequeath to Richard Chamberlain abouesd, and all the Money Goods Chattles & Moveables which I haue at this House of John Clarke, where I am at p^{r}sent, I giue & bequeath to her the said Elizabeth Clarke.

I giue & bequeath to Nathan Bedford Ten pounds to be paid in current pay, and also one ffeather bed with the Bolster Rug and Blanket.

I giue & bequeath to Thomas Swaffer Ten pounds in money.

I giue & bequeath to Robert Tufton aforesaid my best Beaver hat.

I giue & bequeath to John Clark aforesaid my Cow to be kild & spent in his family.

I giue & bequeath to the poor of Great Island aforesaid ffiue pounds to be paid in Money, Corn or Provision.

I do hereby constitute & appoint my said Brother in law Thomas Wiggin, Senr: my full & sole Executor of this my Last Will and Testament, and I desire my good frends, s^{d}. Richard Chamberlain & Cap^{tn} Samuell

Wentworth, to be ouerseers of the same, & do hereby impower them to see the same, & every thing therein contained, to be duly performed. In testimony that this is my Last Will & Testament I haue hereto set my hand & seall the Third day of October in the ffourth year of the Reign of Our Souerain Lord, James the Second, King of England. Annoque Dñi. 1688.

WALTER BAREFOOTE [L. S.]
his W. B. mark.

Signed, sealed &
published, (after
ye erasure of ye 17th &
18th lines [of the original],)
in presence of:
Shedrack Walton
William Godsoe
Henry Trevethan.

We, John Lee & Thomas Swaffer, heard the herein named Walter Barefoote, Esquire, declare that this writing being his Last Will and Testament was read all unto him just as it is herein set down, and did again publish the same October 8th, 1688.

John Lee,
Thomas Swaffer.

[Walter Barefoote came from England, probably between 1650 and 1655. We know that he was a resident of Great Island (Newcastle, the seat, for many years, of the proprietary and provincial government of New-Hampshire), as early as 1660. In 1683, he wrote to the "Lords of the Committee, &c." *(Chalmers Pol. An.)* that he had been a resident of the province more than twenty-five years. Of his previous history or condition we know nothing, unless we give credit to the *ex parte* statement of one Wm. Davis (*ante*, vol. v. p. 358), made before Mr. Secretary Rawson in 1676; but there are obvious reasons for regarding this deposition with suspicion.

Barefoote has not fared very well at the hands of our historians. He is called a "tool of Cranfield;" a "factious person," &c. &c. It is true, he was a staunch royalist and a friend, if not a member, of the Church of England; as were a large number, if not a majority, of the leading men of the province down to the revolutionary war. But he is not the only character who has failed to engage the attention, not to say interest, of our historians, old or new. Conspicuous examples of this neglect, or partizanship, may be found in the case of Capt. John Mason and Sir Ferdinando Gorges; characters of vastly more importance than Barefoote. Had these and other prominent men, who might be named, been of the Puritan party, we might have had from the Mathers, at least, their pedigrees, epitaphs, and exploits set forth at length; and the Hebrew, Greek and Latin tongues would have been taxed for apt words of eulogy.

It is also true, that he was somewhat stern in his official conduct; but he had to deal with many men who were intent upon courses subversive of the rights of the crown, and of its loyal subjects. However, after a careful examination of the printed records, we discover no evidence of peculiar rigor of manner or of misconduct on his part. He was faithful certainly to his oaths, and never played a double part toward the king, or his ministers and agents. He was obnoxious undoubtedly to the authorities and leading men of the Bay, and to their sympathizers and abettors in New-Hampshire; for he was a strenuous opposer of their attempts, finally unsuccessful, to extend the jurisdiction of the Colony of the Bay over New-Hampshire.

Moreover, it should be set down to his credit (and great credit it is), that he never persecuted men for their "opinions," either in matters of religion or politics; and he was one of the few in office who protected the Quakers from the violence of men, both of the laity and clergy, who claimed for themselves rights, and immunities even, which have always been the peculiar property of "tender consciences:" among which is the right to persecute the minority for disobeying the will of the majority; and immunity from punishment for disobedieuce when in the minority.

There is evidence that Barefoote was a man of ability, if not of education. He is styled "Dr. Barefoote" by Judge Bell (*N. H. Hist. Coll.* vol. viii. p. 307); otherwise, we have seen no reason to suppose that he was trained to any profession.

He held various important offices. He was deputy-collector of customs during Pres. Cutt's term; he was named counsellor in Gov. Cranfield's commission, and held that office from Oct., 1682, to Jan., 1683; deputy-governor from Jan., 1683, to May, 1686, and a part of that time was the acting governor; assistant to Mason in the Court of Chancery, for a time; justice of the Court of Common Pleas, by virtue of his office of counsellor; and upon the accession of Pres. Dudley was made a justice for New-Hampshire.

From his letter to the "Lords," above referred to, it appears that he became connected by marriage with many of the leading families of the country, but who his wife was or whether he had any children, we know not. He makes no mention of either in his Will. Savage and Quint state that his sister Sarah was the wife of Thomas[2] Wiggin, son of Thomas[1] of Dover, and the language of the Will tends to support that statement.

Barefoote's Will was proved, in Boston, 21 Feb., 1688–9, and it is probable that he died soon after its execution. It is now first printed, and from a copy, loaned to us by Charles Deane, LL.D., which was made about the time the original was proved. It bears a memorandum referring to another copy in the hands of " Thomas Wigins at Swampscot," among whose descendants was, probably, the late Thomas Wiggin, Esq., of Stratham. Our copy has been carefully corrected by the original.

Considerable documentary matter illustrating Barefoote's official proceedings will be found in "The Provincial Records of New-Hampshire."—Ed. *N. E. Hist. and Gen. Register.*]

MEMOIR OF HON. OLIVER WOLCOTT, SEN., GOVERNOR OF CONNECTICUT, 1796–7.

The following memoir was obtained for the Register by J. Wingate Thornton, Esq., of this city. The original manuscript is now in the possession of G. P. Delaplaine, Esq., of Madison, Wis. When Mr. Delaplaine sent this copy to Mr. Thornton, he wrote that the document had this endorsement upon it in the handwriting of his father: "*Orig'l life of Governor Wolcott, sent me by Gov. Oliver Wolcott, Feb.* 7, 1819, *Sunday.*" The Gov. Oliver Wolcott who sent the document to Mr. Delaplaine, Senior, was the second governor of Connecticut of that name. He was a son of the person whose memoir is given, and was probably the author of the document. A memoir and portrait of him will be found in the Register, vol. iv. pp. 9–10. A genealogy of the Wolcott Family, descendants of Henry Wolcott, the emigrant ancestor, is printed in vol. i. pp. 351–5.

Henry Wolcott, the ancestor of the family of that name in Connecticut, was an English gentleman of Tolland in Somersetshire, who was born in the year 1578. He was the owner of an estate worth five hundred pounds sterling per annum, which, considering the value of money at that period, was a considerable property. His wife was Elizabeth Saunders, to whom he was married about the year 1606. He is represented to have been a man of talents and energy, and, in early life, much addicted to the habits and amusements of a *country gentleman.* Having adopted the principles of the sect of Independents, he became obnoxious to the government, and was thereby determined to remove to America. He first visited New-England in 1628, but returned again to England, and brought over his family in the year 1630, and settled at Dorchester in Massachusetts. Having sold the principal part of his estate in England, he undertook, in the year 1636, the settlement of Windsor in Connecticut. His principal associates were John Mason, a distinguished captain and warrior; Roger Ludlow, a well educated and correct lawyer; Mr. Stoughton, and Mr. Newberry, gentlemen of good estates. These were the chief founders of Windsor, and they defrayed most of the expenses of the settlement. The religious pastor elected by them, was the Rev. Mr. Warham, a man distinguished, at that period, for learning and piety.

In the year 1639, the towns of Windsor, Hartford and Wethersfield associated as a commonwealth, and formed a constitution of civil government. This instrument is understood to have been drawn up by Roger Ludlow, and was approved by the free planters of the settlement. Considered with reference to the period when it was formed, this constitution may be pronounced to be the best system of democratical government which had then been devised. Experience has demonstrated that it was well calculated to promote and perpetuate the views of its founders. The charter granted by Charles II., in 1662, was prepared in Connecticut, and it embraced the principles of this original compact; and they have been recently re-established in the new constitution adopted by the people. It may, therefore, be truly asserted, that the government of Connecticut, since 1639, has been conducted by the free representatives of the people; that its municipal regulations have secured a high degree of happiness and tranquillity, and have hitherto been less variable than those of any other government.

Henry Wolcott was annually elected a member of the assembly, or one of the magistracy, till his death in 1655, in the 78th year of his age.

His eldest son, Henry, succeeded to the principal part of his estate and was annually chosen a magistrate. He was named as one of the patentees, in the charter granted to Connecticut by Charles II. He died in 1680.

Simon Wolcott was the youngest son of the first Henry Wolcott. He was a farmer in Windsor, was born in England in 1625, immigrated to this country with his father's family, married Martha Pitkin in 1661, and died at Windsor in 1687, leaving a numerous issue.

The youngest son of Simon, was Roger Wolcott, who is distinguished in the annals of Connecticut. He was born at Windsor, January 4, 1679.

The impoverished state of the country, occasioned by Indian wars, and the labors and expenses incident to new settlements, deprived him of the advantages of an early education. He was bound as an apprentice to a mechanic, at the age of twelve years. At twenty-one, he established himself at East Windsor, where by industry and frugality, he acquired a plentiful estate. By regular degrees, he rose to the highest military and civil honors. He was commissary of the Connecticut forces, in the expedition against Canada, in 1711, and was second in command, with the rank of major-general, at the capture of Louisburgh, in 1745. He was successively a member of the assembly, and of the council; a judge of the county court, deputy governor, chief judge of the superior court, and from 1751 to 1754, governor. He died May 17, 1767, in the 89th year of his age.

He was free and affable, easy of access, of ready wit and great humor, a sincere Christian, and a zealous advocate for the civil and religious privileges of his country, which he defended with a firm spirit. Though uneducated in early life, his literary attainments were respectable. He published several tracts and a long poem, containing an account of the agency of John Winthrop in procuring from Charles II. the charter of Connecticut, and describing, in the quaint language of that day, the principal events of the Pequot War, as conducted by John Mason.

Oliver Wolcott, the events of whose life are more particularly the subject of this memoir, was the youngest son of Roger Wolcott, and was born the 26th of November, 1726. He was graduated at Yale College in 1747. In the same year he received a commission as captain in the army, from Gov. Clinton, of New York, and immediately raised a company, at the head of which he marched, to the defence of the northern frontiers, where he served for about a year; but the regiment to which he was attached, being disbanded in consequence of the peace at Aix La Chapelle, he returned to Connecticut, and studied medicine, under the direction of his brother, Dr. Alexander Wolcott, then a distinguished practitioner. Before he was established in practice, the county of Litchfield was organized, and he was appointed the first sheriff of the county in 1751. In the year 1774, he was advanced to be an assistant or councillor; to which station he was annually elected till the year 1786. While a member of the council, he was also chief judge of the court of common pleas for the county, and for many years judge of the court of probate for the district of Litchfield. He served in the militia, in every grade of office, from that of captain to that of major-general. On all the questions preliminary to the revolutionary war, he was a firm advocate of the American cause. In July, 1775, he was appointed, by congress, one of the commissioners of Indian affairs for the northern department. This was a trust of great importance. Its object was to induce the Indian nations to remain neutral during the war. While he was engaged in this business, the controversies respecting boundaries between Connecticut and Pennsylvania, and between Vermont and New-York, menaced the tranquillity of the colonies, and exposed them to the seductions of British partisans. Mr. Wolcott's influence was exerted, with great effect, to compromise these disputes, and to unite the New-England settlers in support of the American cause. In January, 1776, he attended congress at Philadelphia, and remained with that body till the declaration of independence was adopted and signed. He then returned to Connecticut, and on the 15th of August was appointed by Gov. Trumbull, and the Council of Safety, to command fourteen regiments of the Connecticut militia, which were ordered for the defence of New-York. This duty he performed, till the force, amounting to more than five thousand men, was subdivided into four brigades. He then returned home for a few weeks. In November, 1776, he resumed his seat in congress, and accompanied that body to Baltimore during the eventful winter of 1777. The ensuing summer, he was constantly employed in superintending detachments of militia, and corresponding on military subjects. After detaching several thousand men to the assistance of Gen. Putnam, on the North River, he headed a corps of between three and four hundred volunteers, who joined the northern army, under Gen. Gates, and aided in reducing the British Army, under Gen. Burgoyne. In February, 1778, he attended congress at York-Town, and continued with that body till July. In the summer of 1779, after the invasion of Connecticut by the British, he was in the field, at the head of a division of the militia, for the defence of the sea coast. In 1780, he remained in Connecticut. From 1781 to 1783, he occasionally attended congress. In 1784 and 1785 he was one of the commissioners of Indian affairs for the northern department, and, in concert with Richard Butler and Arthur Lee, prescribed the terms of peace to the Six Nations of Indians. From 1786, he was annually elected lieutenant-governor; till 1796, when he was chosen governor, which office he held till his death on the first of December, 1797, in the 72d year of his age.

This brief recital of the services of Oliver Wolcott proves, that during an active and laborious life devoted to the public service, he constantly enjoyed the confidence of his fellow citizens; a confidence alike honorable to him, and to the people of the State. He married Laura Collins, of Guildford, in the year 1765, with whom he lived till her death in 1795. In the arduous duties in which he was engaged during the revolutionary war, he was well supported by his wife, who, during his almost constant absence from home, educated their children, and conducted the domestic concerns of the family, including the management of a small farm, with a degree of fortitude, perseverance, frugality and intelligence, equal to that which in the best days of ancient Rome, distinguished their most illustrious matrons. Without her aid, his public services could not have been rendered, without involving a total sacrifice of the interests of his family: with her aid, his house was a seat of comfort and hospitality, and by means of her assistance, he retained during life a small estate, a part of which was a patrimonial inheritance.

The person of Gov. Wolcott was tall and erect, indicating great personal strength and dignity. His countenance manifested a sedate and resolute mind. His manners were urbane, and through life he was distinguished for modesty. Though firm and tenacious of his own opinions, which he distinctly expressed on all suitable occasions, he ever manifested great deference for the opinions of others. The State of Connecticut was, upon principle, well united in support of the revolution, and during the war was second only to Massachusetts, in the effective force furnished for its defence. There were here no British governors, officers, judges or agents. Though a few respectable men were of opinion that the war was premature and indiscreet, yet as their opinions proceeded from their peculiar views of the public interests and policy, their opposition was, in general, limited by moderation. The consequence was that the war of the revolution produced, in this State, few or none of those distressing consequences which usually attend civil conflicts. The subject of these remarks was therefore able to maintain with his political opponents, and to extort from the enemy, the character of an inflexible republican, with the precious commendation of being just and humane in all his conduct. He was indeed a republican of the old school, and his ideas of government and social liberty were derived from the purest sources. He was never idle; dissipation had no charms for him. Though not a learned man by profession, the writings of the most celebrated historians, biographers, poets and orators, both ancient and modern, were familiar to his mind and afforded him the only relaxation in which he indulged from active exertions. He was intimately acquainted with public law, and with the works of the great luminaries of science, who flourished in Europe, subsequent to the reformation. His integrity was inflexible, and never even suspected, his morals were strictly pure, and his faith that of a humble Christian, untainted by bigotry or intolerance.

Gov. Wolcott was personally acquainted with and esteemed by most of the great actors of the American revolution, and his name is recorded in connection with many of its most important events. It is the glory of our country, that the fabric of American greatness was reared by the united toils and exertions of patriots in every State, supported by a virtuous and intelligent people. It is peculiar to *our revolution*, and distinguishes it from every other, that it was recommended, commenced, conducted and terminated, under the auspices of men who, with few exceptions, enjoyed the public confidence during every vicissitude of fortune. It is therefore sufficient for any individual to say of him, that he was distinguished for his virtues, his talents and his services, during the *Age of Men*—

> " Of Men on whom late time a kindling eye
> Shall turn, and tyrants tremble while they read."

That Gov. Wolcott was justly entitled to this distinction, was never disputed by his contemporaries.

ELIOT'S NEW-ENGLAND BIOGRAPHICAL DICTIONARY.

Letter of Rev. John Eliot to Rev. Dr. Wm. Bentley.

[This letter shows some of the difficulties under which Eliot's Dictionary was composed and carried through the press. The first edition of Allen's Biographical Dictionary was published in 1809, the same year as Eliot's. We are indebted to Miss Mary R. Crowninshield for the original letter.—Ed. *N. E. H. & G. Register*.]

Boston, Jan. 11, 1810.

Dear Sir, Last evening I received your letter & packages, had no opportunity to pay for the conveyance which I wished to do, and make the charge either to Dr. Morse or the Historical Society.—For nothing in it was for myself, either letter or scrap of paper.

I thank you for perusing my book—though I think neither your *compliments* nor your *exceptions* (*as the case of some individuals*) have much justness in them. I am very sorry I ever published it. My design was to be preparing it three or 4 years, & then make a job for my son. When Allen published his proposals, I was pressed into a thing I knew to be precipitate & wrong. I was urged by friends who felt or feigned friendship and expressed a higher opinion of my abilities *than I knew* they had. I was sick, hurried, plagued with other affairs. The Gentlemen who undertook to serve, heaped cares without putting a finger to lighten the burden. They engaged *blockheads* for printers, one of whom left it, to print the *Patriot*, and the other was always sure of making mistakes, more so after a proof was corrected, if a figure could be *turned upside down*.

It will never see another edition in my day. The characters I think best drawn, meaning with truth, candour and impartiality, are S. Adams, J. Hancock, Hutchinson, Chauncy, *Hubbard* & *Williams*. A Gentleman from New York says I have *not* done justice to Adams, & that the book is horribly deficient, in not having *James Sullivan*, the glory of our times.—Several Gentlemen in Boston, estimable for Talents & worth, tho' federalists (which may lower them with you), say they would have *not* subscribed for the *book* had they seen what I have said of S. A. & John Hancock.

You say that I have not done justice to two men, who certainly are great favourites with me. I have declared R. W. with "*all his excentricities*," one of the greatest and best men of the Planters. I have plucked a feather from the cap of *Penn*, by declaring that the first writer upon toleration, the first promoter of it in any government was this *great* man. I took my authorities, *not* from Mather or Morton, or Hutchinson, but from Winthrop, Callender, Backus, Bentley & *his* own writings.

As to Hubbard, I believe what Mr. Frisbee said was correct & very consistent with what you relate. I believe that the Clergy of the neighbourhood, & all the wise men of the Province did think and speak *highly* of him. But a generation in the town of Ipswich rose up, who only were witness of his infirmities. I believe in every instance when a minister grows old, and people are put to expense to maintain him, they will treat him with neglect. I fully believe you & I, worthy, learned & respectable as we are, will experience it, if we outlive the days of our vigour, & loiter here after our companions have gone to their long home.

After saying this, I thank you for your hints, and will endeavour to make use of them. I should certainly have quoted the passages which you have done if I had seen them, & will certainly do it if I ever reprint, which I never expect to do.

For the *many*, very many *real* expressions & tokens of your respect & affection, I again heartily thank you. I believe no man's friendship towards myself is more sincere (at times I have thought it extravagant), but all compliments upon my Dictionary I can away with.

And am with high sentiments of esteem & regard
your friend & brother, JOHN ELIOT.

[Addressed to]
Rev. William Bentley, Salem.

NOTES ON EARLY SHIP-BUILDING IN MASSACHUSETTS.

[Communicated by Capt. GEO. HENRY PREBLE, U. S. N.]

A complete List of the Public and Private Armed Vessels belonging to Massachusetts, prior to the Revolution, from 1636 *to* 1776, *and of Armed Vessels built or fitted out in Massachusetts from* 1776 *to* 1783, *inclusive.*

Continued from vol. xxv. page 369.

Vessels.	Class.	Guns.	Swivels.	Men.	Commanded by	Date.
Jason	Ship	10		25	T. Dinsmore	1780
Jason	Ship	16		70	C. Hamilton	1781
Joseph	Brig	8		15	H. Higenson	1782
Joseph	Brig	6		20	P. Wells	1781
Joseph	Brig	8		25	C. Babbidge	1776–7

Also Capts. Field and West. In September, 1776, captured a schooner in ballast; and in November, captured a ship with a valuable cargo. Recaptured three times.

Juliet	Brig	6		16	S. Smith	1781
Julius Cæsar	Ship	14		40	J. Harrendon	1782
Junius	Ship	10		25	N. West	1781
Junius Brutus	Ship	18		100	J. Brooks, &c.	1780
Junius Brutus	Ship	20		120	N. Broadhouse	1781–2

March, 1782, in company with the Holker and two other privateers, sailed on an expedition against Tortola, W. I., where they engaged several armed British vessels, and made two captures.

Juno	Ship	12		25	W. Hayden	1780
Juno	Brig	12		16	J. Felt	1782
Jupiter	Ship	14		40	W. Orm	1782

An American brig of this name, Capt. Watson, captured an Algerine galley of 12 guns, in 1786, and carried her into Malaga.

Lady Washington	Sloop			7	Cunningham, &c.	

June, off Boston, beat off 4 armed barges, killing several of the enemy. October, off Boston, captured a ship, with a cargo of rum, sugar and cotton.

Lady Washington	Brig	6		15	W. White	1782
Landdon	Sch'r	6	10	50	J. Codman, &c.	1776
Languedoc	Sch'r	8		25	R. Yearmans	1781
Languedoc	Sch'r	4		25	Dunn & Hegarty	1781

Vessels.	Class.	Guns.	Swivels.	Men.	Commanded by	Date.
Lark	Brig	4		13	R. Stonehouse	1781
Lark	Sch'r	4		12	J. Tilden, &c.	1781
Lee	Sch'r	8		50	D. Walters, &c.	1776

Captured 3 British transports, and assisted in taking a fourth, with Col. Campbell and part of the 71st Regiment on board.

Lee	Sloop				— Burke	1776

Had an action with a ship and schooner. Finding it rather warm, hauled off.

Lee	Ship	6		25	J. Conway	1782
Lee	Sch'r	6		30	W. James	1782

See also previous to 1776.

Lexington	Brig	14		50	B. Crowninshield	1782
Lexington	Brig	10		20	D. Smith	1781
Liberty	Sch'r	6		25	— Pierce	1776

October, captured a ship or brig, with a cargo of fish and lumber.

Lion	Brig	10		45	J. Mason	1781
Little Bachelor	Sloop	4		20	M. Johnson	1782
Little Dan	Sch'r	4		25	D. Young	1781
Little Porgia	Brig	10		60	W. Armstrong	1781
Little Vincent	Brig	10		16	J. O'Brien	1781
Little Vincent	Brig	8		25	N. Poor	1781
Little Vincent	Sloop	4		6	R. Chaloche	1781
Lively	Sloop	6		30	A. Dunn	1781
Lively	Sch'r	8		35	G. Ashby	1781
Lively	Sloop	6		25	M. Duprey	1782
Lively	Ship	14		30	N. Goodwin	1780
Lively	Sloop	10		35	D. Adams	1776

Rescued the officers and crew of the British frigate "Blonde," wrecked near a barren and desolate island.

Live Oak	Ship	6		20	S. Tucker	1782
Lucy	Brig	12		25	S. Clay	1780
Lynch	Sch'r				— Ayers	1776

Evidently the same vessel recorded in 1775.

Manete	Sch'r	6		16	J. Ducarte	1780
Marlborough	Ship				— Babcock	1778

Reported to have captured 28 prizes, one a slaver with 300 slaves.
"Penn. Packet" for July 14th.

Marquis	Ship	10		20	N. West	1780
Marquis	Ship	16		80	R. Cowell	1781
M. DeLafayette	Ship	16		100	Buffington, Reed	1781–2
Maria	Ship	12		35	S. Hill	1781
Mars	Ship	14		45	J. Webber	1781
Mars	Ship	6		20	S. Dagget	1781
Maria	Brig	7		20	P. Maxfield	1781
Massachusetts	Brig	16			D. Souther	1776

September, captured a brig of 6 guns and 28 men, with a company of dragoons on board.

Massachusetts	Brig	16		30	J. Calef	1780

In 1779, captured a ship with a cargo valued at $100,000.

Massachusetts	Brig	16		30	— Fiske	1777

In company with the privateer "Tyrannicide," captured the barque "Lawnsdale," after resisting 3 hours, and losing 3 killed; also a ship and 6 other vessels, in one of which were 63 Hessian Chasseurs.

Vessels.	Class.	Guns.	Swivels.	Men.	Commanded by	Date.
Medium	Sch'r	4		25	B. Withern	1781
Mercury	Sch'r	6		15	W. Ferris	1781
Mercy	Sch'r	4		10	J. Adams	1782
Minerva	Brig	16		35	A. Hallet	1782
Minerva	Sloop	6		10	N. Buffington	1782
Mohawk	Ship	20		130	E. Smith	1781
Mohawk	Ship	20		80	J. Carnes	1782
Montgomery	Sch'r	4		15	B. Ashton	1782
Montgomery	Brig	8		20	J. Carnes	1780
Monmouth	Brig	6		20	D. Ingersoll	1778–82

In 1778, captured a vessel that was afterwards lost near Portsmouth, with her crew of 11 men. In 1779, captured 2 brigs, 1 schooner and 1 sloop, the latter in charge of a midshipman and 4 men.

Monmouth	Brig	20		160	— Ross	1779

One of the cruisers destroyed in the Penobscot, to prevent falling into the possession of the British Squadron.

Moore	Brig	14		40	E. Burroughs	1782
Morning Star	Ship	8		12	F. Roch	1780
Nancy	Brig	4		13	T. Parker	1780
Neptune	Ship	24		120	W. Friend	1777
Neptune	Ship	7		20	W. Woodbury	1780
Neptune	Ship	14		65	H. Smith	1781
Neptune	Ship	15		60	S. Smith	1781
New Adventure	Ship	6		25	R. Cushing	1780
New Adventure	Brig	14		50	J. Neal	1781
Nimble Shilling	Sch'r	6		15	J. Clover	1781
Nimble Shilling	Sch'r	5		16	S. Hill	1781
Norwich Witch	Sch'r	4		10	A. Minor	1780
Oliver Cromwell	Ship	10	10	60	W. Coit & J. Tilley	1776

Captured by the British sloop-of-war "Beaver," May 11, 1777.

Oliver Cromwell	Ship				— Parker	1779

Captured the tender "St. George," of 10 guns; also a ship and schooner, in all 60 prisoners.

Oliver Cromwell	Ship	16		85	J. Bray	1781

Reported to have been captured by the "Galatea" frigate.

Pallas	Ship	10		20	G. Hodges	1780
Pallas		14		80	— Johnson	1779

Captured a ship, loaded with provisions; was one of the vessels of the Saltonstall Expedition.

Panther	Sch'r	8		35	S. Massury	1781
Panther	Brig	6		15	G. Lane	1782
Patty	Ship	8		20	Derby & Smith	1782
Patty	Ship	4		16	N. Nichols	1777
Patty	Brig	6		16	J. Oakes	1779
Patty	Brig	6		15	J. Bishop	1779
Patty	Brig	8		20	W. Hayden	1782

Vessels.	Class.	Guns.	Swivels.	Men.	Commanded by	Date.
Peacock	Brig	4		12	P. Wells	1782
Peacock	Sch'r	4		16	S. Smith	1780
Peacock	Sch'r	4		10	E. Davis	1781
Peacock	Sch'r	4		15	A. Mackay	1781
Penguin	Sch'r	10		40	S. Foster	1782
Perus	Ship	22		150	S. Crowell	1782
Phenix	Brig	8		16	J. Richard	1780
Phenix	Sloop	10	8	60	— Cunningham	1776
Pickering	Sloop	16		100	J. Harraden	1779

May, had an engagement of 1 hour and 25 minutes with a cutter of 20 guns. June, captured the schooner "Golden Eagle," 22 guns and swivels, and 57 men, which was soon after recaptured by the "Achilles," which the "P." afterwards engaged for several hours, beat her off, and then retook her prize, on board of which she found the 2nd Lt. of the "Achilles."

Pa. Gazette, No. 2619.

October, off Sandy Hook, engaged at the same time, and captured after 1 hour and 30 minutes, ship "Hope," reported to have been armed with 14 guns; brig "Pomone," reported to have been armed with 12 guns; cutter "Royal George," reported to have been armed with 14 guns; and during the same year three other armed vessels.

Vessels.	Class.	Guns.	Swivels.	Men.	Commanded by	Date.
Pilgrim	Ship	18		150	J. Robinson	1779

Captured 3 prizes, one with men, and 2 with cargoes of salt.

Vessels.	Class.	Guns.	Swivels.	Men.	Commanded by	Date.
Pilgrim	Ship	18		150	J. Robinson	1781

January 5th, captured, after an action of several hours, the "Mary," of 22 guns and 83 men; her Captain among the killed; both vessels very much shattered.

Vessels.	Class.	Guns.	Swivels.	Men.	Commanded by	Date.
Pink	Sch'r	4		20	M. Harvey	1782
Polly	Sloop	12	8	100	— Leech	1776

August, 1779, captured a brig, with a cargo of tobacco.

Vessels.	Class.	Guns.	Swivels.	Men.	Commanded by	Date.
Polly	Ship	16		24	S. Lee	1782
Polly	Ship	6		14	G. Leacy	1780
Polly	Ship	20		35	W. Coas	1781
Polly	Ship	8		30	J. Foster	1781
Pompey	Boat			10	W. Thomas	1781
Poppet	Sch'r		4	10	T. Barnard	1782
Poras	Ship	20		140	J. Carne	1781
Porga	Brig	14		40	W. Armstrong	1780
Port Pacquet	Ship	8		20	S. Forrester	1781
Prosper	Ship	6		18	J. Atkins	1780
Protector	Ship	26		200	J. F. Williams	1779

January 9th, at sea, engaged the British ship "Admiral Duff," Capt. R. Strange, of 30 guns, for 1½ hours, when the latter blew up, and 55 only of her crew were saved from the wreck. The "P." subsequently had a running fight for several hours with the "Thames" frigate, and escaped. Midshipman (subsequently Commo.) Preble was attached to the "P." at this time. For an account of this fight, see Vol. II. of N. E. Historical and Genealogical Register. The "Protector" was finally captured by the "Roebuck," a 40 gun ship, and the "May Day," of 28 guns. Her log-book is now in the possession of the N. E. Historic, Genealogical Society.

Vessels.	Class.	Guns.	Swivels.	Men.	Commanded by	Date.
Providence	Sloop	8		15	J. Simmonds	1780
Putnam		2	16	45	— Bayley	1776

Captured a privateer, of 8 guns and 20 men.

Vessels.	Class.	Guns.	Swivels.	Men.	Commanded by	Date.
Putnam		20		170	Waters	1779

Was one of the Saltonstall Expedition.

Queen of Spain	Ship	6		15	T. Barnard	1782
Race Horse	Brig	6		15	N. Thayer	1781
Race Horse	Sch'r	8		25	A. Storey	1782
Race Horse	Sch'r	4		15	T. Oliver	1782
Rainbow	Sch'r	6		25	O. Webb	1782
Rainbow	Sch'r	10		40	W. Webb	1782
Rambler	Ship	16		40	B. Lovett	1782
Ranger	Sch'r	6	10	40	— Robert	1776
Ranger	Brig	10		20	S. Babson	1780
Ranger	Brig	8		15	T. Simmonds	1781
Ranger	Brig	8		20	J. Knight	1781
Ranger	Sch'r	2	4	20	J. Burgess	1782
Ranger	Sch'r		4	20	J. Christopher	1782
Rattlesnake	Ship	20		85	M. Clark	1781

The British claim to have captured a cruiser of this name.

Raven	Ship	10		40	J. Davis	1780
Raven	Sch'r	10		40	G. Olmstead	1780
Raven	Sch'r	10		40	G. Hollister	1781
Raven	Sch'r	10		45	S. Buckland	1782
Recovery	Brig	12		15	S. Ingersoll	1782
Recovery	Brig	6		16	W. Dennis	1782
Reprisal	Brig	8	10	70	— Wheelwright	1776
Reprisal	Brig	10		55	P. Read	1777
Reprisal	Galley	4		25	B. Frizzle	1781
Reprisal	Sch'r	4		30	J. Curtis	1781
Reprisal	Sch'r	6		12	W. Jacobs	1782
Republic	Sloop	12			J. F. Williams	1776

Captured ship "Julius Cæsar," armed ship, with a valuable cargo taken to Boston.

Resolution		6		25	A. Potter, &c.	1781
Resolution	Ship	20		130	S. West	1782
Resolution	Brig	6		18	L. Seare	1780

One of these captured 5 vessels in 1779; cargoes of coal, &c.

Resource	Ship	10		24	R. Ober	1780
Retaliation	Brig	10	9	70	— Giles	1776

Captured a ship armed with 6 guns, after a resistance of two hours. May 14, 1779, was attacked by an English cutter of 16 guns and a brig of 14, and beat them off.

Retaliation	Ship	12		30	J. Goodhue	1780
Retaliation	Ship	10		24	S. Sewell	1781
Retrieve	Sloop	10	16	80	— Stone	1776
Revenge	Sloop	12		80	J. White, &c.	1776

August, captured ships "Anna Maria," cargo of rum and sugar, and "Polly," cargo of wine, &c. Brigs "Harlequin" and "Fanny," cargoes of rum and sugar. Sloop "Betsey," and one other released with prisoners. A ship of this name, 18 guns and 150 men, was in the Saltonstall Expedition, 1779.

Vessels.	Class.	Guns.	Swivels.	Men.	Commanded by	Date.
Revenge	Sloop	4		14	A. Rainey, &c.	1780
Revenge	Sloop	4		14	E. Burrows, &c.	1781
Revenge	Sch'r	8		40	B. Knight, &c.	1781
Revenge	Sch'r	4		35	S. Foster	1781
Revenge	Sch'r	4		35	L. Coat	1781
Revolt	Brig	8		20	H. Phelps	1781
Rising States	Brig	20	16	100	J. Thompson	1776

Also armed with 7 cohorns.

Robin Hood	Ship	14		60	S. Smith	1781
Rochester	Boat		4	20	S. Morton	1782
Rochambeau	Snow	16		35	M. Melally	1781
Roebuck	Ship	14		90	Hemfield, Gray	1779-80

April, off Salem, captured the privateer sloop "Castor," of 8 guns and 60 men.

Romeo	Sloop	10		15	J. Grimes	1781
Romulus	Brig	14		25	J. Grafton, &c.	1781
Rover	Sch'r	6		20	E. Ayre	1781
Rover	Sch'r	12		40	D. Niedham	1782
Rover	Sloop	8	14	80	— Forrester	1776

Engaged the ship "Africa," which soon after blew up, and only 3 lives out of a crew of 26 were saved; captured the snow "Lively," and the brigs "Mary and James," "Sarah Ann" and the "Good Intent."

Rover	Ship	24		100	J. Barre	1781

A packet of this name, carrying 6 guns, was captured by an American privateer, Capt Sweet, in 1779.

Rover	Sch'r	6		30	Z. Young	1782

The enemy claim to have captured a cruiser of this name, carrying 14 guns.

Rover Galley	Sch'r	4		25	L. Carver	1782
Ruby	Brig	6		20	S. Babson	1781

Salem	Brig	12		20	H. Williams	1780
Salem	Sch'r	6		30	E. Stanley	1782
Salem Packet	Ship	12		30	J. Cook	1781
Salem Packet	Ship	9		20	J. Brewer	1782
Sally		20		180	— Holmes	1789?

Destroyed in the Penobscot, to prevent capture.

Sally	Sloop		2	16	E. Crocker	1782
Satisfaction	Sch'r		10	20	M. Smelthurst	1782
Satisfaction	Sloop	14	12	100	— Wheelwright	1777
Scammel	Sch'r	16		40	N. Stoddard	1782

October, was chased on the Jersey shore by two British men-of-war, whose boats were beaten off, and the privateer got off without having sustained material injury.

Scotch Irish	Boat		2	12	J. Wing	1782
Scourge	Ship	20		120	J. Parker	1781
Sea Flower	Brig	6		15	W. Whitcomb	1781
Sea Flower	Sloop	4		30	R. Jones, &c.	1782

Vessels.	Class.	Guns.	Swivels.	Men.	Commanded by	Date.
Sea Flower	Sloop	6		40	D. Nye	1782
Sebastian	Ship	10		30	J. Grooves	1780
Senegal	Brig	10		35	N. Bentley	1781
Shaker	Galley	6		40	S. Stacey	1782
Shark	Brig	14		80	D. Allen	1781
Shaving Mill	Boat				D. Loring	1781
Sherwood	Brig	14		11 ?	J. Tucker	1782 ?
Siren	Sch'r	12		50	D. Stevenson	1781
Sky Rocket	Brig	16		120	— Burke	1779

Probably overrated in guns and men; one of the Saltonstall Expedition.

Vessels.	Class.	Guns.	Swivels.	Men.	Commanded by	Date.
Spanish Fame	Brig	10		25	J. Robb, &c.	1781
Spanish Packet	Ship	10		20	T. Dalling	1782
Speedwell	Sloop	8	12	70	— Greeley	1776

October, captured a snow, and sent her to Boston.

Vessels.	Class.	Guns.	Swivels.	Men.	Commanded by	Date.
Speedwell	Brig	10		50	J. Murphy	1781
Speedwell	Boat	2		20	L. Barbor, &c.	1782
Spitfire	Brig	1	10	20	W. Perkins	1782
St. Mary's	Brig	12		30	J. Leach	1782
Success	Sch'r	2		18	S. Rodgers	1781
Success	Ship	6		15	W. White	1780
Success	Brig	10		30	J. Brown	1781
Success	Brig	16		20	S. Stanwood	1782
Success	Boat	1	4	20	S. Freeman, &c.	1782
Surprise	Brig	14		20	B. Cole	1782
Surprise	Sch'r		8	18	N. Perkins	1781
Surprise	Sch'r	8		35	J. Lengoore	1782
Swallow	Brig	6		20	H. Higgenson	1782
Swift	Brig	14		70	J. Little	1781
Swift	Brig	14		20	J. Johnson	1781
Swift	Brig	8		20	A. Woodbury	1781
Swift	Sch'r	2	10	30	T. Saunders	1781
Tartar	Sch'r	2	8	18	T. Dexter	1782
Tartar	Ship	24		200	— Grimes	1776

Mentioned in Clark's Naval History, p. 50; probably overrated in guns and men.

Vessels.	Class.	Guns.	Swivels.	Men.	Commanded by	Date.
Tempest	Ship	12		40	J. Souns	1781
Thomas	Ship	10		20	F. Boardman	1781
Thomas	Brig	12		35	J. Smith	1780
Thorn	Ship	16		100	Daniel Waters	1778
	Ship	16		60	Daniel Waters	1778

Engaged the brig "Gov. Tyron," Capt. Stebbins, of 16 guns, and at the same time the brig "Sir William Erskine," Capt. Hamilton, of 18 guns, each having a greater number of men than the "Thorn." After an action of 2 hours the "Tyron" struck, and the "Erskine" made sail to escape, but was pursued and captured. Also same year, captured the ship "Sparlin," of 18 guns and 97 men, after an action of 50 minutes; carried the two last prizes into Boston; the first separated in the night and escaped. Capt. Walters was appointed a captain in the U. S. Navy, upon the recommendation of Gen. Washington, March 15, 1777.

Vessels.	Class.	Guns.	Swivels.	Men.	Commanded by	Date.
Thorn	Ship	18		120	S. Tucker	1781
Three Friends	Sch'r	4		25	W. Young	1782
Thrasher	Sch'r	8		30	B. Cole	1781
Tiger	Brig	14		70	S. Crowel	1781
Tiger	Ship	16		74	J. Tucker	1782
Trooper	Ship	8		30	S. Dunn	1781
True American		12			— Buffington	1778

Had a severe engagement with a W. I. privateer.

True Blue	Sloop	6	8	40	O. Allen	1776
Tryall	Sch'r	6		20	S. Rodgers, &c.	1782
Two Brothers	Ship	8		60	T. Chester, &c.	1776
Two Brothers	Sch'r	1		25	W. Gray	1781

Re-enforced by volunteers in April, 1779; captured off Salem, a privateer of 8 guns and 60 men.

Twin Sisters	Brig	16		25	S. Avery	1781
Tybalt	Brig	8		20	P. Howland	1782
Tyrannicide	Brig	14		100	J. Fisk	1776

June 13th, at sea, captured, after a resistance of one hour, the British packet schooner "Despatch," of 8 guns, 12 swivels and 31 men, loss of her Captain (Gutteridge), and 1 man killed and 7 wounded. In July, at sea, captured the armed ship "Glasgow," with 30 prisoners. In August, at sea, captured the brig "St. John" and schooner "Three Brothers."

Tyrannicide	Brig	14		90	A. Hallet	1779

March 29th, off Bermuda, carried by boarding, after an obstinate resistance of more than one hour, the British brig "Revenge," of 14 guns and 85 men, Capt. Kendall; the latter had two of her guns dismounted, and many of her crew killed and wounded. The "T." had 8 wounded.

Tyrannicide	Brig	14		90	S. Harding	1779
Tyrannicide	Brig	14		90	— Cathcart	1779

August 14th, destroyed in the Penobscot to prevent capture.

Ulysses	Ship	10		40	D. McNiel	1780
Union	Sch'r	8		25	J. Blackley	1777
Union	Sch'r	4		20	D. Parsons	1781
Union	Pol'ca	4		15	T. Powers	1780
Union	Ship	4		12	E. Schin	1781
Union	Brig	8		20	J. Gardner	1780
Union	Sloop	10	14	65	— Semes	1786?
Vengeance	Brig	18		100	— Newman	1778

September 17th, captured the packet ship "Harriet," of 16 guns and 45 men, after an action of 15 minutes; had one man killed. September 21st, captured the packet ship "Eagle," of 14 guns and 60 men; resisted 20 minutes and lost several killed and wounded, among the former a colonel; had on board 4 lieutenant-colonels and 3 majors.

Vengeance	Brig	18		190	— Thomas	1779

August 14th, one of the fleet destroyed in the Penobscot.

Venus	Ship	10		80	G. Babcock	1781
Venus	Ship	10		20	T. Nicholson	1782

Vessels.	Class.	Guns.	Swivels.	Men.	Commanded by	Date.
Venus	Brig	6		15	M. Leslie, &c.	1780–1
Virginia	Ship	10		24	W. Claghorn	1782
Viper	Sch'r	2		25	T. Coburn	1782
Viper	Sloop	2		25	B. Hilton	1782
Viper	Ship	14		65	J. Niel	1782
Volunteer	Sch'r	8		20	L. Luce	1782
Volunteer	Galley	1		24	W. Hart	1782
Vulture	Sch'r	4		18	W. Shaloner	1782
Washington	Ship	7		15	E. Lewis	1781
Wasp	Snow				— Harthorne	1776
Wasp	Boat			19	S. Thompson	1782

October, lost 3 killed and 10 wounded in an action of 2 hours with an armed British packet; captured a snow with a cargo of oats. November, captured a ship with a cargo of fish, &c.

Wasp	Sch'r	4		16	E. Pike	1780
Wasp	Brig	6		20	D. NcNiel	1782
Wexford	Brig	20		120	J. Rathburn	1781
William	Ship	8		25	J. Power	1781
Willing Maid	Galley	4		25	J. Savage	1782
Winthrop	Sloop	13		35	Geo. Little	1781

Ed. Preble, afterward commodore in the navy, was her 1st lieut. Captured 2 letters-of-marque on her first cruise, afterwards cut out the British armed brig "Merriam" lying in the Penobscot with a prize sloop, and made numerous other captures, among which was a schooner of 8 guns, that was first chased on shore.

Wolf	Sloop	10	10	90	— Freeman	1776
Yankee	Sloop	9	16	43	— Johnson	1776

July, captured ships "Creighton" and "Zachara," cargoes rum and sugar. The prisoners in these prizes afterwards rose and took "Yankee," and carried her to Dover, where the captain was imprisoned and treated with great cruelty.

Yankee Hero	Brig	14		40	J. Tracy	1776

June, was captured by the English frigate "Lively," after a sharp resistance and the loss of 4 killed and 13 wounded.

Zephyr	Brig	4		15	G. Lane	1780

NOTE.—The classification, &c. of vessels contained in these tables are compiled chiefly from Emmons's Statistical History of the U. S. Navy, or have been copied from official documents; nevertheless, a sloop may have been called a ship, or a brig sometimes a schooner, and perhaps the swivels have sometimes been included in the number of guns given, but in the absence of positive proof, I have confined myself to the record.

The guns on board the privateers fitted out in Massachusetts, during the year 1781, amounted to 500, and the men to upwards of 2300.—(*Penn. Packet*, July 26.)

(To be continued.)

EARLY PRINTING IN VIRGINIA.

[The following correspondence, printed from the originals in the possession of Miss Mary R. Crowninshield, seems to have been begun at the desire of Isaiah Thomas, Esq., who was then engaged upon his *History of Printing in America*, which was published the next year. In that work, vol. ii., pages 41–2, he makes these statements :—

"Lord Effingham, who was appointed governor in 1683, was ordered expressly, 'to allow no person to use a printing press on any occasion whatsoever.' Although these instructions were given to lord Effingham, yet no act of the colonial government of Virginia can be found, after the strictest search by the greatest law characters in the state, which prohibits the use of the press. The influence of the governors was, undoubtedly, sufficient for the purpose without any legislative act."

The expression, "the strictest search by the greatest law characters in the state," in this extract, no doubt refers to that detailed in this correspondence. We are indebted to Col. Thomas H. Ellis, formerly of Richmond, Va., now of Chicago, Ill., for the greater part of the material from which we have compiled the subjoined notes; also, to Thomas H. Wynne, Esq., and Alex. Q. Holladay, Esq., of Richmond, and Conway Robinson, Esq., of Washington, D. C., for assistance.—[Ed. of *N. E. Hist. and Gen. Register.*]

William W. Hening,[1] Esq. to Hon. St. George Tucker.

Dear Sir, *Richmond, 4th July,* 1809.

Your favour of the 28th ult°. was put into my hands this morning. —I will with pleasure, make the examination requested, and inform you of the result.—If a law ever did exist, in Virginia, prohibiting the printing of News Papers, it must have been, I presume, posterior to Purvis's collection of the laws: for at the period of the publication of that book, and for many years afterwards, no such thing as printing of any kind seems to have been contemplated in Virginia.

It is well known that Purvis was printed in London (supposed about the year 1682).—I have an abridgement of the Laws of Virginia printed in London also, in the year 1722; and another, purporting to be a *second edition*, printed in 1728; but, in truth, it is the same book, with only a new title page;—a species of typographical artifice, very common at that period, especially as it related to law-books of every kind.

My Statutes at Large have progressed, in the printing, as far as the March session 1657–8 and from the earliest period of our legislation to that date, I have discovered no law of the kind alluded to in the extract inserted in your letter.—I will immediately examine the intervening period

[1] William Waller Hening is more generally known for his connection with the "Statutes at Large" of Virginia, a series of 13 volumes compiled and edited by him with great learning and ability. In its historical features, also, this exhaustive work is entitled to the highest credit. Mr. Hening also published several law manuals, and, jointly with Mr. William Mumford (a translator of Homer), reported and published several volumes of law-reports.

We have not been able to ascertain anything definite in regard to his ancestors, or early history, and it would seem that his great services to his native State have not secured for his memory the notice he deserved. He died 31 March, 1828, and probably in Richmond. A son, the Rev. Edmund Waller Hening of the Protestant Episcopal Church, was for some years a missionary in Africa.

The name *Waller* was probably the name of his mother. If so, he was perhaps descended from John Waller, one of the first planters at Jamestown in 1607, or from Edmund Waller who is said to have come over early in the 18th century. Mr. H. B. Grigsby, in his "Discourse on the Life and Character of the Hon. Littleton Waller Tazewell" (1860), supposes that this Edmund was a grandson of Edmund the poet. He is in error, however, in stating that this Edmund of Virginia was the first of the name in the colony.

between 1658, and the commencement of Purvis, as well as the MSS. embraced in that book, and as low down as 1733 (when the first Revisal of our laws was printed in Virginia); and if any thing should occur which will throw any light on the subject to which your enquiries have been directed, I will communicate it to you.

I am respectfully, yrs,

[Addressed to] Wm. W. Hening.

The Hon[ble] St. George Tucker,
Williamsburg [Va.]

[Memo. by Judge Tucker.]

St. G. Tucker to his friend Bishop Madison.[1]

Having no recollection of any such law as that which the reverend M[r]. Bentley in his Letter to you, enquires after, I wrote to M[r]. Hening who has made the most ample collection of the Laws of Virginia, which he is now actually engaged in publishing, to make the same enquiries from him. The preceding Letter contains his answer, which you will do me the favor to transmit with my best respects to M[r]. Bentley & Doctor Oliver.

July 10, 1809.

Bishop Madison to Rev. Dr. William Bentley.

Rev. & Dear Sir, *July* 12, 1809.

I transmit the Result of Judge Tucker's enquiries relative to the object of which you wished to be informed. I am sorry that no decisive answer has yet been obtained, but you will find, from Mr. Hening's Letter, that this cannot long be the Case. Mr. Hening's Diligence &

[1] The Rev. James Madison, D.D., first bishop of Virginia, and son of John Madison, clerk of Augusta Co., Va., was born at Port Republic, in the county of Rockingham, Va., 27 Aug., 1749, and died in Williamsburgh, 6 March, 1812. He was descended from the Capt. Isaac Madison (or Madyson) whose name appears as an active agent in the affairs of the colony at Jamestown from almost the first. See Smith's *Hist. of Va.*; Neill's *History of the Virginia Company*, &c.

In 1653, John Madison was settled on Chesapeake Bay. He was the father of John, the father of Ambrose, who was the father of James, the father of Pres. James Madison. The family planted itself on the shores of Chesapeake Bay, but gradually extended its branches through Virginia to the waters of Mississippi, and several of its members were pioneers of the tide of frontier life and adventure in that direction. See *Letter of John Madison*, under date of 1753, in Rives's *Madison*. From the writer of that letter, who was first cousin of Pres. Madison's father, sprang Bishop Madison; Col. George Madison, distinguished in the war of 1812, and governor of Kentucky, and other eminent men of that name.

The bishop was educated at the College of William and Mary, where he distinguished himself as a scholar; elected professor of mathematics in 1773; admitted to orders in the church by the bishop of London in 1775; president of William and Mary from 1777 to 1812; consecrated bishop by the archbishop of Canterbury, assisted by the bishops of London and Rochester, 19 Sept., 1790.

Bishop Madison's studies in mathematics, moral philosophy and natural history were extensive. His published writings are not numerous. Among them is a sermon on the death of Gen. Washington; an elegy on John Madison, 22 Sept., 1809, and a prayer composed (in 1807) for the celebration of the two hundredth anniversary of the settlement of Jamestown. He prepared a map of Virginia, of which a few copies are extant. The Richmond *Enquirer* contains also a communication from him about a mammoth, 14 July, 1809, and one on meteroic stones, 13 Dec., 1810. The same paper contains his obituary, under date of 13 March, 1812, and that of his widow, Mrs. Sarah Madison, under date of 26 Aug., 1815. The degree of doctor in divinity was conferred upon him in 1785, by the University of Pennsylvania.

One of the bishop's daughters, perhaps his only daughter, married the late Robert G. Scott, an eminent criminal lawyer of Richmond, who was some years consul of the United States at Rio de Janeiro—and was succeeded in the same office by his son Robert G. Scott, Jr.; another of Mr. Scott's sons, Charles L., was a representative in congress from California; a daughter married Edwin Harvie Chamberlayne, chief clerk in the office of the James River and Kanawha Company, at Richmond.

Accuracy may be entirely relied upon; & if the Gentlemen engaged in the work mentioned should find it convenient to wait for the Issue of Mr. H.'s researches, I shall lose no Time in forwarding it to you.

I regret, very sincerely, that the Person alluded to in your Letter should be the source of uneasiness to his dearest Friends, as well as to yourself. There was, certainly whilst he was here, a kind of Eccentricity, or strangeness in his manners, which impress'd many with the Belief of some Derangement. It is too probable, I think, that there is more of Reality than mere Pretext, in his situation.

I wrote to our Friend, Dr. Oliver, a few Days past, and mentioned to him, that I should write to you as soon as I rec^d^ Mr. Tucker's Reply. I thought it would be more satisfactory to forward the inclosed. I am, Rev^d^ sir—with the greatest Respect, Yr Friend & Ser't,

J. Madison,
Williamsburg.

[Postmarked W^ms^burg, Va., July 14.]
[Addressed to]
The Rev^d^ Dr. Bentley,
Salem, Massachusetts.

Hon. St. George Tucker[1] to the Rev. Dr. Bentley.

Reverend Sir, *Warminster, Va., August* 3d, 1809.

A few days before I left home, in Williamsburg, I did myself the pleasure to communicate to Bishop Madison the answer which I had received from M^r^. Hening, respecting the prohibition of printing newspapers in Virginia, at some period antecedent to our revolution. By the last post I have received a second Letter from that Gentleman, the contents of which are as follow.

"Not being able to discover in all my researches into the old acts of assembly in my possession, any trace of a law interdicting the publication of news-papers in Virginia, I requested information from M^r^. Jefferson, on the subject: the subjoined is an extract of a Letter just received from him.

1 St. George Tucker was educated at William and Mary College. He read law and began practice. After the revolutionary war, he was appointed by the legislature one of a committee, composed of Edmund Pendleton, Henry Tazewell, St. George Tucker, Joseph Prentis, Arthur Lee, and William Nelson, Jr., to revise and digest the laws of Virginia; one of the judges of the General Court, professor of law in William and Mary, a judge of the Court of Appeals, and district judge of the United States for the eastern district of Virginia. His judgeship in the Court of Appeals he resigned 2 April, 1811. The office of district judge he resigned several years previous to his death, in consequence of feeble health. In 1801, he published a letter on slavery, addressed to a member of the General Assembly of Virginia, which has frequently been quoted in the anti-slavery manuals of later days, taking ground that the effect of domestic slavery on the moral character of the whites was baneful, and inconsistent with the truest principles of republicanism. He prepared an edition of "Blackstone's Commentaries, with Notes of reference to the constitution and laws of the United States, and the Commonwealth of Virginia"; author, also, of various political essays, and of the poetic lines, beginning, "Days of my youth, ye have glided away."

Judge and Mrs. Tucker died, and were buried, at "Edgewood," Nelson county, Va., the seat of Joseph C. Cabell, Esq., who had married his step-daughter.

He was a near relative of the late Hon. Henry St. George Tucker, of London, who was for a number of years, by successive elections, chairman of the board of directors of the East India Company; and also a relative of the late Hon. George Tucker, who was for about six years a representative in congress from Virginia, the first professor of moral philosophy and political economy in the University of Virginia, author of "The Laws of Wages, Profits and Rent, investigated," "Progress of the United States in Population and Wealth," "The Life of Thomas Jefferson," "A History of the United States," &c.

Judge Henry St. George Tucker, his eldest son, an alumnus of William and Mary, was sometime a member of congress, chancellor of the fourth Judicial Circuit, president of the

"'I do not know that the publication of newspapers was ever prohibited in Virginia. My Collection of Newspapers begins in 1741, but I have seen one newspaper of about three years earlier date, as well as I can recollect. The first Laws printed in Virginia, were, I believe, the collection of 1733. Till the beginning of our revolutionary disputes, we had but one press, and that having the whole business of the Government, and no com-

Court of Appeals, professor of law in the University of Virginia, author of Lectures on Natural Law, Lectures on Government, Lectures on Constitutional Law, Commentaries on the Laws of Virginia, &c. &c., and president of the Virginia Historical and Philosophical Society. He married Ann Evelina Hunter, who was a daughter of Moses Hunter and Ann Stephen (a daughter of General Adam Stephen), of Jefferson county; and died in Winchester, Va., 28 August, 1848.

Of his two daughters, the first, Ann, married Dr. T. Magill, formerly professor of the principles and practice of medicine, obstetrics and medical jurisprudence in the University of Virginia; the second, Virginia, married Henry L. Brooke, Esq., an attorney and counsellor-at-law, formerly of Richmond, now residing in Baltimore. Mrs. Magill, assisted by two of her daughters, is the principal of the Valley Female Institute—an admirable and very successful school for the education and training of young ladies, in Winchester. Her eldest daughter married the Rev. J. R. Graham, pastor the Presbyterian Church in Winchester. Another of the daughters, Miss Mary Tucker Magill, has been for several years an accepted contributor to some of the leading magazines of the country—and the Lippincotts have at this time in preparation a story of Virginia Home Life, written by her, entitled, "The Holcombes." One of Mrs. Brooke's daughters married Daniel Lucas, Esq., a lawyer by profession, and the author of numerous poetical productions—among them: "In the land where we were dreaming."

Of Judge Henry St. George Tucker's sons—

David-Hunter, married a daughter of the late Hon. George M. Dallas. His professional education was received at the University of Virginia, the University of Pennsylvania, and in Paris. He is the author of medical works; was for several years a professor in the Jefferson Medical College, Philadelphia, and for a longer period professor of the practice of medicine in the Medical College of Virginia, in Richmond—where he still practises his profession. His eldest son, *Henry St. George*, a very promising and exemplary young man, was the first soldier in the confederate army, of Virginia, who lost his life after the commencement of the late war.

Nathaniel-Beverley, married Miss Ellis. He now resides in St. Catharines, Ontario, Canada. Soon after leaving the university, he settled to agricultural life at "Hazelfield," the former home of his mother and grandmother, in Jefferson county, Va., but subsequently founded and edited the Washington *Sentinel*, became printer to the U. S. Senate, and, during the administration of Mr. Buchanan, was consul of the United States at Liverpool. One of his sons, *Beverley-Dandridge*, partly educated at Vevay, in Switzerland, and who is now preparing for the ministry of the Protestant Episcopal Church in Virginia, is the author of various hymns, among which we recall one, on the words from St. Mark, "Come: Take up thy Cross and Follow me,"—beginning:

> "Yea, Jesu, Lord, at thy command,
> I take the cross and ready stand,
> To follow thee."

One piece of his contains 133 lines on the words of the Psalmist, "And He hath put a new song in my mouth, even praise unto our God," headed LYRA SACRA, beginning:

> "Too long, too long, O Lord, on careless wings
> My song has wandered far from thee."

John-Randolph, formerly attorney-general of the State of Virginia, and at present associate professor of law in Washington and Lee University. He enjoys a remarkable popularity in his native state. Among his published writings is a lecture, entitled, "The Southern Church justified in its support of the War." He will soon have ready for the press a new edition of "Tucker's Commentaries," adapted to the greatly changed laws of this day. He married a daughter of Col. Humphrey Powell, of Leesburg, Virginia.

St. George, who was for some years clerk of the senate, and afterward, of the House of Delegates, and principal of a classical school at Ashland, Hanover county, died during the late war, from disease contracted in the military service of the Confederate States; being at the time the captain of a company of infantry. His contributions to polite literature were numerous, and some of them very graceful and beautiful. Among his poems was "The Southern Cross;" and among his prose works, "Hansford; a tale of Bacon's Rebellion." He married a daughter of the late Governor Thomas Walker Gilmer, of Charlottesville, Virginia.

Judge Nathaniel-Beverley Tucker, the second son of Judge St. George Tucker, was some time district-judge of the United States for the district of Missouri, afterward professor of law in William and Mary, author of "Tucker's Pleadings;" also, of "Lectures on the Science of Government," and among other literary works, of "The Partisan Leader." One of

petitor for public favor, nothing disagreeable to the Governor could be got into it. We procured Kind to come from Maryland to publish a free paper. I do not suppose there ever was a legal obstacle.'"

Such, Sir, is the most satisfactory Information I have been able to procure in answer to your enquiries. Be pleased to accept my best wishes, & respects, & do me the favor to present them also to Doctor Oliver.

I am, Reverend Sir, your most obed[t] sev[t],

The Reverend M[r]. Bentley. ST. G. TUCKER.

his daughters married the late Henry A. Washington, who was also a professor in William and Mary, and, under the authority of congress, edited, with Notes, "The writings of Thomas Jefferson."

Elizabeth, only daughter of Mrs. Coalter, who was the daughter of St. George Tucker, married John Randolph Bryan, the adopted son and one of the legatees of John Randolph, of Roanoke, at one time a lieutenant in the United States Navy, afterwards a distinguished farmer in Gloucester county, Va., but now residing at "Carysbrook," Fluvanna county, with large planting interests also in Alabama. One of his sons, Joseph, a member of the Richmond bar, recently married a daughter of John Stewart, Esq., of "Brook Hill," near Richmond.

An obituary notice of Judge St. George Tucker will be found in Niles's *Register*, vol. xxxiii., 1 Dec., 1827; and a fine biographical sketch in Call's *Reports*, 4th vol. (Richmond, Va., 1833).

PEDIGREE.

HENRY[1] Tucker, of Port Royal, Bermuda, married Anne Butterfield. Their children were:—

1. HENRY, Lt. Gov. of Bermuda; died Feb., 1808.

2. FRANCES, married Henry Tucker, Esq., of Somerset, Bermuda; died 12 Sept., 1825. Their son John was the father of the wife of Dr. Robert Emmet of the University of Virginia.

3. THOMAS TUDOR, a physician in Charleston, C. S.; afterward treasurer of the United States under Washington; which office he held till his death, in the term of the second Adams.

4. ELIZABETH, a resident of Bermuda as late as 1828.

5. NATHANIEL, physician in the town of Hull, Eng.; author of "The Bermudian" and other poetical compositions; died in Dec., 1807.

6. ST. GEORGE, born in Port Royal, 29 June, 1752 (O. S.), and on 23 Sept., 1778, married Frances Bland (see *Note A*), daughter of Theodoric Bland, Esq., of Cawson's on James River and Appotomax River, Va., widow of John Randolph, Esq. (see *Note B*), of Chesterfield, and mother of Richard Randolph, born 9 March, 1769; Theodoric Bland Randolph, born 22 June, 1771, who died and was buried at Bizarre, in Cumberland county, February, 1792; and John Randolph, born 2 June, 1773.

The children of this marriage were:—

(1) Anne Frances Bland Tucker, born 26 Sept., 1779; wife of John Coalter, judge of the Court of Appeals; died 12 Sept., 1813.

(2) Henry St. George Tucker, born 5 Jan., 1781.

(3) Theodorick Tudor Tucker, born 17 Sept., 1782. He died 3 April, 1795.

(4) Nathaniel Beverley Tucker, born 6 September, 1784.

(5) Henrietta Eliza Tucker, born 16 Dec., 1787, and died July, 1796.

Their union was dissolved by the death of Frances Tucker, 18 Jan., 1788, in the 36th year of her age, she being born 24 Sept., 1752 (O. S.). She was interred at Matoax, in Chesterfield county, where a plain black marble monument remains to mark the place.

St. George Tucker and Lelia Carter were married at Currotoman, in Lancaster county, Va., 8 Oct., 1791. She was the daughter of Sir Peyton Skipwith, of Mecklenburg, Va., and widow of George Carter, of Currotoman, was born 9 Feb., 1769.

St. George Tucker, their son, was born in Williamsburg, Va., 29 Aug., 1792; he died 26 Sept., 1795.

Julia Maria Tucker, their daughter, was born 25 Nov., 1793, and died a few days after.

Martha Rutledge Tucker, their second daughter, was born 4 Oct., 1796, and died about an hour afterward.

BLAND (NOTE A.)

ADAM Bland (in the reign of Edward VI.) married Jane Atkyns.

JOHN Bland, m. Susan ——. From them came John, whose son Giles came to Virginia, engaged in Bacon's rebellion and was hanged by Gov. Berkeley; and

THEODORIC, who came to Virginia about 1654; m. Jane Bennett, dau. of Richard Bennett, governor of Virginia, in the time of Cromwell, and died 23 April, 1671.

RICHARD, m. (2) Elizabeth Randolph (see *Note B*). Their eldest son Richard was a leading member of the revolutionary convention of Virginia, and of the continental congress, and styled by Jefferson, "the wisest man south of James River." A daughter, Mary, m.

Isaiah Thomas, Esq., to Rev. Dr. Bentley.

My good Friend, *Aug.* 14, 1809.

I should have sooner noticed yours of the 25th ult., but have been absent from home for three weeks.

I can repay your goodness only by thanks and feelings of gratitude.

It may be that the declaration of Berkeley, and the Instructions to Ld. Effingham, relative to the press in Virginia made that impression on my mind, as led me to believe that a law anciently had been enacted in the colony to prohibit the Printing Press. The mandate of Ld. Effingham was, perhaps, at the time sufficient without a legislative act. I most cordially thank you and your friends in endeavoring to ascertain the fact by so thorough an investigation.

Henry Lee, and their son Henry was father of the celebrated Col. Henry Lee (Light Horse Harry) of the revolutionary war, who was the father of the late Gen. Robert E. Lee.

Theodoric m. Frances Bolling (see *Note C*). Their only son, Theodoric, was colonel of dragoons during the revolutionary war, and afterward member of congress. He died childless. Their daughter

Frances, m. (1) John Randolph (see *Note C*), and they were the parents of "John Randolph, of Ronoake." She m. (2) St. George Tucker.

Randolph (Note B).

William[1] Randolph emigrated from Warwickshire, Eng., to Virginia about 1660, and established himself at Turkey Island, about twenty miles below Richmond, in James River. He m. Mary, dau. of Henry and Catharine Isham, of Bermuda Hundred, Va., of the family of Isham in Northamptonshire, Eng., baronets. He was one of the first trustees of William and Mary College, and died 11 April, 1711. Their children were:—

(1) William[2] (of Turkey Island), a royal counsellor of state.

(2) Thomas[2] (of Tuckahoe), was father of Col. William (of Dungeness), the friend of PeterJefferson, father of Thomas Jefferson, and his son Col. Thomas Mann was a member of the house of burgesses, of the committee of safety, &c., and his son of the same name of Edgehill (who married Martha, daughter of Pres. Jefferson), was a member of congress, colonel of the 20th regt. in the war of 1812, governor of Virginia, &c. One of Thomas's[2] daughters, Judith, married Pres. William Stith, the historian; another, the Rev. William Keith, by whom she had Mary, grandmother of Chief Justice Marshall.

(3) Isham[2] (of Dungeness), member of the house of burgesses, and adjutant-general of the colony, married Jane Rogers, in London, Eng., in 1717. They had five sons and six daughters. Jane, the eldest, born in London in 1720, m. Peter Jefferson. He died in 1742. Several of his descendants held high official positions.

(4) Col. Richard[2] (of Curles) married Jane Bolling (see *Note C*), (gr. gr. granddaughter of Pocahontas), and was treasurer of the colony, &c. He was the grandfather of John Randolph, of Roanoke, and, on the mother's side, of Gov. Thomas Mann Randolph, of Edgehill.

(5) Sir John[2] (of Williamsburg). He was sent to England to obtain a renewal of the charter of William and Mary College, and returned knighted; attorney-general, speaker of the house of burgesses, treasurer, &c. of the colony. His eldest son, Peyton,[3] was also attorney-general and speaker under the crown, and first president of the U. S. congress. His second son John[3] was also also attorney-general, and went to England on the breaking out of the revolutionary war. Edmund, son of John,[3] was aide-de camp to Gen. Washington, governor of Virginia, attorney-general, secretary of state of the U. S., &c. &c.

(6) Henry[2] died unmarried.

(7) Edward,[2] a captain in the British navy.

(8) Mary,[2] married Capt. John Stith. Their child William was rector of Henrico parish, president of William and Mary College, and historian of Virginia.

(9) Elizabeth,[2] married Richard Bland (see *Note A*).

The above is but an outline of this family. All the Randolphs of Virginia are descended from William.[1]

Bolling (Note C).

1. Robert[1] Bolling married: (1) Jane Rolfe, granddaughter of Pocahontas. (2)—Stith. By his first wife he had:—

John, who married Miss Kennon, and their daughter Jane married Richard Randolph, 4th son of William, and became the mother of John Randolph, first husband of Frances Bland, and grandmother of John Randolph of Roanoke.

By his second wife, Miss Stith, he had:

Drury, whose daughter Frances married Theodoric Bland, and their daughter Frances married (2) St. George Tucker, and was the mother of Nathaniel Beverly Tucker, who married a sister of Col. T. H. Ellis.

The line of John Randolph, from Pocahontas, runs thus: Pocahontas,[1] Thomas Rolfe,[2] Jane (Rolfe) Bolling,[3] John Bolling,[4] Jane Bolling,[5] John Randolph,[6] John Randolph.[7]

My work puts on the features of magnitude—at least more so than I intended it should. I have noticed engraving, &c., in which seals are included—thank you for the hint—if I can but once get thro' with the first object,—printing—I can better determine, how far I can proceed with the arts that were its accompaniments.

"The Essex Journal and Merimack Packet" which you mention, was introduced at Newburyport by myself. I set up a press there in 1773.

I return Bishop Madison's Letter, with thanks for the opportunity of perusing it. Y^r obliged friend,

Rev. M^r. Bentley. I. Thomas.

Mr. Hening (in his letter to Judge Tucker) mentions a *second* edition of the Laws of Virginia, printed in 1728, as "a species of typographical artifice." He supposes it the *same* Edition as was printed in London 1682 [1722? Ed.]. It may be the case, but there was a press, that printed for government, at Williamsburg, in 1727.

Judge Tucker to Rev. Dr. Bentley.

Reverend Sir, *Warminster, Virginia, August* 22, 1810.

I do myself the pleasure to subjoin the copy of a Letter which I received from M^r. Hening, a few days before I left home, on the subject of the prohibition of printing in Virginia in the earlier period of the regal Government here. I am very respectfully,

To the reverend Sir,

M^r. Bentley, Salem, Your most obed^t Servt,

Massachusetts. St. G. Tucker.

[Copy.]

Dear Sir, *Richmond*, 21 *July*, 1810.

For several days past I have been engaged in examining the ancient M:S:S: in my possession, with a view to extract from them such documents as tend to elucidate the history of the period embraced by the 2^d: vol: of the Statutes at large. In my researches I have discovered a most important fact, relating to the introduction of printing into this Country. As this is a subject on which you consulted me last spring, &. neither M^r. Jefferson nor myself could give any information, I enclose you a literal transcript from the M:S: that you may communicate it to your friend in Massachusetts.

"February 21st, 1682–3.

"John Buckner called before the Ld Culpeper and his Council for printing the Laws of 1680, without his Excellency's licence;—and he & the printer ordered to enter into Bond in £100, not to print any thing hereafter, until his Majesty's pleasure shall be known." [From a M:S: furnished to the Editor by Thomas Jefferson, late pres^t of the U. S. and purchased by him of the Executor of Richard Bland, dece'd. See page 498., Stat: at Large.]

This paper establishes two important facts, hitherto unknown, or at least, only handed down by tradition; 1st, that there was a printer in Virginia, so early as 1682–3. and 2dly, That he was prohibited from printing *any thing*, till the King's pleasure should be known. It is probable that the King's pleasure was not very early signified, as the first evidence of any printing afterwards, is to be found in the revisal of 1733, which, to the disgrace of our printers, is much better executed than any subsequent revisal. I am, &c.

Directed to [Signed] Wm. W. Hening.

St. George Tucker, Williamsburg."

THE BROMFIELD FAMILY.

[Communicated by Prof. Daniel Denison Slade, M.D.]

Continued from vol. xxv. page 335.

The children of Edward and Abigail Bromfield were :—

(1) Edward, who was born in Boston, Jan. 30, 1723.

This son, from his excellent character and disposition, gave great promise of future distinction. Unfortunately for the world, his life was short. The following account of him was written by Rev. Thomas Prince, and appeared in the *American Magazine* for December, 1746.

. . . . . "He was the eldest son of Mr. Edward Bromfield, merchant of this town—was born in 1723, entered Harvard College 1738, took his first degree in 1742, his second in 1745, and died at his father's house Aug. 18, last, to the deep reluctance of all who knew him. From his childhood, he was thoughtful, calm, easy, modest, of tender affections, dutiful to his superiours, and kind to all about him. As he grew up these agreeable qualities ripened in him, and he appeared very ingenious, observant, curious, penetrating, especially in the works of Nature, in mechanical contrivances, and manual operations, which increased upon his studying the mathematical sciences, as also in searching into the truths of Divine Revelation, and into the nature of genuine experimental piety.

"His Genius first appeared in the accurate use of his Pen, drawing natural landscapes and images of men and other animals, &c., making himself a master of the famous *Weston's* short hand in such perfection as he was able to take down every word of the Professor's lectures in the college hall, sermons in the pulpit, and testimonies, pleas, &c. in courts of judicature.

"As he grew in years with a clear, sedate, unprejudiced and most easy way of thinking, he greatly improved in knowledge, and therewith a most comely sweetness, prudence, tenderness and modesty graced all his conversation and improvements in the eyes of all about him. As monuments of his extraordinary industry and ingenuity, in two or three minutes view I see he has left in his study (1) maps of the earth in its various projection, drawn with his pen in a most accurate manner, finer than I have ever seen the like from plates of copper. (2) A number of curious dials, made with his own hands, one of which is a triangular Octodecimal, having about its centre eighteen triangular planes, with their hour lines and styles standing on a pedestal though unfinished. (3) A number of optical and other mechanical instruments of his own inventing and making, the designs and uses of which are not yet known. (4) A considerable number of manuscripts of his own writing, containing extracts out of various authors, with his own pious meditations, and self-reflections, though almost all in short hand, with many characters of his own devising and hard to be deciphered. (5) As he was well skilled in music, he for exercise and recreation, with his own hands has made a most accurate organ with two rows of keys and many hundred pipes, his intention being *twelve hundred*, but died before he completed it. The workmanship of the keys and pipes, surprisingly nice and curious, exceeded any thing of the kind, that ever came from England, which he designed not merely to refresh his spirits, but with the harmony to mix, enliven and regulate his vocal and delightful songs to his Great Creator, Preserver, Benefactor and Redeemer. He thought the author of Nature and Musick, does by his early choristers of the air with which the day spring rises, teach us to awake with them, and begin our morning exercise with grateful hymns of joy and praises to him. And what is surprising was that he had but a few times looked into the inside work of two or three organs which came from *England*. (6) But what I would chiefly write of is—his clear knowledge of the properties of light, his vast improvements in making microscopes most accurately, grinding the finest glasses, and thereby attaining to such wondrous views of the inside frames and works of nature as I am apt to think that some of them at least have never appeared to mortal eye before. He carried his art and the perfection of his instruments to such a degree as to make a great number of surprising discoveries of the various shapes and clusters contained in a variety of exceedingly minute particles of vegetables, insects, &c., as also of the yet smaller clusters which composed the particles of those clusters, &c., that he seemed to be making haste to the sight of the *Minima Naturalia*, or the very minutest and original atoms of material substances. In short he could meet with no curious piece of mechanism, but he could readily see its deficiencies, make one like it, and happily improve. At one time he told me it seemed as if we might magnify almost unboundedly, or as far as the rays of light preserved their properties and could be visible—at another time, that he saw a way of bringing sun-beams in such a manner and number into a room in the coldest day of winter, as to make it as warm as he pleased without any other medium. I earnestly urged him to write down, delineate and publish his discoveries, for the instruction of men and the glory of God, but his excessive modesty hindered him, and now they are gone without recovery."

An excellent portrait of this young man, probably by Smibert, is still preserved and is now in the possession of Mrs. M. Bromfield Blanchard, of Harvard, Mass. There are also extant several of his drawings executed with the pen.

(2) Abigail, born Jan. 9, 1726; married June 13, 1744, Hon. William Phillips, the 3d son of Rev. Samuel Phillips, settled at Andover, and a descendant of Rev. George Phillips who came out with Gov. Winthrop in 1630, settled at Watertown, and died there July, 1644. Mrs. Phillips died in 1775. Their children were:—1. Abigail, married Josiah Quincy, Jr., and left one child, Hon. Josiah Quincy, mayor of Boston and president of Harvard University. 2. Hannah, married Samuel Shaw, Esq., and died at Dedham, Jan. 24, 1833. 3. Sarah, married Capt. Edward Dowse, and died at Dedham, 1839. 4. William, for many years lieut.-governor of Massachusetts, married Sept. 13, 1774, Miriam, daughter of Hon. Jonathan Mason, and died May 25, 1827.[1]

(3) Henry, born in Boston, Nov. 12, 1727. Of his boyhood and youth we know nothing beyond the fact that he was fitted for mercantile life, in which he was for many years engaged in his native city, and afterwards in London, in connection with his brother Thomas. He formed an early attachment for Margaret, the daughter of Thomas Fayerweather, Esq., of Boston, and to this lady he was married Sept. 17, 1749. During the year following his marriage, Mr. Bromfield went to England, but returned to Boston after a few months absence. In this city were born to him:—1. Margaret, born Oct. 5, 1750, died 1765. 2. Henry, born Dec. 24, 1751, died in Cheltenham, England, Feb. 5, 1837. 3. Abigail, born April 11, 1753, married D. D. Rogers, 1781, died Oct., 1791. 4. Sarah, born May 1, 1757,

[1] Bridgman's *Memorials of the Dead*—King's Chapel Burying-ground.

married 1786, Dr. E. Pearson, died Feb. 12, 1831. 5. Edward, born Feb. 1, 1760, died in infancy.

Mrs. Bromfield died of small pox, while on a journey, in Brookfield, Mass., and was buried there. The papers of the day thus noticed her death:

"On the 3d instant died at *Brookfield* of the Small Pox, in the 30th Year of her age, Mrs. MARGARET BROMFIELD of this Town—She was riding for her Health, and on her Return home, when she was seized with that distemper, so often fatal in what is called the Natural Way, which at once destroy'd an engaging Form, and cut short a valuable Life.

"The external Advantage of her Person was accompanied with a Sweetness of Temper, and an Assemblage of Virtues, that form'd a distinguish'd and very amiable Character; and all who knew her, partake in the deep Regret which the Loss of this Lady has occasioned to her Family and nearest Friends.

"The Serenity with which she met the Approach of Death, tho' attended with Circumstances peculiarly affecting, was derived from that Piety which she early began to cultivate, and of which she was a fair Example; and the Prospects it afforded her in her last Moments, reconciled her to the Dissolution of every tender Engagement in Life."

The following is upon her grave-stone:—"Here lie deposited, in hope of rising to a life immortal, the remains of Margaret, the amiable and virtuous consort of Mr. Henry Bromfield, mercht. in Boston. Born March 19, 1732. She died in this town of the small pox."

A portrait of this lady is now in the possession of her granddaughter, Mrs. Blanchard, of Harvard.

Mr. Bromfield married Sept. 25, 1762, a second wife, Hannah Clarke, eldest daughter of Richard Clarke, Esq., of Boston, born Feb. 27, 1724; died Aug., 1785.

Their only child Elizabeth was born Aug. 19, 1763, married D. D. Rogers, Esq., 1776, and died May 5, 1833, having had the following children: 1. Elizabeth, married J. T. Slade. 2. John. 3. Henry. 4. Hannah, married W. P. Mason, Esq.

The political dissensions which were now agitating the country, and the consequent embarrassments in mercantile affairs, were undoubtedly the chief motives for inducing Mr. Bromfield to seek rural retirement. In selecting the village of Harvard for his future residence, he was probably influenced by the great beauty of its situation, as well as by the peculiar excellence of the mansion,[1] which he purchased April 1, 1765.

The following is an extract of a letter from his brother Thomas Bromfield:

"DEAR BROTHER, "*London*, 2 *Nov.* 1766.

* * * * "I take notice y^{t} you are a move^{g} your things into the country wth a design to move there yourself—I wish you may find

[1] This old mansion, so long the abode of refinement and hospitality, was an object of interest to every one who visited the village of Harvard. Its situation amidst avenues of lofty elms, as well as its venerable appearance with gambrel roof and quaint chimneys, were suggestive of true home comforts, suggestions which few modern structures can offer. It was erected in 1733, by the first minister of the town, Rev. John Secombe. Tradition says that his father-in-law, Rev. Will. Williams, of Weston, Mass., offered to furnish as large a house as he would build. Mr. Secombe came from Medford, and was the author of a witty poem entitled "Father Abbey's Will," recently republished by Mr. Sibley, the worthy librarian of Harvard University. He left Harvard in 1757. Mr. Bromfield occupied the mansion more than forty years. At his death it passed successively into the possession of his son-in-law, Dr. Pearson; his granddaughter, Mrs. Blanchard, and his grandson, Henry B. Pearson. After battling the storms and tempests of a century and a quarter, it fell a victim to fire, Aug. 5, 1854—and its ruins are still the object of melancholy interest to many who have passed days of happiness beneath its shelter.

it agreeable live^{g} there, but I doubt it much. I believe its best to try, & then if you dont find it to be agreeable, pluck up stakes & come over here. As to sister's being any hindrance I believe on ye contrary that before she has winter'd and summer'd Harvard she will be willing to go almost any where rather than remain there, but its possible I may be out in my judgment wth regard to that matter.

"You'l please to give my kind love & regards to her & tell her y^{t} in my opinion, England is far preferable to Harvard, & y^{t} she will hear from her friends almost as often."

From the preceding letter, and from one to his father-in-law, Richard Clarke, as well as from certain memoranda in my possession, we learn that Mr. Bromfield moved with his family to Harvard in 1766—spending the winter of 1767 there, altho' he did not permanently reside in the place until ten years later. During this interval he visited England at least twice, once accompanied by his son Henry. His correspondence with members of the family on both sides of the ocean is interesting, relating as it does to the stirring events of the day. Moving to Harvard in March, 1777, the change from the society of friends and relatives to such utter seclusion must have been great indeed. The concluding lines of a letter from his son then in Philadelphia, truthfully foreshadow the life and closing days of the good man, the last as yet far distant. "I had almost forgot that by this time you are retired to the peaceful abodes of Harvard, and instead of the perplexing arrangement of figures and more anxious dependence on floating treasures are now agreeably employed in assigning to each plant its station, and possess present joy in the bud while contemplating the sure prospect of happiness in plenty. May the tranquil scenes which now surround you be an exact emblem of your future days, produced in the summer of life; may you reap largely of the fruits of virtue in its decline to refresh and delight you in the frigid season of hoary age, and be hereafter restored to fresh vigor and glory in an eternal Spring."

The life pursued by Mr. Bromfield at Harvard, was an uneventful one, but interesting to us in every particular, as showing the occupations of a country gentleman in New-England during the last century. In 1776, he had been appointed justice of the peace, an office which he held at intervals for many years. He busied himself in the affairs of his farm, and from an allusion in a letter to his fall from a horse, he undoubtedly indulged himself in the healthful exercise of the saddle. The loss of his wife in 1785—a severe trial at any time—was the more so in his isolated situation, in the midst of a New-England winter. Under date of Dec. 29, 1785, he writes to his brother Thomas—"I am now solus here, except a negro man."[1] The character of Mrs. Bromfield endeared her to every one about her. In a journal of Aug. 22, 1785, appeared the following notice:

"On the 17th instant died, at Harvard, in the County of Worcester, Mrs.

[1] This was honest, faithful Othello. Every one, man, woman and child in Harvard, and I may say the surrounding country, knew this excellent and devoted servant. Born a slave, he was in the employ of Mr. Bromfield for many years. Several anecdotes are told of his eccentricities, and of the entire dependence that the master had upon his servant. He died about seven years before Mr. Bromfield. Buried in an obscure corner of the grave-yard, his resting-place was neglected, and almost unknown until marked by a neat stone, erected by the late Henry B. Pearson, Esq., with the following inscription upon it:

OTHELLO,
The faithful friend of
Henry Bromfield.
Came from Africa
About 1760—Died 1813,
Aged about 72.

Hannah Bromfield, consort of *Henry Bromfield*, Esq; of that place:—A Lady whose virtues and accomplishments rendered her an ornament to human nature, and a blessing to her family and friends; uniform in her endeavours to alleviate the distresses, and heighten the enjoyments of life, she was equally amiable and beneficent in every situation; and left the world with serenity, in the joyful hope of that immortal felicity, for which afflictions like those her decease occasions, had a happy tendency to prepare her."

In a letter to his son Henry, Feb. 4, 1791, Mr. Bromfield allows us a peep into his domestic life. He writes in the depth of winter—his daughter Elizabeth and friends have just made him a visit of four days, and a great treat this must have been to him in his solitude. "It was a high regale to me." He speaks of the neighboring clergy as his friends. They were so, and in them he found almost the only ones with whom he could sympathise. They always maintained the highest regard for him throughout his long life.

"If the sleighing shall break up soon, I shall have a hopeful prospect for three months to come." Whoever has passed a winter and the early spring in one of our country towns, must well know the condition of our roads at that season of the year. Bad enough at the present day with all our improvements in road making, what must they have been eighty years ago! With scarcely any books, except a few standard authors; no news, except that brought by the weekly newspapers, which in all probability came very irregularly during the winter season, owing to the imperfect mail arrangements and the great distance of the post office (this being in a neighboring town), with only occasional letters from dear relatives and friends—no wonder Mr. Bromfield says, "I am thinking to turn mechanic, and add some conveniences to my outbuilding." During the months of summer he could find abundant and delightful occupation in his garden and fields—and to this he must have looked forward during the inclement season, with much the same feeling as does the captive to his day of deliverance. His daughter, Mrs. Abigail Rogers, had returned from her tour in Europe somewhat improved in health; but was at this time far distant in Virginia.

Under date of Feb. 9, he adds a few lines to the same letter. How vividly from his description can we picture to ourselves the old gentleman sitting by his generous wood fire, all alone in the south-east parlor, writing to his dear son, by the light of two candles, in their silver candlesticks, nothing to break the death-like silence within, but the ticking of the tall old clock in the corner, a souvenir which he has brought from London—and without, the raging of the elements. "Last evening it came on to rain and continued till noon this day, when it came on a tremendous Snow storm, and now (8 o'clock) blows as if all nature was coming to wreck." How the old trees bent beneath the blasts, and how the wintry winds howled around the old mansion that night! No matter, he regards the storm as a friend, for he has formed his plans for "slipping down" to the city upon *runners* to visit his dear daughter and friends—much the easiest and most expeditious way of communication for those days. Still the inclemency of the weather that day has deprived him of enjoying a dinner with the high sheriff at Lancaster, and, what would have gratified him still more, of participating in Divine Service in the afternoon, under the ministration of Dr. Parker.

In the autumn of 1791, Mr. Bromfield was again afflicted, by the death of his daughter Mrs. Abigail Rogers.

In one of the Boston papers appeared this notice of Mrs. Rogers:—"Died in town, on Friday evening, deeply lamented by her acquaintance, Mrs. Abigail Rogers, the amiable consort of Mr. D. D. Rogers, merchant, and daughter of Henry Bromfield, Esq. The exemplary patience, resignation and cheerfulness with which she supported a long and very painful illness, demonstrate the importance even to the present life, of that exalted piety, which is founded in a firm belief of the truths of christianity."

A portrait of this lady, in the possession of H. B. Rogers, Esq., is one of Copley's best efforts.

His son Henry, in a letter to his father from London, Oct. 30, 1802, says: "I participate in the pleasure, with which you relate the circumstances of your farm—a good crop well got in, the finest firuits of the neighbourhood, the cellar stored with vegetables and the barn filled with hay imply an abundance for man and beast, which may well communicate gladness to the heart and praise to that beneficence from whence they proceed. Such circumstances with such sensibilities, combined with the hope of better things to come, is an allotment truly enviable."

Again, in letters written during the year 1813, he says: "Nov. 5.—The weather lately has been very unpleasant for the ingathering, which should be dry for housing of roots, &c. I am now housing mine, and last evening husked my corn and now making my cyder." Nov. 17, he says: in a letter to his daughter, Mrs. Rogers—hoping to have seen her at Harvard during the fine weather: "The reverse of weather has taken place, by a severe storm of snow. I have to fear a solitary winter.—I have had thoughts of keeping Thanksgiving with you, but on reflection find I am not provided with a comfortable surtout for severe cold—mine is too thin and old to appear in Boston. At home and on Sundays I wear a cloak[1] over my surtout, which wont do to appear in at the great town. The fireside is most consonant to my age and my feelings, especially in severity of weather. By the late snow I have been able to get home a good pile of dry wood, cut the last season, to make us comfortable, but shall find the want of my dear children and friends to converse with. In my situation it makes it very dull."

Mr. Bromfield had little or no connection with politics, or even with the village affairs. He led a life, as we have seen, of almost complete retirement, after the death of his wife and the marriage of his daughters. His son had established himself in England. The neighboring clergy and the relatives and friends who came to visit him in the pleasant season, were the only means of social enjoyment. His health was usually excellent, and it was not until his last short sickness that he was confined to the chamber.—He died at Harvard, Feb. 9, 1820, at the advanced age of 92. A funeral sermon was delivered by Dr. Thayer of Lancaster, entitled "The Good Man." From this we make a few extracts:—"Such was his distrust of himself, so profound his reverence of God and so correct his ideas of the terms upon which an erring mortal may have a title to mercy, that he would have pronounced himself unworthy to be held up to the generations of men as a pattern. Cheerful, ardent, social, sympathetic and trusty, he imperceptibly won the affection, commanded the confidence and invited the familiarity of all who knew him. The intelligent and refined were his early

[1] The cloak alluded to was bright scarlet. What a pleasing picture! The old gentleman in scarlet cloak, wig and cocked hat, silk stockings with knee buckles, long staff in hand, accompanied at a respectful distance behind by his faithful negro servant, wending his way on a summer sabbath morning through the long avenue of elms to the village church.—And such was the deference paid to age, and to christian virtues, that no one left his pew until the old man had passed out. All this too at a period quite advanced into the present century. The cloak and other articles mentioned are still in good preservation.

associates. He had within his reach the means of general knowledge. He was conversant with the enlightened of his own country and of other nations. No diversity of taste or fashions in society, and no desire to rank with the unreflecting great, could change or corrupt the disposition and habits of life which happily formed him for domestic scenes. The character of his religion cannot be too highly celebrated. It was formed of such plain practical principles and maxims, as are found in the sermon of the divine Redeemer. It was a religion not of morals merely, but also of deeds. It was a religion unmixed with ostentation, arrogance, and an exclusive spirit. It was alike removed from indifference, apathy and indolence on the one hand, and from intemperate zeal, intolerance and presumptuousness on the other. Of its benign operation we had the best evidence in his temper and life.

[To be continued.]

CHRISTOPHER KILBY, OF BOSTON.

[Communicated by CHARLES W. TUTTLE, Esq.]

THE capacity, public services, wealth and liberality of Christopher Kilby, place him among the worthies of Boston of the last century. While he lived abroad most of his days and died there, and while most of his living posterity are now in England and Scotland, he was, nevertheless, a son of Boston, began his public life here, remembered his native town in its affliction, bequeathed his name to one of its most public streets, and a few of his posterity still live here. Although his name appears frequently in the records of his time, is mentioned by Hutchinson, Drake, and other historians, and is memorably associated with Boston, but little is publicly known of his career and his connections. His personal history derives fresh interest from the fact that his great-granddaughter was the first wife of the seventh Duke of Argyll, the grandfather of the Marquess of Lorne, who recently married Her Royal Highness, the Princess Louise, of England.

Christopher Kilby was the son of John and Rebecca (Simpkins) Kilby, of Boston. He was born May 25, 1705, and bred to commercial pursuits. In 1726, he became a partner in business with the Hon. William Clark,[1] a distinguished merchant of Boston, whose eldest daughter he married the same year. Mr. Clark carried on an extensive commercial trade with England and the West Indies; and Kilby was several times in those countries, on business of the firm, during the continuance of the partnership, which terminated on his return from England in 1735. In this period of nine years he passed three abroad in commercial undertakings. He now formed a partnership with his brother-in-law, Mr. Clark's youngest son, Benjamin, and continued in the same business[2] until he went to England in 1739.

[1] The Hon. William Clark was brother of the Hon. John Clark, of Boston, for many years speaker of the house of representatives, and grandson of Dr. John Clark, an eminent physician, whose portrait is in the *Massachusetts Hist. Society Collections.* Dr. Clark married Martha, sister to Sir Richard Saltonstall, one of the Massachusetts Bay Company. Mr. Clark was a member of the house and provincial council. He was a merchant, and had a large estate. He died in 1742, leaving widow, Sarah, two sons, and two married daughters, Mr. Kilby's wife being dead some years before.—See *Descendants of Hugh Clark,* and *Suffolk Probate Records.*

"Last Saturday died here the Honorable William Clark, Esq., who has been one of the most considerable Merchants in this Town, and has formerly served as a Representative for the Town in the General Court, and was for some years one of the Members of his Majesty's Council."—*The Boston Weekly News Letter,* July, 1742.

[2] Kilby's *Letters.*

In May, 1739, he was chosen representative to the general court from Boston, his colleagues being Thomas Cushing, Jr., Edward Bromfield, and James Allen. The session of the court began near the end of May, and continued, with several intermediate adjournments, to the end of the year, the domestic affairs of the province being in a troubled state. Mr. Kilby served on all the important committees of the house, and took an active part in the business of the session. Important questions relative to the issue of paper money and to the boundaries of the province were discussed and acted upon. Gov. Belcher had received instructions from the king to limit the issue of bills of credit to a period not exceeding in duration those current at the time of a new issue, and the consequence was that all became payable in 1741. The governor declined to recede from his instructions, although the public distress was great. The last of September the house resolved to send a special "agent to appear at the court of Great Britain, to represent to his majesty the great difficulties and distress the people of this province labor under by reason of thus being prevented from raising the necessary supply to support the government and the protection and defence of his majesty's subjects here." Thomas Cushing, a distinguished member of the house, and formerly its speaker, was chosen agent; and a committee of eight, Mr. Kilby being one, was appointed to draw up his instructions. On account of continued ill health, Mr. Cushing declined the office, and Mr. Kilby was, on the second of October, chosen in his place.[1]

The province had always selected its ablest men to act as agents, the functions of the office being of a diplomatic character, requiring ability, sagacity, prudence and a knowledge of public affairs. Mr. Kilby, then only thirty-four years of age, accepted the appointment, and Capt. Nathaniel Cunningham, an eminent merchant of Boston, was chosen to succeed him in the house.[2] Early in December Kilby received his instructions, and immediately sailed for England. He presented to the king in council the petition of the house, praying for a modification of the royal instructions to Belcher concerning the issue of bills of credit; but the king could not be pursuaded to make the change prayed for.[3]

In October, 1741, Francis Wilks, long a standing agent of the province in England, was dismissed, and soon after died, and Kilby was chosen in his place. About this time the province took an appeal from a decision of the commissioners respecting the boundary line between it and Rhode Island. In January, 1742, Robert Auchmuty, an eminent lawyer of Boston, and Christopher Kilby, were chosen joint agents to prosecute the appeal before the king in council. Auchmuty continued in this service till April, 1743, and Kilby did not cease his exertions in the matter of the appeal till 1746.[4]

[1] Drake's *History of Boston.* Hutchinson's *History of Massachusetts.* Journal of House of Representatives, 1739.

[2] Capt. Nathaniel Cunningham was one of the richest merchants in Boston in his day. He died in London, Sept. 7, 1748, leaving wife Susanna and children, viz.: Nathaniel, who married Sarah Kilby; Ruth, who married James Otis, the orator and statesman; and Sarah. His estate was valued at nearly £50,000. To each daughter he gave £10,000, and annuities for their support while minors: to Dr. Sewall's church sixty ounces of silver, to be made into a proper vessel for the service of the Holy Sacrament of the Lord's Supper, the expenses of making to be paid out of his estate: to the poor of the church £500. The rest of his large estate to his only son Nathaniel. He mentions Charles Paxton, Esq., as his brother-in law. Mr. Cunningham was one of the proprictors of the lands in the west parish of Leicester, where he built several fine houses. He gave the town, now Spencer, land for a meeting-house and training field.—See *Hist. of Spencer* and *Suffolk Probate Records.*

[3] Journal House of Representatives. Hutchinson's *Hist. of Mass. Mass. Archives.*

[4] Journal House of Representatives. Arnold's *History of Rhode Island. Mass. Archives.*

The removal of Gov. Belcher was one of the questions which agitated the people here, and in New-Hampshire, when Kilby went to England. He was one of the strong party opposed to Belcher, and he used his influence to displace him, and to secure the office for Shirley, who was appointed governor in 1741.[1]

Mr. Kilby continued to act as standing agent of the province till the middle of November, 1748, performing many important services, among which may be mentioned the procuring from the British government reimbursement to the province for expenses in the famous Pepperell expedition to Louisburg in 1745. William Bollan, a lawyer of Boston, son-in-law of Gov. Shirley, was chosen joint agent with Kilby to prosecute this claim for expenses in "taking and securing the island of Cape Breton and its dependencies." In the prosecution of this claim Kilby labored with untiring industry and energy. His official and private letters show this; and nothing but ignorance or jealousy has kept this fact from being more publicly known. In a letter to Secretary Willard, dated March 10, 1747, he says: "No other affair I am concerned in but what is made subservient to this important and most necessary point of reimbursing the province and relieving it from distress which is not possible to be endured long, for I have an unshaken and immovable zeal for the welfare of my country." He writes to the speaker of the house from Portsmouth, England, where he then was in conference with Admiral Sir Peter Warren, under date of April 6, 1748, that the house of commons passed a bill on the 4th inst., "granting to Massachusetts £183,649 02 7½, the time and manner of payment being left entirely with the treasury."[2]

The Duke of Newcastle promised the governorship of New-Jersey to Kilby, on the death of Morris; but the friends of Belcher persuaded the duke to change his purpose at the last moment, and Belcher got the appointment. While agent of Massachusetts he was member of the firm of Sedgwick, Kilby and Barnard, of London. On the death of Sedgwick, the name was Kilby, Barnard and Parker. The business of the firm was extensive, especially with the American colonies.[3]

In 1755, Boston having some grievances of its own, appointed Kilby its standing agent at the court of Great Britain. He accepted the appointment, and performed the duties required of him to the entire satisfaction of his native town.[4]

In May, 1756, England formally declared war with France. John Campbell, fourth Earl of Loudoun, was appointed commander-in-chief of the king's forces in North America, and governor of Virginia. Kilby was appointed "agent-victualler of the army" under the earl, and sailed from Portsmouth, May 20, for New-York, arriving there about the middle of July. The Nightingale man-of-war, having the earl and his staff, and also Thomas Pownall, soon after appointed governor of Massachusetts, on board, sailed from the same port and arrived at New-York a few days later than Kilby. The organization of the army went forward, and great preparations were made for subduing the French in Canada and elsewhere on this continent. Kilby addressed himself to the furnishing of supplies for the army.[5]

In January, 1757, the Earl of Loudoun and many of his officers came to

1 Hutchinson's *History*. Kilby's *Letters*.
2 *Mass. Archives*. Kilby's *Letters*.
3 Kilby's *Correspondence*.
4 Drake's *History of Boston*. *Boston Gazette*.
5 *Boston Gazette*, July and August, 1756. *Doc. History of New-York*.

Boston to meet the commissioners of the several provinces, to consult about raising an army, and other matters, for the campaign of that year. The *Boston Gazette* of January 24, 1757, after speaking of the arrival of the earl in Boston, adds, "At the same time, and in company with the Earl of Loudon, arrived Christopher Kilby, Esq., who went from hence about 17 years past as Agent for this Province at the Court of Great Britain: the warm affection he has discovered for his countrymen, and the signal services he has rendered this Province during that space, has greatly endeared him to us. The Selectmen of the Town waited upon him as Standing Agent of the Town with their congratulations and Thanks for the Favors he has from Time to Time shown us. A Committee of the General Court has invited him to Dine at Concert Hall this Day—and his townsmen rejoice at the opportunity they now have of testifying the deserved esteem they have for him. With Pleasure we can acquaint the Publick that he is in a good measure recovered from the illness which attended him this Fall while at Albany."

Kilby probably remained in this country till the peace of 1763. He was in New-York when the terrible fire occurred in Boston, in March, 1760, destroying many dwelling-houses and causing much distress. Upon hearing of this calamity Kilby sent two hundred pounds sterling to the sufferers, a sum that was regarded as enormous at the time. The district burnt over embraced both sides of "Mackerill Lane," so called. When this part of the town was rebuilt, and the lane widened and extended, it was called "Kilby Street," by common consent, in compliment to Mr. Kilby for his generous donation, and for his zeal for the interests of his native town.[1]

On his return to England he purchased a large estate in the parish of Dorking, county Surrey, where he "built a curious edifice called the priory, and several ornamental seats." Here he lived many years prior to his death, which took place in October, 1771. He left an immense estate, which he distributed among his seven grandchildren, after providing for his wife.[2]

Mr. Kilby was twice married. His first wife was Sarah, eldest daughter of the Hon. William Clark, whom he married Aug. 18, 1726. Mrs. Kilby died April 12, 1739, about six months before her husband was sent, as agent, to England, leaving two young daughters, Sarah and Catherine.[3] A son William died young. In 1742, his father-in-law Clark died, intestate, leaving a large estate. Kilby being in England, his warm personal friend, Thomas Hancock, an eminent merchant, and uncle to Governor John Hancock, was appointed guardian of Sarah and Catherine Kilby, and secured for them their share of their grandfather Clark's estate. Five years later they were sent to England, their father receiving them at Portsmouth. Catherine appears to have died soon after her arrival.

Mr. Kilby was now married again, but had no other children. His second wife's name was Martha, and she survived him. Her family name is not known here. On Sarah Kilby, his surviving daughter, he bestowed every advantage that wealth could command. She received the best education England could afford; and in 1753, was betrothed to Nathaniel, only son of Capt. Nathaniel Cunningham, a merchant of the greatest wealth of any in Boston. His daughter Ruth married the celebrated James Otis, patriot

[1] *Boston Post Boy*, April 7, 1760. Drake's *History of Boston*. Family tradition.

[2] Allen's *History of Surrey and Sussex*, vol. ii. Whitmore's *Heraldic Journal*.

[3] "Last week dy'd suddenly Mrs. Kilby, Wife of Mr. Christopher Kilby of this Town, Merchant, and Daughter to the Hon. William Clark, Esq."—*Boston Weekly News Letter*, April 17, 1739.

and orator. Sarah Kilby returned to this country just before her marriage, which took place June 20, 1754. Mr. Cunningham settled in the fine mansion-house of his father, now deceased, situated on an eminence in Cambridge, now Brighton. In Price's view of Boston, taken in 1743, dedicated to Peter Faneuil, this house is a conspicuous object, and designated by name, being the finest mansion-house in the vicinity of Boston. Nathaniel Cunningham died near the end of the year 1756, leaving two infant children, Susanna and Sarah.

When the Earl of Loudoun visited Boston, a few months after this event, there came with him his aide-de-camp, Capt. Gilbert McAdam, as well as Kilby, who introduced his widowed daughter to Capt. McAdam. He was of an ancient Ayrshire family, and uncle to John Loudoun McAdam, the inventor of Macadamized roads. In September, 1757, Capt. McAdam married the widow Sarah Cunningham, and took her, and her two children, to New-York, the principal head quarters of the army. At the close of the war, possibly before, Capt. McAdam returned to Ayrshire with his family.[1]

Susanna and Sarah Cunningham were the special objects of Kilby's bounty and solicitude. They were sent to France, and there educated with care. Their domestic lives, and the lives of their descendants, are invested with an air of romance. Susanna was thrice married. Her first husband was James Dalrymple[2] of Orangefield, Ayrshire, the friend and patron of Robert Burns. By this marriage she had one son, Charles Dalrymple, an officer of the British army. Through subsequent marriages, first with John Henry Mills and afterwards with William Cunningham, both of Scotland, she is now represented, in this country, by her grandchildren, Mrs. Frances Maria Spofford, wife of the venerable Dr. Richard S. Spofford, of Newburyport, Mrs. Susanna Varnum Mears, of Boston, and Capt. Thomas Cunningham, of Somerville. Her sister, Sarah Cunningham, married William Campbell, of Ayrshire, and had two daughters, the eldest of whom, Elizabeth, married the seventh Duke of Argyll, grandfather of the present Marquess of Lorne.[3]

The following is a copy of an original letter from Christopher Kilby to Thomas Hancock, before referred to.

DEAR HANCOCK, *Spring Garden*, 18 *July*, 1746.

I am greatly oblig'd for the dispatch in Lumber and Bricks to Newfoundland, and for your advice of the vessels arrival there. The Louisburg affair is not in the deplorable case you have imagined. Capt. Bastide[4] is Engineer, and the thing lays with him and his officers; and I think you cannot fail of a seasonable part if any advantage is to be had; but these officers arriving and a great sum of Sterling money to be spent amongst you I should think Exchange must be constantly lowering till this service is over, and however that may be you'll certainly not want as much of their money as I should think you would be willing to take. I have mention-

[1] Kilby's *Letters*. Family papers.

[2] In one of Burns's letters, he writes thus, of Dalrymple: "I have met in Mr. Dalrymple, of Orangefield, what Solomon emphatically calls, 'a friend that sticketh closer than a brother.'"

[3] Burke's *Peerage and Landed Gentry*.

[4] John Henry Bastide, royal engineer for Nova-Scotia. In April, 1745, Massachusetts granted him £140 for his services in the repairs of the forts in this province. He was made director of engineers in 1748, and afterward raised to the rank of major-general.

To the grandchildren of Susanna Cunningham, above named, I am indebted for permission to examine letters and family papers in their possession relating to the subject of this memoir. I am also indebted to Charles L. Hancock, Esq., for information contained in letters of Kilby and others, in his possession.

ed you to most of the Staff Officers on this Expedition.[1] Mr. Abercrombie,[2] who is Muster Master General, having directions to you in his Pocket-book, and if it should be necessary will introduce you to the General,[3] to whom indeed you'll not need it, but apply to him as easy as possible with the use of my name, and I hope he will receive you as my best Friend. We have been often together since his return to Town, and I believe he has a good opinion of my services in recovering the Expedition after it was laid aside.

Pray do him all the service you can, and if you find it not inconvenient offer him a lodging in your house for a night or two, till he can be otherwise accommodated. His Power is great and may be useful to you, he is honest open and undissembling; you'll like him very well on increasing your acquaintance.

Belcher[4] has got the Government of the Jerseys; it was done by Duke of Newcastle yesterday which neither Dr. Avery[5] nor I expected two days before. I have not seen the Dr. since the appointment, nor shall till his return to Town on Tuseday next. The vessel that brought the News from Boston, was several days below before her bag of Letters came up, and its said the Advice was sent in the mean time to Belcher's Friends. It's a shocking affair, and must destroy any favorable opinion entertained of the Duke of Newcastle by the People of the Colonies; and I am of opinion it will lessen Gov'r Shirley's Influence in his own and in the Neighboring Governments. There is a very worthy set of people in the Jerseys that it will most fatally prejudice. I fear they have been almost ruined by Law without a possibility of getting so far thro' it as to have an appeal home, and I am mistaken if some of them have not defended their possessions by fire and sword; they will be in fine hands under Belcher, who is to be the Tool of the Quakers, as they are one would imagine of Satan. Some time past this seemed to be allotted for me[6] by the desire of the Gentlemen who came from thence who had engaged Dr. Avery's Interest to perfect it, and it was mentioned to, and approved of [by] the Duke of Newcastle. The vacancy has at last happened when it was impossible for me to accept it, and after consulting the Doctor we had laid a Plan for keeping the appointment off till we could hear from our Friends, which neither he nor I have done by the ships that bring the News of Morris's[7] death, nor had many months before. But the Duke[8] differing in this Instance from every other circumstance of this sort during his Administration, has fix't the thing in the greatest hurry (on some other motive certainly, than the Interest of the Quakers). As the thing concerns myself I am in no pain not having been defeated; but as it may be hurtful to the honest people who are to fall under his Government and will stagger and discountenance the very best people in our own and the neighboring Colonies, it gives me much concern. This Letter must be broke off here to go to Portsmouth where the Ships tarry, and [if] anything occurs I shall back it by another, being

Dear Sir,

Your most sincere Friend and obliged humble Servant,

CHRIS. KILBY.

To
Mr. Thomas Hancock,
Merchant in Boston.

[1] This expedition was designed to proceed against Canada. A squadron under Admiral Warren was to go to Quebec by way of the St. Lawrence, and a land force to Montreal by way of Albany under the command of Gen. St. Clair. The English troops collected at Portsmouth, Eng., and sailed several times, but returned. They finally sailed for France, and the Canada expedition was abandoned. Kilby's letter indicates that they were to come to Boston; at least the principal officers.

[2] Gen. James Abercrombie; he was next in command to the Earl of Loudoun in 1756; he commanded the English forces sent against Ticonderoga in 1758.

[3] Lieut. Gen. James St. Clair.

[4] Jonathan Belcher, provincial governor of Massachusetts from 1730 to 1741.

[5] Dr. Benjamin Avery, a man of the greatest influence at court about this time.

[6] Provincial governor of New-Jersey. Kilby's aspirations were not behind those of other Massachusetts agents, who always aspired for royal appointments as soon as they got fairly Anglicized.

[7] Lewis Morris, ancestor of a very distinguished family, was chief-justice of New-York, and afterward governor of New-Jersey. He died May 21, 1746.

[8] Duke of Newcastle, minister of British America, from 1724 to 1748. "Newcastle was of so fickle a head, and so treacherous a heart that Walpole called his name 'Perfidy.'" —Bancroft's *History*.

I suppose This was penn'd by Eld. Green sup. 2/5.

(201)

The Names of the Children that have bin Baptised in the Church in Charltowne Begining at the ninth of January A thousand six hundred and thirty two.

11 mo: day	9	John James the son of Thomas James: and of Elizabeth his wife was babtised.
12: mo: day	23	Joseph Stower: the son of Nicholas Stower: and of Amy his wife: was babtised.
1633		1633.
1: mo: day	16	John Molton: the son of Thomas Molton: and of Jane his wife: was babtised.
3: mo: day	25	Thomas Mousall the son of Ralph Mousall: and of Alice his wife: was babtised.
6: mo: day	31	Loyis whitehand: the daughter of Georg whitehand and of Alice his wife: was babtised.
7: mo: day	14	James Pemberton the son of James Pemperton and of Alice his wife: was babtised.
8: mo: day	2	Mary wade: the daughter of Jonathan wade: and of Susannah his wife: was babtised.
9: mo: day	9	Nathaniell Hutcheson: the son of George Hutcheson: and of Margerite: his wife: was babtised.
10: mo: day	22	Theophilus Richeson: the son of Ezekiell Richeson. and of Susanna his wife: was babtized.
		1634.

The names of such as were baptized in the church of christ in Charlestown: since January, 18: 166$\frac{3}{4}$ that this book came into my hand, to be kept by me, Thomas Shepard.

	166$\frac{3}{4}$	day.		
Sy:	— 12.	7.	[Anna] the daughter of mr Chickring (of Dedham church) —	Chickring.
Sh:	— 12.	14.	[Bartholomew] the son of or bro: mr Jacob Green. —	Green.
		&	[Robert] the son of mr John Long. — — —	Long.
Sy:	— 12	21.	[Samuel] the son of mr John Phillips & of or sister mrs Catharine Phillips his wife —	Phillips.
	1664.			
Sh:	— 2:	10.	[John] the son of or sister mrs Johnson, & Edward her husband.	Johnson.
Sy:	— 2:	17.	[Sarah] the daughter of or sister Lathrop: & Benjamin her husband	Lathrop.
Sy:	— 3:	1.	[Benjamin] the son of of or sister Willson: & Benjamin her husband	Willson.
Sh:	— 3:	8.	[Elisabeth] ye daughter of or sister Elisab: Edmunds & Joshua	Edmunds.
Sy:	— 3:	29.	[John] ye son of or bro: Thomas Rand — — —	Rand.
	—	&	[Thomas] the son of our sister Harris — — — —	Harris.
Sh:	— 4:	5.	[Nathaneel] ye son of or bro: Samuel Haward. — —	Haward.
Sh:	—	&	[Michael] ye son of or bro: Thomas Brigden junr — —	Brigden.
Sy:	— 6.	21.	[Susanna] ye daughter of ye Worshipfull Francis Willoughby.	Willoughby
Sy:	— 7.	4.	[Elisabeth] ye daughter of or bro: William Crouch.	Crouch

— Page 223 (*concluded from vol. xxv. page* 344 *in* Register.) —

Sh:	9.	18.	[Rebeckah] ye daughter of Benjamin Lathrop & [Martha his wife.	Lathrop.
Sy:	10.	9.	[Katharine] ye daughter of Eliſabeth Wyer. —	Wyer.
Sh:	10.	30.	[nathaneel] ye ſon of Thomas Brigden & his wife	Brigden.
Sh:	11.	13.	[Sarai] ye daughter of mr Joſeph Lynd, & Sarai his [wife	Lynd.
	—	&	[Henry] ye ſon of Hannah perkins.	
	—	&	[John] ye ſon of Hannah perkins. } — —	perkins.
	—	&	[Luke] the ſon of Hannah perkins.	
	—	&	[William] the ſon of — —	
	—	&	[Hannah] the daughter of — } Hannah Hurry —	Hurry.
	—	&	[Temperance] ye daughter of	
Sh:	12.	24.	[Mary] ye daughter of Daniel Edmunds — —	Edmunds.
	1667.			
Sy.	1.	17.	[Richard] } twins. ye children of bro: William	Crouch.
	—	&	[Hannah] } Crouch. — — — — — — —	
Sh:	1.	24.	[Luke] the ſon of Hannah perkins. — — —	perkins.
	—	&	[Deborah] the daughter of mr Jonathan Wade & [Deborah his wife —	Wade.
Sh:	2:	7:	[Elizabeth] the daughter of mr Jno Chickring & [Eliſabeth his wife.	Chickring.
Sh:	2.	21:	[Joanna] ye daughter of bro: Edward Wilſon & [Mary his wife.	Wilſon.
Sy:	2.	28.	[Abigail] ye daughter of or bro: mr Laurence [Hammond	Hammond.

— Page 224. —

	yeer: & moreth.	Day.	The Baptized. — — —	
	1667.			
Sh:	3.	19.	[John] the ſon of bro: Abraham Smith. — —	Smith.
Sy:	5.	21.	[Sarai] the daughter of or ſiſter Rebeckah Jenner	Jenner.
Sy:	6.	4.	[Thomas] the son of Capt: John Allen & Sarai his [wife	Allen:
	8.	27.	[John] } ye children of John Knight, & Abigail	Knight.
Sy:	—	&	[Abigail] } his wife	
	—	&	[Alice] ye daughter of or ſiſter Mary Ridgeway	Ridgeway.
Sh:	9.	3.	[John] the Son of our ſiſter Hannah Hurry. —	Hurry.
Sy:	9.	24.	[Rebekah] ye daughter of or bro: Brazier. —	Brazier.
Sh:	11.	12.	[Anne] ye daughter of or ſiſter Anne Taylor —	Taylor.
Sh:	11.	19.	[Elkanah] ye ſon of bro: Thomas Welsh — —	Welsh=
	1668.			
Sh:	1:	1:	[Deborah] ye daughter of mr Will: Foſter & Anne [his wife.	Foster:
	—	&	[Parnel] ye daughter of Mary Winſlow. — —	Winſlow:
Sy:	1.	15.	[Thomas] ye ſon of or ſiſter Mary Webb — —	Webb.
Sh:	1.	22	[Nathaneel] ye ſon of bro: William Clough —	Clough.
	—	&	[Mercy] ye daughter of bro: mr Jno Chickring	Chickring:
Sy:	1.	29.	[John] the ſon of or ſiſter Hannah Griffin —	Griffin.
	—	&	[Mary] ye daughter of mrs Martha March — —	March.
	—	&	[Thomas] } the children of or bro: Thomas White	White.
	—	&	[William] }	
	—	&	[William] ye ſon of or bro: peter Frothingham	Frothinga..
	—	&	[John] } ye children of or bro: John Lowden	Lowden.
	—	&	[Richard] }	
Sy:	2.	5.	[James] ye ſon of mr James Ruſsell, & Mabel his wife	Ruſsell.
	—	&	[Joſeph] ye ſon of mr Jacob Green & Mary his wife	Green.
	—	&	[Mary] ye daughter of or bro: Nathaneel Rand	Rand.

	yeer. & month.	Day.	{ The Baptized. — — — } — Page 225. —	
	1668.			
Sh:	2.	19.	[Robert] y^e^ ſon of bro: Tho: Rand — — —	Rand.
	3.	3.	[Thomas]. } the children of o^r^ ſiſter Sarai Smith.	Smith.
	—	&	[William]. }	
	—	&	[John] — }	
	—	&	[Anna] — } the children of o^r^ ſiſter Anna Fowl.	Fowl.
	—	&	[Eliſabeth] }	
Sy:	3.	24.	[John] the ſon of William Hilton, & Mehetabel his [wife	Hilton.
Sy:	4.	21.	[Nathaneel] ye ſon of G: Eliſabeth Wyer — —	Wyer.
	—	&	[Suſanna] ye daughter of m^rs^ Suſanna Gooſe —	Gooſe.
	—	&	[Zechariah.] }	
	—	&	[Sarai.] — }	
	—	&	[Mary.] — } y~e~ children of m^rs^ Sarai Long	Long.
	—	&	[Eliſabeth.] }	
	—	&	[Ralph.] }	
	—	&	[Mary.] } ye children of Tho: Mouſal, & Mary	Mouſal.
	—	&	[Hannah.] } [his wife	
	—	&	[Grace.] }	
			[Mary.] }	
			[Thomas.] } ye children of o^r^ ſiſter Grace Sheppy	Sheppy.
			[Sarai.] }	
Sy:	6.	2.	[Zechary] y^e^ ſon of o^r^ ſiſter Anna Fowl. — —	Fowl.
	—	&	[Andrew] y^e^ ſon of o^r^ bro: Jno Lowden junio^r^ & [Sarai his wife	Lowden.
Sh:	6.	9.	[Samuel] y^e^ ſon of o^r^ ſiſter Mary King. — —	King.
		&	[Mary] ye daughter of bro: Abraham Smith —	Smith.
Sy:	6.	16.	[Nathaneel] y^e^ ſon of bro: Nathaneel Rand —	Rand.
Sy:	6.	23:	[Eliſabeth] ye daughter of bro: Thomas Lord, & [Alice his wife.	Lord.
Sy:	6 :	30.	[Mehetabel] the daughter of bro: Jno: Call —	Call.

	yeer & moneth.	Day.	{ The Baptized. — — — } — Page 226. —	
	1668.			
Sh:	8.	18.	[James] } the children of or ſiſter m^rs^ Mary	
		&	[Hannah] } [Ridgeway	Ridgeway.
Sy:	10.	6.	[Abigail] the child of m^r^ Jn~o~ Long, & Abigail his [wife	Long:
Sy:	11.	31.	[Eleezar] the ſon of bro: Laurence Dowſe —	Dowſe.
	—	&	[Margaret] ye daughter of m^r^ Joseph Lynd —	Lynd.
Sh:	12.	21.	[William] y^e^ ſon of bro: Nathaneel Hutchinſon & [Sarai his wife.	Hutchinſon.
	—	&	[Joſeph] } (twins) ye children of Tho: Mouſal,	Mouſal.
			[Benjamin] } & Mary his wife — — — —	
	1669.			
Sh:	1.	7	[Nathan] y^e^ ſon of m^r^ Nathan Ranſford, & Mary [his wife	Ranſford.
	—	&	[John.] y^e^ ſon of ye widdow Sarai powel — —	Powel.
Sh:	1.	21.	[Samuel.] y^e^ ſon of Thomas, & Rebekah Jenner.	Jenner.
	—	&	[Eliſabeth] ye daughter of Luke, & Hannah perkins	perkins.
Sy:	2.	4.	[Matthew] y^e^ ſon of Hannah Hurry. — — —	Hurry.
Sy:	3.	2.	[John] y^e^ ſon of Litſt: Laurence Hammond. —	Hammond.
	—	&	[Perſis] ye daughter of bro: Jno. Knight & perſis [his wife.	Knight.
Sh:	3.	16.	[John] y^e^ ſon of m^r^ william Gooſe & ſuſanna his [wife	Gooſe.

— Page 226 (*concluded.*) —

Sh:	4.	6:	[prudence] ye daughter of Jonathan Wade & [Debora his wife.	Wade.
Sh:	5.	25.	[Jonathan] ye fon of Daniel Edmunds & Mary his [wife.	Edmunds.
	—	&	[John] ye fon of Grace Sheppy — — — —	Sheppy.
Sh:	6.	8.	[Ruth] ye daughter of Jofhua & Elifabeth Edmunds	Edmunds.
Sy:	6.	22.	[Jofeph] ye fon of Will: Crouch & . . . his wife	Crouch:
Sy:	7.	12.	[Samuel] ye fon of mary pettiford: bro: Baker's daughter	pettiford:
Sh:	7.	19:	[Abigail] ye daughter of Thomas Orton & his [wife.	Orton.
Sh:	8.	17.	[John] ye fon of Henry & Elifabeth Balcom —	Balcom.
Sh:	8:	31.	[Samuel] ye fon of Thomas White & Mary his wife:	White
Sh:	9:	14.	[Katharine] ye daughter of Edward Wilfon, & Mary [his wife.	Wilfon:
Sh:	9:	21.	[Mary] ye daughter of bro: Jno Cutler & his wife	Cutler.

{ The Baptized. — — — } — Page 227. —

	yeer, & moneth.			
	1669.			
Sh:	ii.	16.	[Samuel] | & [Thomas] | & [Joseph] | & [Jonathan] | & [John] | [Mary] | & [Elifabeth] | & [perfif] ye children of bro: Samuel pierce - - - | & of Mary his wife	pierce.[1]
Sh:	ii:	23.	[Mabel] ye daughter of or bro: mr James Rufsell & [Mabel his wife.	Rufsell.
Sh:	11:	30.	[Mary] ye daughter of or fifter mrs Mary Ranfford	Ranfford.
		&	[Edmund] ye fon of bro: Thomas Rand & Sarai his [wife:	Rand.
Sh:	12.	27.	[John] } ye children of [blot] peter Fowl, & Mary	Fowl.
		&	[Mary] } [his wife.	
	1670.			
Sh:	2.	3.	[Nathaneel] the fon of Nathaneel Cutler. — —	Cutler.
		&	[Sufanna] the daughter of Joseph Frost. — —	Frost.
Sh:	3.	1.	[Richard] the fon of Joseph Kettle & Hannah his [wife.	Kettle.
		&.	[Mary] ye daughter of Samuel Kettle — — —	Kettle.
Sh:	3.	29.	[Abigail] ye daughter of Samuel pierce, & Mary [his wife.	peirce.
Sh:	4.	5.	[Johathan] ye fon of Matthew Griffin, & Hannah [his wife.	Griffin.
Sh:	4.	12:	[Mary] ye daughter of John Fowl, & Anna his wife.	Fowl.
		&	[Margaret] ye daughter of Nath: Hutchinfon, & [Sarai his wife.	Hutchinfon
Sh:	4:	19.	[Abraham] | [Giles] | [Richard] | [John] | [Mary] | ye children of Giles Fifield — — — —	Fifield.[2]

{ The Baptized. — — — } — Page 228. —

	yeer & moneth	Day		
Sh:	4.	19.	[Abigail] ye daughter of mrs Catharine philips	philips.
		&	[John] ye fon of or fifter Hannah perkins —	perkins.
Sh:	4.	26.	[Samuel] | [Ebenezer] | [Abigail] | [Richard] | [Jofeph] | [Benjamin] | ye children of Richard [Asting & Abigail his wife.	Asting.[3]
Sh:	5.	3.	[Mary] ye daughter of Solomon phips, & mary his [wife.	Phips.

[1] Eight lines in the original. [2] Five lines in the original. [3] Six lines in the original.

— Page 228 *(concluded.)* —

Sh:	5.	10.	[Ruth] ye daughter of Ruth Knill — — — — —	Knill.
Sh:	5.	24.	[Iſaac] ye ſon of mary Winſlow — — — —	Winſlow
Sh:	5.	31.	[Mary] ye daughter of John Knight — — —	Knight.
Sh:	6.	14.	[John] ye ſon of mr John Chickring & Eliſabeth his [wife	Chickring.
		&	[Jane] ye daughter of Capt. Lawrence Hammond [& Abigail his wife	Hammond.
Sh:	7.	11.	[Samuel] ye ſon of bro: Nathaneel Rand —	Rand.
Sh:	7.	18.	[Richard] ye ſon of William Hilton & Mehitabel his [wife	Hilton.
Sh:	7.	25.	{ [Joſeph] / [Benjamin] } (twins) ye children of Thomas Lord, & Alice his wife. — —	Lord.
Sh:	8.	2.	[Mary] ye daughter of mr Thomas Ruſsell, & [prudence his wife.	Ruſsell.
		&	[Caleb] ye ſon of bro: John Call, & Hannah his wife.	Call.
Sh:	8.	9.	[Eliſabeth] ye daughter of John Roy, & Eliſabeth [his wife.	Roy.
Sh:	8.	23.	[Deborah] ye daughter of mr Zechary Long, & Sarai [his wife—	Long.
Sh:	9.	27.	[John] ye ſon of mr Elias Roe, & Rebekah his wife	Roe.
Sh:	10.	4.	[Richard] ye ſon of Thomas Sheppy & Grace his wife.	Sheppy.
		&	[Ruth] ye daughter of bro: Samuel Frothingham & [Ruth his wife.	Frothing- [ham
Sh:	10.	18.	[Timothy] ye ſon of Thomas Brigden — — —	Brigden.
		&	[Mercy] ye daughter of or ſiſter Martha Lathrop.	Lathrop.

	yeer & moneth.	Day	{ The Baptized. — — — } — Page 229. —	
	1670.			
Sh:	10.	25.	[Jonathan] the ſon of Thomas Welsh & of—his wife	Welsh.
		&	[Ruhamah] ye daughter of Eliſabeth Wire —	Wire.
		&	{ Sarah / Rebekah. / Rachel. } ye 3 daughters, born at one birth, of Hannah Hurry.	Hurrie.
Sh:	11.	22.	[Mary] ye daughter of Jno Lowden junior, & Sarai [his wife.	Lowden.
Sh:	11.	29.	[Esther] ye daughter of Joseph Kettle & Hannah [his wife.	Kettle.
		&	[Mary] ye daughter of Nathaneel Frothingham & [Mary his wife	Frothing- [ham
		&	[Mary] ye daughter of mrs Eliſabeth Tuck. — —	Tuck.
Sh:	12.	12.	[John] the ſon of Thomas & Sarai Smith —	Smith.
		&	[Elenoe] ye daughter } twins { of Thomas &	
		&	[Eliſabeth] ye daughter } twins { Rebekah Jenner	Jenner.
Sh:	12.	19.	[Joseph] ye ſon of Joſeph Frost & Hannah his wife.	Frost.
Sh:	12:	26:	[Sarah] ye daughter of mrs Abigal Long — —	Long.
	1671.			
Sh:	1:	12:	[Sarah] ye daughter of mrs Ridgeway — —	Ridgeway.
Sh:	2:	2.	[Joſeph] ye ſon of Nathaneel Cutler & of Eliſabeth [his wife	Cutler.
Sh:	2.	16.	[William] ye ſon of William Dady & Martha his wife	Dady.
		&.	[Thomas] ye ſon of Tho: Taylor & Anne his wife.	Taylor.
		&	[John.] | [Thomas.] | [Joſeph.] | & [Benjamin] ye children of Mary Whittamore [1] — — — — —	Whittamore
Sh:	2.	23.	[Edward] ye ſon of bro: Edward Willſon & Mary [his wife.	Wilſon.
		&.	[Samuel] ye ſon of Thomas Mouſal, & Mary his wife.	Mouſal.

[1] Christian names (Whittamore) four lines.

— Page 229 (*concluded.*) —

Sh:	2.	30. &	[William] [James] } the children of Mehitabel Wellsted	Wellsted.
Sh:	3.	21.	[Joſeph] the ſon of Thomas Lynd & Sarah his wife	Lynd.
		&.	[Anna] the daughter of peter Frothingham & Mary [his wife	Frothing- [ham
Sh:	4.	18:	[Nicolaus] ye ſon of Hannah Trerice	Trerice.

	moneth	Day	{ The Baptized. } — Page 230 —	
	1671.			
Sh:	4:	18. &	[John] ye ſon of — — } [Hannah] ye daughter of } John & Hannah Trerice	Trerice.
		&	[Dorothie] ye daughter of John & Hannah Edmunds.	Edmunds.
Sh:	4.	25.	[Katharine] ye Daughter of mr Jno philips & [Katharine his wife	philips.
Sh:	5.	9.	[Nathaneel] ye ſon of Nathaneel Frothingham, & [Mary his wife	Frothing- [ham
Sh:	5.	16.	[Hannah] ye daughter of peter Fowl, & Mary his [wife.	Fowl.
Sh:	6.	13.	[William] ye ſon of Richard Asting & Abigail his [wife.	Asting.
Sh:	6.	27.	[Katharine] ye daughter of mr Jonathan Wade & [Deborah his wife	Wade.
		&	[John] ye ſon of John Edmunds, & of Hannah his [wife	Edmunds.
Sh.	8.	22.	[John] ye ſon of Nathaneel Rand & of Mary his wife	Rand.
Sh.	9.	12.	[Samuel] ye ſon of Joſiah Wood, & of Lydia his [wife.	Wood.
Sh.	9.	19.	[Samuel] ye ſon of mr King & of Mary his wife.	King.
		&	[Ralph] ye ſon of Daniel Edmunds, & of Mary his [wife	Edmunds.
Sh:	10.	3.	[Anne] ye daughter of mr Jno Chickring, & of [Eliſabeth his wife.	Chickring.
Sh:	10.	31.	[Hannah] ye daughter of Samuel pierce, & of Mary his wife.	pierce.
Sh:	12.	4. &	[William] [Mary] } ye children of mrs Mary Marshall.	Marſhall:
		&	[Rebekah] ye daughter of mrs Rebekah Jones. —	Jones.
Sh:	12.	18.	[Sarai] ye daughter of Jno Fowl, & of Anna his wife.	Fowl.
Sh:	12.	25.	[Hannah] ye daughter of Thomas Rand, & Sarai [his wife:	Rand.
	1672.			
Sh:	1.	10.	[Eliſabeth] ye daughter of Thomas White & of Mary [his wife.	White.
Sh:	1.	17.	[Richard] ye ſon of mr James Ruſsell & of Mabel [his wife.	Ruſsell:
		&	[Perſis] ye daughter of bro: John Knight. —	Knight.
Sh:	1.	31.	[Thomas] ye ſon of mr Thomas Ruſsell & of prudence [his wife	Ruſsell.
		&	[Mehetabel] ye daughter of mrs Mehetabel Wellſted.	Wellſted.
Sh:	2.	14.	[Ebenezer] ye ſon of bro: Thomas Welsh — —	Welsh.

	yeer & moneth	Day	{ The Baptized. } — Page 231 —	
	1672.			
Sh:	4.	23.	[Joſeph] ye ſon of Thomas Lord & Alice his wife.	Lord.
Sh:	5.	14.	[Nicholas] ye ſon of mr Joſeph Lynd & Sarah his [wife.	Lynd.

— Page 231 *(concluded.)*

		&.	[Eliſabeth] yᵉ daughter of Captain L. Hammond, [& Abigˡ his wife	Hammond.
Sh:	5:	21.	[John] yₑ ſon of Benjamin Lathrop, & of Martha [his wife.	Lathrop.
Sh:	5.	28.	[James] yᵉ ſon of mʳ James Elſon & of Sarai his wife	Elſon.
		&.	[Abraham] yᵉ ſon of Luke perkins & Hannah his [wife.	perkins.
		&.	[Katherine] yᵉ daughᵗ of mʳ Hunting of yᵉ cʰ of [dedham	Hunting. —
Sh:	6.	18.	[Eliſabeth] the daughter of Henry, & Eliſabeth [Balcom.	Balcom.
Sh:	7.	1.	[Richard] yᵉ ſon of Thomas & Grace Sheppy. —	Sheppy.
Sh:	7.	8.	[Eliſabeth] yᵉ daughter of mʳ Thomas Tuck, & [Eliſabeth his wife	Tuck.
Sh:	7.	22.	[Samuel] yᵉ ſon of Nathaneel Hutchinſon, & Sarai [his wife:	Hutchinſon.
Sh:	8.	6.	[Sarai] yᵉ daughter of Matthew & Hannah Griffin.	Griffin.
Sh:	8.	27.	[Hannah] yᵉ daughter of Joseph Kettle & Hannah [his wife.	Kettle.
Sh:	9.	3.	[Abigail] yᵉ daughter of William Dady, & Martha [his wife.	Dady.
Sh:	10.	15.	[Eleazar] yᵉ ſon of Edward Wier & Eliſabeth his [wife.	Wier.
Sh:	11.	26.	[Elias] yᵉ ſon of Tho: Brigden — — — — —	Brigden.
Sh:	12.	9.	[Rebekah] yᵉ daughter of Will Hurrie, & Hannah [his w.	Hurrie.
Sh:	12.	16.	[Francis] yᵉ ſon of mʳ Nehemiah Willoughby & [Abigail his wife.	Willoughby
		&	[Solomon] yᵉ ſon of Jnᵒ Roy & Eliſabeth his wife.	Roy.
	1673			
Sh:	1.	23.	[John] yᵉ ſon of mʳ Jnᵒ philips & Katharine his wife.	philips.
Sh:	1.	30.	[Eliſabeth] yᵉ daughter of mʳ Jnᵒ Chickring, & of [Eliſabeth his wife.	Chickring:
Sh:	2:	6.	[Katharine] yᵉ daughter of my couſen mʳ Nathaneel Graves & of Eliſabeth his wife — — —	Graves.
Sh:	2.	13.	[Stephen] yᵉ ſon of Joseph Frost, & of Hannah his [wife.	Frost.
		&	[Nathaneel] yᵉ ſon of John, & Mary Whittamore [his wife.	Whittamore

	yeer & moneth	Day	The Baptized. — Page 232 —	
	1673			
Sh:	2.	20	[Eliſabeth] yᵉ wife of John Foſket	Foſket.
	—	&	[John] — The children of John Foſket & of Eliſabeth his wife	
	—	&	[Thomas]	
	—	&	[Joſhua]	
	—	&	[Robert]	
	—	&	[Eliſabeth]	
	—	&	[Mary] —	
	—	&	[John] the ſon of mʳ Will: Marſhal, & of Mary [his wife	Marſhal:
Sh:	2.	27.	[Charles] yᵉ ſon of Couſe Will: Hilton, & of Mehe-tabel his wife. — — —	Hilton.
Sh:	3.	11.	[Eliſabeth] yᵉ daughter of Richard Asting, & Abigail [his wife:	Asting.
Sh:	4.	1.	[peter] yᵉ ſon of peter Fowl, & of Mary his wife.	Fowl.

[To be continued.]

LOCAL LAW IN MASSACHUSETTS, HISTORICALLY CONSIDERED.

[Communicated by WILLIAM CHAUNCEY FOWLER, LL.D., of Durham, Conn.]

Continued from vol. xxv. page 351.

TAXATION AND LOCAL LAW.

MASSACHUSETTS believed that taxation and representation were inseparable; that taxation without representation is tyranny; and that as the colony was not represented in parliament the mother country had no right to impose taxes upon the people of the colony.

"In November, 1703, in answer to the governor's message, the house declared, 'that it had been the privilege from Henry the third, and confirmed by Edward the first, and in all reigns unto this day, granted and now is allowed, to be the just and unquestionable right of the subject, to raise *when* and dispose of *how*, they see cause, any sum of money by consent of parliament; *the which privilege we her majesty's loyal and dutiful subjects here have lived in the enjoyment of*, and do hope always to enjoy the same, under our most gracious Queen Anne and successors, and shall ever endeavor to discharge the duty incumbent on us.'"

Apprehensive that the British cabinet still contemplated raising money in America, by act of parliament, the general court of Massachusetts, in November, 1755, instructed their agent in London "to oppose anything that should have the remotest tendency to raise a revenue in the plantations, for the public use or services of government.

They were willing to be taxed by local laws enacted by their own legislature in which they were represented, but they were not willing to be taxed by the imperial laws of England enacted by parliament in which they were not represented.

THE RELATIONS OF THE CLERGY TO LOCAL LAW.

In the colony of Massachusetts Bay the right of suffrage was enjoyed only by church members. As the clergy practically had the power to determine who should be members of the church, they thus had the power to determine who should enjoy the right of suffrage and who should make the laws. Thus the clergy virtually, by means of the members of their churches, enacted the laws of the colony, and determined the mode of their administration, or their repeal.

From the letter of Governor Winthrop on the formation of the New-England confederacy, and from other facts, we learn that the clergy took an active part in the colonial legislation, especially in that portion of it which related to religious concerns. The clergy were personally and professionally interested to impart such vigor to the local legislation of the colony, as should protect them from the interference of the parliament and the bishops. In other words, under the first charter in the ecclesiastical and civil polity of the colony, the general court made the laws, the members of the church made the generat court, and the clergy made the members of the church. To the influence of the clergy has been attributed the enactment of those local laws under which Episcopalians, Baptists, Quakers, and other denominations were persecuted. It is remarkable when complaints in the name of the king came against the colony for allowing only members of the puritan church to vote, the general court was ready, from fear of losing their charter, to extend the right of suffrage to all of a "good moral character;" and yet they professed to give to the clergy the power of determining who had this "good moral character;" thus practically still leaving to the clergy the right to say who should be voters. Thus in the committee appointed by the general court to make a draught of the fundamental laws of the colony, Rev. Hugh Peter, Rev. John Cotton, and Rev. Thomas Shepard, were members. Thus, too, in 1662, Rev. John Norton with Simon Bradstreet, a leading man in the colony, were sent to England on the important mission to settle the difficulties which had arisen between the colony and the mother country.

Thus, too, in 1688 the Rev. Increase Mather was sent to England, where he was instrumental in procuring the provincial charter under which Plymouth and Massachusetts were united.

The puritan clergy of Massachusetts had all that influence throughout the colony which their brethren, the puritan clergy of England, had in their several congregations, as described by Macaulay in his *History of England*, by Addison in the 317th number of the *Spectator*, and by Sir John Hawkins in his *Life of Johnson.* This influence they exerted in promoting the enactment of the local laws.

The Relation of their Local Laws to the Bible.

The present version of the Bible authorized by King James was published in 1611. It was read with the greatest enthusiasm by many of the puritans, who regarded it as containing the sum of all earthly and all heavenly wisdom. The puritans of Massachusetts Bay were ready to run a parallel between their own experience and that of the Israelites. They had their own Pharaoh, their own house of bondage, their own sea, their own wilderness, their own Canaanites to contend with, and their own Moses and Aaron. And they were willing to assimilate themselves to the Israelites by adopting a portion of their code of laws.

They did not stop to consider that these laws were made for a peculiar people of a different race, in a different age of the world, and living on a different part of the globe; but they only thought them as made for a chosen people of God by God, the great Legislator. It was afterward found on experience and observation that some of these laws were better adapted to a race like the Hebrews, who were to be kept apart from the rest of the world, than for an Aryan race, like these Anglo-Saxons who were destined to become the "universal Yankee nation."

Stamp–Act.

The stamp-act was passed by the British parliament in 1765. The measure was defended by Grenville, by the following arguments:

"That this kingdom has the sovereign, the supreme legislative power over America, is granted; it cannot be denied; and taxation is a part of that sovereign power. It is one branch of the legislation. It is, it has been, exercised over those who are not, who never were, represented. . . . . 'When I proposed to tax America, I asked the house if any gentleman would object to the right. I repeatedly asked it; and no man would attempt to deny it. Protection and obedience are reciprocal. Great Britain protects America: America is bound to yield obedience. . . . . The nation has run itself into an immense debt to give them protection; and now when they are called upon to contribute a small sum toward the public expense, or expense arising from themselves, they renounce your authority, insult your officers and break out, I might almost say, into open rebellion.'"

But these arguments did not satisfy the general court and the people of Massachusetts. They stood upon their rights in refusing to pay the stamp-duty, as Englishmen under the British constitution. Their declaration was, that taxation without representation is contrary to that constitution, and was therefore tyranny, and ought to be resisted. Parliament called this resistance rebellion; but they believed that an unconstitutional law is null, and that resistance to such a law is obedience to God, and justified by the British constitution.

Such was the opposition to the stamp-act, that Oliver, the stamp-master, was hung in effigy, and Governor Hutchinson's house was attacked, because he was supposed to be in favor of the act. The stamp-act was repealed in 1766. Thus Massachusetts contended successfully for her colonial rights and local laws.

External Taxes.

In 1767, parliament laid a duty on tea, paper, glass, and other articles, that thus by an external tax, under the conceded right to regulate commerce, it might accomplish what it failed to accomplish by an internal tax under the stamp-act. The colony had hitherto submitted to the exaction of an external tax in the shape of a duty on imported goods. But knowing well what was the *animus* of parliament in passing the law, there was the same opposition to it as to the stamp-act. "We will," they said, "form an association to eat nothing, drink nothing, wear nothing imported from Great Britain. If our opposition to slavery is called rebellion, let us pursue our duty with firmness, and leave the worst to Heaven." An external tax they regarded as making them slaves if they submitted to it, and hence they resisted it.

When Dr. Franklin, in December, 1774, drew up a plan for settling the difficulties between Great Britain and the colonies, one of the conditions proposed by him, and regarded by Massachusetts as indispensable, was, "that all power of internal legislation should be disclaimed by parliament." This was declared by high British authority to be "inadmissible." Still Massachusetts persistently asserted her right to manage her own internal concerns without the interference of Great Britain. Hutchinson, the royal governor, claimed supremacy for parliament in all cases whatever. This claim Massachusetts resisted, from their strong attachment to their local laws,

The right of Self-Government.

In 1640, Winthrop, page 30, vol. ii., remarks:

"Upon the great liberty which the King had left the Parliament in England, some of our friends then wrote to us advice, to send over some to solicit for us in Parliament, giving us hope that we might obtain much. But consulting about it, we declined the motion for this consideration, that if we should put ourselves under the protection of Parliament, we must then be subject to all such laws as they should make, or at least such as they might impose upon us."

Upon this passage, transcribed for his letter to Baron Van der Capellan, a distinguished Dutch statesman, in 1779, Governor Trumbull, one of the most deliberate assertors of the American revolution, and then custodian of the first two manuscript volumes of this history, remarks:

"Here observe, that, as at this time, so it hath been ever since, that the colonies, so far from acknowledging the parliament to have any right to make laws binding on them in all cases whatsoever, they have denied it in any case."

Chalmers speaks of Massachusetts as "always fertile in projects of independence." "Disregarding equally her charter and the laws of England, Massachusetts established for herself an independent government similar to those of the Grecian republics" (Book I. page 400). It appeared more rational to them (the colonists), that the colony should be governed by those who made it the place of their residence, than by men dwelling at the distance of three thousand miles, over whom they had no control. The object was self-government under their own local laws.

Civil superior to Military Authority.

In 1757, Lord Loudon, in view of a certain act of the general court of Massachusetts, made the declaration that "in time of war the rules and customs of war must govern." This declaration was brought before the general court and condemned in a message which it sent to the governor, in which it declares that "the rules and customs of war were not the rules which the civil magistrate was to govern himself by." Thus Massachusetts took ground against military despotism, and in favor of the supremacy of civil law over military rules, and of civil rulers over military despots.

In 1769, the house of representatives, when the governor (appointed by the crown) refused at their request to remove the troops from the town of Boston, declared:

> "That the use of the military power, to enforce the execution of the law, is, in their opinion, inconsistent with the spirit of a free constitution; for by the nature of a free constitution, the people must consent to laws before they can be obliged in consequence to obey them."

Mobs opposed to Imperial Law.

The determination of Massachusetts to support her colony-rights against the power of parliament and the prerogative of the king, is evident from the speeches of the leading orators; from the sermons of leading preachers; from pamphlets and newspapers. With these the temper of the people was in harmony, as shown by the mobs which rose against the laws, and the officers, and the property of the British government. Witness the mob that hung up Oliver in effigy; the mob that burned the records of the admiralty court; the mob that attacked the house of Governor Hutchinson, and destroyed his furniture, and scattered his plate and books and papers; the mob that pelted the officers of customs with stones and bricks; the mob that tarred and feathered one who gave information against the breaking of the acts of trade passed by parliament; the mob that rose in opposition to the soldiers; the mob that threw the tea overboard. These mobs were symptomatic of the spirit that pervaded Massachusetts in opposition to parliament and prerogative, and the defence of colony-rights and local laws.

The Supremacy of Local Law asserted.

Certain violations of the colony-rights and local laws are mentioned in the report of a Boston committee, November 22d, namely, the imposition by parliament of taxes without the consent of the people; the appointment of officers unknown to the charter, supported by the income derived from such taxes; the introduction of fleets and armies to compel obedience to unconstitutional laws; the extension of the powers of the court of admiralty; the act relating to dock-yards and stores, which deprived the people of the right of trial by their peers in the vicinage, and the assumption of absolute legislative powers.

Massachusetts claimed for her people, as men, as colonists, as subjects of the crown, the right to life, liberty, and property; the sole right to manage their internal institutions and concerns; the sole right of raising money from themselves by taxation; the right of being tried by their peers in the vicinage; the right of freely discussing public measures; the right of being governed by the civil as superior to the military power; the right of being free from unreasonable searches, which was violated by the writs of assistance. These and other rights having been violated by the British parliament or

British king, Massachusetts was ready to declare herself a free, sovereign, and independent state.

The Supremacy of Local Law maintained.

For something like a year before July 4, 1776, Massachusetts, standing on her colony-rights, enjoyed a virtual independence. The supremacy of her local laws she was prepared to maintain.

And in April, 1776, the general court passed a resolve to alter the style of writs and other legal processes, substituting the "people and government of Massachusetts" for "George the Third." Thus Massachusetts, in asserting and maintaining the supremacy of the local law, was the first of the "old thirteen" states independent. Thus was she fully prepared to make a public and formal declaration by her delegates Samuel Adams, John Adams, Robert Treat Paine, Elbridge Gerry, that Massachusetts "was, and of right ought to be, a free and independent state; that she was absolved from all allegiance to the British crown." After a seven years' war in defence of the right to be governed by her own local laws, by treaty with Great Britain she was acknowledged "a free, sovereign, and independent state," in which her own local laws were supreme. Thus Massachusetts having contended strenuously from 1628 until 1776 for colony-rights, and local law, was prepared, when she became a sovereign state, having the right to command, to contend strenuously for state-rights and local law. Acting in concert with the other states, she, before the world, vindicated the right of the people of Massachusetts to abolish a government when in her opinion it becomes destructive of the ends for which it was established, and establish such a form of government as she shall judge best.

Massachusetts a Sovereign State.

Massachusetts in 1776, having become a free, sovereign and independent state, proceeded to exercise its sovereignty or right of command. She raised troops; made war; laid taxes; established a mint, and coined money; required the oath of allegiance; enacted laws against treason; punished such as continued loyal to Great Britain. These principles she incorporated in her constitution in 1780, in which she declared herself a sovereign state.

Articles of Confederation.

When the continental congress in November, 1777, "agreed upon a plan of confederacy, securing the freedom, sovereignty, and independence of the (several) United States," and sent it, under the title of "Articles of Confederation," to the several state legislatures, Massachusetts, by the act of her legislature, readily adopted it. In the second article of that compact are the following words: "Each state retains its sovereignty, freedom and independence." These Massachusetts had contended for successfully, in the halls of legislation, and on the battle-field, and these she retained.

In February, 1787, the subject of a convention for revising the articles of confederation being under consideration in the congress, Nathan Dane, of Massachusetts, opposed the movement. "He was at bottom unfriendly to the plan of a convention, and dissuaded his state from going into it." (Eliott's *Debates*, vol. v. 196.)

Convention for forming a new Federal Constitution.

March 11, 1787. "Massachusetts has also appointed (delegates to the convention). Messrs. Gorham, Dane, King, Gerry, and Strong, compose her deputation." The resolution under which they act, restrains them from acceding to any departure from the principles of the fifth article of confederation. It is conjectured that this fetter, which originated with the senate, will be struck off. Its being introduced at all denotes a very different spirit, in that quarter, from what some had been led to expect. The fifth article, which the legislature of Massachusetts was unwilling to have altered, is as follows :—

"For the more convenient management of the general interests of the United States, delegates shall be annually appointed in such manner as the legislature of each state shall direct, to meet in congress on the first Monday in November, in every year, with a power reserved to each state to recall its delegates, or any of them, at any time within the year, and to send others in their stead for the remainder of the year.

"No state shall be represented in congress by less than two, nor by more than seven members ; and no person shall be capable of being a delegate for more than three years in any term of six years ; nor shall any person, being a delegate, be capable of holding any office under the United States, for which he, or another for his benefit, receives any salary, fees, or emoluments of any kind.

"Each state shall maintain its own delegates in a meeting of the states, and while they act as members of the committee of the states.

"In determining questions in the United States in congress assembled, each state shall have one vote.

"Freedom of speech and debate in congress shall not be impeached or questioned in any court or place out of congress ; and the members of congress shall be protected in their persons from arrests and imprisonment, during the time of their going to and from attendance on congress, except for treason, felony, or breach of peace."

This article is a very strong assertion of the doctrine of state-rights and of the high estimate of the people of Massachusetts of the value of local laws.

The Federal Convention.

The convention for altering the federal constitution, namely, the articles of confederation, assembled May 25, 1787, and continued in session until September 17. On the subject of state-rights, the course of Massachusetts in that convention was not as distinct as that of Connecticut in favor, or as that of Virginia in opposition. She acted sometimes with the larger states for the abridgment of those rights, and sometimes with the smaller states for the preservation of those rights. On the great question, whether the states shall have an equal vote in the senate, the vote of Massachusetts was equally divided and thus lost. Mr. Gerry and Mr. Strong voted in the affirmative, Mr. Gorham and Mr. King in the negative. The reason why Mr. Gorham and Mr. King went against state-rights was, that they were willing that Massachusetts, Virginia and Pennsylvania, on account of their greater population, should be the leading states. Massachusetts in this way would have the pre-eminence in New-England in the senate, just as she wished to have the pre-eminence under the federal constitution of 1643.

On the question of giving to the federal government the power to issue paper money and making it a legal tender, Massachusetts was opposed to giving this power and thus enlarging the power of the federal government. On the motion for striking out from the proposed constitution, "and emit bills of credit," Massachusetts with the majority voted in the affirmative, and probably for the same reason that influenced Connecticut and Virginia, as stated by Mr. Madison, namely : to "cut off all pretext for a paper currency, and particularly for making the bills a tender for public or private debts." Massachusetts had seen the evils of continental money, and she was unwilling to repeat those evils. She was prescient of the future, and was unwilling to give any authority to the federal government to issue bills and make them a legal tender.

[To be continued.]

DESCENDANTS OF COL. RICHARD LEE, OF VIRGINIA.

[SOME time since a genealogy of the Lee Family of Virginia was published, mainly devoted to the English pedigree of the family. A critic in "The Nation," however, has pointed out not only that this English portion is unsupported by proof, but even that it is based on a fatal mistake. It is not the pedigree of the emigrant to Virginia. As the American part of the genealogy was very meagre, two of the descendants of Col. Richard Lee (C. F. Lee, Jr., Esq., of Alexandria, and Joseph Packard, Jr., Esq., of Baltimore) have prepared the following sketch, which we are happy to lay before our readers. It embraces five generations, counting the children of Richard Lee (who emigrated to Virginia in 1641) as the first generation.

All possible care has been exercised in preparing this pedigree, and the names and dates are believed to be correct, being taken from family bibles, wills, tombstone inscriptions, old letters and other manuscripts.

The compilers desire to obtain further authentic information preliminary to a more extended genealogy.—ED.]

1\. RICHARD[1] LEE, emigrated to Virginia in 1641; married Anna ——, and had children; following order given in his Will dated 1663:

- i. JOHN, d. unmarried. (*Old Churches and Families*, Vol. II., p. 136. Bishop Meade.)
- 2\. ii. RICHARD.
- iii. FRANCIS.—iv. WILLIAM.
- 3\. v. HANCOCK.
- vi. BETSEY.—vii. ANNE.—viii. CHARLES.

2\. RICHARD,[2] second son of Richard[1] Lee and Anna ——, born 1647; died March 12, 1714; married Lettice Corbin, daughter of Henry Corbin, gentleman. She died Oct. 6, 1706, æt 49. Children:

- 4\. i. RICHARD.
- 5\. ii. PHILIP.
- iii. FRANCIS, d. unmarried. This fact is mentioned in Wm. Lee's statement, and confirmed by a sentence in Philip Lee's Will, who mentions some land in Gloucester Co. as being the property of his brother Francis, and which was bequeathed to him, in the event of the said Francis dying unmarried. This property Philip left to one of his sons, and hence the above conclusion.
- 6\. iv. THOMAS.
- 7\. v. HENRY.
- vi. MARY, m. Wm. Fitzhugh, of Eagle's Nest, King George Co., Va. (*Old Churches and Families*, Vol. II., pp. 138, note, and 193.)

3\. HANCOCK,[2] fifth son. Twice married: first, Miss Kendall; second, Miss Allerton. Died in 1729, and is buried at Ditchley, Northumberland Co., Va. (*Old Churches and Families*, Vol. II., p. 136.)

- 8\. i. HANCOCK, son by Miss Kendall.

4\. RICHARD,[3] eldest son of Richard Lee[2] and Lettice Corbin, married a Miss Silk, of London, and children were:

- 9\. i. GEORGE.
- ii. LETTICE, twice married: first, Mr. Ball; second, —— Corbin; issue.
- iii. MARTHA, m. Turberville. Issue. The eldest of these sisters married, and had a son called George Lee Turberville.

5\. PHILIP,[3] second son. Twice married: first, —— ——; second, Elizabeth ——. He went to Maryland in 1700, and died in 1744. The names of children given in order named in his Will admitted to probate May 1, 1744; date of Will, March 20, 1743:

10\. i. RICHARD.
11\. ii. THOMAS.
12\. iii. PHILIP.
iv. CORBIN. No issue.
13\. v. HANCOCK.
14\. vi. ARTHUR.
15\. vii. FRANCIS.
16\. viii. GEORGE. No issue.
ix. ELEANOR, m. Fendall; d. April 22, 1759.
x. ANNE, wife of Jas. Russell, merchant, London; also wife of Wm. Potts, grandmother of Geo. W. Potts, Frederick, Md.
xi. ALICE, first husband Thomas Clark; one child born from this marriage, a daughter, who married John Rogers, Chancellor of Maryland; second husband, Meriwether Smith, of Va. Their son, Gov. Smith, was burnt in the Richmond Theatre in 1811.
xii. HANNAH, first husband Bowie: daughters were, Mrs. Bell, of Hagerstown, and Mrs. Taylor; second husband, —— Sprigg. Mrs. Chas. Carroll, of Bellevue, one of the descendants.
xiii. PEGGY.
xiv. LETITIA, first husband Dr. James Wardrop; second husband, Dr. Adam Thompson; third, Col. Jos. Sims. By her first and third husbands she had no children: by her second marriage she had two daughters, Mary Lee and Alice Corbin, the first of whom married Col. Williams, of Maryland, and the second, Capt. John Hawkins, a distinguished officer in the Revolutionary Army, serving with the Virginia troops.
xv. ELIZA, d. Sept. 19, 1752, æt. 22. (From a "mourning ring.")

6\. THOMAS,[3] fourth son, married Hannah Ludwell, granddaughter of Lady Berkeley, who married Col. Phil. Ludwell in 1680. Died in 1751. Date of Will, Feb. 22, 1749, and admitted to record July 30, 1751. In this Will he styles himself, "President, and Commander-in-Chief of the said Colony." Children:

i. RICHARD, b. June 17, 1723; d. unmarried.
17\. ii. PHILIP LUDWELL.
iii. HANNAH, b. Feb 6, 1727–8; m. Gawin Corbin, and had one daughter named Martha, who married George Richard Turberville, and had two sons.
iv. JOHN, b. March, 28, 1728; d. unmarried.
v. LUCY, b. Sept. 26, 1730; d. unmarried.
18\. vi. THOMAS LUDWELL.
19\. vii. RICHARD HENRY.
20\. viii. FRANCIS LIGHTFOOT.
ix. ALICE, b. June 4, 1736; m. Wm. Shippen, Jr., Surgeon in Revolutionary Army, and had several children, of whom only two lived to be of age: i. Anne Hume Shippen, m. Henry B. Livingston; ii. Thomas Lee Shippen, b. 1765, m. March 10, 1791, Elizabeth C. Farley, and had William and Thomas Lee Shippen.
21\. x. WILLIAM.
xi. ARTHUR, b. Dec. 21, 1740; never married; d. Dec. 12, 1792.

7\. HENRY,[3] fifth son, married Miss Bland, daughter of Richard Bland, of Jordan, in Prince George Co., Va. (*Old Churches and Families*, Vol. I., p. 446–7.) Children:

i. JOHN.
22\. ii. RICHARD.
23\. iii. HENRY.
24\. iv. LETTICE, m. a Fitzhugh.

8\. HANCOCK,[3] son of Hancock[2] and Miss Kendall, married Miss Mary Willis, of Willis Hill near Fredericksburg, Va. Children were:

25. i. HANCOCK.
26. ii. JOHN.
27. iii. HENRY.
iv. RICHARD, d. unmarried.
v. SARAH, m. Col. Gilerson of the Revolutionary Army.
vi. MARY, m. Major Ambrose Madison, brother of President Madison; issue, one daughter, Mrs. Nellie C. Willis, of Orange Co., Va.

9. GEORGE[4] LEE, son of Richard,[3] removed from England to Virginia, and married, first, Miss Wormeley, and had one daughter. The second wife was a Miss Fairfax: issue, three sons, names unknown.

10. RICHARD,[4] eldest son of Philip[3] Lee, died 1787 or 1789; married Grace ———, who died Oct., 1789. Children were:

i. RICHARD, d. in 1834. No issue.
28. ii. PHILIP THOMAS.
iii. ELEANOR A., d. May 17, 1806, without issue.

11. THOMAS,[4] second son of Philip Lee, died 1749; married ——; issue were:

29. i. THOMAS SIM.
ii. SARAH. No issue.

12. PHILIP,[4] third son of Philip Lee, died in ——, before his father. Married Grace ———, and had several children, as reference to the will of Philip Lee, Sen. will show, though only the name of one known.

i. PHILIP.

13. HANCOCK,[4] fifth son of Philip Lee, died in 1759.
14. ARTHUR,[4] sixth son, married, and died; issue.
15. FRANCIS,[4] seventh son, married, and died; issue.
16. GEORGE,[4] eighth son, married, and died; no issue.
17. PHILIP LUDWELL,[4] second son of Thomas[3] Lee, born Feb. 24, 1726–7; married Miss Elizabeth Steptoe. Children were:

i. MATILDA, m. Gen. Henry Lee.
ii. FLORA, m. Ludwell Lee.
iii. PHILIP, d. without issue.

18. THOMAS LUDWELL,[4] fourth son, born Dec. 31, 1730–1; married Miss Aylett; died April 13, 1778. Children were:

30. i. THOMAS LUDWELL.
ii. AYLETT. Never married.
iii. GEORGE, m. Eveline Beverly, and had Maria,[6] and George[6] who m. Miss Henderson and left issue.
iv. ANNE FENTON, m. Daniel Carroll Brent, of Richland, Stafford Co., Va., Jan. 3, 1782, and had twelve children. The following named lived to be of age: William Brent, Jr., b. Jan. 13, 1783, d. May 13, 1843; Thomas Ludwell Lee, b. Aug. 9, 1784; Adelaide, b. Dec. 25, 1786; Eleanor, b. Oct. 11, 1787; George Lee, b. August, 1795; Mary Aylett, b. Oct. 3, 1793.
v. LUCINDA, m. John D. Orr, of Prince William Co., Va., and had children: Eleanor, who m. Gen. Asa Rogers, of Virginia; Mary Aylett Orr, d. unmarried; Thomas Ludwell Lee Orr, d. unmarried.
vi. REBECCA, d. unmarried.

19. RICHARD HENRY,[4] fifth son, born Jan. 20, 1732; died at Chantilly, in Westmoreland Co., Va., June 19, 1794. Twice married: his first wife was Miss Anne Aylett, whom he married Dec. 3, 1759, and by her he had issue:

31. i. THOMAS.
32. ii. LUDWELL.

iii. MARY, b. July 28, 1764; christened March 11, 1765; m. Col. Wm. A. Washington, nephew of Gen. Washington: no issue.

iv. HANNAH, m. Corbin Washington, also a nephew of Gen. Washington, and had issue: Richard Henry; John Augustine, proprietor of Mt. Vernon, who m. Miss Jean Charlotte Blackburn, and had issue, three children: Maria, John Augustine and Richard (the first son owned Mt. Vernon, just previous to the war); Bushrod Corbin, m. Miss Blackburn, and had issue; Mary, m. Noblet Herbert, and had issue, two sons.

His second wife was Mrs. Anne Pinkard, *née* Gaskins, whom he married about June, 1769 (*Life of R. H. Lee*, Vol. I., p. 255), and had issue:

iv. ANNE, b. Dec. 1, 1770; christened Jan. 6, 1771; m. Charles Lee, and had issue, four children.

v. HENRIETTA, b. Dec. 10, 1773; christened Jan. 14, 1774; d. in 1803 or 1804; m. first, Richard Lee Turberville, and had issue: Cornelia, m. Chas. C. Stuart, and has issue; George Lee, m. Miss Dobell, d., and has issue; Richard Henry, d., no issue. Her second husband was Rev. William Maffitt, of So. Carolina, and had two children: Anne Lee, d. unmarried; Harriotte, m. Rev. Reuben Post, and has issue.

vi. SARAH, b. Nov. 27, 1775; d. May 8, 1837; m. Edmund J. Lee.

vii. CASSIUS, b. Aug. 18, 1779; d. July 8, 1798.

> "May every Cæsar feel
> The keen, deep searching of a Patriot's steel."
> —*Family Bible of R. H. Lee.*

32. viii. FRANCIS LIGHTFOOT.

20. FRANCIS LIGHTFOOT,[4] sixth son, born Oct. 14, 1734; married Miss Rebecca Tayloe, in 1769, daughter of John Tayloe, of Mt. Airy, whose wife was Rebecca Plater, daughter of Hon. Governor George Plater, of Maryland; no children; died in April, 1797, within a few hours of each other. (*Old Churches and Families*, Vol. II., p. 181.)

21. WILLIAM,[4] seventh son, born August —, ——; married Hannah Philippa Ludwell, eldest daughter of Philip Ludwell, of Greenspring, James City Co., Va., March 7, 1769, in "Parish Church of St. Clement's Dane in the Co. of Middlesex, kingdom of Great Britain," and had children:

i. WILLIAM LUDWELL, b. about 1772; d. unmarried in 1802.

ii. PORTIA, b. 1777; d. Feb. 19, 1840; m. William Hodgson, of White Haven, England, who died in Alexandria, Va., Nov. 7, 1820, æt. 55 years. Their children were: William Ludwell, d. Sept. 27, 1841, æt. 42 years; Cornelia Ludwell, d. June 4, 1846; Caroline Octavia; Charles Henry; Augustus Henry; Julia Augusta; Elizabeth Augusta, d. June 11, 1825, æt. 11 years; Sydney Ludwell, d. in 1869. (?)

iii. BRUTUS, b. Nov., 1778; d. June, 1779.

iv. CORNELIA, b. in Brussells, March 3, 1780; m. John Hopkins in 1806, and died in 1817 or 1818. Children were: Portia, b. 1807; m. Dr. Robert T. Baldwin, of Winchester, Va., in 1830, and has children; Hannah Philippa Ludwell, b. Aug. 3, 1811; m. Cassius F. Lee, Sept. 18, 1833; d. Jan. 25, 1844. Left children. Mary Anna, b. Jan. 8, 1813; m. Rev. Wm. M. Jackson, who died in Norfolk in 1855. She d. November, 1843. Left children. Harriotte Lee, b. 1816; m. Rev. Richard K. Meade in 1837; d. Feb. 14, 1839. Left one son.

22. JOHN,[4] eldest son of Henry[3] Lee, married a Widow Ball: left no children.

23. RICHARD,[4] second son of Henry,[3] married, when 60 years old, Miss Sally Poythress (his second cousin), of Prince George Co., Va.; she was 16 at her marriage. He died 1795; she died 1828. Children were:

i. MARY, m. Thomas Jones, of Chesterfield Co., Va., and left children: Joseph, Richard Lee, Thomas Lee and Benson—all living.
ii. LETTICE, m. Dr. John Augustine Smith, formerly President of William and Mary College, and afterwards President of College of Surgeons, &c., in New York. Children were: Richard Augustine; Sally Poythress, m. John Campbell, of N. Y.; Martha Burwell, m. John Hilchburn, of Philadelphia; Mary Dabney, unmarried.
iii. RICHARDIA, m. Presley Cox. Children: Elizabeth, m. Rev. Mr. Griffith, first Bishop elect of Diocese of Virginia; Sarah, m. Mr. Power.

24. HENRY,[4] third son of Henry[3] Lee, married Dec. 1, 1753, Lucy Grymes, "youngest daughter of Charles Grymes, Gent.," known by tradition as the "Lowland Beauty." He died about July or Aug., 1787, and left issue:

33. i. HENRY.
34. ii. CHARLES.
35. iii. RICHARD BLAND.
36. iv. THEODORIC.
37. v. EDMUND JENNINGS.
vi. LUCY, b. in 1774; never married.
vii. MARY, m. a Mr. Fendall, and had two children: Philip Richard, d. Feb. 15, 1869, æt. 73 years, and left issue; Eleanor, married, and now deceased.
viii. ANNE, b. in 1776; d. Aug., 1857; m. Wm. Byrd Page, and had issue: Mary Ann, m. Roger Jones, and has children; Jane Byrd, d. unmarried; Edmonia, m. Hall Nelson, d., and left children; Wm. Byrd, died unmarried; Charles Henry, twice married: first, Miss Crawford, children—second, Miss Jane Leaton, no children; Mann Randolph, m. Miss Bell, and has children; John Randolph; Richard Lucien, m. Miss Taylor, and has children; Cary Selden, d. unmarried.

25. HANCOCK,[4] son of Hancock[3] Lee and Miss Willis; died in 1815; married Miss Winfred Beale, daughter of Jno. Beale, of Westmoreland Co., Va. Their children were:

38. i. WILLIS.
39. ii. HANCOCK.
40. iii. THOMAS.
iv. ARTHUR, d. unmarried.
v. PAMELA, d. unmarried.
vi. MARY FRANCES, d. unmarried.
vii. ANNE, d. unmarried.
viii. EMELINE, m. Mr. Richards, deceased; no children.
ix. ELIZABETH, m. Capt. Sangster, of Fauquier Co., Va.; no children. She is still living.

26. JOHN,[4] second son of Hancock[3] Lee, married Miss Bell. Children were:

41. i. WILLIS.
42. ii. JOHN HANCOCK.
iii. LEWIS, d. unmarried.
iv. ELIZABETH, m. Dr. Wilkerson, of Frankfort, Ky. No children.
v. ANNA, m. John J. Crittenden, of Kentucky, and had children, one of whom was Gen. Thomas Lee Crittenden, U. S. Army; the other was Gen. Robert Crittenden, U. S. Army.
vi. ———, m. Gen. Call, of Kentucky; no children.
vii. MATILDA, m. Mr. Wallace, of Woodford Co., Ky.; no children.

27. HENRY,[4] third son of Hancock[3] Lee, married and had children: the daughters' names have not been ascertained:

i. WILLIS, never married.
ii. HANCOCK, never married.
iii. JOHN, never married.
vi. ———, m. Mr. Davis.
v. ———, m. her cousin, John Lee.

28. PHILIP[5] THOMAS, second son of Richard,[4] died 1778; married in England, a Miss Russell, and had issue: one son, and four daughters whose names have not been ascertained.

- i. RUSSELL, d. in 1793, a minor and without issue.
- ii. —— ——, m. Mr. Gamble. No children.
- iii. —— ——, m. Mr. Contee; left two sons and a daughter: P. A. L. Contee, Edward H. Contee; the daughter married a Mr. Kent.
- iv. —— ——, m. Mr. Dawson; left children.
- v. —— ——, m. Mr. Clerklee; left children.

29. THOMAS SIM,[5] son of Thomas[4] Lee, born in 1745; died Nov. 9, 1819; married Mary Diggs, only child of Ignatius Diggs, of Prince George's Co., Maryland, and had children, as follows:

- i. IGNATIUS. No issue.
- 43. ii. THOMAS.
- 44. iii. WILLIAM.
- 45. iv. ARCHIBALD.
- 46. v. JOHN.
- vi. MARY CHRISTIAN.
- vii. ELIZA, m. Outerbridge Horsey, U. S. Senator from Delaware, and left children.

30. THOMAS LUDWELL,[5] son of Thomas Ludwell,[4] married Fanny Carter, of Sabine Hall; died about May, 1807. Had children, all daughters:

- i. ELIZABETH, m. St. Leger Landon Carter.
- ii. MARY, m. Tench Ringgold, of Washington, D. C.
- iii. WINIFRED BEALE, m. William Brent, Jr., of Richland, Stafford Co., Va.
- iv. FANNY CARTER. Died single.
- v. ANN LUCINDA, m. John M. McCarty.
- vi. CATHARINE. Died single.
- vii. SIDNEY. Died single.

31. THOMAS,[5] eldest son of Richard Henry,[4] born Oct. 20, 1758; married Nellie Brent, and had one daughter:

- i. ELEANOR, who m. Girard Alexander. One child, Thos. Ludwell, now Col. in U. S. Army, married and has children.

32. LUDWELL,[5] second son of Richard Henry,[4] born Oct. 13, 1760; died in 1833; married in 1788, his cousin, Flora Lee, second daughter of Philip Ludwell Lee, and had three children:

- 47. i. RICHARD HENRY.
- ii. CECILIA, m. James L. McKenna; no children.
- iii. MATILDA, m. Richard Love, has children, and is now living.

His second wife was Miss Armistead, whom he married in 1797. Children were:

- iv. MARY ANN, m. Gen. Robert B. Campbell, of S. C.
- v. ELLEN, m. Rev. N. P. Knapp, of Mobile, Ala.; left children.
- vi. ELIZA, m. Wilson Cary Selden.
- vii. EMILY. Never married.
- 48. viii. FRANCIS LIGHTFOOT.
- ix. BOWLES. Never married; deceased.

32. FRANCIS LIGHTFOOT,[5] fourth son of Richard Henry,[4] born in 1782; died in 1850. He married a Miss Fitzgerald, and had children:

- 49. i. SAMUEL PHILLIPS.
- 50. ii. JOHN FITZGERALD.
- iii. ARTHUR. Died unmarried.
- iv. ELIZABETH, m. H. T. Harrison; left a daughter who died unmarried.
- v. FRANCES, m. first, Goldsborough Robinson; second, —— Pettitt: issue living.

33. HENRY,[5] eldest son of Henry[4] Lee, born Jan., 1756; died March 25, 1818. Popularly known as "Light-Horse Harry." Twice married: first to Matilda Lee. Children were:

i. HENRY. Died without issue.
ii. LUCY, b. 1786; m. 1803; d. 1860; m. Bernard Carter. Children were: Josephine, m. Eugene Fransen; Matilda, m. Thomas M. Willing; Mildred, m. L. de Potestad, and left issue; Charlotte, m. G. W. Featherstonehaw, and left issue; Charles, m. Miss Calvert; Bernard.

His second wife, married July 18, 1793, was Ann, sister of Bernard Carter, above named. She died July, 1829, æt. 56 or 58 years. Ch.:

51. i. CHARLES CARTER.
52. ii. SYDNEY SMITH.
53. iii. ROBERT EDWARD.
iv. ANN CARTER, m. Wm. L. Marshall; died, and left children.
v. MILDRED, m. Edward Childe; died, and left children.

34. CHARLES,[5] second son of Henry Lee,[4] died in 1815; married twice: first to Anne Lucinda, daughter of Richard Henry Lee:

i. CHARLES. Died unmarried.
ii. ARTHUR. Died unmarried.
iii. ALFRED. Died unmarried, in 1865.
iv. ANNE LUCINDA, b. in May, 1791; m. Walter Jones, May, 1808; d. May, 1835. Children were: Virginia Collins, m. Dr. Thomas Miller; Walter, d. unmarried; Nannette Lee, m. Dr. Robert E. Peyton in 1833; Rosina, m. Rev. Jos. Packard in 1838; Elizabeth Mary, m. Henry T. Harrison in 1841; Charles Lee, unmarried; Catherine Ella, d. unmarried; Anne Harriotte, m. Matthew Harrison in 1851; Frances Lee, unmarried; Sarah Cornelia, unmarried; Violetta Lansdale, unmarried; Thomas Walter, d. unmarried.

His second wife was Margaret Peyton, widow of Yelverton Peyton, and daughter of the Rev. John Scott. Children were:

54. v. ROBERT EDEN.
vi. ELIZABETH GORDON, m. Rev. A. D. Pollock about the year 1836, and has children: Thomas Gordon, killed at the battle of Gettysburg, 1863; Margaret, m. Dr. Erasmus Moore; Anne Lee, m. Charles P. Janney; Elizabeth G., unmarried; Roberta Lee, unmarried; Charles Lee, unmarried.

35. RICHARD BLAND,[5] third son of Henry,[4] born Jan. 20, 1761; married Miss Elizabeth Collins, of Philadelphia, Feb. 8, 1794; died March 12, 1827. Left issue:

55. i. RICHARD BLAND.
56. ii. ZACCHEUS COLLINS.
iii. MARY ANN, b. May 11, 1795; d. June 21, 1796.
iv. ANN MATILDA, b. July 13, 1799; m. Dr. Bailey Washington, now deceased: has children.
v. MARY COLLINS, b. May 6, 1801; d. Feb. 22, 1805.
vi. CORNELIA, b. March 20, 1804; m. Dr. James McCrae: has children.

36. THEODORIC,[5] fourth son of Henry Lee,[4] married Miss Hite or White. Children:

57. i. JOHN.
ii. CAROLINE, m. Mr. Walker: children.
iii. JULIANA, m. Jos. Gales, of Washington, editor of the National Intelligencer.
iv. CATHARINE, m. Mr. May: children.

37. EDMUND JENNINGS,[5] fifth son of Henry Lee,[4] born May 20, 1772; died May 30, 1843; married about 1796 to Sarah, daughter of Richard H. Lee. Children were:

58. i. EDMUND JENNINGS.
59. ii. WILLIAM FITZHUGH.
60. iii. CASSIUS FRANCIS.
61. iv. CHARLES HENRY.
62. v. RICHARD HENRY.
vi. ANNE HARRIOTTE, b. March 6, 1800; d. Sept., 1863; m. Mr. John Lloyd, of Alexandria, and had children.
vii. SALLY. Never married.
viii. HANNAH, m. Rev. K. J. Stewart, and has one daughter living.
ix. SUSAN MEADE, b. March 26, 1814; d. Feb. 15, 1815.

38. WILLIS,[5] eldest son of Hancock Lee,[4] married Miss Richards, and left children:

63. i. JOHN HANCOCK.
ii. MARY, m. Mr. Thomas Ashton.

39. HANCOCK,[5] second son of Hancock Lee,[4] married Miss Richards, and left children.

40. THOMAS,[5] third son of Hancock Lee,[4] married Miss Bell, of Louisville, Ky., sister of Samuel Bell, a wealthy merchant of that city. He moved to Missouri, and died there several years before the war. Children were:

i. MATILDA, m. Mr. Gaskins, of Virginia, and had two sons who were killed during the war.
ii. JANE, unmarried and still living.

41. WILLIS,[5] eldest son of John Lee,[4] married.

42. JOHN HANCOCK,[5] second son of John Lee,[4] married.

43. THOMAS,[6] second son of Thomas Sim[5] Lee, married and left children.

44. WILLIAM,[6] third son of Thomas Sim[5] Lee, married and left children.

45. ARCHIBALD,[6] fourth son of Thomas Sim[5] Lee, married and left children.

46. JOHN,[6] fifth son of Thomas Sim[5] Lee, born in 1788; married Miss Carroll, grand-daughter of Charles Carroll of Carrollton; died May 17, 1871, and left children.

47. RICHARD HENRY,[6] eldest son of Ludwell[5] Lee and Flora ——, died about 1863 or 1864; married twice: first wife, Miss Duncan; second wife, Miss Jourdan. Children by both marriages.

48. FRANCIS LIGHTFOOT,[6] son of Ludwell[5] Lee and Miss Armistead, married Miss Rogers, of S. C. No children.

49. SAMUEL PHILLIPS,[6] eldest son of Francis Lightfoot[5] Lee, married Miss Blair, and has children.

50. JOHN FITZGERALD,[6] second son, married Miss Hill, and has children.

51. CHARLES CARTER,[6] second son of Henry[5] Lee and Ann Carter, died March, 1871; married Miss Taylor. Left children.

52. SYDNEY SMITH,[6] third son, born Sept. 2, 1802; died July 22, 1869; married Miss Anne Mason. Left children.

53. ROBERT EDWARD,[6] fourth son, born at Stratford, Westmoreland Co., Va., Jan. 19, 1807; married, June 30, 1831, to Miss Mary Custis, daughter of Geo. W. Parke Custis, of Arlington, near Alexandria, Va.; died Oct. 12, 1870, at Lexington, Va. Left children.

54. ROBERT EDEN,[6] youngest son of Charles Lee, married Miss Margaret Gordon Scott; died. No children.

55. RICHARD BLAND,[6] eldest son of Richard Bland Lee, born July 20, 1797; married Miss Julia Prosser, and has children.

56. ZACCHEUS COLLINS,[6] youngest son, born Dec. 5, 1805; married Miss Martha Jenkins; died Nov. 26, 1859, and left children.

57. JOHN,[6] son of Theodoric[5] Lee, married Miss Prosser; died, and left children.
58. EDMUND JENNINGS,[6] eldest son of Edmund Jennings Lee, born in 1797; married, first, Miss Shepherd, and second, Miss Bedinger, of Jefferson Co., Va. Children by both marriages.
59. WILLIAM FITZHUGH,[6] second son, born May 7, 1804; married Miss Mary S. Chilton; died May 19, 1837. Left children.
60. CASSIUS FRANCIS,[6] third son, born May, 1808; married first, Hannah Philippa Ludwell Hopkins; second, Anne E. Gardner, April 15, 1846. Children by both marriages.
61. CHARLES HENRY,[6] fourth son, born in 1818; married Elizabeth A. Dunbar, and has one daughter.
62. RICHARD HENRY,[6] fifth son, born in 1820; married Evelyn B. Page, and has children.
63. JOHN HANCOCK,[6] son of Willis Lee, born in 1805; married, and has children.

THE WINSLOW FAMILY.

[Communicated by the Rev. LUCIUS P. PAIGE, D.D., of Cambridgeport, Mass.]

Concluded from vol. xxv. page 358.

5. KENELM[3] (*Kenelm*,[2] *Kenelm*[1]), b. about 1667, inherited the homestead in Harwich (now Brewster). He was a clothier, or cloth dresser; and the business which he established at Setucket, or Winslow's Mills, was prosperously conducted both by himself and his posterity. He was selectman three years, town treasurer five years, and representative in 1720. In consequence of the imperfection of records, his domestic relations have heretofore been involved in obscurity; his wife has been supposed to be the second wife of his father, and his paternity to his large family of children has not generally been recognized. Fortunately, he executed a will, 22 Jan., 1728–9, in which his legitimate claim to both wife and children is fully established. He m. 5 Jan., 1689–90, Bethia Hall, and d. 20 March, 1728–9, in the 62d year of his age; his widow was published, 19 March, 1729–30, to Mr. Joseph Hawes, of Yarmouth. The births of Mr. Winslow's children are not found on record; but the dates are estimated partly from the order in which the names are mentioned in the father's will, and partly from inscriptions on head-stones in the "Winslow burying-ground." His children were:—

i. BETHIA, b. about 1691; m. 5 March, 1712–13, John Wing, and d. 19 June, 1720, aged 29.
ii. MERCY, b. about 1693; m. 8 March, 1710–11, Philip Vincent.
iii. REBECCA, b. about 1695; m. 21 March, 1719–20, Samuel Rider; resided in Yarmouth, afterwards in Rochester.
iv. THANKFUL, b. about 1697; m. 4 Feb., 1722–3, Theophilus Crosby, of Yarmouth.
v. KENELM, b. about 1700; a clothier; resided in Harwich (Brewster); m. 14 Sept., 1722, Zerviah Rider, by whom he had thirteen children; she d. 5 April, 1745, aged 41, and he m. 8 May, 1746, Mrs. Abigail Sturgis, of Yarmouth, who d. 17 Sept., 1783, aged 76. Mr. Winslow was selectman three years; also a justice of the peace and of the quorum. He d. 28 June, 1783, in the 83d year of his age.

vi. THOMAS, b. about 1704; resided in Harwich (Brewster); m. 12 Feb., 1722–3, Mehetabel, dau. of his uncle, Maj. Edward Winslow, of Rochester, by whom he had twelve children, nine of whom died, aged less than one year, and their head-stones stand in a sad row in the "Winslow burying-ground." He was a selectman, a colonel, and judge of the Court of Common Pleas. He d. 10 April, 1779, in the 75th year of his age; his wife survived him.

vii. MARY, b. about 1707; m. 9 March, 1726–7, Ebenezer Clapp, of Rochester.

viii. HANNAH, bap. 9 Sept., 1711; m. 14 Dec., 1728, Edward Winslow, Jr., son of her uncle Maj. Edward Winslow, of Rochester, and d. 25 Sept., 1745, in the 35th year of her age.

ix. SETH, b. 1715; resided in Harwich (Brewster), and m. 15 Jan., 1735–6, Thankful Sears, who d. 7 March, 1736–7, aged 18. He was published 11 March, 1737–8, to Priscilla Freeman, who d. 11 Feb., 1776, aged 60. He d. 12 Aug., 1754, aged 39 years, 5 months and 8 days, having had six children; three daughters survived him.

6. JOSIAH[3] (*Kenelm,*[2] *Kenelm*[1]), b. 7 Nov., 1669; received by gift, 27 Feb., 1693–4, one quarter part of his father's lands in Freetown, and 14 Feb., 1702, purchased all his father's lands on the west side of Taunton River, and undivided rights in Freetown, where he resided during the remainder of his long life. He was a clothier, and established the business of cloth-dressing near Assonet Bridge, where it was continued by several generations of his descendants. (*Ante*, xix., 47, 273.) He was frequently selectman and assessor; also a Captain, by which title he was generally designated. His first wife, the mother of all his children, was Margaret Tisdale, to whom he was published 13 June, 1691. According to the Freetown and Middleborough Records, he was subsequently married, 3 Nov., 1738, to Mrs. Hannah Winslow, perhaps widow of his cousin Richard Winslow, of Freetown; 2 March, 1748–9, to widow Hannah Booth, of Middleborough; 30 Nov., 1749, to Martha Hathaway, of Freetown; and published, 6 Sept., 1750, to Mary Jones, of Berkley. He d. 3 April, 1761, in the 92d year of his age. (*Ante*, xviii., 301.) His will, 5 March, 1753, indicates that his wife Mary, and all his children, except the eldest daughter, were then living. They were:—

i. JOSIAH, b. 9 June, 1697; "m. Sarah, dau. of John Hayward, Jr., 1721; lived awhile in East Bridgewater, and afterwards exchanged farms with Joseph Keith, and went up to W. Bridgewater, near to Easton line." (Mitchell's *Hist. Bridgewater*, p. 353.) He was living in 1753, with sons Josiah, Ezra, and John-Hayward.

ii. MERCY, b. 15 Dec., 1700; published 15 Nov., 1728, to James Whitcomb, of Rochester, and d. 20 April, 1729.

iii. EBENEZER, b. 22 Nov., 1705; m. Esther Atwood, was a Major and resided in Berkley. (*Peirce Family*, p. 84.)

iv. EDWARD, b. 11 Aug., 1709; was of Taunton, 2 Jan., 1758, when he received a deed of gift from his father.

v. JAMES, b. 12 Aug., 1712; was a clothier and Major, resided in Freetown. He was published 15 Feb., 1737–8, to Charity Hodges, of Norton, by whom he had nine children. His will, dated 17 June, 1776, was proved 22 March, 1777.

vi. MARGARET, b. 5 April, 1716; m. 5 July, 1733, John King, of Norton.

vii. MARY, b. 24 March, 1720; published 10 July, 1742, to Daniel Hunt, Jr., of Norton.

viii. RACHEL, b. 9 Feb., 1722; m. 1 May, 1746, Edward Winslow, Jr., son of her uncle, Major Edward Winslow, of Rochester, and d. 28 Dec., 1766, "in the 45th year of her age," or 1767 as inscribed on her head-stone.

7. SAMUEL[3] (*Kenelm,*[2] *Kenelm*[1]), b. about 1674, in early life styled cordwainer, and afterwards yeoman, resided in Rochester, 1700, and was Deacon of the First Church in that town as early as 1710. He m. 26 Sept., 1700, Bethia Holbrook, of Scituate; she d. and he m. 11 Nov., 1703,

Mercy King, of Scituate; she d. 16 Feb., 1733, and he was published 15 Sept., 1739, to Ruth Briggs. He was living in 1750, and perhaps followed his sons in their emigration to Hardwick. His children were:—

i. MERCY, b. 16 Aug., 1705; m. 15 Aug., 1721, James Whitcomb, of Rochester, and d. 20 Sept., 1726.
ii. ELIZABETH, b. 29 Jan., 1706–7.
iii. ANN, b. 13 Feb., 1708–9; published 1 May, 1731, to Roland Hammond, of Rochester, and d. 1734.
iv. THOMAS, b. 7 June, 1711; m. 27 June, 1734, Rebecca Ewer, of Barnstable, by whom he had fifteen children; removed to Hardwick about 1752.
v. KENELM, b. 20 Feb., 1712–13; m. 21 June, 1734, Elizabeth Clapp, by whom he had eleven children; removed to Hardwick about 1749, and to Petersham about 1773.
vi. JUDITH, b. 8 July, 1716.

8. NATHANIEL[3] (*Kenelm*,[2] *Kenelm*[1]), b. about 1678; resided early in Freetown, but manifested a more roving disposition than was common to his race. I find traces of him in Freetown, 1701–1705; in Little Compton, 1707–1709; in Rochester, 1710, 1711; and in Middleborough, 1712–1718; he was styled, 9 Nov., 1721, "late of Middleborough," and it is probable that he was the same person who "removed to Damariscotta, 1729, and testified in court at Old York, 1742, then 63 years old." (Mitchell's *Hist. Bridgewater*, p. 390.) He m. 9 July, 1701, Elizabeth Holbrook, of Scituate. Their children, born at Freetown, were:—

i. MARTHA, b. 1 May, 1702.
ii. ELIZABETH, b. 16 Jan., 1703–4; d. 14 March, 1704.
iii. ELIZABETH, b. 16 Feb., 1704–5.

9. EDWARD[3] (*Kenelm*,[2] *Kenelm*[1]), b. 30 Jan., 1680–1, was a farmer, and resided in Rochester. In 1725, together with Ebenezer Lewis, of Barnstable, and Edmund Freeman, of Harwich, he erected "iron-works, to carry on the making and forging of iron," near his dwelling-house, "on the middle branch of the Mattepoisett River." He was selectman, town clerk, town treasurer, justice of the peace and of the quorum; he was also a Major, and was generally known by his military title. He m. Sarah ——, who d. 11 Oct., 1767, aged 85. He d. 25 June, 1760. His children were:—

i. EDWARD, b. 6 Nov., 1703; a farmer and Captain, resided in Rochester and inherited the homestead. He m. 14 Dec., 1728, Hannah, dau. of his uncle Kenelm Winslow, of Harwich; she d. 25 Sept., 1745, and he m. 1 May, 1746, Rachel, dau. of his uncle Josiah Winslow, of Freetown; she d. 28 Dec., 1766,* and he was published 9 Aug., 1767, to Mrs. Hannah Winslow, of Dighton. He d. 7 May, 1780.
ii. MEHITABLE, b. 6 May, 1705; m. 12 Feb., 1722–3, Col. Thomas Winslow, son of her uncle Kenelm Winslow, of Harwich, and was living 20 March, 1779.
iii. SARAH, b. 1707; m. before 1725, Thomas Lincoln; he d. in Rochester, 15 June, 1730, aged 30, and she m. 31 May, 1731, James Whitcomb,† of Rochester, and was living in Western (now Warren), 28 Feb., 1771, when dower was assigned to her.

* The date 1767, inscribed on her head-stone, is a manifest mistake, if she was then "in the 45th year of her age," and if Capt. Winslow's subsequent publishment is correctly recorded.

† James Whitcomb, son of James, was b. at Scituate, 21 Aug., 1697, and d. at Western (now Warren), in 1763. His twin-brother, Nathaniel Whitcomb, was b. two days earlier, 19 Aug., 1697, and d. at Hardwick, 18 March, 1772. Both resided several years in Rochester. Before he was thirty-four years old, James Whitcomb had four wives, three of whom were cousins to each other, as mentioned in the text:—(1) Mercy, dau. of Deacon Samuel Winslow, 15 Aug., 1721; (2) Joanna Spooner, of Dartmouth, 12 July, 1727; (3) Mercy, dau. of Capt. Josiah Winslow, published 15 Nov., 1728; (4) Sarah, dau. of Maj. Edward Winslow, 31 May, 1731.

iv. LYDIA, b. 8 Sept., 1709; m. 10 July, 1729, Dea. James Foster, of Rochester, and d. 7 Jan., 1770. [Her dau. Mary, b. 11 April, 1732, m. 24 Oct., 1754, Col. Timothy Paige, of Hardwick, and d. at New Braintree, 21 July, 1825, aged 93.]
v. MERCY, b. 1 Sept., 1712; m. 10 Oct., 1730, Chillingsworth Foster, of Harwich (now Brewster), and d. 25 Jan., 1757.
vi. THANKFUL, b. 2 April, 1715; m. 10 April, 1735, Josephus Hammond, of Rochester, and d. before 2 Oct., 1758.

10. JOHN[3] (*Kenelm,[2] Kenelm[1]*), b. about 1701, a farmer, resided in Rochester, and was elected Deacon of the church in that town, 5 Aug., 1748. He m. 15 March, 1721–2, Bethia Andrews, who survived him. His will, dated 11 Jan., 1752, and proved 16 July, 1755, mentions all the children named below, except Bethia and Stephen:—

i. JOHN, b. 31 Oct., 1721; m. 3 Aug., 1745, Bethia Sherman.
ii. DEBORAH, b. 8 Feb., 1724–5; m. 15 March, 1743–4, John Sherman.
iii. JEDEDIAH, b. 26 March, 1727; published 24 March, 1750, to Elizabeth Goodspeed, of Barnstable.
iv. NATHANIEL, b. 22 April, 1730; m. 23 April, 1757, Thankful Randall.
v. BETHIA, b. 24 May, 1732; probably d. young.
vi. LEMUEL, b. 3 Nov., 1734.
vii. PRINCE, b. 6 April, 1737.
viii. STEPHEN, b. 5 July, 1739; probably d. young.
ix. ELIZABETH, b.

11. NATHANIEL[3] (*Nathaniel,[2] Kenelm[1]*), b. 29 July, 1667, resided principally in Marshfield, though certain deeds of land indicate that he was in Shawomet, or Swansey, at least a portion of the time, from 1700 to 1709. He is styled "Captain;" but perhaps this was his maritime title, for it is said that he commanded "the sloop Seaflower, engaged in freighting oak wood from Careswell Creek to Boston." (*Mem. of Marshfield*, p. 29.) He m. Lydia, dau. of Josiah Snow; she d. September, 1716, and he m. 17 Feb., 1717–8, Deborah Bryant, of Scituate, who d. 28 Nov., 1778, aged 97, as the Marshfield Records say; but if the date of her birth is accurately given by Deane (*Hist. Scituate*, p. 227), she lived 99 years. Administration on his estate was granted 30 March, 1736. His children, recorded in Marshfield, were:—

i. LYDIA, b. 24 Jan., 1693; m. 10 Dec., 1718, Joseph Thomas.
ii. THANKFUL, b. 3 Feb., 1695; m. 27 Oct., 1725, Nathaniel Kean, of Pembroke.
iii. SNOW, b. 13 May, 1698; m. 6 Nov., 1728, Deborah Bryant.
iv. OLIVER, b. 24 Nov., 1702; "settled in Scituate," and m. Agatha Bryant. "He had a son Oliver, who was killed in the French war in 1758, at the age of 20, a son John, who removed to Nobleboro', Maine, and Major Nathaniel, a man who inherited the bold spirit of his distinguished ancestors." (*Hist. Scituate*, p. 390.)
v. DEBORAH, b. 21 March, 1708.
vi. PATIENCE, b. 29 June, 1710.
vii. NATHANIEL, b. 9 Sept., 1712; m. 3 Feb., 1731, Susanna Bryant.
viii. RUTH, b. 30 Dec., 1718.
ix. ABIAH, b. 4 Dec., 1721; m. 16 July, 1741, Nehemiah Thomas.
x. ALLATHEAH, b. 4 Nov., 1723; probably d. young.

12. JAMES[3] (*Nathaniel,[2] Kenelm[1]*), b. 16 Aug., 1669, appears to have resided in Plymouth, 1699–1701, where the birth of two children was recorded, and in Swansey, 1706–1708. He became a permanent resident in Rochester about 1709, and was town treasurer several years. He m. Mary ——, who d. 4 Dec., 1717, aged 43, and he m. Elizabeth ——, who survived him. His will, dated 11 Feb., 1731–2, proved 20 Sept., 1733, mentions all the children named below, except Nathaniel:—

i. SETH, b. 1799; m. 23 Oct., 1729, Abigail Whittredge.
ii. MARY, b. 1701.
iii. BARSHEBA, b. 11 May, 1705.
iv. JAMES, b. 2 May, 1709.
v. JOB, b. 7 Sept., 1712.
vi. NATHANIEL, b. 4 Nov., 1715; d. 23 Jan., 1725.
vii. PETER, b. 11 April, 1720.

13. GILBERT³ (*Nathaniel,*² *Kenelm*¹), b. 11 July, 1673, resided in Marshfield, and m. 7 Feb., 1698, Mercy, dau. of Josiah Snow, who survived him. He d. 12 June, 1731. His will, dated 26 May, 1731, mentions all the children named below, except Lydia:—

i. ISSACHAR, b. 19 Feb., 1699.
ii. BARNABAS, b. 24 Feb., 1701.
iii. GILBERT, b. 26 July, 1704.
iv. ANTHONY, b. 24 April, 1707.
v. MERCY, b. 1 Aug., 1710.
vi. REBECCA, b. 3 Jan., 1712.
vii. JOB, b. 2 June, 1715; m. 20 March, 1740, Elizabeth Macomber.
viii. BENJAMIN, b. 28 Aug., 1717.
ix. LYDIA, b. 25 April, 1720; d. 5 Oct., 1723.

14. KENELM³ (*Nathaniel,*² *Kenelm*¹), b. 22 Sept., 1675, inherited the homestead in Marshfield, and was justice of the peace. He m. Abigail Waterman, who d. 15 Aug., 1729, aged 47. He d. 10 June, 1757, aged 82. His children were:—

i. SARAH, b. 3 Dec., 1704.
ii. ABIGAIL, b. 25 June, 1707; m. 25 June, 1730, Rev. Isaiah Lewis, of Wellfleet.
iii. NATHANIEL, b. 21 April, 1709.
iv. FAITH, b. 2 Feb., 1712.
v. KENELM, b. 5 Nov., 1716; m. Abigail Bourn, of Barnstable, who d. 21 Dec., 1761, aged 32. He d. 13 Aug., 1780. Their son Kenelm, b. 24 July, 1756, alienated the homestead of his fathers, and removed to Kennebec Co., Maine. (*Mem. Marshfield*, p. 28.)
vi. ELEANOR, b. 17 June, 1718.
vii. JOSEPH, b. 30 Oct., 1724.

15. JOHN² (*Nathaniel,*² *Kenelm*³), b. 13 Jan., 1683–4, appears to have resided successively in Marshfield, Swansey and Wareham. He m. Mary ——, who survived him. His will, dated Wareham, 5 Dec., 1755, and proved 3 April, 1758, mentions all the children who are named below. The birth of the first three is recorded in Marshfield:—

i. FAITH, b. 3 Nov., 1706; m. —— Randall.
ii. ELEANOR, b. 15 April, 1709; m. —— Besse.
iii. WILLIAM, b. 5 Dec., 1713; d. at Wareham, about 1759.
iv. SARAH, b. ——; m. —— Turner
v. MARY, b. ——; m. —— Wood.

16. RICHARD³ (*Job,*² *Kenelm*¹), b. ——, resided in Freetown, and m. Hannah ——, who was living a widow, 19 Aug., 1737. His will, dated 7 Aug., 1727, and proved 16 April, 1728, describes him as a "practitioner of physick and chirurgeon," and mentions all the children who are named below:—

i. RICHARD, b. 19 Aug., 1711.
ii. HEZEKIAH, b. 9 Dec., 1713; m. 30 May, 1737, Betsey Paine.
iii. SARAH, b. 8 May, 1716; m. 30 May, 1737, Ichabod Eddy.
iv. WILLIAM, b. 24 Sept., 1718; m. 7 July, 1743, Elizabeth Merrick.
v. HANNAH, b. 14 April, 1721.
vi. EDWARD, b. 10 Oct., 1723; m. 20 Oct., 1748, Phebe Winslow.

17. JAMES[3] (*Job*,[2] *Kenelm*[1]), b. 9 May, 1687, resided in Freetown. His children, by wife Elizabeth, were:—

i. MARY, b. 20 June, 1709.
ii. NATHAN, b. 1 April, 1713.
iii. JOB, b. 30 March, 1715.
iv. BENJAMIN, b. 19 June, 1717.
v. ELIZABETH, b. 6 May, 1721.
vi. JAMES, b. 6 Aug., 1725.
vii. SYBIL, b. 3 Oct., 1727.

18. GEORGE[3] (*Job*,[2] *Kenelm*[1]), b. 2 Jan., 1690–1, a carpenter, resided in Freetown, and m. Elizabeth ——, who survived him. His will, 5 May, 1757, proved 15 June, 1757, mentions all the children named below, except Elkanah:—

i. HOPESTILL, b. 9 Jan., 1722–3; m. —— Cook.
ii. ABIGAIL, b. 26 Dec., 1724; m. —— Aiken.
iii. PHEBE, b. 2 Oct., 1726; m. 20 Oct., 1748, her cousin Edward Winslow.
iv. GEORGE, b. 19 June, 1728.
v. ELIZABETH, b. 28 July, 1730; published 14 June, 1754, to Jacob Strange, Newport.
vi. ELKANAH, b. 13 Jan., 1732–3; probably d. young.
vii. BARNABAS, b 30 Sept., 1734; m. 6 July, 1761, Sarah Terry.
viii. REBECCA, b. 6 Sept., 1736; m. 15 Dec., 1757, Richard Kirby, of Dartmouth.

19. JONATHAN[3] (*Job*[2], *Kenelm*[1]), b. 22 Nov., 1692, resided in Freetown, and m. 25 Nov., 1722, Sarah Kirby, probably of Dartmouth. Their children were:—

i. REBECCA, b. 26 Aug., 1723; d. 18 Dec., 1731.
ii. JONATHAN, b. 22 Nov., 1725.
iii. JOHN, b. 22 Nov., 1725; d. 3 Sept., 1742.
iv. THOMAS, b. 5 July, 1729.
v. SARAH, b. 19 July, 1731.
vi. NATHANIEL, b. 20 May, 1733.
vii. RUTH, b. 1 Feb., 1735–6.
viii. REUBEN, b. 18 May, 1738; published 2 July, 1763, to Mary Webster.
ix. BENJAMIN, b. 14 Feb., 1740–1; published 6 Nov., 1767, to Content Webster.
x. HANNAH, b. ——; m. 21 Nov., 1765, to John Valentine.
xi. HOPESTILL, b. ——; m. 19 July, 1767, Stephen Taber.

20. JOSEPH[3] (*Job*,[2] *Kenelm*[1]), a cordwainer, resided in Swansey, and was representative in 1721. Administration on his estate was granted, 4 Sept., 1727, to his widow Hannah; but she d. before 22 Feb., 1727–8, when an inventory was presented. Distribution was made 15 Jan., 1733–4, to the children, viz.:—

i. OLIVER, ii. JOSEPH. iii. JOB. iv. RUTH. v. MARY.
vi. HANNAH. vii. SUSANNA. viii. PRISCILLA.

21. JOHN[3] (*Job*,[2] *Kenelm*[1]), b. 20 Feb., 1694–5, resided in Freetown, was representative 5 years, and m. 9 Oct., 1729, Betsey Hathaway, to whom administration on his estate was granted, 7 Oct., 1755. All the children named below, except Andrew, received portions of their uncle William Winslow's estate, 1 May, 1781.

i. HULDAH, b. 10 March, 1729–30; m. —— Chase.
ii. ABNER, b. 7 May, 1732; m. 16 Aug., 1759, Rebecca Hathaway.
iii. SYLVIA, b. 10 March, 1733–4; published 10 Sept., 1757, to Samuel Barnaby.
iv. LUCY, b. 20 Feb., 1735–6.
v. ANDREW, b. 19 Feb., 1737–8.
vi. LEMUEL, b. 25 Dec., 1739; m. 7 Jan., 1762, Abigail Hathaway.
vii. LOIS, b. 16 March, 1741.
viii. EUNICE, b. 25 April, 1744.
ix. OLIVER.
x. WILLIAM.
xi. JOSEPH.

ELIZABETH[3] (*Job*,[2] *Kenelm*[1]), b. 1696–7; m. John Marshall, of Freetown. Their dau. Ruth, b. at Freetown, 1 April, 1737, m. 13 Feb., 1754, Capt. James Green, of East Haddam, Conn., and d. 27 Nov., 1816.

[For some of the facts relative to the Winslows of Freetown, I am indebted to Gen. Ebenezer W. Peirce; most of the other facts embodied in the foregoing sketch were obtained by a personal examination of Town and County Records. I shall be glad to receive any additional information; especially in regard to Damaris ——, who m. Kenelm Winslow, of Harwich, about 1690, and *more* especially, as to the parentage of Sarah ——, who m. Maj. Edward Winslow, of Rochester, about 1702. L. R. P.]

THE PAGE FAMILY.

[Communicated by WILLIAM PRESCOTT, M.D., of Concord, N. H.]

JOHN PAGE, born at Dedham in England in 1586, came to New-England with Gov. Winthrop in 1630, and settled in Dedham, Mass. He had, by his wife Phebe, John, Jr., Roger, Edward, Robert, Samuel and David. He died Dec. 18, 1676, aged 90.

The only detailed record in the possession of the writer, of the descendants of the above sons, is that of the descendants of Samuel, of which, Rev. D. Lancaster, in his history of Gilmanton, has recorded most that is to be found, and to which the reader is referred.

ROBERT PAGE, born in Ormsby, County of Norfolk, England, in 1604, emigrated to New-England in 1637. He was son of Robert of that place, who, by his wife Margaret, had:

1. i. ROBERT, b. in 1604; m. Lucy ——, b. in 1607. ii. THOMAS, b. 1606. iii. REBECCA, bap. May 16, 1608. iv. HENRY, b. 1610. v. FRANCIS, b. 1612.

Robert Page, Sen., d. in England, July, 1617. His will was dated July 1, 1617, and proved July 23d, in which he mentions wife Margaret, and the five children above named.

ROBERT PAGE, the emigrant, with wife Lucy, four of his children and two hired servants, Wm. Moulton and Ann Wadd, emigrated to America in 1637; at which time he was 33, and Lucy 30 years of age. He settled in Hampton, N. H., and was among the first settlers of that ancient town, where he d. Sept. 22, 1679, aged 75. Lucy, his wife, d. Nov. 12, 1665, aged 58. From the records in Hampton we learn that he was one of the most active, energetic and influential men in town. He was elected a member of the first board of selectmen, and again in 1647, 1652, 1655, 1659, 1667 and 1670. He was a member of the general assembly in 1657, and again in 1668.

He was also marshal of the old county of Norfolk, in which Hampton was then included. He was granted the privilege, by a vote of the town, of building the first saw-mill, which he was required to do within a year, but by reason of his being engaged in constructing a parsonage the time was extended to two years.

In 1659, when 76 persons were taxed, Robert Page's tax was the highest, and amounted to one twentieth of the whole sum. A committee was appointed to assign to each person the seat in which he was to sit, and a penalty was attached for a violation of the order. The people were seated in accordance with their social position and standing in the community. The front seat was considered the most honorable place. In this seat Robert

Page and a few others were placed on one side, while to their wives was allotted the front seat on the opposite side. Mr. Page was the only deacon of the church for more than 20 years, and was succeeded in that office by his son Francis.

Notwithstanding the many offices which he filled, and the multiplicity of business which he performed, he was unable to write his name and always made use of a *mark* for a signature, and a late town clerk of H. gave it as his opinion that the mark was uniformly made with the left hand.

1. ROBERT[1] and Lucy had the following children:

i. MARGARET, b. in England, 1629; m. 1651, Wm. Moulton, who came over as the hired servant of her father, and they were the ancestors of many of the Moultons in this country. He d. in 1664, and she m. for her second husband, John Sanborn, Sen., as his second wife; she d. July 13, 1699, a. 70.
ii. SUSAN, b. 1631.
2. iii. FRANCIS, b. 1633; m. Dec. 2, 1669, Meribah Smith.
iv. REBECCA, b. 1636; m. Oct. 15, 1652, Wm. Marston, Jr., b. 1622, d. Jan. 22, 1704, aged 82. She d. June 27, 1673, aged 37. They had: 1. Rebecca, b. 1654; m. June 3, 1676, John Smith, *the Tailor*. 2. Hannah, b. Aug. 21, 1656; m. Oct. 19, 1676, Samuel, son of Samuel and Ann Fogg, b. Dec. 25, 1653. 3. Mary, b. April 4, 1659; d. Dec. 2, 1660. 4. Samuel, b. Sept. 8, 1661; m. Sarah, dau. of Wm. Sanborn, Sen., b. 1663. He d. Nov. 8, 1723. She d. of palsy, April 17, 1738, aged 75. 5. Triphena, b. Dec. 28, 1663; m. 1685 or 6, Joseph, son of Joseph and Ann Philbrick. 6. Lucy, b. April 21, 1665. 7. William, b. 1667; d. in 1667. 8. William, b. 1669; m. Susanna ——. 9. Mariah, b. May 16, 1672; m. March 1, 1695, James Prescott, Jr., son of James Prescott, Sen., the emigrant of 1668, b. Sept. 1, 1671, and had Jeremiah, Samuel, Elisha, Sarah, Lucy, Ebenezer, James and Rebecca. (See *Prescott Memorial*, pages 233–5.)
3. v. THOMAS, b. in Hampton, 1639; m. Feb., 1664, Mary Hussey. He d. Sept. 6, 1686.
vi. HANNAH, b. in Hampton, 1641; m. June 15, 1659, Henry Dow, Jr., b. in England, 1634; was marshal of the province of New-Hampshire in 1680, mandamus counsellor in 1702; d. May 6, 1702, aged 68. She d. Aug. 6, 1704, aged 63. They had: 1. Samuel, b. Nov. 4, 1661. 2. Joseph, b. Oct. 20, 1663. 3. Simon, b. March 4, 1667. 4. Jabez, b. Feb. 8, 1672.
vii. MARY, b. 1644; m. Dec. 28, 1665, Samuel Fogg, an early settler of Hampton, as his second wife. She d. May 8, 1700. They had: 1. Seth, b. 1666; m. 1693 or 4, Sarah, dau. of Richard Curwin. 2. James, b. Feb. 16, 1668; m. Mary ——, three children. 3. Hannah, b. April 6, 1672.

2. FRANCIS[2] (*Robert*[1]), b. in England in 1633; m. Dec. 2, 1669, Meribah Smith, settled in Hampton; d. Nov. 15, 1706. They had:

4. i. SAMUEL, b. March 3, 1671; d. Dec. 6, 1764, aged 93 yrs. 9 mos. 3 days.
ii. LUCY, b. Sept. 22, 1672; m. Jan. 4, 1694, Ichabod, son of Henry Roby, b. Nov. 26, 1664. Ten children.
iii. SUSANNA, b. Dec. 2, 1674; m. Dec. 25, 1696, Benjamin Bachellor, b. July 19, 1673. They had six children. Their fourth, Susanna, b. in 1702, m. Ebenezer Webster, and they were the grand-parents of Hon. Daniel Webster.
5. iv. FRANCIS, b. Dec. 14, 1676; m. Jan. 27, 1698, Hannah Nudd.
v. MERIBAH, b. March 17, 1679; m. Samuel Tilton; d. Dec. 14, 1723, aged 44.
vi. REBECCA, b. Feb. 24, 1681; m. March 2, 1706, Samuel Palmer.
6. vii. JOSEPH, b. Nov. 25, 1686; m. Dec. 14, 1721, Sarah Moulton; d. Feb. 5, 1773, aged 86 yrs. 2 mos. 11 days.
viii. THOMAS, b. 1684; m. first, ——; m. second, Mary, dau. of Benjamin Towle, b. May 20, 1695, and d. 1783, aged 88.

3. THOMAS[2] (*Robert*[1]), b. in Hampton in 1639; m. Feb. 2, 1664, Mary Hussey. He d. in Hampton, Sept. 6, 1686. They had:

i. MARY, b. May 21, 1665; m. 1690, Samuel, son of Henry Robie, b. Aug. 15, 1659, and d. Jan. 21, 1733. She d. Sept. 5, 1750, aged 85 yrs. 4 mos. 4 ds.
ii. ROBERT, b. July 27, 1667; d. 1686.

7\. iii. CHRISTOPHER, b. Sept. 20, 1670; m. Nov. 14, 1689, Abigail, dau. of Daniel and Mehitable (Sanborn) Tilton, one of the early settlers of Hampton; she was b. Oct. 28, 1670. He d. Oct. 4, 1751, aged 81.

iv. JOHN, b. Nov. 15, 1672: m. and sold his farm to John Swett, who married his sister, and removed to Cape May; d. young.

v. THEODATE, b. Feb. 8, 1675; d. young.

vi. STEPHEN, b. May 14, 1677; m. Jan. 3, 1701, Mary Rawlings. He d. Feb., 1714, in his 37th year.

vii. BETHIA, b. May 23, 1679; m. Dec. 9, 1696, John Swett, son of Benjamin. (The son of the first John, and Hester, daughter of Peter Weare. He, the first John, was b. 1620, and m. 1647.) John Swett bought the farm of his brother-in-law John Page, as above. He was born in 1670, and d. in Kingston, N. H., Jan., 1753, aged 83, leaving a widow Sarah (second wife). REGISTER, vol. vi. p. 57. Bethia had, Huldah, b. 1699, Sarah, John, Elisha, Benjamin, Joseph, and Samuel Winslow, b. 1712.

4\. SAMUEL[3] (*Francis*,[2] *Robert*[1]), b. March 3, 1671; m. first, Jan. 1, 1696, Hannah Williams, who d. Dec. 24, 1701. He m. second, Nov. 18, 1702, Anne Marshall. He d. Dec. 6, 1764, aged 93 yrs. 9 mos. and 3 days. Samuel and Hannah had:

i. HANNAH, b. Oct. 31, 1696; d. in infancy.

ii. SAMUEL, b. May 3, 1698; d. in infancy.

iii. MERIBAH, b. Dec. 18, 1699.

Samuel Page and Anna had:

iv. SAMUEL, bap. Oct. 3, 1703. v. HANNAH, bap. Sept. 3, 1704.

vi. PRUDENCE, b. Sept. 2, 1706; m. first, Samuel, son of Samuel and Meribah (Page) Tilton, b. Nov. 1, 1703. He d. and she m. second, John Marston, (probably son of Caleb), b. Dec. 19, 1787. He d. and she m. third, Capt. Wm. Branscomb. She d. Oct 28, 1796, aged 90.

vii. ELIZABETH, b. Jan. 12, 1708; m. Isaac Tobey.

viii. BENJAMIN, b. March 6, 1709; d. young.

ix. SOLOMON, b. March 16, 1710; grad. at Harvard, and m. Dorothy ——.

x. JEREMIAH, b. Sept. 9, 1711.

xi. JOHN, bap. Nov. 18, 1712; m. March 14, 1751, Sarah Sanborn, dau. of Reuben, b. June 12, 1732; settled in Epping.

xii. BENJAMIN, bap. Nov. 21, 1714; m. Mary Sanborn, dau. of Shubael, bap. June 19, 1720.

xiii. STEPHEN, bap. Jan. 22, 1716; m. first, Nov. 11, 1740, Annie Perkins, dau. of James and Huldah (Robie) Perkins, and b. Aug. 24, 1720, d. May 28, 1752. He m. second, Mary Burnham.

xiv. ANNA, bap. Dec. 7, 1718. xv. SIMON, bap. March 17, 1721.

5\. FRANCIS[3] (*Francis*,[2] *Robert*[1]), b. Dec. 14, 1676; m. Jan. 29, 1698, Hannah Nudd, and d. Aug. 19, 1755, aged 79 yrs. and 8 mos. They had:

i. SARAH, b. Oct. 18, 1698; m. Josiah Bachelder, son of Nathaniel, by second wife, widow Wyman, and b. about 1690–92.

ii. ANNA, b. Nov. 17, 1700; d. young.

iii. HANNAH, b. April 16, 1704; d. young.

iv. MERIBAH, bap. Feb. 2, 1707.

v. ELISHA, b. March 3, 1708. vi. JOSIAH, b. July 22, 1709.

vii. ANNA, b. July 26, 1711.

viii. CHARITY, b. Oct. 13, 1713; d. June 30, 1715.

ix. HANNAH, b. Feb. 17, 1716. x. MARY, bap. Feb. 9, 1718.

6\. JOSEPH[3] (*Francis*,[2] *Robert*[1]), b. Nov. 25, 1686; m. Dec. 14, 1721, Sarah Moulton; d. Feb. 5, 1773, aged 86 yrs. 2 mos. 11 days. They had:

i. DOROTHY, b. Sept. 9, 1722.

ii. FRANCIS, b. April 19, 1724; m. Mary, dau. of Reuben and Sarah (Leavitt) Marston, b. Sept. 14, 1728. He d. May 1, 1802, aged 78.

iii. THEODATE, bap. Feb. 6, 1726. iv. MERIBAH, bap. Feb. 11, 1728; d. young.

v. JOSEPH, bap. March 1, 1730.

vi. DANIEL, bap. June 4, 1732; settled in Deerfield, N. H.

vii. MERIBAH, bap. April 13, 1735; d. Feb. 4, 1736.
viii. LUCY, bap. Sept. 4, 1737.
ix. MARY, bap. Dec. 9, 1739; m. Benjamin Brown.

7. CHRISTOPHER[3] (*Thomas,*[2] *Robert*[1]), b. Sept. 2, 1670; m. Nov. 14, 1689, Abigail Tilton, b. Oct. 28, 1670. He d. Oct. 4, 1751, aged 81 yrs. 1 mo. They had:

i. ROBERT, b. Sept. 8, 1690; d. July 20, 1706.
ii. ABIGAIL, b. Feb. 21, 1693; m. Dec. 23, 1715, William Moulton. She d. Jan. 22, 1776, aged 83.
iii. MARY, b. Dec. 13, 1695; m. Sept. 12, 1717, Samuel Dow. She d. March 10, 1760, aged 84 years and 4 months.
iv. LYDIA, b. Aug. 3, 1698; m. Nov. 15, 1721, John Towle, son of Joseph, b. 1694, and d. Dec. 5, 1786, aged 92. She d. May 22, 1772, aged 73¾.
v. JONATHAN, b. Feb. 25, 1700; m. Jan. 4, 1724, Mary Towle, dau. of Joseph, b. March 11, 1701. He d. 1770, aged 70.
vi. DAVID, b. Nov. 1, 1703; m. Jan. 27, 1728, Ruth Dearborn, b. May 21, 1705, and d. of fever, Jan. 8, 1741, aged 35 yrs. 7 mos. 18 days.
8. vii. SHUBAEL, b. Feb. 15, 1707; m. Jan. 21, 1731, Hannah Dow, b. Jan. 10, 1709. He d. May 16, 1791, aged 84 yrs. 3 mos.
viii. JEREMIAH, b. May 28, 1708; m. Dec. 17, 1730, Elizabeth, dau. of Abraham and Theodate (Robie) Drake, b. Feb. 28, 1712. He d. Sept. 18, 1786, aged 78 yrs. 4 mos.
ix. TABITHA, b. Aug. 21, 1711; m. Oct. 5, 1740, Caleb, son of Caleb and Ann (Moulton) Marston, b. July 3, 1699, as his second wife, and had nine children. She d. May 30, 1792.

8. SHUBAEL[4] (*Christopher,*[3] *Thomas,*[3] *Robert*[1]), b. Nov. 1, 1707; m. Jan. 21, 1731, Hannah Dow, b. June 10, 1709. They had:

i. ABIGAIL, b. Nov. 27, 1731; m. Jan. 31, 1753, Joseph Hobbs. She d. Dec. 28, 1790, aged 59 yrs. 1 mo.
ii. SARAH, b. April 12, 1734; m. Dec. 15, 1751, Benjamin Philbrick. She d. July 19, 1831, aged 97 yrs. 3 mos. 7 days.
iii. REUBEN, b. May 24, 1736; lost at sea in 1769, in his 34th year.
iv. MARY, b. April 6, 1738; m. Jan. 27, 1757, Christopher Smith. She d. March 28, 1778, aged 40.
v. SAMUEL, b. Dec. 12, 1741; m. Feb. 7, 1770, Sarah Sherburne. He d. Dec. 6, 1821, aged 80.
vi. NATHANIEL, b. Jan. 26, 1746; m. Betsey Leavitt. He d. Sept., 1806.
9. vii. ABNER, b. Nov. 15, 1748; m. Nov. 13, 1785, Abigail Moulton.
viii. and ix. Twins, b. 1750; d. in infancy.
x. JOSIAH, b. Oct. 17, 1753; d. Nov. 14, 1754, aged 1 year 1 mo.

9. ABNER[5] (*Shubael,*[4] *Christopher,*[3] *Thomas,*[2] *Robert*[1]), b. Nov. 15, 1748; m. Nov. 13, 1785, Abigail Moulton. They had:

i. JOHN, b. Aug. 21, 1786; m. March 7, 1817, Betsey Tucke.
ii. JOSIAH (the genealogist), b. Sept. 24, 1788; m. Dec. 19, 1826, Susan Leavitt. He has ever taken a great interest in genealogical investigation, and was, in his day, better acquainted with the family records of Hampton than any of his contemporaries, and has probably furnished and supplied others with more record and other matter, than any other, if not more than all others in Hampton. The records of Hampton were as familiar to him as household-words, of which he was very liberal in furnishing copies to all who applied to him. He could relate many anecdotes and transactions of the early settlers which he had gathered from persons much older than himself. His knowledge of the records of Hampton was much facilitated by his being for many years town-clerk. It is greatly to be regretted that his usefulness has been cut off by reason of blindness, which has laid him by for many years. It is also stated, that, more recently, his mental faculties are failing. He has ever been a modest, unassuming and useful citizen. If living, he is now (Dec., 1871), in his 84th year.
iii. DAVID, b. Oct. 17, 1791; m. Feb. 27, 1816, Harriet Norwood.
iv. ABIGAIL, b. Nov. 11, 1795; m. Dec. 8, 1815, Thomas Leavitt.

NOTES AND QUERIES.

GOV. BAREFOOT.—[After our note to Gov. Barefoote's Will (*ante*, pp. 13–16) was printed, we discovered in the ancient records of Portsmouth, N. H., the following memorandum, for a copy of which we are indebted to Marcellus Bufford, Esq., the efficient and courteous city-clerk. Gov. B. is also styled *chirurgeon* in the court-records in Exeter, N. H. This settles the question as to his profession.—ED.]

"At a meeting of the selectmen the 11th June, 1678,

"Agreed with Capt. Barefoote for the curing of Rich; Harvey who lately broke his leg, and if s[d] Barefoote make a perfect cure providing and finding all means at his own cost excepting Rhum for stupes [bandages, &c. ED.] (which the town is to find), and if said Barefoote shall perfect the cure he is to have for the same twentie pounds all into money or merch[t] white oak pipe staves at £3:10*s*. per m., and if in case he perform not a perfect cure, he agrees to have nothing for his pains more than 20*s*. in money already p[d] him for what he has done for him to this day."

"Mr. Ric; Harvey deceased the 13th day of this instant June 1678."

OXNARD FAMILY.—In addition to what is given on pages 3–10 of this number of the REGISTER, data respecting this family will be found in Capt. Preble's *Genealogical Sketch of the First Three Generations of Prebles in America.*

BATTLES.—John Battles, of Plympton, was appointed administrator on the estate of his father, John Battles, of Plympton, in probate at Plymouth, Sept. 5th, 1745; inventory presented Sept. 17, appraisal £50. 16s. 1½d.—(*Records*, vol. viii. p. 314.)

In Mitchell's *Bridgewater* it is stated that John Battles settled at Stoughton Corner, where he had children, the youngest of whom, Susannah, married Benjamin Washburn in 1742. (Page 113.)

Deane's *History of Scituate* mentions Joseph Battles as there from Hingham in 1738, the marriage of his son Joseph in 1758, and speaks of descendants of the latter living still at Hoop-pole Neck. Deane refers the origin of this family to Robert Battile, of Boston (by him written Battles), 1658. The inventory of Battile's estate and a list of his creditors are mentioned in *His. and Gen. Register*, vol. x. p. 175, the dates severally 1660 and 1663. P. B.

LEBARON.—Elizabeth LeBaron, daughter of Lazarus LeBaron, of Plymouth, born 1745–6, married Rev. Ammi R. Robbins, of Norfolk, Conn., 1762. (See *His. and Gen. Register*, vol. xxv. p. 181.) Her family was large—among them Rev. Thomas Robbins, D.D., of Hartford, and was doubly connected with Plymouth as the home of the relations of Mrs. R., and of Rev. Chandler Robbins, D.D., minister of Plymouth, her husband's brother. In her family the tradition was preserved that her grandfather, Dr. Francis LeBaron, was of Huguenot origin; that he was held in confinement as a student in a Jesuit college to be educated as a priest; that he escaped over the wall of its enclosure to the sea-coast, and found refuge upon a ship, and may have become its surgeon. The writer has himself heard this tradition from the lips of Mrs. Robbins in her family in Norfolk, where she survived until 1829. It tallies certainly with the history of the period referred to, preceding 1696, when the severest affliction of the Huguenots was from the abstraction and confinement of their children and youth to be educated in the faith of the state. In the neighborhood of Rochelle and Bordeaux, as elsewhere, maritime enterprise was largely in Protestant hands, and furnished an opportunity of escape to the refugees. So the Jesuit style of education for the priesthood might in many cases include a knowledge of surgery. The youthful refugee, LeBaron, was received as surgeon on a privateer, and when shipwrecked on the New-England coast was content to make himself a home by such means of a professional livelihood as he could command, among strangers. His religious opinions may not have been disclosed. Thatcher states that he wore a cross upon his breast to the last, and was a "Catholic." But who saw the cross, and who interpreted it, if any but rumor reported it? If not a symbol of his own faith, was it a keepsake cherished by another's? The Huguenot was not a Puritan, the French exile not English, the stranger not in his heart altogether one with his neighbors. The family tradition, as held by Mrs. Robbins, is confirmed as such in the sermon preached at her funeral by Rev. Ralph Emerson, September 30, 1829, printed in Hartford, of which an extract is given below. Mr. Emerson, the successor of her husband in the pastorate, had boarded many months in her family, and lived in most intimate habits of association with herself and her kindred. He subsequently was professor of ecclesiastical history in Andover Seminary, and was personally and as a scholar worthy to speak the eulogy of one of the most venerable of women:—"She was born January 1, 1746, in Plymouth in Massachusetts—a spot forever so sacred to every true child of the Pilgrims who there found a refuge from the hand of oppression. Her father was Dr. Lazarus LeBaron, a respectable and beloved physician, and a descendant of those persecuted Huguenots whose prayers are still signally answered by a covenant-keeping God, in spiritual mercies on their posterity. . . . Where the prayers of the suffering pious from two nations unite, and their blood flows in the same veins, what blessings may meet—what responsibilities concur!" P. B.

PUFFER.—Mathias Puffer married in Braintree, 12 March, 1662, Rachel Farnsworth. Can any one give me information about her? And was she possibly the same with either Rebecca or Ruthy, daughters of Joseph Farnsworth, of Dorchester? Ruth is made to appear wife of *William* Puffer in Dorchester Church Records? Is this a mistake?

I want information about Mrs. Elizabeth Gregory, who was admitted to the church of Milton, b. 6 May, 1694. W. S. APPLETON.

THE FIRST WEDDING IN NEW-ENGLAND.—[The first wedding ever celebrated in the New-England colonies, took place May 12th, 1621, 250 years ago, and five months after the landing of the Pilgrims on Plymouth Rock. The names of the happy pair were Mr. Edward Winslow and Mistress Susanna White.

The late Miss Frances M. Caulkins, the historian, celebrated the event in the following lines which we print from her autograph.—ED.]

First bride, first bridegroom of the land,
  Under the Christian banner;
The straitest of a strait-laced band,
  Young Winslow and gentle Susannah.

Hail to the nuptials, shining fair,
  At the head of our puritan story!
It brightens all New-England air,
  With a stream of wedding glory.

No bells, no pomp, but side by side,
  Pure in soul and prim in manner,
Such methinks was the wedding tide,
  Of Winslow and his fair Susannah.

O could I sway the countless years,
  Downward o'er our country flowing,
All the weddings of all the spheres,
  Should with these pattern tints be glowing.

Such weddings with such groom and bride,
  So linked with grace and duty,
Ten thousand fold be multiplied,
  In all their homely beauty.

Not games or banquets mark the day,
  Plain robes, not costly dressing:
Solemnities and not display,
  Few friends, and hearty blessing.

When faith is pledged and hearts unite,
  'Tis a type of heavenly union;
Sacred should be the nuptial rite
  To home born heart-communion. [F. M. C.

THE OLD FORT ON CONANICUT ISLAND, NEAR NEWPORT, R. I.—In some late publications, particularly in the tale of Newport, lately published by Ticknor & Fields, under the name of "Malbone," this old fort, which commonly bears the name of Fort Dumplin, is called Fort Louis. Is this merely the fancy of the novelist, or is there any authority for the name?

There is a map extant which bears the following title:—*A Topographical chart of the Bay of Narraganset in New-England, taken by Charles Blaskowitz, and dedicated to Lord Percy, Lt. Gen. of his majesty's forces, showing the several works and batteries raised by the Americans, with the banks, shoals and rocks.* London, 1777. This chart, which seems to have an official character, shows no batteries at the Dumplins or the Beaver-tail, though both these points are laid down by name. It shows the north Battery, now called Fort Greene, and a fort on Goat Island, which are all the works laid down.

We have also seen a French atlas, called *Pilote Americain Septentrional A Paris, Geographie du Roi*, 1776–7. This contains a map or chart of Narraganset Bay, which shows no fort at the Dumplins, though the north battery and a fort on Goat Island are represented. . . . . As neither of these French and English charts, drawn for the use of the fleets and armies of those nations, showed any fort at the Dumplins, it seems probable that none existed there in 1777.

Now General Pigot, the British commander on Newport Island in 1778, in his despatch of Aug. 31st, of that year to Sir Henry Clinton, describing the battle which took place in that month by sea and land, near Newport, writes thus:—"The next morning the guns on the Beaver-tail and Dumplin batteries . . . were rendered unserviceable, as the (French) fleet entering the harbor would cut off all communication with that island (Conanicut). On the 8th inst., at noon, the French fleet standing in under a light sail, kept up a warm fire on Brenton's Point, Goat Island, and the North Batteries."

It thus appears, that in 1777, there were no fortifications except at Dyer's Point (the North Battery), and at Goat Island. That in 1778, there existed works at Brenton's Point, Beaver-tail, and the Dumplins. These latter forts must have been built in that year by the British, who held the islands, and we have seen that the last named work was known to Gen. Pigot by the same name which the fishermen give to it to-day, viz., Fort Dumplin. We certainly cannot believe that a fort built in war time by the British, would have been named for the king of the hostile nation. That would be, as if during our late war the forts around Washington had been named for Jeff. Davis or Napoleon. If Fort Dumplin ever had its name changed to Fort Louis, it must have been after the British left these shores, and the work fell into American hands. Is there any record of such a change of name? C.

Henry Short and Anne Longfellow, of Newbury, Mass., and an Ancient piece of Furniture.—Not long ago my attention was directed, at a neighbor's house, to a curious piece of antique furniture, which on examination reminded me of a description of one similar which I saw in a former number of the Register, and which was supposed to have once belonged to Eliot, the apostle to the Indians.

This one has shared the varied fortunes of one of our oldest families for nearly two centuries. The owner says it used to be called a dressing-case. When it came into her possession, age and neglect had shorn it of its completeness and greatly marred its beauty. The top or cover was gone, which in all probability added much to its appearance; and evidently much of the inside furnishing is gone also. I wish I could give as good a drawing of this as you had of the Eliot cabinet.

It is made of oak, and stands on turned feet about two inches from the floor. As it now is, it is about 19 inches in height, 20 broad and 14 in depth. The shallow box in the upper part has several partitions curiously arranged, for what purpose we hardly know. Next below are two drawers, which are fastened by a slide passing down through a groove from the top, into a mortise-hole in the top of the drawers. These are divided one into two and the other into three parts. Below these at the bottom of the chest is a long drawer which is fastened by a spring underneath. The whole is handsomely carved. The present owner, Miss Abby S. Short, has had a plain lid attached to the top, as the most fitting under the circumstances. As it is, it is quite an ornamental piece of workmanship. On the strip between the drawers is carved in large figures "1694," and on the lower drawer are these initials placed in this style $\mathrm{H}^{\mathrm{S}}\mathrm{A}$. These with the date give the article an historic place.

The town records of Newbury give the marriage of Henry Short and Anne Longfellow May 11, 1692. She was widow of William Longfellow, and daughter of Henry Sewall. He was born March 11, 1652, and married for his first wife Sarah Whipple, March 30, 1674. He was quite a prominent man in the town; was town clerk for many years, and taught the school, as his account book gives a list of the boys of the period who attended. He was son of Mr. Henry Short, who came with the first settlers in 1635, and died May 5, 1673. His first wife was Elizabeth ——. His second wife, and the mother of his children, was Sarah Glover, whom he married Oct. 9, 1648. M. T. Little.

Query.—I find the following in the *Gentleman's Magazine*, 1776:—

"Oct. 2, 1776. A French ship of 62 guns, arrived at Boston, said to be purchased at Toulon by Mr. Silas Dean; she had her guns in her hold." Query—what ship was this, and was she so purchased? P.

Hamlin, James.—Any one who has given any attention to, or has been engaged in perfecting a record of the descendants of *James Hamlin, of Barnstable, Mass.*, will confer a favor by addressing "*F. H. Hamlin*, Box 915, Albany, N. Y."

Expenses of the First Celebration of the 4th of July, by Congress, in 1777.—\$832.47-90. "In consequence of an adjustment by the commissioners of claims the auditor-general reports, that there is due to Daniel Smith, of the city tavern, for his bill of Expenses of Congress on the 4th of July last, including the balance of an old account 729.68-90 dollars; also a bill for materials, workmanship, &c. furnished for the fireworks on the 4th July, 102.69-90 dollars; amounting in the whole to 832.47-90 dollars."—(*Journals of Congress*, Friday, August 8, 1777.)

Why is the fraction expressed in *ninetieths* and not hundredths? P.

STANDISH (Myles) AND REV. DR. PARISH.—In referring to the descendants of Captain Myles Standish, to whose memory it is contemplated to erect a monument at Duxbury, and none of the early pilgrims more richly deserves one, as no allusion has been made to it, I infer it is not generally known that the Rev. Dr. Parish, of Byfield, was his lineal descendant. Dr. Parish alludes to the fact in his *History of New-England*, in which he says that a son of Standish died in Duxbury—a grandson, Deacon Joseph Standish, moved to Norwich, Conn., of whom he was the great grandson. Dr. Parish inherited many of the characteristics of the great puritan captain. M.—(*Newburyport Herald*, Aug. 25, 1871.)

GOV. SAMUEL ALLEN.—In April, 1691, The heirs of Capt. John Mason sold their interest in the various patents of land granted to Captain Mason, to Samuel Allen, of London, who about the same time procured of the crown a commission for the government of the province of New-Hampshire. In 1698, Gov. Allen came to this country and assumed the government. He died in 1705, leaving widow Elizabeth, one son, and three daughters. In 1708, administration was granted on his goods and chattels in the house of his widow then living in Charlestown, Mass. Among the items inventoried are, Gov. Allen's picture, and the pictures of his three children. One daughter married Lieut Gov. Usher.

Can any one tell me where Gov. Allen's picture may be seen? Also, who his other two daughters married? Also, where are his papers relating to his New-Hampshire interests? C. W. T.

G. F. G.—(*ante*, xxiv. 192). The writer of the memorandum bearing this signature was George F. Guild, who died in Havana, June 24, 1853, a. 42 (*ante*, vii. 375).

His library, which was rich in American history, was sold at auction by Clark & Son, at Boston, Oct. 12, 1853. J. W. D.

WAYTE.—In the REGISTER, vol. xxv. p. 39, John Wayte, son of Gamaliel, of Boston, "is supposed to be the same who was settled in Malden." Except in similarity of names, grounds for this supposition are not apparent.

JOHN WAYTE, of Malden, was son of Samuel and Mary (Ward) Wayte, of Wethersfield, co. Essex, Eng. (Dean's *Memoir of Nathaniel Ward*, p. 129), and was born about 1618. He accompanied, or followed, to N. Eng., his father-in-law, Joseph Hills, who came in the "Susan and Ellen," of London, in 1638. They were leading men in the settlement of Malden, and together represented the town in the house of deputies for a period of thirty-four years, and both attained the speaker's seat. John Wayte was prominent in town and colonial affairs, and had the honor of notice by Randolph in his "Articles of High Misdemeanor." (*Hutch. Papers*, vol. ii. p. 266, Prince So.) He died Sept. 26, 1693. He married in England, Mary, daughter of Joseph and Mary (Dunster) Hills, of Malden, co. Essex, who died Nov. 25, 1674. He married, August 4, 1675, Sarah Parker, who died Jan. 13, 1707–8, aged 81. John and Mary Wayte had:—

i. JOHN, m. June 12, 1674, Sarah Muzzy; removed to Rumney Marsh, where he d. in 1722.

ii. JOSEPH, m. Aug. 7, 1672 Hannah, daughter of Thos. and Elizabeth Oakes, b. in Cambridge, May 4, 1657. He m. Oct. 24, 1688, Mercy, daughter of Peter and Mary (Pierce) Tufts, who survived him, and m., June 11, 1694, Lemuel Jenkins, of Malden, and d. July 19, 1736. He d. in 1692.

iii. SAMUEL, b. in Malden, Oct. 11, 1650; m. Mehitable, daughter of Wm. and Sarah Bucknam, b. Aug., 1654, d. Sept. 17, 1734; and d. Sept. 20, 1720.

iv. MARY, b. Aug. 31, 1653; d. Aug. 9, 1667.

v. HANNAH, b. Sept. 9, 1656; m. Oct. 11, 1676, Wm. Bucknam, of Malden, who d. Sept. 16, 1693; m. Jan. 12, 1693–4, Joseph Hasey, of Rumney Marsh, who d. June 28, 1707. Place and date of death unknown.

vi. MEHITABLE, b. Sept. 15, 1658; m. Deliverance Parkman, of Salem, and d. before 1686.

vii. THOMAS, b. Sept. 1, 1660; m. Mary ——, who d. Jan. 6, 1763, aged 96; and d. Dec. 23, 1742.

viii. REBECCA, b. Nov.22,1662; m. in Charlestown, March 31,1681, Jonathan Tufts.

ix. SARAH, m. April 25, 1684, Nathaniel Stone, of Sudbury.

x. NATHANIEL, b. May 27, 1667; m. Elizabeth ——; was selectman in 1707; and d. about 1714. D. P. COREY.

THE UNITED STATES FLAG.—*Query*—When and where did our federal flag obtain the name of "*Old Glory*"? P.

THE SKINNERS OF COLCHESTER, CONN.—(*Answer to* "*E. H., Chicago, Ill.*," p. 388, REGISTER, 1871.)

The Skinners of Colchester, Conn., went from Hartford or vicinity, probably. The following is also probable.

John[1] Isham, of Barnstable, Mass.; m. 16 Dec., 1677, Jane Parker.
John[2] " b. at " " 25 Aug., 1681.
John[3] " called 2d of Colchester, b. 1720; m. 19 Dec., 1751, Dorothy Foote.

Yonkers, N. Y. H. N. O.

TRULL, as a surname.—The subjoined communication, of the Lord Bishop of Bath and Wells, writing from Trull, one of the oldest parishes in England, suggests the origin of the family bearing that surname.

"*Trull, Sept.* 8, 1871.

"MY DEAR SIR,

"I duly received your letter of July 7th, and lost no time in making such enquiries from learned friends as might assist me in answering your question, as to the etymology of the name Trull. Happening in the course of my diocesan duties to be staying in the parish, I have begun to write to you from hence, but shall finish my letter after my return to Wells. The friends whom I have asked to assist me are Mr. E. Forrman, the learned historian, and Mr. Justice Willes, who, besides being the ablest judge on the Bench, has extensive acquaintance with many branches of literature.

"I. It is to be presumed that your name is derived from this parish of Trull; possibly you may have the means of knowing whether your ancestors came from Somersetshire. If they did, we might take it as certain that they derived their name from that place. I am informed that Trull has existed and still exists as a proper name, and a friend tells me, that in Edward IIId's reign, a Walter de Trill gave certain rents in the parish of Marnhull near Blandford to found a chaplaincy in that parish. Trull is pronounced *Trill* by the common people to this day, which looks as if Trull were a Welsh word. The Welsh always pronounce *u* like y, or i.

"II. The enquiry remains, what is the derivation of Trull as the name of a place. Mr. Seller, the rector of Trull, tells me, that he considers it a contraction for Treudle; that there are two tithings in Trull and the adjoining parish of Titminster, still called Treudle, and that Dugdale speaks of Treudle or Trull. Treudle means a bowl, which seems suitable to the situation of the church or village in a hollow.

"The name has nothing whatever to do with the Shakspearian Trull, which is Teutonic and connected with our root, *Stroll*. We speak of a strolling player; the idea would be a vagabond woman of unsettled habits. Or it might be connected with the Trolls, which play such a prominent part in the Norse popular tales. (Vide Dasent's *Norse Tales*.)"

We are glad to be able to add, that the letter of our distinguished correspondent closes with an intimation that something more upon this interesting archæological subject will be furnished hereafter.

Brookline, Mass., 23 *Oct.*, 1871. W. B. TRULL, M.D.

THOMAS'S HISTORY OF PRINTING IN AMERICA.—The American Antiquarian Society propose to issue a new edition of this rare and valuable work from a revised copy left by the author. An appendix will contain entirely new articles upon early printing in Spanish America and the United States; a list of publications in the United States prior to 1776; and other matters of later information relating to printers and printing on this continent. A finely engraved portrait of the author will accompany the work.

This edition will make two vols., 8vo., of about 500 pages each, and will be printed in a manner worthy of its subject, and creditable to the American press. The price will be, to subscribers, $7.50 in cloth, $10 in half turkey morocco.

As a large edition is not contemplated, it is desirable to learn how many copies are likely to be called for beyond those required for the immediate uses of the Society.

THE BAGG FAMILY.—Mr. Lyman H. Bagg, of West Springfield, Mass., is engaged in preparing a genealogy of this family, and solicits information from all sources.

MARSHALL—WINSLOW.—Can any one give the ancestry or any facts about John Marshall who married Elizabeth Winslow? (Vide REGISTER, vol. xxv. p. 358). He died in May, 1772, in his 70th year; she Nov., 1768, in her 72d year. Their daughter Ruth was born in Freetown, Mass., April 1, 1737, but married and lived in East Haddam, Conn.

Early Paper Making in Massachusetts. Advertisements.—"Some years ago the art of Paper Making was set up in this Province, tho' for want of Persons, that understood the Business, it failed; but lately one Mr. *Clark*, has carried it on at the Mills in *Milton*, to as great Perfection as at *Pennsylvania;* And all the discouragements the Manufacture at present meets with is the want of RAGS. . . . . If the Heads of Families would therefore order their Children and Servants to collect and save the Rags that are often thrown away, they would not only receive a valuable consideration therefor, but promote a Manufacture whereby the Exportation of some Thousands of Pounds a Year would be saved this Province.

"Cash for RAGS of Linen, coarse and fine, old Sail Cloth, Cotton or Checks, will be given by Mr. *Boice*, near the South Battery in *Boston* or at the Paper Mills in Milton."—(Nath'l Ames's *Almanack* for 1764.)

"*Many of these Almanacks were printed on paper made at Milton, those who are desirous of encouraging our own Manufactures, are requested to save RAGS:—for linnen and cotton linnen Rags, finer than Oznaburgs two Coppers a pound will be given; and one Copper for coarse whites and checks: They are taken in at John Boyes, near the South Battery in Boston, and at the Paper Mills at Milton.*"—(Ames's *Almanack for* 1776).

"*Mr. Mascoll Williams gives Cash for Linen Rags coarse and fine at his Shop in Salem.*"—(*Philo's Essex Almanack for* 1770.)

"F. Russell *at his printing office next the bell tavern in Danvers carries on the printing business in its several branches; where travelling trades &c. are desired to call and supply themselves with a number of new books, some of which are on the times, and will be sold cheap.*

"*In compliance with a late resolve of the general assembly of this State*, 6*d. lb. will be paid for white lin. and cot. lin. rags*, 4*d. lb. for coarse and check do. or old canvas and sail cloth*, 2*d. for old junk delivered at the printing office, or to the four paper Mills at Milton. Weaver's thrums and shoemakers and taylors linen shreds will make good paper.*

☞ *Said* Russell *has to sell cheap, Bibles, with Dr. Watts's Psalms in them. Testaments. Watts and Tate's and Brady's Psalms. Psalters, Spelling Books, Primers, Watts Divine Songs for children. Writing paper, Quills, Wafers, &c.*"—(Bickerstaff's *Boston Almanack* for 1779.)

Queries—who was the predecessor of Mr. Clark in the art of paper-making in Massachusetts, and what is known concerning him and his enterprise?

Who was Mr. Clark—and are any of the four paper mills, at work in 1779 in Milton, now in existence?

Is the *Bell* Tavern at Danvers, of which there is a rude cut in the almanack for 1779, still standing? P.

NEW-ENGLAND HISTORIC, GENEALOGICAL SOCIETY.

NECROLOGY.

[Communicated by Rev. Dorus Clarke, D.D., Historiographer.]

Rev. Joseph Addison Copp, D.D.—The ancestry of Dr. Copp, for six generations, was as follows:

1. *William Cope*, born in England in 1609, and emigrated to Boston, in New-England, in 1635. He was the first proprietor of "Copp's Hill." He joined the First Church in Boston, June 20, 1640.

2. *David* (now called) *Copp*, the eldest son of William Cope, was born in 1635; was an elder in the North Church, and died in Boston, Nov. 1715.

3. *Jonathan*, second son of David and Obedience (Topliff) Copp, was born in Boston, Feb. 23, 1664, and died in Montville, Conn., Nov. 9, 1746.

4. *Jonathan*, son of Jonathan and Catharine (Lay) Copp, of Lyme, Conn., was born June 12, 1694.

5. *Joseph*, son of Jonathan and Margaret (Stanton) Copp, was born in Stonington, Conn., in 1732, and died in 1815.

6. *Daniel*, son of Joseph and Rachel (Dennison) Copp, was born in New-London, Conn., Aug 4, 1769, and died Jan. 10, 1822.

The subject of this sketch was the third son of Daniel and Sarah (Allyn) Copp, and was born in Groton, Conn., now called Ledyard, July 4, 1804. When he was yet a boy, he went to St. Mary's, Geo., and to St. Augustine, Fla., where he spent several years, and the education he received there was conducted by two Roman Catholic priests, and wholly in the Spanish language. He was employed by the priests as an altar-boy at the mass in the Roman Catholic Church, and it was their intention to fit him for the priesthood of that church.

At about the age of sixteen his father died, and relinquishing all claims upon the paternal estate, he went to New-Orleans to seek his fortune. But, without friends and without fortune, he was unconsciously under the protection of his Father in heaven. On his arrival in New-Orleans, he embarked in an English ship for Liverpool. As the ship passed down the Mississippi, it was ascertained, by arrivals coming in from Europe, that England was on the eve of a war with France, and the danger of impressment into the British service was so imminent, that he left the ship at the Balize and returned to New-Orleans. The ship, instead of being boarded by British cruisers, as was feared, foundered at sea.

An unknown hand still directed his steps. It was now midsummer, and fearing to remain in New-Orleans at that season of the year, he took passage up the river, intending to return in the autumn. Here his plans were again overruled. On his slow passage up the Mississippi, he was taken sick, and after intense suffering, he was put on shore on the banks of the Cumberland River, without earthly friends, in a state of great bodily prostration, and almost entirely without money. He at last found a temporary home among entire strangers, who took him in, cared for him in his sickness, and provided for his immediate wants. He finally succeeded in obtaining a school, where he remained a year in the bosom of a Christian family who were interested in his case. He was skeptical and irreligious, and often silenced others by his skilful dialectics, in their efforts to reclaim him from his infidelity. By and by, however, his heart began to relent, and he at last yielded to the force of truth. His intentions and aspirations were now suddenly changed, and from that hour on to the close, he was an intrepid defender of the faith which before he had scorned. A new plan of life now opened before him. He had laid himself irrevocably upon the altar of duty. Immediately he commenced study preparatory to college and to the Christian ministry. He soon entered Cumberland College in Princeton, Ky., was early licensed to preach, and often walked fifteen or twenty miles on Saturday to supply some neighboring congregation, and returned to his studies on Monday. A year after his graduation, he was called to assist the president of the college for a short period in the instruction of the higher classes, and about twenty-five years afterward, and soon after his settlement in Chelsea, he was invited to the presidency of that institution. For three or four years he performed ministerial service in Winchester, Tenn., where his labors were signally blessed.

The summer of 1835 he spent in New-Haven, attending the theological lectures in Yale College, and in the autumn he was called to the pastorate of the Presbyterian church in Sag Harbor, L. I. There, for sixteen years, his consistent life, his glowing, persuasive eloquence, his urbane manners, and his profound knowledge of human nature, contributed largely to his usefulness.

In 1851 he was invited to take the charge of the newly formed Broadway church, in Chelsea, Mass., where for twelve years he labored with his wonted measure of success. But in Nov. 1863, he was suddenly smitten down by paralysis, and though he lived six years afterward, he was never able to resume the active duties of his much-loved profession. A repetition of the paralytic attack, on the evening of the Sunday, Nov. 7, 1869, suddenly terminated his scholarly, useful, and somewhat eventful life, at the age of sixty-five years.

The Rev. Samuel E. Herrick, his successor in the pastorate of the Broadway church, delivered a highly appropriate address at the funeral of Dr. Copp, and subsequently a discourse more minutely commemorative of his life and character, to which I am largely indebted for the facts contained in this article.

In 1856, the University of Tennessee honored itself and him by conferring upon him the degree of Doctor in Divinity. He was admitted a resident member of the N. E. Historic, Genealogical Society, Sept. 21, 1858, and on one occasion he read an interesting paper before the society, on the "Collections of the Library of Mr. Teft," of Savannah, Ga. But we shall enjoy the results of his literary taste, and see his genial face no more in this hall. He was frequently present at its monthly meetings, and though he rarely took a very active part in the proceedings, his occasional remarks will long be remembered for their good sense, and his gentlemanly manners were worthy of universal imitation.

Dr. Copp was married July 13, 1836, to Miss Fedora Frances Isham, daughter of Ralph and Laura Worthington Isham, of Colchester, Conn. He had four children, two of whom died in infancy, and two, with their mother, survive their father, namely: Laura Worthington, born in Sag Harbor, L. I., March 28, 1847, and Lucretia Burr, born in the same place, July 25, 1849.

Hon. Joshua Victor Hopkins Clark.—Mr. Clark was admitted a corresponding member of the New-England Historic, Genealogical Society, March 21, 1855. He died in Onondaga, N. Y., June 18, 1869, aged 66 years.

He was the son of Thomas and Ruth (Morse) Clark, and was born at Cazenovia, N. Y., Feb. 6, 1803. He was descended paternally from Thomas Clark, of Plymouth, who came in the Ann in 1623; and maternally from Samuel Morse, an early settler of Dedham, Mass.

In very early manhood, he commenced writing for the agricultural papers, and subsequently he was a large contributor to the columns of the *Genesee Farmer* and the *Albany Cultivator*.

He remained upon the homestead until he was twenty-five years of age, when he removed to Eagle village, where he resided until 1838, when he removed to Manlius, where he continued to reside, and cultivated a large farm until within the last ten years, with scientific skill and pecuniary success.

After his removal to Manlius, his taste for historica research began to develope itself. It was there that he composed the only two works which he ever published, namely: *The History of Onondaga*, in two large volumes, and *Lights and Lines of Indian and Pioneer Life*. The latter work was spoken of by the *London Times*, as containing legends which bear on their face the stamp of genuineness, without revealing the interpolations of the interpreter or the translator. During the last ten or twelve years of his life, Mr. Clark published in the *Syracuse Journal* a number of articles of great historical value. His rare combination of the labors of a practical farmer with those of an author, and his various efforts to promote the cause of education in the state of New-York, attracted the attention of the public, and he became the recipient of many honorary testimonials. He was elected a corresponding member not only of the N. E. Historic, Genealogical Society, but of several literary and scientific societies in New-York, New-England and the Western States. Geneva College conferred upon him the honorary title of Master of Arts. Residing in the vicinity of the Onondaga tribe of Indians, he took a deep interest in their social and religious prosperity, and was elected and duly installed an honorary civil chief in January, 1850, with the title of Go-yah-de-Kae-na-has, signifying, the Friend and Defender. He was also deeply interested in the cause of universal education, and did not a little to improve the common school system of the state of New-York. For nearly thirty years he was an active and efficient trustee of the Manlius Academy, and secretary to the board of trustees the most of the time.

He was a member of the Protestant Episcopal church for forty years, and vestryman and warden at different times. He was sincere in his belief, and thorough as an officer. He was a member of the New-York legislature for the year 1855, and, in consequence of his civil relation to the "Six Nations," he was made chairman of the committee on Indian Affairs. His reports upon the condition of the Indians of New York, and the Anti-Rent question then agitating the public mind, are remarkable for their clearness and erudition. He was for several years the president of the village corporation, and in every way possible gave his aid and influence to make Manlius one of the prettiest villages in central New-York.

He was the first president of the Manlius and Pompey Agricultural Society, and the first president of the Onondaga Historical Association. His numerous translations from French authors, concerning the missions of the Jesuits and their occupancy of the country, his biographical sketches of Indian chiefs and other prominent men, and his compilations of facts and figures, which embrace hundreds of proper names and thousands of dates, are so many testimonials to his intense assiduity and great accuracy.

When Mr. Schoolcraft published his *Notes on the Iroquois*, he did not give Mr. Clark that credit which it is believed he should have done, for his legend of Hi-a-wat-ha; and when Prof. Longfellow published his celebrated *Song of Hi-a-wat-ha*, the curiosity of the public was considerably excited in regard to some of the incidents referred to in that elaborate and popular poem. A warm controversy arose between Mr. Clark and Mr. Schoolcraft, in which Mr. Clark asserted his claims to the honor of having first published the legend, which had suddenly assumed such prominence in the public mind, and which he had obtained from two aged chiefs of the Onondaga tribe. Mr. Schoolcraft, in reply, imputed to Mr. Clark motives unworthy of a gentleman, and superciliously ignored his claim to that honor; and Mr. Clark, in turn, clearly convicted Schoolcraft of plagiarism, if not of untruthfulness. It is not my province to enter into that controversy, nor even to express any opinion upon the merits of the case only so far forth as the interests of historic truth evidently require.

That Mr. Schoolcraft did Mr. Clark great injustice in that matter is made quite clear by Mr. Francis Parkman in his late work, *The Jesuits in North America in the Seventeenth Century*, a work which presents the Indian traditions more fully, perhaps, than any other now before the public. Mr. Parkman says, "In all Mr. Schoolcraft's productions, the reader must scrupulously reserve his right of private judgment." He also says of Mr. Schoolcraft's six large quarto volumes, entitled, *The History, Condition, and Prospects of Indian Tribes*,[1] "It is a singularly crude and illiterate production, stuffed with blunders and contradictions, giving evidence on every page of a striking unfitness either for historical or philosophical inquiry, and tasking to the utmost the patience of those who would extract what is valuable in it from its oceans of pedantic verbiage." From this view of Mr. Schoolcraft's historical work, it is almost an unavoidable inference, that Mr. Clark had altogether the best side in that controversy, and that his claim to the honor of having first published the legend of Hi-a-wat-ha, is just. Several years ago, Mr. Clark sent this Society a long account of this unpleasant affair, which may be found among the Society's manuscripts.

The last five years of Mr. Clark's life were rendered sad by a cancerous affection which attacked his face, and for the last year kept him almost constantly in a state of physical and mental torture.

As a farmer Joshua V. H. Clark was sagacious, scientific and successful; as a public man he was honest and upright; as a Christian, zealous and hopeful; as a friend, devoted and firm; as a neighbor, kind and obliging; as an essayist, instructive and entertaining; as a historian, faithful and truthful; and take him, for all in all, he possessed a union of qualities not often found in the same individual.

Mr. Clark was married Feb. 10, 1830, to Phebe A. Sims, by whom he had five children: William Thomas, b. March 11, 1831, and resides in Omaha, Neb.; Albert Gallatin, b. Jan. 6, 1833; resides in Osceola, Mo.; Louise Helen, b. June 27, 1839, now Mrs. C. W. Henning, of Golconda, Ill.; Sophia Adaline, b. Dec. 11, 1841, resides in Manlius, O.; and Cornelia Sims, b. July 20, 1847, resides in Manlius, O.

Gen. Appleton Howe, M.D.—Dr. Appleton Howe was born in Hopkinton, Mass., Nov. 26, 1792, and died in South Weymouth, Oct. 10, 1870, aged 77 years. His earliest American ancestor, on his father's side, was James Howe (son of Robert, of Hatfield Broad Oak, Essex, England), who emigrated from England and settled in Ipswich, Mass. He was born about 1605, and died May 17, 1702, *ante*, viii. 148. He had a son by the name of Abraham Howe, who also had a son by the name of Abraham Howe. Gen. Howe's ancestor, of the fourth generation, was Dea. Abraham Howe, who married Lucy Appleton, of Ipswich, whose grandfather's name was John Appleton, and who died Jan. 4, 1794. John Appleton was a remote descendant of Samuel Appleton, who was born at Little Waldingfield, Eng., and emigrated to Ipswich, Mass., in 1635-6. This Samuel Appleton was also the ancestor of the Appletons of Boston.

Dea. Abraham Howe was the father of Rev. Nathaniel Howe, of Hopkinton, Mass., who was born in Ipswich, Mass., Oct. 6, 1764, and graduated at Harvard College in 1786. The Rev. Nathaniel Howe, of Hopkinton, the father of Dr. Howe, was settled over the Congregational church in that place, Nov. 26, 1791, and retained that position till 1830, a period of thirty-nine years.

Dr. Howe, on his mother's side, descended from Col. John Jones, who received his military commission from one of the Georges before he left England. Col. John Jones was the father of Olive Jones, who was the mother of Dr. Howe. She was a native of Ashland, then a part of the town of Hopkinton.

Dr. Appleton Howe graduated at Harvard College in 1815. Among his classmates were the Rev. Richard M. Hodges and the Hon. John G. Palfrey. He took his medical degree at Harvard in 1819, after pursuing a course of study with Drs. John C. Warren and John Ware. He soon commenced practice in South Wey-

[1] Introduction, p. 80.

mouth, Mass., and for many years maintained a distinguished standing in his profession. His mind was highly vigorous, and his love of medical science was enthusiastic. He early acquired great influence in the town, and for many years he was an acknowledged leader in all public improvements and reforms. Military and political honors also clustered upon him. In 1839, he was chosen major-general of the first division of the Massachusetts militia; and again, under the new law, he was appointed to the same office in 1841. He was also chosen captain of the Ancient and Honorable Artillery Company in 1840. In 1841 and 1842 he was elected senator in the state legislature from Norfolk county by the whig party, of which he was a zealous advocate, until the anti-slavery movement commenced, when he as warmly seconded the efforts for the emancipation of the slaves in the southern states. He was also a decided temperance man, and earnestly advocated the principle of entire abstinence from intoxicating liquors, both by precept and example. For twenty years Dr. Howe was a member of the school committee of South Weymouth, and labored indefatigably for the improvement of the schools, and also of the roads and of the general sanitary and moral interests of the town. He was a man of sound judgment, and unswerving, tenacious and unyielding in his opinions in all matters where great interests were involved. He was also distinguished for his large-hearted benevolence. Though he never made a public profession of religion, he was a firm and liberal supporter of the parish with which he was connected, and the pastors of the church can attest that they have frequently been sharers in his unostentatious beneficence. In his last days, when the hand of death was evidently upon him, he expressed his trust in the Saviour and his submission to the Divine Will.

Dr. Howe was twice married. His first wife was Harriet Loud, daughter of Eliphalet and Hannah (Blanchard) Loud, both of Weymouth. They were married Dec. 12, 1822. Harriet was born Feb. 28, 1795, and died childless, Nov. 15, 1848. His second wife was Eliza Loud, of Weymouth, daughter of Joseph and Thankful (Bates) Loud, and was born May 9, 1812. They were married Aug. 12, 1851. Joseph Loud was the son of Eliot and Sarah (Pratt) Loud, of Weymouth, and Eliot was the son of Francis aud Honor (Prince) Loud. By his last marriage, Dr. Howe had two children—a daughter, Harriet Appleton Howe, born Dec. 13, 1852, who still lives; and a son, Appleton Loud Howe, born Feb. 20, 1854, and who died Nov. 23, 1856.

Dr. Howe was admitted a resident member of the New-England Historic, Genealogical Society, Jan. 20, 1867.

Winthrop Sargent, Esq.—Mr. Sargent was born in the city of Philadelphia, Sept. 23, 1825, and died, of a gradual decline, in Paris, France, May 18, 1870. His remains were brought home and interred in the family vault at Laurel Hill, near Philadelphia. He was the son of George Washington and Margaret (Percy) Sargent. His mother was the daughter of Lieut. Robert Percy of the Royal Navy, and his father was the son of Winthrop Sargent, a distinguished revolutionary officer of the Massachusetts line, adjutant-general of the United States army at the time of St. Clair's defeat, and first governor of Mississippi. (*Ante*, xviii. 379; xxv. 210.) Gov. Winthrop Sargent and his son George W. Sargent were graduates of Harvard College, and Winthrop Sargent received the degree of Bachelor of Laws at the Harvard Law School in 1847, but graduated at the University of Pennsylvania in 1845. He practised law for a few years in Philadelphia, and for a brief period in New-York, but his health did not permit prolonged attention to the fatiguing duties of his profession. His taste was altogether in the line of literary pursuits, and it was very early developed.

He edited the "Journal of the Officers engaged in Braddock's Expedition," from original manuscripts in the British Museum, with an "Original Historical Memoir"; and also a "Journal of the General Meeting of the Cincinnati in 1784," from the original manuscripts of his grandfather, Major Winthrop Sargent. These were the productions of an age so youthful, that most men at that time only give promise of future excellence, but they occupy places of very considerable distinction among the standard works on American history. Washington Irving, in his "Life of Washington," says: "In narrating the expedition of Braddock, we have frequently cited the Journals of Captain Orme and of the Seamen's Detachment; they were procured in England by the Hon. Joseph R. Ingersoll, while Minister at the Court of St. James, and recently published by the Historical Society of Pennsylvania, ably edited and illustrated by an admirable introductory memoir by Winthrop Sargent, Esq., member of that society." Mr. George Grote, the historian of Greece, also speaks of this work in terms of high commendation. The Westminster Review, too, says, "It is a book of considerable merit, and it deserves far more respectful treatment" than many similar American productions.

At a later period, Mr. Sargent published a collection of the "Loyalist Ballads of the Revolution," and the "Loyal verses of Joseph Stansberry and Dr. Jonathan Odell," relating to the American revolution. He also edited "The Letters of John Andrews, of Boston, from 1772 to 1776." His "Life and Career of Major John Andre" is a more elaborate work, and, like all his productions, shows his patient research for materials, and his discriminating and graceful use of them. The following articles from his facile, fruitful pen, have appeared in the North American Review:

April, 1853,	page	273.	Bibliomania.
Oct. 1853,	"	267.	Society of the Cincinnati.
Oct. 1853,	"	409.	Dickens's Bleak House.
Jan. 1854,	"	67.	M. Gironiere's Philippine Islands.
Jan. 1854,	"	105.	Life and Death of Louis XVII.
Jan. 1854,	"	251.	Esther de Berdt.
April, 1854,	"	305.	Literary Impostors. A. Dumas.
July, 1854,	"	158.	Chinese Rebellions.
Oct. 1854,	"	314.	Bibliopegia.
Jan. 1855,	"	236.	Lord Mahon's last Volume.
Oct. 1855,	"	346.	Flanders's Lives of the Chief Justices.
Jan. 1857,	"	122.	Beaumarchais.

Mr Sargent's style is distinguished for vivacity and brilliancy. Had he confined himself to the field of literary criticism, he would have reached eminent distinction. His inclinations, however, were strongly in the line of historical investigation. He reverenced the past and loved it. He was fond of its actors, and he delighted to reproduce them in their ordinary garbs, and modes of thought, and daily actions.

At a memorial meeting of the Pennsylvania Historical Society, Mr. Jordan said of Mr. Sargent, "He was of Revolutionary descent, and he could do justice to the motives and feelings which made a man a Tory."

"He was eminently a citizen of the world in his knowledge of men and manners, and his various and discursive reading made him familiar with men of different periods and of different countries. A mind so versatile and varied, united to studious habits and a genuine fondness for literature, would, almost of necessity, have resulted in some work which would have taken its place among the classics of American literature. But he was called away, leaving much accomplished, but with the promise of greater usefulness unfulfilled."

Mr. Sargent was married in April, 1851, to Sarah, daughter of Ignatius Sargent, Esq., of Boston. She died in 1852, leaving one child, a son, Ignatius, born in April, 1852, who now resides in Brookline, Mass.

Mr. Sargent leaves one brother, George Sargent, of Natchez, Mississippi, and two sisters, namely: Mrs. Henry Duncan, and Mrs. William Butler Duncan, both of New-York.

Mr. Sargent's connection with the N. E. Historic, Genealogical Society, as a corresponding member, dates from Sept. 11, 1855.

It may assist the society to form a proper conception of the high estimation in which Mr. Sargent was held by his friends and the literary public, to state, that no less than *thirty-two* different obituary notices of him have already appeared; some of them from England, others from France, and one from California.

Proceedings.

Boston, Massachusetts, Wednesday, Sept. 6, 1871.—A meeting was held this afternoon at 3 o'clock, at the Society's House, No. 18 Somerset street, the president, Hon. Marshall P. Wilder, in the chair.

Samuel H. Wentworth, Esq., the recording secretary, read the record of the proceedings at the June meeting, which was approved.

James F. Hunnewell, Esq., the librarian, reported that, since the last meeting, 105 volumes and 503 pamphlets had been presented to the library.

Charles W. Tuttle, Esq., the assistant historiographer, read biographical sketches of the following deceased members, viz.: Charles Henry Woodwell, Esq., William Reed Deane, Esq., and Joseph Palmer, M.D.

The board of directors nominated fourteen candidates for membership, who were elected.

William B. Trask, Esq., offered the following resolutions, which were unanimously adopted:

Whereas, William Reed Deane, Esq., for many years chairman of the Committee on Papers and Essays, and a member of the board of directors, has, since the last meeting of our society, been taken from us by death,

Resolved, That we mourn in him the loss of a devoted member and an active and efficient officer of this society, a student well read in the literature of England and America, an able and ready writer, and a diligent antiquary, full of the local lore, and familiar with the customs and usages of the early settlers of New-England.

Resolved, That we bear witness to his virtues as a man, to his genial manners and large heart, ever ready to serve others and ever adding to the favors conferred by his sympathy and kindness; and to the Christian fortitude and patience with which he bore a painful illness during the last years of his life.

Resolved, that we tender to his children our sympathy for their loss, and that an attested copy of these resolutions be sent to them by the secretary.

Rev. Increase N. Tarbox, D.D., read a paper, entitled *An Item in Personal History, and Reminiscences of the Stackpole House.* Thanks were voted and a copy requested.

William B. Towne, Esq., gave notice that he should, at the next meeting, move to amend Article 17 of the By-Laws.

Boston, Oct. 4.—A meeting was held this afternoon at 3 o'clock, Winslow Lewis, M.D., in the chair.

The recording secretary read the record of the previous meeting, which was approved.

The librarian reported that, during the last month, 28 volumes and 68 pamphlets had been presented to the society.

The Rev. Edmund F. Slafter, the corresponding secretary, made his report of acceptances and other correspondence since the June meeting.

Biographical sketches of deceased members were read, viz.: of Hon. John A. Poor, of Portland, Me., by the assistant historiographer; and of Jeremiah P. Jewett, of Lowell, by Robert B. Caverly of that place.

The directors nominated two members, who were elected.

On motion of Mr. Towne, the By-Laws were amended so as to read:

Article 17. The society shall, at the quarterly meeting in October in each year, choose a standing committee on publication; and, at the annual meeting, four additional standing committees, each committee to consist of not less than five members; and said committees shall hold monthly meetings for the transaction of business, viz.:

1st, on Publication;
2d, on the Library;
3d, on Papers and Essays;
4th, on Finance;
5th, on Heraldry.

Boston, Nov. 1.—A meeting was held this afternoon, President Wilder in the chair.

The recording secretary read the record of the last meeting, which was approved.

The corresponding secretary made his monthly report.

Rev. Dorus Clarke, D.D., the historiographer, read a biographical sketch of the Rev. Henry Longueville Mansel, B.D., Dean of St. Paul's, London, a corresponding member, recently deceased. Remarks upon the philosophy and writings of Dean Mansel were afterwards made by Rev. Wm. P. Tilden.

The directors nominated two members, who were elected.

The Rev. E. F. Slafter offered the following resolutions, which were unanimously adopted:

Resolved, That we have learned with profound sorrow of the great loss sustained by the Chicago Historical Society in the recent desolating fire in that city—of its valuable building, of its large library of historical works, and particularly of its rare collection of original documents and manuscripts, illustrative of the history of the great West, which cannot be duplicated and are irretrievably lost.

Resolved, That we fully approve the action of the Board of Directors in offering to receive from historical societies or private persons all books that may be given to restore, as far as may be, these losses, and to furnish store room for the same until the Chicago Historical Society shall be ready to receive them.

Resolved, That we heartily concur in the proposition of the directors to forward to the Chicago Historical Society, as a gift, such of our publications and such other duplicate volumes as may properly be spared from the shelves of our own library.

Hon. James D. Green presented to the society valuable steel engravings of Isaac Watts, Joseph Addison, Sir Richard Steele and Archbishop Tillotson.

Boston, Dec. 6.—A meeting was held this afternoon, Pres. Wilder in the chair.

The recording secretary read the record of the last meeting, which was approved.

The librarian reported as donations to the society since the last meeting, 25 vols. and 205 pamphlets. Some valuable pamphlets were presented by C. W. Tuttle, Esq., among which was one printed in 1647, entitled, *A Word to Mr. Peters and Two Words for the Parliament and Kingdom*, attributed to the Rev. Nathaniel Ward, author of the *Simple Cobler of Aggawam*, the gift of James B. Robb, Esq.

The historiographer read biographical sketches of two deceased members, namely, Rev. Joseph Richardson, of Hingham, one of the oldest members, probably the oldest, and Henry Oxnard Preble, of Charlestown, one of the youngest.

The directors nominated candidates for membership, who were elected.

Charles W. Tuttle, Esq., read a paper on Christopher Kilby, of Boston, agent of the province of Massachusetts in England, for whom Kilby street, in Boston, was named. This paper is printed in the present number of the REGISTER, p. 43.

The following persons were chosen a committee to nominate officers at the annual meeting, viz.: Frederic Kidder, Esq., Rev. Lucius R. Paige, D.D., William B. Trask and Jeremiah Colburn, Esqs., Col. A. H. Hoyt and William B. Towne, Esq.

BOOK-NOTICES.

The Memorial Volume of the Edwards Family Meeting at Stockbridge, Mass. Sept. 6–7, *A.D.* 1870. Boston: Congregational Publishing Society. 1871. 8vo. pp. 206.

This meeting differed from ordinary family reunions, insomuch that it was to do honor to the memory of famous Jonathan Edwards, one of the fourth generation in the family, instead of a more remote ancestor. The book is composed of tributes to his character and works, and although as the father of nine married children, Jonathan Edwards has many living descendants, and though they were largely in attendance, this volume gives no genealogical facts worth notice. One page is all that is given to the family record, and not even a foot-note tells us of the number of his progeny present or absent. As a record of an interesting meeting it loses much of its value from the want of some spectator ready and able to notice the genealogical value of the occasion. W. H. W.

The History of the Descendants of Elder John Strong, of Northampton, Mass. By BENJAMIN W. DWIGHT, author of "The Higher Christian Education," and of "Modern Philology" in 2 vols. Albany, N. Y.: Joel Munsell. 8vo. In two vols. together. pp. lxii. and 1586.

The first sensation of the examiner of this book is one of wonder at its extent. It is in itself a library of genealogy, an eloquent testimony to the progress which this science has made in America. Turning over the pages and noting the care with which facts have been sought, and especially dates have been recorded, the reader is willing to concede that the author has been laborious, careful, zealous and persevering. A high degree of praise must be given him for what he has done, and we are the more ready to give this encomium because a more sober judgment fails to confirm the first impression. It can hardly be said that the author has written a great genealogy. It is an immense collection, but it lacks some essential qualities which lesser books contain. An analysis shows a failure to treat successfully the vast bulk of material, and on some points the critical acumen of the author is felt to be sadly deficient.

The plan of arrangement is opposed to the experience of the great body of genealogical writers. The author makes a merit of this, but he can hardly hope that his results will prove us all wrong. Our theory is that a family history should be built on the plan of confining the notation to the bearers of the family name; to the male lines. This Strong genealogy owes much of its size to the addition of female branches. These are carried into the text in a way that destroys any attempt to understand the proportion of the Strongs to the other families. Instead of being a novelty, it is an imitation of the worst feature of English genealogies. It may be termed the *parenthetical* arrangement, since the author hastens to put down consecutively all the items he collects relative to one branch, before he proceeds to the next. For example, he begins on p. 20 with the oldest son of the emigrant, and traces John,[2] John,[3] Jonathan,[4] Jonathan,[5] Hannah,[6] Clarissa (Sawyer),[7] Esther (Nason),[8] Hannah (Sawyer),[7] Calvin and Hill (Chandler),[8] and Hill Chandler's children of the ninth generation, all comprised on pp. 20–23. Thus in the first four pages he has covered eight generations and traced through Hannah Strong, her daughter Hannah Sawyer, and her grandson Hill Chandler to her great-grandson George Washington Chandler. And all this without any use of the exponent for the generation such as we have used above, and without any plan of numbering except straight on for each person, so that George W. Chandler is 147.

Surely this is genealogy run mad. Take this very item, which we choose simply because it is the first, and because all the rest of the book is like it. This great-grandson of Hannah Strong, great-great-grandson of Jonathan Strong, has of course seven other persons to whom he is as nearly related as to her, and fifteen other ancestors as near as Jonathan. In what view can he be considered a part of the Strongs? If every one is to be recorded in every genealogy to which he can be traced by any line of descent, he must be recorded in over one hundred families, even in the eight generations covered by New-England history. Common sense is against any such view. Let family feelings have full power, let all the possessors of a common name draw closer the ties of kindred, but do not make genealogy ridiculous by tracing every ramification after it ceases to bear any reasonable proportion to the whole.

Had Mr. Dwight confined himself to a history of such persons as bore the name of Strong, he would probably have adopted the usual convenient and clear mode of arrangement. As it is, we can only say that the material collected with so much zeal is as poorly arranged as it well could be.

The ancestor of the family here was John Strong, concerning whom something is said, pp. 14–18, which justifies our distrust of the author's critical ability. He says that John Strong was born in Taunton, England, in 1605, and had a sister Eleanor; that they were children of Richard Strong, of Caernarvon, who was born in 1561, moved to Taunton in 1590, and died in 1613. Also that Eleanor married Walter Deane, of Taunton, Mass. All these statements seem to lack the necessary proofs. The most that can be said is that Gov. Caleb Strong, in 1777, prepared a sketch of the family stating something like this, but without the dates. We complain therefore that Mr. Dwight should print any such traditions as *facts*, or else that he should withhold any farther information since received. One would hardly imagine that Mr. Savage, a few years ago, pointed out the deficiencies in the evidence, when the story is here repeated so glibly. We maintain on the contrary, and beg Mr. Dwight to prove the error, that nothing is known of the ancestry of John Strong, and that there is no more reason to imagine that he was born in Taunton than in York, or London.

All the discussion about coats-of-arms, crests and mottoes is equally puerile. The descendants of John Strong have no ascertained right to any; and it would have been well for the author to impress this distinctly upon his readers.

Another matter in which Mr. Dwight has been deceived and led into the repetition of confuted errors, is in regard to the Jones pedigree on p. 161. In relating the ancestry of Hon. Anson Jones, Mr. Dwight repeats the old mistake of saying that William Jones, of New-Haven, was the son of Col. John Jones, by his wife Henrietta, sister of Oliver Cromwell. He emphasizes the mistake by printing the Cromwell pedigree.

Now Mr. Savage has clearly stated that William Jones came from London in 1660, having already married there Hannah, daughter of Gov. Theophilus Eaton. He died Oct. 17, 1706, in his 82d year, but nothing is known of his parentage. It is clear that he was not the son of Henrietta Cromwell, for though the exact date of her marriage is unknown, it was at least after 1649. She could not be the mother of William, who was born in 1624. In fact there is not a single reason to suppose that William Jones was a relative of Col. John Jones; but as so little is known of the Col., it is hard to *prove* that he was not.

We must therefore reluctantly conclude that this genealogy cannot be ranked among the best. The results of many years' experience have convinced us that there is but one good plan of arrangement, the one familiar to our readers, and we hope Mr. Dwight may adopt it for his future works. It is better to have one complete family record than many pages of slightly connected facts. If the collector is loth to suppress the facts he has slowly accumulated, it is better to print a hundred brief genealogies in appendices. All of Mr. Dwight's materials might have been thus preserved, and the gain in clearness would have been immense. No one objects to such fragments, in fact they are most eagerly sought for. Bond's *Watertown* is a collection of the records of a neighborhood, but its very disconnectedness makes it of value to a wide circle of readers. W. H. W.

Fletcher Genealogy: An Account of the Descendants of Robert Fletcher, of Concord, Mass. By EDWARD H. FLETCHER, of New-York City. Printed for the Author, by Alfred Mudge & Son. Boston: 1871. 8vo. pp. 279.

A good specimen of the simpler form of genealogy. There is hardly any biography; very probably the individuals mentioned, a large proportion of whom were farmers, led unpretending lives. The dates seem carefully collected, and the volume has a good index. The plan is not very good, the first four generations being traced, and then the great-grandsons consecutively are taken as heads of lines. But these families are collected into eleven parts without any plan except such as govern the chapters of books, viz., some regard to length. In some, only one family is traced; in others, two or more are added together. There is no confusion of plan, but the cause of this arbitrary connection is not explained.

Still the author has done a work for which he should receive the thanks of his relatives. He mentions that, in 1848, he published a genealogical chart of the family. On p. 64 is a cut of Emerson arms, but no authority is given for it. A portrait of Calvin Fletcher forms the frontispiece. W. H. W.

Memoirs of the Wilkinson Family in America. Comprising Genealogical and Biographical Sketches of Lawrence Wilkinson of Providence, R. I.; Edward Wilkinson of New Milford, Conn.; John Wilkinson of Attleborough, Mass.; Daniel Wilkinson of Columbia Co., N. Y., &c., and their Descendants from 1645–1868. By Rev. ISRAEL WILKINSON, A.M., Jacksonville, Ill. Davis & Penniman, Printers. 1869. 8vo. pp. 585.

In this genealogy will be found a great mass of information relative to the Wilkinsons, though treated in a somewhat desultory way. The first 32 pages are given to various matters, including a brief record of the descendants of Roger Williams, and also some papers relative to the early settlement of Rhode-Island. Pages 32–312 are devoted to the descendants of Lawrence W.; pages 313–541 to biographies of members of the family; pages 542–576 to the other families of the name specified in the title.

Lawrence Wilkinson, the emigrant, was one of the settlers at Providence, and was there in 1657 certainly. His name is appended to a document dated 19th of 11th month, 1645, but it is also clear that the names were signed to this agreement after its date, whenever the writers came into town fellowship.

It is also quite clear that a Lawrence Wilkinson of Lanchester, either in 1645–47 or in 1652, an officer in arms, had property sequestered and was allowed to go to New-England. This matter is stated on Mr. Somerby's authority and may be accepted as fact, though the discrepancies in date should be remedied. It is further said that this officer is the man with whom the known pedigree begins, which is probable; and an attempt to show that the officer was son of William Wilkinson, of Harperly House, Lanchester, co. Durham, but this is problematical. In brief, the pedigree is probable but by no means proven, and the family ought not to accept it or use the arms until the facts have been made out.

The book contains a great deal of biographical matter, and may fairly be entitled a good genealogy. It may be noted that the author says, on page 279, that he has much material for a Sayles genealogy. W. H. W.

Orthodox Congregationalists and the Sects. By Rev. DORUS CLARKE, D.D. Boston: Lee & Shepard. 1871. 12mo. pp. 169.

The object of this work is to compare the orthodox or conservative congregationalists with other denominations of christians—to show the causes which prevent that denomination from increasing in numbers as rapidly as some of the others—and to suggest methods for removing the obstacles which retard its progress. The book is divided into three parts. The first is devoted to proving the claims of the church polity of the congregationalists to be the best and most scriptural pattern—the second to ascertaining the peculiarities of different denominations which promote or retard their increase—and the third to pointing out the things to be done by orthodox congregationalists to advance their cause and give greater efficiency to the efforts of those who are laboring to promote that cause, in the ultimate triumph of which Rev. Dr. Clarke has full faith.

The book bears traces of deep thought and is a very suggestive one in many respects. The author has evidently investigated his subject carefully, and if he has in any instance failed to represent the opinions of his opponents fairly, we think it has been done inadvertently.

Our readers who do not belong to the author's denomination may object to the assumption in the title-page, which possibly may be intended as an offset to rival assumptions. They, no doubt, will find something in the book to which they will not assent; nor will all his conclusions, probably, be admitted by them. They will find, however, a number of important questions discussed in an able manner. Such discussions, treated in a candid spirit and in an impartial manner, cannot fail to advance our historical as well as our theological knowledge. J. W. D.

General Conference of the Congregational Churches in Maine, 1871. The County Conferences and Report of the Maine Missionary Society; being a portion of the Minutes of the General Conference for 1871.

This pamphlet does not give the name of the printer or place of its publication, but we presume we are indebted to E. F. Duren, Esq., of Bangor, for our copy.

It is neatly printed, and is valuable to us for its statistics and necrology.

A Commemorative Discourse on Rev. Alonzo Hill, D.D., of Worcester. Read before the Worcester Association at Sterling, Feb. 15. Repeated at the Meeting of the Worcester Conference in Clinton, May 3. By JOSEPH ALLEN, D.D., of Northboro'. Reprinted from "The Religious Magazine." Boston: Leonard C. Bowles. 1871. 8vo. pp. 8.

We tender to the venerable Dr. Allen our thanks for a copy of his tribute to the public services and personal worth of one, who, for more than forty years, was his friend and co-laborer. Dr. Hill, the pastor of the Second Congregational Society of Worcester, was an able minister, a faithful pastor, and a scholar of varied acquirements.

El Averiguador. Correspondencia entre Curiosos, Literatos, Anticuarios, &c. &c. Madrid, 1° Agosto, 1871. No. 15, Segunda epoca. 8vo. pp. 16.

The above is the title of a magazine, printed in Madrid, semi-monthly, in the Spanish language and in the interests of Spanish literature, which treats of a great variety of topics, and in a manner at once brief, erudite and instructive.

The character of the serial will be clearly seen by a simple statement of some of the subjects discussed under their proper heads, in the present number.

Preguntas. Under this head questions are raised relating to history, engravings, moral science, philology, geography and philosophy.

Respuestas. Replies are given to former queries upon the etymology of geographical names, the origin of dramatic operas, the use of titles, literature, with a discussion of the origin of the song, "Marlborough has gone to the war."

Curiosidades. An unfinished article under this head treats of "Spectacles of better sight," or aids to the perception of things as they are.

Philatelia. Here we have something on the origin and science of postage stamps.

Bibliografia. Under this department we have an extended notice of the Quarter Century Discourse delivered before the New-England Historic, Genealogical Society by the Rev. Mr. Slafter. The article contains many important statements and suggestions, especially noticeable as reflecting Spanish ideas in regard to the objects for which our society was established. Believing that it will be read with great interest not only by the members of the society but by all students in the same line of historical research, we transfer a translation of it to our pages.

"*Discourse delivered before the New-England Historic, Genealogical Soceity*, by the Rev. Edmund F. Slafter, A.M. Boston, MDCCCLXX. (En. 4°, 59 pagines.)

"Ever since the month of March, 1845, an association has existed in Boston, under the title of "New-England Historic, Genealogical Society," whose chief object is to collect carefully all data and items of information relating to the families and ancestors of the first settlers who passed over from Great Britain to establish themselves on the American continent. The Rev. Mr. Slafter is careful to state, in his remarkable discourse, that "*we desire not to be distinguished by titles or honors unearned by ourselves, and which belong only to those who have gone before us*;" from this statement, and from their recognizing that,—genus et proavos, et quæ non fecimus ipsi; vix ea nostra voco,—it is easy to see, that the character of this English society is unlike that of certain Spanish books and writings (modern enough, indeed) which, by means of meagre notes and of coats-of-arms, often the products of a beginner's fancy, gratify the harmless vanity of him who sums up his whole happiness in the fact, that his ancestors were governors of a castle, or members of the Orders of Alcântara and Santiago.

"The purpose of the *Historic, Genealogical Society* is useful and philosophical, as it is the outgrowth of the good sense which is a matter of course in the English race. By studying the history of the individual, that of the family, that of the most insignificant town, that of the house, that of the lands or estate; by this synthetic process valuable data are collected, true and important to the general chronicles of the nation.

"The Boston society publishes a periodical, the series of which now amounts to twenty-three volumes, embracing learned and curious notices of 281 families. These reviews begin with the ancestor who emigrated from England to North America. Naturalization papers, wills, private notes relating to important events, discourses, academic degrees, war papers, sepulchral inscriptions and a multitude of analogous documents accompany these narratives "*neither discolored by the stupidity, nor distorted by the ingenuity of any modern art*," as Mr. Slafter aptly says.

"It enters into the design of the society to promote the publication of local histories, ninety-six of which have been published, through its influence, between the years 1845 and 1870.

"The library of the corporation consists now of eight thousand volumes, printed or in manuscript, each containing a greater or less store of useful data for any one who may desire to study the history of New-England. The generosity of the members shows itself in donations, legacies and foundations of a permanent kind. Among these last there is one, the income of which must necessarily be expended in the binding of books. The edifice where the society holds its meetings, and which contains the offices and appurtenances, was purchased for the sum of $20,000. The library contains an apartment which is fire-proof. In the discourse that we are examining there is cited a full and curious history of the successive proprietors and the different vicissitudes of the estate from its first possessor in 1634 to the date of its purchase by the society in 1870. The purchase-money was obtained by subscription among the members whose names are given, and this list shows the sum contributed by each, from $1000 for the largest down to $100 for the smallest.

"I deem it not out of place to note here (let those forgive me who think otherwise) that there is a Spanish writer, whose works, historical, political and geographical, and whose magazine-articles upon various subjects, and even his private letters, must stand as lofty land-marks among the chief literary productions of the nineteenth century. Well, then: the most excellent Senor Don Fermin Caballero, the person to whom we refer, has said (see his *Discourse read before the Royal Academy of History, Madrid*, 1866) that, in order to secure a general history of Spain, worthy of the cultivated world, it is necessary that we should possess the special histories of the notable cities and towns where not a few data remain to be collected and sifted out as well in the edifices, objects and relics that still exist upon the ground, as also in the civic archives; in the customs, the traditions, the festivals, the amusements, the topographical names of the region and the language of the natives. We must use every endeavor and employ every possible stimulus to secure the production and publication of particular descriptions. Every year, in the programmes of the Academy, let powerful inducements be offered anew to such persons as shall write works of this kind. Let us strive to awaken the natural desires of gain and glory in those who can successfully undertake the task; let a taste for this line of studies be spread in a thousand ways, and the pursuit of them be facilitated by furnishing a sure basis, and practical rules to painstaking writers.

"What I have transcribed, clearly reveals the Spanish *theory* of that which, for years past, the Boston society has been carrying into effect. Let us now look at the *practice*.

"In the '*Life of the most illustrious Melchor Cano*' (Madrid, 1871), Don Fermin Caballero devotes the whole of the fourth chapter of his remarkable work to the *Genealogy of the Canos.* Although the author tells us that such study has wearied him excessively, because it is little to his taste, he nevertheless recognizes its importance, when it is pursued according to rule and in a suitable manner. Accordingly that very portion of the work is as delightful and erudite as it is useful and interesting.

"I think that Senor Caballero has no knowledge either of the existence or character of the New-England Historic, Genealogical Society; and I am sure, therefore, that if he has practised the principles which form the basis of the said association, it has been because his own judgment showed him that they were good and advantageous. And if, on the one hand, this may well be a gratification to the Spanish author, on the other hand it must also be a ground of self-gratulation to the estimable English society, that one of the most distinguished Castilian writers has paid it so public a tribute.

"Returning now to the discourse of the Rev. Mr. Slafter, I would say that I find it written in an English as chaste as it is classical and graceful. However, by reason of this very sobriety of words, which marks the Germanic languages, it is difficult to give a full idea of the work without transcribing it almost entire, or without at least devoting to it a more extended article than the nature of this periodical, THE AVERIGUADOR, allows.

"Let these lines, therefore, be regarded not as a critique, but rather as the three or four words placed on the back of a book merely to indicate the subject-matter with which the volume concerns itself.

"Ever since the year 1738, there has been in Spain a Royal Academy of History, which has been in correspondence with the most distinguished literary societies of Europe and of America. Its largeness of mind and its generosity have kept pace with its learning and renown. The character of its statutes bears a resemblanee to those of the *New-England Historic, Genealogical Society.* We have the conviction, nay almost the evidence, that if the Boston society (as being the younger) should address the one of Madrid, it would meet with a pleasing reception, mutual correspondence would be established, fraternal intercourse inaugurated, and exchanges of books made. For, beside the advantages which this might produce to both countries owing to the numberless points of contact which there are between the histories and literatures of nearly all the nations of the world, that noble utterance of the Spanish academician, Cavanilles, must very speedily come to be realized, when he said '*that in the world of letters there should be no strangers save the ignorant.*'

"To the latter class unfortunately belongs, as he has fully proved by the foregoing writing, Dr. Th.—TANGER, July, 1871."

The reader will bear in mind that the Rev. Mr. Slafter's discourse was delivered in 1870. The Historic, Genealogical Society has expended upon its estate over $40,000. The society's library also contains about 28,000 pamphlets, many of which are rare and valuable.

California. By MARSHALL P. WILDER. Boston: Wright & Potter Printers. 8vo. pp. 31.

This address or lecture of Col. Wilder, is a comparative view of the climate, resources, and progress of California, with observations made in a tour to the Pacific coast, in the summer of 1870, the special objects of his visit being the examination of the agricultural and horticultural resources of that state. The lecture was prepared at the special request of and delivered before the Boston Mercantile Library Association. It has been repeated by request before the Massachusetts Board of Agriculture, the Massachusetts Agricultural College; the faculty and students of Amherst College and Dartmouth College, respectively; the Pennsylvania Horticultural Society, the merchants of Philadelphia, &c.

We were among the many gratified and instructed listeners to the lecture, on the occasion of its first delivery, and a perusal of it in print has but served to deepen the impressions then received. California is certainly the marvel of this age, whether we consider its political or social history and career, or its climate, soil, mines, scenery and productions. If this lecture were the work of a stranger, we should be delighted with its eloquence, and its poetry of thought and imagery, and, while amazed at its statements and statistics, we should feel justified in suspecting that they are highly colored if not greatly exaggerated; but there can be no room for any suspicions of the sort, when we know whose practised eye, sound judgment, and mature experience saw and carefully weighed the facts here presented.

An Official Inaccuracy respecting the Death and Burial of the Princess Mary, daughter of King James I. Read at a Meeting of the Historical Society of Great Britain on Monday, June 12, 1871, by Col. JOSEPH LEMUEL CHESTER, Fellow of the Historical Society. 8vo. pp. 8.

In this brief but comprehensive essay Col. Chester has proved that a mistake of three months occurs in the date of the death of this infant princess, as recorded on her monument in Westminster Abbey, and in the registry of burials there. She died on the 16th *September*, 1607, not on the 16th *December* as recorded in both places. The proof is ample and conclusive. The fact thus shown, relieves James from the accusation of heartlessness, in authorizing and sharing the Christmas festivities of that year. After three months mourning for this child of two and a half years of age, the usual routine of the court was to be resumed.

Col. Chester points out that the Registers of the Abbey were mutilated after the Restoration in 1660, and that the officer who was installed in Feb., 1660-1, put the fragments together and transcribed them into a new volume. They are therefore not to be relied on as of great authority. W. H. W.

A Discourse on the Life and Services of the late Gulian Crommelin Verplanck, LL.D. Delivered before the Numismatic and Antiquarian Society of Philadelphia, on the evening of May 5, 1870, by CHARLES HENRY HART, Historiographer of the Society, and Corresponding Member of the N. Y. Genealogical and Biographical Society; the N. E. Historic, Genealogical Society; the Long Island Historical Society [&c.]. Reprinted from the "New-York Genealogical and Biographical Record" for October, 1870. New-York: 1870. Quarto, pp. 20. [Reprinted for private distribution.]

The late Mr. Verplanck of New-York was one of the last conspicuous representatives of the Knickerbocker families. He was eminent for his social and civil virtues, for his literary acquirements and writings, and for his public services. He failed to be as eminent in the profession of the law, only because he abandoned it at an early period of his life. Confessedly, he was one of the best men this country has produced, and his individuality was made up of rare qualities most rarely mixed. The death of such a man awakens fresh regret that the good old patriarchial days have gone forever—" days" when men are said to have lived for hundreds of years.

Mr. Hart has happily added to his already long list of biographical sketches this one of Mr. Verplanck. He gives an outline of his family genealogy, and a brief but skilfully and tastefully executed portraiture of his character. The pamphlet is especially worth preserving.

Memorial to the Men of Cambridge who fell in the First Battle of the Revolutionary War. Services of Dedication, Nov. 3, 1870. Cambridge: Press of John Wilson & Son. 1870. 8vo. pp. 40.

This memorial contains a detailed account of the proceedings of the city government of Cambridge, Mass., relating to the erection and dedication of a monument in honor of those sons of Cambridge who fell in defence of the popular cause, on the 19th of April, 1775, within the territorial limits of the town. The names of these martyrs are as follows: John Hicks, William Marcy, Moses Richardson (buried in Cambridge), and John Russell, Jabez Wyman and Jason Winship (buried in Menotomy).

The Rev. Alexander McKenzie, pastor of the First Church in Cambridge, in his oration at the dedication, in 1870, of the monument to the soldiers of the late civil war, called attention to the fact that no effort had ever been made to suitably honor the memory of the earlier patriots; and, on the 14th of September following, Horatio G. Parker, Esq., submitted to the board of aldermen an order, providing for the erection of a monument at the expense of the city.

The service of dedication consisted of a prayer by the Rev. Pliny Wood, of the Methodist Episcopal Church; music by a select choir under the direction of George Fisher, Esq.; remarks by the mayor, the Hon. H. R. Harding; the singing of hymns composed by Mrs. A. C. Wellington and Miss Sarah S. Jacobs, respectively, and a historical address by the Rev. Alexander McKenzie.

All the exercises were in excellent taste, and worthy of the occasion and of the city.

An Oration delivered at Lexington on the Dedication of the Town and Memorial Hall, April 19, 1871, *being the* 96*th Anniversary of the Battle of Lexington.* By Dr. George B. Loring. With the Proceedings and a Historical Appendix. Boston: Press of T. R. Marvin & Son. 1871. 8vo. pp. 76.

This pamphlet is a memorial volume of the enterprise which has resulted in the erection of a new Town Hall in Lexington, Mass., embracing within its walls a town hall for municipal purposes; a memorial hall, in honor of the citizens of the town who fell on the 19th of April, 1775, and of residents, and others serving on her quota, who lost their lives during the civil war, 1861–1865; and of the establishment of the free town library (or the Cary Library). It recites the action of the town, the Lexington Monument Association, Mr. William H. Cary, of Brooklyn, N. Y., a native of Massachusetts, and his wife, Mrs. Maria Cary, a native of Lexington, and others. Mrs. Cary's donations amount to over twenty thousand dollars.

The undertaking, from 1869 to its completion, was in the hands of a committee, of which Hon. Charles Hudson was the chairman. He was also one of the committee of publication of this volume, a copy of which we received by his kindness.

We commend this example of Lexington to other towns or cities that may hereafter erect memorials to the patriotic dead, and to individuals who would perpetuate the memory of their deceased friends. Monuments of stone or bronze are better than none; but the best monuments, because they may be permanently useful, are free libraries, museums of art or science, public halls, churches or chapels, and hospitals. And we hope that the day will soon come when the public taste, now in many instances expressed in ostentatious and extravagant memorials, as seen in our cemeteries, shall have been educated to a higher standard.

Scribner's Monthly Illustrated Magazine for the People. Conducted by J. G. Holland. Scribner & Co., 654 Broadway, N. Y. Price, $4.00 per annum, in advance. [A. Williams & Co., agents, 135 Washington st., Boston.]

The third volume of this ably conducted magazine began with the November No., and the issues for Nov., Dec. 1871, and January, 1872, show that no efforts are spared to make this magazine, in respect to reading matter, illustrations and dress, worthy of the best taste and culture of the day.

The Manual of the First Lutheran Church of the City of Albany. Albany: Joel Munsell. 1871. 12mo. pp. 128.

This beautifully printed manual contains the liturgy used by this ancient religious society; the history of the society; lists of pew-holders in 1788, 1792, 1871; a list of communicants from 1786 to 1871, and other matters of value.

It is illustrated with wood-cuts of the church edifice in 1816 and 1871; a plan of Albany in 1695; the corporate seal; and several autographs of someof the more prominent members of the church in former years.

In Memoriam. John Cox, 1795–1871. *Henry Oxnard Preble,* 1847–1871. 8vo. pp. 27.

This pamphlet, from the press of D. Clapp & Son of Boston, was privately printed by its author, our esteemed friend, Capt. Geo. Henry Preble, U. S. N., and is a brief biographical sketch of his father-in-law, John Cox, a highly respected citizen and eminent merchant of Portland, Me., where he was born on the 13th of Feb., 1795, and died on the 25th of Jan., 1871; also a series of tributes in prose and verse, from various sources, to his deeply lamented son, Henry Oxnard Preble, who on the 25th of May, 1871. Capt. Preble has also caused copies of these memorials was born in Portland, on the 4th of Jan., 1847, and died in Charlestown, Mass., to be bound up separately.

A memoir of Henry O. Preble will shortly appear in the Register.

Bibliography of the Local History of Massachusetts. By Jeremiah Colburn. Boston: Wm. Parsons Lunt. MDCCCLXXI. 8vo. pp. 119.

This handsome volume is a reprint from the Register, where it appeared in instalments, beginning in 1867, and will be found to be a very convenient as well as very complete index to a great number of books and pamphlets relating to Massachusetts; and all the more convenient, because only a fraction of the publications, whose titles are here given, can be found in any one library.

The matter is placed under the names of the towns and cities arranged in alphabetical order; a plan, perhaps, as good as any for a work of this kind. A valuable addition to the book would have been an index of authors' names, and it is very probable that this will be introduced into another edition of the book, which undoubtedly will be called for within a few years.

Of course, every work of this nature is more or less incomplete, and is susceptible of indefinite enlargement; each successive edition taking up the publications as they appear from time to time.

In these one hundred and nineteen pages, Mr. Colburn has given us a survey by titles of an immense mass of history and literature, testifying to the fecundity of our local press and pen; and he has rendered invaluable service to collectors, librarians and students.

This edition of the *Bibliography* was privately printed, and but few copies remain unsold. The work was a "labor of love" on the part of the compiler, and if any compensation should ever come to him it must be from future editions.

1. *Provincial Papers. Documents and Records relating to the Province of New-Hampshire, from* 1722 *to* 1737; *Containing Important Records and Papers pertaining to the Boundary Lines between New-Hampshire and Massachusetts.* Published by authority of the Legislature of New-Hampshire. Volume IV. Compiled and edited by NATHANIEL BOUTON, D.D., corresponding secretary of the New-Hampshire Historical Society. Manchester: John B. Clarke, State Printer. 1870. 8vo. pp. viii. and 891.
2. *Provincial Papers. Documents and Records relating to the Province of New-Hampshire from* 1738 *to* 1749; *Containing very valuable and interesting Records and Papers relating to the Expedition against Louisbourg,* 1745. Published by authority of the Legislature of New-Hampshire. Volume V. Compiled and edited by NATHANIEL BOUTON, D.D., corresponding secretary of the New-Hampshire Historical Society. Nashua: Orren C. Moore, State Printer. 1871. 8vo. pp. viii. and 962.

Upon the appearance of the former volumes of this historical series, we called attention to the wise liberality which New-Hampshire is manifesting in the steady support she has given and still affords to the work of rescuing her provincial records and papers from decay, by printing them. This support comes from no party, sect or clique, but seems to be due to the general sense of the propriety and desirableness of the thing itself. It is well, too, that the historical society of the state, which prompted and still zealously encourages the work, should be recognized as it is by the continued employment of Dr. Bouton, as the compiler and editor.

We have heretofore expressed the hope that New-Hampshire will not halt in this work until every part of her strictly historical records have been printed, at least down to the beginning of the present century. Undoubtedly a few more volumes will suffice for that purpose. It is an honor to the state, and generations yet unborn, as well as the living, will hold the names of all connected with the undertaking and all who fostered it, in high esteem. The paltry sum expended on such a noble work, will never be missed from the treasury, while these priceless records of the past history of the state will be preserved from every possible vicissitude, for the instruction of the people in virtue and patriotism, as well as for evidence of the highest value in matters affecting the right and title of property.

Volume IV. of the Provincial Papers includes the latter part of the term of John Wentworth, lieutenant-governor and commander-in-chief in the absence of Gov. Shute; the brief term of Gov. Burnet, 1729, and that of Gov. Belcher, 1730 to October, 1737. The "records of council," here printed, extend from June 21, 1722, to Nov. 2, 1728, and are all, probably, from the first date named to April 2, 1742, that can be found. A portion of the missing records very likely, as the editor supposes, were destroyed by the fire which consumed Mr. Sec'y Waldron's house in 1736. They may yet be found in private hands, whither have strayed too many of our provincial and colonial papers.

The specially valuable portion of this volume, however, is that which relates to the memorable, little understood, and often misrepresented dispute between New-Hampshire and Massachusetts, respecting their boundary line.

The compiler has appropriately put into this volume, also, the correspondence of Gov. Belcher with Mr. Secretary Waldron, 1731–7, in which the governor uses great directness and plainness of language regarding men and measures of that day; also the correspondence between John Tomlinson, Esq., agent of the province in England, with Theodore Atkinson, Esq., and others of New-Hampshire, 1733–7. This latter correspondence, which relates chiefly to the boundary controversy, should be carefully studied by all who would gain an accurate idea of the public affairs of the province during that period.

Volume V. whose title is also given above, contains all the official records and documents found in the office of the secretary of state, and elsewhere, relative to the important part New-Hampshire took in the expedition against Louisbourg, in 1745. (For a partial list of officers and soldiers in the expedition, see *ante*, vol. xxii. p. 116; vol. xxiv. p. 368; and vol. xxv. p. 3.) It is of little consequence who was the first to suggest this expedition (whether it was Gov. Shirley or Capt. William Vaughan, son of Lt. Gov. Vaughan of New-Hampshire, who acted a conspicuous and meritorious part in the reduction of the fortress), but it is certain that the province through her governor, Benning Wentworth, her council and assembly, and her leading men, ably seconded the enterprise, furnished more than her quota of men and supplies to that object, and by her land forces, carpenters and sailors, materially and brilliantly contributed to the success of the undertaking. These letters, papers, memorials and reports will greatly aid the future historian of the expedition.

This volume also contains further documents relating to the determination of the vexed question of the boundary line between New-Hampshire and Massachusetts, and other able papers of Mr. Tomlinson, the agent above-named, relating to that subject. The miscellaneous papers, the agreement for the purchase of the Masonian claims (now first printed from a copy prepared by Col. Joshua W. Peirce of Portsmouth, N. H., one of the few surviving heirs and assigns of the original Masonian proprietors, and who has the original in his possession); incidents of Indian warfare; the failure of the projected expedition against Canada in 1746 and 1747, and other papers, are of value and interest.

This volume is not as well printed as the previous volumes; the type being of a different and less attractive style, and there are a few marks of carelessness on the part of the printer. The editorial work has been done, as in the former volumes of the series, with ability, true historical fidelity, and, as one can readily see, with care and industry.

The peculiar labor and difficulties attending the transcribing and editing of ancient, moth-eaten, worn, disfigured and mutilated records, such as are most of the originals in many of our state-archives, can be truly appreciated only by the select, the divine few, who delight to go to original sources for information; but we most fervently hope that the results of Dr. Bouton's toil will not fail to gain the attention they deserve from his fellow citizens; that all who can obtain them will buy, read and keep copies of these volumes, and that one copy, at least, will be placed and its custody secured in every town library. If we would have our children become good citizens they must be made to read and understand our laws and our histories, both local and general; and our duty, in the same respect, is no less plain and imperative toward the invading hosts from Canada and Europe.

The Story of a Famous Book: An Account of Dr. Benjamin Franklin's Autobiography. By Samuel A. Green, M.D. Boston: For private distribution. 1871. 8vo. pp. 14.

This is a reprint, for a few friends of the author, of an article which originally appeared in the *Atlantic Monthly* for February, 1871, under the title of "The Story of a Famous Book."

Of Franklin's autobiography, it is undoubtedly true, as Dr. Green says, that it was the earliest American book that acquired and sustained a great popularity; and few books of the same class are to be compared with it in style and interest. Its history is both eventful and remarkable, and this is set forth in detail by Dr. Green in this interesting pamphlet. He traces the history of its composition, of it translations into the French language, and of its retranslation into English; an account of the singular vicissitudes that attended the original manuscript; and also an account of many of the various editions of the work, and a statement of their peculiarities.

This pamphlet is a valuable addition to our bibliographical history.

Historical Memoranda relating to the Discovery of Etherization, and to the connection with it of the late Dr. William T. G. Morton. Prepared by a Committee of Citizens of Boston chosen to raise a Morton Testimonial Fund. Boston: Printed by Rand, Avery & Frye. 1871. 8vo. pp. 16.

Who was the discoverer of etherization is a question that has vexed the souls of not a few men on both sides of the Atlantic Ocean. In this case, as in almost all instances of great inventions and beneficial discoveries, the final result was reached by degrees, to which many men and many ages, perhaps, contributed; but he was the true discoverer who seized upon admitted facts, principles, forces, or properties of matter, and applied them to practical and beneficial ends. It is established beyond serious controversy that Dr. Morton first successfully proved that ether is an *inevitable, complete* and *safe* agent for the alleviation of physical pain. This occurred in the Massachusetts General Hospital, in Boston, on the 16th and 17th of Oct. 1846.

Dr. William Thomas Green Morton was born in Charlton, Mass., 9 Aug. 1819, and died in the city of New-York 15 July, 1868.

A Memorial of Anson Burlingame, late Envoy Extraordinary and Minister Plenipotentiary from the Chinese Empire to the Treaty Powers. Boston. 1870. 8vo. pp. 23.

This pamphlet, City Document, No. 66, contains a full account of the proceedings connected with the funeral of Mr. Burlingame, which took place Saturday, 23 April, 1870, at the expense and under the direction of the city of Boston.

Anson Burlingame was the son of Joel Burlingame, and was born in New-Berlin, county of Chenango, N. Y., 14 Nov., 1820, and died in St. Petersburg, Russia, 23 Feb., 1870. He was educated at the public schools of Ohio and Michigan, at the Branch University of Michigan in Detroit, and at the Harvard Law School. In 1852 he was a member of the general court of Mass.; in 1853, a member of the committee for revising the state constitution, and in 1854 was elected a member of the federal congress, where he served for the next six years, but was defeated in 1860. In 1861, he was appointed resident minister at Vienna, but the emperor of Austria refused to receive him, on personal and political grounds; and while yet in Europe, was appointed ambassador to the court of Pekin. In 1867, the emperor of China appointed him chief of an extraordinary mission to the principal western nations. He was in the successful discharge of this mission when he died. He married a daughter of Isaac Livermore, Esq., of Cambridge, Mass., who with several children survives him.

Myles Standish, with an Account of the Exercises of Consecration of the Monument Ground on Captain's Hill, Duxbury [Mass.], Aug. 17, 1871. Prepared by STEPHEN M. ALLEN, Corresponding Secretary of the Standish Memorial Association. Boston: Alfred Mudge & Son, Printers. 1871. 8vo. pp. 76.

At last, the memory of doughty and redoubtable Myles Standish is to be perpetuated by a monument upon or near the spot where his ashes rest. This is well. And yet it is hardly needed; for, if we look about us, we shall see everywhere monuments, far nobler and, as we hope, more enduring than brass or stone, to the civic as well as private virtues, the martial skill and courage, the self-denying labors, and the far-seeing and far-reaching prudence of Standish and his contemporaries.

The pamphlet under notice contains a sketch of the life and character of Standish; a history of the organization and proceedings of the Monument Association; the oration of Gen. H. B. Sargent, and the after-dinner speeches of Gen. B. F. Butler, Hon. Geo. B. Loring, Hon. N. B. Shurtleff, and the Rev. A. A. Miner, D.D.; poems by Justin Winsor, Esq., of Boston, and the late S. F. Streeter, of Baltimore, &c.; and is embellished with cuts representing a front view of Standish's house built in 1666, and still standing; also a view of his kitchen, and a *fac-simile* of his autograph.

The pamphlet is well printed, and the contents well arranged by Mr. Allen, to whom we are indebted for a copy.

RECENT REPRINTS FROM THE REGISTER.

1. *A Memorial of Josiah Barker, of Charlestown, Mass.* By HARRY HERBERT EDES, Member of the New-England Historic, Genealogical Society, and Corresponding Member of the State Historical Society of Wisconsin. Boston: Privately printed. 1871. 8vo. pp. 25. [D. Clapp & Son.]
2. *William Pitt Fessenden: A Memoir prepared for the New-England Historical and Genealogical Register for April,* 1871. By GEO. HENRY PREBLE. Reprinted for private distribution, with additions. Boston: David Clapp & Son, Printers. 1871. 8vo. pp. 24.
3. *Reminiscences of Lucius Manlius Sargent: with an Appendix containing a Genealogy of his Family, and other matters.* By JOHN H. SHEPPARD. Boston: Printed by David Clapp & Son. 1871. 8vo. pp. 51.
4. *Old Cambridge and New.* By THOMAS C. AMORY. Reprinted from the New-England Historical and Genealogical Register, for July, 1871, with additions. Boston: James R. Osgood & Co., 124 Tremont Street. [David Clapp & Son, Printers.]

We give the titles of some of the more recent reprints from our pages mainly for the purpose of putting the fact of their re-issue on record. They are printed on heavy paper, and are valuable contributions to our local and genealogical history. With the exception of the last, which is for sale at Osgood & Co.'s, they were printed for private distribution among the authors' friends.

MARRIAGES AND DEATHS.

MARRIAGES.

FORSTER=LYON. In Charlestown, Mass., Sept. 5, Edward Jacob Forster, M.D., to Anita Damon, dau. of Henry Lyon, M.D., all of Charlestown.

GERKEN=ALOFSEN. In Paris, France, Nov. 7, at the Protestant Church, M. Jean Adolphe Gerken, of Amsterdam, Holland, to Miss Frances Alofsen, dau. of S. Alofsen, Esq., of Jersey city, N. J., honorary vice president of the N. E. Historic, Genealogical Society.

TROUP=WHEELER. In Ayer, Mass., June 27, 1871, by Rev. Elias Nason, Mr. Charles A. S. Troup, of Boston, and Miss Clara E. A., daughter of George T. Wheeler, of Ayer.

DEATHS.

COREY, Solomon Pendre, in Malden, Sept. 11, 1871, of heart disease. He was born in Kingston, Mass., Jan. 28, 1813, and was son of Capt. Solomon and Charlotte Delano (Winsor) Corey. He married May 6, 1835, Martha S., daughter of Thomas and Hannah (Cheever) Waite, of Malden. His paternal ancestry is given in REG. xix. 174. In the maternal line he was descended from Pilgrim stock, through his grand parents Peter[8] and Charlotte (Delano) Windsor, Sam'l and Rhoda[7] (Delano) Winsor, Joshua[6] and Hopestill (Peterson) Delano, Ebenezer and Martha[5] (Simmons) Delano, John and Mercy[4] (Pabodie) Simmons, William and Elizabeth[3] (Alden) Pabodie, John and Priscilla[2] (Mullins) Alden, William[1] and—— Mullins. The last four were the well-known passengers in the "Mayflower," 1620. Other ancestors in the same line are Philip de la Noye and Moses Symonson (Simmons) of the "Fortune," 1621, Stephen Tracy of the "Ann," 1623, Rev. Ralph Partridge, first minister of Duxbury, and his son-in-law Rev. Thomas Thacher, first minister of the Church now known as the Old South in Boston.

COX, Rev. S. J. (of the Philadelphia Methodist Episcopal Conference), in Zanesville, Ohio, August 23, 1870, aged 80 years. He was a son of Hon. James Cox, who was a member of congress from New-Jersey in the years 1809 and 1810, and uncle of Hon. Samuel Sullivan Cox, now of congress from New-York.

DANIELL, Otis, a well known member of St. Paul's parish in this city, March 7, 1871, aged 66 years. He was buried March 11, at Mount Auburn Cemetery. The funeral service was conducted at St. Paul's Church, by Rev. Dr. Nicholson. A large number of citizens, and many of the children of the Church Orphan's Home, of which Mr. Daniell was a substantial benefactor, were in attendance. We take the following just tribute of respect from the *Advertiser* :—

"We are seldom called upon to record the decease of a private citizen who will be more greatly missed by his associates, nor of any of greater moral worth than him whose name heads this notice. Of a most retiring and unobtrusive disposition naturally, he was from principle so averse to having his name connected in a public manner with the philanthropic and religious movements of the day, that his real services and labors were hardly known to the world at large. And yet from the time he came to Boston, about the year 1818, until the day of his death, his whole life was one of self-denial and religious consecration. He was born in Needham, in 1805, and came to Boston as clerk for the late Moses Grant. So acceptable and valuable were his services that he was admitted general partner in the business before becoming of age. The firm of Grant & Daniell was formed in 1826; Mr. Daniell's connection terminated in 1855. The house thus founded was always known for the probity and high commercial character of its business transactions. The strictest principles of rectitude, honor and prudence alone guided their councils. Mr. Daniell was possessed of more than ordinary caution; and, although he had a capacity that enabled him easily to grasp and control to a successful result large transactions, yet he was ever averse to those hazards which imperil fortunes while promising great pecuniary gains. These qualities gave great value to his services as a bank officer and as an administrator of fiduciary estates.

"He early in life connected himself with the Episcopal Church, and was always a consistent and earnest supporter of the churches and institutions maintained by that order. He was one of the founders and for many years one of the wardens of Grace Church, in Temple Street, until the church edifice passed to another denomination. He was also an officer and a constant benefactor of the Church Home for Orphans. But it was in private life that he was best known and loved. His charities were constant though unobtrusive, and were always regulated by principle. He seemed to regard himself as a steward to manage his estate for his Master, as one that must give account. Those who came to know him intimately knew not whether to prize him most for his wisdom or for his kindly courtesy. To all such his loss is irreparable."

DEAN, Dr. Oliver, at Franklin, Mass., Dec. 5, aged 87. He was a son of Seth Dean, of Franklin, where he was born Feb. 18, 1783; and was descended from John[1] Dean (who settled at Dedham as early as 1677), through Ebenezer,[2] Ebenezer[3] and Seth,[4] his father. He was educated a physician, and was a member of the Massachusetts Medical Society. In 1811 he married Miss Caroline Francœur, who died in 1866, and in 1868 he married Mrs. Louisa C. Hawes, of Wrentham, who survives him. In the war of 1812 he removed to Medway, and practised there until 1817, when his health failed and he withdrew forever from his profession. For nine years he was superintendent of the Medway Cotton Manufactory, and eight years Superintendent and to the time of his death president of the Amoskeag Manufacturing Company in Manchester, N. H. For ten years subsequent he resided on a large farm in Framingham; in 1844 he became one of the prominent men in the School Street Church in Boston, and in 1851 purchased his late residence in Franklin

He was the founder of the Dean Academy at Franklin, on which he bestowed about $250,000, during his life, and to which he left by his will property estimated at $300,000. He also made bequests to Tufts College, of which institution he was president of the board of trustees, and to which he had been a liberal benefactor. He leaves a bond of $20,000 towards the erection of a new Universalist church at Franklin. The Universalist denomination has lost in him one of its best friends. He left no children.

HAYES, Susan, widow of the late Hon. Wm. A. Hayes, in South Berwick, Me., September 20, 1870, aged 80.

JAMESON, John, Esq., in Cornish, Me, April 2, 1870, aged 70 years. He was a member of the bar of the county of York.

Jameson, Elizabeth Jewett, wife of the late John Jameson, Esq., in Cornish, Me., April 7, 1870.

Minor, Capt Robert D., died suddenly on the morning of Nov. 25, 1871, in Richmond, Va. The deceased was born (as we have been informed) in Fredericksburg, in the year 1826. During President Tyler's administration he received his warrant as a midshipman in the United States navy, and, by reason of gallant service and a faithful and honorable discharge of duty, he won the rank of lieutenant.

At the commencement of the late war, he resigned his commission and at once entered the naval service of the confederate states as a captain, and bore himself with great bravery. He acted a prominent part in the memorable fight in Hampton Roads, and was in that engagement wounded in the shoulder, while bearing a flag of truce to save the crew of one of the frigates disabled by the iron-clad ram, Virginia.

When the scheme for the improvement of the navigation of the James River had been perfected, he was called in his capacity of engineer to take charge of the work. The present condition of that improvement bears high testimony to his efficiency and activity, and in his death the city has met with a loss it can illy afford to bear.

As an officer and a gentleman, Capt. Minor was *sans peur et sans reproche*. As a husband, a father and a friend, he was loving, kind, gentle and true.

Sanford, Solomon White, in Taunton, Ms., December 29, 1870, unmarried, aged 41 years, 3 months and 3 days.

He was the second son of Reverend Enoch Sanford and Mrs. Caroline White, his wife (*ante*, vol. xxv. p. 104). He was born at the parsonage in Raynham, Ms., September 26, 1829, and resided in Taunton, Milford, New-York city, and Providence, R. I., where he was the junior partner in the manufacturing firm of Homer, Black and Sanford.

About a year before his death, on account of failing health, having met with considerable success, he retired from active business, and returned to his father's residence in Raynham.

He was the paternal grandson of Capt. Joseph Sanford, of Berkeley, Ms., a soldier of the revolution, born 1761, died 1834, and his wife Mrs. Eleanor Macomber, born 1763, died 1845. Paternal gr. grandson of Lieut. George Sanford, born 1724, died 1820, and his wife Mrs. Mary Phillips, died 1793: and paternal gr. gr. grandson of John Sandford, died 1747, and his wife Mrs. Abigail Pitts, born 1689, the granddaughter of Peter Pitts and Edward Babbitt, of Taunton, and gr. granddaughter of of Miles Tarne, of Boston.

Some account of his maternal ancestors is given, *ante*, vol. xxv. pp. 103, 104.

Mr. Sanford was endowed with many pleasing traits of character, and his genial companionship endeared him to a large circle of friends. He was buried in Raynham in the family inclosure.

Sayward, Joseph, Esq., in Alfred, Me., 11 August, 1869, aged 82 years.

Spooner, Samuel, of Southampton, Ms., May 26, 1870, aged 71 years, 1 mo. 27 days. He married, 19 Dec., 1822, Sarah L., daughter of Abraham and Hannah (Morse) Losey. She was born September 21, 1797.

He was son of Samuel and Zeriah (Hale) S., of Somers, Conn., grandson of Samuel and Elizabeth (Parker) S., of Douglass, Ms.; gr. grandson of Joshua and Freelove (Westcott) S., of Providence, R. I.; gr. gr. grandson of Benjamin and Joanna (Tobey) S., of Middleboro', Ms.; gr. gr. gr. grandson of William and Sarah S., of Dartmouth; gr. gr. gr. gr. grandson of William and Hannah (Pratt) Spooner of Dartmouth.

s.

Sullivan, Capt. James, in Portland, Me., March 18, 1871. He was the son of Capt. John and Mary (Yeaton) Sullivan, and grandson of Ebenezer, son of master John Sullivan, of Berwick, Me. He was born in Portsmouth, N. H., Jan. 23, 1810; married, Aug. 1842, Anne M., daughter of William Shaw, Esq., of Boston.

For many years he commanded a ship in the New-Orleans and Havre trade; afterward in the New-York and Liverpool trade. During the war of the rebellion he sailed the steamer Conqueror, a transport, between New-York and southern ports. He leaves a widow and two children, Anne Josephine and James William.

He was a kind husband and father, an affectionate brother, a faithful friend, a noble man.

Yeaton, Mrs. Eliza S., wife of Mr. Orlando Yeaton, in Brooklyn, N. Y., Oct. 23, 1870, aged 65 years 7 mos. She was sister of Capt. James Sullivan above named.

H. W. Smith.

Samuel Tucker

NEW-ENGLAND

HISTORICAL AND GENEALOGICAL REGISTER

AND

ANTIQUARIAN JOURNAL.

VOL. XXVI. APRIL, 1872. No. 2.

COMMODORE SAMUEL TUCKER.

[Communicated by JOHN H. SHEPPARD, A.M.]

SAMUEL TUCKER was born in Marblehead, Mass., Nov. 1, 1747, as appears on a leaf in the old family bible, and was christened in the First Church of Christ in Marblehead, Nov. 8th, of the same year, according to the record of said church. He was the third child of Andrew and Mary Tucker, who had eight children, viz.: Andrew, Mary, Samuel, William, Nathaniel and Elizabeth, twins, and Sarah.

Andrew Tucker, his father, according to tradition, was one of three brothers, who emigrated together from Dundee, Scotland, when young men, one of whom settled in South Carolina, one in Virginia, and one, Andrew, in Marblehead; but this tradition is probably incorrect, as there was an Andrew Tucker at Marblehead as early as 1663. His mother's maiden name was Mary Belcher,—an English lady, handsome, fashionable and of a refined education. She was fond of social life. Her figure was tall and majestic, and from her style of dress, stately appearance, and winning manners, she was called "The Lady Mary." This maternal gaiety descended to Samuel, as a precious heirloom, which he cherished during a long life.

His father followed the sea; was a skilful shipmaster, and much respected. Before the revolution, he was in affluent circumstances and lived in style. The house which he built more than a hundred years ago, on Rowland Hill, near the bay in Marblehead, is still standing, changed from a gable roof to the modern fashion. He is said to have laid out much cost on this building, and decorated his rooms with rich paper-hangings imported from France. Here the writer saw some fragments of this paper, thick as cloth and figured with vermilion and black stripes. This house must have been stylish in its day, and is still a substantial and convenient tenement.

Of the boyhood and education of Samuel, we only know that at an early period he was sent to school, and was well grounded in reading, writing and arithmetic. His father seeing that he was a bright boy and apt to learn, wished to send him to college, but the youth had no taste for the groves of the academy: his element was the sea, and to so great a degree was his soul kindled by the songs and stories of the Marblehead mariners, who seemed like descendants of the ancient sea-kings, that at eleven years of age he ran away and embarked on board of the Royal George, an English sloop-of-war, which was bound on a cruise to Louisbourg. He was afterward apprenticed to the captain by his forgiving and prudent father. It was there he acquired much nautical knowledge, and became acquainted with British signals,—a source of great value to him in his future career.

At seventeen, he enlisted as second mate on board of a vessel from Salem, of which his brother was first mate. When she was within a few hours' sail of Lisbon, she was pursued by two Algerine corsairs. The captain was frightened, as he gazed at them from the companion way; and to quiet his fears he retreated to his bottle, and hid himself in the cabin. Samuel's brother was at the helm, and becoming also alarmed, gave it up to our young hero, who, as night was approaching, boldly sailed toward the pirates, as in token of surrendering. Darkness came on, he put out the lights, crowded sail, and in the morning arrived safely in Lisbon. The base captain, ashamed of his cowardice, put Samuel out of sight on board an English frigate; but the story of this daring escape, it is said, got wind, and Samuel was then promoted to the berth of midshipman. How long he continued in this frigate, is unknown,—probably for a short period; for he was afterward mate of a vessel in the merchant service, and subsequently master of a ship.

He was married Dec. 21, 1768, soon after he became of age. His wife was Mary, daughter of Samuel and Ann Gatchell, of Marblehead. Mr. Gatchell was deacon of the Congregational Church of that place,—a worthy and estimable man. On his marriage, Capt. Tucker took part of his father-in-law's house, which was a double one, and afterward moved to his father's on Rowland Hill, in order to take care of him, now old and a victim of disease. The latter who had been unfortunate, and was now reduced in property, must have died during the war with England, as the son refers in a future letter to taking care of his mother, "who had no other to look up to for either succor or aid in the least, during more than thirty years." This venerable widow died in Bristol, Maine, at her son's house, in 1808, over ninety-one years old,—an example of maternal love and filial affection ever sacred and ever honorable. She is said to have been a woman of strong and superior mind.

In 1774, he commanded the brig Young Phenix, on a voyage to Bilboa, Spain, where amidst breakers and great peril he saved the vessel. But we must pass over his voyages and accompany him to London when the revolutionary war was breaking out. He was there urged by a recruiter to enlist as an officer in the king's service, and in his haste he cursed "his most gracious majesty." This hard-shelled patriotism exposed him to trouble and danger of imprisonment, and he was obliged to leave London secretly, and making his escape by the aid of friends, he obtained a passage in a ship belonging to the celebrated financier and patriot, Robert Morris, of Philadelphia. On the voyage a furious storm arose, and the preservation of the ship was due to the skill and coolness of Capt. Tucker. This incident made Mr. Morris an efficient and permanent friend, who was instrumental in procuring the notice and patronage of Gen. Washington for the brave seaman. From his tent at Cambridge the General sent him a commission as captain of the armed schooner Franklyn. It was dated Jan. 20, 1776. This was one of the earliest commissions issued by the commander-in-chief on the formation of an infant navy. Capt. Tucker was then at home in Marblehead, and his interview with the officer who announced to him the honor, has come down to us as a tradition, well authenticated and full of humor. His armed vessel lay at Beverly, and the next day Tucker was on board of her and scouring the seas.

He made several cruises in the Franklyn, and was so successful in taking prizes as to receive the thanks of Gen. Washington. His patriotic wife made the banner under which he fought; the field of which was white, with the figure of a pine tree in green. He captured the ship George, laden with troops and munitions of war. In the spring of 1776 he was transferred to the command of the armed schooner Hancock, in which he also made many captures. There is an interesting account of one capture in the summer of that year, which occurred in the vicinity of Marblehead, when his wife and sister stood on the top of a lofty hill in that place and saw through a glass the smoky encounter, heard the roar of the artillery and witnessed the arrival of the prize in the harbor. The captures in 1776 were very numerous and annoying to the enemy. An English work, the "Remembrancer," speaks of 342 vessels captured; of this vast number, Capt. Tucker took very many. In his life-time he had a complete list of them, but it was lent and lost.

Such were his services and success that, on the 15th day of March, 1777, he was appointed by congress commander of the frigate Boston, by a commission, bearing the signature of John Hancock, president. In this ship he took several prizes. On one occasion the encounter was very bloody; for he boarded the enemy and lost the brave Magee, his lieutenant, who headed the marines and fell a sacrifice. Having a presentiment of his fate, this intrepid officer handed to Capt. Tucker, just before the attack, a ring, watch and miniature to be sent, if he were slain, to his only sister.

Command of the frigates and armed vessels was frequently changed; but on the 27th of December, 1777, Capt. Tucker again was appointed master of the frigate Boston; and, Feb. 10, 1778, he was ordered to convey the Hon. John Adams as envoy to France. He was authorized to fit her out for this purpose at his own discretion; and consequently he supplied her with additional spars and canvass, which it was said, were of peculiar and original construction, having reference to swift sailing. As the object of Mr. Adams's mission was important, it was so well known to the enemy that a British seventy-four and two frigates at Newport had been watching the motions of the Boston and the time of her departure. To escape a force so formidable and avoid the numerous men-of-war which infested the track across the Atlantic to France, Capt. Tucker had been selected to the command on account of his nautical skill and well-known intrepidity. So great was the confidence of Mr. Adams in this naval officer, that he committed not only himself, but his young son, the since celebrated John Quincy Adams, then eleven years old, to his charge.

On the 17th of February, 1778, at seven o'clock in the afternoon, Capt. Tucker weighed anchor at Nantasket Roads, and went to sea with colors flying, firing a salute of seven guns on the occasion.

The log-book of this momentous voyage is preserved, and has furnished material for an accurate account of this era of his life. It begins with these words in his own handwriting: "Pray God, conduct me safe to France and send me a prosperous cruise." It was a sweet memorial of the care and influence of a pious mother, who thirty years before had offered, in baptism, her infant Samuel to the protection and guidance of the Almighty.

On the 19th of February, at 6 P.M., he saw in the east three large ships of the enemy and hauled his wind to the south. He then, on consultation with Mr. Adams and his officers, wore ship and run an hour to the northward, and saw two of these ships under his lee with short sail,—one ship of 20 guns, the other as large as his own; the third was far off. Immediately the man at mast-head cried out that there was a ship on the weather quarter. Though continually exposed to these frigates, he avoided them by frequent changes of his course,—sometimes approaching them, and sometimes distancing them, till they were diminished to the view as a mere speck. Thus he made his escape, till a furious storm arose, which drove them out of sight, and left him to fight a terrible battle with the winds and waves. The storm was gathering at 10 P.M., on the 21st, and at twelve midnight, it blew a tempest. The thunder drowned the roaring of the waves. The lightning struck the mainmast and topmast, wounding three men, and knocking down several others. Capt. Tucker remarks in his journal: "We were in great danger, the sea very cross and high." Heavy rains came on, and they were obliged to scud before the wind. They were in north latitude 38° 33′, and longtitude, west, 60° 30′. The scene on board the ship at this time must have been terrific. In the noon of night, in the "dead of darkness,"—to borrow a similitude from the awful imagery of Prospero in the Tempest,—the rattling of ropes and crackling of timbers and spars; the dread roar of the angry winds; the gleaming sheets of fire, at times flashing over the sea and sky; the sight of three wounded sailors and the fall of others by a stroke of lightning; the tall masts trembling beneath the blast; and, add to all this, the dismal echo from the pumps that there was water in the hold: these were enough to appal the boldest veteran that ever faced the cannon's mouth in battle. Well might the captain in his distress, alarmed for his anxious passengers and crew,—while before him and around him a terrible storm of rain, thunder and lightning threatened every moment to sink him and them,—well might he, in such a mass of sorrows, pour forth that short and simple prayer from his heart, which stands recorded in his journal of that day: "Pray God protect us and carry us through our various troubles." Gladly must every serious mind contemplate such a precious example of faith, uttered by one of the noblest seamen of the revolution. What must have been the sufferings of that man at that dark hour, when he thought of home, of his family, and of his bleeding country struggling with the mightiest nation on the globe, and then beheld the grand mission on the very verge of destruction! for it seemed as though the artillery of heaven was pointed against him.

Yet, when we gaze in imagination at this awful picture, and summon up the scene to our view through a vista of nearly a hundred years, as we sit by our cheerful firesides in this happy land, there seems to be a moral grandeur and sublimity in this event. We see the dark outline of his stalwart form on the deck of the frigate,—at spells illuminated by a blaze of lightning,—erect and commanding, and hear him issuing his orders to the intrepid seamen with a voice rising above the tempest. He alone is calm and collected, like Æneas of old,

Curisque ingentibus æger,

concealing his deep anxieties, peering through the black clouds for one ray of light, and cheering his brave companions with hope of weathering the storm; while near him stands the sturdy patriot of Braintree, ready to cry aloud: "This is the Hand of God, stretched out to shield us from the enemy."

We could never look on the face of one of those heroic men, who fought in the armies of the revolution, or gained renown in the navy, without sensibility. The warm emanations of gratitude were excited. In these survivors of '76 we saw the vestiges of a race of patriots in whose hearts the vestal fire of freedom burned with an undying flame. They belonged to an immortal band,—a Theban phalanx,—which Providence had raised up to lay the foundation of a republic, which now stretches across a vast continent.

The storm and boisterous weather held on for several days, and a squall on the 24th of February carried the main-top-mast over. "Thanks to God," wrote Tucker, "no man was lost or wounded." After twenty-two days of exposure to such tempestuous weather, and, with skilful manœuvring to avoid the prowling enemy, they reached lat. 44°, and long. 16° west, and on the 11th of March, they saw a distant ship on the south east, standing west, and soon discovered she was armed. Capt. Tucker, having consulted with Mr. Adams, who favored his views, immediately shook out a reef in his topsail and gave chase.

"What should you do," said Mr. Adams to him one day, when three ships were pursuing him, "if you could not escape and they should all attack you?" He replied: "As the first would be far in advance of the others, I would carry her by boarding, and would myself head the boarders. I should take her, for no doubt a majority of her crew, being pressed men, would turn and join me. Having taken her, I should be matched, and could fight the other two."

A gentleman related these facts to the writer, as he heard them directly from Mr. Adams himself a few months before his decease. The venerable patriot was at the time in his mansion in Quincy, sitting by the fireside. Something appertaining to the bravery of Com. Tucker, coming up in their conversation, drew out several anecdotes of the naval hero. Mr. Adams described the voyage to France; the escape of the Boston from three English privateers; the terrible storm, and the particulars of the capture. As soon as they perceived she was an armed vessel, Capt. Tucker, after consultation, prepared for action and boldly sailed up to her. The drum beat to arms, and in the mean time Mr. Adams seized a musket and joined the marines, standing by a gun ready for battle. The captain stepped up to him, put his hand on his shoulder, and in a voice of authority said: "Mr. Adams, I am commanded by the continental congress to deliver you safe in France, and you must go down below, Sir." Mr. Adams smiled, and went down into the cabin. Tucker, by this time, had contrived to get his frigate into the position he wished. His guns were all shotted; each man was at his post, the match-stocks smoking; and yet he hesitated to give order to fire. At this delay his men grew impatient, and seeing so fine a chance to strike a decisive blow, they began to murmur bitterly, when he cried out in these memorable words: "Hold on, my men. I wish to save that egg without breaking the shell." Nor were they compelled to hold on long; for the enemy seeing at once the advantage he had gained, and that his own chance of conquest or escape was desperate, immediately struck his colors.

The authenticity of this account of the capture of the Martha is unquestionable, though it may differ in some particulars from that of some others which have been published. The narrative of the conversation with Mr. Adams, did not refer to a broadside fired by the Martha; but Capt. Tucker in his lifetime remarked that she had fired three guns. One statement of this capture appeared in print, wherein it was said that the enemy discharged a broadside as the Boston approached, and shivered off a piece of the mizen yard, which in falling, struck Capt. Tucker on the head, and knocked him down; but that he quickly recovered from the stunning blow and resumed his command. This is in part confirmed by a letter he wrote to the navy committee of the eastern department, dated March 11, 1778; and he there states that the enemy, discovering that he hoisted his colors, "bore away, firing a broadside, which carried away my mizen-yard and did no other damage." And further, the captain of the Martha said: "he did not think himself able to get his colors down soon enough;" for, says Capt. Tucker: "he was horribly scared." The prize ship, Capt. M'Intosh, bound from London to New-York, with a valuable cargo, was sent to Boston under two officers, Mr. Barron and Mr. Reed; but was recaptured by the enemy.

On the 17th of May, he weighed anchor, saluting the Castle of Bordeaux as he passed. He joined a fleet of Frenchmen, in company with the celebrated Paul Jones, who was then cruising with a brig of 10 guns. During June, he cruised among the beautiful islands in the Bay of Biscay, captured the John and Rebecca, a Scotch brig, the brig Britannia, the Elizabeth and others. With the ship of war Ranger, Capt. Simpson, he united with the Providence under Com. Whipple. In September, this squadron began to sail homeward, took several prizes on their cruise, and Oct. 15, all three arrived safe in Portsmouth.

There is an anecdote in the correspondence of John Adams (vol. x. pp. 26–27), where Mr. Adams speaks of the remarks of Capt. M'Intosh, commander of the prize ship Martha, while he was a prisoner. The captain was curious to examine the frigate, and Tucker allowed him to see every part of her. He frequently expressed to Mr. Adams his astonishment; he had never seen a completer ship. "However," he added, "you are a rising country of the world, and if you send to sea such ships as this, you will be able to do great things."

Judge Sprague, late justice of the district court of the United States, in a splendid eulogy, at Hallowell, Me., on Adams and Jefferson, July 26, 1826, says: "The public ship, on board which he embarked, was commanded by the gallant Commodore Tucker, now living and a citizen of this state, who took more guns from the enemy, during the revolutionary war, than any other naval commander, and who has been far less known and rewarded than his merits deserve."

In 1779, he joined the Masonic Fraternity. During that summer, the Deane, Capt. Nicholson, and the Boston, Capt. Tucker, went to sea in company. They took many prizes, and returned Sept. 18, after a successful cruise.

There is a letter among his papers, from John Paine, Esq., late of Thomaston, Maine, referring to one terrific fight in which Tucker captured an armed vessel. The scene of the conflict was appalling. It was in the dead of night. The dashing of the waves, the gleaming and thunder of the artillery, and the uncertainty and horror of an engagement between two hostile war ships in darkness or only the glimmering of star-light, were enough to make the stoutest heart tremble. That he did fight such a battle, there can be no doubt; but neither the time, the name of the ship he commanded, nor the name of the prize, can now be summoned from oblivion in the silent grave where he lies, by any spirit or table-mover.

The various prizes he took, excited much admiration in the papers of the day. The Sandwich packet,—the privateer Glencairn 20 and Thorn 18 guns,—were among his valuable captures.

After his return from this cruise, the Boston frigate, Capt. Tucker, and Confederacy, 32 guns, Capt. Harding, were sent out to intercept the British cruisers and convoy the Eustatia fleet of merchantmen, with supplies of clothing from Holland to the American army; and notwithstanding the frigates of the enemy hovered about the fleet like eagles after their prey, he conducted them unharmed to Philadelphia.

It was on this cruise of June, 1779, that he acquired the title of commodore. He was directed to proceed, in company with the Deane, Capt. Nicholson, who being a junior captain, Tucker took by usage and custom the command with that title.

Our space will not allow a description of the battles he fought in taking some of his prizes. But, one was so remarkable it deserves a brief notice in this sketch. On his cruise with Capt. Nicholson, the report of his bravery had reached New-York, and excited much talk among the officers of the British navy who were there. They fitted out a frigate to take him. The news reached Tucker; and in a few days he saw the English ship of war in the distance and knew her well. He then hoisted English colors, and as the two vessels approached each other within hailing distance, the British captain hailed him with "What ship is that?" "Capt. Gordon's," said the Commodore; for Capt. Gordon commanded an English ship, modelled and built much like the Boston, and had taken many prizes. "Where are you from?" "From New York," said Tucker. "When did you leave?" "About four days ago." "I am after the Boston frigate, to take that rebel Tucker, and am bound to carry him dead or alive to New York," said the captain; "have you seen him?" Tucker rejoined, "Well, I have heard of him: they say he is a bad customer."

In the meantime, Com. Tucker was manœuvring to bring his ship into a raking position, so as to sweep the decks of the English frigate. He had every man at his post, his guns shotted, his gunners stationed with lighted matches in their hands, and all waiting orders of the commander. There was a man in the maintop of the enemy's frigate, who had formerly known the Commodore, and he cried out to his captain. "That is surely Tucker; we shall have a hell-smell directly."

Tucker, having got his ship in a raking position, ordered the American flag to be hoisted; and then said in a voice of thunder to the British captain, "The time I proposed talking with you has ended. This is the Boston frigate,—I am Samuel Tucker, but no rebel. Either fire or strike your flag." Seeing the advantage his adversary had, he struck his flag. Not a gun was fired. Ex-Pres. John Adams, June 13, 1779, says: "Tucker has sent in a twenty-four gun ship this afternoon, which did not fire a shot at him before striking. It is at the Capes, with the Confederacy, one of the finest in any service, as it is said by foreigners." It was the frigate Pool. Among the papers of the deceased there is an enumeration of his captures of the Boyd, Pool, Patsey, Tryall, Flying Fish, Adventure and Thorn, most of them armed, the last a privateer.

In September, 1779, Com. Tucker was ordered to the defence of Charleston, S. C. The squadron consisted of the Providence, Com. Whipple; the Boston, Capt. Tucker; the Queen of France, Capt. Rathbone; and the Ranger, Capt. Simpson. They arrived there shortly before Christmas. On the invasion by Sir Henry Clinton at the head of a large body of troops, and a powerful fleet under Admiral Arbuthnot, the city was compelled to surrender, after a siege of thirty days, to an overwhelming force: but the little squadron, before it fell into the hands of the enemy, formed a retreat up the river, and did essential service; for no small part of the heavy guns, which bristled on the ramparts, was supplied from Com. Whipple's squadron, manned by his marines and directed by his officers. This fact is unnoticed by Mr. Simms in his history of South Carolina, and seems to have escaped the notice of Mr. Lossing in his Pictorial Field Book, so deservedly a favorite of the public.

When a special order came from the Admiral to the commander of the Boston frigate to strike his flag, Tucker replied, "I do not think much of striking my flag to your present force; for I have struck more of your flags than are now flying in this harbor."

The 26th of June, 1780, he arrived in Boston on parole; but he was soon exchanged for Capt. William Wardlow, whose sloop-of-war, Thorn, he had captured a year ago. He asked the command of her from the Navy Board, and it was granted him. In 1780 and '81 he made a number of cruises in her, and captured a great many prizes. Among his men was Josiah Everett, who had served on Dorchester Heights, was in the battle of Saratoga, and died in New-Portland, Me., some years ago. Shortly before his death he gave a glowing detail of a sanguinary battle between the Thorn and the Lord Hyde. The description is in the *Life of Com. Tucker.* So terrible was the conflict, that Tucker, tho' victorious, looking round on the dead and wounded, and on the clots of blood on the deck, cried out, "Would to God I had never seen her!" There was also a severe battle with the Elizabeth, a 20 gun ship, in which the English captain, Timothy Pine, was mortally wounded.

Prosperity, however, will not last forever. His little, triumphant Thorn,—indeed, for a time, a thorn to the British lion, like the sword-fish to the whale,—was at last captured near the mouth of the St. Lawrence by the British frigate, Hind, and the prisoners were landed on the island of St. John's; from whence, with Dr. Ramsay and a few others, Com. Tucker made his escape in an open boat, crossed the bay of Massachusetts, and arrived in Boston in the middle of August, 1781. There was some complaint afterward about his breaking his parole, which was subsequently healed. Peace followed within a year and a half, during which time, though in the public service and liable at all times to do duty, it does not appear that he was ordered to the command of any ship of war.

In the beginning of 1780 he had removed his family to Boston, where he purchased a brick three-story house with a cupola and front yard in Fleet street,—then the fashionable and court-end of the town,—on the southern side near Hanover street. Numerous prizes had made him rich. Not far from the west side, stood the large and spacious domicile of Gov. Hutchinson, with a garden full of fruit trees. His widowed daughter, Mrs. Hinds, the mother of Col. Hinds, of Bremen, Me., resided with him, and the Colonel often heard his mother remark that sitting on the Sabbath, at the open window, on the western side, she frequently listened to the preaching of the Rev. John Murray, in his church in Hanover street, as there was no building then on the corner to intercept the voice. On the other side of Fleet street, opposite his house, there was a large mansion, where several naval officers had their lodgings. All these buildings have vanished under the march of improvement.

As he was deemed a man of wealth, he associated with the first society of Boston; for riches, then as now, always opened the doors of hospitality in this place. He was polite, genial and popular, and indeed too generous for his own good. His personal appearance in the mid-day of life was striking,—of more than average height, bright complexion, fine features, and with deep blue eyes, which, when animated, seemed to grow dark and piercing.

He was stout, with a very broad chest, and usually wore the brilliant dress of a naval commander,—a blue coat with lapelles, scarlet vest and dark-blue small-clothes; as one of his old friends described his costume to the writer, and as agreeing with the account by Mrs. Elizabeth Perkins, who died in Boston in 1853, aged 99,—a niece of the eminent Samuel Adams. She remarked to the writer, "The Commodore kept open doors, was hospitable and fond of company and of gladsome spirits." She said, "he was a goodly man to look upon, so handsome, so animated,—I often danced with him in the minuet, and we girls were after him as a partner, his foot was so light on the floor. Commodore Tucker was truly a noble man."

From his expensive habits of living, and reckless loans in lending without security, he soon wasted his fortune and was reduced to narrow circumstances. In August, 1786, he left Boston and returned to Marblehead, where he purchased two-thirds of the Gatchell Mills and grainery, situated near the confines of Salem. But it was in vain our hero tried to support a family accustomed to style and extravagance by grinding of corn. He probably thought this was only a temporary resource; for hearing that some revenue cutters were to be built by the government, he applied to Mr. Alexander Hamilton, secretary of the treasury, for the command of one. The reply to his petition for this humble office was, in the words of Hamilton, "*it is too late;*" others had secured the prize. He had repeatedly petitioned congress for payment of his arrears in the naval service, and he was unsuccessful; because,—can posterity believe that an omnipotent legislature could resort to such an infamous defence?—because *his claims were outlawed! It was too late!*

Disappointed, mortified, unfortunate, and now poor, with his wife and venerable mother and children, he sold his grist-mill, and emigrated to Maine, where he settled down on a wild, rough farm in a small, old house at Bristol (now Bremen), near Muscongus harbor, and within sight of the blue mountains of Camden, there to labor with his hands, and pass through deprivations for thirty years. There he lived, industrious and respected. Year after year he was chosen a selectman, four times sent to the Massachusetts general court, and after Maine became a state, twice to her legislature.

In his official visit to Boston in 1816, as a representative, many old acquaintances called upon the noble veteran. His kind and illustrious friend Ex-Pres. Adams received him at his mansion in Quincy with much cordiality.

His numerous applications to congress, either to pay the arrears justly due him, or allow him a pension, is a history of injustice and of the proverbial ingratitude of republics. Seven times, at different sessions of congress, were his petitions for relief presented by influential members, viz.: in 1790, 1800, 1806, 1812, 1816, and 1820,—and in 1821, when Hon. Mr. Walker, of Georgia, offered in his favor a most able report in the senate, stating that justice and gratitude unite "in his call upon government." On which the senate passed a bill for his half-pay as captain; but the house of representatives rejected it by a majority of one. In June, 1832, a general act was passed, and a pension of $600 a year was settled on him.

On the 20th of December, 1820, the electoral college appointed him, being one of their number, a special messenger to carry on to Washington the votes for president and vice-president.

When he first appeared in the house of representatives among the strangers who stood outside the bar, his commanding figure, naval dress and silvery locks excited much attention. It was soon whispered about, that

Com. Tucker, one of the very few surviving naval officers of the revolution, was there; and all eyes were fixed upon him. Was it not a moment, even to the great men in the congress, of sublime recollections of American history? And did not his position at that time remind them of a more exalted personage before the queen and nobles of Carthage, as he stood alone in his glory?

"Restitit Æneas, claraque, in luce refulsit."

There were many in that august assembly, fifty years ago, who had heard of the man, his bravery, his nautical skill, his battles and success on the ocean, while his deeds were yet fresh in the minds of the older members. It was quickly reported in the capitol that there was one among them, who had taken from the enemy sixty-two sail of vessels, more than 600 pieces of cannon, and 3000 prisoners in the revolutionary war. Let not the writer of this sketch be thought to exaggerate. Such was the averment in the *National Intelligencer* of Dec. 16, 1820. The Hon. Mark L. Hill was about to move that Com. Tucker be admitted on the floor, when, upon examination, it was found that soon after the revolutionary war, congress had passed an unanimous vote of thanks to him for services rendered and according to usage he was admitted.

In this brief account, many exciting events and particulars of his sea-fights have been reluctantly passed over, for they form part and parcel of his life on the ocean. Nor is there space more than to allude to the important lead he took in favor of law and order, when Maine was on the verge of a civil war between tenants and proprietors, in what was called the "Squatter Insurrection." It was terminated in the wisdom of the legislature by buying the rights of the proprietors and quieting the tenants by a satisfactory and equitable provision.

And we can but touch on the last naval exploit of the venerable Commodore in the war of 1812 with England. With forty-four daring young men, who had armed a wood coaster, he captured a British armed vessel, and brought her safely to port. But, is there not a record of this in his Life, before alluded to? Such was our noble patriot, to whom Mr. Hamilton wrote, that it was too late to give him the command of a revenue cutter; but this meritorious officer, even in his old age, proved that it was *never too late to defend his country!*

After his pension as captain was granted, the aged veteran lived not many months. It should be remarked that he had received a small pension under the pension law of 1816, and in 1820 he built a house where his old one stood, more convenient and suitable to his rank. But his last relief came too late. He had become an old man. His beloved wife, who had shared with him the weal and the woe of fortune for sixty-three years, had gone to her rest. She was a talented, brave, and noble woman. Such a just provision for his comfort and delightful feeling of independence, had it been made earlier in his life, when she was with him, would have been a real boon and a blessing, especially when he mused on his rugged acres and reflected that his cattle must be housed seven months of the year in that Siberian climate.

And here it may be well to remark, that after 1816 the pensions of the revolutionary soldiers added greatly to the length of their days, whenever they were not shortened by accident or intemperance. This fact stands out upon their graves in bold relief. The cause of such longevity may be ascribed to the comfort and well-being of the mind, even where a small annuity dispels the anxiety of to-morrow's sustenance and keeps the wolf from the door. For nothing corrodes an honorable man like penury. It deprives him of his freedom; he is a slave and a fugitive from happiness; all hope is gone,—hope, the spirit of the soul; he feels a chill on the life-blood of his heart, and he dies because he has no motive to live. So justly did the celebrated Junius once remark to a young man: "Let all your views in life be directed to a solid, however moderate independence. Without it no man can be happy or even honest." But to conclude.

He died in Bremen, after a short, but sharp sickness, under the watchful care of his widowed daughter, Mrs. Hinds, and her son Col. Samuel Tucker Hinds, March 10, 1833, aged 85 years and four months. He saw death,—the greatest of mysteries,—coming toward him like a spectre at whose approach almost all men tremble; and he looked him in the face with an eye undimmed by age and unblanched by fear, as he had often done when death hovered over him in the day of battle. A few hours before his departure, he said to his friend Denny McCobb, Esq., then collector of the port of Waldoborough, who stood in tears at his bed-side:—"Well, general, I am about to pass away to that world, from which no traveller has returned. You are soon to follow me. I hope and trust, we shall meet there, where no pain nor sorrow will disturb us, and be happy in the smiles and favor of heaven. My trust is in Christ. Farewell." Gently and calmly he then breathed his last.

The obsequies of this eminent naval officer were performed in a manner honorable to his character and evincing the love and respect of his neighbors. Though it was a bleak and stormy day, and the travelling exceedingly dreary and uncomfortable, hundreds came from a distance to attend his funeral and follow his remains to the grave in the Bremen cemetery, where they rest by the side of his wife. Only a simple slate-stone tells where he lies; no marble nor monument honors the memory of this pioneer of the American navy.

EDWARD OXNARD'S JOURNAL.

Continued from page 10.

[1775.]
[Nov.] 27.. Messrs. Bliss Green, Taylor, Silsbee & Quincey spent the evening with me. good wine, bread & cheese. They stayed till past twelve o'clock.
29.. At home till one, & then called on Mr. Silsbee. At 2 went to the Queen^s Arms to dine. Agreed to go with Mr. Taylor to see Garrick in the character of Hamlet. At 4 we set out, tho' an hour before the play began. On our arrival at the theater we found full five hundred people waiting for the Doors to be opened. When they were, the crowd was so great that I was in great danger of being squeezed to death. Notwithstanding I was so early, when I got into the 2*s* gallery, it was full, all to four seats, and I suppose it will hold near five hundred people. I had here an opportunity of seeing the character of the English nation for justice. A man came in after the gallery was full & pushed a Frenchman out of his place. The Frenchman being unable to speak English was obliged to put up with it, but as soon as the people found the man to be a foreigner & unacquainted with the language, they began to resent the behaviour of the other, and

ordered him to give way or take the consequences, which would have been throwing him over the gallery, a term often made use of when persons are unruly, but a threat seldom performed. I returned highly entertained. Garrick acted to admiration, considering his age, which is nearly 65.

In his younger years, I think he must have been entitled to all the merit, which is ascribed to him in Tragedy. In respect to the other performers, I can say but little in their favor. It is said the reason that the players are so poor at this house is owing to the avarice of Garrick, who will not pay the price required for good performers. The Entertainment after the play was called "The Lottery," the sentiment of which was poor, highly reflecting on the nobility. Mr King shone in this, as he does in all comic parts. The house was so full, that it was impossible to obtain a place after the curtain was drawn up. Three thousand people were present.

7th Dec. Went to Lord George Germaines office with Mr. Berry. From thence to the Park, where we had the pleasure of seeing Lord North. He is of middle stature & round favored, & may be called handsome.

Passing through the palace at St. James, we saw the Queens page of honor, Lord Norths son. He looks about twelve years of age & of an agreable countenance.

8th This morning went with Mr Silsbee to Guildhall to see Judge Nares preside in one of the courts. He has greatly the look of Fitch, the lawyer. We dined in Ivy Lane. From thence went to Westminster Hall, where the Court of King's Bench was sitting, Lord Mansfield sole judge. I was not a little surprised to see with what decision the causes were determined.

I was there not above thirty minutes and three causes were delivered to the Jury & determined, one to the amount of £240. Lord Mansfield appears very authoritative, & will not bear any contradiction. He does not suffer the Jury to leave their stands but stay & determine as he advises, tho I must say the three verdicts I heard rendered, appeared to be very just. His Lordship is of middling stature, something stern in his countenance, that strikes one with awe: of about sixty five years of age. On his leaving the Bench, there is a person whose duty is to hold his train till he arrives at the place where he unrobes.

Mem: see good sermons offered, four for a penny.

11th The weather still continues remarkably mild and pleasant, so much so that Messrs Berry, Silsbee & myself took a walk to Hyde Park, where we had an opportunity of seeing her Majesty. The Coach windows were down & I stood so near that I could touch the carriage with my hand. She is a small sized woman with very regular features, except her nose which has something of the turn up to it. Her whole countenance is engaging. She was in a coach drawn by six fine black horses, with two of the horse guards before & twelve behind. Dined at Queens Arms, & after called on Mr Blowers. From thence went to Covent Garden theatre to see their majesties. The play was the Duenna.

18th Mr Silsbee called on me & informed me of the disagreeable news of the burning of the town of Falmouth. Oh my poor heart, how can I support the tidings; my tenderest connections driven to the extremes of poverty & distress by the arts of designing villains. I spent a most melancholy day

19th Dined at "The three Tuns" in the Strand, took a stroll with Mr Amory & took tea with him.

22th Went to the house of Lords, in hopes of getting in but was disappointed. Admitted to the Princes Chamber to see the king robed before he goes into the house. A party of the yeomen lined the passage from the street door to the chamber where he robes. Present, four mace bearers, Sir Francis Molineaux, usher of the Black rod, Heralds at arms &c. &c. The Lord Chamberlain after the king enters puts on the robes, but the king himself puts on the crown, after which he goes into the house of Lords, sends the usher of the Black rod to acquaint the House of Commons that he is ready to give his assent to such bills as are then to be approved, on which they deputize a committee to carry them up. His majesty then touches the several Bills with his sceptre, which are then immediately recorded & become laws.

27.. Col. Pickman & Mr. Cabot called on me this morning. Dined at Mr Curling's. Dinner leg of mutton & capers, roast turkey & mince pies, considered a grand dinner by persons of large estates. Mr Laurence gave me a cast in his coach to Cheapside. Spent the evening with Mr Watson; there heard of the arrival of Gen. Burgoyne.

29.. Mess[rs] Noble & Page called upon me & we dined together, after which I went to Mr Silsbee's, who gave me very disagreeable accounts from America. went to the play house in hopes of diverting my mind, but could not be admitted at half price ticket, & so went to Mr Watson's & spent the remainder of the evening. Yesterday arrived Mess[rs] Rodgers, Lee & Roberts from Boston.

31st. Drank tea at Mr. Blowers in company with Mr & Mrs. Amory, Mr G. Harrison, & Mess[rs]. Green & Quincey.

3[d]. Jan 1776. rose at 10. Dressed & called upon Mr Bliss, dined at the Queen's Arms on fish. The length of time that fish is kept here renders it soft, & a disagreeable taste given it, which they try to conceal by rich sauces of catchup, oyster & anchovy.

In the evening went to hear a famous disenting minister whose name is Riley, the most noisy, ranting blade I ever heard.

6.. went into the Park where I met Mr Flucker & Mr Bliss, with whom I took a turn, when we met Mess[rs]. Green & Quincey. After which I went to dine with Mr Blowers on salt fish. I stayed till 7 o'clk & then went to Drury Lane to see the performance of Shakespeare's Jubilee, as performed at Strafford, in which Mr Garrick has shown the greatest taste & fancy by the happy disposition throughout all the characters.

16.. It still continues to snow & the roads are impassable, so that no mails can arrive from any part of England.

18.. This morning being pleasant waited on Mr Blowers who invited me to dine with him, after which went to S[t]. James Palace to see the nobility & gentry congratulate their majesties on the Queen's birthday, which is observed on this day, whereas in reality, it soon succeeds the King's. It is however kept on this day for the benefit of the manufacturers & others for the reason that were it kept on her real birthday, the nobility would make one suit answer the purpose of both, but being kept with so great an interval between, they are obliged to procure new dresses. The Lord Chamberlain will allow no one to be admitted, who is not in full dress with sword & bag. A scotch nobleman lost his star set in brilliants, supposed to have been stolen. Taking into view the number who attend on these occasions, it may be called a genteel mob, for there is no opportunity of passing each other, the crowd is so great & the room so small. The dresses of the ladies were exceedingly rich, their heads being covered with diamonds of very great value. some, I have no doubt had at least £5000.

19.. Mr Laurence sent his servant to acquaint me of the death of his son, which required me to bespeak a suit of new clothes. It is customary to go into mourning for the most distant relation. Dined at the Queen[s] Arms & spent the evening with Mr Watson.

27.. Last evening was as cold as any I ever experienced in America. It deprived me of sleep. Subscriptions have been opened to relieve the many miserable objects who are perishing from the inclemency of the weather, to which the nobility have contributed large sums. The city of London has voted £1500. The Ice has clogged the river to that degree, that colliers & other ships are prevented from coming up.

31st. clear & cold, but not so violent as for ten days past. Before I was well up, Gov. Hutchinson called to invite me to dinner, which invitation I accepted.

He gave a good dinner & treated me in a friendly manner.

Feb 1st. Weather moderate. Went to Westminster Abbey with Mess[rs]. Silsbee, Rogers & Berry. From thence to Westminster Hall to see the Judges presiding in their several courts, Chancery, King's Bench & Common Pleas.

In the Court of King[s] Bench, Lord Mansfield, Sir Richard Ashton, Sir W. H. Atherton, Edward Willis. Common Pleas, Sir W[m]. De Grey, Sir G. Naines, Sir W[m]. Blackstone, Sir Henry Gould.—Court of Chancery, Lord Bathurst. Dined at the Queen[s] Arms, & spent the evening at home. Yesterday many persons passed from Wapping to Ratcliffe on the Ice.

4.. went this morning to hear the famous Dr Leuscy who gave up his living because he could not in all respects subscribe to the Litany. He has abridged it of many of the prayers & thus reads it to his followers,—about 150 persons. In the afternoon went to hear the famous Toplady, who has written against Mr Wesley, concerning good works. He by no means came up to my expectations. Is exceedingly fond of introducing allusions in his sermons, which in general are in bad taste. Spent the evening at Mr Blowers.

7.. warm & pleasant. went to hear a cause tried before Justice De Grey in Westminster Hall. The serjeant's at law are, I think allowed too much freedom in their interrogations to witnesses. Oftentimes they came to contradict themselves through confusion. From thence went with Mess[rs]. Green, Smith & Quincey to dine at the Mitre Coffee house. found it poor enough. I drank tea at Mr Curlings, who gave me a kind reception.

8.. rain & sunshine alternately, somewhat as in April at home. Dined with an American club. nineteen were present. Mr Flucker took tea with me & we afterwards went to see the performance of the famous juggler, Breslau, a German.

His tricks are wonderful, and it would almost seem that he was aided by the Devil.

9.. weather rainy. dined with Mr Small at Hampton Row, & was most sumptuously entertained

15.. clear & pleasant. went into the city as far as Aylitt Street & called on Gov. Hutchinson, who was not at home. Dined with the club at the Adelphi. Sir Francis Bernard & his son did us the honor of a visit. spent the evening at home.

22[d]. went this morning to the Hustings at Guildhall to witness the polling for City Chamberlain. The mob in favor of Mr Wilkes were very noisy in shewing their approbation of any one who supported him, but when any one appeared who preferred Mr Hopkins, he was received with groans & hisses, & every mark of disrespect they could shew. At the close of the polls, it appeared that a majority of 150 was in favor of Mr Hopkins whereupon the mob were greatly enraged & were with difficulty prevented from insulting him. Two persons did so, for which they were apprehended, but released on promise of good behavior. Dined at the Crown & Anchor in Arundell Street with the Club. 21 were present. Heard there of the news of the defeat at Quebec. Eighty were killed, among whom was Montgomery. Three hundred were taken prisoners, among whom was Col. Arnold.

March 5— strolled into the Park & drank some fresh milk. many poor people keep cows there for the purpose of furnishing it to visitors. Saw the Guards perform a few evolutions before the Prince of Wirtemburgh, who is a man of middling stature & well featured, but has a remarkably red face. Went to Messr. Langfords to witness a sale of pictures. The pleasure one receives from viewing the productions of the ancient masters is not easily to be expressed; the mind is lost in admiration and for the moment, nature appears to be rivalled by art. I never spent three hours with more pleasure. Dined at the Three tuns, Strand. Spent the evening with Mr Bury.

7— continuation of rain. at home till 4 o'clk. dined with the Club at the Crown & Anchor, 28 present. Intended to go to the Opera, but could not get in, & so went to Drury Lane Theatre, Mr Garricks last night. The loss to the stage is irreparable. The words he applied to Shakespeare in the Jubilee may aptly be said of him, "we ne'er shall look upon his like again."

12— pleasant all day. Went with Mr Blowers to see the scaffolding being erected at Westminster Hall for the trial of the Dutchess of Kingston for bigamy. Dined at Mr Blowers, & afterwards went to Drury Lane, it being Mr. King's benefit. The play was "woman a riddle." Mr King supported his character, as he always does, with great spirit.

18— clear & pleasant. Went with Judge Sewall to the house of Lords, but were refused admittance by an old hag, who pretended that she paid the land tax. From thence we went to the house of Commons. It is a small & mean looking room, by no means as fitting, as the house of Commons of England, ought to have. The speaker's seat is greatly inferior to that of the speaker in the house of representatives in Massachusetts. dined at the Queens Arms. In the evening to Covent Garden, Mrs Barrys benefit. She is a woman of about 40 years of age, common size, with an agreeable person. Her voice is rather weak of which she is sensible & speaks accordingly. There is no actress at either of the Theatres, who has so much control over the passions of the audience, as Mrs Barry. In comedy she plays equally as well as in Tragedy. It is impossible to form a correct judgement of what Barry was, from what he now appears. He is old & his constitution seems broken by debauchery.

1776

March 21— Weather clear & pleasant. The Messrs. Sewalls, Curwen, Wickham, Cabot, Smith & myself went to the Chapter House, Westminster, to see the Dooms Day Book, which is 790 years old. In this book, William, the Conqueror, ordered the names of all the proprietors of lands in England to be recorded and the value of them, by which they were to be taxed. At that time, it appears that there were but eight hundred proprietors in the whole county of Kent, which I suppose is one of the largest counties in England. It is written in Latin, but so greatly abreviated, as to render it difficult to be read, unless one is familiar with it. The leaves are of vellum and notwithstanding its great age, it is almost as entire, as if it had been written but a few days back. A person is now engaged in transcribing it for publication.

22^d^. This day the Lord Mayor John Sawbridge, Esq., attended by a few of the nearest of the Common Council of London, went in procession to S^t^. James to present his majesty a petition praying that a specification of the terms, which his majesty & both Houses of Parliament would grant the Colonies, should precede the dreadful operations of the armament. His majesty gave them for answer the reply, "that when the Americans laid down their arms, & peacefully retired to their respective homes, he would immediately withdraw both his own troops and the auxiliaries."

27th strolled with Mr Flucker in S^t^. James Park until 2 o'clk. Took a dish of Chocolate at the Coffee house & read the papers until 3. Dined at the Crown & Anchor on Cronip Cod & oyster sauce & had *to pay for it.* In the evening went to Drury Lane to hear the Oratorio of the Messiah, composed by Handel. It is impossible for me to express the pleasure I received. My mind was elevated to that degree, that I could almost imagine that I was being wafted to the mansions of the blest. There were more than one hundred performers, the best in England. The chorus "Hallelujah! for the Lord God omnipotent reigneth," is the most sublime piece of music in the whole world.

May 2^d^. This morning the 11th Reg. of Dragoons left London to take up their quarters at Blackheath. Breakfasted at 10. Mr Bliss received a line from Mr Coffin Jr. with the disagreeable intelligence that General Howe had been obliged to evacuate Boston. My feelings on this occasion are such that I lack words to express them. To divert our melancholy we strolled to Cashaltin, one of the pleasant villages in England.

14th This morning Mr Curwen breakfasted with me. Dined & spent the afternoon at Mr Blowers. Brampton heard that nine Jamaica ships had been taken by the Provincials, and the defeat of the same by Gen. Burgoyne at Trois Reveres, where two hundred were taken prisoners. In the evening engaged in writing home letters to be taken by Mr Searl, a son in law of Mr Jonathan Gore.

4th Aug. worshipped in the morning at the Temple: dined at the Queen' Arms. In the evening drank tea with Mr Cox at Newington Green. Heard of the arrival of a vessel from Genl. Howe, and from the great secresy, I fear that it has brought some bad news. A report prevails that he has been defeated near New York, and that the Hessians were all killed.

18th In the morning went with Dr. Oliver to hear the Rev. Dr. Fordyce. His text was Act 10th verse 42. Dined at the Crown with Messrs. B. & P. Watson, after which we set out for Turnham Green, but at Kensington it began to rain, & we sought shelter in the Church. On examining the tomb stones in the Church yard, I found the following erected to my worthy friend Mrs. Eustis.

"Here lyeth the body of Mrs. Jane Eustis, late of
Boston, New England, who departed this life 21 Jan
1771, aged 48 years. She was Good."

The rain continuing, after waiting three hours for a coach, we were under the necessity of walking home in the rain.

22^d^. This day the news came of Gen. Clinton' ill success in south Carolina, the loss of two hundred killed & wounded & the burning of the ship Actæon & another vessel. at 12 with Messrs. Taylor & Silsbey set out to walk to Highgate to call on Mr Paddock. He & Mr Gore seem to be much dejected at the appearance of things in America. I wish my own spirits were good, but they have been much depressed for ten days past.

26th. at 11 went with Mr Silsby to Mr Taylors, & stayed there till 1 o'clk & then set out to see Bliss, & with him visited St. James Park, where we met many of our countrymen, who seem to have taken possession of it. Judge Sewall invited me to dine with him & I did myself the pleasure of accepting the same. Good haddock & roast beef for dinner, after which Mr Blowers was sent for, & we had a fine bottle of Florence together. Mr Bliss & Treasurer Gray dropt in, & from Mr Gray we learnt that he was likely to suffer as Provincial Treasurer, having been threatened with a prosecution for a provincial note of £1400, if he should refuse to pay it himself. stayed till 8 o'clk & then Mr Blowers & Chipman accompanied us home through the Park.
23d. at home till 12. then to Mr Sewalls & there heard that Gen. Howe had landed at York on the 15th Sept. & the provincials endeavoring to retreat, meet with great slaughter. It is further stated, that he had taken post half a mile from their strong works. This news came by a ship which had spoken the Galatea frigate, which had left New York on the 19th Sept. The frigate had retaken two Jamaica ships which had been previously captured. returned home & acquainted Messrs. Murray, Leonard, Danforth, & Chandler with the news, and there was great joy thereat. spent the afternoon at Mr Sewalls, & the evening at the Treasurers with the Club, in addition to which were Mr & Mrs. Robinson, & Mrs. Oliver.
25th. went with Messrs. Willard & Danforth to see the Park Guns fired, it being the seventeenth anniversary of the kings accession to the throne: from thence to the Guard room of St. James Palace to see the Company go to the Levee, where were the handsomest women I have seen in England. remained about an hour, & then sat out for home.

Just as we had entered the Park from the Palace, observed a boat in which was the Prince of Wales & the Bishop of Osnaburgh: we went back & got so near as to have an exceedingly fine view of them. The Prince of Wales has a full countenance like his father, & in heighth of medium size. The Bishop is rather thin faced & of a sprightly expression, his features resembling those of the king.
29th. Mr Sewalls child being suddenly taken ill, the club spent the evening with us. Yesterday evening a very hot press: 1500 men were taken & nearly a dozen persons were killed or drowned. The rumors of a war with France gain ground. The citizens are much alarmed & stocks are falling fast from the great fears of a French War.
Nov. 3d. Col. Murray called on me at 10. & informed me that he had been to see Lord Amherst, & that he had told him that war with France was doubtful & yet it was prudent to prepare for the worst. Went with Mr Blowers into the city. received advices from Boston that the inhabitants were in a very melancholy condition, and that paper money was refused to be taken. returned home to dine. spent the evening at the club.
7th. Went with Mr Blowers as far as Mr Storeys. From thence went to the New England Coffee house to read the papers. Am much surprised to see how the NE papers misrepresent matters of fact, as for instance the battle of Long Island. The Club at Col. Murrays. Won 1*s*.
10th. started with Messrs. Willard & Gray for Westminster Hall, on our way saw the King & Queen coming from Kew. In the Park, met Capt. Rogers, who informed me that my friends in general were all well in America. Leaving him went to the Court of Chancery the other courts being shut, & saw the Lord Chancellor Bathurst. spent the evening at home until 6 Then to Col. Murrays. Lost 6d.

[To be continued.]

ATKINSON ACADEMY.

Communicated by William C. Todd, Esq.

The first four academies incorporated in New-Hampshire were Phillips, at Exeter, incorporated in 1781; New-Ipswich, incorporated in 1789; Chesterfield, incorporated in 1790; and Atkinson, incorporated Feb. 17, 1791. As the one at Atkinson, however, was instituted, and went into operation, some time before it was incorporated, it is in point of age the second in the state.

The people of the little town of Atkinson, originally a part of Haverhill, Mass., now a border town of New-Hampshire, seem early to have directed their attention to education. Special efforts had long been made to render their grammar schools of a high order, and in 1788 a suitable building was prepared and an academy was organized. Three individuals were especially prominent in its establishment, Hon. and Dr. Nathaniel Peabody, Rev. Stephen Peabody, and Dr. William Cogswell, all of whom deserve more than a passing mention.

Nathaniel Peabody, the first physician of the town, was born in Topsfield, that cradle of the Peabodys, March 1, 1741. He was son of Dr. Jacob Peabody, and by his mother, Susannah Rogers, daughter of Rev. John Rogers, of Boxford, was a descendant from Rev. Nathaniel Rogers, of Ipswich, Massachusetts. As a physician he was very successful, and was prominent in the organization of the New-Hampshire Medical Society. He was active in the cause of his country at the outbreak of the revolutionary war, and was appointed, Oct. 27, 1774, Lieut. Colonel of the 7th New-Hampshire regiment. March 25, 1779, he was elected a delegate to the continental congress. Subsequently he was speaker of the New-Hampshire house of representatives, state senator and councillor, and major-general of the militia. Towards the close of his life he became involved in debt, and was confined in the jail in Exeter, having what was called "the limits of the jail yard,"—that is, allowed to walk and reside within a certain distance from the jail, embracing quite a portion of the town. There he died June 27, 1823. He was a man of much energy and ability, and prominent in the early history of New-Hampshire. He was much interested in education, and in 1791 received the degree of master of arts from the trustees of Dartmouth College.

The Rev. Stephen Peabody, the first settled clergyman in Atkinson, was born in Andover, Mass., Nov. 11, 1741; was graduated at Harvard College 1769, a classmate of Theophilus Parsons; and ordained at Atkinson, Nov. 25, 1772. He was to receive £160 as settlement money, and £66 13*s.* 4*d.* the first year, increasing 40*s.* annually till it amounted to £80, and ten cords of wood a year. He remained pastor of the church till his decease, May 23, 1819. He was chaplain in the army during the revolutionary war. His second wife was the widow of Rev. John Shaw, of Haverhill, Mass., daughter of Rev. John Smith, of Weymouth, and sister of Mrs. John Adams, a lady of great accomplishments, and whose influence in refining the people of her husband's parish is felt to this day. By her first husband she was the mother of William Smith Shaw, long connected with the Boston Athenæum, and of Mrs. Abigail Adams Felt, wife of the late Joseph B. Felt (see Register, xxiv., 1–5), so well known by his historical and antiquarian investigations.

To Mr. Peabody was mainly due the establishment of the academy. He became personally liable for its debts, and to secure funds obtained an act of the legislature of New-Hampshire authorizing a lottery, no unusual method in those days to procure aid for charitable purposes. Application was made to the legislature of Massachusetts for permission to sell tickets in the limits of that state, as by an act in Feb., 1801, the sale of lottery tickets from other states was forbidden except by legislative consent. Permission was not granted, not from any moral scruples, but from a desire to protect home industry, a trait the people of that day handed down to their children.

"Parson Peabody," or "Sir Peabody," as he was usually termed, was a pastor of the old school, kind and affable, yet always in dress and manner preserving the dignity of his profession. Every Sunday he announced what families he would visit during the week and "catechize the children," and at the appointed time with much trembling the little ones were gathered by their parents, in their Sunday clothes, into the best room, to pass the trying ordeal of an examination in their Westminster Catechism; happy if successful, covered with shame unutterable if they failed. At church the whole congregation rose when the good pastor entered, and at the close of the services all stood reverently while he with his wife passed bowing down the aisle and out of the sanctuary. He kept open house, and was known to all the countrymen who passed through his village once a year to exchange their produce for groceries. A large fire burned at night in his sitting room, and often, it is said, the stranger would enter and warm himself at the grateful fire, talk with his entertainer in the adjoining bed room, and depart, the face of the guest unseen, and, with the courtesy of the days of chivalry, his name not asked. The memory of this good minister is still green in the town of his long labors.—*Requiescat in pace.*

Dr. William Cogswell was born in Haverhill, Mass., July 11, 1760. He was a descendant of John Cogswell, who came from London and settled in Ipswich in 1635. He was appointed surgeon's mate at West Point in 1781, and continued in the service till the close of the revolutionary war. In 1784 he was promoted to the charge of the hospital at West Point, where he remained till Sept. 1, 1785, when he commenced practice in Atkinson. He was active in his profession, in the cause of education and in public affairs. An excellent citizen, he was decided in his opinions, and energetic in every good work. He tolerated no wrong in the community around him, and trained up a large family of children by obedience at home to be good men and women. Among his children still living, are Francis Cogswell, late president of the Boston and Maine Railroad; Dr. George Cogswell, of Bradford, and Rev. Nathaniel Cogswell, of Yarmouth; and of the deceased were the wife of Gov. William Badger, of New-Hampshire, and Rev. Dr. William Cogswell, the first editor of the REGISTER, distinguished for his labors in the cause of education, and for his antiquarian and genealogical researches. There are many grandchildren, among whom are William C. Clarke, attorney-general of New-Hampshire, Gen. William Cogswell, of Salem, and J. B. D. Cogswell, of Yarmouth.

But to return to Atkinson academy from this notice of its founders.

The original building was burned in 1802, and in 1803 the present much larger structure was erected on the model of Phillips Academy, in Exeter, so recently burned.

In the scarcity of such institutions the Academy soon gained a high reputation, and was largely patronized even from a distance. It early became a mixed school, at a time when but little attention had been paid to female education, and has so continued to the present time, being the first Academy in the country where, according to Rev. Dr. Felt, himself one of its pupils, the sexes were educated together in the higher branches.

It is interesting to note, in comparison with present educational expenses, how low were all the charges at this school in its early history. The tuition for the first two years was only 6*s.* a quarter of three months; then 9*s.*; in 1797, it was $2; 1805, $3; 1839, $4.00; 1848, $4.80. Board at first, including lodging and washing, was 4*s.* 6*d.* a week; then, for many years, 6*s.*; in 1830, 7*s.* 6*d.* for the whole week, 6*s.* for those who spent the Sabbath at home; in 1850, from $1.50 to $2 per week, including lodging and washing.

The academy has until recently had no funds, and the only salary of the teachers has been the tuition of the students. In 1855 Mr. James Atwood, of Westchester, Pa., a native of the town, gave to it $1000, and his son-in-law, Dr. Almon Z. Barden, $500; and in 1868, Rev. Joseph B. Felt left it a legacy of $2000; which constitute its only funds. There is an opportunity for some wealthy and benevolent individual to do good, and build for himself an enduring monument, by endowing this ancient institution, and giving it his name. It is not a little remarkable that a self-supporting institution should have so long maintained itself, which is due to its healthy location, the wants of a large rural surrounding population, and its convenience of access.

Among the many pupils of this old academy can be named not a few of eminence. There occur to the writer the names of Levi Woodbury, noted in boyhood as in manhood, for his untiring industry, Gov. Kent of Maine, Jonathan and Joseph Cilley, President Brown of Dartmouth, Gen. James Wilson, Judge White of Salem, Rev. Dr. Benjamin Hale, president of Hobart College. Grace Fletcher, the first wife of Daniel Webster, was here educated, and has been described to the writer by her schoolmates as a pale, modest, retiring girl.

The following is a list of the different principals of the Academy:—

Moses Leavitt Neal, of Londonderry; H. C. 1785; attorney; clerk of house of representatives of New-Hampshire legislature; register of deeds of Strafford county; lived at Dover, and elsewhere; died 1829, aged 62.

Daniel Hardy, of Bradford, Mass.; D. C. 1789; studied divinity; tutor at Dartmouth; taught at Chesterfield, N. H., and Bradford, Mass.; a distinguished linguist; died at Dracut, Mass., Nov. 25, 1833, aged 60.

Samuel Moody, of Byfield, Mass.; D. C. 1790; teacher at Hallowell, Me., where he died April 6, 1832, aged 67.

Silas Dinsmore, of Windham; D. C. 1791; purser of U. S. navy, Indian agent, with the rank of colonel, to the Choctaw and Cherokee Indians, and collector at the port of Mobile; a man of much energy and integrity. It was to him that a cabinet secretary wrote to ask, "How far does the Tombigbee run up into the country?" His reply was, "It runs down, not up at all." The correspondence resulted in his dismissal. He died at Bellevue, Ky., June 17, 1847, aged 80.

Stephen Peabody Webster, of Haverhill, Mass.; H. C. 1792; was the first person that entered College from the Academy; clerk of the courts of Grafton county; representative, senator, and councillor, of the state of New-Hampshire; taught at Haverhill, N. H., where he died, 1841.

John Vose, of Bedford; D. C. 1795; preceptor of Pembroke Academy; representative and senator of the general court; author of several addresses and of two valuable and original works on astronomy; died at Atkinson, May 3, 1840, aged 73. He taught at Atkinson twenty-three years, and at Pembroke eleven years. He was a worthy man, a devout Christian, a superior teacher, with more than ordinary ability and scholarship. He was offered the position of judge, but declined it.

MOSES DOW, of Atkinson; D. C. 1796; settled as a clergyman in Beverly, Mass., and York, Me.; died in Plaistow, May 9, 1837, aged 66.

WILLIAM COGSWELL, of Atkinson; D. C. 1811; preceptor of Hampton Academy; clergyman; settled in Dedham, Mass.; secretary of the American Education Society; professor in Dartmouth College; president of Gilmanton Theological Seminary; editor of the American Quarterly Register, and author of many religious publications; died in Gilmanton, April 18, 1850, aged 62.

FRANCIS VOSE, of Francestown; D. C. 1817; preceptor in Colchester, Ct., Hampton, N. H., Newburyport, Topsfield, and Haverhill, Mass., and Bloomfield Academy, Me.; died in Pembroke, Aug. 8, 1851, aged 62.

JACOB CUMMINGS, of Warren, Mass.; D. C. 1819; preceptor in Hampton; clergyman; settled in Stratham, N. H., Sharon and Southborough, Mass., and Hillsborough and Exeter, N. H.; died in Exeter, June 20, 1866, aged 73.

STEPHEN FARLEY, of Hollis, N. H.; D. C. 1804; clergyman; settled in Claremont and Atkinson, N. H.; wrote several theological volumes; died in Amesbury, Mass., Sept. 20, 1851, aged 71.

ENOCH HALE, of Alstead, N. H.; was not a college graduate; died in Atkinson.

JOHN KELLEY, of Plaistow, N. H.; A. C. 1825; preceptor in Derry, N. H., Female Academy; attorney at law in Plaistow, Chester and Atkinson, N. H.; resides in Atkinson.

JOSEPH PECKHAM, of Westminster, Mass.; A. C. 1837; clergyman; settled in Kingston, Mass.

JOSEPH ALLEN TAYLOR, of Granby, Mass.; H. C. 1839; died in Atkinson, 1842, aged 28.

BENJAMIN A. SPAULDING, of Billerica, Mass.; H. C. 1840; a missionary in Iowa.

MALACHI BULLARD, of West Medway, Mass.; D. C. 1841; clergyman; settled in Winchendon, Mass.; died May 10, 1849, aged 31.

JOHN WASON RAY, of Auburn, N. H.; D. C. 1843; teacher in Manchester, N. H., Eastport, Me., and Derry, N. H.; clergyman; settled in Vernon, Ct., and Goffstown, N. H.

EDWARD HANFORD GREELEY, of Hopkinton, N. H.; D. C. 1845; clergyman; settled in Haverhill and Nashua, N. H., and Methuen, Mass.

JOSEPH GARLAND, of Hampton, N. H.; B. C. 1844; physician in Gloucester, Mass.

CHARLES DARWIN FITCH, of Greenfield, Mass.; D. C. 1837; teacher in Phillips Academy, Andover, and elsewhere.

WILLIAM CLEVES TODD, of Atkinson, N. H.; D. C. 1844; principal of Newburyport Female High School; visited Europe in 1848, and again in 1867, remaining nearly three years; resides in Boston.

CHARLES PRESCOTT PARSONS, of Gilmanton, N. H.; D. C. 1853; teacher in Gilmanton, N. H., and elsewhere.

JOHN WEBSTER DODGE, of Newburyport, Mass.; A. C. 1857; clergyman.

JUSTIN WHITE SPAULDING, of Plainfield, N. H.; D. C. 1847; teacher in West Boscawen and Meriden, N. H., Bradford, Vt., and Taunton, Mass.; died in Atkinson, Sept. 28, 1865, aged 42.

NATHAN BARROWS, a graduate of Western Reserve College, 1850; studied medicine in Cleveland, Ohio, and the city of New-York, and practised in various places; teacher in South Berwick, Me., Claremont, N. H., and in Kimball Union Academy, Meriden, N. H.

WILLIAM ELLINGWOOD BUNTEN, of Dunbarton, N. H.; D. C. 1860; teacher in Dunbarton, N. H. and Gloucester, Mass.; lawyer; captain in the war of the rebellion.

For most of the facts stated in this article, the writer is indebted to a sketch of Atkinson by the Rev. William Cogswell, D.D., in the *New-Hampshire Historical Collections*, and to that most valuable work, *Alumni of Dartmouth College*, by Rev. George T. Chapman, D.D., of Newburyport.

RUTLAND COUNTY INSURRECTION—1786.

By Rev. FREDERIC W. HOLLAND, A.M., of Cambridge.

HUMAN nature is ever the same. Heavy burdens produce bitter groans. The absence of any means of relief tempts suffering men to despair. Desperation does not stop to reason whether the chosen means of extrication are the best. Immediate, temporary escape is enough. At such emergencies a few reckless men, ordinarily of no account, rise into notice. A recent war leaves military weapons in possession of those who are directed by no principle in their use, and reverent of no law. At the close of our revolutionary struggle the causes of discontent were greater than they can ever be again; were sufficient to have utterly overthrown government among a people less conscientious, intelligent, revering than ours. Besides the usual offence of people who had become ostentatiously rich by preying upon the public; by flood after flood of irredeemable paper currency, the expenses of government had been needlessly multiplied, as if by some spendthrift heir anxious to be rid as soon as possible of the accumulations of patient labor. Before 1780, congress had issued two hundred millions of dollars of continental money, which was received in Vermont at par, until Sept. 1777, when it sunk rapidly; and kept on sinking, until paper dollars were of little more value than copper cents, at which rate congress actually funded the remaining two millions.

In 1781 the first bank was established in Philadelphia; and four years after, close upon the time of which we are to speak, the first bank appeared in New York, and also in Boston, but with a circulation confined to those towns. A year after, i. e. in 1786, a national mint was established, whose business was only the coinage of copper; gold and silver coins being an importation from Europe. The present generation will not believe how recently the currency of the United States was chiefly in English and Spanish pieces,—those which were most circulated being the smallest silver coins from the peninsula, fourpences and ninepences.

In the derangement of currency through the depreciation of what the people would not receive as a legal tender, congress did as nearly as possible nothing from fear of giving offence by doing too much. Such pitiable weakness, as was never before seen in a government which survived a crisis, was mingled with bitter divisions and sectional animosities. Without an army, without a navy, without funds or means of creating revenue, living from day to day by borrowing (the most expensive way of living), having no friends on earth but Holland and France, one of them not willing, the other not able to help so far away from home, state-rights were generally recognized as supreme; state-jurisdiction was in fierce controversy; state-interests were infinitely more engrossing than abstract idolatry to the general good. Prophetic souls have always been few, and seldom heeded till the slow arm of Providence has realized their prognostics. One might as well try to get listeners to a discussion of the best principle of ballooning to-day, as have expected thus to enlighten the American people upon the superb destiny opening before them, and thus have inspired patience under their temporary calamities. Besides this general derangement and destitution of a circulating medium, some states were suffering from local causes,—suffering as they thought without sympathy and beyond necessity.

It would need a Shakspearian inspiration to cast oneself back into those scenes, and bring up before the mind's eye the lowering skies which overhung our fathers wherever they looked.

Vermont, not responsible for any portion of the national debt, because not admitted into the confederation, had managed its own debts quite tolerably by the sale of state-lands and by confiscation of tory property; but, with peace, came in upon her a whole sea of troubles. Every kind of property depreciated; foreign goods flowed in and foreign specie flowed out; the fisheries were not born; the manufactories were still-born, and abandoned by the nurse; large landed estates were unable to pay a small debt in specie (that debt being at least double what it was when contracted); habits of dissipation were never so prevalent, some of our fathers counting it a disgrace not to have their guests carried drunken to bed; the freshly-resumed courts threatened to exact the uttermost farthing of principal and interest, the mere costs of a suit at law being more than some industrious farmers could pay; the listlessness of despair presaged ruin to thousands.

Shays's rebellion is popularly regarded as the only open attempt at insurrection. Its purpose was to prevent the holding of courts in Worcester county, at which actions were pending that threatened ruin to men who would in ordinary times have been prosperous. Its interest centres at the heart of Massachusetts. Its history has been minutely written, nothing having been extenuated nor aught set down in malice. It was really terminated by a somewhat heroic march of thirty miles to Petersham by Gen. Lincoln, during a night of awful cold; when the insurrectionists were surprised, their organization dispersed, and their leaders captured. This was in the fall and winter of 1786. These rebels were as much to be pitied as condemned. When they held Worcester they had no money to buy food, they had nothing to eat for twenty-four hours; shelter even was grudgingly given. Old Dr. Bancroft, I remember, sat on his door-step with his key in his pocket, and when Shays commanded him to open his house to the regulators, as they were called, the minister replied that if they entered his house they must do it over his prostrate body. Shays bade the regiment march on. So they were nothing less than beggars with arms in their hands; they were objects of compassion rather than of malignant hate. When they retreated, having accomplished nothing, 'twas through storm and snow; some badly frozen and some stricken with death: their own sufferings so uncomplainingly borne, their sacrifices so freely made, being greater than the miseries visited by many revolutionists upon conquered communities. As the grievances under which they groaned were perfectly real, as no other means of relief but stopping the courts seemed within reach, as they carefully forebore committing any injuries upon property or persons, I think we shall sooner lament their blindness than censure the malice of this last attempt at rebellion in old Massachusetts.

More than any other New-England State, Massachusetts has enjoyed the advantage of having its history amply written. Events of like moment in other quarters have passed into oblivion. The men have not been found to record what was worth preserving as a picture of the times until the period had nearly passed for recovering the most indispensable facts.

Vermont has very much the same spot on her escutcheon with Massachusetts. The same debts were pressed by the same legal processes to the same cruel, unjust, ruinous results. Courts, judges, sheriffs, attorneys, were no less dreaded and detested in the Green Mountain than the Bay State. Nor do I think the affair so infamous in purpose or savage in method or pernicious in effect, that a true New-Englander should desire every vestige of the movement to be blotted out.

The first outbreak of angry feeling has already passed into oblivion. In 1784, a convention was held at the "Edge of Wells," where discontent muttered itself aloud; and judges, lawyers and sheriffs received hearty execrations from some who were suffering unjustly, as from many suffering justly at their hands.

The next summer but one, the distress increasing, and general bankruptcy impending, Gov. Chittenden published an address to the citizens, counselling the cultivation of the necessaries of life, particularly wool and flax, urging industry, economy and non-importation, praying for mutual forbearance and good will between creditor and debtor. When in Oct., 1786, the legislature met at the little court house in Rutland, now a very humble private dwelling, it was found that the popular feeling so pervaded their body they were ready to jump to the most radical measures of relief. A law was passed authorizing the defaulting debtor to pay the same articles which would have been good in the life of the contract; and another that debtors should pay creditors in other states on specific articles according to the laws of those states. Other and more ultra legislation was in prospect, when Nathaniel Chipman persuaded four other members of the house to unite with him in staving off all action, by referring the settlement of debts to the January meeting of the respective towns. This was done; and the same day, October 31, 1786, a mob attempted to break up the court in Windsor.

After the legislature arose, some evil spirits were busy as the very father of mischief, misrepresenting the legislative action, and summoning the people to armed resistance of the plots of lawyers and the cruelty of judges. Col. Thomas Lee, a resident upon Otter Creek, three miles from Rutland, somewhat distinguished in the war, where he had served as captain in Warner's regiment, but a bankrupt, dissipated, anxious to escape withal from pecuniary liabilities, was the head and front of this offending.

On the third Tuesday, November, 1786, the county court was about to open its usual session under Chief Justice Increase Moseley. Rutland was not at all what it is to-day. Having now ten thousand inhabitants, it had not then two thousand. Having at this hour over two score of inhabited streets, it had not then more than two score buildings, half of which were built of logs. The principal street called Main, was north and south as to-day. The relics of a picket fort were still visible,—visible now no more. Fort Ranger, a little west, had been mostly removed to repair mills and feed the winter fires. The cardinals did so to the Coliseum, and the Pashas to the pyramids. The court house or state house, now occupied not very comfortably as a dwelling, by Goodnow, was divided into two rooms, the east without a floor for the jury, the west for the court, with an elevated platform to the north-west for the judge. The log-jail, with two rooms, stood handy to the north. During the session of court, the chief-justice was wont to wear a three-cornered hat, and the sheriff a sword. There seemed to have been at this time two churches, two school-houses, and certainly three taverns; a large proportion for the schools, and some explanation of the restlessness, poverty and recklessness of part of the inhabitants. No doubt these inns were very small, story and a half log-huts, I imagine; no doubt, in the poor means of locomotion then enjoyed, people had to rest longer on their way, a day's journey being less than thirty miles from inn to inn. Still, the fact is striking that "old Jamaiky" was freely dispensed at either place, and during winter evenings liberally imbibed,—a red-hot iron like the modern poker being the acknowledged sceptre of the little kingdom, and a punch-bowl the emblem of the accepted libation to the deity of the scene.

As the judges entered the village Nov. 21, on their way to the court house, a mob of men and boys waylaid them, demanding that they should adjourn. At eleven, however, the court was opened and adjourned till two. In the interim, certain persons representing themselves as a committee of the people waited upon the judge with a petition that the session be postponed. The answer was that in the afternoon, when the docket had been called, and the business of the day attended to, their petition would be considered.

In the afternoon, as this programme was about to be observed, Col. Lee rushed in at the head of a hundred men, in a tumultuous manner, and began to harangue the court for not granting the people's request. So few friends of the court were present the sheriff could not be sustained in enforcing order; and the judges (unable to proceed) satisfied themselves by appointing a reopening the next morning at nine o'clock. This was in fact a defiance of the mob. The crisis came. Arms were instantly procured at a neighboring house, distributed among the people, and the court house so effectually guarded that the law and order party were actually imprisoned. The mob, styling themselves "regulators," then resorted to intimidation, without effect; but, after two hours' menace, they released judge, jury, sheriff and attorney without injury. At the judge's lodgings a written petition for redress of grievances was presented, which was met with this reply: "The judges of the C. C. in and for the C. of Rutland, having taken into consideration the petition of a number of the inhabitants in which it is requested that this Court adjourn without doing any business, find on examination of the docket, that a large number of cases are in suit in which plaintiffs and defendants are mutually agreed to come to a decisive trial this session; and some other matters of such importance to the peace, dignity and interest of the good people of this County, that the Court cannot (agreeable to the tenor of their oaths and the general good) comply with the aforesaid requisition. Notwithstanding the Court would not wish to try any causes at this time but such as in its opinion are necessary to preserve the peace, interest and dignity of this County and the State."

This of course accepted the challenge of battle. The Lee party were now to show what stuff they were made of. They announced their determination to break up the court by violent measures; stationed guards within the court house; misrepresented the judges' reply; accused them of acting deceitfully, and did (what ought to have been their beginning, middle and end) send for reinforcement to the neighboring towns.

The government party did not of course fold their hands. Jonathan Bill of Rutland, sheriff, sent orders to Col. Isaac Clark of Castleton, Col. Pearl of Pawlet, and Lt.-Col. Spofford of Tinmouth, to raise the county militia without delay, and march with firearms and three days' provisions to assist him in sustaining the court. This order was promptly obeyed. Before any assistance came to the rebels they were in fact overpowered. By nine o'clock of Wednesday morning Cols. Clark and Pearl arrived with such force that the court house was evacuated and no farther insult was offered to the majesty of the law. A Tinmouth company came under Captain Orange Train. At noon western men began to pour in: Capt. Gregory's command from Hubbardston, Capt. Israel Hurlbut and others from Castleton, Capt. Titus Walton and others from Poultney: proving that the rebels had reckoned without a host: illustrating Burke's figure that a few insects (buzzing about) can make more sensation than a whole herd of oxen feeding. Approaching the field of action the militia halted, were addressed by Capt. Watson, ordered to load their guns and be ready.

Meanwhile the judges had been escorted by the sheriff from their houses to the tribunal of justice, and proceedings duly opened; but adjourned on account of the excitement to the next morning. The regulators, on the other hand, trusted their cause to words: they marched about the streets discussing their grievances, insisting that the lawyers were bent on ruining the country, that the Irishman, Matthew Lyon, had been elected a judge, that one lawyer was strutting about in kid gloves, ruffled shirt and gold bracelets; and that there ought to be a general amnesty act. Evidently they were not up to the occasion. At dusk Col. Cooley with fifty others from the north retired to the house of Lieut. Post. In the evening seven or eight of the ringleaders were arrested, but Col. Lee had fled. At midnight orders were issued to seize the Cooley party. Capt. Lee and Lieut. Sawyer, both of Clarendon, with sixteen horsemen and a small body of infantry, approached Post's house cautiously—surrounded it—and captured its sleeping inmates. Some pistols and muskets were discharged—no one knowing who fired first. The only man really shot, Nicholas Hopkins, a mobite, lost his arm by amputation; the rest of the captives, with but three escapes, being conducted to the jail, where very soon there was not room to sit up. Thursday morning commenced the trial of the conspirators: five of whom were acquitted; twenty-one pleaded guilty, and were fined from nine shillings upwards with costs; fourteen were fined from £3 to 25, and required to recognize for good behavior through one year.

Some of them were exceedingly worthy persons. Benjamin Whipple (fined £10) had the June before sat on the bench as assistant judge; young Hopkins was swept along with the mob merely by a boy's love of adventure. As usual, the chiefly guilty person, the originator of the hopeless scheme, the Lee first mentioned, escaped.

On Saturday afternoon, the troops were assembled, addressed by Col. Clark and dismissed,—starting for home the next morning. But, the western militia arriving at Pine Hill (which borders the village of Rutland), found that two hundred men, who had not been engaged in the preceding riot, stuffed with the double falsehood that those who were captured suffered cruelly, and that success was still possible where it had never been, lay in their homeward path. The court directed the raising of the county for their relief. This was so effectually done (notwithstanding unfounded charges of severity and double dealing against the court), that the rebel gathering listened patiently to an appeal by the Rev. Jacob Wood (a popular revivalist of that vicinity), who turned the scales so entirely that members of the regulators went over to the other side; and by Monday all was quiet again.

Finally, on Monday morning the militia received the thanks of the court and were dismissed to their homes. Nothing ruffled the judicial dignity any more; and on Tuesday evening the court adjourned without day. The militia were compensated by the state; the muster-roll is still to be seen at Rutland. On the 2d of March, 1787, the general assembly passed the following resolution:

"That this House entertains a high sense of the services done the state by the officers and soldiers whose spirited exertions crushed the late daring insurrection against government in the counties of Rutland and Windsor; and does hereby return the said officers and soldiers their hearty thanks."

Thus died into silence the northern echo of Shays's rebellion: a faint but genuine reverberation of that summer thunder and heat-lightning. The respectability of the persons engaged in the insane enterprise of plunging society into anarchy proves how general, deep-seated, substantial were the grounds of discontent; how hard it is after a grand convulsion to get the state machine into harmonious running again; how much more we owe our continuance as a republic to the trust in the integrity of Washington than is popularly imagined; for at the bottom of the cup lay everywhere these fierce discords, besides sectional hostility and overhanging bankruptcy, which nothing save the magic of his name made the people endure in confidence of a peaceful solution at last. It need not be added that the people of Vermont did themselves credit by meeting this sore trial of infant institutions with profound reverence for law, with thorough respect for individual rights, with holy fidelity to conscience; proving that no future strain can ever rend asunder our nation's cable, nor drive our good ship of state from that safe anchorage where she defies the storm, nor even permanently darken our political horizon.

Puffer, Mathias.—In the Jan. No. of the N. E. Hist. and Geneal. Register, p. 80, is an inquiry about the wife of Mathias Puffer.

May 22, 1662, a Mathias Puffer, of *Braintree*, was accepted by the Committee (Messrs. Eleazer Lusher, Roger Clap and William Parke) empowered to assist in settling the Plantation granted at Netmocke (Mendon), as an inhabitant. From the Mendon records, I learn that Mathias Puffer and *family* were settled in this town in Nov. 1664. Mathias Puffer and family were living in this town in 1675, at the breaking out of King Philip's war. During the war the town was abandoned, and the inhabitants did not return until Jan. 1680. Puffer did not return, as I do not find his name afterwards in our records. While at Braintree, and during the Indian war, he petitioned the Council to be allowed to remain there (he had been summoned to return to Mendon), to take care of his children; his *wife* and eldest son having been *slain* by the "barbarous Indians." I do not find the name of Puffer among our record of Births, Marriages and Deaths, in fact no such records until *after* the war.

If this Mathias was the *one* who married Rachel Farnsworth, unless he had married again before 1675, Rachel Puffer was killed by the Indians in this town, July 14, 1675.

John G. Metcalf.

Mendon, Mass., Jan. 14.

THE NEW-HAMPSHIRE GAZETTE.

THE OLDEST NEWSPAPER IN AMERICA.

Communicated by FRANK W. MILLER, Esq., of Portsmouth, N. H.

PORTSMOUTH, the only port worthy the name on New-Hampshire's eighteen miles of sea-coast, was originally planted as a mercantile settlement, and not a religious colony. And this peculiarity of her origin has impressed itself on every phase and period of her history. Accordingly we find her, and the province of New-Hampshire, of which she was at once the head and the largest member, getting along without a press from 1623 until 1756; and when at length the press did come, it was first used to print an almanac and newspaper; and indeed this first press was never used in printing many books.

The history of printing in Portsmouth is thus mainly the record of newspapers and editors; although considerable book work was done at one time, about the close of the last century, including a heavy edition of Rollin's Ancient History, by Treadwell & Brother, in 8 vols. Charles Tappan, Charles Peirce, Gray & Childs, T. H. Miller and C. W. Brewster also issued several works, at a later date; and Mr. Miller also printed music, and his were the only specimens ever issued in the state, so far as I can ascertain, except the publications of Henry Ranlet (and possibly others) at Exeter, which were considerable.

Daniel Fowle, the first printer in New-Hampshire, who established the New-Hampshire Gazette in Portsmouth, Oct. 7, 1756, was a native of Massachusetts, and his record shows him to have been a fair printer, and able editor; successful in business; a true patriot, and good man. He commenced business in Boston, in 1740, and in 1750 published the Independent Advertiser, in connection with Gamaliel Rogers. Fowle afterward opened a bookstore and printing office in Boston; and in 1754 was arrested by order of the Massachusetts house of representatives, on suspicion of having printed a pamphlet entitled "*The monster of monsters;* by Tom Thumb Esq.," which contained severe animadversions on some of the members. Fowle denied the printing, but acknowledged the sale of the pamphlets. After the rudest and most insolent treatment, he was taken to the common jail, and confined in the same cell with a notorious thief, and next that of a murderer awaiting execution. After three days he was set at liberty, but refused to go; he had been confined, uncondemned by the law, and demanded that the authority which had imprisoned, should release him. But after staying with the jailor three days longer, and learning that his wife was seriously ill from anxiety on his account, he returned home. He afterward published an account of these arbitrary proceedings in a pamphlet entitled "The total eclipse of liberty."

In vain endeavoring to obtain satisfaction or indemnity for his illegal detention, and disgusted with the provincial government of Massachusetts, he determined to leave Boston; and sought the freer soil of New-Hampshire. Accepting the invitation of several "respectable" gentlemen of Portsmouth, he removed to this town; and early in October, 1756, issued here the first number of the Gazette, on a sheet which, laid open, measures seventeen inches by ten—an exact *fac simile* of which is furnished in each copy of this number of the REGISTER. The Gazette, now in its one hundred and sixteenth volume, is still published at Portsmouth, being now issued in quarto form, on a sheet 29 × 42 inches. The present office is on the same street, and not many rods above the original location, but there have been numerous other sites occupied in the mean time.

It will be seen that no place of issue is stated in the publisher's imprint or elsewhere; but a daughter of the late John Melcher, Esq. (Fowle's successor and heir), still living, states positively that the singular and quaint old wooden building, of which we present an exact picture on p. 139 (from a photograph by Davis Brothers, of Portsmouth), was Fowle's original office, and so the site of the first printing in New-Hampshire. It is located on the corner of Pleasant, Washington and Howard streets, and opposite the beautiful and famous old Wentworth mansion; in the near vicinity of the original meeting-house, and in what was then the business centre as well as the "court end" of the town. The office (that is the material and the business,—not the building) was after a few years removed by Fowle to Fore or Paved street, now Market; but had it been retained in the first location, it would have escaped the fires which have several times visited it in various others, but which have never devastated the south end of the town.

Fowle's opening address is pronounced by Rev. Dr. Peabody to be a masterpiece of its kind; and no one can inspect the volumes of the paper under his management, without conceiving a most favorable idea of his ability and discretion, integrity and honor, public spirit and patriotism. He continued in business in Portsmouth for about thirty years, until 1784, for a portion of the time having a less worthy nephew connected with him; but for the most part assisted chiefly by his negro slave, Primus, an excellent pressman, although he did not know a letter, and who lived to the age of ninety. Dr. Peabody also remarks "that the N. H. Gazette is believed to be the only newspaper in this country which has had a continuous existence for a century, without a change of name." But this was said in 1856, at the centennial celebration of the Gazette; and since that time, at least two others have completed their hundred years, The North American in Philadelphia, and The Newport Mercury in Rhode Island.

Pictorial illustrations were perhaps as popular then as now, but engravings were scarce, and engravers scarcer. Fowle had brought with him, from his Boston printing office, a set of wood-cuts, probably of Æsop's fables; and with that of the fox and the crow, as will be seen, the head of the Gazette was at first adorned. Whether the public was the crow, and Fowle the fox, we cannot say, nor how the emblem or device was to be taken; but this cut was soon broken, and was replaced by that of Jupiter and the peacock. Some time afterward the royal arms took their place in the head, and kept it until displaced by the American revolution.

Mr. Fowle did little else than print his paper, the province laws, and a few pamphlets. The governor appointed him a justice of the peace soon after his arrival. He was a correct and industrious printer, and an agreeable man, and succeeded in accumulating a considerable property. He published the Gazette, alone or with a partner, till 1785; when he transferred it to John Melcher and George Jerry Osborn, two of his apprentices. Mr. Fowle died in 1787, aged about seventy years, leaving most or all his estate to John Melcher, according to his agreement when young Melcher went to live with and work for him. Melcher died in 1850, aged nearly ninety years, and his highly respectable descendants are still enjoying the competency thus gained from Fowle, and increased by himself.

The exact chronology of the Gazette is as follows: Daniel Fowle printed it from 1756 to 1764, when Robert Fowle became associated with him. They continued till 1773, when Robert went to Exeter and started the first paper there. In 1776, Benjamin Dearborn became publisher; but two years after, Mr. Fowle again resumed the publication, and continued it to 1785, when Melcher & Osborn took it. A part of the old wooden building, then standing on what is now Market street, which was occupied as a printing office by Fowle and his successors, is now a dwelling on Russell street.

Mr. Osborn soon left the firm, but Melcher continued the business of printer and bookseller till 1802, when he sold out to Nathaniel S. & Washington Peirce, who changed the politics of the Gazette from federal to republican. Melcher was the first state-printer of New-Hampshire, and the only Portsmouth citizen who has ever filled that office. He imported a fount of pica type upon which to print the laws of the State, and it was in regular use for more than sixty years. The writer now has in his possession, the original press used in printing the Gazette, also a large earthen inkstand, a settee, and several founts of type, which descended from Fowle to Melcher, and were bestowed by his family on the writer's father, the late Rev. Tobias H. Miller, himself a prominent editor in this city for nearly fifty years past, until 1870. Mr. Melcher filled the high office of coroner for many years, was a very exact and accurate printer and business man, and having made a snug property in his trade, lived in the best of health and spirits almost half a century after he retired from it. The writer of this well remembers his nice, prim appearance as a veritable gentleman of the old school, in our streets, during his last years.

N. S. & W. Peirce, in connection with Benjamin Hill and Samuel Gardner, published the Gazette about three years, and in 1805 sold it to William Weeks, who came from Portland, Me. Up to this time very little editorial matter had appeared in the paper, except a little political writing at certain periods. The scissors (or, rather, penknife) did most of the work, as they often do the best of it now. The "news" and selected matter were all that was expected—and it was of no consequence if the news from Washington was several days, or from Europe several weeks old, instead of hours or minutes, as now. Mr. Weeks held an able pen, and wrote more than his predecessors. He remained editor for more than four years of a stormy period, and at the close of 1813 was succeeded by Beck & Foster. This firm continued until dissolved by the death of David C. Foster in 1823. From that time till 1834, Gideon Beck was the publisher; then Albert Greenleaf was admitted partner, and the next year, 1838, Mr. Beck left the business. Now appear the names of Thomas B. Laighton (afterward well known at the Isles of Shoals), and Abner Greenleaf, Jr., in the imprint, for a year or less; when Mr. Greenleaf alone conducts the paper up to 1841. Then Joel C. Virgin and Samuel W. Moses published it until 1843; then Mr. Moses for a year. After this, Abner Greenleaf (senior) is named as editor, then A. Greenleaf & Son. This year, 1844, closes without any imprint, and for the next two years there was none, the paper being then owned by prominent democrats, and managed by them and their friends.

In 1847, William P. Hill, a son of Isaac Hill, came from Concord, in this state, and bought the Gazette, and also another opposition sheet which had been started; and uniting the two, enlarged the Gazette, and called it "The N. H. Gazette and Republican Union." He was unsuccessful, and lost several thousand dollars in the publication; and after in vain attempting to establish a daily Gazette in connection therewith, he left the paper in 1850, and was succeeded by Gideon H. Rundlett, of Portsmouth, who ably and faithfully edited and published the paper for its owners, who were leading members of the democratic party.

Edward N. Fuller, from Manchester, relieved Mr. Rundlett after his two years' service, in 1852, and remained in charge of the business until 1858, when, after making another creditable but unsuccessful attempt to establish a daily Gazette, he left the state, and was for several years connected with the Newark Journal in New-Jersey. Mr. Fuller was an able man and skilful journalist, but had a difficult field to work in here. He was succeeded in the management of the Gazette, by Amos S. Alexander, Esq., from Fisherville,—a man of more ability than discretion in the use of his pen; a most social and agreeable gentleman, of Falstaffian personal proportions. This "Alexander the Great" (as he was sometimes called by rival editors) was obliged to vacate his position as custom-house officer and editor, in favor of Mr. Samuel Gray, of Portsmouth, who now bought the office, in February, 1859. Mr. Gray was a good printer, and capable business man, and conducted the paper to the satisfaction of its patrons, until Sept. 14, 1861, when he sold out to Frank W. Miller, who united the Gazette with the Chronicle (a daily and weekly paper established in 1852 by these same men, with others, then partners, as Millers & Gray), in which connection it is still published, the daily being known as "The Portsmouth Chronicle," and the weekly as "The New-Hampshire Gazette."

In 1857, the firm of Millers & Gray (the third member having been Thomas W. Miller who deceased in 1856) was dissolved, F. W. Miller remaining as sole owner and publisher. In 1858, he purchased the New-Hampshire Phenix, a temperance paper printed at Concord, and put the titles of both at the head. This cannibalistic performance of swallowing numerous other papers, has been the experience of many old publications.

Mr. George W. Marston was admitted partner with Mr. Miller, April 13, 1868, under the style of Frank W. Miller & Co.; and Mr. Miller sold his interest to Mr. Washington Freeman Oct. 13, 1870, since when the business is well conducted by Marston & Freeman.

The Gazette was strongly loyal for many years; so much so, that in 1765 it was feared the editor would not oppose the stamp act vigorously enough, and another paper called the Portsmouth Mercury was started, but after three years it ran out. In 1802, the Gazette was changed to republican, but about Jackson's time espoused the democratic cause, and followed the fortunes of that party until united with the Chronicle. Thenceforth, with T. H. Miller continuously, and three of his sons at different times as editors (with whom Jacob H. Thompson, now of the New-York Times, was for several years a valuable assistant), and later under Mr. Marston's management, the Gazette has been and is a supporter of the republican party.

It must not be supposed that the printers of the Gazette enjoyed a monopoly of the business in Portsmouth during all these years. Far from it. Nearly or quite thirty other different papers have been started, and for the last eighty years there have been commonly three weeklies issued, and within twenty years two dailies have been established in addition,—the Daily Times in 1868. Of these, up to the time of the very successful Chronicle, in 1852, only one had succeeded with any great degree of permanence,—the Oracle, now Portsmouth Journal.

In 1793, Charles Peirce commenced a semi-weekly called the "United States Oracle of the Day," but in about two years changed it to a weekly, and in 1801 sold it to William Treadwell; and after passing through other hands, the name was altered to "Portsmouth Journal" (which it still retains), by N. A. Haven, Jr., who became editor in 1821, and it was in 1825 sold to Charles W. Brewster and Tobias H. Miller, both recently deceased. In 1835, Mr. Brewster bought out Mr. Miller, and the paper is still published by his son, Louis W. Brewster, for several years his partner, and is one of the most substantial and highly esteemed family journals in the State. As a characteristic, it has the same small, neat heading which it has borne for a large portion of its whole existence of three-quarters of a century.

Mr. Brewster, senior, made one or two efforts, many years ago, to start a small daily, but not immediately receiving what he deemed adequate encouragement, he declined to go on. His two volumes of valuable and interesting local history, known as "Rambles about Portsmouth," and his noble essay entitled "Fifty years in a Printing Office," are, in addition to his weekly Journal, an ample record of a well-spent life. Verily, his works do follow him, and his children rise up and call him blessed.

His old partner, Tobias H. Miller,—printer, editor, publisher, and minister of the gospel,—was for more than half a century prominently connected with the press of his native state; and no doubt, at one time or other, was interested in more different newspapers than any other man who ever lived in New-Hampshire. As an editor, few have shown more ability or been more popular, though he was as outspoken as Fowle; but, unlike Fowle, he cared not to amass wealth. He was a clergyman of good standing, first in the Orthodox Congregational, and afterward in the Universalist denomination; and keeping both pen and voice active almost to the day of his death, he was a year or two since gathered with our list of worthies, of whom he was proud to be accounted one. His six sons have all had more or less connection with the printing office, four of them being editors of newspapers.

It is curious to look at the ages of the first printers of Portsmouth. Fowle lived to be about 70 years old, working nearly fifty; Primus, his slave, to be 90, working more than fifty; Melcher, Fowle's apprentice, to be 90, working nearly thirty years; Samuel Whidden, Melcher's apprentice, and in part his successor, to be 70, working forty-five; and T. H. Miller, who first worked with Whidden, to be 68, working fifty-five years. Of all these men, probably the first, Daniel Fowle, made more money by the printing business, than has ever been made by any other in this state, even to the present day; although Mr. Melcher, who inherited Fowle's property and increased it in other ways than by printing, doubtless gathered a larger estate than he. Fowle held the office of justice of the peace, a position conferring power and emoluments in those days; Melcher was for years the coroner, a respectable and profitable office; and in later times, even to the present, the publisher or editor of the Gazette has usually been the recipient of some profitable government office, in the customs or postal department. Before the year 1800, eight several and distinct papers competed with the Gazette, at different times; since that time, at least twenty of all sorts have begun and ended. Of the men, besides the Gazette pioneers, and their near followers, Charles Peirce, who started the Oracle (now Journal), and the late lamented Charles W. Brewster, also of the Journal, all of whom accumulated a comfortable competency, few if any of their numerous competitors and followers, except the Chronicle publishers, have added much to their substance by their hard labors, though some of them were very able and worthy men. The Oracle and Journal throughout have had able writers. The Gazette, from the time Mr. William Weeks took it, in 1805, has been actively edited, and usually with ability.

It is fitting and proper here to note the fact that the antiquity of the N. H. Gazette has been disputed and denied by some, especially by the Newport Mercury of Rhode Island, which was started two years after the Gazette, by Benjamin Franklin's less worthy brother James. The form, size and entire make-up of the little Mercury (as shown by the *fac simile* issued at the time of *their* centennial celebration, in 1858), clearly evinces that it was patterned, as near as might be, after Fowle's Gazette; and the Mercury bases its claims to greater antiquity than the Gazette, on the statement that the Gazette was for a year or more, about 1775, suspended from publication, or else published under a different name. But neither of these statements are true, as the files and all the records of history show. For although there have at various times been several other titles connected with that of New-Hampshire Gazette, this has never been omitted, nor has the paper ever failed of regular and continuous issue. There appears at one time to have been another New-Hampshire Gazette, printed at Exeter, fourteen miles distant from Portsmouth, by one Robert Fowle, whom Dr. Peabody alludes to as an unworthy nephew of the great Daniel; this was issued irregularly for a year or two, first called "A New-Hampshire Gazette," and afterwards "The New-Hampshire Gazette," and its brief existence may have caused the misapprehension as to the veritable Gazette. At any rate, the bound files of the Gazette, which still exist, almost complete if not entirely so, in the Athenæums of Portsmouth and Boston, show that this charge is not correct, and the evidence is good and sufficient of the superior age of the paper. Rev. Dr. Peabody, in his address, sustains this view; and the late Rev. T. H. Miller, who had thoroughly studied the subject, also insisted on it. Thomas, in his *History of Printing*, more than half a century since, said "The New-Hampshire Gazette is the oldest paper in New-England,"—and it is very certain that it has not grown any younger, nor any of its cotemporaries relatively any older since. The files show that the name of N. H. Gazette and Historical Chronicle was, on May 25, 1776, changed to Freeman's Journal or N. H. Gazette; and about one year afterwards was again changed to N. H. Gazette, or State Journal and General Advertiser. But the original title of New-Hampshire Gazette, which Fowle gave it, has always been sustained at the head of the paper, and this is beyond question the oldest paper, not only in New-England, but in the United States. And there is only one other paper, so far as I can discover, that at any time, within many years back, could have disputed successfully the claims of the N. H. Gazette to priority in the Union. We allude to the Virginia Gazette, which was established at Williamsburg in 1736, twenty years before Fowle's, and was the third paper started in the country. The publishers most of the time during the last twenty years have been two brothers of the name of Lively, to whose courtesy I am indebted for some information concerning the paper, and for copies of the last issues, as late as 1869, which show them to be able journalists. Mr. Lively states that he has valuable bound files of the paper, sufficient to fill a horse-cart; but that its publication has been suspended and resumed several times during its long career,—if, indeed, such an interrupted and broken series of existences can be termed and counted as one and the same life. In one case, at least, Messrs. Lively abandoned the old historic name, but resumed it again after a few months. In 1862, this Virginia Gazette was necessarily discontinued for a while, by reason of the U. S. forces occupying the town of Williamsburg,—and a sheet was issued from the office by some of the printer "boys in blue." At the close of the war, the former publishers resumed the old Gazette, but did not continue to print it long, and it is now enjoying one of its silent or hibernating periods. But as its last able and gentlemanly editor informs me that there is now a good opening for a paper in Williamsburg, let us hope that this, one of the earliest of all our many "Gazettes," may soon be resuscitated to new and long-continued life.

As for the New-Hampshire Gazette, the worthy subject of this brief and imperfect sketch, which yet has grown far beyond the limits I intended,—this is still alive indeed, and is now published by Messrs. Marston & Freeman, in quarto form of eight pages of six columns each; and is one of the largest, best and most flourishing papers in the state. It was issued in its present shape for the first time, by the writer of this article, Nov. 16, 1867. The long-continued support of this old newspaper by the people of Portsmouth and vicinity, would seem to be another evidence of their noted steadfastness, enterprise and thrift in the olden times.

Rev. Dr. Peabody also states in his address, that "this town can claim the distinction of having issued the first religious newspaper in the country, and I am inclined to think in the world." This was the "Herald of Gospel Liberty," which was started by Rev. Elias Smith, the very able founder here of the Christian Baptist or Christian sect; and his son, Rev. Matthew Hale Smith, has for years been the spicy New-York correspondent of the Boston Journal. The paper, after several changes of name and location, is still published under its original title, in Dayton, Ohio. I am well aware that some persons attempt to disprove this claim of priority likewise. Dr. Peabody further says, "I am also led to believe that the earliest religious magazine published in America was 'The Piscataqua Evangelical Magazine,' issued in Portsmouth four or five years, beginning in 1805."

A very interesting celebration of the one hundredth anniversary of the introduction of printing into New-Hampshire,—really the celebration of the establishing of the Gazette,—was held in Portsmouth, October 6, 1856. The movement was originated by the New-Hampshire State Historical Society, and was largely indebted for its success to the intelligent and untiring efforts of Edward N. Fuller, Esq., then publisher of the Gazette, and his brother, now Frank Fuller, Esq., of Utah. Mr. E. N. Fuller published at the time, a pamphlet of sixty pages, containing a full account of the proceedings on the occasion,—the street procession and decorations, and the indoor festivities,—the oration, poem, &c. in the Temple, originally the church built for Elder Elias Smith; the dinner in the old historic Jefferson Hall, with the after-feast of speeches, sentiments, &c. The oration of Rev. Dr. A. P. Peabody, then pastor of the Unitarian Church in Portsmouth, and editor of the North American Review, although written at very short notice, was of course an able and eloquent production, and no less a glowing tribute to the art personated, than a valuable compilation of and contribution to the general and local history of the craft, the devotees of which perhaps have proved themselves generally less crafty than most other guilds. Benjamin P. Shillaber, Esq., well known as Mrs. Partington, delivered the poem on the occasion; and Albert Laighton, who has been styled the poet of New-Hampshire, and Thomas B. Aldrich, wrote odes which were sung by a select choir,—all the three poets being natives of Portsmouth.

The famous battalion of Amoskeag Veterans, from Manchester, N. H., under command of the late Col. Chandler E. Potter, the well-known historian, performed escort duty for the imposing street procession, which embraced the fire department and military and civic organizations of the city, and a small mechanical department. The great attraction was the old wood and stone printing press (often called Ramage, but of course much older[1] than that pattern), which had been owned and worked by Franklin J. Draper, of Boston, and Daniel Fowle and John Melcher, of Portsmouth, and upon which the New-Hampshire Gazette was first printed. This historic press was set up in a hayrack in the most *outre* style, and was operated as the procession moved along the streets, with the old inkballs and all; and *fac-similes* of the first newspaper printed in the state (like that presented herewith), were distributed to the eager populace, just a century from its appearance from the very same press.

The first Printing Office in New-Hampshire, still standing in Portsmouth.

Of the numerous and significant decorations of buildings, we can only refer to two. At the corner of Howard and Washington streets, and very near Pleasant, still stands the queer shaped old wooden building which was used by Fowle for the first printing office in the state, and of which we present an engraving with this article. This structure was decorated agreeably to the suggestions of the writer hereof, with a large painting of the Draper printing press, behind which was seen the rising sun, and over all, the words, "Let there be light!" Underneath all, the inscription, "Success to the craft which puts down kingcraft and priestcraft." Flags were suspended across the street at this point, and the bands as they passed saluted

1 Mr. George W. Bazin, of Boston, who was an apprentice in the Portsmouth Oracle office about 1814 (and while there gave the late Rev. Mr. Miller his first lessons in type-setting), and who now, at the age of 78 years, is making full weekly bills as compositor at the office of Rand & Avery, thinks this is incorrect; but I am sure the late Mr. Miller held the view stated above. Mr. Bazin is correct in stating that an old press was brought from Portsmouth to Boston to join in the great Franklin statue celebration, and that this bore the name of A. Ramage; but Mr. Isaac Frye, also an old Portsmouth and Boston printer, remembers two presses in the Melcher office, and thinks the oldest was not a Ramage. It has long been claimed that "Franklin worked on this press," as it is for scores of others; and possibly he did pull a sheet or two, when travelling as Postmaster General, and calling at printing offices—to please the boys.

the sacred spot. At the office where the Gazette was then published, on Daniel street, there was erected a fine national arch, surmounted by an eagle and flags, on the pillars of which appeared thirteen stars, and on the keystone, "Daniel Fowle, 1756:"

"To him whose memory our art endears,
We yield the homage of a hundred years."

There was also a colossal bust of Franklin, the wooden figurehead, we think, of the old U. S. ship Franklin, and which is now displayed in the grounds of Portsmouth Navy Yard.

The after-dinner speeches at Jefferson Hall, were especially interesting. Mayor Richard Jenness presided, and Hon. Frank Fuller was toast-master. Among the sentiments responded to, was one to "Daniel Fowle," by the Rev. Tobias H. Miller, who has recorded nearly all of the scanty knowledge we have of Fowle's history, and that of John Melcher his next successor. Benjamin P. Shillaber also read a humorous poem, and Mr. Charles W. Brewster worked into ingenious rhyme many of the names of the numerous poets of Portsmouth. Father Boylston, of the Amherst Cabinet, and the veteran Father John Prentiss, long of the Keene Sentinel (who is still living at the age of ninety-four years), entertained the company with anecdotes and reminiscences of their times. E. N. Fuller, Esq., spoke for the Gazette, and named many whose able pens had enriched its columns. The whole celebration was one of the most interesting ever held in the city, and was in every respect worthy of the important event it commemorated. There were present many scholars and literary men from abroad, and the number of newspaper editors and reporters in attendance was probably larger than was ever gathered on any other occasion in the state. In the procession, the car containing the circulating printing office was labelled, "The Press," and a large carriage filled with Boston and New-York editors, was inscribed, "The Quill." Besides the exercises already alluded to, the visiting multitudes were entertained with a rowing regatta on the Piscataqua river, and a grand centennial ball was given at Congress Hall in the evening, which was pronounced the most brilliant affair of the sort ever given in this noted old city. And thus began and ended the first centennial celebration of the art of printing in America. For the expenses, the city council appropriated $500, one half of which only was expended, the balance being made up by subscriptions from public-spirited citizens.

Tarbox.—In Hanson's History of Gardiner, Me., page 107, it is stated that Joseph Tarbox was a descendant of a French Huguenot family which spelled its name Tabeaux. Can this statement in regard to the corruption of Tabeaux into Tarbox be verified? C. Woodman.

Cambridge, Mass.

Treworgye.—In connection with this name in New-England (see Register, vol. v., pp. 345–47) the following is of interest:—"April 8, 1651, a warrant was issued to John Treworgie and Walter Sykes, ordering them to sail in the Crescent to Newfoundland and to sequestrate for the benefit of the Commonwealth, all ordnance, ammunition, houses, boats and other articles belonging to Sir David Kirke, and to collect the taxes paid by strangers for the right of fishing."—*Interregnum Entry-Book*, cxvii., 114, quoted in Henry Kirke's First English Conquest of Canada, London, 1871, pp. 177–8. J. W. T.

THE BROMFIELD FAMILY.

Communicated by Prof. Daniel Denison Slade, M.D.

Concluded from page 43.

An excellent portrait of Mr. Henry Bromfield, by Morse, the telegraph inventor, adorns the parlors of his granddaughter, Mrs. Blanchard, of Harvard.

Mrs. Margaret Bromfield died at Brookfield, May 3, 1761.

Henry, the eldest son of Henry and Margaret Bromfield, accompanied his father to England in 1768, where he entered into mercantile life under the supervision of his uncle Thomas, in London. After a short residence there, he returned to this country and engaged in business with his father in Boston. In the autumn of 1775 he was in Andover, to which place some of the members of the family had temporarily retired. Several letters to his father in Boston, dated at Andover, and Charlestown Ferry, accurately portray the stirring events occurring at this time. During the years 1777 and '78 Mr. Bromfield undertook a journey with a partner in business, Mr. Gibbs, going as far as the Carolinas. In October, 1787, he left the country for England, having just previously made one or more voyages to Europe in business pursuits.

Making London his home, he there married Margaret Letitia Fox. In 1812, however, leaving the metropolis, he retired to Cheltenham, where he passed the remainder of his life. The following extracts from a sermon[1] preached at his death, by his pastor, best portray his character:—

"Our object is neither to conceal defects nor to heighten excellencies, but to draw the character of our deceased friend just as it was in truth and reality."

"He had entered upon his eighty-sixth year, in the enjoyment of a much greater degree of bodily health, and mental energy, than is usually experienced at so advanced a period; but it must be remembered that he was active, temperate, and pious. He used the world as not 'abusing it.' He neglected neither the health of his body nor that of his soul; though he preferred the latter to the former. Hence he absented not himself from public worship, either morning or evening; and was as constant in his attendance on the week-day services, as on those of the Sabbath; and that, too, during the whole winter season, when his advanced age might have justified his absence. His old age, like that of the patriarch Abraham, was a *good old age;* that is, a morally good and truly happy old age; not merely living, nor what the epicure and voluptuary would style 'living while we live;" but living as God would have us live—in that rational and lawful enjoyment of the comforts and blessings of this life, which is really beneficial to ourselves and to others, and promotive of his glory."

"Our aged friend was permitted to stand till he had arrived at the richest degree of autumnal maturity, 'like as a shock of corn cometh in, in his season.'"

"His understanding was sound, and his mind had been imbued with scriptural knowledge from early youth; and after his removal from America to London, for the more convenient transaction of his commercial concerns, the means of his spiritual improvement were considerably enlarged."

[1] "The Matured Christian: a Sermon preached in Cheltenham Chapel, on Sunday Morning, February the 19th, 1837, on occasion of the lamented Death of Henry Bromfield, Esq. By the Rev. John Brown, Minister of the above Chapel. Cheltenham: 1837."

"About twenty-five years ago he withdrew from his mercantile pursuits in the metropolis, and took up his residence in this town, through the whole of which period he was in communion with us; and very grateful to your minister, was the remark of one of his most intimate friends, that during his continuance at Cheltenham Chapel, he made still further advances in the knowledge and practice of religion."

"Here we must likewise remark, that in addition to the public means of religious instruction, our friend was in the daily perusal of the sacred scriptures, which he accompanied with earnest prayer and devout meditation. Thus he had obtained a clear and comprehensive knowledge of the great truths and doctrines of Christianity, all of which were well arranged in his mind, and laid up in order, so as to be easily recalled by the memory as the occasion might require, whether for instruction, direction, or consolation. On all the essentials of religion, his mind was fully made up, so that he was never in quest of novelty. He had none of that restless Athenian curiosity, which is constantly inquiring after some *new thing*."

"His character for liberality and benevolence is well known; and that he was no bigot, the religious and charitable objects to which his bequests were made, both in the Establishment and out of it, place beyond the possibility of doubt. He was a practical Christian, humbly devoted to the benefit of man, and the glory of God."

Sarah, the second daughter of Henry and Margaret Bromfield, was a person of superior intellect and cultivation, of an extremely sensitive nature, quick perception, great refinement and delicacy of feeling, together with a warm-hearted benevolence. She was a most exemplary Christian.

She was married in October, 1785, to Eliphalet Pearson, LL.D., who was the first preceptor of Phillips Academy in Andover, which office he held eight years, when he was called to Cambridge to assume the professorship of oriental languages and English literature in Harvard University. By his distinguished learning and ceaseless efforts, Dr. Pearson essentially elevated the standard of education during his connection with the University, where he remained twenty years. He was subsequently professor of sacred literature in the Theological Seminary in Andover. Resigning all public offices, he passed the remainder of his life in quiet domestic enjoyment, for which he was peculiarly fitted by the tenderest sensibility. He was, however, actively interested in the advancement of all educational and christian schemes to the close of his life. He died Sept. 12, 1826. Mrs. Pearson died Feb. 12, 1830.

Their children were:—1. Margaret Bromfield, born Nov. 10, 1787; married May 30, 1825, Rev. I. H. T. Blanchard (H. C. 1817), who was settled as minister in Harvard, Mass., 1823. Ill health compelled him to resign in 1831. Recovering in a measure, he was settled over a small parish in South Natick, Mass., where he remained about five years. Removing to Weymouth, he passed the remainder of his days with his widowed mother. His death occurred April 9, 1845, after a life which exhibited strong fidelity in duty, and great patience in suffering. Mrs. Blanchard still lives in Harvard, beloved and respected by a very large circle of friends. 2. Edward Augustus, born July 4, 1789; died Dec. 14, 1853. 3. Abigail Bromfield, born May 17, 1793; died in infancy. 4. Henry Bromfield, born March 29, 1795; married, 1841, Elizabeth McFarland; died June 29, 1867.

(4) Sarah, born April 21, 1732; married Hon. Jeremiah Powell, of North Yarmouth; died March, 1806, aged 74. The following is from a newspaper of the day:—

"The mild and amiable disposition of Mrs. Powell, endeared her to the whole circle of her acquaintance. Her modest, affectionate and friendly behaviour was uniformly displayed, and the christian graces were always in lively exercise. Her piety was unostentatious, but it was deeply rooted, and brought forth much fruit. She lived by faith, and the hopes and promises of the gospel cheered her to the last moment of her existence and produced a calm but glorious triumph over the *king of terrors*."

(5) Thomas, born Oct. 30, 1733. Went to England, and was engaged there in mercantile pursuits during a long life. He died May, 1816, a. 83.

(6) Mary, born Oct. 7, 1736; married William Powell, of Boston; died 1786. Their daughter, Anna Dummer, born 1770, married, 1800, Thomas Perkins, and died Sept. 11, 1848, aged 78. Their children were: 1. William Powell. 2. Anna Powell, married Henry Bromfield Rogers (H. C. 1822), Sept. 12, 1832. 3. Miriam, married F. C. Loring.

(7) Elizabeth, born Nov. 5, 1739; died April, 1814, aged 75. "In the character of Miss Bromfield were united the mild virtues of meekness, patience and good will, a disposition to make others happy, and a readiness to acknowledge the kindness of friends. Her tranquil and benevolent life was guided by the rules of the gospel. This was her staff and refuge, and as it afforded support and solace by the way, it rendered death welcome and the prospect beyond infinitely desirable."

(8) John, born Jan. 6, 1743; married in Newburyport, May 3, 1770, Ann, the second daughter of Robert Roberts, a native of Wales. He died February, 1807. Mrs. Bromfield died Jan. 20, 1828. The second son of this marriage, and the fourth child, was John Bromfield, born in Newburyport, April 11, 1779. He spent his school days chiefly at Dummer Academy, Byfield, and was there fitted for college. Circumstances, however, preventing him from entering the University, he commenced a mercantile apprenticeship, and afterwards sailed as supercargo for several merchants, making voyages to Europe and to the East Indies. By this means, and by making judicious investments, and practising an exact economy, he was enabled to increase his property to such an extent as to be able to give twenty-five thousand dollars to the Boston Athenæum, an institution which his love for literary pursuits induced him to select, as worthy of his liberality, and at his death he by will distributed one hundred and ten thousand dollars among various public institutions, besides legacies to relatives. He died Dec. 8, 1849. Of his brothers, Edward was educated at Andover Academy, went on several voyages, and died on his return from Paris. Thomas died at sea. His sister, Mrs. Ann Tracy, was a person of superior intellectual powers, and highly cultivated. She died Sept. 9, 1856.

Morris, Charles. On page 462 of the Memoirs of the Wilkinson Family, published in Jacksonville, Florida, 1869, in the biography of Commodore Charles Morris, U. S. N., it is stated that his eldest son Charles fell nobly contending for the Union, during the "Great Rebellion," in Missouri. That is a mistake. His son Charles was shot in the neck while in a boat in the Tobasco river, on an expedition against Tobasco, during the Mexican war, 1846–7, and was taken to Anton Lizaillo, where he shortly after died on board the Flag-ship, from the effects of his wound.

Dr. William Bowen Morris, a son of the Commodore, is now a practising physician in Charlestown, Mass. There is another son in the Army, and Commander George, of Cumberland notoriety, in the Navy. Geo. Henry Preble.

Charlestown, Mass.

THE NEW MASONIC TEMPLE.

Prepared, at request, by John H. Sheppard, A.M.

Among the costly edifices which adorn the city of Boston is the New Masonic Temple, situated on Tremont & Boylston streets. This magnificent structure was erected by the Grand Lodge of Massachusetts, on the site of the Freemason's Hall, destroyed by fire in 1864, and was dedicated June 24, 1867, under Chas. C. Dame, Esq., Grand Master, in presence of Andrew Johnson, president of the United States, the members of his cabinet, and a large assemblage of the fraternity. So rapidly and yet thoroughly was the new temple wrought, that it seemed like the fabled Phœnix to rise from its ashes.

The first object which strikes the mind of the spectator is the splendid location and the surroundings of this fine edifice. Standing at a corner of a capacious sidewalk, where two wide and leading streets intersect each other, facing our beautiful Common, and upon a central spot of the business and travel of the public, this structure amidst the modern buildings around looms up in the architecture of a distant age.

The front on Tremont street is about 90 feet in width and 80 in height to the coping beneath the roof. The style is Gothic of the 14th and 15th centuries, modified in the ground story for commercial purposes. It is four stories to the Mansard roof which makes a fifth; and is divided into three sections: the central division is 25 feet wide, projecting a foot from the main body, the other two 33 feet.

In the projection is a porch with a lofty entrance, over which are two large windows: the first a canopied window with a sharp gable opening on a balcony, and in the third story, an arched one. The sides are supported by massive and flying buttresses, reaching to the third story, between which on each side of the door, there is a niche filled by a symbolic pillar of Winooski marble, with sculptured emblems on the capital which is surmounted by a globe. The entrance is under a grand archway, and the vestibule with a marble flooring is tastefully finished, with a panelled and arched ceiling; and through this a wide flight of stairs leads to the second story.

The window over the door in the third story is embellished with the Cross of Malta, having on each side one narrow and pointed. Rising on the left of the turret above the parapet stands a round tower, 7 feet in diameter, and 16 in height, designating the flag or watch tower of a castle in the feudal times; and on the right side there is a smaller square tower to preserve uniformity. Between these a gable extends from each tower, containing within it a rose window, terminating in a pinnacle. From the grand arch door between the buttresses to the gable tower and pinnacle, a gracefulness and grandeur of expression set off the façade in a striking manner.

At the extreme of the left division, a slender round tower, on account of symmetry, ascends to 15 or 16 feet above the coping; and at the base of the column on which it rests appears the Gate of the Temple.

At the southern corner of the right hand division, a lofty turret springs from five arches upon six round pillars of an octagon, 9 feet in diameter on the ground floor, with buttresses at the angles. This majestic turret contains a balcony with windows from the coping to the top of the roof; then a smaller one above; and from thence, gradually narrowing, tapers to a point 30 or 40 feet from the 4th story. At the base there is a door of the octagon, and also balconies with pointed windows in 2d and 3d story. The elevation of this turret so high above the whole building, with its arches, gables, finials, and niches for future statues, and adorned with rich tracery, makes it a prominent feature, unique and pleasing to the eye.

The first story contains four large arched windows and doors on each side of the entrance; that on the right opening on the Home Savings Bank. The 2d and 3d have six large pointed windows, and the fourth story twelve of narrower size; the roof has also four small pointed windows.

The façade on Boylston street is about 100 feet in length, and with the windows and decorations well comports with the front. A small projection 40 feet in width is walled up to the second story, having near the top of it four small semi-circular windows. In the third story there is one large window flanked with arched panels. The parapet is surmounted by pinnacles, and at the south-east corner a turret rises from the coping. Left of the middle section in the front story there are three large windows, and to the right of the section a door and two windows; and all those in the other stories harmonize in their construction with the front of the building.

The whole exterior exhibits a rich and picturesque model of mediæval architecture, graceful in its proportions and highly ornamented; yet it is unavoidably subjected to some deviations in the ground story, and especially by the introduction of changes and emblems peculiarly adapted to an ancient institution. Modern architecture requires many such innovations from the simple and wonderful beauty of the pure orders of antiquity; yet this simplicity should never be lost. "Denique sit, quid vis, simplex duntaxat et unum." Neither the Parthenon on the Acropolis of Athens, nor the Temple of Jupiter or Theseus, if they could rise from their ruins, could accommodate an assembly of christian worshippers; and therefore originated the Gothic style; such as the stately Trinity Church in Summer street. Yet there are some exceptions; St. Paul's Church, on Tremont street, is a beautiful specimen of the Ionic order.

The above is but a brief and meagre account. For a minute and elegant description of this building, with its gables, pinnacles, arches, finials, spandrils and tracery, the reader is referred to the "Dedication Memorial of the New Masonic Temple in Boston, by William B. Stratton," and to Moore's Freemason's Magazine, to which this brief outline owes many obligations.

The material of the exterior is white granite from Concord, N. H., which, to a stranger standing a few rods off on the Common, presents the illusion of white marble. We now proceed to the interior.

Landing on the wide corridor of the second story, you find on the left side the apartments of the Grand Master and Grand Secretary, which are frescoed, tinted and handsomely fitted up with furniture of black walnut and carpets. The secretary's room is capacious, in view of the Common, and supplied with two large and lofty book cases with glass doors, which, since the loss of the old library by fire, have been replenished by the aid of the brethren, and the indefatigable researches and liberality of Dr. Winslow Lewis, P. G. Master. He has already collected and catalogued five hundred volumes of rare and precious masonic works. On the same side are the coat-room and ante-room.

On the right side of the corridor is the reception-room, facing Tremont street, with two small rooms adjacent. East of them is the Corinthian Hall, where the Grand Lodge holds its communications and the blue lodges confer their degrees. This splendid apartment is worthy of Solomon in all his glory. It is 40 feet by 70, and 22 feet in height, adorned with columns, pedestals, modillion cornices and coved ceiling, on which is portrayed a superb pictorial centre piece, emblematical of the genius of Masonry, designed by Charles W. Moore, P. G. S., to whose taste the ornamentation of the building is much indebted. The hall is lighted by two massive chandeliers, and the furniture is of black walnut with chairs in green plush and costly Wilton carpets. A gorgeous altar, ornamented with sculptured devices of the Art, reflects the sacredness of the place; for Masonry is a religious institution. Three cunningly carved chairs on a dais, the middle one of which, ornamented with two columnar supporters, is for the grand master — three canopies with masonic designs hanging over them, above which the rising sun is delineated on the ceiling; Ionic, Doric and Corinthian pillars of a perfect order before the stations of the three first officers in the east, west, and south; the picture of the meridian sun, and the setting sun above the seats of the grand wardens; the marble statues of Faith, Hope, Charity and Wisdom, placed on pedestals in niches at the four corners of the room, a gift of Gen. William Sutton, past S. G. W.; the four columns in the west serving as an ornament to the hall and a screen before the organ; a representation of Tacita, Goddess of Silence, an emblem worthy of a conspicuous place in the halls of congress; four portraits in panels above the niches, viz.: of Washington, Warren, Lafayette and Franklin; four pictured seals, particularly that of Lord Viscount Montague, Grand Master of England, from whom, in 1733, this Grand Lodge derived its charter to Henry Price its first G. M.,— all these are among the ornaments, emblems and memorials, thus briefly grouped together in this outline of Corinthian Hall, where more than two hundred lodges are represented in the sessions as a masonic legislature.

The Egyptian Hall, which with the GOTHIC above it is of similar dimensions with the Corinthian, is in the third story. It is a picturesque piece of architecture, and allures the eye by its novelty and elaborate finish, with massy columns surmounted by bell-shaped capitals on which are sculptured the palm-leaf, the lotos, and faces of Isis. The ceiling is blue, sparkling with golden stars; from the centre of which hangs a large chandelier of forty lights. Sculptures of various objects, and emblems in the Egyptian style predominate; and two pillars in the east adorn the sides of the throne of the high priest, on which are inscribed some hieroglyphics, which, since the wonderful discovery of a key by Champollion, are found to be the letters used by the ancient priesthood of Egypt. A translation of this inscription accompanies them. The words are written in perpendicular lines,—such was the ancient Egyptian, and is the Chinese mode of writing. The inscription on these pillars is a copy from one on the obelisk of Luxor now standing in the Place de la Concord in Paris. The furniture and fittings of this hall are in character with the rest.

A bird's eye glance must suffice to look at the halls of the three commanderies—the Boston, De Molay and St. Bernard in the fourth story; the two last of which are ornate with chivalric emblems and rich furniture. But the Gothic Hall, with its arched ceiling, foliated bosses, deep mouldings and columns; its panels portraying the escutcheons of knighthood; its pictorial banners representing knights on horse-back or the cross of Palestine; and the gallant form of the last commander of the Knights Templars, Jaques de Molay, on a conspicuous panel, must awaken sublime emotions in the bosom of the beholder, who is familiar with the history of the crusades, which, Hume says, "shook all Europe to its foundations."

The Banquet Hall only remains to be noticed. It occupies the fifth story, is well arranged and furnished for the accommodations of those crowded festal gatherings consecrated to the two holy St. Johns.

Had space allowed, it would have been gratifying to have recurred to those, who gave their time, talents or credit to this great work; but their names are written not only on the records, but on the hearts of the brethren. Already we see, in Corinthian Hall, the marble busts of Charles W. Moore and William Sutton; and on the walls are hung the portraits of past Grand Masters, Winslow Lewis, John T. Heard, William Parkman and Charles C. Dame; also of past D. G. M. Marshall P. Wilder.

THE FIGHT AT DIAMOND ISLAND.

Communicated by the Rev. B. F. DeCosta, of New-York.

Standing upon one of the heights near the head or southern end of Lake George, the tourist looks down on the placid waters, and sees at his feet a little island covered with verdure, and glowing like an emerald in the summer sheen. This is Diamond Island,[1] one of the best known of the many exquisite isles that gem the little inland sea.

From time immemorial it has borne its present name, derived from the exquisite crystals with which the underlying rock abounds. Here is the scene of the fight which took place on this lake, Sept. 24, 1777, an occurrence that appears to have been purposely overlooked by the Americans at the time, and which has since failed to find a chronicler.[2]

[1] Silliman, who was here in 1819, says: "The crystals are hardly surpassed by any in the world for transparency and perfection of form. They are, as usual, the six-sided prism, and are frequently terminated at both ends by six-sided pyramids. These last, of course, must be found loose, or, at least, not adhering to any rock; those which are broken off have necessarily only one pyramid."—*Silliman's Travels*, p. 153.

[2] This affair was alluded to by the English, though the Americans said nothing. Among recent writers, I have found no notice beyond that by Lossing in his Field Book, vol. i. p. 114. When the present writer composed his work on Lake George he had not found the official account by Col. Brown.

But before proceeding to give the narrative of this event it may be well to speak of several other points, and to make a brief statement of the military situation at that time.

First comes the question of the discovery of Lake George by the Europeans. According to the best knowledge that we possess, its waters were first seen by a white man in the year 1646.[1] It is true Champlain tells us that he saw the falls at the outlet of the lake in 1609, yet there is nothing whatever to indicate that he visited the lake itself, though the Indians had informed him of its existence. It is reasonable, therefore, to conclude that Lake George was seen for the first time by a European, May 29, 1646,[2] when it received its name, "Lake Saint Sacrament," from the Rev. Isaac Jogues, S. J., who, in company with Jean Bourdon, the celebrated engineer, was on his way south to effect a treaty with the Mohawks. Arriving at the outlet of the lake on the evening of *Corpus Christi*, they gave it the above name in honor of this festival, which falls on the Thursday following Trinity Sunday, and commemorates the alleged Real Presence of Christ in the Great Sacrament.

From this time until 1755 the lake was rarely visited by Europeans. At this period the French commenced the fortifications of Ticonderoga, while the English met the advance by the construction of Fort William Henry at the opposite end of the lake.

We pass over the struggles that took place on these waters during the French wars, and come to the period of the revolution, when a feeble English garrison held possession of Ticonderoga, while Capt. Nordberg lived

[1] See *Relations des Jesuites*, 1646, p. 15.

[2] Mr. Parkman, in his work on *The Jesuits in America* (p. 219), has indeed stated that Father Jogues ascended Lake George in 1642, when, in company with Père Goupil, he was carried away a prisoner by the Indians.

The opinion of Mr. Parkman is based on a manuscript account of that journey, taken down from Father Jogues's own lips by Father Buteux. The account, after describing the journey southward and over Lake Champlain, which occupied eight days, says that they "arrived at the place where one leaves the canoes" *(où l'on quitte les canots)*, and then "marched southward three days by land," until they reached the Mohawk villages. But there is nothing whatever in the description, by which we can recognize a passage over Lake George, nothing about the portage, the falls, nor the outlet. Everything turns chiefly on the fact that they *arrived at the place where one leaves the canoes.* This place, it is assumed, was the head of Lake George, from whence there was a trail southward. Now in regard to the existence of such a trail at that period, there can be no doubt; yet unquestionably it was not the *only* trail followed by the Indians. The old French map shows two trails to the Mohawk villages, one from the head of Lake George, and the other from the South-west Bay.

It is true that Champlain, in 1609, intended to go to the Mohawk country, by Lake George, yet at the period of Jogues's captivity we have no account of any one taking that route. Father Jogues himself clearly did not cross the lake in 1646. It is distinctly said that they arrived at the end of the lake *(bout de lac)* on the eve of the Festival of *St. Sacrement*, when they named the lake, and the next day went south *on foot*, carrying their packs on their backs. This is the view given by every one who has treated the subject in print, including Mr. Parkman himself.

To this it has been answered that *bout de lac* alway means the *head* of the lake, and that the terms are so used in the Relations; yet if we return to the *Relation* of 1668 (vol. iii. p. 5), detailing the journey of Fathers Fremin, Pieron and Bruyas, we find that this is not the case. The writer there says that while he and others delayed on an island in Lake Champlain, the boatmen went forward, "landing at the *end* of the Lake *(bout de lac)* du St. Sacrement, and preparing for the portage." At this place, the north end of the lake, there is a heavy portage, in order to get around the Falls of Ticonderoga. In the next sentence he again calls this end of the lake, which is the north end or outlet, *bout de lac.* But we have also to remind the reader, that the place where Father Jogues *left his canoe*, in 1646, was at the north end of the lake (the foot), which he, like the others, calls *bout de lac.* The language is so translated by Parkman and others who have mentioned the circumstance. *Bout de lac*, in the Jesuit *Relations*, therefore does not mean the *head* of the lake. We see, then, that we have not sufficient reason for supposing that "the place where one leaves the canoes" meant the head, or south end of Lake George, and consequently that the alleged passage over the lake by Jogues, in 1642, is indefensible.

in a little cottage at the head of the lake, being the nominal command of tenantless Fort George. With the commencement of the struggle for liberty, Lake George resumed its former importance as a part of the main highway to the Canadas, and by this route our troops went northward, until the tide turned, and our own soil, in the summer of 1777, became the scene of fresh invasion. Then Burgoyne's troops poured in like a flood, and for a time swept all before them. It was at this period that the fight at Diamond Island took place.

Burgoyne had pushed with his troops, by the Whitehall route, far to the southward of Lake George, being determined to strike at Albany, having left but a small force at Ticonderoga, a handful of men at Fort George, and a garrison at Diamond Island to guard the stores accumulated there. Seeing the opportunity thus broadly presented, Gen. Lincoln, acting under the direction of Gates, resolved to make an effort to destroy Burgoyne's line of communication, and, if possible, capture his supplies. To this end, he despatched Col. John Brown with a force to attack Ticonderoga, an enterprise which, though attended with partial success, failed in the end. To this failure he subsequently added another, which resulted from the fight at Diamond Island.

But since the printed accounts of the attack upon Ticonderoga are almost as meagre as those of the struggle at the island, we will here give the official report, which is likewise to be found among the Gates Papers, now in the possession of the Historical Society of New-York, prefacing the report, however, with the English statement of Burgoyne.

In the course of a vindication of his military policy, Gen. Burgoyne writes as follows:

"During the events stated above, an attempt was made against Ticonderoga by an army assembled under Major-General Lincoln, who found means to march with a considerable corps from Huberton undiscovered, while another column of his force passed the mountains Skenesborough and Lake George, and on the morning of the 18th of September a sudden and general attack was made upon the carrying place at Lake-George, Sugar-Hill, Ticonderoga, and Mount-Independence. The sea officers commanding the armed sloop stationed to defend the carrying place, as also some of the officers commanding at the post of Sugar-Hill and at the Portage, were surprised, and a considerable part of four companies of the 53d regiment were made prisoners; a block-house, commanded by Lieutenant Lord of the 53d, was the only post on that side that had time to make use of their arms, and they made a brave defence till cannon taken from the surprised vessel was brought against them.

"After stating and lamenting so fatal a want of vigilance, I have to inform your Lordship of the satisfactory events which followed.

"The enemy having twice summoned Brigadier General Powell, and received such answer as became a gallant officer entrusted with so important a post, and having tried during the course of four days several attacks, and being repulsed in all, retreated without having done any considerable damage.

"Brigadier General Powell, from whose report to me I extract this relation, gives great commendations to the regiment of Prince Frederick, and the other troops stationed at Mount-Independence. The Brigadier also mentions with great applause the behaviour of Captain Taylor of the 21st regiment, who was accidentally there on his route to the army from the hospital, and Lieutenant Beecroft of the 24th regiment, who with the artificers in arms defended an important battery.[1]

Such is Burgoyne's account of the attack upon Ticonderoga; next to which comes that of Col. Brown, who for the second time in the course of his military experience has an opportunity of exhibiting his unquestioned valor. His report to Gen. Lincoln runs as follows:

[1] State of the Expedition from Canada. By Burgoyne. p. xciv. Ed. 1780.

"North end of lake George landing.
"thursday Sep 10th 1777

"Sir,

"With great fatigue after marching all last night I arrived at this place at the break of day, and after the best disposition of the men, I could make, immediately began the attack, and in a few minutes, carried the place. I then without any loss of time detatched a considerable part of my men to the mills, where a greater number of the enemy were posted, who also were soon made prisoners, a small number of whom having taken possession of a block house in that Vicinity were with more difficulty bro't to submission; but at the sight of a Cannon they surrendered. during this season of success, Mount Defiance also fell into our hands. I have taken possession of the old french lines at Ticonderoga, and have sent a flag demanding the surrender of Ty: and mount independence in strong and peremptory terms. I have had as yet no information of the event of Col^o. Johnsons attack on the mount. My loss of men in these several actions are not more than 3 or 4 killed and 5 wounded. the enemy's loss; is less. I find myself in possession of 293 prisoners. Viz^t 2 captains, 9 subs. 2 Commissaries. non Commissioned officers and privates 143. British 119 Canadians, 18 artificers and retook more than 100 of our men. total 293, exclusive of the prisoners retaken.—The watercraft I have taken, is 150 batteaus below the falls on lake Champlain 50 above the falls including 17 gun boats and one armed sloop. arms equal to the number of prisoners. Some ammunition and many other things which I cannot now ascertain. I must not forget to mention a few Cannon which may be of great service to us. Tho: my success has hitherto answered my most sanguine expectations, I cannot promise myself great things, the events of war being so dubious in their nature, but shall do my best to distress the enemy all in my power, having regard to my retreat—There is but a small quantity of provisions at this place which I think will necessitate my retreat in case we do not carry Ty and independence—I hope you will use your utmost endeavor to give me assistance should I need in crossing the lake &c—The enemy but a very small force at fort George. Their boats are on an island about 14 miles from this guarded by six companies, having artillery —I have much fear with respect to the prisoners, being obliged to send them under a small guard—I am well informed that considerable reinforcements is hourly expected at the lake under command of Sir John Johnson—This minute received Genl. Powals answer to my demand in these words, 'The garrison intrusted to my charge I shall defend to the last.' Indeed I have little hopes of putting him to the necessity of giving it up unless by the force under Colonel Johnson.

"I am &

"Genl Lincoln."[1]

"John Brown.

We now turn to the fight at Diamond Island, giving first the English version, simply remarking as a preliminary, that in the postscript of a letter address, by Jonas Fay to Gen. Gates, dated Bennington, Sept. 22, 1771, is the following:

"By a person just arrived from Fort George—only 30 men are at that place and 2 Gun Boats anchor'd at a distance from land and that the enemy have not more than 3 weeks provision."[2]

Writing from Albany after his surrender, Gen. Burgoyne says, under the date of Oct. 27, that

"On the 24th instant, the enemy, enabled by the capture of the gunboats and bateaux which they had made after the surprise of the sloop, to embark upon Lake George, attacked Diamond Island in two divisions.

"Captain Aubrey and two companies of the 47th regiment, had been posted at that island from the time the army passed the Hudson's River, as a better situation for the security of the stores at the south end of Lake George than Fort George, which is on the continent, and not tenable against artillery and numbers. The enemy were repulsed by Captain Aubrey with great loss, and pursued by the gunboats under his command to the east shore, where two of their principal vessels were retaken, together with all the cannon. They had just time to set fire to the other bateaux and retreated over the mountains."[3]

[1] Gates Papers, p. 194. [2] Ibid. p. 208.
[3] State of the Expedition from Canada, p, 53,

This statement was based upon the report made by Lieut. Irwine, the commander at Lake George, whose communication appears to have fallen into the hands of Gates, at the surrender of Burgoyne.

Lieut. Geo. Irwine, of the 47th, reports thus to Lieut. Francis Clark, aid-de-camp to Gen. Burgoyne:

"Fort George 24th Septr. 1777.

"Sir

"I think it necessary to acquaint you for the information of General Burgoyne, that the enemy, to the amount of two or three hundred men came from Skenesborogh to the carrying place near Tyconderoga and there took seventeen or eighteen Batteaus with Gunboats—Their design was first to attack the fort but considering they could not well accomplish it without cannon they desisted from that scheme, they were then resolved to attack Diamond Island (which Island Capt. Aubrey commands) and if they succeeded, to take this place, they began to attack the Island with cannon about 9 o'clock yesterday morning, I have the satisfaction to inform you that after a cannonading for near an hour and a half on both sides the enemy took to their retreat. Then was Gun boats sent in pursuit of them which occasioned the enemy to burn their Gun boats and Batteaus and made their escape towards Skenesborough in great confusion—we took one Gun boat from them with a twelve pounder in her and a good quantity of ammunition—we have heard there was a few kill'd and many wounded of them. There was not a man killed or hurt during the whole action of his Majesty's Troops. I have the honor to be Sir your most obedient and most humble Sert

"Geoe Irwine Com at Fort George
"Lt 47th" [1]

We now turn to the hitherto unpublished report of Col. Brown, who reports as follows, not without chagrin:

"Skeensboro Friday 11 o'clock, a m. Sept 26th 1777

"Dear Sir

"I this minute arrived at this place by the way of Fort Ann, was induced to take this rout on act of my Ignorance of the situation of every part of the continental Army——

"On the 22 inst at 4 o'clk P.M. I set sail from the north end Lake George with 20 sail of Boats three of which were armed, Viz one small sloop mounting 3 guns. and 2 British Gun Boats having on Board the whole about 420 Men officers included with a Determined resolution to attack Diamond Island which lies within 5 miles Fort George at the break of Day the next Morning, but a very heavy storm coming on prevented—I arrived Sabbath Day point abt midnight where I tarried all night, during which time I [sic] small Boat in the fleet taken the Day before coming from Fort George, conducted by one Ferry lately a sutler in our army, I put Ferry on his Parole, but in the night he found Means to escape with his Boat, and informed the Enemy of our approach, on the 23d I advanced as far as 12 Mile Island, the Wind continuing too high for an attack I suspended it untill the Morning of the 24th at 9 oclock at which Time I advanced with the 3 armed Boats in front and the other Boats, I ordered to wing to the Right and left of Island to attempt a landing if practicable, and to support the Gun Boats in case they should need assistance, I was induced to make this experiment to find the strength of the Island as also to carry it if practicable—the enemy gave me the first fire which I returned in good earnest, and advanced as nigh as I thought prudent, I soon found that the enemy had been advertised of our approach and well prepared for our reception having a great number of cannon well mounted with good Breast Works, I however approached within a small Distance giving the Enemy as hot a fire as in my Power, untill the sloop was hulled between wind and Water and obliged to toe her off and one of the boats so damaged as I was obliged to quit her in the action. I had two men killed two Mortally wounded and several others wounded in such Manner as I was obliged to leave them under the Care of the Inhabitants, who I had taken Prisoners giving them a sufficient reward for their services.

I Run my Boats up a Bay a considerable distance and burnt them with all the Baggage that was not portable—The Enemy have on Diamond Island as near as

[1] Gates Papers, p. 218.

could be collected are about three hundred, and about 40 at Fort George with orders if they are attacked to retreat to the Island—Gen[l] Borgoine has about 4 Weeks Provision with his army and no more, he is determined to cut his Road through to Albany at all events, for this I have the last authority, still I think him under a small mistake—Most of the Horses and Cattle taken at Ty and thereabouts were left in the Woods. Gen[l] Warner has put out a party in quest of them.

"I am Dear S[r] wishing you and the
"Main Army
"great Success your most ob[t]
"huml[l] Ser[t]
"Jno Brown

"Gen[l] Lincoln

"NB You may Depend on it that after the British Army were supply with six Weeks provision which was two weeks from the Communication between Lake George and Fort Edward was ordered by Gen[l] Burgoine to be stor'd and no passes given——

"The attack on the Island continued with interruption 2 Hours."[1]

Thus ended the fight of Diamond Island; a fight which, if attended with better success, might have perhaps hastened the surrender of Burgoyne, and resulted in other advantages to the American arms. As it was, however, the Britsh line of communication on Lake George was not broken, while the American leaders took good care to prevent this failure from reaching the public ear through the press. Thus Col. Brown's reports to Gen. Lincoln remained unpublished. They have now been brought out to be put on permanent record, as interesting material for American history.

To-day the summer tourist who rows out to this lovely isle, which commands delightful views of the lake far and wide, will see no evidences of the struggle, but will find the very atmosphere bathed in perfect peace. Of relics of the old wars, which for more than a hundred years caused the air to jar, and echoing hills to complain,—there are none. The ramparts that once bristled with cannon have been smoothed away, and the cellar of an ancient house is all the visitor will find among the birches to tell of the olden occupancy of man.

Scripture Names in Baptism.—The following, from the 1599 London Edition of the Geneva Bible, shows the origin of the custom of using Scripture names in baptism.

J. W. T.

"Whereas the wickednesse of time, and the blindnesse of the former age had beene such that all things together have beene abused and corrupted, so that the very right names of divers of the holy men named in the Scriptures, have beene forgotten, and now seeme strange unto us, and the names of infants, that should ever have some godly advertisements in them and should be memorials and markes of the children of God received into His household, have beene hereby also changed, and made the signes and badges of idolatry and heathenish impietie, we have now set forth this Table of the Names that be most used in the Old Testament, with their interpretations, as the Hebrew importeth, partly to call backe the godly from that abuse when they shall know the true names of the Godly Fathers and what they signific, that their children now named after them, may have testimonies by their very names, that they within that faithfull familie in all their doings had ever God before their eyes, and that they are bound by these their names to serve God from their infancie and have occasion to praise Him for His works wrought in them and their fathers."

[1] Gates Papers, p. 220.

— Page 232 (*concluded from page* 54 *in* Register). —

Sh:	4.	15.	[Suſanna] ye daughter of mr Blaney & of Sarah his [wife:	Blaney.
Sh:	4.	22.	[Katharine] ye daughter of mr Jonathan Wade, and of Deborah his wife. — — —	Wade.
Sh:	4.	29.	[John] ye ſon of mr James Ruſſell & of Mabel his wife.	Ruſſell.
	—	&	[John] ye ſon of mr Jno Jones & of Rebekah his wife.	Jones.
	—	&	[Hannah] ye daughter of Jno Call & of Hannah his [wife.	Call.
Sh:	5.	6.	[Joſhua] ye ſon of bro: John Kent, & of Hannah [his wife.	Kent.
		&	[Deborah] ye daughter of mr Giles Fifield — —	Fifield.
Sh:	5.	20.	[Nathaneel] ye ſon of mr Nath: Wade, & of Mercy his wife (i.e. ye daughter of ye Worſhipfull Simon Bradſtreet) of ye ch in Andover:	Wade.
Sh:	6:	3:	[Eliſabeth] ye daughter of Nathaneel Cutler —	Cutler.
Sh:	6:	31.	[John] ye ſon of mr Zechary Long & Sarah his wife	Long.
Sh:	7.	14.	[Rebekah] ye daughter of mrs Hannah Trerice.	Trerice.
Sh.	7:	28.	[mercy] ye daughter of Thomas Mouſal & mary his [wife:	Mouſal:

	yeer & moneth. 1673.	Day.	The Baptized. — Page 233. —	
Sh:	8.	19.	[John] ye ſon of Nathaneel Rand & of Mary his wife.	Rand.
Sh:	8.	26.	[John] | & [Henry] | & [Richard] | & [Nicholas] ye children of Henry Salter, & Hannah his wife.	Salter.[1]
Sh:	9.	2.	[Mary] ye daughter of Daniel Edmunds & of Mary [his wife.	Edmunds.·.
	—	&	[Eliſabeth] ye daughter of Zechariah Johnſon. ~~	Johnſon:
Sh:	9.	9.	[Anne] ye child of mr Hunting. of ye ch of Dedham.	Hunting.—
Sh:	9.	16	[Richard] ye ſon of Richard Taylor & of Anne his [wife.	Taylor.
	—	&	[Sarai] ye daughter of John Lowden, & Sarah his [wife.	Lowden.
Sh:	9.	23.	[John] ye ſon of John Knight, & of his wife.	Knight.
Sh:	10.	14.	[Hannah] ye daughter of Luke perkins & Hannah [his wife.	Perkins.
Sh:	10.	28.	[Hannah] ye daughter of Nathaneel Frothingham [and Mary his wife.	Frothing- [ham.
Sh:	11.	18.	[Abigail] ye daughter of John Fowl & Anna his [wife.	Fowl.
Sh:	12.	1.	[Eliſabeth] ye daughter of Edwd Wilſon & Mary [his wife.	Wilſon.
Sh:	12.	22	[Elenor] ye daughter of mr Tho: Jenner & of [Rebekah his wife.	Jenner.
		&	[Thomas] -- | & [Eliphelet | & [Dorothe] ye children of Thomas Hitt & of Dorothie his [wife.	Hitt.
		&	[Eliſabeth] ye daughter of Saml Frothingham, & of [Ruth his wife.	Frothing- [ham.
	1674:			
Sh:	1.	8.	[Elenor] ye daughter of mr W Wellsted & Mehitabel [his wife.	Wellsted.
Sh:	2.	26.	[Eliſabeth] ye daughter of mr phil: Knell & Ruth [his wife.	Knell.

[1] Salter, entry in four lines MS.

— Page 233 (*concluded*). —

Sh:	4.	28.	[Elifabeth] ye daughter of mr neh: Willoughby & [Abigail his wife	Willoughby
	—	&	[Abigail] ye daughter of mr James Elfon & Sarai [his wife.	Elfon.·.
Sh:	5.	26.	[Anna] ye daughter of mr Joseph Lynd, & of Sarai [his wife.	Lynd.

	yeer: & moneth.		The Baptized. — Page 234. —	
	1674.	day.		
Sh:	5.	26.	[Elifabeth] ye daughter of mr Timothy Symmes, & [of Elifabeth his wife.	Symmes.
	—	&	[Abigail] ye daughter of bro: Thomas Lord, & of [Alice his wife.	Lord.
	—	&	[Abigail] ye daughter of William Hurrey & of [Hannah his wife:	Hurrey.
Sh:	7.	13.	[William] ye fon of Thomas Rand & of Sarai his [wife.	Rand.
Sh:	8.	11.	[Thomas] ye fon of mr Jno Jones & of Rebekah his [wife.	Jones.
Sh:	8.	25.	[Elifabeth] ye daughter of mr Jno Chickring & of [Elifabeth his wife.	Chickring.
Sh:	9.	1.	[Jonathan] ye fon of John Fofket, & of Elifabeth [his wife.	Fofket:
Sh:	9.	15.	[Mary] ye daughter of Matthew Griffin, & Hannah [his wife.	Griffin.
Sh:	9.	22.	[Thomas] ye fon of Thomas Moufal & of Mary his [wife:	Moufal.
Sh:	i0.	20.	[Joseph] ye fon of Henry Balcom & of Elifabeth [his wife.	Balcom.
Sh:	i0.	27.	[Jofeph] ye fon of Jofiah Wood, & of Lydia his wife:	Wood.
Sh:	ii.	10.	[Solomon] ye fon of Solomon Phips & Mary his wife.	phips.
Sh:	ii.	31.	[Jofeph] ye fon of Jofeph Kettle, & of Hannah his [wife.	Kettle.
Sh:	i2.	28.	[Jofeph] ye fon of mr Henry Philips & Mary his [wife of Bofton ch.	Philips. —
	—	&	[John] ye fon of peter Frothingham & of Mary his [wife.	Frothing- [ham.

	1675. moneth	day.		
Sh:	1.	7.	[mercie] ye daughter of John Roy, & of Elifabeth [his wife.	Roy.
Sh:	1.	14.	[Mary] ye daughter of mr John Phillips & of [Katharine his wife.	Phillips.
Sh:	1.	21.	[Abigail] ye wife of mr Daniel Davifon — —	Davifon:
Sh:	1.	28.	[prudence] ye daughter of mr Tho: Ruffell & [prudence his wife.	Rufsell.
Sh:	3.	9.	[Abigail] ye daughter of John Fowl & of Anna his [wife:	Fowl.
	—	&	[John] } ye children of Alexander Steward & of Hannah his deceafed wife.	Steward.
	—	&	[Samuel] }	
	—	&	[Hannah] }	
	—	&	[Margaret] }	
Sh:	3.	23.	[John] ye fon of bro: John Dowfe & of Relief his [wife.	Dowfe.
	—	&	[William] ye fon William Brown, & of Mary his [wife.	Brown.
	—	&	[Aaron] ye fon of Aaron Way & of Mary his wife.	Way.

	yeer & moneth 1675.	day	The Bapitized. — Page 235 —	
Sh:	4.	6.	[Jſaac] ye ſon of couſ. mr John Long, & of Mary [his wife.	Long.
Sh:	5.	4.	[Edward] } ye children of John Larkin ^ & of Johanna his wife — — —	Larkin.
	—	&	[John] }	
	—	&	[Robert] }	
	—	&	[philip] ye ſon of mr philip Knill, & of Ruth his wife.	Knill
Sh:	5.	18.	[Sarah] ye daughter of mr Jno Blaney & of Sarah [his wife:	Blaney.
Sh:	6.	15.	[Benjamin] ye ſon of Samuel & Mary pierce. —	pierce.
Sh:	6.	22.	[Elias] } ye children of Elias Maverick & of Margaret his wife. —	Maverick.
	—	&	[Margaret] }	
	—	&	[Eliſabeth] }	
	—	&	[Samuel] ye ſon of Thomas Hitt, & of Dorothe his [wife.	Hitt.
Sh:	7.	12.	[Samuel] ye ſon of John Knight. — — — —	Knight.
Sh:	7:	19.	[Timothy] ye ſon of Nathaneel Cutler, & of Eliſab: [his wife.	Cutler.
Sh:	7.	26.	[Benjamin] ye ſon of ye Rd mr Samuel Whyting & of Dorcas his wife } of Billerecai.·. — — —	Whyting.
Sh:	8.	3.	[Job] ye ſon of William Brown, & of Mary his wife:	Brown.
Sh:	8.	10.	[Jacob] ye ſon of peter Fowl & Mary his wife. —	Fowl.
	—	&	[Eliſabeth] ye daughter of Timothy Cutler, & Eliſa-[beth his wife.	Cutler.
Sh:	8.	17.	[Joseph] ye ſon of John Walker & of Anna his wife.	Walker.
	—	&	[Joseph] ye ſon of John Kent & of Hannah his wife.	Kent.
Sh:	9.	14.	[Thomas] ye ſon of John Marſhall & of Mary his [wife, of Billerecai ch	Marſhall:
Sh:	9.	28.	[Jephts] ye ſon of Zechariah Johnſon & of Eliſabeth [his wife.	Johnſon.
Sh:	10.	5:	[Thomas] ye ſon of Nathaneel Frothingham & of [Mary his wife.	Frothing-[ham.
Sh:	11.	9.	[Thomas] ye ſon of mr Giles Fifield. — — —	Fifield.
		&	[Samuel] ye ſon of Samuel Frothingham & Ruth his [wife:	Frothing-[ham.
Sh:	12.	6.	[Zechariah] ye ſon of Zechariah Ferris & of [his wife.	Ferris.
Sh:	12.	13.	[Abigail] ye daughter of mr Daniel Daviſon & [Abigail his wife.	Daviſon.

	yeer: & moneth. 1675.	day.	The Baptized. — Page 236 —	
Sh:	12.	20.	[Samuel] ye ſon of Nathaneel Rand — — —	Rand.
Sh:	12:	27.	[Joſeph] ye ſon of John Lowden & of Sarah his wife.	Lowden.
		&	[Eſther] ye daughter of bro: John Call & Hannah [his wife.	Call.·.
16 mo	76. neth.	day.		
Sh:	1:	12:	[Eliſabeth] ye wife of Zechariah Johnſon. — —	Johnſon.
		&	[Johanna] ye daughter of Jno Larkin & of Johanna [his w.	Larkin.
Sh:	1:	19:	{ [Hannah] } the children of Samuel Bickner, & of Hannah his wife. — — —	Bickner.
			{ [William] }	
Sh:	1:	26.	[Zechariah] ye ſon of Edward Wier & of Eliſabeth [his wife.	Wire.

— Page 236 (*concluded*). —

		&	[Nathaneel:] } ye children of Jno Goodwin & of	
		&	[Martha:] } Martha his wife — — — — —	Goodwin.
Sh:	2.	2.	[Katharine] ye daughter of couſ. mr Zech: Symes [& Suſanna his wife.	Symmes.
		&	[Alice] ye daughter of Richard Taylor & of Anne [his wife:	Taylor
Sh:	2.	9.	[Simon] } twins: ye children of mr Nathaneel Wade & of	
		&	[Suſanna] } Mercy his wife (worſll Simō Bradstreets dtr } of Andover.	Wade.
		&	[Mary] ye daughter of Luke perkins & of Hannah [his wife.	Perkins.
		&	[Relief] ye daughter of John Dowſe, & of Relief [his wife.	Dowſe.
Sh:	2.	16:	[Edward] ye ſon of mr Will: Marſhall, & of Mary [his wife.	Marſhall.
		&	[Anna] ye daughter of Jno Walker & of Anna his [wife.	Walker.
Sh:	2.	23.	[Nathan] ye ſon of mr Nathan Heman, & of Eliſabeth [his wife.	Heman
		&	[Sarai] }	
		&	[Abigail] } ye children of Jacob Cole & of Sarai his wife. } — —	Cole.
			[Hannah] }	
Sh:	2.	30.	[Mary] } ye children of Chriſtopher Goodwin	
		&	[Hannah] } & of Mercy his wife.	Goodwin.
		&	[Thomas] ye ſon of Jno Wilder: of Lancaſter: yet not in full communion there. but only renewing [covenant.	Wilder.
Sh:	3.	7.	[Nathaneel] ye ſon of bro: Joſeph Frost & of Hannah [his wife.	Froſt.

yeer & moneth 1676		day	The Baptized. — Page 237 —	
Sh:	3.	14.	[Samuel] ye ſon of Samuel Dowſe & of Hannah his [wife.	Dowſe.
		&	[Edward] ye ſon of Moſes Newton & of Joanna his wife. of ye ch of xt in Marlburrough.	Newton.
Sh:	3.	21.	[Joſhua] }	
		&	[Robert] } ye children of Samuel Lord. & of Eliſabeth his wife.	Lord.
		&	[Eliſabeth] }	
Sh:	3.	28.	[Mary] ye daughter of Abel Benjamin, & of Amethia his wife. — — —	Benjamin.
		&	[Rachel] ye daughter of Richard Aſting, & of Abigail his wife. — — —	Aſting.
Sh:	4.	4.	[Ruth] ye daughter of Josiah Wood, & of Lydia his [wife	Wood.
Sh:	4.	11.	[Abigail] ye daughter of Iſaac Fowl & of Beriah [his wife.	Fowl.
Sh:	4.	25.	[Maud] ye daughter of mr James Ruſsell, & of [Mabel his wife.	Ruſsell.
		&	[Samuel] ye ſon of Edward Willſon, & Mary his wife.	Willſon.
Sh:	5.	9.	[Joanna] ye daughtr of mr Joſeph Lynd, & of Sarai [his wife.	Lynd.
Sh:	5.	23.	[Katharine] ye daughter of mr Tho: Tuck, & of Eliſabeth his wife: —	Tuck.
Sh:	6.	20.	[Sarai] ye daughter of mr Timothy Symmes, & of Eliſabeth his wife. — —	Symmes.

— Page 237 *(concluded)*. —

Sh:	6.	27.	[Ebenezer] y^e ſon of m^r Samuel Hunting & of Hannah his wife of ye c^h of x^t in Dedham:	Hunting.
Sh:	7.	3.	[Iſaac] y^e ſon of Iſaac Fowl, & of Beria his wife.	Fowl.
Sh:	7.	24.	[Abigail] ye daughter of Elias Maverick & of [Margaret his wife.	Maverick.
Sh:	8.	1.	[Deborah] ye daughter of Thomas Rand & of Sarai [his wife.	Rand.
Sh:	8.	8.	[Jonathan] y^e ſon of m^r Zechary Long & of Mary his wife a member of ye c^h in Newbury.	Long: —
Sh:	8.	29.	[Alice] ye daughter of Thomas Mouſal & of Mary [his wife.	Mouſal.
Sh:	9.	12.	[Sarai] ye daughter of Zechary Ferris, & of his [wife.	Ferris.
Sh:	9.	26.	[Thomas] y^e ſon of Solomon Phips & of Mary his [wife.	Phips.
Sh:	10.	31.	[Eleazer] y^e ſon of Iſaac Johnſon & of Mary his [wife.	Johnſon.
		&	[Mary] ye daughter of Iſaac Johnſon & of Mary his [wife.	

	yeer, & moneth. 1676.	day.	The Baptized: — Page 238 —	
Sh:	11.	21.	[John] y^e ſon of Abel Benjamin & of Amethia his [wife.	Benjamin.
Sh:	12.	11.	[John] y^e ſon of m^r William Wellſteed, & of [Mehetabell his wife.	Wellſteed.
Sh:	12.	18.	[Jacob] y^e ſon of Jacob Cole, & of Sarai his wife.	Cole.
Sh:	12.	25.	[Eliſabeth] ye daughter of m^r Nathan Heman & of [Eliſabeth his wife.	Heman:

16 mo	77. moneth.	day.		
Sh:	1.	18.	[Eliſabeth] ye daughter of Joseph Kettle & of [Hannah his wife.	Kettle.
Sh:	2.	1.	[Samuel] y^e ſon of Samuel Bickner & of Hannah his [wife.	Bickner.
Sh:	2.	15.	[Samuel] | & [John] | & [Stephen] | & [Thomas] | & [Jonathan] the ſons of John Foſdick	Foſdick.[1]
		&	[Mary Branſon] ye daughter in law of Jno Foſdick.	Branſon.
		&	[Anna] ye daughter of John Foſdick:	Foſdick.
		&	[Hannah] ye wife of o^r brother James Miller:	Miller.
		&	[Mary George] ye daughter of Goodwife Harbour:	George:
		&	[Nathaneel] y^e ſon of Nathaneel Davis & of Mary [his wife	Davis.
Sh:	2:	29.	[Joanna] ye daughter of m^r Daniel Daviſon & of [Abigail his wife.	Daviſon.
		&	[Iſaac] y^e ſon of Iſaac Johnſon & of Mary his wife.	Johnſon.
Sh:	3.	27.	[Anna] ye daughter of m^r Jno Blaney & of Sarah [his wife.	Blaney.
		&	[Mary] ye daughter of Aaron Way & of Mary his [wife	Way.
Sh:	4.	3.	[Katharine] ye daughter of couſ. m^r John Long & [of Mary his wife.	Long.·.
		&	[Rebekah] ye daughter of G Allen: of ye c^h of Lancaſter:	Allen:
Sh:	4.	10	[Suſanna] ye daughter of m^r Jonathan Wade, & of [Deborah his wife.	Wade.

[1] In the MS. five lines.

	yeer & moneth 1677		The Baptized: — Page 239 —	
Sh:	4.	10.	Mrs Sufanna Tompfon, ye wife of mr Benjamin [Tompfon.	Tompfon.
		&	[Abigail] } ye children of mrBenjamin Tompfon & of Sufanna his wife.	
		&	[Sufanna]	
		&	[Anna]	
		&	[Hannah] } ye children of John Baxter & of Hannah his wife. — —	Baxter.
		&	[Sarai]	
		&	[John]	
		&	[William]	
		&	[Mary]	
		&	[Elifabeth] ye daughter of Willm Vine, & of [Elifabeth his wife.	Vine.
		&	[Samuel] } ye children of Edward Counts & of Sarai his wife — — —	Counts.
		&	[Sarai]	
		&	[Elifabeth]	
Sh:	5.	1.	[Mary] ye daughter of G: Joseph Stowers.	Stowers.
		&	[John] ye fon of mr Jno Goofe & of Sarai his wife.	Goofe.
Sh:	5.	8.	[Joel] ye fon of John Whittamore & of Mary his [wife.	Whittamore
		&	[Mary] ye daughter of mr Jno Goofe, & of Sarai [his wife.	Goofe.
Sh:	5.	22.	[Hannah] ye daughter of James Miller & of Hannah [his wife.	Miller.
Sh:	6.	5.	[John George] (a young man ye fon of Goodwife [Harbour)	George.
		&	[Mary] ye wife of James Millar. — — — —	Millar.
		&	[James] | & [Mary] | & [Robert] | & [Job] | & [Abraham] | & [Ifaac] | & [Mery] | & [Jane] | } the children of James Millar & of Mary his wife.·.	Millar.[1]

	yeer & moneth. 1677.	day.	The Baptized. — Page 240 —	
Sh:	7.	2.	[Elifabeth] ye daughter of Edwd Willfon & of Mary [his wife.	Willfon.
		&	[Jacob] ye fon of peter Fowl & of Mary his wife.	Fowl.
		&	[Hannah] ye daughtr of Jofeph Froft & of Hannah [his wife.	Froft.
		&	[John] } the children of William Everton & of Sarai his wife:	Everton.
		&	[Founel]	
		&	[Samuel]	
		&	[Jofeph]	
		&	[Sarai]	
Sh:	7.	9.	[Thomas] ye fon of Thomas Larkin, & of Elifabeth [his wife.	Larkin.
		&	[John] } ye children of ye widdow Elifabeth [Dean.	Dean.
		&	[Katharine]	
Sh:	7.	16.	[Samuel] ye fon of Thomas Carter & of Efther his [wife.	Carter.
Sh:	7.	23.	[David] ye fon of mrs Katharine Anderfon.	Anderfon.
		&	[Eliezer] ye fon of John Fowl, & of Anna his wife:	Fowl.
		&	[John] ye fon of John Goodwin, & of Martha his [wife.	Goodwin.
Sh.	8.	7.	[John] ye fon of mr Jno Jones, & of Rebekah his [wife.	Jones.

[1] In the MS. eight lines.

CORRESPONDENCE RELATIVE TO "THE HISTORY OF MASSACHUSETTS BAY," BETWEEN ITS AUTHOR, GOV. THOMAS HUTCHINSON, AND REV. EZRA STILES.

Communicated by Hon. WILLIAM A. SAUNDERS, of Cambridge.

The following interesting correspondence is printed from a copy in the hand-writing of the Rev. Abiel Holmes, D.D., author of *The Annals of America.* Our readers will appreciate its value. A memoir and portrait of Gov. Hutchinson will be found in the REGISTER, vol. i. pp. 297–310. For notices of the Rev. Ezra Stiles, D.D., the Rev. Dr. Holmes and most of the other persons mentioned, see Drake's new *Dictionary of American Biography.*—J. W. D.

[THOMAS HUTCHINSON.]

Boston 15 Feb. 1764.

REV^{d}. SIR,

My good friend M^{r}. Chesebrough mentioned to me some time ago that you was employing some part of your time in a History of the Country; but whether it was a general history of the Colonies or of any one in particular, and whether your plan was large and circumstantial, or compendious and more general, he did not acquaint me. I have spent some time in a work of this nature, which I have now ready for the press, but is very much confined to the Massachusetts Bay. The other colonies which sprang from it I have touched upon to shew their rise and have there left them, except when their affairs were connected with those of Massachusetts. I have at first been more minute in the characters and other circumstances relative to our first Settlers, but afterwards have confined myself pretty much to our political history, having for some years been collecting what materials I could for this purpose. I have come down no lower than 1692, the time of our settlement under our present charter. I have a chapter upon the ecclesiastical constitution of the colony, another upon the system of laws, and conclude with an account of the natives and the condition they were in, and their customs and manners when the English first arrived. I have endeavoured for as much new matter as I could from manuscripts and such authors as are quite forgot to render a work so little interesting as this must be from the nature of it, as entertaining as possible. The whole including several original letters and other manuscripts will make a volume of near 500 pages in quarto. How far it will interfere with your design you will be able to judge. If I had known that a gentleman of your talents was engaged in a work of this nature, I should not have thought there would have been occasion for my employing myself in the same way. My materials would have been better improved in your hands than in my own. I intended to have published the work here, but as there is some probability of my going to England in a few months, I shall suspend the publication until that matter is determined. I am, with great esteem,

Sir,
Your most obedient servant
THO. HUTCHINSON.

[Ezra Stiles.]

Newport May 7, 1764.

Sir,

I wish I had as good an excuse for deferring the acknowledgment of the honor you did me in your Letter of 15th. of February last, as Selden, who for a year delayed an answer to the celebrated Vossius with the book *De Historicis Romanis*, that he might remit him the Chronological Inscriptions on the Marmora Arundelia then lately arrived from Asia. I had thought indeed to have taken the liberty of suggesting some things to your Honor, which it becomes the modesty I ought to possess, and especially the confidence due to your abilities, to suppress. You have done me an unexpected condescension in writing me a plan of your work, apprehending I was employed in the same or a like design. You do not know, sir, with how much pleasure I understood the History of the Massachusetts Bay was written by an English native of New England, a Descendant of the first accession, and a Gentleman of your eminence, but above all of your Honor's abilities—if I should not be deceived in conceiving you, like Mr. Agent *Dummer*,[1] a friend to Charter Liberties: for such an one only, in my opinion, can justly write the History of New England. It is not to be expected that an European of the present age (or until the third generation) can do justice to the history of the American Provinces, especially their Infant Plantation, the *Initia tantæ oriundæ Rei tantique futuri Imperii*, as I think Livy expresses it. This was a principal inducement to my employing the leisure of a few years past in collecting materials for a part or the whole of the British American History. But on what particular plan to form it, to what comprehension to extend it, I had not fully determined. In general I designed something, that in doing justice to my native Country might have survived the oblivion which swallows up many historical productions. My first view (whether I had stopped here or proceeded) was to write the History of New England as of one entire emigration, people and settlement, to deduce it through the civil, military, commercial, rural and ecclesiastical changes and revolutions, to the late memorable and glorious war, less glorious Peace, and I fear more inglorious loss of Charter Privileges: this, which in future History will be distinguished as the *Period of Liberty*, I purposed to have written. But I had rather been discouraged for some time before I heard your Honor was engaged in a thing of the kind—partly because I greatly doubt my possessing the true historic genius, as to perspicuity of narration, and precision of ideas in adjusting and connecting the several parts so that the whole might rise to view without intricacy or confusion; I doubted also my purity of mind and impartiality for some interesting descriptions and accounts. I was also partly and principally dissuaded from the unavoidableness of personal and provincial offences in tracing recent events to their sources, and deriving them up to the true springs of action (a thing, I presume, which has dissuaded your Honor from deducing your history [no] lower than about the Revolution). Add to this an immensity of labor, I believe too great for a feeble and slender constitution to encounter. Perhaps the most I may ever complete may be an Ecclesiastical History; and yet even this is uncertain.

You readily see, Sir, that to complete my plan of a political or civil History I must necessarily wish to see the particular histories of each of the Colonies well and amply written, and the facts sufficiently vouched and

[1] Jeremiah Dummer, author of the *Defence of the New England Charters*.—J. W. D.

authenticated for a transmission to future ages. I wish you may find inclination and leisure to resume and bring down your History of the Massachusetts beyond 1692 to the present time, at least to prepare it a posthumous work. And as the Massachusetts is the greatest part or half of New England, which collectively and in their original were very much one people, you might easily enlarge your plan to a comprehension of the four New England Governments, the *primordiæ* of all which you must have already written. In which case I will endeavor to procure you some materials for Connecticut and Rhode Island, if your Honor shall condescend to accept any assistance from me. You would thus write a complete history of an intire people, or of one intire emigration and settlement during the period of its purest liberty. Your work would review and pass down to succeeding ages with a perpetuity of honor and utility which would repay your labors. The Grecian Emigration, settled at *Syracuse*, in a century or two equalled and surpassed New England for numbers, perhaps polity, till the Age of Tyrants. We should with more pleasure read the intire History of that whole settlement at the age of 150 years, than of one principal District, or only the greater half. There is a pleasure in comprehending a whole. There are a few modern events that require purity of judgment and great delicacy, yet even these I believe would pass your pen with felicity. In the most tumultuous period, Confucius wrote the civil wars of China with success, and traced them to the invidious hereditation of provinces and principalities 500 years before, the spirit of which wrought with tumultuous efficacy in the age he lived. If you can persuade yourself to encounter the risque of a little temporary displicency, to which a faithful modern though well vouched account may be liable, we may hope you will gratify the public with 2 quarto volumes instead of one. I shall purchase your work as soon as it is printed, and promise myself great satisfaction in it. I am, may it please your Honor, with the greatest respect,

Your Honor's most obedient and very humble servant,

EZRA STILES.

Hon. Lieut. Govr. Hutchinson, Boston.

[THOMAS HUTCHINSON.]

REVEREND SIR, Boston 4 July 1764.

Your obliging letter of 7th May I did not receive until yesterday. It happened to find me at leisure, which I do not expect to last long, and therefore embrace the first opportunity of answering it. I am sorry you have conceived so favorable an opinion of my performance. I remember the old line, *Magnus mihi paratus est adversarius expectatio.* I shall certainly disappoint you in every thing but the historical facts, many of which I fancy will be new to you, and yet you will think ought to be preserved. I have let the manuscript rest for 4 or 5 months, expecting an answer to my request for leave to go to England where I intended to have printed it, but I cannot yet obtain an answer, and am in doubt what it will be when it comes. I have therefore laid aside the thoughts of my voyage if our Assembly should be disposed to renew their request to me, and shall begin to think of printing it here.

Among other original papers, which I had laid by to print at large at the end of my History, is the trial of my Ancestress.[1] It is a curious piece, and

[1] *The Examination of Mrs. Anne Hutchinson at the Court at Newtown*, November, 1637, was printed by Gov. Hutchinson as Appendix No. II. in his second volume.—J. W. D.

I would not destroy it for ten guineas; but I doubt whether it is not too minute to be favorably received by the world in general. I take the liberty to send it to you by my nephew. If you advise to it I will print; if you should think it best not to print it, I am sure it will please you to read it. The original is so defaced, that it cost me some pains to copy it. When you have convenient opportunity please to return it to me.

If God spare my life I think I shall put together other materials I have collected, and when I set about it will ask the favor of any you are possessed of, but I have had too great a share myself in our publick affairs for 30 years past to think of publishing that part of our History. I threaten M^r^. Otis[1] sometimes that I will be revenged of him after I am dead. I am,

Sir,

Your very humble servant

THO. HUTCHINSON.

[EZRA STILES.]

SIR, Newport, Jany 8, 1765.

I take this first opportunity to acknowledge the honor you have done me in sending me the volumes of your *History of the Massachusetts Colony.* You will not doubt I read it with great pleasure, though as I received it but yesterday I have but half finished the first volume. Some perhaps may think that more of the margin might have been interwoven in the body of the history. Some things I could wish you a little more copious in: and among other things I wish to see the original Instrument, if in being, of the Seacoast Partition among the Lords before the Plymouth Company surrendered their Charter 1635. I think Milford and New Haven were settled together, but neither from Hartford. The Hartford and Connecticut settlers begun their western settlement at Stratford river, and so along to Greenwich and Rye, &c. The East end of Long Island and Towns west from Stratford always sent Deputies to Hartford. The Pequots were never extinguished, as was said: to this day they subsist a distinct body of about 300 souls, but without a Sanjumman—they are little less than the Narragansetts and Mohegans, and larger than the Nihantucs. I have from New Haven Records a List of the rateable Estate of that Town about 1643, when the number of souls was 420, and the total Estate was £36,307, of which Governor Eaton possessed £3000, M^r^. Davenport £1000, and seven persons with these possessed one quarter of the whole. Guilford was a distinct Colony or Government at first, they incorporated by a civil as well as Church Covenant.

I do not know whether M^r^. Wheelwright's Sermon 1636 or 7 was ever printed.[2] I have a MS. copy, I believe in M^r^. Wheelwright's own hand writing, brought off by M^r^. John Coggeshall, and still preserved in that family. I have also a copy of the Election Sermon preached by the minister of Cambridge, I think M^r^. Shepard, when M^r^. Vane was dropped.[3]

[1] The patriot, James Otis.

[2] The famous fast-day sermon of Rev. John Wheelwright, Jan. 19, 1636-7, remained in manuscript till 1867, two hundred and thirty years after it was preached, when it was printed in the April number of Dawson's *Historical Magazine*, and in the *Proceedings of the Massachusetts Historical Society*. The article in the *Historical Magazine* was reprinted in pamphlet form.—J. W. D.

[3] This sermon was evidently that printed in the REGISTER, vol. xxiv. pp. 361-6. After the number containing this sermon was published, Hon. J. Hammond Trumbull, LL.D., of Hartford, Ct., wrote to the editor as follows:

"I was very glad to see in the REGISTER for October, Mr. Shepard's own notes of the

Your account has increased my veneration of M^r. Cotton's character. He was a Father of New England, and a kind of Numa Pompilius in Church and State. Governor Winthrop's character reviews well—had been perfect but for being too much addicted to persecution: he led this people like another Moses, and, like him, was treated ill. It is a delicate thing to hit off characters with justice. Most have their good and ill. The business of an historian is so to paint, that we may know the man and see him as he is. You have sometimes taken occasion to contrast the good and evil of character, without pointing out the result, the prevailing and ultimate complexion. Is Sir Harry Vane's memory to be honored on the whole because of what he did in 1644? After describing the blemishes, adducing a great and good action may strike with so much force as to obliterate the sense of ill, and vice versa. It is wise to speak with caution and prudence, but a Genius that discerns justly pronounces with boldness. In recent characters it is prudent, may be necessary, to leave the reader to comparisons and deductions. Endicot, Vassal, &c. are distant. A spirit of dominion secretly and covertly operated with too much strength in the Clergy, even in good M^r. Cotton, &c. and their power and influence were prodigious—the whole power of the Magistrates, as a distinct body, depended on them; and between the power of the People and that of the Clergy the Magistrates had a perpetual struggle, and sometimes were scarce firm enough. The case is now altered, since two branches of the Legislature in effect depend on the Crown.

Though you seem to show cautiousness in characters and motives, yet actions personal and public are narrated with perspicuity, and, I believe, good intelligence, justice, and impartiality—which is the most essential part of history. Pardon and forgive me, Sir, in these remarks, which, I fear, are too assuming: and accept my thanks that you have so early as in its second Century done your Country the honor to write its History; and that in a manner which will transfuse your name with glory through all the Histories and Ages of America.

I am your Honor's
most obedient and devoted servant,
EZRA STILES.

To the Hon. THOMAS HUTCHINSON, Esq.
Lieut. Governor of the Province of Massachusetts.

[THOMAS HUTCHINSON.]

REV^d. SIR, Boston 15 January 1765.

I am very much obliged to you for your favorable opinion of my book, and more so for your observations upon it. The same remark

Election Sermon of 1638. The substance of this sermon I found, some twenty years ago, among the papers of President Stiles in the Library of Yale College, 'extracted with abbreviations from an ancient MS. in the possession of the Rev. Mr. Townshend [Thompson ?] of Warren.' The 'ancient manuscript' cannot have been Shepard's own, but was probably an abstract of the sermon written out from the short hand notes of some one of his hearers. Pres. Stiles, as I have intimated, preserved only the substance of these notes, on four small quarto pages, with the caption: 'Mr. Shepard's Sermon on the Day of Election, in Boston, May 2, 1637.' Here is an error in the date, 1637 for 1638, which the given day of the month enabled me to correct. In Mr. Shepard's own notes, as appears by the publication in the Register, there is an error in the *day*. The Court of Election in 1638 was held on May 2d, not May 3rd."

The discrepancy between the date of the Court of Election and Mr. Shepard's memorandum (which is plainly 3) was noticed when the sermon was printed; but it was thought possible that the sermon might have been delivered the day after the meeting of the Court.

J. W. D.

has been made by others, which you make, of many things being brought into the Notes, which might better have come into the body of the page, and I am satisfied it is just. I am ashamed to give you the reason of this fault, but really it was to save me trouble, finding it easier to insert things which occurred to me, after I had passed by the time they related to, in this way, than by altering the page. I had, from the beginning, determined to have large notes, something in the same manner as Mr. Harris[1] has in his Life of Cromwell, &c., but I carried it too far. Indeed I wonder more fault is not found with the whole performance. I think from my beginning the work until I had compleated it, which was about twelve months, I never had time to write two sheets at a sitting without avocations by publick business, but was forced to steal a little time in the morning and evening, while I was in town, and then leave it for weeks together; so that I found it difficult to keep any plan in my mind. I have an aversion to transcribing, and except the three or four first sheets and now and then a page in which I had made some mistake, the rest of the work is rough as I first wrote it.

I find I have very improperly expressed myself as to Mr. Prudden's removal from Hartford. He came with his company from Hertford in England; but the reader will be likely to suppose I intended Hartford in America. I believe I am right as to Southold. After some time they might be included with Connecticut, but the reason given in my manuscripts for their uniting is that some of New Haven were owners of the lands at Southold, and would not sell them unless the purchasers would unite with them.

The Pequods were never considered in any public transactions as a tribe after the war with them. I did not know that any considerable number remained distinct at this day. I fancy they may with propriety enough be said to have been extinguished.

Sir Harry Vane had hard measure in 1662. Compassion might lead me to too strong an expression.

I have no talent at painting, or describing characters. I am sensible it requires great delicacy. My safest way was to avoid them and let facts speak for themselves. I was astonished after reading Robertson's History of Scotland, and having settled Mary Stewart's character in my own mind as one of the most infamous in History, to find him drawing her with scarce a blemish.

I hope you will be so good when you have gone through as to point out to me any errors. Mr. Condy[2] to whom I gave the copy, finding the book was in demand here, ordered immediately a large impression in England. I am sorry for it, because I had not opportunity enough to make several amendments, I should have chosen to have made. Care is taken of the typographical errors which are numerous, as also some inaccuracies.

I did not enough consider the present taste for anecdotes. I could have enlarged the volume, or made it large enough for two.

I am with esteem, Sir,

Your very humble servant

THO. HUTCHINSON.

Wheelwright's sermon I have. Shepard's like all others of that day I fancy would be but little relished now.

[1] Rev. William Harris, D.D., of Honiton, Eng., author of the lives of James I., Charles I., Oliver Cromwell and Hugh Peters.

[2] Jeremiah Condy. See REGISTER, xix. 254; xxiv. 114.—J. W. D.

[To be continued.]

NEW-ENGLAND HISTORIC, GENEALOGICAL SOCIETY.

Proceedings of the Annual Meeting.

The annual meeting was held at the Society's House, 18 Somerset street, Boston, on Wednesday, January 3, 1872.

The Hon. Marshall P. Wilder, the president, called the meeting to order at three o'clock in the afternoon.

The following reports were then submitted.

Report of the Librarian.

The whole number of bound volumes in the library, as reported last year, was	8653
Added during the year 1871, ...	561
Whole number of volumes at the present time,	9214
The number of pamphlets reported last year, .	26943
Added during the year 1871, ...	1172
Whole number of pamphlets at the present time,	28115

The number of bound volumes added is three hundred and thirty-two and of pamphlets three hundred and four, in excess of last year. This does not include a large collection of both books and pamphlets presented by Mr. Benjamin H. Richardson, of Boston, but which have not yet been placed upon the shelves, and are not included in the above enumeration.

A large collection belonging to the Dorchester Antiquarian Society, has been placed with the library of this society. A great number of newspapers, photographs, engravings, impressions of colonial seals, framed portraits and manuscripts have been received.

Of the volumes acknowledged above, 250 were bound volumes of newspapers, the gift of Messrs. Addison and Isaac Child, with a carefully prepared and beautifully executed index of titles, names of editors, publishers, etc., by the latter gentleman.

The bound volumes and many of the pamphlets presented, include matter of much value for the purposes for which the library was formed. A full list of donors is appended to this report.

The librarian abstains from remarks in regard to the much needed additions to the library that would promote its efficiency and tend toward a desirable completeness. In the very competent care to which it will be entrusted, these ends will receive all practicable attention.

Jas. F. Hunnewell,
Librarian.

Names of donors of books, pamphlets, etc., during the year 1871.

		Bound vols.	Pamph-lets.
Adams, Simeon P.,	Boston		1
Adams, Hon. Charles Francis,	Boston	10	
Adams, Rev. Edwin G.,	Templeton		2
Allen, Stephen M.,	Boston	1	
Almack, Richard S., F.R.S.,	London, Eng.	1	
American News Co.,	New-York, N. Y.	2	6

		Bound vols.	Pamphlets.
American Unitarian Association,	Boston	1	
Amory, Thomas C.,	Boston		1
Andrews, Gen. Samuel,	Boston		1
Antiquarian Society,	Worcester		1
Association Cong. Churches,			1
Austin, Hon. Arthur W.	Boston	1	
Baker, Amos	Boston	2	
Baldwin, Byron A.	Chicago, Ill.		1
Bancroft, J. M.,	New-York, N. Y.		1
Barrett, Hon. James,	Woodstock, Vt.		1
Bates, Mrs. J. A.,	Charlestown		25
Bicknell, Thomas W.,	Providence, R. I.	1	
Bill, Ledyard,	New-York, N. Y.	1	
Board Public Charities,	Harrisburg, Penn.	1	
Boltwood, Lucius M.,	Hartford, Ct.		1
Brewer, Prof. Fisk H.,	Chapel Hill, N. C.		1
Bright, Jonathan B.,	Waltham	1	38
Brigham, William F.,	Boston	1	1
Brooks, Rev. Charles,	Medford		1
Buffalo Historical Society,	Buffalo, N. Y.		13
Bush, Francis, Jr.,	Boston		1
Butler, Prof. James D.,	Madison, Wis.		1
Cattell, Rev. William,	Easton, Penn.		1
Caverly, Robert B.,	Lowell	1	
Chicago Historical Society,	Chicago, Ill.	2	17
Child, Messrs. Addison and Isaac,	Boston	250	
Clapp, David & Son,	Boston		2
Clarke, Robert,	Cincinnati	2	28
Clarke, Rev. Dorus, D.D.,	Boston	1	
City of Boston,		4	
City Auditor,	Boston	1	
City of Chelsea,		1	1
Colburn, Jeremiah,	Boston	7	16
Cope, Gilbert,	West Chester, Penn.	1	
Corey, D. P.,	Malden	2	
Cornell, Dr. Wm. M.,	Boston	3	62
Cutter, William R.,	Woburn	1	
Cutler, Mrs. B. C.,	Brooklyn, N. Y.	1	
Cutler, Rev. Samuel,	Hanover	9	
Dawson, Henry B.,	Morrisiania, N. Y.		1
Dean, John Ward,	Boston	3	18
Deane, Rev. J. Bathurst, F.S.A.,	Bath, Eng.	1	
De Bernardy, C. W.,	London, Eng.	1	
De Costa, Rev. B. F.,	New-York, N. Y.		1
Dixon, B. Homer,	Toronto, Canada	1	
Dorr, J. A. (Estate of),	Boston		3
Dion, J. O.,	Chambly Basin, Canada		1
Drake, Samucl G.,	Boston		13
Dudley, Dean,	Boston	1	
Duren, Elnathan F.,	Bangor, Me.		1

		Bound vols.	Pamph-lets.
Durrie, Daniel S.,	Madison, Wis.		2
Duyckinck, Evert A.,	New-York, N. Y.		1
Dwight, J. S.,	Chicago	1	
Edes, Harry H.,	Charlestown		2
Edwards, Henry,	Boston	1	
Ellis, William Smith,	London, Eng. (folios)	27	
Emery, Rev. S. H.,	Taunton		2
Essex Institute,	Salem		9
Falls, A. J.,	Washington, D. C.	1	
Futhey, J. Smith,	West Chester, Penn.	1	
Garrison, Wendell P.,	New-York, N. Y.		1
Gibbs, Prof. Wolcott,	Cambridge		1
Goodman, A. T.,	Cleveland, Ohio		5
Goodell, Abner C.,	Salem		2
Goss, Elbridge H.,	Melrose		3
Green, Dr. Samuel A.	Boston		10
Hart, Charles H.,	Philadelphia, Penn.	1	2
Handley, Rev. Isaac,	Mt. Sidney, Va.		2
Hayes, John L.,	Boston		5
Hebard, Hon. Learned,	Lebanon, Ct.		1
Hemenway, Miss Abby M.,	Ludlow, Vt.	1	
Higginson, Thomas W.,	Newport, R. I.	2	5
Hill, Clement H.,	Washington, D. C.		1
Homes, Henry A.,	Albany, N. Y.		1
Holland, Rev. Frederic W.,	Cambridge		26
Holbrook, Albert,	Providence, R. I.	1	
Hotchkiss, Frank E.,	New Haven, Ct.	4	69
Howe, Elias,	Boston		1
Hoyt, Albert H.,	Boston		2
Hoyt, David W.,	Providence, R. I.	1	
Hudson, Hon. Charles,	Lexington		1
Huntingdon, Rev. E. B.,	Stamford, Ct.	1	
Iowa State Historical Society,	Iowa City, Iowa	12	3
Jackson, Dr. Charles T.,	Boston	1	1
Jenks, George C.,	Concord, N. H.	1	
Jordan, John, Jr.,	Philadelphia, Penn.	1	
Kidder, Frederic,	Melrose		4
Kip, Rt. Rev. Wm. Ingraham, D.D.	San Francisco, Cal.		1
Latrobe, Hon. J. H. B.,	Baltimore, Md.		2
Lawrence, Wm. R.,	Longwood (Brookline)	1	29
Lewis, Dr. Winslow,	Boston		140
Lincoln, Hon. Solomon,	Boston		1
Lincoln, George,	Hingham		1
Lippincott, J. B.,	Philadelphia, Penn.	2	
Little, William,	Manchester, N. H.	1	
Mass. Horticultural Society,	Boston		1
Maryland Historical Society,	Baltimore, Md.		1
Massachusetts Historical Society,	Boston	3	
McKenzie, Rev. Alexander,	Cambridge	1	1
Meigs, Gen. M. C.,	Washington, D. C.	2	

		Bound vols.	Pamphlets.
Miles, Rev. Henry A., D.D.,	Longwood		1
Minnesota Historical Society,	St. Paul, Minnesota		1
Moore, Mrs. Mary,	Milford, N. H.	1	
Mountfort, George,	Boston		1
Mudge, Alfred & Son,	Boston	2	
New-York State Library,	Albany, N. Y.	21	
New-York Gen. and Biog. Society,	New-York		3
New-Hampshire Hist. Society,	Concord, N. H.	2	
North, James W.,	Augusta, Me.	1	
Nelson, Charles H.,	Newbern, N. C.		1
Paige, Rev. Lucius R., D.D.,	Cambridgeport		1
Paine, Nathaniel,	Worcester		6
Peirce, Gen. Ebenezer W.,	Freetown	1	
Pennsylvania Hist. Society,	Philadelphia, Penn.	1	
Perry, Rev. Wm. Stevens, D.D.,	Geneva, N. Y.		1
Pease, Richard L.,	Edgartown, Mass.		1
Pease, Austin S.,	Springfield	1	
Pearce, Stewart,	Wilkesbarre, Penn.	1	
Poor, Alfred,	Salem		68
Potter, Hon. E. R.,	Kingston, R. I.	1	7
Preble, Capt. George H., U. S. N.,	Charlestown	30	151
Public Library,	Boston		2
Public Library,	Cincinnati, Ohio	1	
Rapid Writer Association,	Mendon		1
Reed, Charles,	Bridgewater	34	119
Richardson, Jeffrey,	Boston	1	
Richardson, Hon. William A.,	Boston		10
Robb, James B.,	Boston		4
Rollins, Hon. J. R.,	Lawrence	4	
Russell, Edward,	Boston	1	1
Rhode-Island Hist. Society,	Providence, R. I.	1	
Register Club,	Boston	2	
Sandham, Alfred,	Montreal, C. E.	5	
Sawyer, F. W.,	Boston	2	
Scott, Benjamin,	London, Eng.	3	4
Sedgwick, C. F.,			1
Slafter, Rev. Edmund F.,	Boston	8	39
Sheppard, John H.,	Boston		1
Simmons, George A.,	Boston	3	
Smithsonian Institution,	Washington, D. C.	2	
Smith, Samuel,	Worcester	1	
Snow, Rev. T. W.,	Jamaica Plain	1	13
Society of Antiquaries,	London, Eng.	3	1
State of Massachusetts,	Boston	2	
Strong, Alexander,	Boston	2	
Swett, Hubbard,	South Boston	3	52
Temple, Rev. J. H.,	Framingham	2	
Thacher, Peter,	Boston	13	
Thornton, J. Wingate,	Boston	1	43
Town Clerk of Wenham,		1	

		Bound vols.	Pamphlets.
Tobey, Edward S.,	Boston	1	
Trustees Town of Melrose,			1
Trustees of Hingham Library,			1
Tuttle, Charles W.,	Boston		1
Tuttle, Rev. Dr. J. F.,	Crawfordsville, Ill.		4
Upham, Roger F.,	Worcester		1
Vermont Hist. Society,	Montpelier	1	1
Vermont State,	Montpelier	4	
Washburn, Hon. Emory,	Cambridge		1
Warren, G. Washington,	Charlestown	1	
Weisse, Mrs. Jane L.,	New-York	1	
White, Ambrose H.,	Boston	1	
Whitmore, William H.,	Boston	2	3
Wilder, Hon. Marshall P.,	Boston		1
Williams, J. F.,	Boston		3
Williams, Robert S.,	Utica, N. Y.		5
Wilbur, Asa,	Boston	1	
Winthrop, Hon. Robert C.,	Boston		7
Winchester, Caleb T.,	Middletown, Ct.		1
Wisconsin State Hist. Society,	Madison, Wis.	1	1
Woodman, Cyrus,	Cambridge		1

Ballard, Joseph,	Boston	1 file newspapers.
Black, James W.,	Boston	Photographs.
Chaplin, Charles,	Boston	1 map.
Cobb, Jonathan H.,	Dedham	Photograph.
Cutler, Rev. Samuel,	Hanover	3 maps.
Davenport, Henry,	Boston	Impression seals.
Ellery, Harrison,	Boston	Newspapers.
Gay, Eben F.,	Boston	Engrav'd plates, old tax bills.
Green, Hon. James D.,	Cambridge	Several engraved portraits.
Hall, J. B.,	Portland, Me.	Weekly newspapers.
Hotchkiss, Frank E.,	N. Haven, Ct.	2 maps.
Matchett, William F.,	Boston	Newspapers.
Sandham, Alfred,	Montreal, C. E.	Newspaper cuttings and Photographs of Montreal.
Trask, William B.,	Boston,	Photographs.
Williamson, Hon. J.,	Belfast, Me.	Newspapers.

Report of the Committee on the Library.

During the first three months of the past year the library remained in the rented rooms of the society, at No. 17 Bromfield street, where it had been during the preceding twelve years and a half, having been deposited there early in October, 1858. In the last days of March it was removed to the Society's House. The books were classified under the direction of the librarian, and such as are in more constant use were placed in the library proper, and those that are more rarely called for, together with the duplicates and the books left to the society by the late Lieut. Gov. Cushman, were placed on the shelves in the gallery of the hall. While this removal with a better classification of the books has rendered our entire collection easily accessible for the use of our members, it has also made it more obvious to your committee how many valuable and important volumes are still to be added before the library will be as full as we could desire it, even in the present stage of our progress. The departments of family and local history, if we restrict the terms to works relating to whole families and to the history of towns and cities of New-England, are nearly complete. A few additional volumes would render them entirely so.

The books in these two departments have been contributed mostly by their authors, or by persons in some way interested in the volumes themselves. There is a feeling of loyalty to historical studies on the part of most writers and publishers of local or family history, which leads them, often unsolicited, to place their productions in our library. They desire, very properly we think, that the results of their studies should be made useful to all other investigators in the same field. It is a proper and natural method of acknowledging, and in some measure of repaying the obligations which they owe, if not to this society, at least to scores of helpers in the progress of their work.

But the other departments of the library are by no means as full as the two to which we have referred. We have a limited amount of historical matter relating to nearly all of the several states of the Union. As these are mostly gifts from the friends of the society, coming from altogether independent sources, they are to a great extent miscellaneous, and do not embrace any large part of what has been written in reference to any one of the states in question. It will be obvious that an accumulation of books in this manner, while they are exceedingly valuable in themselves, and not to be spared from our collection, cannot be supposed to cover the whole subject to which they relate, since they have not been selected with that end in view. There are consequently many deficiencies in the departments which relate to the general, local, and family history of all the states of the Union. As the local and family history of New-England is closely wrought into and interwoven with that of all the other states, the importance of having, for reference, all books relating to them, cannot well be over-estimated. They are quite indispensable to the completeness of our library, as well as to the convenience of those who are making the investigations, which it is our especial aim to promote.

There is another class of books which the committee regret to say are still wanted to a large extent in the library. We refer to the extensive series of works relating to America, published in Great Britain at different periods, from the discovery of the continent down to the present time. These are far more numerous and important than the casual observer would suppose. It would be easy to specify a large number of volumes containing historical matter of the greatest importance to the investigators who frequent our library, and new ones are coming from the press every year. Some of these works, even those recently published, contain important references and original documents never before printed, throwing light upon interesting and important points in our history. These works are of peculiar and special value to us, and almost indispensable in the present stage of our progress.

On the removal of the library to the Society's House, and the arrangement of the books under more exact classification, it was found that the number of duplicates belonging to the society is not large. With the exception of Bond's Genealogies of Watertown, The Cushman Family, and a few genealogies by our late associate, the Rev. Abner Morse, the number is small. We presume that the impression has prevailed among our members and others, that duplicates were not wanted. This is by no means the case. They can always be exchanged for volumes needed, and consequently are of great value. We have made this reference in order to state distinctly that all books and pamphlets whatever, relating to localities, societies or persons connected with New-England, or throwing light in the remotest manner upon our history, will be cordially welcomed, as they will contribute essentially to enrich and enlarge the library.

The fire-proof apartment in the Society's House, constructed for the accommodation and protection of manuscripts and rare volumes, which cannot be duplicated, against the casualties and ravages of fire, has been completed. Its double walls, resting upon solid foundations, arched above and beneath with iron girders, it is believed, render it entirely safe. And your committee beg leave to state that it offers new inducements for the permanent deposit in our archives of family papers and letters, and original documents both private and public, where they may be carefully preserved for the perusal and instruction of the generations that shall come after us. It is to be hoped that those who have the custody of family or other manuscripts, will not regard them as safe in private houses, or be willing to trust them to the chances of being neglected, scattered, lost or destroyed, but will, more wisely, place them in the archives of this society, where they will be properly indexed, and arranged for the inspection and use of such persons, as at any future time, however remote, may be interested in the subjects to which they relate.

Your committee have solicited gifts to the society of historical works, by correspondence and otherwise. As the fruit of these efforts many valuable additions have been made by our members and friends, both in this country and in England. While the thanks of the society have been cordially returned to all the donors by the proper officers, it will not be regarded as inappropriate to mention here the gift of twenty-six folio volumes of great value for historical reference, by our associate, William Smith Ellis, Esq., of London, England.[1]

During the past year the Dorchester Antiquarian Society has placed its library, embracing books and pamphlets, together with a collection of engravings and other articles of antiquarian interest, in the archives of this society, and the books and pamphlets, when distributed into their proper classes, will add greatly to the richness and copiousness of our collections. As a catalogue of them has not been completed, the number of books and pamphlets amounting to several hundreds, and a more particular description of them, are necessarily deferred to our successors in office. The gift of a large number of bound volumes and pamphlets has recently been made to the society by our associate, Benjamin H. Richardson, Esq., of Boston. This collection has not yet been arranged or classified, and, as it is not included in the enumeration of books added in the librarian's report, a more definite statement touching its extent and character must likewise be referred to our successors.

As your committee is charged with the duty of increasing the library, we are happy to state that the number of bound volumes and pamphlets received during the past year is greatly in advance of the preceding year, and the historical value of the works, we believe to be, much greater. The additions have all been made as gifts, by the members and friends of the society.

The several classes of books referred to in the earlier part of this report,

[1] Donations to the library from Great Britain should be sent to Mr. W. Wesley, 28 Essex street, Strand, London, marked, "*A gift to the N. E. Historic, Genealogical Society*, 18 *Somerset street, Boston, care of the Smithsonian Institution, Washington, U. S.*"

as greatly needed, are such as will not, to any considerable extent, ever come to the library as simple donations. These deficiencies must be supplied by purchase. To meet this want there should be expended annually a sum of not less than five hundred dollars. This amount will be needed yearly in all future time, to add such volumes, relating to America, as have been and are to be published in this country and in Great Britain. The establishment of a foundation, the income of which shall be devoted to this object, is a subject which must soon occupy the attention of the society.

For the committee,

EDMUND F. SLAFTER.

REPORT OF THE COMMITTEE ON PAPERS AND ESSAYS.

During the past year nine papers were read before the society, namely:

February 1.—By the Hon. Joseph White, LL.D. on the "Derivation of the Names of some of the Towns in Massachusetts."

By Prof. John Johnston, LL.D., of the Wesleyan University at Middletown, Ct., on "Abraham Shurt and John Earthy, two prominent actors in the Early History of Maine."

March 1.—By Mr. Frederic Kidder, on "Cabot's First Voyage of Discovery to North America."

By Mr. J. Otis Williams. Subject: "A Chat with the Puritans."

April 5.—By the Rev. Elias Nason, on "The Model Town of Massachusetts."

May 3.—By Thomas C. Amory, Esq., on "Sir William Pepperrell and the Pepperrell and Sparhawk Mansions in Kittery, Me."

June 9.—By the Rev. Daniel P. Noyes, on "John Winthrop and his Influence on the Early History of Massachusetts."

September 6.—By the Rev. Increase N. Tarbox, D.D. Subject: "Reminiscence of the Stackpole House."

December 6.—By Charles W. Tuttle, Esq., on "Christopher Kilby, of Boston, agent of the Province of Massachusetts in England."

Of these papers, those by Prof. Johnston and Mr. Tuttle have been printed.

For the committee,

SAMUEL BURNHAM.

REPORT OF THE COMMITTEE ON PUBLICATION.

The only matter on which the committee were called to take official action, during the past year, was the editing, printing and distribution of the *Historical and Genealogical Register*. Four numbers, constituting the twenty-fifth volume, have been promptly issued, and the number for January, 1872, being the first number of the twenty-sixth volume, has just been published.

It must be a source of satisfaction to the surviving members of the society who were instrumental in originating this periodical, and to the several committees of publication, to witness its continued prosperity, and to realize that it has already reached an age which may justly be regarded as venerable The Register was started in order to meet a real want, and it has filled a place still unoccupied by any other publication. The chief design of its projectors was to create an organ of communication between this and other societies, and the public, and for the further and more important object of printing, and by that means of preserving a portion, at least, of the great mass of papers, records, documents, and other manuscripts relating to the early history of the people of the United States: to present, as it were, in photographic likeness and with exact fidelity the habits, customs, thoughts, words and deeds of our ancestors.

In the prosecution of this work, the successive committees of publication and editors have been greatly favored by the free-will offerings of valuable and dearly prized family-papers, and have had access to and the most liberal use of the richest collections of ancient papers and records to be found in the country. And it is worthy of note, that while the series of volumes now makes almost a library of itself, and is confessedly the most valuable historical series of the kind extant, the literary work on not one of its more than 13000 pages has ever been paid for; nor has payment ever been asked or expected.

There has not been in the past any lack of material for its pages; and though, for many years to come, we should seemingly make but little progress in the work of publishing even the most valuable portion of our ancient manuscripts, yet we hope by showing, as we already have done, the value of such material,—which too often is considered worthless and consigned to the fire or other uses,— to do not a little toward creating a general interest in its preservation.

The desire and purpose of the founders of the Register was to make it a strictly historical work; and that it should not be in any sense, or in any degree, the organ of a sect or party or clique, of any kind. This desire and purpose has been almost uniformly respected and approved. It may be that the success of the publication, and its general approval and support by our most intelligent historical students is due as much to this feature of its management as to its varied, interesting and valuable contents.

This society has never had, and has not now, any quarrels with any other society. It has no prejudices to disseminate; no jealousies to cherish; no griefs to avenge. It regards all other societies, and all candid, truthful and intelligent historical inquirers as friends and brethren; and it cordially welcomes them to a common field of investigation. It desires to ascertain the facts of our early history; to pursue its investigations with judicial calmness and impartiality; and to hold the truth in all charity, as well toward the living as the dead. In their management of the Register the committee have strenuously sought to be guided by the same spirit.

It may gratify the subscribers to the Register to learn that its circulation is steadily extending, and, if we may judge from the numerous testimonials which come to hand, that it is now regarded, both abroad and at home, with no less favor than it has been at any former period. This result is owing in part to a plan, recently adopted by the committee, of procuring contributions upon historical subjects of general interest. Many of these papers are very valuable, and have commanded the attention both of the general reading-public and of critical students of American history.

In the volume just closed, besides a great mass of miscellaneous papers of more or less interest and value, will be found genealogies, or genealogical notes, of the Allen, Appleton, Baldwin, Bird, Bromfield, Bowne, Browne, Coffin, Deane, Foster, Gardner, LeBaron, Leffingwell, Lucas, Mosely, Neill, Sargent, Weir, Winslow, Vassall and other families; memoirs and portraits of Gov. William Plumer, William Pitt Fessenden, David Reed and Lucius Manlius Sargent; the discourse delivered by Mr. Charles H. Bell at the dedication of the Society's House on the 18th of March, 1871; Mr. Thomas C. Amory's paper entitled Old Cambridge and New; Mr. William C. Fowler's paper on Local Law in Massachusetts Historically Considered; Capt. Geo. Henry Preble's articles on Early Ship-building in New-England; Mr. Charles Hudson's very complete lists of the colonial soldiers engaged in the Louisbourg Expedition, in 1745; and other articles of scarcely less merit; all of which cost their authors much time and labor.

In the number just issued from the press will be found articles of interest to persons and families both in and out of New-England; such as sketches of the Oxnard Family by Mr. E. S. Moseley, and of the Bromfield Family by Dr. D. D. Slade; genealogies of the Winslow Family by the Rev. Dr. Paige, of the Page Family by Dr. William Prescott, and of the Lee Family of Virginia; an article on Christopher Kilby, by Mr. C. W. Tuttle; poems of the Rev. Michael Wigglesworth; continuations of Capt. Preble's paper on Early Ship-building in Massachusetts, of the Record-book of the First Church in Charlestown, Mass., by Mr. James F. Hunnewell, and of Mr. Fowler's article on Local Law in Massachusetts; a memoir of Gov. Oliver Wolcott, Sen., written by his son Gov. Oliver Wolcott, Jr.; and other papers of value.

The portrait, accompanying the sketch of the late Mr. Benjamin P. Richardson, furnished by his family, and the other illustrations in the same number contributed by Mr. Moseley and Mr. Hunnewell, respectively, exceeded in cost the sum of $225.

Hitherto no systematic plan has been used in extending the circulation of the Register. It is now proposed to make an effort in that direction, and at a recent meeting of the Register club it was voted to recommend to the society to appoint a committee for that purpose. The members of the society, each subscriber to the Register, and all who may read this report are earnestly invited to aid the committee in procuring subscribers. We desire to double our list of subscribers, and to use the income that may thus be obtained in enlarging and otherwise improving the Register.

It would seem desirable that all the publications of the society, and all circulars issued and blank forms used by the different officers of the society in their official capacity, should pass through the hands of some one committee before they are printed, so as to secure a reasonable degree of uniformity. To this end it is recommended to the society to direct the committee on publication to prepare such forms as may be needed from time to time and supervise the printing of the same, and of all the publications of the society.

For the committee,

ALBERT H. HOYT.

REPORT OF THE CORRESPONDING SECRETARY.

Besides the more strictly official correspondence of the year, which has just closed, numerous letters have been received relating to historical questions, and to the interests of the society; some of them conveying valuable information on subjects of interest and importance. Such as were of more general interest have been read at the monthly meetings of the society. Replies have been sent to all communications requiring answers, and, as far as possible, with the information desired. Letters accepting membership from one hundred and three gentlemen have been received and placed on file. Three corresponding, and one hundred resident members have been added to the society during the year; a list of their names is herewith submitted.

Corresponding Members added in 1871.

The Rt. Rev. William-Ingraham Kip, D.D., San Francisco, Cal.
James-Ross Snowden, A.M., Philadelphia, Pa.

Resident Members added in 1871.

Edward-Livingston Adams, Watertown, Mass.
Oakes Ames, North-Easton, Mass.
Samuel Atherton, Boston, Mass.
Walter-Titus Avery, A.B., New-York, N. Y.
Edmund-James Baker, Boston, Mass.
Elisha Bassett, Boston, Mass.
William-Carver Bates, Newton, Mass.
Frank-Forbes Battles, Lowell, Mass.
James-H. Beal, Boston, Mass.
Francis-Everett Blake, Boston, Mass
The Hon. Charles Bradley, Providence, R. I.
John-Miner Brodhead, Washington, D. C.
David-Henry Brown, A.B., Boston, Mass.
Alexander-Claxton Cary, Boston, Mass.
Ebenezer Clapp, Boston, Mass.
The Rev. George-Faber Clark, Mendon, Mass.
William-Smith Clark, A.M., Ph.D., Amherst, Mass.
Benjamin-Pierce Cheney, Boston, Mass.
Edward-Russell Cogswell, A.M., M.D., Cambridgeport, Mass.
James-Cogswell Converse, Southborough, Mass.
James-Wheaton Converse, West-Newton, Mass.
Albert-Forster Damon, Philadelphia, Pa.
Daniel-Edwin Damon, Plymouth, Mass.
Ebenezer Dale, Boston, Mass.
The Hon. John-Calvin Dodge, A.B., Boston, Mass.
The Rev. Jonathan Edwards, A.M., Dedham, Mass.
Warren Fisher, Jr., Boston, Mass.
John-Smith Fogg, South-Weymouth, Mass.
Herman Foster, Manchester, N. H.
Alfred Fawcett, Chelsea, Mass.
Marcus-Davis Gilman, Auburndale, Mass.
William-Taylor Glidden, Boston, Mass.
Henry-Augustus Gowing, Boston, Mass.
Andrew-Townsend Hall, Boston, Mass.
Leonard-Bond Harrington, Salem, Mass.
Ezra Hawkes, Chelsea, Mass.
Charles-Amasa Hewins, West-Roxbury, Mass.
Horatio-Hollis Hunnewell, Boston, Mass.
Franklin Hunt, Boston, Mass.
James-F.-C. Hyde, Newton-Centre, Mass.
Francis-Marshall Johnson, Newton-Centre, Mass.
Frederick Jones, Boston, Mass.
Josiah-Moore Jones, Boston, Mass.
Leonard-Augustus Jones, A.B. LL.B., Boston, Mass.
The Hon. Elbridge-Gerry Kelley, Newburyport, Mass.
James-Reynolds Knott, Boston, Mass.
Franklin King, Boston, Mass.

William-Richards Lawrence, M.D., Brookline, Mass.
George-Thomas Littlefield, Charlestown, Mass.
John-Staples Locke, Boston, Mass.
John-Emery Lyon, Boston, Mass.
George-Henry Martin, Bridgewater, Mass.
Jonathan Mason, Boston, Mass.
Frederick-Warren-Goddard May, Boston, Mass.
The Rev. Alexander McKenzie, A.M., Cambridge, Mass.
Charles Merriam, Boston, Mass.
Thomas Minns, Boston, Mass.
Levi-Parsons Morton, New-York, N. Y.
Edward-Strong Moseley, A.M., Newburyport, Mass.
Enoch-Reddington Mudge, Boston, Mass.
Lyman Nichols, Boston, Mass.
Charles-Edward Noyes, Jamaica Plain, Mass.
Prof. Edwards-Amasa Park, D.D., Andover, Mass.
Samuel-Russell Payson, Boston, Mass.
Avery Plummer, Boston, Mass.
John-Alfred Poor, A.M., Portland, Me.
Jonathan Preston, Boston, Mass.
William-Gibbons Preston, Boston, Mass.
The Rev. George Punchard, A.M., Boston, Mass.
Benjamin-Heber Richardson, Boston, Mass.
Nathan Robbins, Arlington, Mass.
Royal-Elisha Robbins, Boston, Mass.
John-Prentice Rogers, Boston, Mass.
Oliver-Webster Rogers, Woburn, Mass.
James-Edward Root, Boston, Mass.
Stephen-Preston Ruggles, Boston, Mass.
Edward Russell, Boston, Mass.
Daniel-Waldo Salisbury, Boston, Mass.
The Hon. George-Partridge Sanger, A.M., Cambridge, Mass.
Benjamin Shreve, Salem, Mass.
Clinton-Warrington Stanley, A.B., Manchester, Mass.
Daniel-Baxter Stedman, Boston, Mass.
Alexander Strong, Boston, Mass.
Joseph-Teel Swan, Boston, Mass.
Cyrus-Henry Taggard, Boston, Mass.
John-Gallison Tappan, Boston, Mass.
Rear Admiral Henry-Knox Thatcher, U. S. N., Winchester, Mass.
George-Newton Thomson, M.D., Boston, Mass.
William-Cleaves Todd, A.B., Boston, Mass.
Henry-Elmer Townsend, M.D., Boston, Mass.
Joseph-Warren Tucker, Boston, Mass.
Nathaniel-Wing Turner, West-Newton, Mass.
Supply-Clap Thwing, Boston, Mass.
Jonathan Towne, Milford, N. H.
The Rev. Alexander-Hamilton Vinton, D.D., Boston, Mass.
Moses-Conant Warren, Brookline, Mass.
Charles-Cotesworth-Pinckney Waterman, Sandwich, Mass.
Ambrose-Haskell White, Boston, Mass.
Eben Wright, Boston, Mass.
John-Stratton Wright, Boston, Mass.

Early in the year blanks were sent to our corresponding members asking for personal information, and many of them have been, and it is hoped that all of them will soon be returned amply filled out. As the information desired consists of facts and statistics which are simple matters of history, there cannot properly be any breach of delicacy or anything self-eulogistic in giving them on account of their personal character. The memoirs prepared by this society of its deceased members are intended to be strictly accurate and true to the facts of history. They will prove to be eminently so, if the information asked of our members is full and specific. The statements, which are made by them, are the foundation on which the personal narratives of their life and character will be constructed, and they will comprise the principal material of a biographical dictionary of the members of the society, which it is intended to publish at a future day. It is therefore important that the personal information should be given with as much accuracy and fulness as possible.

The corresponding secretary begs to state that blanks will be furnished to any members who may desire to add to the information which they have already given, and when returned to him they will be filed or bound in volumes, properly indexed and preserved in the archives of the society.

EDMUND F. SLAFTER,
Corresponding Secretary.

REPORT OF THE HISTORIOGRAPHER.

The historiographer has prepared and read before the society during the year 1871 memorial sketches of the following named members:

Winthrop Sargent, A.M., who died May 18, 1870, aged 44 years.
Gen. Asa Howland, who died June 24, 1870, aged 82 years.
Mr. Benjamin-Parker Richardson, who died Nov. 7, 1870, aged 68 years.
The Rev. Ebenezer Burgess, D.D., who died Dec. 5, 1870, aged 80 years.
Mr. James Read, who died Dec. 24, 1870, aged 81 years.
The Hon. Buckingham Smith, who died January 5, 1871, aged 60 years.
The Hon. David Sears, A.M., who died January 14, 1871, aged 83 years.
The Hon. Oliver-Bliss Morris, A.M., who died April 6, 1871, aged 89 years.
Mr. Elmer Townsend, who died April 13, 1871, aged 64 years.
Mr. Henry-Oxnard Preble, who died May 24, 1871, aged 24 years.
The Rev. Henry-Longueville Mansel, B.D., who died July 13, 1871, aged 50 years.
The Rev. Joseph Richardson, A.M., who died Sept. 25, 1871, aged 93 years.

The assistant historiographer, Charles W. Tuttle, Esq., has prepared and read during the year 1871, memorial sketches of the following named members:

Col. James-Warren Sever, A.M., who died January 16, 1871, aged 73 years.
Mr. Charles-Henry Woodwell, who died January 31, 1871, aged 42 years.
The Rev. Romeo Elton, D.D., who died Feb. 5, 1871, aged 79 years.
Joseph Palmer, M.D., who died March 3, 1871, aged 74 years.
Mr. William-Reed Deane, who died June 16, 1871, aged 61 years.
The Hon. John-Alfred Poor, A.M., who died Sept. 5, 1871, aged 63 years.

The number of members whose decease, during the past year, has come to the knowledge of the society, is twenty. This, considering the present large membership, is a very favorable exhibit, and calls for special gratitude to the Preserver of our days, for our "times are in His hands."

The following is the necrology for the year:—

Necrology for 1871.

The figures on the left indicate the date of admission to the society.

1863. The Hon. Buckingham Smith, of New York, N. Y., born Oct. 31, 1810; died January 5, 1871.

1846. The Hon. David Sears, A.M., of Boston, Mass., born Oct. 8, 1787; died Jan. 14, 1871.

1869. Col. James-Warren Sever, A.M., of Boston, Mass., born July 1, 1797; died January 16, 1871.

1867. Mr. Charles-Henry Woodwell, of Worcester, Mass., born March 18, 1828; died January 31, 1871.

1845. Samuel-Holden Parsons, A.M., of Middletown, Conn., born Aug. 11, 1800; died Feb. 23, 1871.

1852. Joseph Palmer, M.D., of Boston, Mass., born Oct. 3, 1796; died March 3, 1871.

1846. The Hon. Oliver-Bliss Morris, A.M., of Springfield, Mass., born Sept. 22, 1782; died April 9, 1871.

1868. Mr. Elmer Townsend, of Boston, Mass., born March 3, 1807; died April 13, 1871.

1857. Mr. And Emerson, of Boston, Mass., born Feb. 3, 1803; died May 3, 1871.

1870. Mr. Henry-Oxnard Preble, of Charlestown, Mass., born Jan. 4, 1847; died May 24, 1871.

1845. Mr. William-Reed Deane, of Mansfield, Mass., born Aug. 21, 1809; died June 16, 1871.

1859. The Rev. Henry-Longueville Mansel, B.D., of London, England, born Oct. 6, 1820; died July 31, 1871.

1871. The Hon. John-Alfred Poor, A.M., of Portland, Me., born Jan. 8, 1808; died Sept. 5, 1871.

1855. The Hon. William-Saxton Morton, A.M., of Quincy, Mass., born Sept. 22, 1809; died Sept. 21, 1871.

1857. The Rev. Joseph Richardson, A.M., of Hingham, Mass., born Feb. 1, 1778; died Sept. 25, 1871.

1846. Gen. Guy-Mannering Fessenden, of Warren, R. I., born March 30, 1804; died Nov. 3, 1871.

1853. Mr. Nathaniel Whiting, of Watertown, Mass., born —— —, 1802; died Nov. 18, 1871.

1859. Joseph-Green Cogswell, LL.D., of Cambridge, Mass., born Sept. 27, 1786; died Nov. 26, 1871.

1871. Mr. Ebenezer Dale, of Boston, Mass., born April 2, 1812; died Dec. 3, 1871.

1858. Henry-Theodore Tuckerman, A.M., of New-York, N. Y., born April 20, 1813; died Dec. 17, 1871.

Dorus Clarke,
Historiographer.

Report of the Treasurer.

The total income derived in 1871 from annual assessments, admission fees, the income of the life-fund, including a balance of $32.80 from the account for 1870, amounts to $1688.82, and the ordinary expenses have been $1634.70; leaving a balance in the treasury of $54.12. During the same period, the sum of $1090 has been received for life-memberships, and in accordance with the by-laws of the society added to the life-fund.

B. B. Torrey,
Treasurer.

Life-Members.

The following named members constituted themselves life-members in 1871.

Mr. Samuel Adams, Milton, Massachusetts.
Mr. Samuel Atherton, Boston, Massachusetts.
The Hon. Oakes Ames, North Easton, Massachusetts.
The Hon. Roger Averill, Danbury, Connecticut.
Mr. Walter-Titus Avery, A.B., New-York, New-York.
Mr. Elisha Bassett, Boston, Massachusetts.
Mr. James-H. Beal, Boston, Massachusetts.
Mr. Austin-Williams Benton, Brookline, Massachusetts.
Mr. Benjamin-Peirce Cheney, Boston, Massachusetts.
Mr. Ethan-Nelson Coburn, Charlestown, Massachusetts.
Mr. James-Wheaton Converse, West Newton, Massachusetts.
Mr. Deloraine-Pendre Corey, Malden, Massachusetts.
The Rev. David-Quinby Cushman, Bath, Maine.
*Mr. Ebenezer Dale, Boston, Massachusetts.
Mr. George Daniels, Milford, New-Hampshire.
Mr. Alfred Fawcett, Chelsea, Massachusetts.
Mr. Warren Fisher, Jr., Boston, Massachusetts.
Mr. John-Smith Fogg, South Weymouth, Massachusetts.
Mr. William-Taylor Glidden, Boston, Massachusetts.
The Hon. William Greene, East Greenwich, Rhode Island.
Mr. Andrew-Townsend Hall, Boston, Massachusetts.
The Hon. Hiland Hall, LL.D., North Bennington, Vermont.
Mr. Leonard-Bond Harrington, Salem, Massachusetts.
Mr. Ezra Hawkes, Chelsea, Massachusetts.
Mr. Horatio-Hollis Hunnewell, Boston, Massachusetts.
Mr. Francis-Marshall Johnson, Newton Centre, Massachusetts.
Mr. Frederick Jones, Boston, Massachusetts.
Mr. Josiah-Moore Jones, Boston, Massachusetts.
Mr. Franklin King, Boston, Massachusetts.
Mr. Williams Latham, Bridgewater, Massachusetts.
The Hon. Solomon Lincoln, A.M., Boston, Massachusetts.
Mr. John-Emery Lyon, Boston, Massachusetts.
The Hon. Silas-Nelson Martin, Wilmington, North Carolina.
Mr. Charles Merriam, Boston, Massachusetts.
Mr. Levi-Parsons Morton, New-York, New-York.
*Mr. William-Saxton Morton, Quincy, Massachusetts.
Edward-Strong Moseley, A.M., Newburyport, Massachusetts.
The Hon. Enoch-Reddington Mudge, Boston, Massachusetts.
Gen. Josiah Newhall, Lynnfield, Massachusetts.

Mr. Lyman Nichols, Boston, Massachusetts.
The Rev. David-Temple Packard, A.M., Brighton, Massachusetts.
Mr. John-Wells Parker, Boston, Massachusetts.
Francis Parkman, LL.B., Boston, Massachusetts.
The Rev. Albert-Clarke Patterson, A.M., Buffalo, New-York.
Mr. Samuel-Ruggles Payson, Boston, Massachusetts.
The Hon. Asahel Peck, Montpelier, Vermont.
Mr. Avery Plumer, Boston, Massachusetts.
The Hon. Jonathan Preston, Massachusetts.
Mr. William-Gibbons Preston, Boston, Massachusetts.
Mr. Nathan Robbins, Arlington, Massachusetts.
Mr. Royal-Elisha Robbins, Boston, Massachusetts.
Mr. Stephen-Preston Ruggles, Boston, Massachusetts.
Mr. Edward Russell, Boston, Massachusetts.
Mr. Benjamin Shreve, Boston, Massachusetts.
Mr. Daniel-Baxter Stedman, Boston, Massachusetts.
Mr. Alexander Strong, Boston, Massachusetts.
Mr. John-Gallison Tappan, Boston, Massachusetts.
Mr. Edwin Thompson, Charlestown, Massachusetts.
Mr. James-Brown Thornton, Scarborough, Maine.
Mr. Supply-Clap Thwing, Boston, Massachusetts.
William-Cleaves Todd, A.B., Boston, Massachusetts.
Mr. Nathaniel-Wing Turner, West Newton, Massachusetts.
The Hon. Amasa Walker, LL.D., North Brookfield, Massachusetts.
The Rev. Joshua-Wyman Wellman, D.D., Newton, Massachusetts.
Mr. Eben Wright, Boston, Massachusetts.
Mr. John-Stratton Wright, Boston, Massachusetts.

Report on the Bond Fund.

Dr. Henry Bond, of Philadelphia, left a testamentary gift to this society of about 800 copies, in sheets, of his work entitled "Genealogies and History of Watertown," together with certain manuscripts.

At a meeting of the society held July 6th, 1859, a board of trustees consisting of three persons, was appointed to manage this bequest, under the following restrictions.

It was ordered "that it shall be the duty of said trustees to prepare the unbound copies of Bond's Genealogies and History of Watertown for sale, and to dispose of them from time to time as they may think best;—that after paying the necessary charges, the money received shall be faithfully invested by them for the benefit of the society, and that they shall report to the society the condition of the funds and the property at the annual meetings."

It was also ordered "that the money so invested shall be called the Bond Fund, the principal of which shall always remain intact; and the annual income shall be disposed of in the manner following, viz.:—not less than one-eighth of said income shall be annually added to the principal of the fund, and the remainder shall be expended in the purchase of local histories and genealogies, reserving however a sufficient amount to bind and preserve the manuscripts left us by Dr. Bond."

The sale of books has been slow, but a certain number of copies has been disposed of yearly, and the fund has been constantly increasing. Five copies have been sold during the last year, for the sum of $25.

At the present time we have $250, in government bonds, and a balance in the hands of the trustees of $79.07.

It will be seen that all the moneys accruing from the sale of books, are required to be invested, and that one-eighth of the interest on said investments must be annually added to the principal. Seven-eighths of the interest on the principal may be expended in the purchase of books. In this way the amount of the fund is constantly increasing, and when our books are all disposed of, it will amount to a very important sum. We may now expend about fifteen dollars yearly, from this source, for the purchase of books.

For the trustees,

ALMON D. HODGES.

REPORT ON THE BARSTOW FUND.

This fund was founded by a gift of $1000 to the society in 1860, 1862, and 1863, by the late John Barstow, Esq., of Providence, R. I., then a vice-president of the society for that state, the income of which is devoted to the binding of books. From the income of the past year forty-five volumes have been bound, leaving a balance of $68.07.

For the trustees,

WM. B. TOWNE.

REPORT ON THE TOWNE MEMORIAL FUND.

This fund was founded by a gift of $1000, Jan. 1, 1864, from Wm. B. Towne, Esq., then of Brookline, in this commonwealth, but now of Milford, N. H., which sum was to be placed in the hands of trustees, the principal and the interest to be kept separate and apart from the other funds of the society, and the income thereof to be devoted to the publication of memorial volumes of deceased members, whenever the society should deem it expedient. In the year 1870 the founder added another $1000, subject to the same conditions. The income has been permitted to accumulate, and the fund now amounts to $2861.68. A memorial volume has been commenced, but not completed.

For the trustees,

CHARLES B. HALL.

REPORT OF THE BUILDING COMMITTEE.

As the object for which your committee was appointed has not been entirely consummated, they are not able to make a full report. They would however state that the work is substantially completed, with the exception of procuring and inserting the mural tablet, and fitting the audience-room for the reception of books. When the committee entered upon their duties they did not contemplate fitting this room for such use, for some years; but in view of the activity that prevails in the society, and the work that is expected to be accomplished at an early day, they recommend that this be done immediately.

The amount of subscriptions thus far received is $42,575.00; and the amount paid for the purchase of the estate, alterations, repairs and furniture, $42,438.63.

Certain subscriptions were made with the understanding that they were not to be paid till the commencement of this year. When these are received there will be ample means for completing the duty assigned to the committee; and perhaps a small balance as a nucleus for a publication fund.

For the committee,

WILLIAM B. TOWNE.

Portrait of the late Treasurer of the Society.

The committee appointed, at the last annual meeting, to procure a portrait of William B. Towne, Esq., as a testimonial on his retirement after a service of ten years as treasurer, report that they have performed the duty assigned to them, and herewith present a life-like likeness, executed by Mr. Adna Tenney.

Long may this memorial continue to adorn these walls, and perpetuate a grateful remembrance of our associate's ardent devotion and faithful service to the society.

Marshall P. Wilder,
Edmund F. Slafter,
Henry Edwards.

The Sears Medals.

At the request of the president, Charles W. Tuttle, Esq., secretary of the board of directors, reported, that at the stated meeting of the board, held January 2, 1872, a sealed box inscribed to the "President and Officers of the Historic, Genealogical Society, Boston, 1854," left in the custody of the society at that date, by the late Hon. David Sears, with directions that it be opened after his decease, was unsealed in presence of the directors. It contained eighty bronze medals; also, a sealed package on which is written: "To be delivered to the eldest lineal male descendant of David Sears and Ann Winthrop Sears in 1954."

Only two of the packages, which are seven in number, were opened. The medals in these two packages, with a single exception to which I will presently refer, were alike.

On the *obverse* of the medal is a monument surmounted by a crest, whose main feature is an open helmet with the hilt of a dagger on its right. On the left stands an American Indian, with his right hand resting on the monument, with a bow in his left hand, a tomahawk slung at his side, and several arrows on his back, the ends visible above the left shoulder. On the right is a figure in mail, with the left hand resting on the monument, a sword at his side, holding a shield in his right hand charged with armorial bearings.

On the monument is this inscription: SCEARSTAN SAYER SEARS COLCHESTER Over the whole is a scroll on which is inscribed, ST PETERS CHURCH In the exergue is H. DE LONGUEIL.

On the *reverse*, the field is left blank, while between a beaded circle and the extreme edge, is this circumscription: DESCENDED FROM RICHARD SEARS THE PILGRIM. * PLYMOUTH ROCK 1630.*

The exception, to which reference has been made, is a medal enclosed in a wrapper, inscribed "Model. Richard Sears of Chatham, . . . reverse engraving." This medal is from the same die as the others, but the following inscription has been cut on the blank field of the reverse:

RICHARD SEARS OF CHATHAM SON OF DANIEL II OF CHATHAM BORN 1750 MARRIED MEHITABLE MARSHALL DIED 1839 IN LINEAL DESCENT FROM KNYVET OF YARMOUTH ELDEST SON OF THE PILGRIM

In a case of the same size as the package to be delivered in 1954, are two medals having the same obverse as that already described, but the reverse is from a different die. One of them has the same circumscription as that before described, with the following in the field:—

DAVID SEARS I OF BOSTON SON OF DANIEL II OF CHATHAM BORN 1752 MARRIED ANN WINTHROP DIED 1816 IN LINEAL DESCENT FROM KNYVET OF YARMOUTH ELDEST SON OF THE PILGRIM

The other medal has in the field a shield on which are various quarterings of arms which we need not describe. On a circular band surrounding it is this inscription: EXALTAT HUMILES On a scroll beneath is HONOR ET FIDES The whole is surmounted by an eagle. The medal has this circumscription: PLY. COL. 1630 BOS. MASS. 1770

A paper fastened to the inside of the lid of the box, has the following written on it:—"Monumental Memorials, Bronze Medals. To be given by the President of the Historic, Genealogical Society to the members of the Sears Family. Any individual of the name of Sears applying for a medal, must prove his descent from Knyvet, Paul or Sylas Sears, the three sons of Richard Sears the Pilgrim, and must promise to have engraved on the reverse the inscription ordered by the President."

"Richard Sears landed at Plymouth on the 8th of May, 1630."

After the reading of the foregoing reports, Mr. Frederic Kidder, in behalf of the committee appointed at a previous meeting to nominate the officers of the society for the current year, submitted a report. A ballot was taken, and the gentlemen nominated for the respective offices were declared duly elected, as follows:

PRESIDENT.

The Hon. MARSHALL P. WILDER, of Boston.

VICE-PRESIDENTS.

The Hon. GEORGE BRUCE UPTON, of Boston .	Massachusetts.
The Hon. ISRAEL WASHBURN, Jr., of Portland . .	Maine.
The Hon. IRA PERLEY, LL.D., of Concord . .	New-Hampshire.
The Hon. HAMPDEN CUTTS, A.M., of Brattleboro' .	Vermont.
The Hon. JOHN RUSSELL BARTLETT, A.M., of Providence	Rhode-Island.
The Hon. WILLIAM A. BUCKINGHAM, LL.D., of Norwich	Connecticut.

HONORARY VICE-PRESIDENTS.

The Hon. MILLARD FILLMORE, LL.D., of Buffalo .	New-York.
The Hon. JOHN WENTWORTH, LL.D., of Chicago .	Illinois.
The Rt. Rev. HENRY W. LEE, D.D., LL.D., of Davenport	Iowa.
The Hon. INCREASE A. LAPHAM, LL.D., of Milwaukee	Wisconsin.
The Hon. GEORGE P. FISHER, of Washington .	Dis. of Col.
SALOMAN ALOFSEN, Esq., of Jersey City . . .	New-Jersey.
The Hon. JOHN H. B. LATROBE, of Baltimore .	Maryland.
WILLIAM DUANE, Esq., of Philadelphia . . .	Pennsylvania.
The Rev. WILLIAM G. ELIOT, D.D., LL.D., of St. Louis	Missouri.
The Rev. JOSEPH F. TUTTLE, D.D., of Crawfordsville	Indiana.
The Hon. THOMAS SPOONER, of Reading . . .	Ohio.

CORRESPONDING SECRETARY.

The Rev. EDMUND F. SLAFTER, A.M., of Boston . Massachusetts.

RECORDING SECRETARY.

SAMUEL HIDDEN WENTWORTH, A.M., of Boston . Massachusetts.

TREASURER.

Mr. BENJAMIN BARSTOW TORREY, of Boston . Massachusetts.

HISTORIOGRAPHER.

The Rev. DORUS CLARKE, D.D., of Boston .	Massachusetts.

ASSISTANT HISTORIOGRAPHERS.

CHARLES W. TUTTLE, A.M., of Boston . . .	Massachusetts.
JOHN WARD DEAN, A.M., of Boston . . .	Massachusetts.

LIBRARIAN.

JOHN WARD DEAN, A.M., of Boston . . .	Massachusetts.

DIRECTORS.

The Hon. GEORGE BRUCE UPTON, of Boston .	Massachusetts.
The Hon. EDWARD S. TOBEY, A.M., of Boston . .	Massachusetts.
CHARLES W. TUTTLE, A.M., of Boston . . .	Massachusetts.
Mr. JOHN CUMMINGS, of Woburn	Massachusetts.
Mr. JOHN FOSTER, of Boston	Massachusetts.

COMMITTEE ON PUBLICATION.

ALBERT H. HOYT, A.M., of Boston	Massachusetts.
JOHN WARD DEAN, A.M., of Boston . . .	Massachusetts.
WILLIAM H. WHITMORE, A.M., of Boston . .	Massachusetts.
WILLIAM S. APPLETON, A.M., of Boston . .	Massachusetts.
WILLIAM B. TOWNE, Esq., of Milford . . .	New-Hampshire.

COMMITTEE ON THE LIBRARY.

Mr. JAMES F. HUNNEWELL, of Charlestown . .	Massachusetts.
JEREMIAH COLBURN, A.M., of Boston . . .	Massachusetts.
The Rev. EDMUND F. SLAFTER, A.M., of Boston .	Massachusetts.
Mr. HARRY HERBERT EDES, of Charlestown . .	Massachusetts.
Mr. DELORAINE P. COREY, of Malden . . .	Massachusetts.

COMMITTEE ON PAPERS AND ESSAYS.

Mr. FREDERIC KIDDER, of Boston . . .	Massachusetts.
SAMUEL BURNHAM, A.M., of Boston	Massachusetts.
The Rev. INCREASE N. TARBOX, D.D., of Boston .	Massachusetts.
WILLIAM S. GARDNER, Esq., of Boston . . .	Massachusetts.
DAVID GREENE HASKINS, Jr., Esq., of Cambridge	Massachusetts.

COMMITTEE ON HERALDRY.

WILLIAM H. WHITMORE, A.M., of Boston . .	Massachusetts.
ABNER C. GOODELL, Jr., A.M., of Salem . . .	Massachusetts.
AUGUSTUS T. PERKINS, A.M., of Boston . .	Massachusetts.
WILLIAM S. APPLETON, A.M., of Boston . .	Massachusetts.

COMMITTEE ON FINANCE.

WILLIAM B. TOWNE, Esq., of Milford . . .	New-Hampshire.
Mr. HENRY EDWARDS, of Boston	Massachusetts.
The Hon. CHARLES B. HALL, of Boston . .	Massachusetts.
Mr. PERCIVAL LOWELL EVERETT, of Boston . .	Massachusetts.
The Hon. JOHN A. BUTTRICK, of Lowell . .	Massachusetts.

After the election of officers the president addressed the society, as follows:

Gentlemen of the Society:

I thank you for your kindness which has again called me to this chair. When I accepted the presidency of this institution four years since, it was at the urgent solicitation of personal friends, but with no expectation or desire to hold it save for a brief season, and until the breach made by the sudden decease of your lamented president, Gov. Andrew, could be filled by a person more competent than myself for the discharge of its duties. I appreciate most highly this renewed testimony of your confidence as well as the honor which it confers, yet I am fully aware that this distinction is bestowed, not on account of any merit which I possess as an historian, but rather as a token of your appreciation of my efforts to promote the usefulness of the society, and to aid in establishing, with pecuniary means, its various departments on a more sure and permanent basis.

In my former addresses I alluded to certain measures as necessary to the progress and well-being of the society. The first and most important of these was the erection of a suitable edifice for its accommodation. This has been accomplished, and as anticipated in my last address, the Society's House was dedicated to the interests of New-England history by formal and appropriate services on the 18th day of March, being the anniversary of the incorporation of the society. On that occasion the Honorable Charles H. Bell, of New-Hampshire, our associate member, delivered a discourse replete with interesting suggestions in relation to the future of American history. This has since been published in the pages of the New-England Historical and Genealogical Register, and will soon be issued also in pamphlet form. But, what is especially grateful to our feelings, as you have heard by the report of the building committee, our house has been paid for by the generous contributions of our own members, and stands today as a free-will offering without any encumbrance whatever. Here let it stand for many years to come, as an honorable memorial of the munificence of those who aided in its erection.

By the reports which have been submitted, it will be seen that the strictest economy has been observed in all the departments, and that the services of all the officers and committees have been performed without compensation. Nor would I fail here to record the fact that the supervision and direction of the New-England Historical and Genealogical Register has been rendered for many years without pay, and in a manner to redound to the honor of its editor and his associates. The Register has been published regularly and is increasing in interest and patronage. The ability with which it is conducted is generally acknowledged and most gratefully appreciated. Its volumes have contributed largely to promote the objects and to extend the influence of the society, and are justly esteemed by other societies both at home and in foreign lands.

Soon after the public opening of our house the library was transferred to its proper department, and the books suitably classified. Since that time no member of the society has found any difficulty, as in former years, in obtaining all the aid in his historical investigations which the bound volumes belonging to the society could furnish. The library has been under the supervision of our associate, Mr. James F. Hunnewell, as librarian. Mr. Hunnewell kindly consented to accept this office for one year at some personal inconvenience, and now declines a reëlection on account of the pressure of his business. Most heartily do I rejoice with you in the election of a gentleman to fill his place who has long been identified with the society, and who is in all respects qualified to discharge the duties of the office.

The Society's House, in all its appointments, is eminently adapted to the purposes of the institution, and meets with universal approbation. We may, therefore, regard the attainment of this solid structure, so convenient in its arrangement and so tasteful in its architecture and finish, as marking an important stage or crisis in our progress. But, when I say that this marks a stage in our progress, I mean distinctly to announce that we cannot stop here. We have not yet achieved all that is to be desired. Other steps are to be taken before our enterprise will be crowned with success.

Our first great want has been supplied. Our next is a permanent curator, under the official title of librarian,—a man of generous, scholarly culture, and familiar with the whole range of New-England history,—who shall devote his whole time to the interests of the society, in the arrangement and cataloguing of our books, pamphlets and manuscripts, and in such ways as shall promote the growth and improvement of the library. Fortunately we possess this officer in our new librarian, and it only remains for us to secure the means for his support. This is not a new subject; it has been upon my mind for several years. I have long seen that an officer possessing these high qualifications, wholly consecrated to the service of the society, and generously paid, would be indispensably necessary to our well-being and future success. I alluded to this subject in the remarks I had the honor to submit last year. I then said, "if we accomplish all we hope to in the future, it will be necessary to have connected and unbroken, intellectual and scholarly labors in the general superintendence of the institution, which we cannot ask and which we cannot obtain from the occasional attention which gentlemen engrossed with any important business can render. The services of a person of culture, learning, and capacity for the higher duties to which I have referred, cannot be obtained without a suitable salary; and I make these remarks in order to call your attention to the importance of increasing our fund so as to provide for this exigency in the future."

And allow me to repeat with emphasis what I said then. I regard this as the great and crowning want of the institution. I cannot see how we can make any permanent or satisfactory progress without such an officer. With this acquisition a new impulse will be given to our purposes and our work; and I doubt not that, in a reasonable time, not only every bound volume in the library will be made accessible, but our twenty-eight thousand pamphlets will be properly classified, and the subjects treated by them will be so fully known that any one of them could be brought forward for examination without any loss of time; and our manuscripts will be so disposed and indexed that they can all be made useful to the historical student.

There is another relation in which such an officer as I have described will be of great importance, not only to the members of the society, but to all who visit the library for the investigation of the local or family history of New-England. It will often happen, as it has in the past, that the investigator will come to us in the early stages of his work, when he is in a large degree uninformed as to the sources, and sometimes as to the character of the information to which his researches should be directed. The suggestions of a competent librarian would in such a case be invaluable. And, while it should not be his duty to make investigations for members, or others who are permitted to use the library, he could so fully point out and lay open the sources of information, without occupying too much of his time, as greatly to facilitate their labors.

And here permit me to say another word on the importance of preserving, arranging and classifying our collection of pamphlets and manuscripts. I regard this as one of the most imperative duties of all historical and genealogical societies. No institution with which I am acquainted has bestowed sufficient care on this subject. Something has been done, but not enough. The collecting of pamphlets without providing for their preservation, and arrangement for use, is but of little advantage to historical study. Without this, they are quite as accessible in the possession of individuals or families, as in public repositories; because, when stored away in masses, they are no better than so much waste-paper.

Ordination, funeral, and election sermons, centennial discourses, Fourth of July orations, and speeches at public celebrations are full of historical matter. A fact can sometimes be found in them which may be sought for elsewhere in vain. The spirit of the times is reflected in them. The tone of thought, the sentiments, the principles of the contemporary age are to be found in them. Not all, not any one, perhaps, is of the highest value in all respects; but all in a greater or less degree furnish facts, thoughts and sentiments which are the natural growth and illustration of the progress of the age.

With these considerations, I never think of our large collection of pamphlets but I feel a great desire that they should be arranged, classified and catalogued, without which they are inaccessible, and are of little benefit to the cause of history. Bound volumes of history, biography, and travels, are easily seen and distinguished on the shelves of a library. Pamphlets in bundles not arranged, not catalogued, are utterly useless. But when carefully classified they constitute a rich source of historical information.

I am aware than when a society or an individual obtains the possession of an old, rare pamphlet it is regarded as a very important feat accomplished; but, when a collection of such pamphlets is made, the first duty is to take care of them, so as to render their use easy, and hence valuable to the student. While I thus speak, I acknowledge the great improvement in the building in which our valuable library is located, and also the greater safety of our collections, stored in our fire-proof apartment. But, in my opinion, our imperative duty, is to look to our pamphlets as soon as the means of doing so can be obtained. They are invaluable and, if arranged as I have suggested, will of themselves constitute a valuable collection to which students will resort for information in all the departments of history and biography. A catalogue of these and of our books cannot much longer be dispensed with. It would be a key to our treasures, and would place it in the power of the humblest inquirer to make himself acquainted with an immense number of facts of which he had been ignorant; and at the same time open an inexhaustible source from which he may enlarge his historical acquisitions,—a collection of the richest treasures, which are now like pearls buried in the depths of the ocean.

For these reasons, gentlemen, and for others which will doubtless occur to your minds, I trust we shall soon secure a fund, the income of which shall enable us to meet the expenses of the librarian's salary, and to accomplish such other objects as are necessary to the success and prosperity of the society.

Permit me to call your attention to another object, viz.: the adoption of such measures as will add to the interest and value of the papers to be read at our monthly meetings. As this is a New-England society, it is important that every part of New-England should be represented both by the authors and in the subjects of the papers brought before us. The most important historical questions, which are appropriately discussed before this society, are local in their character; therefore the investigation of the facts which relate to them must be made in the locality where the events transpired. Hence if we aim to illustrate the history of the whole of New-England, we must have writers and investigators of the facts from every part of it, historical scholars, whose residence in the locality of which they treat has enabled them to carry on their investigations from original sources and public records for years, and from which they can bring to us things literally new and old. We should have papers read here by residents of Maine, New-Hampshire, Vermont, Rhode Island, Connecticut and the remoter parts of this commonwealth. Even were it convenient to obtain papers from month to month from gentlemen in the city of Boston, or its immediate vicinity, it would by no means achieve the object we desire to accomplish. We must therefore extend broader invitations and secure the services of our members, and other historical scholars, who reside at a distance. In doing this we have not the means to meet the necessary expenses, which surely ought not to be incurred by those who prepare the papers in question. A permanent fund, yielding two or three hundred dollars, would enable us to pay all expenses incurred by the journey of our guests, and to procure papers of rare interest and great value from students of New-England history, far and near. I earnestly hope we shall be able to secure this object during the present year.

The society is now advancing on the second quarter of a century since its incorporation. It is firmly established and is constantly extending its field of operations. It is working harmoniously with kindred associations, both in this and other countries, and it is receiving the aid and sympathy of numerous friends.

In reviewing the work of the society, I am satisfied that our present plan of operations is judicious and good. And now that we are permanently located in a house of our own, and have secured the services of a librarian whose time will be devoted wholly to our work, I feel that no change is necessary except the further acquisition of funds to secure the continued prosperity of the society.

To accomplish this most desirable object, I recommend the appointment of a special committee for the purpose of soliciting the means of establishing a fund, the income of which may be devoted to the payment of the librarian's salary and other expenses not prospectively provided for. The importance and duty of sustaining our society in a flourishing condition needs no further argument from me.

But, when I reflect on the influence of New-England principles and New-England examples in the cause of freedom, civilization, and humanity, and in whatever tends to the comfort, happiness, and advancement of the human race, I am deeply impressed with a sense of the obligation which rests on us to preserve and transmit their history unimpaired, which so clearly redounds to their honor and the welfare of mankind. Our society was organized for this special purpose; but, as I have often addressed you on this topic, I shall not tax your patience by enlarging upon it at the present time.

No branch of human research can have a more salutary influence on the mind than the study of New-England history; and, next to the training of the spirit for the life eternal, I know of no more noble employment than that of treasuring up and perpetuating the deeds, principles, and virtues of a noble ancestry. Like the cheering rays of the morning, they have pierced the darkest portions of the earth; they have lit up the paths of Christian civilization around the globe; they will illume the broad highway of the future with beams of hallowed light; and their teachings will forever constitute the true means of maintaining free governments, individual rights, and the highest happiness of mankind. Day by day, and step by step, their principles are revolutionizing the empires of the earth; and, as time advances, they will be more and more appreciated for their wisdom and virtue. These principles will live forever to bless the world; and will continue to march on in triumph toward that grand millennial era, when the governments of this world shall form one great circle of free republics, and when peace on earth and good-will to men shall prevail. Let us, then, recover all that is great and good from the history of the past, and let us also treasure up all that is valuable and of good-report in the present. He that would not do this can have but little reverence for his ancestry, home, or country, and but little interest in the welfare of those who are to follow him. Well did Burke remark: "People who do not look back to their ancestry will not look forward to their posterity." How imperatively does the Bible enforce this injunction on all generations of men: "Hear this, ye old men, and give ear, all ye inhabitants of the land. Tell ye your children of it, and let your children tell their children, and their children another generation."

Gentlemen: I congratulate you on the increasing prosperity and usefulness of our society, and the cheering prospects before us. Let these excite us to renewed diligence, and let us labor with greater zeal for the promotion of its objects. Let us be active while our day lasts. Soon, he who now occupies this chair and all those who now surround him will have passed from time into eternity. But our institution will survive, and millions of grateful hearts shall rise up and bless the memory of the men who laid its foundations and labored for its advancement.

May the society continue to be more and more appreciated for its labors and usefulness. May it receive the sympathy and favor of the public, and the generous munificence of noble-hearted men; and go on prospering until the final day, when the histories of this earth and of our race shall be transferred to the great record above, eternal in the heavens.

On the conclusion of the president's address, the Rev. Edmund F. Slafter offered the following resolution, which was adopted:

Resolved, That a special committee, consisting of the following gentlemen, viz.: the Hon. Marshall P. Wilder, Wm. B. Towne, Esq., the Hon. George B. Upton, John Cummings, Esq., and John Foster, Esq., be appointed to solicit subscriptions to establish a fund, the income of which to be appropriated to the payment of the salary of a librarian, and to such other purposes as may be necessary for the efficiency and prosperity of the society.

William B. Towne, Esq., offered the following resolution, which was adopted:

Resolved, That the thanks of the society be tendered to Mr. James F. Hunnewell for his services as librarian during the past year.

On motion of Col. Albert H. Hoyt, the following named members were appointed a special committee, for the purpose of extending the circulation of the New-England Historical and Genealogical Register, viz.: Mr. Deloraine P. Corey, Capt. Geo. Henry Preble, U.S.N., Charles W. Tuttle, Esq., and Mr. Harry H. Edes.

On motion of Mr. Harry H. Edes, it was

Voted, That the president's address and the reports submitted at this meeting, together with the record of the other proceedings, be referred to the standing committee on publication, with authority to prepare for the press and print one thousand copies of the same, for distribution among the members.

THE FAMILY OF RALPH SMYTH, OF HINGHAM, MASS.

Communicated by THOMAS SMYTH, of Boston.

THE early settlers of the present town of Hingham, Mass., were mostly from Hingham, County of Norfolk, Eng., and Cushing in his statement of those early settlers, mentions RALPH, as coming "from Old Hingham," in 1633, and against the name Cushing puts the figure (1), clearly indicating that he came alone. His name first appears upon the Hingham records in 1637, when he drew a house lot on "Bachelor street," now Main street. The colony records call him "Ralph Smyth," and as late as Sept. 22, 1652, the probate records for Suffolk Co. say "Ralph Smyth," "of Hingham." (N. E. HIST. AND GEN. REGISTER, vol. viii. p. 61.)

He was of Eastham, in the Plymouth colony, in 1657, in which year he took the "oath of fidelity." See Plymouth Colony Records, Lib. 8, folio 184. The name is here and ever after on the Records, "Smith." Was constable of Eastham in 1660, and in 1664, was trading with "Josias Hubbert, of Hingham."

Volume 6, folio 175, Plymouth Colony Records, has the following "court order." Oct. 27, 1685.—"Administration is granted by this court to Grace Smith, the relict of Ralph Smith, and Samuell Smith, son to the s^d^ Ralph Smith, all of the town of Eastham, in the colony of New-Plymouth, in New-England, deceased, on all the goods and chattells of s^d^ Ralph Smith."

The record of the marriage of Ralph, is not to be found, and the indications are that Grace was not the mother of his children. Hobart, in his diary of Hingham affairs, gives valuable information concerning this family; viz.:

2. i. SAMUEL Smith, bap. July 11, 1641.
3. ii. JOHN, son of Ralph Smith, bap. July 23, 1644.
4. iii. DANIEL Smith, bap. March 2, 1647.

There can be but little doubt that Thomas, of Eastham, who in 1690, June 24, took at Barnstable, "ye oath of a freeman," was also a son of Ralph, but having made very careful examination and finding no documentary proof of the same, we omit a record of his family, simply stating for the benefit of any person that may be interested, that his eldest son, Ralph, was born in Eastham, Oct. 23, 1682, and Thomas, Jan. 16, 1687, also at Eastham; this last settled in Truro, from whom come, Gamaliel 1715, Barzilla 1717, Gamaliel 1744, Gamaliel 1772, Barzilla 1775, and numerous others, the family being highly respectable and influential in the affairs of Truro for many years.

2. SAMUEL[2] (*Ralph*[1]), baptized in Hingham, July 11, 1641, married in Eastham, Jan. 3, 1667, Mary, daughter of Gyles Hopkins, who

came over with his father Stephen in the Mayflower, 1620; was a trader; died at Eastham, March 20, 1696. Children:—

5. i. SAMUEL, b. May 26, 1668; d. Sept. 22, 1692.
ii. MARY, b. June 3, 1669; m. Daniel Hamilton.
iii. JOSEPH, b. April 10, 1671.
6. iv. JOHN, b. May 26, 1673.
v. GRACE, b. Sept. 5, 1676. vi. DEBORAH, b. Dec. 10, 1678.

This Samuel's estate was settled April 22, 1697, by order of the probate court of Barnstable Co. Joseph, Grace and Deborah, not mentioned. John had "ye half of two farms at Monomoy," and Mary had "ye half of two farms at Monomoy, with her brother John." Lib. 2, folio 47. Estate, Real and Personal, £1,275.12.9.

3. JOHN[2] (*Ralph*[1]), baptized in Hingham, July 23, 1644; married in Eastham, May 24, 1667, Hannah, daughter of Thomas Williams, who was of Plymouth in 1637. He there married Elizabeth Tate, Nov. 30, 1638, and died in Yarmouth about 1692. In his will, dated May 10, 1692, he gives to

7. i. "JOHN SMITH, my grand child, a lot of meadow land in Eastham."

The date of the birth of the last named John, cannot be ascertained, and if there were other children, the record is so uncertain that it is not safe to follow.

4. DANIEL[2] (*Ralph*[1]), baptized in Hingham, March 2, 1647; married in Eastham, May 3, 1676, Mary, daughter of John Young. Children:

i. DANIEL, b. Jan. 8, 1678. (Eastham Records.)
ii. CONTENT, b. June 8, 1680. " "
iii. ABIGAIL, b. April 30, 1683. " "
iv. JAMES, b. April —, 1685. " "
v. NATHANIEL, b. Oct. —, 1687. " "
vi. MARY, b. Jan. 8, 1692. " "

Will of Daniel Smith, Sen., of Eastham, dated May 11, 1716, entered on probate Jan. 20, 1720 (Probate, Lib. 3, folio 63), mentions: wife Mary; children, Daniel, James, Abigail, Content Howes, and Nathaniel, who received "the homestead," and was appointed administrator.

5. SAMUEL[3] (*Samuel,*[2] *Ralph*[1]), born in Eastham, May 26, 1668, and married Bathshuba Lathrop, May 26, 1690. Children:

8. i. SAMUEL, b. Feb. 13, 1691. 9. ii. JOSEPH, b. Oct. 9, 1692.

They had, in the distribution of their grandfather Smith's estate in 1697, equal shares with their uncle and aunt, as follows: "Samuel Smith, and Joseph Smith, issue of said eldest son Samuel, shall have to them or their heirs forever, a farm at Monomoy, that "Cahoon lives on." (Lib. 2, f. 59.)

6. JOHN[3] (*Samuel,*[2] *Ralph*[1]), born in Eastham, May 26, 1673, and married there, May 14, 1694, Bethiah Snow, daughter of Stephen, a brother of Mark, sons of Nicholas, who married Constance, daughter of Stephen Hopkins the Pilgrim. The mother of Bethiah was Susanna Deane, daughter of Stephen and Elizabeth Deane, early of Plymouth. The widow Deane married Josias Cook, and soon after they removed to Eastham. John and Bethiah had Samuel, born in Eastham, May 21, 1696. For the rest of the family, we refer to the probate court files (M. Bourn, judge of probate), Lib. 5, folio 204. "Now it appears to me, that when s[d] John Smith deceased, he left surviving, six sons; viz., Sam[l] ye Eldest, Deane, John, Stephen, David and

Seth, and Three Daughters: viz., Mercy, Mary, and Bethiah." "S[d] Dean Smith is Since Deceased, leaving four children; viz., Dean, Heman, Aseph, sons, and Merriam a daughter." The date of this settlement is July 31, 1734. The guardians of the minor children of John and Bethiah, were appointed in July, 1722, and Samuel, the eldest son, appointed administrator, Feb. 25, 1717. Bethiah had not married in 1734; she is then mentioned as "the widow and Relict of ye said John Smith, deceased." The article on the "Deane Family" in the *N. E. Hist. and Gen. Register*, vol. 3, p. 378, has a detailed account of the line of that family from which Bethiah descended. See also, *Register*, vol. 18, p. 266. The will of Miriam Wing, widow of John Wing, Jr., of Harwich, dated May 24, 1701, and proved Jan. 8, 1702–3, gives all her property to Dean Smith, "son of my Kinswoman, Bethiah Smith, of Monomoy." Thus in the absence of a record of the births of the children on the town books, we ascertain their names by combining other documents.

Lib. 5, folio 204. "An account of Debts Due from estate of Jn° Smith, Late of Chatham, Deceased, and paid out by Samuel Smith, Administrator; viz.,

Paid to Saml. Sturgis, Esq.,	29	1	7
paid to madam Reliance Stone,	08	9	6
paid to Mr. John Mayo,	02	11	10
Sett out to the Widow,	54	15	0
P. Mr. Nath'l Stone,	4	0	0
P. Constable Thomas Nickerson,	02	1	4
P. Madam Elizabeth Greenleaf,	0	14	10
P. Daniel Hamleton,	1	1	0
P. ye Commissioners for Interest money,	23	2	6
Sett out to my mother,	4	1	6
Dean Smith, time and expense,	0	10	0
P. to myself for expense and time as administrator,	3	15	0
Money due unto the Bank,	102	10	0

Allowed by the Court July 19, 1722,
The total amt. al'd £254 10 0."

Cattle mark assigned to Samuel Smith, March 23, 1716; to Dean Smith, Feb. 5, 1721, by vote of the town of Chatham.

We can connect of these sons only Dean and Seth, with any of the numerous family of this name in Chatham or Harwich.

10. i. DEAN. 11. ii. SETH.

In the year 1715, "Elisha Hedge, John Smith, son and heir to Samuel Smith, late of Eastham, deceased, David Meloit, and Hugh Stuart, of Monomoy, alias Chatham," presented a petition to the "General Court," asking "that lands purchased of the Indians, John and Josephus Quason, in 1694, called Monomoy Beach, with some pieces of meadow, &c., may be confirmed to them."

7. JOHN[3] *(John,[2] Ralph[1])*. The Eastham town records show this family as follows, viz.: children of John and Sarah Smith:—

	i.	HANNAH,	born	March 18, 1695.
	ii.	JOSEPH,	"	Dec. 28, 1697.
	iii.	SARAH,	"	Nov. 6, 1699.
	iv.	WILLIAM,	"	Sept. 8, 1702.
	v.	LYDIA,	"	April 24, 1704.
12.	vi.	SETH,	"	Jan. 28, 1705.
	vii.	ELEAZER,	"	Mar. —, 1708.
	viii.	REBECCA,	"	May —, 1709.
	ix.	JOHN,	"	Mar. 13, 1712.

His will, dated Dec. 1, 1742, and entered Lib. 6, folio 250, mentions son Joseph to whom he gave land "on the southerly side of the cedar swamp in "Little Skatett," and my tenement lot in Rock Harbor neck and all my land at the Harbour's mouth neck." "Also my carpenters tools." Joseph, administrator. "I give and bequeath to my son Williams Smith, the land that I possessed him of heretofore." "I give and bequeath to my son Seth Smith, the one half of the upland of my homestead," and after describing the same, and several other lots of land, he gave him "a lot of meadow, which I had of my Grandfather Williams." "To my son John Smith" all and singular my tenement homestead, wherein I do dwell," but reserves "the West room and Buttery" for his "loving wife Bethiah."

The conditions upon which the above bequests are made, are that the three sons, Joseph, Seth and John, shall maintain "my daughter Hannah Smith in sickness and in health during her natural life," and furnish certain named articles, such as wood, hay, corn, wheat, &c. "to my loving wife Bethiah Smith," "To my daughter Elizabeth Brown," "To my daughter Rebecca Brown."

8. SAMUEL[4] (*Samuel,*[3] *Samuel,*[2] *Ralph*[1]), born in Eastham, Feb. 13, 1691; married in Eastham, Oct. 9, 1712, Abigail Freeman (Eastham T. R.). Children:—

	i.	MARY,	born	Jan. 23, 1714.
13.	ii.	ZOHETH,	"	Dec. 11, 1716.
	iii.	ABIGAIL,	"	Dec. 17, 1718.
	iv.	MARTHA,	"	Aug. 23, 1721.
	v.	BATHSHUBA,	"	May 9, 1723.
	vi.	GRACE,	"	June 15, 1725.
	vii.	SUSANNA,	"	Aug. 25, 1727.
	viii.	SAMUEL,	"	Feb. 21, 1729.
	ix.	JOSEPH,	"	Sept. 9, 1731.

His will is dated at Wellfleet, April 18, 1768, proved Oct. 11, 1768: wife Sarah; gives "to heirs of son Zoheth, deceased, viz.: Zoheth, Richard, Elizabeth, Samuel, and Ruth;" "to heirs of daughter Bathsheba Atwood, deceased, viz.: Abigail, Martha, John, William, Bathshuba, Thankful, Anna and Zoheth;" "to heirs of daughter Martha Rich, deceased, Martha Rich and Abigail Young;" "to daughter Abigail Eldridge, wife of Jessee Eldridge;" "to daughter Susanna Atwood," and "to son Joseph Smith," whom he appointed administrator.

9. JOSEPH[4] (*Samuel,*[3] *Samuel,*[2] *Ralph*[1]), born in Eastham, Oct. 9, 1692; married in Eastham, June 24, 1715, Mary Hopkins, daughter of Joshua. Joseph Smith appointed guardian of Bashua, Samuel, and Huldah Smith, children of Mary Smith, late of Eastham; property in right of their "grandfather Joshua Hopkins." (Probate, Lib. 6, folio 30 and 31, June 22, 1741.) The will of Joseph is dated: Eastham, Dec. 7, 1778; proved, June 10, 1779. It gives "to Mary Hickman my daughter, wife of James Hickman," "to daughter Bathshuba," "to my grand children, children of son Joseph deceased," viz.: Samuel, Joseph, Josiah, Abraham and Mary, and "to daughter Rebecca Ford." The town books have

i.	BETHIAH,	born	April 17, 1716.
ii.	MARY,	"	Oct. 4, 1718.
iii.	BATHSHUBA,	"	Aug. 8, 1724.
iv.	SAMUEL,	"	Dec. 21, 1729.
v.	HULDAH,	"	July 29, 1732.
vi.	REBECCA,	"	July 23, 1739.
vii.	JOSEPH,	"	Oct. 17, 1743.

10. DEAN[4] (*John,*[3] *Samuel,*[2] *Ralph*[1]), born in Chatham, married Hester. Children:—

14. i. DEAN.		See *Probate*, Lib. 5, folio 204, of the same family, No. 6.
ii. ASEPH.		
iii. HEMAN.		
iv. MIRRIAM.		

11. SETH[4] (*John,*[3] *Samuel,*[2] *Ralph*[1]), born in Chatham, about 1713; see the following: (Probate, Lib. 4, folio 69.)

"To Sam[l] Smith, of the town of Chatham and County of Barnstable, Yeoman, Greeting.

Whereas, Seth Smith, a minor being aged about nine years, son of John Smith late of the town of Chatham, now deceased, hath occasion for a guardian in his minority, I do therefore hereby authorize and appoint you guardian to the said Seth Smith, with full power to receive and take into your custody all such estate as belong to the said Seth Smith, and the same to keep for his use, until he shall arrive to full age." "July 8, 1722. John Otis, Judge."

The following is from the Chatham town records:—

"Children of Seth, Sr. and Elizabeth Smith:"

i. HUGH, born Jan. 8, 1739; died young.
ii. MARY, born Aug. 22, 1740.
15. iii. SETH, born Aug. 22, 1743.
iv. ENOS, born Feb. 21, 1745; accidentally shot.
v. ELIZABETH, born Feb. 6, 1748; married Moses Mayo.
16. vi. HUGH, born July 21, 1751.
vii. ZILLAH, born Sept. 7, 1753; married Miller Paine.

His second wife was Mary Nickerson, whom he married in Chatham, Nov. 18, 1756. She is not mentioned in his will, which is dated March 10, 1787. He gave "to son Seth," "to grandchildren, children of my daughter Mary Nickerson, deceased," "to daughter Elizabeth Mayo, wife of Moses Mayo," "to daughter Zillah, wife of Miller Paine," "to son Hugh, and to his heirs and assigns all my estate," except what was given to the other heirs. Hugh, administrator.

Mary married Seth Nickerson, of Provincetown, March 19, 1761. He was a native of Chatham. Their descendants in part were, children: (1) Nathan, born Dec. 11, 1763; (2) Elizabeth, born 1766, married Edmund Smith; (3) Enos, born Sept. 19, 1770; (4) Ebenezer, born Aug. 17, 1768, who married Salome Collins, daughter of Cyrenius of Chatham, and settled in Boston; died in Waltham, Mass., Oct. 25, 1855. Maria, a daughter of Enos, married John Young, of Provincetown; children: Enos, now of Provincetown, aged about 35; Nathaniel, of Chicago, Ill., aged about 29; John, Jr., of Provincetown, aged about 24.

12. SETH[4] (*John,*[3] *John,*[2] *Ralph*[1]), born in Eastham, Jan. 28, 1705; there married, Oct. 3, 1728, Anna Knowles. Children:—

i. BARNABAS,	born	May 30, 1731.	Eastham Town Records.
ii. REBECCA,	"	May 19, 1734.	" "
17. iii. SETH,	"	May 22, 1737.	" "
iv. EDWARD,	"	Aug. 2, 1739.	" "
v. ANNA,	"	May 1, 1741.	" "
vi. ELIZABETH,	"	Oct. 10, 1745.	" "

13. ZOHETH[5] (*Samuel,*[4] *Samuel,*[3] *Samuel,*[2] *Ralph*[1]), born in Eastham, Dec. 11, 1716; and there married, Hannah Sears, Feb. 23, 1737. Children:—

i. ZOHETH, born Oct. 12, 1739; Eastham Records.
ii. RICHARD, " Mar. 18, 1741. " "
iii. ELIZABETH, " Feb. 6, 1745. " "
iv. HANNAH, " Mar. 9, 1746. " "

For the other children see the following extracts from Probate records, Lib. 20, folio 377. "Samuel Smith, 3d, of Wellfleet," made his will Jan. 5, 1779, proved June 11, 1779, "to Joshua Mayo Smith, son of my late Bro. Zoheth Smith," "to Hannah Sears Smith, daughter of my late Bro. Richard Smith," "to Samuel and Elizabeth Arey, children of my late sister Elizabeth Arey;" "to Hannah Greene, the daughter of my only sister Ruth Greene, wife of Joseph Greene," &c.

14. DEAN[5] (*Dean,*[4] *John,*[3] *Samuel,*[2] *Ralph*[1]), children of Dean and Rachel Smith:—

i. RACHEL, born Dec. 12, 1747. Chatham Records.
ii. ESTHER, " June 1, 1750. " "
iii. ASEPH, " June 6, 1753. " "
iv. MARTHA, " Aug. 10, 1755. " "

15. SETH[5] (*Seth,*[4] *John,*[3] *Samuel,*[2] *Ralph*[1]), born in Chatham, Aug. 22, 1743; and there married Elizabeth Eldridge, April 26, 1764. Their children, born in Chatham, were:—

18. i. EDMUND, born Jan. 25, 1765.
ii. JOSHUA, " April 19, 1766. iii. ENOS, born April 19, 1768.
iv. BETTY, " 1796.
v. REUBEN, " 1778, at Provincetown, where they settled 1780.
vi. SETH. vii. DAVID. viii. LIZZIE.
ix. HANNAH. x. ELDRIDGE. xi. ABIGAIL.

16. HUGH[5] (*Seth,*[4] *John,*[3] *Samuel,*[2] *Ralph*[1]), born in Chatham, July 21, 1751; there married Lydia Paine, the town records say Jan. 19, 1775, but the family record fixes the date at June 17, 1775. This family left Chatham about 1794, and settled at Buckstown, now Bucksport, Me. Children:—

19. i. SETH, b. Oct. 4, 1777.
ii. ANDREW, b. Oct. 28, 1779, whose son Eugene Theodore, born in 1816, is now living in Brooklyn, N. Y.
iii. THOMAS, b. Jan. 25, 1782; married Phebe Tappan and moved West.
iv. MARY, b. Sept. 24, 1784; married Jessee Bassett, of Bucksport, Oct. 22, 1807; ch. John Sheppard, b. Aug., 1808, Benj. Franklin, b. 1810.
v. EBENEZER, b. Oct. 21, 1786; married Zulina Handy, June 13, 1807; died at Bucksport, Dec. 23, 1846. Widow died, April 9, 1849; their ch. Andrew, Mary, Ruth, Lydia and Levina.
vi. and vii. SUSAN and LYDIA, born Feb. 2, 1789.
viii. ZILLAH, b. Feb. 22, 1792; married Randall Burrill, of Bucksport, April 23, 1814. Children: James, born March 25, 1815, now living in Central City, Colorado. Randall Gardner, born July 24, 1816, married at Boston, May 12, 1845; his son Herbert Leslie, born April 27, 1856. Harvey Miller, born March 25, 1818, and died at sea on board ship "New World," 1840. George Whitefield, born April, 1820. Nancy, died an infant; and Alfred, born June 20, 1827, died unmarried Nov. 6, 1860.
ix. LYDIA, born Aug. 29, 1794; married first, James Maddocks, Aug. 1, 1816, and second, John Tillock, Dec. 9, 1824. Children: Joseph,[1] born Oct. 24, 1825, who married Dec. 9, 1844, Flora D. Ryder. Phebe[2] S., born Feb. 26, 1827, unmarried. John[3] N., born Dec. 20, 1828, married Lizzie Clay, Dec. 19, 1849; their children are, Edwin L., born 1851; John Charles, born 1867. Caroline[4] L., born April 22, 1833, married Joshua Smith, of Bucksport, Feb. 1, 1853; children are, Julietta, born Sept. 27, 1857, Willie Tillock, born Sept. 23, 1867. Lydia,[5] born June 17, 1836; married G. H. Snow, April 24, 1859; live in New York; their son Emery born 1866.

17. SETH[6] (*Seth,*[4] *John,*[3] *John,*[2] *Ralph*[1]), born in Eastham, May 22, 1737; there married Thankful Baker, Jan. 18, 1759. The town records give children of Seth and Thankful Smith, as follows:—

i. BARNABAS, b. Feb. 22, 1762. ii. WILLIAM, b. July 1, 1764.
iii. SARAH, b. Jan. 10, 1767. iv. JESSE, b. Jan. 28, 1769.
v. and vi. SETH and EBENEZER, b. May 12, 1772.
vii. SAMUEL, b. Jan. 15, 1775.

18. EDMUND[6] (*Seth,*[5] *Seth,*[4] *John,*[3] *Samuel,*[2] *Ralph*[1]), born in Chatham, Jan. 25, 1765; married at Provincetown, Elizabeth Nickerson, daughter of Seth and Mary, 11 (ii.). Children were:—

i. JOHN, died, aged about 18. ii. FREEMAN, died in 1869, aged about 75.
iii. MARY. iv. EDMUND. v. LIZIE. vi. OLIVE, who married John Stone, deceased, no children.
20. vii. JOHN, born March 9, 1809.

19. SETH[6] (*Hugh,*[5] *Seth,*[4] *John,*[3] *Samuel,*[2] *Ralph*[1]), born in Chatham, Oct. 4, 1777; married at Bucksport, Me., Hannah Pratt Albee, April 23, 1806; d. at Bucksport, March 19, 1853. His widow is yet living at Bucksport; very old. Children:

i. HARRIET, died a babe.
21. ii. SETH HALL, b. April 27, 1809.
iii. ALFRED PRATT, died aged 4 years.
iv. ENOS, b. April 4, 1813. His son Henry born 1851.
v. CAROLINE KALSO, b. 1814; died 1828.
vi. ELMIRA ALBEE, b. 1817; married Henry Benson, and live in Blackstone, Mass. Their son, Seth Hall Benson, born 1850, now a student at West Point Military School.
vii. SARAH ELDRIDGE, b. 1820; married Henry Eldridge, and "went West."
viii. HANNAH ADAH, b. Jan. 22, 1823; married first, George Taft, second Elnathan Handy; children are: Abby L. Taft, born 1851, Martha E. Handy, born 1862.

20. JOHN[7] (*Edmund,*[6] *Seth,*[5] *Seth,*[4] *John,*[3] *Samuel,*[2] *Ralph*[1]), born in Provincetown, Mass., March 9, 1809; there married Mehitable Cook Ghen, daughter of Thomas Ghen and Sarah Cook, and granddaughter of Samuel Ghen and Sabra Gross, of Truro. Samuel was a brother of Thomas and James Genn, or Ginn, whose descendants now live at or near Bucksport, Me. The three brothers came from Virginia, where the family is quite numerous. Josias Cook, of Eastham, who married the widow Dean, was the ancestor of Sarah Cook. Children of John and Mehitable:—

i. EDMUND, born in Provincetown, Jan. 26, 1832; now living there, unmarried.
22. ii. ALONZO, born in Provincetown, July 27, 1833.
23. iii. THOMAS, born in Clinton, Me., July 13, 1837.

The father died in Clinton, in the spring of 1837, and the mother returned to Provincetown, that year, where in 1846 she married Samuel Parker, son of the late Rev. Samuel Parker, of Provincetown, deceased. Their daughter Isadora, born Jan. 26, 1848, now living in Boston.

21. SETH HALL[7] (*Seth,*[6] *Hugh,*[5] *Seth,*[4] *John,*[3] *Samuel,*[2] *Ralph*[1]), born in Bucksport, Me., April 27, 1809; there married Eliza Handy, widow of Ebenezer; her maiden name was Morgan. Their children:—

24. i. ALFRED LEWIS, born 1835.
ii. HATTIE ELIZA, born 1838; she married, May, 1866, Capt. J. H. Chipman, of Bucksport, and in October of the same year, he died in Palermo, Sicily.

22. ALONZO^8 (*John,^{7} Edmund,^{6} Seth,^{5} Seth,^{4} John,^{3} Samuel,^{2} Ralph^1*), born in Provincetown, July 27, 1833; there married Nancy, daughter of Joshua Smith. Children:—
   i. CLARA, born Aug. 6, 1855, in Provincetown, Mass.
   ii. LIZZIE, born Aug. 20, 1857, in " "
   iii. FRANK WILLIS, born July, 1869, in Cohasset, Mass.

23. THOMAS^8 (*John,^{7} Edmund,^{6} Seth,^{5} Seth,^{4} John,^{3} Samuel,^{2} Ralph^1*), born in Clinton, Me., July 13, 1837; married in Lincoln, Mass., Aug. 15, 1866, Mary Frances, daughter of Maj. Daniel Weston and Mary Wheeler, of L. Mary Isabel, their daughter, born in Charlestown, Mass., March 26, 1868. The family now live in Boston.

24. ALFRED LEWIS^8 (*Seth Hall,^{7} Seth,^{6} Hugh,^{5} Seth,^{4} John,^{3} Samuel,^{2} Ralph^1*), born in Bucksport, Me., 1835. His son, Frank Elmer, born in 1866.

NOTES AND QUERIES.

A BRANCH OF THE AVERY FAMILY.—The following facts covering an important branch of the Avery family in this country (*ante*, vol. xxv. p 191) have been furnished me for publication by Henry W. Avery, Esq., a lineal descendant of Christopher Avery of England, who first settled in this country, in Gloucester, Mass., in 1630.

While this material lacks something of completeness, it still will be found of much service to genealogists and antiquaries generally. LEDYARD BILL.

Norwich, Conn.

CHRISTOPHER AVERY^1 was born in Salisbury, England, and came to America in the ship "Arabella," in the year 1630, and settled in Gloucester, Mass. He died in 1679.

JAMES AVERY^2 (*Christopher^1*) was b. in England about 1620. He was with his father in Gloucester, but moved to New-London, Conn. in 1651. He m. (1) Joanna Greenslade, (2) Sarah Miner.

JAMES AVERY^3 (*James,^{2} Christopher^1*), the son of the preceding James, was b. Dec. 15, 1646; m. Deborah Sterling.

JAMES AVERY^4 (*James,^{3} James,^{2} Christopher^1*), son of the foregoing James Avery,^{3} was b. April 20, 1673, and m. Mary Griswold.

EBENEZER AVERY^5 (*James,^{4} James,^{3} James,^{2} Christopher^1*), son of James Avery,^{4} was b. March 29, 1704. He m. (1) Lucy Latham, (2) Rachel Denison (widow).

EBENEZER AVERY^6 (*Ebenezer,^{5} James,^{4} James,^{3} James,^{2} Christopher^1*) was b. March 7, 1732. He was killed in Fort Griswold, Sept. 6, 1781, at the massacre of a portion of the garrison by the British troops under Arnold.

EBENEZER AVERY^7 (*Ebenezer,^{6} Ebenezer,^{5} James,^{4} James,^{3} James,^{2} Christopher^1*) was b. Aug. 8, 1762, and m. (1) Hannah Morgan, by whom he had six children. She d. Sept. 27, 1792. (2) Mary Eldridge, by whom he also had six children. She d. Jan. 19, 1854. Mr. Avery was a colonel of militia about 1798, and a justice for over thirty years, during which time he married over eighty couples. He died Aug. 8, 1842. The children by first wife were: Lucy,^{8} Ebenezer,^{8} Fanny,^{8} Egbert,^{8} Clarissa^8 and Jonathan.^{8} By second wife: Charles Eldridge,^{8} Henry William,^{8} Mary Eldridge,^{8} Sidney,^{8} Amasa^8 and Jared R.^{8}

(First wife's children:)

   i. LUCY,^{8} b. June 11, 1784; m. Oct. 10, 1802, Capt. Daniel Mitchell. They had eleven children. She d. Nov. 4, 1852.
   ii. EBENEZER,^{8} b. April 2, 1786; m. (1) Nancy Avery, by whom he had seven children; (2) Catharine L. Avery, by whom he had four children. He d. March 19, 1863.
   iii. FANNY,^{8} b. April 22, 1788; m. Daniel Avery, Feb. 25, 1808. She had three children. She d. March 30, 1869.

iv. Egbert,[8] b. July 26, 1789; m. Feb. 2, 1815, Eunice Wood. They had five children. He d. Dec. 3, 1854.

v. Clarissa[8] and Jonathan,[8] d. in infancy.

(Second wife's children:)

vi. Charles E.,[8] b. March 6, 1794; m. March 6, 1820, Asenath Cheadell, They had eight children. He d. Sept. 5, 1854. He was settled in the ministry at Auburn, N. Y.

vii. Henry W.,[8] b. Oct. 12, 1795, in Groton, Ct.; m. Nov. 27, 1817, Betsey Denison, dau. of Frederick Denison. She d. May 11, 1866. He resides in Belvidere, Ill. They had children: 1. Frederick Denison,[9] b. Oct. 30, 1818; m. (1) Julia S. Smith. She d. June 24, 1855. (2) Charlotte Mauny. He is a minister in Columbia, Ct. 2. Henry W.,[9] b. May 31, 1823; m. (1) Lydia G. Avery, (2) Rachel P. McCord, Nov. 16, 1848. They reside in Belvidere, Ill.

viii. Mary E.,[8] b. May 15, 1798; m. Nathan F. Denison, of Groton, Ct. They had four children. She d. Dec. 3, 1858.

ix. Sidney,[8] b. March 23, 1800; m. Mary Dickey. They reside in Belvidere, Ill., and have had seven children.

x. Amasa,[8] b. Oct. 18, 1801; m. (1) Betsey Dye, by whom he had two children; (2) Eleanor Atwell, by whom he had one child. He d. Sept. 21, 1869.

xi. Jared R.,[8] b. Sept. 17, 1804; m. Sarah Ann Agnew, by whom he had seven children. This family reside in Groton, Ct., where he has been settled in the ministry.

Admiral William Henry Smythe, a Descendant of Capt. John Smythe [or Smith].—I recently purchased, in New-York, a set of books, in twelve volumes, entitled "Royal Naval Biography, or Memoirs of the Services of all the Flag-Officers, Superannuated Rear Admirals, Retired Post Captains and Commanders whose names appeared on the Admiralty List of Sea Officers at the commencement of 1823, or who have since been promoted. Illustrated by a Series of Historical and Explanatory Notes, which will be found to contain an account of all the Naval Actions, and other important Events, from the commencement of the late reign, in 1760, to the present period, with copious Addenda. By John Marshall (B), Lieutenant in the Royal Navy." Longman, Rees, Orme, Brown, Green & Longman.

The publication of the work was begun in 1823, but not completed until 1835, about a volume a year. It is valuable to American readers and inquirers, from containing the lives and services of a large number of the officers (all certainly who were living in 1823) who were employed against us during the wars of 1775–83, and 1812–14. Looking over my purchase, I find in one of the volumes the book plate and arms of "Capt. William Henry Smyth, R. N.," and that the work was a presentation copy from the author to him. Observing a strange similarity in the arms (three Turk's heads, &c.) on the book plate, with those of the redoubtable Capt. John Smith of American and Pocahontas fame, I turned to a sketch of the Life of Capt. Wm. Henry Smyth in vol. v. of the work, and to the same in O'Byrne's "Naval Biographical Dictionary," pages 1094–96, and found that distinguished and scientific officer was not only a direct descendant of the redoubtable Capt. John, notwithstanding his spelling his name with a "y," but also the grandson of an American loyalist of New-Jersey.

Admiral Wm. Henry Smyth, R.N.; D.C.L.; Knight of Royal Sicilian Order of St. Ferdinand and of Merit; Fellow of the Royal, the Antiquarian, the Astronomical and the Geographical Societies of London; Member of the Society for the Statistics and Natural His. of Tuscany, and of the Academy of Sciences of Palermo; Vice-Pres. R.S.; Pres. R.A.S.Do., &c. &c. &c., was the only son of Joseph Brewer Palmer Smyth, of New-Jersey, a descendant in the paternal line from Capt. John Smith (whose armorial bearings he bore), and Georgina Caroline, granddaughter of the Rev. M. Pilkington.[1]

[1] Letitia, the *dau.* of Dr. Van Lewen, a physician of Dublin, was born in 1712. She became the wife of the Rev. Matthew Pilkington, from whom she was separated on account of the irregularity of her conduct. After this, she settled in London, where she subsisted partly by writing and partly by the bounty of her friends. She wrote "The Roman Father, a Tragedy," "The Turkish Count, or London Apprentice, a Comedy," "Memoirs of her Life," and various poems, &c., and died in 1750. (*Godwin's Univer. Biography.*) Probably Georgina Caroline Smyth was *her* granddau.

During the American Revolution, Joseph Brewer Palmer Smyth took up arms as a loyalist, and was with Burgoyne at the battles which preceded his surrender at Saratoga. The peace which established the independence of the colonies, depriving him of very considerable landed property, he returned to America, by permission, to substantiate his claims on the British Government, but suddenly died. The lords of the treasury, however, assigned a small annuity to Mrs. Smyth and her two children. He is not mentioned in Sabine's American Loyalists.

Wm. Henry Smyth, the only son, was born at Westminster, Jan. 21, 1788, and after a cruise in the E. I. Co.'s service, entered the Royal Navy as a midshipman in 1805. It is unnecessary to follow him through his honorable and gallant naval career, which is detailed in the two sketches from which I have extracted these notes. He was promoted a Lieut. in 1813, a Commander in 1815, and attained Post rank as Captain Feb. 7, 1824; was made a Rear Admiral on the retired list, May 28, 1853; Vice Admiral, Feb. 13, 1858; Admiral, Nov. 14, 1863. He is perhaps best known for his very eminent hydrographic services in the Mediterranean. In 1821, he received from Mehemet Ali an offer of "Cleopatra's Needle," intended as a present to George IV., but had no means or opportunity to embark in it; and the same year, for his prompt but unavailing efforts to save from destruction a ship on fire, he received the thanks of the U. S. Consul at Gibraltar, and of the masters of eleven American merchantmen. He was retired from active service in 1846. The Emperor of Austria presented him with a gold snuff-box set with brilliants. In 1815, about the same time, he obtained two honorable augmentations to his family arms, and was admitted by Sir Wm. Sidney Smith into the "Anti-Piratical Soc. of Knights Liberators of the Slaves (white and black) in Africa," instituted by the allied Sovereigns at Vienna in 1814. He was one of the Committee for Improving and Extending the Nautical Almanac, and was a member of the National Institute at Washington, the Academy of Sciences at Boston, and the Naval Lyceum, New-York. He was also the author of several scientific, professional and literary works.

He married at Messina, Oct. 7, 1815, Annarelle, only daughter of T. Warington, Esq., of Naples, by whom he had a numerous family. His second son, Charles Piozzi, was Astronomer Royal for Scotland. His name appears for the last time in the Royal Navy List, 1865, and he died during that year or the beginning of 1866.

George Henry Preble.

Pitkin.—Mary Pitkin (*Register*, xvii. 39), daughter of Joseph Bishop Abrams, of Saratoga Springs, N. Y., and his wife Lucy, daughter of Thomas White Pitkin (and granddaughter of Hon. Joseph Marsh, first Lieutenant Governor of Vermont), married, first, James Edward Poole Stevens, gent., son of Hon. Godfrey Stevens of Claremont, N. H., Oct. 5, 1852, the service being conducted by the late Rt. Rev. Carleton Chase, D.D., Bishop of New-Hampshire. By this husband, who died Dec. 9, 1865, at Somerville, Mass., she had issue:

Charles Ellis, born in Tremont place, Boston, Mass., July 5, 1853; baptized by the Rt. Rev. Manton Eastburn, D.D., Bishop of Massachusetts, in Trinity Church, Boston; at present (1871) a student in the University of Pennsylvania.

Lucy Pitkin, born in Boston, Mass., May 20, 1855; baptized by the Rt. Rev. Thomas March Clark, D.D., LL.D., Bishop of Rhode Island; at present (1871) pursuing studies at Maplewood Young Ladies' Institute, Pittsfield, Mass.

Mary Abrams, born June 19, 1857, in Boston, Mass.; baptized by Rev. Edward N. Kirk, D.D.; died in Philadelphia, Pa., Sept. 10, 1870.

James Edward Poole, born in Philadelphia, Pa., May 27, 1861; baptized by Rev. William P. Breed, D.D.

She married, secondly, Rev. Henry Boardman Ensworth, Nov. 1, 1866, at Andover, Mass., the service being performed by the Rev. Edwards A. Park, D.D., Professor in the Andover Theological Seminary. They have one child:

Samuel Cassius, born Feb. 26, 1868, at Pittsburgh, Pa.; baptized by his father.

Note.—Mrs. Ensworth is descended from the celebrated Major John Mason, of Connecticut, from the Hobarts, the Whitings, and the St. Johns. See New England Historical and Genealogical Register, vol. xiv. pp. 61, 62; vol. xv. pp. 117, 217, 318; vol. xvii. p. 32.

C. Ellis Stevens.

Paoli, Chester Co., Penn.

STANDISH, MYLES. (*Register*, vol. xxvi. p. 82.)—In this note are two errors: one of the types in substituting *Joseph* for Josiah; and an error of Dr. Parish in stating that Josiah was a grandson of Myles.

Josiah Standish, the second son of Capt. Myles, went to Norwich in 1686. (See Mitchell's *Bridgewater*, page 308; Winsor's *Duxbury*, page 321; Caulkins's *History of Norwich*, page 118, 1st Ed.) He was Ensign Josiah, afterwards Capt. He had children: Myles, Josiah, Samuel, Israel, Mary, Lois, Mehitable, Martha, Mercy. In Pilgrim Hall is a package of thirteen letters of the Standish family, and among them are autograph letters of Josiah, Samuel and Lois, three of the grandchildren of the redoubtable Myles.

From Josiah, Dr. Parish was descended. Josiah, 2d, had a daughter Hannah, who married Nathan Foster, of Stafford, Conn., whose daughter Eunice was the mother of Dr. Parish, of Byfield, and of the mother of the writer, as may be seen by the following epitaph in the old graveyard at Andover, Mass., which I will, with your permission, copy entire:—

"Sacred to the Memory of
Mrs. EUNICE PARISH,
Consort of Mr. Elijah Parish, who died
13 December, 1799, ætat. 66.

"She was the daughter of Mr. Nathan Foster, and granddaughter of Dea. Josiah Standish, who was grandson of Capt. Myles Standish, Military Commander of the Colony, who landed at Plymouth Decr. 1620.

"Her eldest son is the Rev. Elijah Parish, of Byfield; her second son was the late Rev. Ariel Parish, of Manchester, who died 20 May, 1794, ætat. 30. Her only daughter is Mrs. Philomela Thurston, wife of Mr. Stephen Thurston, of this town. Her son Asa died 20 Feb., 1772, aged 3 years.

"Her faithful aid relieved the woes of life,
No husband e'er enjoyed a kinder wife;
With holy zeal she taught each list'ning child,
Persuasive goodness spoke in accents mild.
Content to stay, but not afraid to go,
Her parting words forbid our tears to flow."

I will simply add that Hannah Foster née Standish was the grandmother of Lafayette Standish Foster, of Norwich, Conn., former Senator, and for some time president of the United States Senate.

Elmira, N. Y., Jan. 15. ARIEL STANDISH THURSTON.

MARSHALL, JOHN.—(*Register*, vol. xxvi. pp. 74, 83.) Of his children were:

RUTH, wife of Capt. James Green.

WILLIAM, b. Freetown, June 5, 1733; m. July 26, 1761, Lydia Warner. She d. Oct. 18, 1766, in her 24th year. He d. March 24, 1806, aged 73, in East Haddam, Conn.

ELIZABETH, b. Freetown, Feb. 9, 1741; m. Asa Willey, of Litchfield, Conn.

THOMAS, b. Freetown, May 17, 1744; m. Feb. 6, 1770, Rebecca Ackley; settled in East Haddam, and had ten children. D. W. PATTERSON.

Newark Valley, N. Y., Jan. 13.

TRAVELLING ON THE LORD'S DAY.—I copy the following from the original.

J. COLBURN.

"To the Constables of Boston or either of them.

Complaint being made to me that a Certain Sailor whose name is Supposed to be Isaac Hambleton late of Boston did yesterday profane the Lord's Day travailing from Dedham to this Town in contempt of the Law. These are therefore in Her Majesties Name to command you forthwith to apprehend the s'd Sailor Isaac Hambleton or by what other name he may be called, and him bring before me or some other of Her Majesties Justices to make Answer.

"Hereof you are not to fail. Given under my hand and seal in Boston this seven and twentieth day of July 1702. Annoque Regni Anna Regina Angliæ &c. Primo.

SAM. SEWALL.

"July, 28. 1702. Constable Edward Oakes brought Isaac Hambleton before me, and he confessed the Fact: owns ye Capt. Dwight charged him not to travell. He alleged he had two Indians and he was afraid he should lose them. Sentenced him to pay 20*s*. w'ch he immediately did in Gold. S. S.

[Endorsed] "Isaac Hambleton fined 20*s*. for Travelling last Lord's Day, July 26. July, 28. 1702. Const. Edw. Oakes."

LETTER OF BENEDICT ARNOLD TO MRS. KNOX.—

[We are indebted to Rear Admiral Henry Knox Thatcher, for a copy of this letter. He remarks that "the original is among the miscellaneous papers of Major-General Henry Knox. It is written upon a sheet of foolscap of the largest size, and coarse enough for musket-ball cartridge paper, which it probably was designed for. The letter was written at a time when Arnold stood high in the estimation of Washington, and it is said that he was at this period one of the most accomplished officers in the army."—ED.]

Watertown, 4 March, 1777.

Dear Madam, I take the liberty of Inclosing a Letter for the Heavenly Miss Deblois, which [I] beg the favor of your delivering, with the trunk of Gowns &c. which Mrs. Colburn promised me to send to your House, I hope she will make no objection against receiving them, I make no doubt you will soon have the pleasure of seeing the Charming Mrs. Emery, and have it in your power to give me some favorable Intelligence—I shall remain under the most Anxious Suspence until I have the favor of a line from you, who if I may Judge will from your own experience, conceive the fond Anxiety, the Glowing hopes and Chilling fears that Alternately possess the breast of

Dear Madam Your obedt and most

Humble Servt

Mrs. Knox. B. ARNOLD.

MINISTRY RATE, CAMBRIDGE, 1728.—

Cambridge Nov. ye 14, 1728.

To Dea^c. Samll. Bowman, Receiv^r of ye Ministry Rate in s'd Town. This May Certifie unto You the Sums Totall of the Lists of the Ministry Rate Committed to ye Respective Constables of s'd Town (vizt)

John Cutter Sam^ll Andrews Gershom Davis	Assessors	To Henry Prentice	48	10	6
		To Thomas Dana	27	3	9
		To Thos Willington	24	5	9

PURITAN PORTRAITS.—One of the results arising from the Bicentenary commemoration in England, August 24, 1862, of Bartholomew day 1662, when two thousand ministers resigned their livings, for conscience sake, rather than comply with the Act of Uniformity (*ante*, xx. 192), was the determination to erect a large building in London to commemorate the event, which should be practically useful also for several religious purposes. Last May an advantageous site was obtained in Faringdon street, and a "MEMORIAL HALL" will soon be commenced. Mr. Gustavus E. Sintzenich, an artist residing at Exeter, England, has conceived the idea of adorning this hall with the portraits of the great men who suffered, in past times, in England, for their nonconformity,—"skirmishers in the great fight for religion and liberty,"—and for the last four or five years has been devoting his time as well as his artistic talent to the realization of his design. In the course of his researches, he has discovered, in the possession of private individuals, several original portraits, the existence of which was not suspected. His collection of portraits of Puritan and Nonconformist ministers is now quite numerous, comprising many of the most celebrated names. He wishes to include also the portraits of the puritan ministers, who were driven by persecution from our mother country, and settled in New-England, and has furnished the following hints about costume, to enable us to test the authenticity of paintings which are claimed to be portraits of these ministers:

"During the reigns of Queen Elizabeth and James I., ministers wore the round frill; in that of Charles I., a change took place, and the large square collar or bands supplanted the frill; this continued during the protectorate, and on, through the reigns of Charles II. and James II., till about the revolution, 1689, when these large bands were modified into a smaller size, not much larger than those of the present day. Again, the puritans wore the hair in moderate curls, and a small black skull-cap, from about 1600 till 1690, when the black cap gave way to the large curled wig of the fashion of Louis XIV. These are guides about dates, which have helped me to correct errors about the names of portraits, which are sometimes miscalled. I find that John Cotton died in 1652. He might have either the frill or large square collar (most likely the latter), and the black skull-cap. A print has just been lent me, called John Cotton, but it is at least 70 years later, having the large wig of 1700 and after, therefore it is of no use."

Further information may be obtained of

18 *Somerset St., Boston.* JOHN WARD DEAN.

BENJAMIN BAGNALL.—From the treasurer's book of Charlestown, Mass., we learn that Benjamin Bagnall of Boston was paid for cleaning the town clock, August 22, 1724. He was of Cambridge, and had a wife Elizabeth, in 1729. These facts I have from T. B. Wyman, Esq. A clock in the possession of the New-England Historic, Genealogical Society bears on its face, "BEN. BAGNALL, BOSTON." What more is known of this person? QUERIST

SACO IN 1779.—THE CONTINENTAL ARMY.—
"To the Selectmen of Pepperrellboro.
Gentlemen.

We the Subscribers Inhabitants of said Pepperrellboro, request you to Call a Meeting of the Inhabitants of s^{d} Pepperrellboro, as soon as Possible to see if they will agree to Hire Six Men to Reinforce the Continental Army agreeable to a Resolve of this State of June 9th 1779, and to Hire Six Men more to go to Rhode Island agreeable to a Resolve of s^{d} State of June 9th 1779 also to see whether the said Inhabitants will for the future agree to Hire men to Reinforce the Continental army if any more requested.

Also to see whether they will raise money sufficient for one or both of s^{d} Purposes. Pepperellboro, June 21, 1779.

THOM^{s} CUTTS.	JOSEPH BRODBURG.	JAMES GRAY.
NATHA^{LL} SCAMMON.	JAMES JOSE.	RICH' BURKE.
HUMPHREY PIKE.	SAM^{LL} BOOTHBY.	SAMUEL DENNET."

The original is in the hand-writing of Col. Cutts. J. W. T.

VIRGINIA,—ITS HISTORICAL TREASURES.—Up to the beginning of the late war, no state had been more fortunate than Virginia in the faithful care with which her general and local records and documentary files had been guarded and preserved from decay or spoliation. The court records of the eastern counties in particular were rich in materials of an historic character, and it had long been hoped by many in and out of the state, that the day would soon come when the state or some of its citizens would cause these *disjecta membra* to be brought together and published in the form of a documentary history, worthy of this venerable commonwealth.

Early in the late war, orders were issued to the clerks of the courts to send all their records and files, or at least the more ancient of them, to Richmond for greater safety. This prudent order was, for the most part, complied with, and the congregated treasures were stored there, in a building supposed to be safe from fire or other danger. But during the war (at what precise period we have not learned), this building and its precious contents were destroyed by fire. By this calamity an irreparable loss ensued to the state and to the cause of history; for these records and files were full of historical matter dating from the first settlement of the colony, or from an early period of its history.

But this is not the whole of the calamity that has befallen the state. It appears that during the war and the year following its close, both the state-library and the state-archives suffered greatly from pillage and mutilation. After the war closed and soon after the appointment of a military governor, a stranger, said to be from the north, obtained permission to examine the records and files in the secretary-of-state's office, and upon subsequent examination it is found that he carried away many documents and papers of great value and interest, and mutilated others!

For such vandalism there can be no excuse, and no punishment sufficiently adequate, unless it be to print the names of the villains where they will continue to be seen and read for ages to come. It is to be hoped that their names will be ascertained. It will give us unalloyed pleasure to contribute our aid toward their perpetual disgrace.

We are gratified to see that at its present session the legislature of Virginia has passed an act, prepared and introduced by the Hon. Thomas H. Wynne, providing for the assorting, arranging and indexing of what remains of its records and files, and for the publication of such of them as the Historical Society of the state may select. Dr. William P. Palmer, a gentleman eminently well qualified, has been chosen to superintend the work.

The state has done a praiseworthy act, and it is to be hoped that future legislatures will encourage and promote what has thus been begun. We congratulate Mr. Wynne, and his associates, upon the honor of being the pioneers of a movement so timely and meritorious.

The same legislature has passed another act, in promoting which, we see by the newspapers that Mr. Wynne took an active interest, namely, in restoring to use the ancient and beautiful seals of the state, adopted in 1779 and used down to the year 1865, when new seals were illegally employed. In our next issue we propose to print an interesting paper on this subject.—[EDITOR.]

Fort Louis on Conanicut, R. I.—The Question is asked (N. & Q., Register, *ante*, p. 80), whether the name of "Fort Louis," in the story of "Malbone," is merely "the fancy of the novelist." To this the novelist answers emphatically, No. He first saw the name in a little book called "Sketches of Newport and Vicinity," published in 1842, and giving a graphic account of Newport as it then appeared. The fort is there mentioned as "the old Fort Louis." The author of the book, Sarah Cahoone, was either from Conanicut herself, or had relatives there, and she used the name which is still, I am told, traditional on that island; though in Newport the name of "Fort Dumpling" is more common.

I am told by our best antiquaries, that it is impossible to ascertain definitely,—unless by searching the records of the war department at Washington,—the date at which the present fort was built. The tradition is, that it was built during the administration of John Adams, and on the site of the batteries of which your correspondent speaks, and which were, perhaps, mere earthworks. It may very probably have been built by a French engineer. I am informed by Commander Matthews, U. S. N., now in charge of the Torpedo station on Goat Island, that he has recently found a stone with an inscription, giving the name of the engineer who built part of those fortifications, as La Roche Fontaine. He may also have built the fort on Conanicut, and the name of the French king may have been the result of his personal attachment, or of the popularity of the French nation among the islanders, after our revolution. At all events it is a traditional name; and a novelist, choosing between two such names, has a right to take the more pleasing. It is also in this case the less inappropriate, as the fort is not on the Dumpling islands, but on a Peninsula of Conanicut, overlooking them. T. W. Higginson.

Newport, R. I., March 18.

NEW-ENGLAND HISTORIC, GENEALOGICAL SOCIETY.

NECROLOGY.

Communicated by Rev. Dorus Clarke, D.D., Historiographer.

Gen. Asa Howland.—He was the son of John and Grace (Avery) Howland, of Conway, Mass., where he was born Oct. 25, 1781, and where he died June 24, 1870. He was a descendant in the seventh generation from John Howland and his wife Elizabeth, daughter of John Tilley, all of whom came in the Mayflower in 1620. The Plymouth Records, in recording the death of John Howland, the Pilgrim, Feb. 23d, 1672, state that he was the "last man that was left of those that came ouer in the shipp called the May Flower, that liued in Plymouth."

The descent of Gen. Howland from *John*[1] *Howland*, was through his eldest son *John*,[2] who married Mary Lee, Oct. 26, 1651; *John*,[3] born in Barnstable, Dec. 31, 1674, and second wife Mary Crocker; *Job*,[4] born June 18, 1726; *John*,[5] born March 31, 1757, and *John*,[6] his father, who married, June 1, 1786, Grace Avery, born in Dedham, Aug. 17, 1755, died Feb. 12, 1841, and who died himself June 17, 1843.

His maternal descent was from William Avery, who was of Dedham, 1653, and removed to Boston, where he died March 18, 1686, (See Bridgeman's *King's Chapel Epitaphs*, p. 301); through *William*,[2] Capt. *William*,[3] and Dea. *William*,[4] who married Bethia Metcalf, and had four sons and three daughters, one of whom was *Grace*,[5] the mother of Gen. Howland.

He was twice married: first, to Phebe Thompson, of Heath, Mass., Oct. 25, 1813; and in the second instance, to Mrs. Nancy Tilton, March 1, 1861. He left no children.

Gen. Howland had several marked characteristics. He was a *self-made man*; his early educational advantages were not of a high order, but he was one of those men, who find compensation for such defects in their own natural and cultivated taste for reading and study. He was a carpenter by trade, and while he plied his profession with great assiduity, his brain was still more actively employed. He early acquired a thirst for knowledge, and he assiduously cultivated it, through his long and useful life.

He was a man of *great industry;* when he was not engaged in his professional vocation, he employed his time in reading, writing and other litarary labors, and thus accumulated a large fund of valuable information,—a fund so large that no scholar could long be in his presence, and not perceive that he was quite at home upon all matters of history, of geography, of public improvement, and upon affairs generally.

He was a benevolent man. He freely used the pecuniary means at his command in the establishment of schools and libraries in his native town, and in aiding indigent young men to obtain an education, especially if they intended to devote themselves to the christian ministry. It was an evidence of the high estimation in which he was held, that for many years he was almost uniformly chosen to preside at the anniversaries of the benevolent societies in Franklin county, and his deep interest in the success of those institutions, as well as his personal dignity and courtesy, rendered him very popular as a presiding officer.

Gen. Howland had a decided taste for *military affairs*. For several years he was colonel of a regiment, in which capacity he responded to the call of the governor of the commonwealth in 1812, and served in a campaign of three months in the defence of Boston. Subsequently he rose to the rank of brigadier-general, and afterwards to that of major-general. He was a thorough disciplinarian, and his dignified and commanding presence on the parade ground will long be remembered by those who had the good fortune to see him on those great military occasions. But the brightest gem in the character of Gen. Howland was his *consistent piety*. Descended from Pilgrim stock, he inherited much of the sound principle which has given the Pilgrim a name almost above every other earthly name. He made a public profession of his faith in Christ, July 7, 1822, and on Nov. 20, 1828, he was chosen a deacon in the orthodox Congregational Church in Conway, an office which he held and honored for forty years. Though he was not destitute of deep emotion, the leading characteristic of his piety was *principle* rather than *impulse*.

Gen. Howland had very considerable taste for historical pursuits, and this society honored itself, as well as him, by electing him to a resident membership, which he accepted Feb. 20, 1861.

Hon. Ezekiel Bacon.—The Hon. Ezekiel Bacon, who was elected a corresponding member of this society Sept. 18, 1847, was born in Boston, Mass., Sept. 1, 1776, and died in Utica, N. Y., Oct. 18, 1870, at the advanced age of 94 years. He descended from an honorable ancestry. The line can be traced back to William Bacon, of Stratton, in Rutlandshire, Eng., about the year 1600. William Bacon had two sons, Henry and Nathaniel. The latter emigrated to this country in 1640, and settled in Barnstable, Mass. He was a councilman in the Plymouth colony. From him descended John first; from him, John second; and from him, John third, who was the father of Ezekiel. John Bacon, the third John in the series, and the father of Hon. Ezekiel Bacon, was a man of so much distinction, that it seems proper briefly to state the more salient points in his history. He was born in Canterbury, Conn., in 1737, graduated at Princeton College, N. J., in 1765, was settled as a Presbyterian minister in Maryland, in 1768, was installed pastor of the Old South Church in Boston, Mass., in 1772, was dismissed in 1775, when he removed to Stockbridge, Mass., and established himself there as an agriculturist. He still preached occasionally, but was almost constantly engaged in some civil office. He was several times a member of both branches of the legislature. He was president of the senate in the year 1803-4, a member of congress from 1801 to 1803, and a judge of the county court of Berkshire for more than twenty years. He was a man of strong powers of mind, a warm politician of the Jefferson school, and died at Stockbridge in 1820, at the age of 83.

This gentleman, the Rev. John Bacon, or Judge Bacon (it is difficult to say which is the more appropriate designation), was a member of the legislative convention of 1777-1778, which drafted a constitution for Massachusetts, presented it to the legislature, by which it was approved and submitted to the people, by whom it was rejected. George H. Moore LL.D., the able librarian of the New-York Historical Society, has rescued from oblivion, and preserved in his "History of Slavery in Massachusetts," a terse and unanswerable speech delivered by Mr. Bacon in that convention, in favor of admitting "negroes, Indians and mulattoes," to the right of suffrage. It would be pleasant, if this were the appropriate time and place, to present some extracts from that able address; but I can only say that Mr. Bacon took the most advanced ground of the present day, as to the extension of the franchise, and ably advocated the most liberal views on that subject. The tone of that speech is the tone to which our ears have so lately become accustomed, and not the ring of a century ago.

The Rev. John Bacon married Elizabeth Goldthwaite, daughter of Ezekiel Goldthwaite, an eminent citizen of Boston, and widow of Rev. Alexander Cumming, his predecessor in the pastorate of the Old South Church. While they were on a visit to Boston, Ezekiel, their only son, the subject of the present memoir, was born; and he was taken home to Stockbridge in a chaise, which was the first pleasure carriage that ever crossed over the Blandford mountains, between the Connecticut and the Housatonic rivers. Hence it passed into a proverb in the family, that "Ezekiel went to Boston to be born."

Ezekiel Bacon entered Yale College at the age of 14, and was graduated in the class of 1794, read law in Judge Reeves's law school in Litchfield, Conn., studied afterwards in the office of the celebrated Nathan Dane, of Beverly, Mass., and practised for several years in Berkshire county. He was a member of the Massachusetts legislature in 1806 and '7; was the representative of Berkshire in the congress of the United States from 1807 to 1813, serving on the committee of ways and means, and for one year during the war of 1812 its chairman. He was then appointed to the office of chief justice of the Circuit Court of Common Pleas for the western district of Massachusetts, which he held, when he received the appointment from Mr. Madison of comptroller of the treasury of the United States, which, owing to ill health, he was soon after obliged to resign, and removing to the State of New York, settled in Utica in the year 1816, where he has since resided. During this period he had represented the county of Oneida one year in the legislature, held the office of judge of the Common Pleas two years, and was a member of the constitutional convention of 1821. He was nominated for congress in opposition to Henry R. Storrs about the year 1824, and was defeated by a majority of less than 100 votes in a poll of several thousand. Since that period he has lived in private life, and during a large portion of the time suffered from protracted ill health and manifold bodily infirmities. He was, at the time of his death, the oldest living graduate of Yale College, the oldest surviving member of congress, and undoubtedly the only living representative of the administration of Mr. Madison. He gave his first vote for Mr. Jefferson, in 1800, and his last for Mr. Lincoln, in 1864, voting at every intervening presidential election between these two periods.

Mr. Bacon, like his father, was an ardent democrat of the Jeffersonion type. When, in early life, he was a member of the celebrated law school in Litchfield, Conn., he formed the acquaintance of Miss Abby Smith, daughter of the Rev. Reuben Smith, D.D., of Litchfield, who was an equally prominent federalist. So high did politics run at that period, that Dr. Smith had very decided objections to have "la petit democrat," the little democrat, as Mr. Bacon was called, for a son-in-law. But at last his scruples were overcome, love triumphed over political prejudice, and Mr. Bacon married the daughter, on the 6th of Oct., 1799. They lived together in the most affectionate manner for the period of 63 years, when she died at the age of 83. Another fact, illustrating the intense political feeling which prevailed in that day, it may be proper to state. Mr. Bacon was invited to deliver an oration on the Fourth of July, in Williamstown, and a copy of it was obtained and publicly burnt by the students of the college.

A public life, like that of Judge Bacon, stretching over nearly half a century, could not fail to be connected with many important incidents in our national history. At the one end, it touched our revolutionary history, and at the other, the war of the rebellion. His youthful enthusiasm was kindled by the one, and at the other, though in very advanced age, he gave the cause of the union his wisest counsels, his devoted labors and his most fervent prayers. His long public life brought him into close connection with many distinguished men, such as President Madison, Albert Gallatin, Wm. H. Crawford, Mr. Monroe, John Quincy Adams, John C. Calhoun, Henry Clay, William Lowndes, Elbridge Gerry, Chancellor Kent, Ambrose Spencer and De Witt Clinton, and with Judge Story he was especially intimate.

Judge Bacon was not a fluent debater, and when he spoke extemporaneously it was with evident embarrassment: but when he prepared himself, he conducted an argument in which it was difficult to say which predominated, his ample information, his sound logic, his transparent statements, or his scathing sarcasm. His power of retort often made his opponent wince under the stroke, and in his cooler moments he sometimes found occasion to apologize for the severity of the infliction.

Judge Bacon was, withal, something of a poet. He published, principally for private circulation, a small volume of poetical effusions, entitled "*Egri Somnia.*" He also published a lecture, which he had delivered at several places, entitled, "*Recollections of Fifty Years Ago.*" Some fugitive pamphlets, and many articles in the public papers, particularly in the Oneida Whig and the Utica Daily Gazette, also emanated from his pen.

He was also a man of great liberality, and an enthusiastic worker in many branches of humane and christian labor. His instincts were high, pure, noble. A puritan by descent and by education, he exhibited many of the best traits of the puritan character,—a character which has given such power to the education, the civil liberty, and the religion of this enlightened land.

Judge Bacon had five children, namely: *John Henry*, who died in 1834; *William Johnson*, now aged 67, who resides in Utica, N. Y., and who was, for 16 years, a Judge of the Supreme Court of the state of New-York; *Francis*, now aged 63, and who is a banker in the city of New-York; *Elizabeth Goldthwaite*, aged 58, and the wife of Henry Colt, Esq., of Pittsfield, Mass.; and *Fdnny Smith*, the wife of Theodore Pomeroy, Esq., also of Pittsfield. She died without issue, in 1851. John Henry, the oldest of Judge Bacon's children, has two sons still living. Judge William Johnson Bacon, of Utica, the third in the series of judges in the family, who have preserved the purity of the judicial ermine of our country, had one son only, Adjutant William Kirkland Bacon, a young man of rare promise, who laid down his life upon the altar of patriotism, in the battle of Fredericksburg, Va., in the late war. The present Judge Bacon has favored the world with an excellent "Memorial" of that beloved son, published by the American Tract Society of Boston.

Rev. Ebenezer Burgess, D.D.—The Rev. Ebenezer Burgess, D.D., of Dedham, Mass., departed this life Dec. 5, 1870. He was born in Wareham, Mass., April 1, 1790, and consequently he was 80 years of age. He graduated at Brown University, in the class of 1809, and at the Theological Seminary in Andover in 1814. He taught in the high school in Providence, R. I., one year; was tutor in Brown University 1811–13, and professor of mathematics and natural philosophy in the University of Vermont, 1815–17. He accompanied the Rev. Samuel J. Mills, that devoted servant of Christ, to Africa, as an agent of the American Colonization Society, to explore the western coast of that continent, and joined the colony of Liberia. They sailed from Philadelphia on that important mission, Nov. 1, 1817, and Mr. Burgess arrived home again Oct. 22, 1818. On their homeward voyage, Mr. Mills was taken sick and died, and his associate performed for him the last offices of personal friendship and ministerial duty, and committed his remains to the ocean.

On the 14th day of March, 1821, Mr. Burgess was ordained pastor of the First Church of Christ in Dedham, and after a highly judicious and successful ministry of 40 years, he resigned the active pastoral duties March 13, 1861.

In 1840, Dr. Burgess published "*The Dedham Pulpit*," an octavo volume of 517 pages. It contains a complete collection of the sermons which were published by the ministers of the First Church in Dedham, from 1638 to 1800. The Rev. John Allin was the first pastor of that church. He was born in England, in 1596, was settled as pastor April 24, 1639, dismissed by death Aug. 26, 1671, at the age of 75 years. The Rev. William Adams was the second pastor. He was ordained Dec. 3, 1673, and died Aug. 17, 1685, after a ministry of less than twelve years. The next pastor was the Rev. Joseph Belcher, who was chosen Nov. 29, 1693, and died suddenly April 27, 1723, in the fifty-third year of his age, and in the thirtieth of his ministry. The Rev. Samuel Dexter was next ordained over that church May 6, 1724, and after a pastorate of nearly thirty-one years, died May 6, 1755. The Rev. Jason Haven was the next pastor. He was chosen Feb. 5, 1756, and died May 17, 1803. He was succeeded by the Rev. Joshua Bates, who was ordained colleague-pastor with Mr. Haven, March 16, 1803, and after a ministry of fifteen years, he resigned the office to accept the presidency of Middlebury College, Vt. Dr. Burgess was his successor.

In 1865, Dr. Burgess published the "*Burgess Genealogy*," an octavo volume of 196 pages. It is confined to one branch only of the great Burgess family, namely, to that of Thomas Burgess, of Plymouth colony. He was the earliest American ancestor of Dr. Burgess, and came to this country about the year 1630. The "Burgess Genealogy" is a work which shows great research and accuracy of detail. The subject of this sketch was not a man who did anything at hap-hazard. His mind was distinguished for comprehensiveness and order. Whatever he undertook was sure to be executed thoroughly, and with good judgment. His mental operations were distinguished for calmness and caution, rather than for rapidity of movement. Hence, his views of all subjects to which he had given his attention were eminently judicious, and he was a bold man who presumed to call them in question. He was a firm believer in the evangelical system of faith, so called, and he held it and preached it in its broadest and most comprehensive relations. Next to the Bible, the Westminster Confession of Faith was his favorite theological textbook, and though he held what he regarded to be the truth with an uncompromising spirit, it was still done with as broad a charity as he conceived to be consistent with fidelity to Christ. His preaching was distinguished, perhaps, for breadth and comprehensiveness, rather than for pointedness and closeness of application. His labors in the Christian ministry were crowned with Divine benedictions, and many at the last day will "rise up and call him blessed."

Dr. Burgess had a remarkably fine *physique*. Dignified and graceful in his manners, with, perhaps, some appearance of preciseness, he would attract attention and command respect in any circle. His general bearing was decidedly of the "old school" type, specimens of which have already become so exceedingly rare, that they are regarded by the present generation almost as curiosities. He had a great deal of that peculiar and indescribable quality which we term *presence*. Though he was affable, and sometimes even playful, every man was impressed with the feeling that he was not to be approached too familiarly,—that his words were weighty, and that they were entitled to the gravest consideration.

May 22, 1823, Dr. Burgess was married to Miss Abigail Bromfield Phillips, daughter of the Hon. William Phillips, of Boston. They were blessed with a family of seven children, namely :—

William Phillips, b. June 8, 1824, and d. Dec. 3, 1827.
Miriam Mason, b. July 19, 1825.
Ebenezer Prince, b. July 2, 1826.
Edward Phillips, b. June 28, 1827.
Martha Crowell, b. May 9, 1829.
Theodore F., b. June 23, 1830; d. April 27, 1835.
Henry Martyn, b. Nov. 5, 1831; d. Feb. 7, 1832.

Miriam Mason was married to the Rev. Dr. A. C. Thompson, Boston Highlands, June 1, 1870.

Ebenezer Prince graduated at Amherst College in 1852, and was married, 1st, to Caroline F. Guild, Nov. 30, 1853, who died June 3, 1859. He is a physician in Dedham.

Their children were:—Abbie Phillips, b. Aug. 26, 1854, d. April 24, 1855; Francis Guild, b. Feb. 17, 1856.

He m., second, Ellen D. Holman, March 1, 1860.

Their children were:—Lucy Holman, b. May 20, 1862; Theodore Phillips, b. Dec. 23, 1864.

Edward Phillips graduated at Amherst College in 1852. Mar. Mary B. Kingsbury, daughter of John Kingsbury, Providence, R. I., Dec. 13, 1855, who was b. June 13, 1835.

Their children were:—William Phillips, b. May 13, 1857; Sarah Kingsbury, b. Jan. 29, 1860; John Kingsbury, b. Jan. 20, 1863; Edward Phillips, b. March 19, 1868.

Dr. Burgess became the possessor of very considerable wealth; and both himself and his estimable wife have long been distinguished for their judicious and large-hearted benevolence. Never, till the records of this earthly history are unrolled at the final day, will the numerous objects which have been blessed by their liberal charities, or the amounts they have received, be fully known. This world has but few worthier men to lose than the subject of this imperfect sketch.

Dr. Burgess was elected a resident member of this society, Dec. 5, 1862.

Hon. David Sears. The Hon. David Sears was born in Boston, Oct. 8, 1787, and died at his residence on Beacon street, in that city, Jan. 14, 1871, at the age of 83. He was a descendant, in the sixth generation, from Richard Sears, "the Pilgrim," who, driven by persecution from his native land, sought refuge among the Pilgrims in Holland, came to this country, landed at Plymouth, Mass., in 1630, and died in 1676. His eldest son, Knyvet Sears, was born in Yarmouth, Mass., 1635, married Elizabeth Dymoke, and died in 1686.

Daniel Sears, 1st, of Chatham, Mass., the elder son of Knyvet, was born in 1682, married Sarah Hawes, and died in 1756. Daniel Sears, 2d, of Chatham, son of Daniel 1st, of Chatham, was born in 1712, married Fear Freeman, and died in 1761. David Sears, 1st, of Boston, son of Daniel, 2d, of Chatham, was born in 1752; removed to Boston in 1770; married Ann Winthrop, a lineal descendant of John Winthrop, the first governor of Massachusetts, and died in 1816. He left an only son, David, the subject of the present sketch. David, 2d, inherited from his father the largest estate which had descended to any young man in Boston, amounting to some eight hundred thousand dollars, which his father had accumulated in the China trade. David graduated at Harvard College, in the class of 1807, of which there are on the triennial catalogue, the names of but two survivors, namely, Mr. David Bates, and Mr. William Thomas. Subsequently he studied law in the office of the Hon. Harrison Gray Otis, but he never practised his profession. In early life, he took a deep interest in public affairs, and for a while was commander of the Cadets. In politics he was a whig and wrote many articles for the papers of the day, upon topics of national interest. He was a member of the state senate in 1851, an overseer for many years of Harvard College, and was also president of the Massachusetts Humane Society. At the last presidential election, he was a member of the electoral college, and was the temporary president of that body.

In business affairs, Mr. Sears was enterprising, though he rarely engaged in any undertaking, unless he was quite sure that it would be pecuniarily successful. He was one of the corporators who built India wharf in this city, and the State street block, and was one of the largest proprietors of the Fifty Associates. His mansion house on Beacon street, recently purchased for a club house, by the Somerset Club, was erected by him nearly fifty years ago, and is said to have been the first dwelling-house of hewn granite ever erected in this city, and at the time of its erection was regarded as the finest residence in Boston.

Mr. Sears was benevolent. His benefactions for the relief of the destitute and for public purposes were numerous, and bestowed with much discrimination; but considering his vast wealth, which had long been accumulating by his judicious investments, his benevolence has perhaps been exceeded by others of comparatively less pecuniary means. It is understood that most of his large estate was bequeathed to his relatives and friends.

Mr. Sears's religious views were both outspoken and peculiar. He built and supported a church at Longwood, for the purpose of carrying out his favorite plan for promoting christian unity.

The wife of Mr. Sears, who died but a few months ago, was a sister of Jonathan Mason, and another sister married Dr. John C. Warren. Four daughters were married respectively to Mr. Wm. Amory; Count d'Hauteville, a Swiss nobleman; Mr. Rives, a son of Hon. Wm. C. Rives, of Virginia, and Mr. George C. Crowninshield. Three sons survive him, David, Jr., Frederick R., and Knyvet W.

Mr. Sears was elected an honorary member of this society and accepted, Sept. 13, 1846.

Proceedings.

Boston, Massachusetts, Wednesday, February 6, 1872. A monthly meeting was held at the Society's House, No. 18 Somerset street, this afternoon, at three o'clock, the president, Hon. Marshall P. Wilder, in the chair.

Samuel H. Wentworth, the recording secretary, read the record of the proceedings at the annual meeting, which was approved.

John Ward Dean, the librarian, reported that during the month of January, 64 volumes, 304 pamphlets, 19 Roman coins, some ancient documents and a large quantity of genealogical manuscripts had been presented to the society.

Thanks were voted to Lewis Slack, of Brookline, for the present of two volumes of a newspaper printed at Boston, entitled *The Independent Chronicle and Universal Advertiser*, for five years, from 1777 to 1781, inclusive; to William H. Whitmore, of Boston, for eight volumes of the *Boston Evening Transcript*, from August, 1858, to July, 1863; to William Duane, of Philadelphia, for a manuscript translation by himself of a journal kept in French, from 1782 to 1785, by his uncle, Benjamin Franklin Bache, then a youth, at Geneva, Passy and Paris, and on his return to this country; and to the Prince Society, for the manuscript copy of John Dunton's *Letters from New-England*, from which their volume was printed, and a manuscript copy of *Mercurius Anti-mechanicus*, attributed to Rev. Nathaniel Ward.

Rev. Edmund F. Slafter, the corresponding secretary, reported letters accepting membership; but as a full list of the members admitted during the year will be printed with the proceedings at the next annual meeting, their names will be omitted here.

The board of directors nominated seven candidates for resident membership, and one candidate for corresponding membership, who were balloted for and elected.

Rev. Dorus Clarke, D.D., the historiographer, read biographical sketches of two deceased members, namely, William Saxton Morton, of Quincy, and And Emerson, of Boston.

Samuel G. Drake read a paper entitled, *Sir Alexander Cuming among the Cherokees, or Facts in the early History of Georgia.* This paper, it is expected, will shortly appear in the Register.

The Hon. Benj. A. G. Fuller, of Boston, read an interesting paper, founded upon a collection of documents and autograph letters of Benjamin Franklin and his sister, Mrs. Jane Mecom, and also from Josiah Flagg and Richard Bache, which he read to the meeting and presented to the Society. Thanks were voted for the paper and for the donation.

The Hon. James D. Green, of Cambridge, presented a volume of family documents, consisting of deeds, wills, inventories and other papers, pertaining to the estates of James Green, of Malden, and his descendants, for five generations and a period of two hundred years; for which valuable present thanks were voted.

Boston, March 6. A monthly meeting was held this afternoon, president Wilder in the chair.

The recording secretary read the record of the proceedings of the last meeting, which was approved.

The librarian reported as donations during the month of February, 128 volumes (including 10 bound volumes of newspapers and 2 manuscript volumes), 138 pamphlets, 5 ancient coins, and a fac-simile in plaster of an early wax medallion of Washington.

The corresponding secretary reported letters accepting membership from several gentlemen.

A biographical sketch of the Rev. James Thurston, of West Newton, a member of the society recently deceased, was read.

The board of directors nominated seven candidates as resident members, and one as corresponding, who were elected by ballot.

The president read a letter from John Wells Parker, of Boston Highlands, a member of the society, promising the society a series of Massachusetts newspapers for about one hundred years.

Frederic Kidder, of Melrose, read an interesting paper entitled *Flora McDonald in America*, in which he gave the history of her American life from her arrival in North Carolina, in the ship Baliol, in 1774, to her departure in 1779 or 1780, mostly collected during Mr. Kidder's residence in North Carolina many years ago, and largely from the recollection of aged persons who had known the heroine.

BOOK-NOTICES.

Dictionary of American Biography, including Men of the Time; containing nearly Ten Thousand Notices of Persons of both Sexes of Native and Foreign Birth, who have been Remarkable or Prominently Connected with Arts, Sciences, Literature, Politics, or History of the American Continent. Giving also the Pronunciation of many of the Foreign and Peculiar American Names, a Key to the Assumed Names of Writers, and a Supplement. By FRANCIS S. DRAKE. Boston: James R. Osgood and Company. 1871. Royal octavo. pp. xvi. & 1019.

There is no one class of reference-books for which the careful student or the intelligent reader has more frequent use, than biographical dictionaries; and the benefit as well as satisfaction to be derived from such aids, is proportioned to their fulness and accuracy. By the word fulness, we mean the number of the biographies and the amount of information collected; but whether the number be great or small, or whether the biographies be brief or extended, their main value depends upon their accuracy, especially in the matter of names and dates. Failure in this respect is subversive of all confidence. We need not, and do not, pay much heed to an author's opinions, or to his judgments upon men or measures, if we find him careless in his facts. If the framework of his edifice is defective, no amount of painting, or gilding, or literary upholstery can render his structure either safe or inviting.

To most persons it may seem to be a light task, in these days of a teeming press, and in view of the vast accumulation of books, pamphlets and newspapers in public and private libraries, to compile a good biographical dictionary, which shall embrace the most important part of the personal history of the eminent dead, and scarcely more difficult to collect the history of the most distinguished among the living; but it will require only very little experience in labor of this sort, to satisfy any one, that, while it is comparatively easy to collect the more general facts in most men's lives, it is far more difficult, and often quite impossible, to ascertain with exactness even the dates and places of their birth and death. This is true of even many distinguished characters. *Hic labor, hic opus est.*

A biographical dictionary should contain the biographies of the most eminent and useful men and women in every calling or profession, and it should present the facts in as condensed a form as may be consistent with clearness of statement and justice to the subject. Discussions, opinions, theories, elaborate criticisms and eulogies are of little use here, for at best they generally embody the opinions of the author only; and while his judgments upon some subjects might be readily taken and accepted, yet it could not be claimed for any man, with a reasonable degree of candor, that he is fully competent to render a critical judgment, or to fairly interpret the judgment of others, outside the sphere of his own special studies. Still less of practical value, and always out of place in works of this class, is whatever savors of political or religious prejudice. The temptation to indulge in this, which may be called one of the natural habits of the mind, is peculiarly strong in biographical writing, where it is often seen in its most offensive forms. Few men are so constituted as to be able to grasp and give due weight to all the facts and circumstances of another man's life, and to exercise that "charity" which "never faileth" toward men from whom they differ. Especially is this true of one's own contemporaries; in our judgments of whom, we often forget that the verdict of posterity is not as yet made up; and that,— because the jurors who are to pronounce that verdict, will pass upon acts, motives and characters, in a more dispassionate temper, and from a wider survey and fuller knowledge of the facts, than we can possibly have,—our present judgments are more likely to be reversed than otherwise. This is a self-evident truth, and ought to serve as a warning; but is is seldom heeded; and so, every day, we are called upon to accept the judgments of others, and they to accept ours, in regard to men and events, as if there were to be no appeal to distant ages, or to calmer times.

A truly serviceable biographical dictionary, then, should be comprehensive in subjects, accurate in details, and candid in style and temper. Two general plans will naturally suggest themselves for such a work; both based upon what we may designate as territorial considerations, namely: the *universal*, and the *national* or *continental*. Of biographical dictionaries prepared upon the universal plan, the Biographie Universelle, Ancienne et Moderne; the Nouvelle Biographie Universelle, *Lempriere's* Universal Biography and *Appleton's* Cyclopædia of Biography; and of the national, The Biographia Britannica and *Allen's* Dictionary of American Biography, are familiar examples.

The more limited the territory covered by a biographical dictionary the greater the chances are that it will be carefully prepared, and especially so if the author is of the same race and country as the persons about whom he writes. Besides, the universal dictionary must necessarily be a voluminous work, and therefore less likely to be the subject of such frequent revisions as are desirable.

A dictionary of American biography, constructed upon the plan and in the style of which we have given an outline, has long been a desideratum. Such a work cannot be the creation of a day or of a year. It must be the product of large reading, great industry and conscientious research: all of which require time, energy, zeal, and critical ability. Few men have been competent to the task, and fewer yet have had the almost infinite patience requisite for such an undertaking.

There have been numerous attempts in the United States to supply this want. The first was *Dobson's* edition of the Encyclopædia Britannica, published in Philadelphia in 1798. This was followed, in 1802, by *Hardie's* New Universal Biography and American Remembrancer, in 4 volumes. In 1809, *Eliot's* New-England Biographical Dictionary, and *Allen's* American Biographical and Historical Dictionary appeared, each in one volume. Both were confined to notices of deceased persons. Eliot's is a work of great merit, but it was hastily prepared, and failed to satisfy even its author (see his letter to Dr. Bentley, *ante*, vol. xxv. p. 20). The first edition of Allen's dictionary contained notices of about 700 persons. The second edition, published in 1832, contained over 1100 articles, and this edition was remarkably free from errors. In 1857, a third edition, shorn of much of the strictly historic matter of the first, was issued, and the title of his book was changed to "Dictionary of American Biography." This contains about 7000 articles, and abounds in errors. Dr. Allen's dictionary is a very useful work, but it is characterized by its author's well-known peculiarities and robust prejudices. One of the humors of the day is that Dr. Allen fervently and equally disliked Unitarians and federalists, and that this appears quite as much in what he excluded from his dictionary, as in his manner of treating these two classes of persons.

The American edition of *Rees's* New Cyclopædia, in 47 volumes, next appeared; this was followed, in 1825, by an American edition of *Lempriere's* Universal Biography, edited and furnished with additional articles, relating to deceased citizens of the United States, by Eleazar Lord. The Encyclopædia Americana, in 13 volumes, a portion of which was devoted to biography, was published between the years 1829 and 1833. *Blake's* General Biographical Dictionary, in one volume, was published in 1836, and a revised and enlarged edition of the same was issued in 1856. *Appleton's* Cyclopædia of Biography, edited by the Rev. Dr. Hawks, assisted by Dr. Robert Tomes, appeared in 1856. This is a valuable and scholarly work. *Appleton's* New American Cyclopædia, in 16 volumes, was published in 1858–62; and *Appleton's* Annual Cyclopædia was begun in 1861. Nine volumes of the latter have been published. Each of the works above named contains a large amount of biographical matter, but neither can properly be styled a dictionary of *American* biography.

Besides the works already cited, there have appeared from time to time, during the last one hundred years, numerous collections of biographies, such as *Belknap's* American Biography, in 2 volumes; *Sparks's* American Biography, contained in two series of 10 and 15 volumes respectively; *Sabine's* Loyalists (a work of extraordinary research and of the highest authority); the National Portrait Gallery of Distinguished Americans, in 4 volumes, commenced by Longacre and Herring, in 1833, and completed in 1839; the National Portrait Gallery and Eminent Americans, in 2 volumes, by E. A. Duyckinck, published in 1862; and other similar works of various degrees of merit. There have also been numerous publications devoted to biographies of some one distinct class of persons, as lawyers, &c.

These works are limited in scope, and confined, almost exclusively, to deceased persons, and to those who were either citizens, or in some way connected with the history, of the United States only. No one of them, certainly, is continental. They are almost all of them restricted to a very few classes of persons, and do not include the names of many men whose labors and achievements have contributed to the progress of the country in the arts and sciences, and other productive industries.

The work whose title is at the head of this notice, is the first attempt at a complete hand-book of American biography. The author has consumed many years in its production, and has had the aid of the labors of all who preceded him, and of larger and more accessible libraries than they enjoyed. He aimed, it appears, to furnish precisely such a reference-book of biography as we have stated to have been a pressing need of the times. He aimed to make his book continental in its range; to give at least an outline of the lives of his subjects, and to embrace in his list, as far as possible, all who have been or now are distinguished for general public services, for special acts of importance to mankind, for eminence in the professions, for marked ability in any direction, and for special usefulness in any and all the departments of human labor.

The best test of such a book as this is its use; but applying the rules we have laid down to this book, we are satisfied that the author has very successfully accomplished his purpose, and placed the literary public, and especially students and editors, under great obligations for this timely help.

In the first place, we find that names and dates are given in full when known; and that a great multitude of errors which have passed without contradiction, and almost without question, from book to book, for years, are here corrected. The author seems to have generally followed the sound rule of going to original sources for his information; and while he has in a very few instances been misled by his authorities, the wonder is, that, amid the frequently discrepant statements which he has had to consult, he has been able to ascertain the facts with so much precision. In his more extended sketches of statesmen, politicians, theologians and soldiers, with very few exceptions, he has succeeded in avoiding the expression of his own religious or political opinions.

We have said that the book is continental. We find, for the first time in a single American book, articles relating not only to persons once or now residents or citizens of, or at some time connected with, the United States, but articles concerning persons prominently connected with the history of Canada and other British American Provinces, Mexico, the South American States, and the West Indies.

Among the many articles concerning celebrities, not found elsewhere, are those relating to Laudonniere, French explorer of Florida; Capt. Robert Gray, the discoverer of Columbia River; Ulloa, the discoverer of California; Menendez, the founder of St. Augustine, the oldest city in the United States; Liguest, founder of what is now the city of St. Louis; Armand, Fleury, Dillon, Deuxponts, and other French officers who served with distinction in our war for independence; and Gens. Grant, Frazer and other British officers opposed to us in that war. There are articles also upon the Rev. Elias Smith, founder of the first religious newspaper in the United States; upon Edwin, Longacre and other engravers; Frazee and others among sculptors; Du Simitière and other painters; Latrobe and others among architects. Of inventors we also find, for the first time in any dictionary, the names of Babbitt,—from whose inventive skill has flowed greater benefits in the direction of our ocean steam-navigation than from any other source,—Burden, Blanchard, and others. Interesting articles are also given upon Ralph Lane, Sir Thomas Dale, Count Frontenac, Don B. De Galvez, James Hardie, Chev. Gerard, Henry Ellis, Gen. Greaton, Josiah Harmar, Stephen Higginson, William Lee (brother of Arthur), Eleazar Lord. There are also new facts as to the birth-place of Columbus (unknown to Irving), and articles upon Capt. John Mason, founder of the province of New-Hampshire, De Kalb, Arthur St. Clair, Dr. Edward Bancroft, Sir George Downing, Sir Ferdinando Gorges, Silas Deane and hundreds of others: educators, authors, poets, engineers, inventors, artists, lawyers, physicians, clergymen, editors, politicians, statesmen, manufacturers, agriculturists and soldiers, living and dead. We find also the names of many Indian chiefs, and that the true pronunciation of the most difficult names is indicated. The book embraces the names of many of the most able or conspicuous officers in the late war, both of the army and navy. The latter has generally been too much overlooked in works of this kind.

Although this book contains nearly ten thousand articles, yet we quickly miss the names of not a few persons whom we think ought to have been included. However, when we bear in mind that the object was to produce a *hand-book* of biography, we see that not only the number of articles, but the space allotted to each, must be limited. In view of the fact that this book is not only intended for the use of people of purely historical or literary tastes, but of those of a wide diversity of tastes,—not for those of one state of our union only but for all,—it is no easy matter to determine what persons should be included in a work of this kind, and what excluded. We presume the author has found this one of his most difficult tasks. To say that he has never erred, would be fulsome flattery; for it would be to attribute to him a degree of knowledge and judgment that is not to be found in the wisest mortal. It will be objected against this dictionary that it is too local; but every such work is so and always will be, no matter by whom prepared or from what part of the country it emanates. For our part, we would not exclude a single article from this volume, and only regret that it is not fuller.

The author evidently did not intend this book to be simply a biography of heroes, nor of the most eminent personages only; but a guide to the names of persons who have rendered public or private service worthy of being specially noted. Those who desire fuller information of the more distinguished personages, are referred by the author to the sources from which it can be obtained.

We had marked a few errors in names and statements for notice here, but no one of them is really vital, and nearly all are such as will be apparent to most persons of ordinary intelligence.

A Memorial of Francis L. Hawks, D.D., LL.D. By EVERT A. DUYCKINCK, Esq. Read before the New-York Historical Society, May 7, 1867. With an Appendix of Proceedings, etc. New-York: 1871. 8vo. pp. 166.

A Memorial of Henry Theodore Tuckerman. By EVERT A. DUYCKINCK. Read before the New-York Historical Society, Jan. 2, 1872. With an Appendix of Proceedings. New-York: Printed for the Society. 1872. 8vo. pp. 15.

In the works before us, Mr. Duyckinck has paid a tribute of affectionate respect to two of his literary and personal friends, both of whom had been his associates as members of the New-York Historical Society. To the Rev. Dr. Hawks, that society is particularly indebted. He found it, some twenty-five years ago, in a languid state, and by the exertions of himself and friends, infused into it new vigor, gave it the aid of his great personal influence, and by his pen and public lectures, created a sympathy for its objects among the community. Mr. Tuckerman was also active in the service of the society and for many years was a member of its committee on fine arts. The lives and characters of these two authors, and the talents of their biographer, are too well known to the readers of the REGISTER to need our eulogy. J. W. D.

Catalogue of the Historical Society of Delaware. With its History, Constitution and By-Laws and List of Members. Wilmington: 1871. 8vo. pp. 23.

The Historical Society of Delaware was organized in 1864. An account of the proceedings on this occasion will be found in the REGISTER, vol. xix. p. 191. Hon. Willard Hall, a native of New-England, has been the president from its organization to the present time. The society is collecting a valuable library; and we trust that a long career of usefulness is before it. Two historical societies had previously been formed in this state, but both were short-lived. J. W. D.

The Semi-Centennial Memorial of the Universalist Church, Roxbury. Boston: Universalist Publishing House. 1871. 8vo. pp. 108.

A Semi-Centennial Discourse before the First Congregational Society in Bridgewater, delivered on Lord's Day, 17th September, 1871. By RICHARD MANNING HODGES, a former Minister of the Society. With Historical Notes. Cambridge: Press of John Wilson & Son. 1871. 8vo. pp. 59.

Centennial Address delivered on the One Hundredth Anniversary of the Organization of the First Baptist Church, South Chelmsford, Mass. By the Pastor, GEORGE H. ALLEN. *With the Poem written by* Mrs. M. B. C. SLADE, *of Fall River, Mass., together with the Original Hymns, and an Account of the Centennial Celebration.* Lowell: Marden & Rowell. 1871. 8vo. pp. 33.

Semi-Centennial Discourse delivered on the Fiftieth Anniversary of the Organization of the Baptist Church in East Haverhill, Mass., Jan. 3, 1872. By EDMUND WORTH, Pastor of the Baptist Church, Kennebunk Village, Me. Haverhill: Woodward & Palmer, Printers. 1872. 8vo. pp. 40.

Much historical information is preserved in commemorative publications like these, and it gives us pleasure to chronicle their appearance. The tasteful volume, whose title is given first in the above list, contains the services at the fiftieth anniversary of the dedication of the Universalist Church in Roxbury. That church was dedicated Jan. 4, 1821, and has since had six pastors, namely, Revs. Hosea Ballou, 2d, D.D., Asher Moore, Cyrus H. Fay, William H. Ryder, D.D., J. G. Bartholomew, D.D., and Adoniram J. Patterson. Portraits of all of these clergymen are given, and all of them, except the first, survive, and took part in the exercises on this occasion.

The second book commemorates the fiftieth anniversary of the author's settlement in 1821, as pastor of the church in the South Parish of Bridgewater, then the second in that town, but by the separation the next year of the West Parish, in which the church organized in 1664 was located, this church, organized in 1716, became the First Church in Bridgewater.

The First Baptist Church in Chelmsford, to whose history the third pamphlet is devoted, was organized in October, 1771. The church has had eight pastors, namely, Revs. Elisha Rich, Abishai Crossman, John Peckins, J. C. Boomer, J. E. Wiggin, J. P. Farrar, and George H. Allen, the present pastor, who is the preacher of this centennial discourse.

The last publication whose title we print contains the services at the celebration last January, of the fiftieth anniversary of the Baptist Church in East Haverhill. During these fifty years, twelve pastors have been settled here, namely, Revs. William Bowen, Caleb Clark, Asa Niles, Otis Wing, B. Knight, Isaac Woodbury, J. M. Harris, Addison Brown, Edward Humphrey, W. H. Dalrymple, Andrew Dunn and C. P. Melleney, the present pastor. Like the other works noticed in this article, this pamphlet preserves much material which will be found of service by the state or town historian. J. W. D.

Lyman Anniversary. Proceedings at the Reunion of the Lyman Family, held at Mt. Tom and Springfield, Mass., August 30*th and* 31*st,* 1871. Albany: Joel Munsell. 1871. 8vo. pp. 60.

An Account of the Silver Wedding of Mr. and Mrs. F. P. Draper, at Westford, N. Y., Friday Evening, June 16, 1871, *including the Historical Essays on the Draper and Preston Families, read on the occasion; and also the Poem, Addresses and other Exercises.* Albany; Joel Munsell. 1871. 8vo. pp. 32.

We rejoice that family gatherings of every variety are increasing, and that they are made, as is the case with those to which these pamphlets relate, the occasion for preserving historical and genealogical information. J. W. D.

City of Boston. Annual Report of the Chief of Police, for 1871.

The author of this report, Edward H. Savage, published, in 1865, a *History of the Boston Watch and Police* from 1631 to that year. A noticeable feature of this report for the genealogist is the full lists which are given this year of the members of the police, with their birthplaces and the terms each member has served.

J. W. D.

Public Ledger Almanac, 1872. Geo. W. Childs, Publisher, Philadelphia. 12mo. pp. 56.

This publication, which has now been issued three years, is annually distributed, as a Christmas present, among his subscribers, by the publisher of the *Public Ledger*, the well-known Philadelphia newspaper. It is a hand-book of political and statistical information concerning the general government and that of Pennsylvania, and is particularly full concerning the city of Philadelphia. It will prove a useful gift to its recipients. J. W. D.

Chronicles of the Town of Easthampton, County of Suffolk, New-York. By David Gardiner. New-York: 1871. 8vo. pp. 121.

This is a valuable contribution to the local history of Long Island. It treats mostly of the period anterior to the American revolution, in only a few points bringing the chronicles down to a later period. The account of the aborigines is full and apparently thorough. The history of several of the early English families is well developed and very interesting, The appendix contains copies of original documents of great value, which are thus preserved, we may say forever, from the hazards of time and fire. The printing is creditably done by Brown & Co., New-York. We are glad to see that, though a thinnish book, its pages are in the generous octavo, so much more suitable and convenient for local history than the dwarfish duodecimo.

E. F. S.

Spalding Memorial: a Genealogical History of Edward Spalding, of Massachusetts Bay, and his Descendants. By Samuel J. Spalding, Newburyport, Mass. Boston: Alfred Mudge & Son, Printers, No. 34 School Street. 1872. 8vo. pp. 619.

Whoever carefully examines this voluminous family history will, we think, agree with us, that Dr. Spalding has brought to this work unusual industry, care and judgment, and that his efforts have been crowned with eminent success. His style is clear, compact and simple. These qualities go far to inspire a belief that the work is accurate in detail, as well as scholarly in style and systematic in arrangement. The experience of the last twenty-five years presents a series of gradual improvements in the structure of family histories, rising from great crudeness into scientific exactness and simplicity. There can be no possible excuse at this time for publishing a work of this sort that is either complicated or confused in its arrangement. It is entirely feasible to weave together the names of five thousand persons, or any larger number if you please, all bearing a kindred relation to each other, in such a manner, that any one of them can be found without the slightest inconvenience, and his relation traced to any of the others. A child that can read with facility and has a fair capacity, can, we venture to say, be taught in ten minutes to master the system of arrangement in the volume before us. There are but two or three things to be observed. We do not think any system can be more simple than this. The names are all numbered from first to last consecutively, and, if the name appears twice, it is followed by the number in brackets, where it may be found again in the consecutive line. As soon as the eye falls upon a name you may know, if no number in brackets follows it, that it does not appear again; if it is followed by a number in brackets, then you may know precisely where in the consecutive line it is again to be found. The references are both ways. Where a name first appears as a child you are referred forward to where it appears as the head of a family; and where it appears as the head of a family you are referred back to where it appears as a child. The indexes all refer to consecutive numbers, so that when you have got the number wanted from the index, you are carried directly to the name, and are not compelled to look through a whole page before you find it.

As nearly all of the members of the family for whom books of this class are designed are wholly unacquainted with the subject, when the book comes to their hands it should be as simple as possible, and not so complicated as to be a never-ending source of annoyance. The writers of these histories should remember that the system of reference which they adopt, is not for those who are already familiar with them, but for such as are entirely ignorant of them, and moreover are not experienced or skilful in finding out intricate and complicated arrangements.

The introduction in the volume before us contains much valuable information in relation to the name of Spalding in England, but does not aim to connect the American with any English branch.

The entire contents of the volume are put within the reach and ready use of the reader by very full and well arranged indexes. The work is illustrated by ten excellent steel engravings of some of the more prominent members of the family, and embellished with the coat-armor of several European families of the name, exquisitely done in heraldic colorings. The letter-press is excellent, and the mechanical execution is every way satisfactory.

There are some suggestions relating to matters of minor importance which we think may be properly made.

The pedigrees thrown into parentheses, a very important item in a family history, would strike the eye more agreeably, if they were printed in Italics.

The graduates of colleges, if arranged according to the date of graduation, would show at a glance the early movement of the family towards a liberal education, and its progress and growth in this direction. Every thing in a family history should contribute to illustrate the family.

The names of those who have been in the military service do not appear to be arranged with the author's usual care, and it does not appear that all of them are descendants of Edward Spalding. But these defects are after all as spots on the sun, and are only more apparent from the excellence of the work as a whole. E. F. S.

Records of the Proprietors of Narraganset Township, No. 1, *now the Town of Buxton, York County, Maine, from August* 1, 1733, *to January* 4, 1811. With a Documentary Introduction by WILLIAM F. GOODWIN, Captain U. S. Army. Concord, N. H. Privately printed. 1871. pp. xx. 40.

This is the title of a remarkable volume, reflecting the highest credit on its editors, Mr. Goodwin and Mr. Cyrus Woodman of Cambridge.

It is proverbial that even with men of honest purpose of accuracy, no two narratives of a transaction will be without differences growing out of imperfect observation or memory, or the coloring of statement which each may unconsciously give to the case, and therefore it is, that in court, out of court, or wherever prudent men are called upon to pass judgment, they demand the production of the original documents as the best evidence: and not even in the halls of justice is this principle more insisted upon or needed than in the investigations which challenge the scrutiny of the careful antiquary, or the student of history. This is the secret of the satisfaction in the possession of original or documentary papers; they inspire confidence, and on them we found our conclusions free from the dangers of secondary evidence. Prompted by these considerations and quickened by natural sentiments of loyalty and love to the place of nativity, and veneration for the pioneers, the rude forefathers of the hamlet, these gentlemen present this book, a most important addition to general as well as local history, and not less a memorial of generous zeal.

King Philip's war, 1676, "clothed all New-England in mourning;" twelve or thirteen towns were utterly destroyed, and Trumbull—good authority—"affirms that about one fencible man in eleven was killed and every eleventh family burnt out." (P. v.) Sixty years after, there were living witnesses "that there was a Proclamation made to the Army in the name of the Government when they were mustered on Dedham Plain, where they began their march, that if they played the man, took the Fort and Drove the enemy out of the Narraganset Country, which was their great seat, that they should have a gratuity of land beside their wages" (p. 16); and 840 representatives of these Narraganset soldiers, "who were of ye best of our men, the Fathers and Sons of some of ye Greatest and best of our families," met on Boston Common—Autumn of 1733—and formed seven independent associations for possessing and improving the lands promised their heroic fathers on Dedham Plain, and now granted to them by the Province,—"Townships six miles square" to each. The proprietary records of "No. 1" of the "Townships" are exactly printed in the present volume which has ninety pages of "Documentary Introduction."—Here the editor finds "the origin of the system of donating the public domain in recompense for military services" (p. vi.).

This is the historical foundation of Buxton, Maine, "No. 1;" Westminster, Massachusetts, "No. 2;" Amherst, New-Hampshire, "No. 3;" Grafton and a part of Manchester, New-Hampshire, and Greenwich, Massachusetts, "No. 4;" Bedford, part of Manchester and part of Merrimack, New-Hampshire, "No. 5;" Templeton, Massachusetts, "No. 6;" and of Gorham, Maine, "No. 7," dating back to 1676, when the best of the land ventured their lives to save the colonies from annihilation. Only fourteen years later, 1690, the same parties and ideas were again opposed at Quebec, the head-quarters of the influence whose Indian emissaries visited our frontiers with almost ceaseless dread of the hatchet and firebrand, consecrated by Romish priests to the extermination of protestant New-England. The editor says (p. 141*), this "Canada Expedition in 1690, unsuccessful because wicked, like all such indiscreet and puritanical warlike exploits, either at home or abroad, involved the Province in financial ruin." Whether this is the place and occasion for flings—they hurt only one—we let pass; but we see no difference between the military expeditions of 1676 and 1690. They were defensive, not aggressive. Nor do we believe Mr. Goodwin can produce particular or probable evidence "of a dissipated and extravagant people and a more dissipated and extravagant Government" in 1690. It disfigures an admirable volume whose contents, collected by indefatigable labor, are skilfully arranged, and enriched with valuable notes on men and things. This book, we hesitate not to say, is a notable addition to our historical resources, deserving grateful recognition. It has been printed at private expense, but it will be held a lasting disgrace to the present Buxtonians at home—or abroad—who will not share in the cost. Mr. Goodwin promises more good things, of which the present is only the *basis*. He says (p. x.): "These documents are selections from a great mass of valuable papers, accumulated in the hands of the compiler, in the course of historical researches, looking to a history of his ancestral towns of Buxton and Berwick."

Some of the most interesting of these pages are "from the Papers of the Hon. George Thatcher, which were found in a tin-pedler's barn in Concord, New-Hampshire." Judge Thatcher's papers were of great and varied interest. What words can do justice to the custodians of such papers who could so little appreciate the treasures, or be so indifferent as to find for them no better destiny than a tin-pedler's cart, and the paper mill! *Proh pudor!* It is full time for the York Institute to be very busy gathering in, before such shameful destruction, the work of ignorance, goes further.

Mr. Goodwin closes with a general suggestion which cannot be acted upon too soon: he says—"Researches into the foundation of American History are constantly disclosing such errors and perversions creating distrust in the representations of the whole body of our annals as every conscientious and exact student in the field of American history painfully understands; and until this branch of literary work receives a higher recognition than has hitherto been accorded to it at the chief seats of American learning, there is little reason to expect any substantial change for the better. It is strange and astonishing that in all the liberality of the American people in founding and fostering educational institutions, so unworthy consideration has been given to the accurate authoritative preservation and transmission of our history. There is no department of American History worthy of the name, and scarcely any pretension to such a department in any university or college in the land; and what is still more deplorable there is manifested, among the great body of our educational classes, no deep-seated anxiety to correct the grave and acknowledged deficiency. Until there shall be a professorship of American History amply endowed, thoroughly organized and appropriately filled, in each of our great leading universities, no *revolution* in this matter can rationally be expected."

J. W. T.

A Sermon preached in the Second Congregational Church, Keene, N. H., April 12, 1871, *at the Funeral of Rev. A. W. Burnham, D.D.* By Rev. Z. S. Barstow, D.D. Boston: Alfred Mudge & Son, Printers, 34 School St. 1871. 8vo. pp. 20.

Memorial Discourse on the Life and Character of Rev. A. W. Burnham, D.D., delivered in the First Congregational Church, Rindge, N. H., April 23, 1871. By Rev. Dennis Powers. Boston: Alfred Mudge & Son, Printers, 34 School St. 1871. 8vo. pp. 24.

The late Rev. Dr. Amos Wood Burnham, of Rindge, N. H., brother of the late Rev. Dr. Abraham Burnham, of Pembroke, N. H., and father of Mr. Samuel Burnham, one of the editors of the Congregational Quarterly, was a marked member and representative of a family which has long been prominent in the learned professions, and in good service for the people in many public emergencies from a very early date in our colonial history.

The subject of these two discourses was born in Dunbarton, N. H., 1 Aug., 1791; graduated at Dartmouth college, in 1815; pursued his theological studies at Andover seminary, and in 1818 was licensed to preach the gospel. He was the first principal of Blanchard Academy in Pembroke, an institution which owed its origin to his brother, Dr. A. Burnham. He was ordained pastor of the first congregational church in Rindge, 14 Nov., 1821, the first and only place in which he preached as a candidate; and his pastoral relation was dissolved at his own request, at the close of the forty-sixth year of his ministry.

Rev. Dr. Barstow says of him :—

"In thorough and practical knowledge of theology, in ecclesiastical law and usages of the churches, he was well skilled, his counsel was widely sought, and he was much esteemed for his wisdom, judgment, and impartial decisions. He was always prominent in all measures pertaining to the welfare of society : and the town of Rindge owes much of its good name to the influence of his faithful labors. In 1858, the trustees of Dartmouth college honored him with the degree of *Sacræ Theologiæ Doctor*, and though never seeking, but rather shunning public life, he has filled many positions of honor with fidelity and efficiency. He served his town two years in the legislature of the state, where he was highly influential. He contributed many articles to the religious press, and several of his occasional sermons and addresses have been published. He was the author of that very useful tract, "The Infidel Reclaimed," which has been translated into several languages, and which has been widely circulated.

"He published an obituary discourse on the life and character of Samuel L. Wilder, Esq., and of the Rev. Ebenezer Hill; and also extended biographical sketches of the clergymen belonging to the Hollis Association of ministers; and an address which he delivered at the centennial celebration in Dunbarton. The Historical Discourse delivered by him on the occasion of the 40th anniversary of his pastorate, and printed together with other addresses, is a very valuable and able production.

"His style of sermonizing was simple, lucid, direct, logical, scriptural, and instructive in a high degree; and his appeals to the consciences of men were solemn and effective. He followed the advice given by Dr. Harris,—to "hit the nail on the head, then drive it through and clinch it;" during his ministry, ten seasons of special interest were enjoyed, bringing into the church many who have adorned the doctrine of God our Saviour. Nearly six hundred persons were received into the church by him during the first forty years of his ministry, and many others were received in the six succeeding years; but the speaker has not definite information of the number.

"Dr. Burnham was remarkable for the punctuality with which he officiated in every appointment, and men might set their watches correctly by noting the time at which he presented himself as ready to fulfil his engagements.

"His household demeanor and influence were of the tender and affectionate, yet dignified type. He there 'opened his mouth with wisdom, and in his tongue was the law of kindness.' 'His children arise and call him blessed;' and 'his friends do praise him!' Integrity and candor were prominent characteristics, while a keen relish for the humorous continually enlivened his conversation, which, united with his varied knowledge, rendered him one of the most genial and enjoyable of companions."

Collections of the History of Albany, from its Discovery to the Present Time, with Notices of its Public Institutions, and Biographical Sketches of Citizens Deceased. Vol. IV. Albany, N. Y. J. Munsell, 82 State Street, 1871. Quarto, pp. iv. and 556.

About a quarter of a century ago, Mr. Munsell began to publish documentary, statistical and biographical matter relating to the history of Albany, and the series, including the volume under notice, consists of ten volumes of Annals and four of Collections. Few towns or cities in the United States could supply such a mass of the materials of history, and few men could have hoped even to excavate, translate, transcribe and arrange the immense amount of matter which Mr. Munsell has brought together, edited, indexed and printed. The people of the State of New-York, and especially the citizens of Albany, owe to him a debt of gratitude which the progress of time must increase, for his great expenditure of time, patience and money. His name is borne upon the title page of thousands of volumes and pamphlets, found in every one of our principal public and in hundreds of private libraries,—publications in every department of history, art and science, many of which are of great value; but none, we venture to predict, will in the future be more prized than the series of Annals and Collections above referred to.

The volume under notice, which we regret to learn is the last of the series, contains notes of important events from the newspapers, and obituaries of Amos Dean, Richard Varick DeWitt, Rev. William James, John S. Van Rensselaer, Stephen Van Rensselaer, James Edwards, Peter Cogger, Rev. I. N. Wyckoff, Alden March, &c.; Key to the names of persons occurring in the early Dutch Records of Albany; contributions to the Genealogies of the First Settlers of Albany; Albany County Records, &c. A very full Index is appended.

The volume is illustrated with portraits of Amos Dean, James Wade, Erastus Corning, Alden March, William B. Sprague, Ariæentie Coeymans and Bernardus Freeman, and with numerous wood-cuts.

The Rights and Dangers of Property. A Sermon delivered before the Executive and Legislative Departments of the Government of Massachusetts at the Annual Election, Wednesday, January 3, 1872. By ANDREW P. PEABODY. Boston: Wright & Potter, State Printers, 70 Milk Street. 1872. 8vo. pp. 32.

This is a most timely discourse upon matters of vital interest to every member of the community, from the text: "Thou shalt not steal." Dr. Peabody, with his usual power of analysis and statement, points out the manifold ways in which, under the shield of legislative encroachments, this command is violated by individuals, by communities, by public and private corporations, by states, and by the general government. He says that there is in a large portion of the community a strong tendency to the invasion of the rights of property,—a tendency which lies at the foundation of various *quasi* political parties or factions, and which has in numerous instances shaped the action of our national and state legislatures. The general government has ceded the public lands with wasteful prodigality; and yielded to the demand for the legal reduction or cancelling of all debts, by the passage of the legal-tender-act during the late civil war.

He shows how groundless is the growing jealousy of large estates, and that such estates are needed safety-funds and movement-funds for the whole community.

Among the modes in which the incessant war against capital is waged, is the reckless creation of public debts upon the plea,—in many instances a most fallacious as well as mischievous plea,—that posterity should help bear the burdens; when the most reasonable presumption is that posterity will have outgrown the improvements and will have needs of their own equal to their tax-paying capacity. In this relation Dr. Peabody urges the legislature to establish a proportion to the valuation of property beyond which no debt hereafter contracted shall be lawful.

In regard to loans by towns and cities, he suggests that some legislative restraint should be put upon the influence of mere numerical suffrage, so that owners may have some voice in mortgaging their property. He also cites the evils growing out of excessive taxation; one of which is the rapid and injurious extension of executive patronage.

In this view the whole system of municipal knavery results from the fact that the property of every community is at the disposal of a majority, made up in greater part of persons who do not feel the burden of taxation, but hope to profit by its disbursements, and that by the action of this majority in many of our towns and cities taxation has already begun to trench upon reserved capital, the inevitable result of which must be decline and ruin.

Seldom within our knowledge has so much good sense and practical wisdom been crowded into an election sermon, and we hope it will bear an hundred fold of fruit. The entire newspaper press, religious and secular, can do no better service than to publish this discourse and bring it home to the people.

Memoir of Nathaniel Gookin Upham, LL.D. Read at the Annual Meeting of the N. H. Historical Society, June 14, 1871. By DANIEL J. NOYES, D.D., Professor in Dartmouth College. 8vo. pp. 58.

We are indebted to Mr. Samuel Burnham, brother-in-law of the late Judge Upham, for a copy of this elegant volume, which was privately printed and not published. The volume contains, in addition to the memoir, extracts from the funeral sermon preached by the Rev. Mr. Blake, of Concord, N. H., and a very good photographic likeness of the deceased.

As a sketch of Judge Upham will soon appear in the REGISTER, among the necrologies of the New-England Historic, Genealogical Society, we will not here anticipate it by such an extended notice of the deceased and of this volume as we should otherwise desire to present.

We must content ourselves, therefore, with calling attention to Dr. Noyes's memoir, which, though brief, is an eloquent, concise and discriminating portraiture of one whose attainments, public services, life and character deserve the most honorable mention and affectionate remembrance.

The Foster Family. One Line of the Descendants of William Foster, son of Reginald Foster, of Ipswich, Mass. By PERLY DERBY, of Salem, Mass. Boston: David Clapp & Son, Printers. 1872. 8vo. pp. 35.

We are indebted to John Foster, Esq., for a bound and interleaved copy of this volume, which was prepared and printed at his expense, as we infer from the imprint, and for private distribution only. It traces one line of the descendants of William, fourth son of Reginald, of Ipswich, 1638—1681, to the seventh generation.

The volume contains much information derived from town records and the registries of wills, and seems to have been carefully prepared. It will strike the reader as somewhat remarkable, in view of the loss, in numerous instances, of our early town records, that seemingly not a child has been born in the "line" here traced, covering a period of more than two hundred years, about which some fact is not given. This, in itself, is pretty good evidence of what may be done, in the way of family records, by careful and persistent searching.

The edition is limited to 200 copies, and is neatly printed on tinted paper.

Border Reminiscences. By RANDOLPH B. MARCY, U. S. Army; Author of "The Prairie Traveller," "Thirty Years of Army Life on the Border," etc. New-York: Harper & Brothers, Publishers, Franklin Square. 1872. 12 mo. pp. 396.

Gen. Marcy, the present Inspector General of the Army, to whom years ago the public was indebted for important official reports of scientific surveys and explorations in the Western and South Western portions of the United States, has been induced by the solicitations of friends to publish this miscellany of fugitive recollections of persons and incidents in his long military experience of frontier life.

Those who were fortunate enough to read his Thirty Years of Army Life on the Border, will readily enough anticipate what his quick and accurate eye for the facts of nature would see, and what his evidently keen sense of the humorous would appreciate in the strange types of character and remarkable developments of humanity which formerly were and no doubt even now can be found in the Far West.

The book is very entertaining, and is rendered all the more so by its numerous illustrative wood-cuts, which need no key to explain their meaning. Years hence such books as these will have no slight historical significance and value, especially to those who should have occasion to study the peculiar influences that largely moulded the character of early Western pioneer life.

Grammar-School History of the United States; from the Discovery of America to the present time. By BENSON J. LOSSING. Illustrated by Maps and Engravings. New-York; Sheldon and Company. 1871. 12mo. pp. 292.

A Primary History of the United States, for Schools and Families. By BENSON J. LOSSING, Author of "The Pictorial Field Book of the Revolution," "Illustrated Family History of the United States," "Pictorial History of the United States for Schools," "Eminent Americans," &c. &c. Illustrated with numerous Engravings. A new edition, including a History of the Great Rebellion. New-York: Sheldon and Company. 1871. 12mo. pp. 239.

These two volumes form a portion of a series of school histories by Mr. Lossing. They are profusely illustrated, and furnished with questions. Tables giving the pronunciation of the proper names used, are also supplied. The style is well adapted to interest the youthful mind and fix in the memory the events narrated.

It is always difficult to prepare a child's book of history. It must be free from verbiage, and from too detailed statements. The danger is, that the writer will state his facts without sufficiently mentioning the circumstances that qualified them. Mr. Lossing has succeeded remarkably well in avoiding this danger, and we notice but few errors, and few instances where an erroneous impression will be conveyed.

The Monks of the West, from St. Benedict to St. Bernard. By the COUNT DE MONTALEMBERT, Member of the French Academy. Fide et Veritate. Boston: Patrick Donahoe. 1872. 8vo. Vol. I. pp. xii. and 699. Vol. II. pp. xxi. and 757.

These two large and handsome volumes, reprinted from the English version, and recently placed before the public, challenge the attention of all special students of European history, of theologians and religious teachers, and of all, in fine, who aim to acquire an intelligent understanding of one of the most remarkable agencies that ever influenced the religious and secular life of Europe. They open to us the lives, the character, the acts and the motives of a class of persons of whom, for the most part, the world at large of the present day has but little knowledge. This work is the first connected and collected history of the different monastic orders and special schools for training and educating men for various religious offices, which prevailed in Europe from the time of St. Benedict, who was born near the close of the fifth century of the christian era, to and including the memorable career of St. Bernard in the twelfth century.

We who live in the full blaze of a material, intellectual and religious development, such as the world has never before seen, are prone to give less credit than we ought to those agencies and those men who, at a critical period of history, saved the church from the repeated assaults of false faith, fostered learning, encouraged the arts, and far oftener saved Europe, not only against repeated deluges of Asiatic ferocity and heathenism, but more than is generally supposed, or at least acknowledged, served as bulwarks against the absolute power or brutal tyranny of the princes of Europe, and helped to keep alive the spirit of rational liberty. Monasticism was not free from evils or abuses. The system was far from being, in theory or practice, perfect; but that is simply saying that it was of human origin, and the monks were human and not angelic beings. But, if it is too much to affirm that the monastic orders wrought in Europe a work which no other agencies could have done, this at least, we may truly say, that they effected what no others attempted; and that the results of their labors, though not unmixed with imperfections, have made the Europe of to-day possible. The system, its members, and their work, must be judged of by the light of the times in which they served their allotted function.

It is hardly necessary to make special mention of the style and temper of these volumes. To say that they are crowded with proofs of exhaustive research and learning, and are models of style, is not extravagant praise. The late Count de Montalembert, whose decease occurred about two years ago, was well known to all intelligent readers of this generation, not only by his published writings and his devotion to the cause of learning and the civilizing arts, but, no less, by his earnest championship of constitutional liberty. He was a devoted son of the Roman Catholic Church, but not a blind or unreasoning zealot. He was an unflinching advocate of civil and religious liberty, and at the same time a chivalrous foe to all forms of wanton license, in religious, intellectual and political life and thought. This was the author's latest and ablest composition. The work is not likely to lead us to become monks, nor to desire the establishment of the monastic orders in the United States: for they have accomplished the work for which they were fitted and now are out of time; but it will serve to correct many erroneous prepossessions, and to kindle and deepen the spirit of true charity.

Sixteenth Annual Report of the Directors of the Public Library of the City of Newburyport. Boston: Solon Thornton, Printer. 1872. 8vo. pp. 30.

It is a source of much gratification to see the increasing attention paid in our large towns and cities to the praiseworthy and useful object of providing entertaining and instructive reading for the people, by means of libraries and reading-rooms.

This object is being greatly promoted by the coöperation of the best men and women in the community, and by the free expenditure of money contributed by them.

In Newburyport, a free reading-room, furnished with the leading newspapers and periodicals, has been opened in connection with the city library. It is supported by the annual gift of a handsome sum of money by William C. Todd, Esq. Our impression is that this is the first instance of an absolutely free public reading-room in New-England, if not in the United States.

A Sermon preached in the First Universalist Church, Charlestown, Mass., Sunday, Jan. 21, 1872. By William T. Stowe. With an Appendix. Published by request. Charlestown: Abram E. Cutter & Co. 1872. 8vo. pp. 19.

This sermon is a memorial discourse on the life and character of the late Barnabas Edmands, a deacon in the religious society above referred to, who was born March 1, 1778, and died January 13, 1872.

In the appendix are selections of obituary notices of Mr. Edmands which appeared in various religious and secular papers. Among them is one from the Charlestown Chronicle of January 20, written by Abram E. Cutter, Esq. This gives the leading facts in the life of Mr. Edmands.

PERIODICALS.

The New-York Genealogical and Biographical Record. Devoted to the Interests of American Geneaology and Biography. Issued Quarterly. January, 1872. Vol. III. No. 1. Published for the Society. Mott Memorial Hall, No. 64 Madison Avenue, New-York City. $2 per annum. 8vo. pp. 56.

The Record continues to be well edited and conducted. The last number contains a memoir of its late editor, John Stagg Gautier, a gentleman of great intelligence, of purity and loveliness of character, of old and widely extended family and social relations. He rendered valuable aid to the N.Y. Genealogical and Biographical Society from the day it was projected to the day of his lamented death.

The other articles are: American Family of Woodhull, The Heraldry of St. Paul's Chapel, Notes on the Lawrence Pedigree, The Humphreys Family, The Wright Family, Marriage Records of the Society of Friends in the town of Harrison, N. Y., New-York Marriages from the Friends' Records of Philadelphia, &c. &c.

The Eclectic Magazine of Foreign Literature. W. H. Bidwell, Editor. New-York. E. R. Pelton, Publisher, 108 Fulton Street. Yearly subscription, $5. [January, February, March and April Nos., 1872.]

The Eclectic is a monthly, devoted chiefly to the republication from foreign sources of the most able essays and reviews. Each number is embellished with a portrait or other engraving. It is well edited, and is printed in clear type, easy to be read by night as well as by day. The work was begun about thirty years ago, and that it is still prospering is creditable to the reading public.

The American Historical Record, and Repertory of Notes and Queries concerning the History and Antiquities of America and Bibliography of Americans. Edited by BENSON J. LOSSING. Philadelphia: Chase & Town, Publishers.

Since the issue of the January number of the REGISTER, three numbers of the above entitled periodical have been published. It is a monthly, in quarto form, and each number contains about fifty pages in double columns, printed in handsome type, on tinted paper. The price is three dollars per annum.

As its title indicates, it is to be devoted to the history, antiquities, and bibliography of America. Mr. Lossing is eminently well qualified to conduct such a work to the benefit and satisfaction of subscribers, and it is probable that he will be able to furnish them from his own collections, and from other sources, much valuable and interesting matter. The numbers issued are illustrated with wood-cuts, *fac-similes* of autographs, &c. The articles, on account of the limited number of pages of each number, are necessarily short, which enables the editor to give variety to the contents.

We cordially welcome this new periodical, and bespeak for it the generous support of the public.

The Bibliotheca Sacra, and Theological Eclectic. Edited by EDWARDS A. PARK, Andover, Mass., and GEORGE E. DAY, New-Haven, Ct., with the co-operation of Dr. J. P. THOMPSON, of Berlin, and Dr. D. W. SIMON, of England. January, 1872. Andover: Published by W. F. Draper. New-Haven: Judd & White. London: Trubner & Co.

This quarterly is in its forty-second year, and maintains the high rank it has always had for ability and learning.

The contents of this number are:—The Physical Basis of our Spiritual Language; English Eloquence and Debate; Revelation and Inspiration; The Weekly Sabbath; The Organic and Visible Manifestations of Christ's Kingdom, and the Human Agency in its Advancement; The Three Fundamental Methods of Preaching; The Public Reading of Sermons, and the Preaching of them Memoriter; Notices of Recent Publications.

The Congregational Quarterly. January, 1872. Editors and Proprietors: ALONZO H. QUINT, CHRISTOPHER CUSHING, ISAAC P. LANGWORTHY, SAMUEL BURNHAM. Boston: Congregational Rooms.

Contents:—Samuel Haven Taylor; The Supply of Ministers; The Conservative Elements in Protestantism; The National Council; Congregational Necrology; Literary Review; Editor's Table; Congregational Quarterly Record; American Congregational Association; American Congregational Union; The Annual Statistics of the American Congregational Ministry and Churches; Congregational Missionaries; Summaries and Statistics; Lists of Congregational Ministers in North America; The National and State Organizations of the Churches.

About half of this number is taken up with valuable denominational statistics, prepared with evident care. The very able and interesting memoir of the late Dr. Taylor, by Prof. Park, accompanied by a portrait, is worthy of special mention.

The Methodist Quarterly Review. January, 1872. D. D. WHEEDON, LL.D., Editor. New-York: Carlton & Lanahan. Cincinnati: Hitchcock & Walden.

Contents:—Conservation, Correlation, and Origin of the Physical, Vital and Mental Forces; The Methodist Book-Concern and its Literature; The Apocalypse a Dramatic Allegory; German Explorations in Africa: Two Systems of Ministerial Education; The Methodist Episcopal Church in the Southern States; Synopsis of the Quarterlies; Foreign Religious Intelligence; Foreign Literary Intelligence; Quarterly Book-Table.

The character of this Quarterly is constantly improving, and its editorial departments are especially valuable.

DEATHS.

BOWMAN, the Hon. Francis, died suddenly in the railroad depot in Portland, Me., Dec. 21, 1871, aged 98 years, 7 mos. 29 days. He was a resident of Cambridge, Mass., and a son of the late Francis Bowman, of Somerville, where he was born April 23, 1792. He was a member of the senate of Massachusetts in 1837. H. W.

DAWSON, Abraham, in Ithaca, N. Y., Jan. 13, aged 76. He was born in Wisbeach, Cambridgeshire, Eng., July 10, 1795, and settled in Gosberton in Lincolnshire. In 1834 he came with his family to this country, and settled in New-York city, whence three years afterward he removed to Ithaca, and resided there till his death. He was by occupation a gardener. No more sturdy champion of the truth, as he understood it, ever lived, and no one died more generally lamented by those who knew him. He was a faithful husband, an affectionate father and an honest man. He had six children, two only of whom survive, namely, Henry B. Dawson, the editor of the *Historical Magazine;* and Mrs. Mary, wife of Rev. F. Dunsenbury, of Ithaca, N. Y. J. W. D.

EWING, Hon. Thomas, in Lancaster, O., Oct. 26, 1871. He was born in Ohio county, Virginia, Dec. 28, 1789. He entered the Ohio University after he had attained his majority, and the degree of bachelor of arts was there conferred upon him in 1815. The next year he was admitted to the bar. In 1831 he was appointed United States senator, and became associated with Clay and Webster in their opposition to the so-called encroachments of the executive. He supported Mr. Clay's protective tariff bill. In 1837 he resumed the practice of law. He supported General Harrison for the presidency during the campaign of 1840, and became secretary of the treasury, in which position he was retained by President Tyler, but he afterward resigned. In 1851, having held other official posts, he retired from political life and devoted himself to the practice of his profession.

MORGAN, Jonathan, in Portland, Me., between Nov. 3 and 6, 1871, aged 93. He was b. at Brimfield, Mass., March, 1778, and was the son of Jonathan Morgan, whose father, David, was one of the first settlers of that town. He entered Brown University 1799, but changed to Union College, where he grad. 1803. He studied law with William Teler, of Schenectady, removed to Waterford, N. Y., afterwards to Brimfield, Ms., then to Cincinnati, studying with Ethan Allen Stone, and was admitted to the bar. He removed to Shrewsbury, Ms. in 1812, thence to Alna, Me. in 1820, and finally to Portland, where he lived about half a century. He had a taste for mechanics and speculative philosophy, spent much time in endeavoring to obtain perpetual motion, and wrote a large book, still in MS., opposing the Newtonian system of philosophy. He published some years ago a translation of the New Testament.

MORSE, Sidney E., Esq., in the city of New-York, Dec. 23, 1871, aged 78 years. He was one of the sons of the Rev. Jedediah Morse, D.D., and for many years one of the owners and publishers of the *New-York Observer*.

PEIRCE. In Portsmouth, N. H., Mar. 9, 1871, Mrs. Emily Sheafe, wife of Col. Joshua W. Peirce, daughter of the late William Sheafe, Esq., and great-granddaughter of Mark Hunking Wentworth, Esq., aged 75 years. She was buried from St. John's church; the Rev. Rufus W. Clark, Jr. rector, officiating.

RILEY, Mrs. Phebe (Miller), on the 7th of March, 1871, after a short illness, at the residence of her daughter, Mrs. Dr. Murdoch, in Urbana, Ohio, at the advanced age of 94 years.

Mrs. Riley came of good old Puritan stock, being the daughter of Mr. Hosea Miller, of Middletown, Conn., a stanch patriot of the revolutionary war. She was born 30 Jan., 1777; her childhood passing amid the turbulent scenes incident to the forming of a great nation, many of which thrilling adventures came fresh to her mind during our late struggle with another and greater despotism. In 1802, she was married to Capt. James Riley, whose shipwreck off the coast of Africa in the brig Commerce, in the year 1816, and subsequent sufferings while held as a slave by the Arabs in the Desert of Sahara, were familiar to every one at the time. After that terrible disaster, Capt. Riley determined to quit the sea, and from that period the course of Mrs. Riley's life is so interwoven with her husband's that a sketch of the one will answer for both. Capt. Riley, having taken large contracts from the U. S. Land Department for surveying the north-western part of Ohio and Northern Indiana, removed his family from New-York City and settled in Van Wert County, Ohio, on the St. Mary's River, then an almost unbroken forest, and much more inaccessible than our remotest territories are now. This frontier life continued eight years, when, the climate being unfavorable to his constitution, they returned to New-York City, where they resided till after his death, which occurred at sea, March 13, 1840. Since that event, Mrs. Riley has lived with her children (who all resided in Ohio), and by her kind, unselfish, useful life, endeared herself to all with whom she came in contact. Possessing a remarkable memory and fondness for reading, her mind became a store-house of useful knowledge and entertaining story. By a happy Providence she retained her eyesight to the very last, and was in the practice of reading daily, particularly in the Bible, which latter was regularly perused from the beginning to the end each year.

She early united with the Congregational Church, and throughout her long and eventful life delighted in Christian charities. J. J.

WOODWORTH, Selim E., Esq. The death of Selim E. Woodworth, which occurred on Sunday evening, Jan. 29, 1871, at the Union Club Rooms, occasioned general regret in San Francisco. The cause of death was typhoid fever, engendered by a cold caught in Liverpool a few months before. In 1834, Mr. Woodworth embarked from New-York, his native city, on an expedition, under Captain Norrell, to the South Seas, as captain's clerk. The vessel, after a long cruise, was wrecked near the Island of Madagascar, and Woodworth remained among the natives for several months, and became familiar with their language. He left the island and made his way with some sailors, in a launch, to Mauritius, and thence returned home after an absence of four years. He was subsequently appointed midshipman, and would have joined the South Sea Expedition, under Wilkes, but did not receive his orders until after the expedition sailed. He afterwards joined the *Ohio*, and spent three years in the Mediterranean, and on returning was appointed to the West India station, where he spent four years. In 1846, he started overland for the Pacific coast, and reached the Columbia river after a trip of sixty days. After a stay of some months in Oregon he came to San Francisco, and soon after the reports of the sufferings of immigrants in the mountains near Donner Lake, caused a few noble-minded men to form a party and attempt their rescue. After performing this service he returned to San Francisco, and afterwards joined the *Warren*, from which he was promoted to the *Anita*, a transport on the coast until the end of the war with Mexico. In 1848 Mr. Woodworth received the grant of the 100-vara lot at the head of Montgomery st., paying therefor the usual price $16. It was afterwards transferred to F. A Woodworth, who willed it to his brother Selim and his sisters. The first business house built on the bay was erected by him early in 1849, he laying the foundations with the assistance of a few sailors. It stood where the Clay-street Market now stands, and had escaped so many fires that it was considered fire-proof, but it was burnt up in 1852. The firm was Roach & Woodworth. In November, 1849, Mr. Woodworth was elected senator of Monterey and Santa Cruz, and served two terms. On the breaking out of the late war he applied for a position in the Navy, from purely patriotic motives, and served on the lower Mississippi with distinction, being promoted twice. At the close of the war he resigned as commander and occupied himself with private business. The deceased was a son of Samuel Woodworth, well known as author of "Old Oaken Bucket," "The Hunters of Kentucky," etc., and at the time of his death was aged 56 years. He leaves a widow and several children, and sisters and other relatives. The deceased was of a most singular disposition, the development of which originated in the adventurous career of his early life. He was self-reliant, fertile in expedients, never at a loss for a reason or an excuse, was as brave as a lion, and possessed a fund of anecdote that made him the shining light in any circle in which he appeared. He died worth half a million of dollars.

B. F. Mason

Daniels Pr. Boston.

// NEW-ENGLAND
HISTORICAL AND GENEALOGICAL REGISTER

AND

ANTIQUARIAN JOURNAL.

VOL. XXVI. JULY, 1872. No. 3.

BENJAMIN FRANKLIN MASON.[1]

Communicated by PHILIP BATTELL, A.M., of Middlebury, Vt.

BENJAMIN FRANKLIN MASON, a favorite artist in Vermont, was born in Pomfret, county of Windsor, in that state,—a few miles distant from the birth-place of Powers,—March 31, 1804. His father, Marshall Mason,[2] was a farmer, originally from Woodstock, Conn., and his grandfather was Elias Mason, who married Lydia Brown in Watertown, Mass. His mother was Polly Sessions, also of Pomfret, Vt., whose mother was Sarah Dana, both of Pomfret, Conn., families. His parents had ten children, of whom Benjamin Franklin was the seventh. Three died in the epidemic of 1812; two sons and four daughters lived to adult age; two of the daughters, one older, one younger than himself, survive him.

He died at his home in Woodstock, Vt., Sunday morning, January 15, 1871, after a few months illness, which began while he was engaged in his professional work in Middlebury.

[1] This memoir is the substance of a paper which was read at a meeting of the Middlebury Historical Society, January 30, 1871. The works of the painter alluded to, comprise a variety extending through a long professional career, to which those present at the reading had familiar access, an opportunity rare with those to whom the usual appeal of criticism is made, as was that personal acquaintance also by which the quality of the man is made answerable for the claims presented for his work.

[2] Marshall Mason, son of Elias and Lydia Brown Mason, born in Woodstock, Conn., October 15, 1765: married first, Polly Sessions, daughter of Simeon and Sarah Dana Sessions, of Pomfret, Vt.; he was born January 30, 1770:—

1. Sarah Dana, b. April 22, 1789.
2. Polly, b. March 29, 1791; d. December 29, 1811.
3. Louisa, b. June 11, 1793; d. September 22, 1815.
4. Augusta, b. March 22, 1795; d. January 22, 1821.
5. Marshall, b. June 4, 1797; married.
6. George Francis, b. January, 1800; d. January 3, 1812.
7. Benjamin Franklin, b. March 31, 1804; d. January 15, 1871.
8. Francis Sessions, b. February 25, 1806; d. September 1, 1812.
9. Harriet, b. Aug. 18, 1808; m. Thomas Chrystie, Feb. 8, 1838.
10. George Francis, b. December 13, 1814; d. Feb. 15, 1815.

Marshall Mason married, second, Christian Bartholomew, June 17, 1817. He died July 11, 1836; Polly Sessions Marshall, his first wife, died December 29, 1816.

Elias Mason, of Watertown, Mass., married Lydia Brown, May 3, 1753, removed to Woodstock, Conn., about 1762. He was in the fourth generation of descent from Hugh Mason, of Watertown. His wife was of the fifth generation from Abraham Browne, who appears in Bond's *History of Watertown* (page 116) to have been of the same family with Robert Browne, the projector of Independency in England.

As we trace his career, we see in it the growth of a fine spirit, nurtured for the honor and advancement of a community drawn like himself to the breast of nature by its loveliness, invigorated by its healthfulness, and illustrating its strength. Pomfret is a rural town, adjoining Woodstock on the north, and it had a merely rural society, with the opportunities peculiar to such towns. The district-school was well cared for, the religious order was sustained, a select social library was enjoyed, and the spirit of reflection in his father's family, particularly, was stimulated by that. The muse found Burns, it is said, at the plough, and saved him to her service from the errors of his passions. Nature had moulded young Mason as a model of symmetry to attract by the sense, rather than to be over-mastered by the spirit of beauty. When this symmetry was assailed by disease, she commended him to art as fitted to appreciate and represent her perfection.

When he was nine years old, necrosis of the lower part of one of his legs manifested itself, and compelled him to undergo a surgical operation. This event was the turning point in his life. During his confinement after this operation, books were brought him from the library by his father. "In these," said his mate, Tom Ware, "are your copies. Why don't you draw? I do. You can draw as well as I can." In this manner the engravings of animals in books, and afterward the portraits of authors, became his copies, and the effort, as his friend had assumed it might, entertained him. They might both have tried their hand before. At school the practice proceeded, at recess and intermissions, with chalk and coal, Ware taking to it more boldly as a pleasure, Mason perhaps more carefully as a study. At home the ceilings began to witness similar efforts in seclusion, and the thought occurred to him to be a painter. Various books became the helps of this period. Buffon was least exhaustible and most worn. Even the skeleton in the Almanac was not slighted, though showing its spindling proportions sadly from year to year. Doddridge offered a handsome face, Franklin submitted to his name-sake a reverend brow, and Johnson, in a wood-cut in Rasselas, was nothing but the blinking Sam which Reynolds painted him. All this was labored at the best in pen and ink. A lead pencil was discovered full two years afterward at a store. A school-mistress advised map-drawing; his father procured him paints and brushes, and his accuracy in geography was justly to be credited to this opportunity. And so the knowledge of water-colors. At fourteen the grateful boy proposed to his teacher to paint her portrait, as a recompense for the facility she had furnished him. The offer was accepted, but the favor was embarrassing. She was handsome and intelligent, he bashful and young. But in painting he was her master, and his method was his own. She was to sit where he could see to paint her face, reflected in a glass. And so the work was duly done, approved by the sitter and pronounced a likeness when finished.

Ware in the interval had met with Abram Tuttle, a portrait painter, of whom both must have heard, a native of Pomfret, once with West in England, who had returned for an interval and was painting among his friends. Ware had talent, the painter was obliging, and what the lad learned of the master he taught in turn to his more studious friend. At sixteen Mason painted his first oil painting, a likeness of his father. It was preserved till 1830, when the same canvass was used for another likeness, which is still preserved. In the succeeding winter he taught a district school in Rochester, where his crutch proved a useful protection against a disorderly youth older than himself. Once *settled*, the mutineer submitted heartily, and standing firm by the master afterward the school became a model. This pupil is believed to have died while in congress from one of the territories. The teacher in another season attended the Academy at Randolph in one of its best periods, gave some attention to Latin, and was associated with several students who became leading men in different departments of life. In 1823–25, he was with Ware in Woodstock, at school and painting. His friend already was making a local reputation, and had begun to go out. In 1825 Mason painted in some families in Pomfret, subsequently in Thetford, Hartland, Peacham, and in Newport, Croydon and other towns in New-Hampshire, as well as Vermont. In 1828 he painted in Montpelier, and occasionally in other towns. In January, 1831, he met in Burlington, J. G. Cole, of Newburyport, Mass., a true artist, who told him all he knew. Of him he gained a knowledge of methods unattainable before, worked under his eye, and under this influence came first to Middlebury in May. After a few days at the Vermont Hotel he received his first order from Nelson Rogers. Others followed freely, and remaining fifteen or sixteen months he had painted more than twenty portraits. Several of those are retained in town, and well declare the artist's promise of forty years ago. All were esteemed likenesses, none were repulsive ones. Several were good as pictures in their class, correctly and chastely executed. In one or two the refinement of art appears, that catches and records the finest expression, however evanescent, however rare, and so repays to nature the charm she gives in return for the gift to grasp it.

The drapery, however various, is followed in imitation from wave to wave, as each color is repeated in clearness and beauty of tint. The texture of the skin invites the touch, the hair betokens youthful sweetness, and glows with or dissolves the fleeting gleam of light. For a shrine of beauty Mason would always bring the offering of his choicest power, no matter what the work might cost.

From here he went to Vergennes. It was the cholera year. His errand was to take the lineaments of a lovely youth, who had perished as was thought by cholera, and the dread of the community was in strange contrast with the devotion of family love and the reverence of genius for the immunity of art. Visiting Montpelier and Woodstock, again he returned to Vergennes, and for two years mingled in the enjoyments of society there, as he had every where been solicited by his cotemporaries to do. They were gay times, he sometimes said, and he was of the gayest.

From Vergennes the artist went to Rutland in 1836, and painted all summer. Friends here from Boston, advised him to go there. Rev. Mr. Fay, of Vergennes, gave him a letter to Judge Fay, of Cambridge, Mass., his brother, and in the fall he went. He painted a portrait of Judge Fay, took a letter from him to Harding, and was introduced by Mrs. Fay to Alexander. The latter was full of cordial courtesy. He made the acquaintance of Franklin Dexter, the distinguished lawyer, who was a painter by choice, and painted every day. He was introduced to Allston, and found him the kindest of all. He met one day, at Allston's studio, Jeremiah Mason, the chief among lawyers, and endowed with all the senses needful for an amateur in painting. Judge Fay continued his friendship, introduced him to collections as well as artists. He painted at his house a Miss Laman, a Southern lass. He had other work, but the conclusion of his judgment was to go out again for practice and make himself a painter.

In the summer of 1836, he was at Rutland painting every body. From here again he was offered by a lady a commission in Troy, which he accepted. She introduced him to her friends. He took rooms in Cannon place, and remained three years, painting Jonas C. Hart, Mayor Tibbetts for the city, D. L. Seymour and wife, and many others. He visited New-York and saw the works of other artists. Among them was Durand, whom he respected, and in his style somewhat resembled.

He had returned again to Montpelier and Woodstock, when on the invitation of the Rev. Mr. Tilden, at that time principal of the seminary, in the winter of 1840–41, he came again to Middlebury. His style was much matured. His work at this visit included his group of Mr. Tilden's three daughters, portraits of Mr. and Mrs. Tilden, of Mr. Rufus Wainwright's family, a half dozen or more pictures; Olivia Norton, General Hastings Warren, Mrs. Battell and children, and numerous others, usually excellent as likenesses, some of the groups bold as well as graceful in arrangement, and fine or vigorous in execution.

At the invitation of Edward Warren, he resided for a year or two in Buffalo, and then went farther west for observation; was at Boston again, with warm commendation from his friend Alexander as the best painter of hair in America, as in color and fibre he might earlier have seemed to be. His teacher, Cole, had been successful here, but had afterward lost all. He returned to Middlebury in 1844. In life and color he has not surpassed his portrait of Joseph Warren, which represents him to the friends of every period of his life, in that mood in which he soonest won them. The pictures of Mrs. John Wainwright and daughter were each masterly, and if he fell short of them at any time, it was only that the mood and power of genius are one, and that study and effort cannot always ensure it. His skill was not unequal; his knowledge was not equally seen, perhaps, in every style of work. He did not vary violently in this, but now and then affected something shadowy in style, when a fuller tone was truer and better.

In 1846, his chief works of local historical interest were done here: the portraits of Rev. Dr. Merrill,[1] Mr. Seymour,[2] Judge Swift,[3] Mr. Ira Stewart,[4] Mr. Starr;[5] perhaps the latter with that of Mrs. Seaver, a little later. His fame may rest securely on these admirable portraits of the men who have so largely given their reputation to the place, and fully represent the strength of character and cordiality of feeling with which their subjects adorned it.

[1] Thomas Abbot Merrill, son of Thomas and Lydia Abbot Merrill, who removed to Deering, N. H., in 1785, born in Andover, Mass., Jan. 18, 1780, grad. Dart. Col., 1801; tutor Mid. Col., 1804–5; pastor Cong. Ch. Middlebury, 1805–42; trustee Mid. Col., 1806–55; S. T. D.; married first, Eliza Allen, of Bradford, Mass., June 17, 1812; second, Lydia Boardman, of South Reading, Mass., Nov. 18, 1837. Died April 29, 1855.

[2] Horatio Seymour, son of Moses and Mary Marsh Seymour, born in Litchfield, Conn., May 30, 1778; grad. at Yale Col. 1797; admitted attorney in Middlebury 1800; U. S. senator 1821-33; judge of probate 1847–55; trustee Mid. Col. 1810–55; LL.D. Yale 1847; married Lucy Case, of Addison, Vt., May, 1800. Died Nov. 21, 1857.

[3] Samuel Swift, son of Job and Mary Ann Sedgwick Swift, b. at Amenia, N. Y.. Aug. 5, 1782; removed to Bennington Co., Vt., 1783; grad. Dart. Col. 1800; tutor Mid. Col. 1801–3; admitted attorney at Middlebury, 1804; in both branches State Legislature, county clerk 1814–46; judge of probate 1819–41; trustee Mid. Col. 1827–55; LL.D.; married Mary Bridgman Young, of Middlebury, Nov. 17, 1817. Judge Swift is the oldest living graduate of Dartmouth College; president of Middlebury Historical Society; author of *History of Middlebury and Addison County.*

[4] Ira Stewart, son of John and Huldah Hubbell Stewart, born in Pawlet, Vt., July 15, 1779; merchant in Middlebury, 1810; state secretary; trustee Mid. Col. 1819–55; married Betsey Hubbell, of Lanesboro', Mass., Oct. 29, 1814. Died Feb. 13, 1855.

[5] Peter Starr, son of Peter and Sarah Robbins Starr, born in Warren, Conn., June 11, 1778; grad. Wms. Col. 1799; admitted attorney at Middlebury 1805; in both branches of state legislature; trustee Mid. Col. 1819–60; LL.D. Married first, Elizabeth Jones, North Adams, Mass., May 8, 1808; m. second, Eunice Sergeant, of Stockbridge, Mass., July 16, 1812. Died Sept. 1, 1860.

About 1856 his painting of Julius A. Beckwith was executed; it excels in drawing and color. In 1865 Elza Stewart was painted, a child two and a half years old, and here also we see the highest attainment of the painter's skill. At about the same time the portrait of Paris Fletcher was painted; as good a subject as the painter was likely to have, and as good a picture as he could make it. President Kitchel and lady are among the artist's best pictures and among his last here.

Rutland, Montpelier, Woodstock have all received the painter, with a similar cordiality and liberality. In Vergennes, St. Albans, Burlington, Brattleboro', Bennington, his appreciation was in like manner flattering.

Were his course traced step by step in order to catch the impress of his personal character upon his friends, or the public, it would be found to accord with the ideal of the part he chose to fill. No whisper of suspicion attended or taint of dishonor survived him. He was free, bold, and even untrammelled. His purpose was above the prescription of sect or party. He impersonated it. Rather, the secret of his consistency was, it impersonated him.

He was an enthusiastic lover of nature in all her moods and manifestations. He communed with her. The blaze of sunlight, and the chant of flowing or falling waters was a relief; still more, the illusions of beauty, serenity and power. The scenery of many portions of Vermont invited this study and communion: scenery which language vainly strives to represent, such as Woodstock Valley, and the gorge in Bristol. But neither mountain, nor vale, nor forest alone instructed or inspired him; science itself was invoked. The rocks, even, were his tutors. Geology, chemistry and botany, all contributed to the rich lessons which nature had taught him. The questions of the schools followed him from his walks to his closets, where art, physics, language and philosophy were diligently and successfully studied.

The artist harmony of qualities and powers was in his person: in elegance of countenance, in symmetry and force of structure. His frame was compact, full-chested. There was no languor or littleness in his voice or manners; but both were hearty, bold, solid; chastened not changed by deference, toned by his earnestness, warmed by interest or attachment.

His secret of success was in labor. He knew no shame of this. It was the just condition of what his hand might do. The gleam of his reward grew patiently under it. His habit in early life was free, in later life careful, always provident, never exacting. He was diligent, because true to the spirit of his calling: an example to youth when tempted by dissipation, or when solicited to indulgence; persistent in labor even as he fronted the grave.

He never married. If ever he loved it must seem to have been, as in the first effort of his art, the counterfeit presentment, the shadow rather than the substance of a woman. There was once a story that two friends once met at the same house on the same errand, and, guessing the object, mutually deferred to each other, and rapidly left the house together. A sister[1] of Mr. E. D. Barber, whose accomplishments as well as amiableness he valued, painted for him a portrait in exchange for one of herself.

In firmness of friendship he was as a rock, gentle, too, and kind to kindly courtesy. He liked not, but he could bear a solitude of heart. No man more admired what is excellent in woman, or loved better to vindicate the

[1] Miss Mary Elizabeth Barber, an accomplished and beloved teacher of drawing and painting in Miss Sheldon's (Mrs. Nott's) Seminary in Schenectady, and Miss Sheldon's Seminary in Utica. Her death occurred, September, 1852.

character of one he admired. In social intimacy he was accustomed to be valued by the best. He was sensitive to apparent slight sometimes, where attention seemed uncalled for, and indifferent to the society of persons to which patience might have reconciled him. Politeness was a principle with him, the humble he would have disdained to overlook. He sought society for intelligent entertainment. He brought more than his equal stores, and when he imparted of them his tone and expression both bespoke a noble style of man. His profession had not misplaced him. He had his cast by nature, and wore the accomplishment which cost him so much, as the ornament only of equal and genial companionship.

In religious affections, he was deeply reverent, in feeling and in principle. He had prejudices but he had charity. He held no exclusive opinions; he studied, he revered, incidently perhaps he doubted; in essentials, he is thought to have believed. His preference in regard to religious order was for the Episcopal church.

Such in brief was the career and character of one who contributed manifestly to educate and elevate the taste and thoughts of the people, among whom he lived and labored—not alone by his art, but also by his life and conversation. He sought to lead them into that higher sphere of thought which is essential to social health and strength. For this how vain a substitute is needless display! how low a substitute the pretensions of station! These are but the offspring, and, in turn, the progenitors of vulgarity, emptiness, treachery and voluptuousness.

It was well that his grave should be placed amid the scenes of his studies and labors, and so a broken and delicately wrought column near the Queechy appropriately marks the spot where he rests.

CORRESPONDENCE RELATIVE TO "THE HISTORY OF MASSACHUSETTS BAY," BETWEEN ITS AUTHOR, GOV. THOMAS HUTCHINSON, AND THE REV. EZRA STILES.

Communicated by Hon. WILLIAM A. SAUNDERS, of Cambridge.

Concluded from page 164.

[EZRA STILES.]

Newport May 29, 1765.

SIR,

Your letter of 15 January I received 22 February, and wrote an answer 25 March, which displeasing me, I have protracted the delay of an answer until I might have waited upon you at Boston; which I intended at the election this week, had not sickness in my family prevented.

You suggested that you was desirous that among others I should remark to you any errors that might occur in your History. In point of Facts, I believe they are very few; yet upon your desire I had noted a few, that were to me doubtful, on a paper now mislaid.

Considering the certain news of the Revolution in England, I had thought whether the spirited intrepidity in the just seizure of Sir Edmond Andross was *rashness?* needed censure, or even apology? Whether it was not rather a glorious effort for liberty.

I was principally charmed with the three first chapters, which indeed comprehend the main of the History. The three last on *Religion*, *Laws*, and *Aboriginals*, did not seem to me to equal the rest of the composition. To say nothing of the ecclesiastical Constitution, as to which I may be prejudiced; the judicial decisions and examples in Legislation which you selected to illustrate the spirit of Laws for that age, perhaps are not the most happily chosen—many are beneath the dignity of Laws; and taken collectively communicate a lower idea of the abilities of our Ancestors in Legislation, than in any other part of their conduct; while generally their jurisprudence and political proceedings were founded in and conducted by an accuracy and justness of sentiment which would have honored them in Parliament. When I review the Massachusetts Law Book before Andross, I doubt if Lycurgus could have delivered better Regulations for an Infant Colony; it is certain M^r. Locke could not—his Plan both of Polity and Legislation failed for Carolina. The faithful Historian is to narrate Truth, and if not all yet so much of the Truth, as that the mind is enabled to a summary and just judgment on complex action. On the subject of Massachusetts Law which is complex, those are to be selected in example, which give the true genius and spirit of the Laws *considered as a System.* The *sanguinary* and *futile* Laws in New England are in my opinion Exceptions, and not of the Genius of our Legislation. Nor do you say otherwise; however I thought they made too great a figure in the Chapter of Laws.

[The remainder of this Letter relates to Colonel WHALLEY, mentioned in Governor Hutchinson's History; and states the traditionary inormation, that Whalley died in Narragansett. But for Dr. Stiles's mature opinion on this subject, see his History of Three of King Charles's Judges.]

[THOMAS HUTCHINSON.]

Boston 6 June 1765.

SIR,

I am obliged to you for your Letter by M^r. Ellery, and for your remarks upon my History. You doubt whether the seizure of Sir E. Andros was rash considering the certain news of the Revolution in England. I fancy you have overlooked the reason I give for my pronouncing it rash, viz. because they had no certain news; and it appears by a multitude of Papers that they were in terror some time after lest the Prince should not be supported, but forced to quit his design.[1]

In going through the many letters and other manuscripts I had occasion to make use of when I was writing the chapter upon Laws, I saw cause to abate from the high opinion I had conceived of the legislators. They discover, I think, a weak attachment to Moses's Plan, I mean when they were considering a Plan which was not perfected until after 20 years after they came over, during which time the greatest part of the laws were established one after another, pro re nata, and these, collected together, made up their code.[2]

As to Whaley, my friend is certainly mistaken. I will inclose to you a

[1] The reader who is curious in regard to this portion of our history should consult *The Andros Tracts*, the last two volumes of the publications of the Prince Society, consisting of rare contemporary pamphlets and documents relating to the inter-charter period. J. W. D.

[2] Gov. Hutchinson evidently had not seen the *Body of Liberties*, compiled by Nathaniel Ward, and adopted in 1641, by the colony. J. W. D.

copy of one of Goffe's letters to his wife in 1674, where he gives a particular account of Whaley's condition, and in one of his next letters speaks of her friend "now with God" &c.[1] I send you the letter the rather because the other parts of it will entertain you. It is Goffe's own hand. He calls his wife his mother; his children, his brothers and sisters, which will be enough of the key to make the letter intelligible. I have said that I could find nothing of Goffe after 1679. There is only a tradition that he and Whaley were buried at Hadley. I therefore think it very possible that Goffe might be the person supposed to be Whaley. I hope before long to see my old friend M^r^. Willett and to converse with him on this and other subjects; if I should be prevented I will write to him upon it. If ever I go to Narraganset, I should not think much of riding a few miles to see the old woman you mention.

When you have convenient opportunity please to send me back Goffe's letter. When you see M^r^. Chesebrough, pray make my compliments to him.

I am, with much esteem,

Sir, Your most humble servant

THO. HUTCHINSON.

[EZRA STILES.]

Newport Oct. 5, 1765.

SIR,

I should have immediately answered your Honor's Letter of 6th. which I received 19th. June ult. but that I intended a visit to Narraganset, and to compare with the autography of the reputed Col. Whaley the letter you inclosed. Sickness in my family postponed my visit last summer, and particularly prevented my attending our Association on that side the Water the first week in September. I beg leave to retain Col. Goffe's letter a little longer, as I intend next week a journey to Connecticut. I was much pleased with the curiosity of that piece of Antiquity, elucidated by your Notes. If the aged person therein mentioned was Col. Whaley, as seems almost certain, the Narraganset Tradition is a mistake.

I thank your Honor for your remarks on the public temerity in Sir Edmund Andros's affair; I had thought they had certain intelligence of the Revolution — and on the New-England Legislators, who might adhere to the Mosaic polity more closely than either the climate, or the spirit of Britons required.

I beg leave most sincerely to condole with your Honor under the injuries, desolations and distresses you have suffered; and lament that the Annals of New-England should be stained with ingratitude to its worthiest best friend, a patriot who merits the esteem of America, and particularly of New-England, whose name and memory will not fail of reverence and applause through all American ages. Happy, that you are possessed of a jewel which it is not in the power of events to despoil or defraud you of. Your Antiquities, Family Pieces, Coins, antient MSS. your own Compositions, and especially your Continuation of the Massachusetts History to 1730, are too irrecoverably lost: how happy are we, that you had printed to 1692! Reparation may be made for some things; for others it is impossible. How detestable is Ochlocracy! I imagine your virtue never had a severer trial. You need all the philosopher,

[1] Some of the correspondence of the Regicides is printed in the *Massachusetts Historical Collections*, xxxviii. 122-225; but this letter is not there. A letter of Goffe to his wife in 1662, is printed in Hutchinson's *Massachusetts*, vol. i., Appendix, No. xiv. J. W. D.

the hero, the Christian. Deity is Immobility and eternal Calmness—may He minister to you, Sir, fortitude, serenity, dignity in sufferings.

It is much beyond me to see how violences can be vindicated in opposing the Stamp Act, or any other Act of Parliament, whether constitutional or not, till every other method has been used. In all parliamentary Resolutions respecting the Colonies (excepting on Religion) so long as the alternatives are *submission* or *civil wars*, I shall not hesitate to chuse and declare for non-resistance till the consequences of the latter are far less tremendous, than the effects of public oppression. . . . . .[1]

I am, Sir, with great esteem and profound respect,

Your most obedient,

very humble servant,

Hon. L^t^. Gov. HUTCHINSON. EZRA STILES.

[EZRA STILES]

Newport, 26 Nov. 1767.

SIR,

Be pleased to accept my most respectful acknowledgments for the second volume of your History, which you did me honor to send me last July.[2] I have read it with great pleasure. Fidelity in narrating *Facts* is a great and principal thing: but then only is this species of writing perfect, when besides a well digested series of authenticated transactions and events, the motives and *Springs of Action* are fairly laid open, and arise into view with all their effects about them, when characters are made to live again, and past scenes are endowed with a kind of perpetual resurrection in History. In both these, sir, you have happily succeeded—I could only wish you to have been more copious on some matters respecting the internal Police.

Your writings, like those of the great Lord Bacon, will receive greater justice and applause from posterity and distant ages, than from the present. The subject of your History is interesting and important, especially in the view of Americans. The arrangement and composition are excellent. . . . . . . Amidst that caution and delicacy, which the Times and your Situation in political life inspire, your profound knowledge of the subjects you discuss, perspicuity in description, love of Truth and your Country, and your happiness at investigating the efficient causes of events, appear with great dignity. . . . . . Permit me, Sir, to wish you every blessing, not "the glorious Independence" of a British nobleman—dangerous to virtue; but a final participation in the exalted, though *dependent*, honors of Immortality, in the splendors of which, all sublunary glory evanishes and is lost.

I am, may it please your Honor,

Your Honor's most obliged

And most obedient servant,

Hon. THOMAS HUTCHINSON, Esq. EZRA STILES.

Lieut. Governor, &c.

[1] The omissions here, and elsewhere in this series of letters, are in the MS. of the Rev. Dr. Holmes, from which we print.

[2] The second volume was published in 1767. We find here an approximation to the precise date of its issue. For a bibliographical account of Hutchinson's *History of Massachusetts*, by Charles Deane, LL.D., see the *Historical Magazine* for April, 1857, vol. i. pp. 97–102. The article was reprinted for private circulation the same year, under the title of *A Bibliographical Essay on Governor Hutchinson's Publications*. J. W. D.

DEED FROM CAPT. THOMAS WIGGIN TO CAPT. RICHARD WALDERN AND THOMAS LAKE, OF A PORTION OF THE SQUAMSCOT PATENT.

Communicated by J. Wingate Thornton, Esq.

[The Squamscott patent, granted March 12, 1629, is printed in full in the Register, vol. xxiv. pp. 264–6. Appended to it will be found the division of the patent in 1656 by the colonial authorities of Massachusetts.]

This Indenture, made the eighteenth day of nouember, in the yeare of our Lord one Thousand six hundred fifty eight, betweene Capt. Richard Walderne & Thomas Lake both of Boston in new England merchants of the one part & Capt: Thomas Wiggins, one of our Honored magistrates on the other part witnesseth that whereas the Generall Court of the massachusetts Jurisdiction of new England in the yeare of our Lord one Thousand six hundred fifty six, in setelling the diuissions or Limmitts of the Two Pattents of Quamscott & Douer, allotted & assigned to the sayd Capt. Thomas Wiggin & partners who had interest in Eight shares & one quarter, of which sayd Eight shares & one quarter, the sayd Capt. Thomas Wiggin, was then owner & possessor of three shares & one quarter, which hee purchased of said Thomas Lake (the timber Excepted) as appeareth by a deed of sale dated the fourth day of nouember, in the yeare one Thousand six hundred & fifty one & one quarter of a share the sayd Captaine Thomas Wiggins had of his owne, the other two shares & three quarters, then belonging vnto mrs. Susanna ffitch: Captaine Ric. Walderne & Thomas Lake since, which the sayd Richard Walderne & Thomas Lake haue purchased ye said ffitch's part with all hir right & interest therein, all which said eight shares & one quarter being one third of the whole diuission or Limmitts of the said Two Pattents of Quamscott & Douer which the said Generall Court allotted & assigned vnto the said Capt: Thomas Wiggins & partners at Quamscott houses the place where the said Captaine Wiggin now dwelleth, beginning at a Certaine Clump of Trees standing upon a peice of old planting Land about ffortie Poles below a place called Sandy point & soe runns vp the Riuer vpon a straight line towards Exiter to the vppermost head line of the second Diuission, being three miles square the lowermost line beginning at the said Clump of Trees, & runns three miles into the Land vpon Southeast line by the Compas as by the said Order of the said Court appeareth, now Know all men by these presents, that wee the sayd Richard Walderne & Thomas Lake, for & in Consideration of one-hundred & ffifty pounds, secured to bee paid by the said Captaine Thomas Wiggin, & the grant of Timber on a quarter part of a share of his hereafter mentioned, Haue giuen granted bargained sold Enfeoffed & Confirmed, & by these presents doe giue grant bargaine sell Enfeoffe & Confirme vnto the said Capt. Thomas Wiggins, his heires & assignes foreuer, the said two shares, & three quarters of the said Diuission, with all our right Title interest clayme & demand of & into the same & euery part & parcell thereof, with all the houses, orchards, Gardens, marsh, Land stock, proffitts, priueledges & accommodations thereunto belonging or in any wayes Apperteyning in as full & ample manner in euery respect as wee ourselues haue can may or of right ought to haue, Also three Acres of Land at Douer neck, which three Acres is by the said Richard Walderne & Thomas Lake to bee layd out to the said Capt. Thomas Wiggins Excepting & foreuer reseruing vnto vs the said Richard Walderne & Thomas Lake, our heires Executo^{rs} Administrato^{rs} & assignes, all the timber now standing growing & being, or that hereafter shall stand grow and bee, vpon all & euery part of the said bargained premisses, such timber in this reseruation not to bee included, as shall at any time hereafter by the said Capt. Thomas Wiggin's, his heires Executo^{rs} assignes or successo^{rs} bee vsed for fyring fencing or building vpon any part of the said bargained premisses, And that wee the said Richard Walderne & Thomas Lake, our heires Executo^{rs} assignes or workmen shall and may from time to time & at all times hereafter haue free libertie of passage or repassage by Land or water for cutting or fetching the said timber from off the said Land & euery part thereof not doing any damage in any corne feilds, or meadowes without making just or due recompence, also Excepting & foreuer reseruing unto vs the said Richard Walderne & Thomas Lake, our heires Executo^{rs} & assignes one parcell of vpland & marsh at Sandy point aforesaid from the mouth of a Creeke called Walls Creeke, about the aforesaid Sandy point vpon a straight line to the lowermost south East line, beginning at the said Clump of Trees fifteene rodd from high water marke, And in case the said Southeast line from Sandy point aforesaid, should take in all or part of the ffifty Acres formerly sold to Captaine Champernoone on the west side of Winnicott Riuer the same is by these p^{r}sents also Excepted & foreuer reserued unto vs the said Walderne & Lake our heires & assignes as aforesaid, To Haue hold and posses and enjoy the said two shares & three quarters with all & euery the proffitts, priueledges & Appurtenances thereunto belonging (Except before Excepted) vnto the said Capt: Thomas Wiggin his heires & assignes to the only vse of the said Captaine Thomas Wiggin his heires & assignes foreuer, And wee the said Richard Walderne & Thomas Lake doe for our selues our heires Executo^{rs} & Administrato^{rs}, Couenant & grant to & with the said Captaine Thomas Wiggins his heirs Executo^{rs} Administrato^{rs} & assignes, by these p^{r}sents that the afore-bargained p^{r}misses, shall bee & Continue to bee the proper right & Inheritance of the said Captaine Thomas Wiggin's his heires & assignes foreuer, without any the lest molestation trouble Expulsion or Euiction of vs the said Richard Walderne & Thomas Lake, our heires Executo^{rs} or assignes, or any clayming any Title clayme or interest to the same, or any part thereof, by from or under vs or either of vs, or ye heires Executo^{rs} or assignes of vs or either of vs, And that wee the said Richard Walderne & Thomas Lake, our heires Executo^{rs} or assignes, or some or one of vs shall & will, vpon reasonable demand deliuer or Cause to bee deliuered vnto the said Captaine Thomas Wiggins, his heires or assignes true copies of all such deeds Euidences or writtings which Concernes the afore-bargained p^{r}misses remaining in either of our hands, the same copies to bee written out & attested, at the only cost & charge of the said Capt. Thomas Wiggins his heires & assignes—And the said Capt. Thomas Wiggins doth by these p^{r}sents for him selfe his heires Executo^{rs} & assignes (in Consideration of the aforesd bargaine) giue & grant unto the aforesaid Richard Walderne & Thomas Lake their heires & assignes foreuer, all the Timber that now is or hereafter shall bee standing growing or being vpon the said one quarter part of a share of his owne afore mentioned, with Libertie from time to time, & at all times hereafter to cutt fell & carry away the same as aforesayd, also the said Capt: Thomas Wiggins vpon the aforesayd consideration, doth by these p^{r}sents resigne vp vnto the said Richard & Thomas Lake their heires & assignes, all his right & interest in the Land called or knowne by the name of the

Owners Land lying & being in Douer neck, As also his interest in the aforementioned Land at Sandy point. In Witness whereof the parties to these p^r^sent Indentures, haue Enterchangably put their hands & seals the day & yeare first aboue written.

THOMAS WIGGIN: [his seale]

Signed sealed & deliuered
in the presence of
Henry Webb:
Ita Attests, Robt Howard, not: Pub:

This deed of sale was Aknowledged before mee this 8th: of the 9th month: 1658: Symon Willard.

This is a true Copie of the Originall word for word as it stands vpon Reccord, in the: 59: 60: & 61: pages of the 3^d^ Booke of the notary Publike of the massachusetts Colony of new England, & out thence drawne & Examined, the first day of June, 1669 as p^r^dict: Robt: Howard, not: Publ: Coloniæ Predict Vera Copia Taken out of the Reccords of the Countie Court of Douer, & Portsmouth: As Attests:

ELIAS STILEMAN, cleric.

Vera Copia Attest. p' Edw. Rawson, Secre^t^.

JOURNAL OF DANIEL LANE,

A PRIVATE SOLDIER AT THE SIEGE OF QUEBEC, IN 1754, WITH A BRIEF ACCOUNT OF THE WRITER.

Communicated by WILLIAM B. LAPHAM, A.M., M.D., Augusta, Me.

THE ancient manuscript of which the following is a *fac-simile*, was found among some loose papers in the office of the secretary of state, in Augusta, Me., the first of January of the present year. No one has been found who had any knowledge of its existence, and how it came to be with old state papers in the state department is a mystery. It may have been deposited with the state for safe keeping, when the state archives were kept at Portland; and on their removal to this city, it may have got mixed up with them and remained undiscovered till now. This was more than fifty years ago, and the public men of that day have nearly all passed away; and the question of how this valuable relic came among the mass of loose and waste papers where it was found, will probably never be fully and satisfactorily answered.

Internal evidence, as will be seen by those who read this journal, goes to show that this is not the original diary kept by the soldier, during the siege, but is a copy made by him, with the addition of new matter, a few years after his discharge.

This document was put into my hands soon after it was found, and I at once began to work up the case, and have at length succeeded in establishing the identity of the writer, beyond a reasonable doubt. The only clue I had to the authorship was furnished by the paper itself, in giving the place of residence of the soldier as Narraganset Number One. Two of the ancient Narraganset townships were located in the state of Maine, viz.: Number One, now Buxton; and Number Seven, now called Gorham.

John Lane was a celebrated Indian fighter between 1730 and 1750, and lived at various places on the coast of Maine,—at York, St. George, and Broad Bay now Waldoborough. He was at the engagement with the Indians at Norridgewood, under Col. Harmon; and when the province granted bounties for scalps, he was out after the St. John Indians all the year before the expedition to Louisburg. He enlisted a company, and served as captain in that expedition. After the surrender of that stronghold, he was mustered out. Broken down in health, he removed to York, his former place of residence, and from time to time, for several years, he was voted sums of money by the government of the Massachusetts Bay, in consequence of his former valuable services and present destitute condition. He died soon after, though I am not able to give the precise date of his death. He left three sons: John, jr., Daniel and Jabez; and one daughter, Joanna.

Daniel Lane's name appears on the muster-roll of Capt. Woodman's militia company, in 1756; he is set down as sixteen years of age, and his residence Biddeford. In the following year his name appears on the roll of his brother John Lane's company, and his residence is set down as Narraganset. In 1757, when he was but nineteen years of age, having been born at Broad Bay, now Waldoborough, in 1740, he enlisted for the campaign against Canada, and was the only soldier from Narraganset Number One, who was at the siege of Quebec. Hence he must have been the author of the following journal. There are persons, now living, who remember hearing him relate many incidents connected with the siege and surrender of Quebec, and among others, that he helped gather the balm (always pronouncing the *l*) that was used about the body of Gen. Wolfe. After having been discharged from this service, it seems that he again enlisted, and went to Halifax, N. S., to aid in the erection of fortifications at that place. Oct. 21, 1762, he was married to Mary, daughter of Capt. Joseph Woodman. Their children were: Mary, married David Redlon; Alice, married Ezekiel Edgcomb; Rebecca, married John Merrill; Charlotte, married John Palmer; Hannah, married Paul Woodman; Susan, married William Merrill; Esther, married John Darrah; Isaac, married Ruth Merrill; Jabez, married Mary E. Knowlton; Olive, married Nathaniel Dunn; and Daniel, jr., born 1783, married Juliette Fernald, of Kittery, and is now living and resides in Newtonville, Mass. The only surviving daughter is Olive (Dunn), who resides at Salmon Falls, Hollis, Me.

Daniel Lane, and his brothers John and Jabez, all served during the revolutionary war, and each had the rank of captain. They are said to have been "splendid looking men," and possessed of great physical powers and personal bravery.

Daniel lived and reared his numerous family at the lower corner in Buxton. His house was burned prior to 1789, when some of his children were yet young. He then moved to Salmon Falls, and subsequently across the river into Hollis, where his son owned and operated a large mill for the manufacture of lumber. He deceased in June, 1811, very suddenly, as he was entering the house of his son-in-law, Paul Woodman, in Bar Mills.

While serving in the revolutionary army, he kept a journal, similar to the following, which is now deposited in the collections of the Maine Historical Society, in Brunswick, Me. He was for a time with the troops opposed to General Burgoyne, and in a skirmish was captured and carried a prisoner to the British general's head quarters. At his earnest solicitation he was paroled, and when sent through the lines was made the bearer of a memorandum, in the hand-writing of Burgoyne, of which the following is a copy.

The original is in the possession of Mrs. Jane Bradley, of Hollis, Me., daughter of Col. Isaac Lane and grand-daughter of Capt. Daniel Lane.

"A MEMORANDUM FOR MR. LANE RETIRING TO HIS OWN HOME AT HIS EARNEST REQUEST AND UPON HIS PAROL."

Hd. Qurs. near Fort Edward, Aug. 9—1777.

"A letter has been received directed to Major General Burgoyne and purporting to be written by General Arnold, accusing General Burgoyne of letting loose the Savages to murder scalp and destroy the human species involving the innocent with the guilty in one sad catastrophe.

"As that letter neither bears a signature, nor has any other marks of authenticity, Lieut. Gen. Burgoyne is not called upon to give it any answer, nor were it otherwise, would he deign to enter into a particular justification against an imputation so foreign to his nature as that of inhumanity.

"Among general facts, the Generals of the Enemy will first accept the testimony of Capt. Lane in his own case; they will also understand that two of their officers who deserved and provoked severity of treatment by the most indecent behaviour after they were prisoners were nevertheless delivered unhurt by the Indians together with a wounded man brought off the field by their special humanity through a sharp fire. Lieut. Genl. Burgoyne has the select of seventeen Indian Nations under his direction. He has made use of them and shall continue so to do as one arm to subdue the enemies of Great Britain, and the Genl. Commanding against him might complain of his availing himself of Artillery, of Cavalry or Bayonets, if they are not possessed of these arms in the same proportion with as much reason as they entertain, when they expect him to withold the service of these auxiliaries.

"As to the rest of the letter, that the progress of this army is to be stopped somewhere, it is acknowledged as the author states it that we are in the hands of God, but will find our way through every other power as far as the king's orders direct, or leave our bones in the attempt."

The remains of Daniel Lane, with those of his wife and two brothers, repose in the old burying ground, near the church, at the Lower Corner in Buxton, and no stone or other monument marks their last resting-place.

The following Journal is printed *verbatim*, the heading with the first two paragraphs constituting its title-page in the manuscript, with a neat pen-and-ink border.

REGIMENTS AT QUEBEC.

Nos.	Names.	Nos.	Names.
15th.	Amherst's	48th.	Webb's
28th.	Bragg's	63d.	Fraser's
35th.	Otway's	68th.	Anstruther's
43d.	Kennedy's		

Lawrence & Monckton's | Battalions. 3 Companies of | Granadiers, Exclusive of 6 | Companies of Rangers & | Lascells Regimt. | under Command of major | Genl. JAMES WOLFE. | at the Reduction of Quebec. | Anno 1759.

July 8th.[1] Our Men of Warr & Bomb Ships began to play upon the French, the same day General Wolfe with about 3000 Regulars & Captain Dankie [*sic.* Qu. Durkee?[2]] with his Company of Rangers; as Captn.

[1] Capt. John Knox, of the British army, published in 1769 an *Historical Journal of the Campaigns in North America*, 1757–60, containing a diary of the military operations during the siege of Quebec. Extracts from this diary are given in the appendix to Sabine's *Address before the N. E. Historic, Genealogical Society, Sept.* 13, 1859, *on the* 100*th Anniversary of the death of Wolfe*, pp. 72–89.

[2] The words in brackets and the foot-notes, except that on the name Epaminondas, are by John W. Dean.

Dankie march'd into the wood the Indians fired upon him, Killed 15 of his Men and wounded him and his Captn. Lieut. Armstrong.

the 10th, this Day General Murray Cross'd the River and Join'd Genl. Wolfe with about 150 Regulars & Captn. Hazzens Company of Rangers.

the 12th, General Monckton opened a Battery on point Levi consisting of about 30 pieces of Cannon and 5 Mortars within one Mile of the Town.

July 15th. About 4 o'Clock this Morning as our Company were alone the French and Indians Engag'd us, it Lasted about one Hour, in which we had one Man Killed and 2 wounded.

16th. General Monckton set the Town on Fire, by throwing Carcases & Shells therein; the fire Lasted about 3 or 4 hours.

17th. this day were attack'd by a Party of French & Indians they took Three Granadiers Killed five Regulars & Scalp'd four of them.

18th. In the Night of this day Captn. Rous in his majestys ship Sutherland,[1] with the Diana of 36 Guns, & Squirrel of 20 Guns, 2 Sloops & 2 Catts hove up, and Slipt by the Town The Squirrel got by first, without being perceived, but as the Sutherland of 50 Guns came abreast the Lower Town the Enemy Perceived her and gave fire; one Shot went thro' her Main Topsail, and another thro' her Mizen topsail, and a Ball Pass'd between her Main & Mizen Masts, and did no other damage; The diana run aground, and thereby broke her Back.—The Captains of these Vessells were Hamilton of the Squirrel and Schomberg of the diana.—Captn. Schomberg was tried by a Court Martial & acquitted.

the 22d. July. Lieut. Butler was order'd to march up Montmorency River; as we were marching by the River Side, the Enemy fired upon us and wounded Lieut. Butler and one John Miller; this Night our Battery at Point Levi Hove 130 Shells into the town, and Several Carkasses & Set the Town on fire about 10 o'Clock at Night, which Continued until Morning Burning.

July 24th. this day Captain Hazzen march'd from this Place with 50 men in order to get Prisoners or Scalps and the same day we returned, and brought 8 with us, and one of our men got wounded.

25th. Lieut. Patten being about a mile from this Place with 7 men the French fired upon them, & run, took one man & the rest made their Escape.

26th. General Wolfe march'd from this Place with about 1200 Men up Montmorency river and when they got about 3 miles the Enemy Attack't them, and we drove them into their Trenches; The Same day Captn. Hazzen took 6 Prisoners.

July 26th. This day Colonel Welch march'd about Six Miles down the River.

27th. As Col. Welch was on the Return, the Enemy fired upon them and killed two and wounded 5; At Night the Enemy Sent down a Large fire Raft in order to destroy our fleet, but by the Vigilancy of our Seamen they were disappointed in their Aims, our Boats towing them On Shore where they consumed.

July 31st. Anstruthers Regimt. Coll: How with the Light Infantry and Captn. Hazzens Compy. of Rangers march'd up Montmorency River, About one Mile, the Enemy gave us one or two fires and Run, but doing us no hurt we returned to Camp. abt. 4 in the afternoon the Army March'd Some by Land & Some by Water[2] in Order to Storm the Enemys Lines,

[1] For a list of the vessels of war which assisted at the reduction of Quebec, with their commanders and the number of guns, see the appendix to Sabine's *Address*, pp. 93–5.
[2] The words "in boats" erased here.

The Granadiers march'd within Musket shot of their Lines, but the Hill being so steep & their Intrenchments so Strong, that it was thought best to retreat tho' with Some Loss. 900, Killed & Wounded.

Augst. 2^{d}. Captn. Hazzen imbark'd on board 2 flat bottom'd boats with about 90 Men in order to go about 15 Miles down the River.

4th. We Landed on the N^{o}. Side of the River ab^{t}. 15 Miles down.—— we took one prisoner, the Enemy presently Attack'd us Killed one Lieu^{t}. one Private & wounded another. We Soon drove them & ret^{d}. to Camp the Same day.

the 9th. Augst. About 2 oClock in the Morning the City was set on fire by Carkasses that was Hove from P^{t}. Levi & Cont^{d}. so until the 10th. at Night.

11th. The Enemy attacked a Number of our Regulars in the Woods and Killed and Wounded about 30 of them.

22^{d}. we Embark'd on board our flat bottom'd boats with 100 Rangers & 150 Light Infantry, Captn. Montgomery Commanded, went 20 Miles down the River that Night and Augst. 23^{d}. We Landed at S^{t}. Jerkins [Joachim?] & there we met Captn. McDonald with 140 Highlanders, & burnt about one Mile, the Enemy Attack^{d} us, we Killed 11 got 3 Scalps & Came off without Loss.——this day we march'd and Burnt about 10 miles towards our Incampment.

24th. We march'd home to Our Incampment.

25th. Captn. Hazzen went from this Place to P^{t}. Levi with all the Rangers that was at Montmorency & Encampt there.

31 Augst. Major Scott imbark'^{d} With all the Rangers.

September 1st.—1759. This day we Sailed down the River.

2^{d}. Came to Anchor near Isle Madame.

3^{d}. General Wolfe Left Montmorency & Encampt on the Island of Orleans.

4th. Lieut. Richardson ariv'd At General Wolfs Quarters from Genl. Amherst.

6th. Came to Sail from Isle Madame.

Septr. 8th. Came to Anchor within 5 Leagues of Comoresco.

9th. Captn. Hazzen's Company Landed at Comeresco.

10th. Major Scott Landed wth. 200 Rangers & 100 and 40 Regulars.

12th. We March'd and on the March we burnt about 70 Mile.[1]

13th. This day General Wolfe Attack'd Montcalm And drove him on the Plains of Abram, in which Engagement he rec^{d}. 3 Wounds and was oblig'd to be carried out of the field & in a short time Expired of his Wounds. Thus fell that Brave young officer in the Field of Glory in his countrys Cause in the 32 year of his Age, being this day Aged 32 years 7 [8] months and 13 [11] days.

In this Engagem^{t}. Genl. Monckton Also got wounded & we had Ab^{t}. 4 or 500 Men Killed & Wounded, We Killed Genl. Lere of the French and took Genl. Levi Prisoner and the french Genl. & Chief comm^{r}. Montcalm, died of his wounds & they had about 2000 killed And taken Prisoners.

Thus Ended that fatal day to both Parties, but Wolfe And Englands Immortal Glory.

17th. Embark'd in order to go up to the Town.

18th. Quebec surrender'd.

21st. Major Scott and the Rangers incampt 2 miles from the Town.

[1] The words, "up the River" erased here.

26th. We Embark'd on board 2 Catts.

28th. We Landed on the Isle of Orleans.

Octob^{r}. 4th. We Embark'd on board the Catts & the Same day Landed at Quebeck.

7th.—We Sailed from Quebec And Came to Anchor off Point Levi.

8th. Came to Sail and the Same day Anchor'd at Isle Madame.

9th. Got under Way & the Same day Came too at the Isle of Coudre.

11th. Got under way and the 12th. Anch^{d}. by the Island of Comoresco.

October 15th. 1759. Got und^{r} way, and the

21st. made Cape Gaspe, the Same day had some Snow.

25th. We Came up with the Island of Cape Breton.

November 7th. we came in sight of Penobscot Hills.

8th. Arrived at Boston.

30th. Captn. Rogers, Captn. Storks [*sic.* Qu. Stark?] & Captn. Brewer with their Companys of Rangers were dismissed.

Decr. 5th. I Left Boston and Arriv^{d}. at Narraganset N°. 1 the 14th. day of the Same Month & ye year 1759

Thus ends a few remarks upon the very remarkable Seige of that Important City of Quebec in that Part of New France called Canada. Now in full Possession of his Britannick Majesty George the 3^{d}.
But Conquer'd in the Reign of his Majesty George the Second.

On General Wolfe

Whilst George in Sorrow bows his Laurell'd head,
And bids the Artist Grace the Soldier dead,
We raise no Sculptur'd Trophy to thy Name,
Brave Youth the fairest in the list of Fame.
Proud of thy Birth we bless the Auspicious Year
Struck with thy Fall we Shed a Gen'ral Tear
With humble Grief inscribe one Artless Stone
And from thy Matchless honors date our own.

On General Monckton

When Briton's lov'd Epimanondos[1] dy'd,
Thou fell unconquer'd bleeding by his Side,
Thy wounds a Pass-port to the Rolls of Fame,
Blazons the Hero & adorns thy Name.

Journals of Various other Remarks.

Ent^{d}. under Captn. Jefferds the 19th. day of May 1761.

August 4th. 1761. March'd from Narraganset in Order to Embark for Halifax.

6th. Embark'd from Kittery for Boston.

7th. Arriv^{d} at Boston & Sailed for Hallifax the 13th. day

17th. Arriv^{d}. at Hallifax September 9th. Captn. Parker & 3 Commissioned officers arr^{d}. here from Boston wth. 28 Private Men.

having obtain'd Leave to be Absent Accordingly Sailed from Hallifax the 19th. of October.

20th. Ab^{t}. 8 O'Clock got under way.

21st. Wind S. E.

22^{d}. Arriv^{d}. at Saco.

23^{d}. d^{o}. at Narraganset

[1] Gen. Wolfe.

28th. Went from d^{o}. in the Pursuit of John Mitchel and the Same day arriv'd At Saco.

29th. hired a Horse & went to Wells.

30th. Went to Colonel Sparehawk & got the deserters inlistment same day went to Portsmouth, and was Stopt by a Snow Storm untill

Novr. 3^{d}. when I got to Wells.

4th. Took a deserter & got as far as Saco.

5th. at Night got to Falmouth & Confin'd him in Goal.

6th. Set out for home

7th. got home.

13th. Set out from Home for Falm^{o}. in order to Send John Mitchel to Halifax.

14th. got there and found he had run away.

17th. Set out from Falm^{o}. for Narraganset.

18th. Got home.

19th. Set out for falmouth and got there the Same day.

November 20th. About Noon Set Sail for Halifax From Falm^{o}.

23^{d}. This Morning came Abreast of Cape Sables the same day about 4 o'clock came to Anchor in Point Rosway [Port Roseway?].

24th. Got under way & the same day Anchor'd in Liverpool.

25th. Got under way & the Same day Anch^{d}. in Halifax

Decr. 12th. Imbark'd on board the S^{t}. Andrea a ship of about 200 Tons and Decr. 14th. Set Sail from Hallifax.

21st. Arrived at Nantasket 7 Mile from Boston & there we Anch^{d}. one Night.

22^{d}. Hove up & run within 5 Miles of the Town

24th. Got underway & the Same day Arriv'd in Boston, & the

25th. disembark'd & every Man, proceeded to His Home.—and this day I went on board of a sloop Belonging to Cape Orpos [Porpoise?] one M^{r}. Huff Master and the

26th. of Decr. Sailed from Boston and Arriv'd at Cape Ann.

28th. Sailed thence & the Same day reach'd C. Orpos.

29th. Reach'd Narraganset

Anno 1762

May 8th. 1762

March'd from Boston the same day reach'd Marblehead & Beat up for Men

11th. Listed one Man.

12th. March'd to Salem, beat up met wth. no Success.

13th. March'd to Newbury.

15th. d^{o}. to Old York.

18th. d^{o}. to Wells.

19th. d^{o}. to Biddeford.

20th. d^{o}. to Falmouth, & there Enlisted 3 Men.

23^{d}. March'd to Goram Town & from thence to Narraganset.

May 25th. 1762 March'd to Biddeford.

29th. to Narraganset again.

June 1st. March'd from Narraganset to Wells.

2^{d}. Took up John Mitchell a deserter.

3^{d}. Carr^{d}. him to York.

5th. Went from york to Saco.

6th. Went to Narraganset.
10th. March^{d}. from d^{o}. to Falm^{o}.
11th. Sailed from d^{o} for Boston.
14th. Arriv'd at Boston.
18th. Sailed from Boston.
20th. Arriv^{d}. at Falmouth.
21st. Took up a deserter and y^{e}
25th. Arriv^{d} home at Narraganset.

SALEM LOYALISTS.—UNPUBLISHED LETTERS.

Communicated by John J. Latting, Esq., of New-York.

The original letters, of which the following are literal copies, were found among the effects of Samuel Porter, at the time of his death in London, in 1798. They subsequently came into the possession of James Orchard Halliwell, Esq., the distinguished Shakspearean scholar and antiquary, by whom they were presented to the Astor Library of New-York.

Samuel Porter, before the revolutionary war, was an eminent lawyer in Salem, Massachusetts; graduated at Harvard College in 1763. With many of his townsmen he committed the unpatriotic and unpardonable offence of signing the address to Gov. Hutchinson on his retirement from office, and embarkation for England, May 30, 1774. In the following year, he with other loyalists fled from Salem, and took refuge in England, where he resided most of the time during the war. He was proscribed in the banishment act of 1778.

He was a gentleman of culture and refinement, and by his cheerfulness contributed greatly to the enjoyment and enlivenment of the band of "refugees" at the weekly dinners and meetings of the New-England Club in London during the war. His fellow townsman, Col. William Brown, then in England, writing to Judge Curwen in 1780, says of him:—"I lately received a line from Mr. Porter, describing in the most gaudy colors imaginable, the happiness to which his situation has introduced him, encouraging all the world to come to Shrewsbury, and promising every felicity that the golden age could ever boast of. What strange mortals we are! Some men are always happy where they are, some where they have been, and some where they shall be; and yet, we are none of us satisfied with past, present, or to come."

At a subsequent period of his residence in England, 1783, Judge Curwen makes the following entry concerning him in his journal:—"My townsman Samuel Porter, also came to see me; neither time, climate, change of place or circumstances, will ever alter this man's character; I never knew one whose characteristic qualities are so deeply impressed as his."

He appears to have visited Salem in 1788, but soon returned to England and died in London in June, 1798.

Mrs. Mehitable Higginson, to whom the first of these letters is addressed, was a daughter of Dr. Thomas Robie, of Salem, and the third wife of John Higginson, of that town, a descendant in the sixth generation from Rev. Francis Higginson.[1]

[1] A biographical account of Mrs. Higginson and her only daughter Mehitable, who is well remembered as a teacher in Salem, we are obliged to omit; but it will appear in the October number of the Register.—[Editor.]

The Mr. Blaney referred to in Mr. Ashton's letter was Joseph Blaney, born in Marblehead, Feb. 12, 1730; was a graduate of Harvard College, in the class of 1751; married, May 19, 1757, Abigail, daughter of Samuel and Catharine (Winthrop) Browne, of Salem. After his marriage he removed to Salem, and resided in Washington street, on the estate owned by his wife, where Dr. Fisk, dentist, now resides. He was a merchant, and one of the selectmen for several years. He died in Salem in June, 1786.

Jacob Ashton was the son of Jacob and Mary (Ropes) Ashton; graduate of Harvard College, 1766; married Susanna, daughter of Capt. Richard Lee; was a merchant, and president of Salem Marine Insurance Co.; lived in the house now owned and occupied by the Misses Bachelder, No. 200 Essex street; died Dec. 28, 1829, aged 85, leaving a son William, and four daughters.

Rufus Chandler, a lawyer of Worcester, and William Jackson, a merchant of Boston, were noted tories and fled to England at the commencement of the war. They were both proscribed by the act of 1778. Chandler died in London, Oct. 11, 1823, at the age of 76. Jackson died in 1810, at the age of 79.

[SAMUEL PORTER.]

London, March 15, A.D. 1777.

DEAR MADAM,

I hope I shall in a Measure be entitled to your Pardon when I have assured you that I never saw or heard of your obliging Letter of ye 17th Augt. last till the last day but two in last month, for having been abst. in F. & other Dom'ns on ye Contin't, from ye first Day of July & Mr Sewall into whose hands it came having the direction of any Concerns of mine here, thought it needless to post it after me (& indeed ye latter part of the year, I was so continually on ye wing, did not know how to hit me with it) but meant to & says did mention it in his, but if so t'was some one I missed off. Which I would beg leave to offer you as some apology for my neglect to have Earlier gratefully acknowledged it. I am sorry if you can imagine my writing to you can afford me the least semblance of trouble further than shame for an inelegant & impertinent Performance, or that you Ma'm should Ever think to apologize for your Epistolary Faculty. I can but admire as well as at ye same time applaud your hearty Loyalty untainted amid such misfortune, wish it may at some time receive its ample Reward.

News hence I don't pretend to burden you with as John the Painter[1] seems to have been of late Burthen of the Song, a better accot. of whome, his operations here & Exit, I can't transmit you than contained in my Newspapers some of which will take the Liberty to Engross ye Bundle with tho suppose you'll have by reprinting as soon as this may reach you. Could wish Hallifax more agreeable but hope you will continue to Enjoy Peace there with Every necessary of Life; at least think you need fear no more Molestation at Fort Cumberland or otherwise as ye Ensuing Campain must carve out more necessary Employ for the rebellious that way, for which preparations here at Home as well as in ye foreign States in Pay are making with ye utmost Dispatch. Genl. Clinton for Rhode Island and Burgoyne for Canada return in about 10 Days. Tho' I can't be so sure of that speedy consumation of that affair as are most of our Countrymen here, for France has now given ye strongest assurance against their Interference, or Ever suffering any one Prize to be by any American Vessell bro't to any seaport of theirs; & Prussia, whereto Dr. Franklin finally pretended to repair, has made it instant Death to any officer who shall presume to Engage himself to their service. I yet can flatter myself in all confidence, with ye happiness of meeting you with your Daughter, sometime within this three years, in Salem, again a Land of tranquility, should it not in ye meantime suffer utter Perdition & our Lives be continued which may God grant us & that forbid.

Am sure Ma'm you need never be anxious of your Child's Education at least the more essential & delicate part thereof, should no other advantage offer seperate or deprived of her Mother.

[1] For an account of James Aitkin, *alias* John the Painter, see Gordon's *American Revolution*, vol. ii. p. 184.—[J. W. D.]

I most gratefully sense the Honour of any confidence you seem ready to do me respecting her, and you & she Ma'm may rest assured that should I return & make Salem my residence (which at present to me is quite a mote point) any the minutest opportunity to distinguish myself in rendering her or you every possible service in my power will be most cheerfully embraced by Ma'm both your & her affectionate & sincere Friend as well as obd't and faithful servant,

To Mrs. Higginson. SAM[l] PORTER

P. S. Mr Sewall a couple of miles hence has been so unhappy as to bury his daughter suddenly while I was abroad of wh. perhaps you are already apprized. Col. Browne just returned from Paris daily expects Mrs Browne with her Inft Dau from Rhode Island. Mr Curwen has been resident for this 8 months about 150 miles in ye West.

Col. Pickman intends going to his Sis[r]. Gardiner at New York soon, & other Essex Friends are all well here, and like to be where & how to pass my ensuing sum'r I am not at all yet resolved, not probable long in a Palace till Winter brings me up.

[Addressed]
To Mrs Mehitabel Higginson, Hallifax.

[JACOB ASHTON.]

Salem, 20 March 1787.

DEAR SIR,

I wrote you in Octo. last, in which I informed you that your Friend Mr. Blaney was Dead & that I had administered on his Estate, since which I have had no convenient opportunity to write you—at that time I had just received his Books & papers, and did not know enough of them to give you any information respecting your affairs—in my Letter I desired you to appoint some Person here to receive your papers & to give me a discharge—but I have not received a line from you 'till a few days ago when your favors of the 26th Augt. 11th Sept. last came to hand in which you desire I wou'd attend to your concerns in this part of the world 'till you shall find it convenient to come this way yourself.—As I am willing to do you any service in my power, I will for the present take care of your Bonds & Notes, & any thing else belonging to you which I can find, & follow as far as I am able, the directions in your Letters.

Inclosed you will find a state of your affairs as far as I can now give them.—With respect to the ability of the several persons indebted, to make payment, I will inquire & let you know the next opportunity, which I hope will be soon—the only Bond missing is one from Barna. Dodge, which he says he paid Mrs Blaney & took the Bond in the year 1775.—there are also two Notes of hand missing, viz. Phila. Perkins' & Adam Brown's one of which (Brown's) you will find you are credited for in Mr Blaney's account, the other I don't know any thing of, but will Enquire & let you know in my next—the particular state of your Book-debts I must also leave 'till I have more opportunity to inform myself respecting them—Just before your Letter came to hand I received of Jerch. Page £11.15.0, being the principal of his Note, & wrote a Rec[t]. therefor on the Note, which sum I will remit you, as soon as I can collect so much as to make a sum worth sending—it is unfortunate for you that Mr. Blaney received so much on your Bonds, as it is highly probable his Estate will fall short of discharging the demands upon it, tho' as yet I can form no opinion how much, as his Estate is principally in Lands & it is very uncertain at what rate they can be disposed of—it is not likely I shall be able to collect much money for you soon, as the disturbances in our State have for the present put a stop to all Law proceedings—however as I receive money, I will send it to you in the way I shall think safest & most for your interest.—Bills here on London are considerably above par & therefore shall send money whenever I collect it, & shall get it insured from hence to London, unless I receive directions from you to the contrary—it is likely commissioners will soon be appointed to examine the claims on Mr. Blaney's estate, whenever that shall take place, I shall present them with your demands on the Estate.—I have found in the Brick store which Mr. Blaney sold Five years ago, your Library, but whether there is the whole number of Books you left is uncertain, however if you will send me a list of them, & any are wanting I will endeavour to look them up.—I have not found leisure to Examine the Books since I received them, but in my next will send you a list of them.

No process was Ever commenced on any of your Bonds or Notes—Mr. Blaney put several of the Bonds into Mr. Pynchon's hands & desired him to call on the Persons indebted, for Payment—Mr. Pynchon accordingly wrote to them, and soon after the Persons to whom he wrote applied to Mr Blaney & he took the Bonds from Mr. Pynchon again & nothing since has been done by Mr Pynchon respecting them—Agreeable to your desire I enclose a copy of your acct. against Col. Frye which I have taken from your acct. on file. I shou'd have sent the one left by you on file, but I fear'd a miscarriage & I should not have known where to find the acct. as only a part appears in your Book.

I am Dear Sir Your Friend & Servt.

JACOB ASHTON.

P. S. As I have waited some time expecting some vessel wou'd sail from this neighbourhood for London & can't hear of any one going soon I shall send this by a Brig[n] bound to Bilboa as it will probably reach you much sooner than any other way I know of at present and I imagine you will be very anxious to hear from me—I shall write again the first opportunity I have to England.

Samuel Porter Esq.

[Addressed] Samuel Porter Esq.
to the care of Thomas Graham Esq.
No. 10 Serle's Court, Lincolns Inn
London.

{M.A. 17 87}
{SHIP-LRE BRISTOL 12}

Pr Capt. Weeks, via Bristoll.

[Endorsed, in Saml Porter's hand]
[. . . . torn . . . .] ton's of March 20, 1787.
re May 18, pd 1*s*. with Colo[l] Frye's Acct.

MR. PORTER,

Sir when I administered on Mr. Blaney' Estate and received his Books & Papers I found in his Trunk the following Bonds & Notes belonging to you—On which Bonds was due May 1775, agreeably to your Memo. as follows—

On Archs. Rea's Bond	£84 3 4	On John Brown's	£42 0 6
John Rea's	386 16 0	Saml. Andrews's	31 15 3
Asa Peabody's	105 5 0	Thos. Andrews's	47 4 4
Jedh. Chapman's	63 2 0	Jona. Bickford's	20 16 6
Ezekl. Adam's	41 18 5	Joseph Porter's	100 5 0
Saml. Fairfield's	20 3 8	Asa Perley's	20 19 2
Thos. Andrew's	105 5 0		
			£1069 14 2
Enoch Putnam's Note for	£5 11 10½	Israel Dane's	1 18 6
Dr. Joseph Manning's	3 16 6	Joseph Blaney Esqr.	20 0 0
Timothy Fuller's	3 12 0	Willm. Putnam's	7 0 0
Jacob Perkins's	7 4 0	Tarraut Putnam's	50 0 0
Nathl. Harraden's	2 16 0	Jereh. Page's	11 15 0
Paul Dodge's	13 16 8	Danl. Cheever's	3 14 8
Jacob Dodge's	1 15 1		
		Car'd over	£132 10 3½

Amount of Bonds bro't over		£1069 14 2
Amount of Notes bro't over	£132 10 3½	
John Wells's note for	12 8	
Willm. Dodge Junr.	1 7 3	134 10 2½
		£1204 4 4½

Also Samuel Larrabee's Note to Perkins.

The Endorsements on the Bonds since May 20, 1775, are as follows, viz.—

On Archs. Rea's Bond, Mar. 23, 1786,	£7 9 7	in part of Principal by J. Blaney Esq.
On John Rea's Aug. 9, 1785, 10 mos. interest,	44 12 6	in part do. " "
On the same March 4 '86	30 0 0	" " "
On Asa Peabody's June 30, 1785	43 0 0	" " "
On the same Sept. 29, 1785	42 0 0	" " "
On Jedh. Chapman's, June 24, 1776	31 4 0	" by N. P. Sargent Esq.
On the same March 24, 1785	5 12 0	" J. Blaney Esq.
" " May 3, 1785	16 0 0	" "

On the same April 28, 1786	6 0 0	in part by J. Blaney, Esq.
" Joseph Porter's April 18, 1786	25 0 0	" "
" Ezekl. Adams's March 26, 1785	6 13 6	" "

The above are all the endorsements on the Bonds, but there is a Memo. in Mr. Blaney's Book of having "Recd. of Major Parley £10 towards his Bond to Mr. Porter May 19, 1785."

Judge Sargeant paid for you at Ipswich Court in June 1776 in Sundry Actions per his acct.	£5 0 0
He paid W. B. Townsend, Esqr. on Note	18 4 8
He also paid Jona. Andrews Colr. Taxes your Tax	8 0 0
	£31 4 8

All which amount to 8d. more than he received for you on Chapman's Bond as above. Yours J. ASHTON.

[RUFUS CHANDLER.]

DEAR SIR. Its now more than six months since I arrived in this disagreeable country, the weather has been so Extreme Cold that we have continued froze up the whole time and are heartily tired of Nova Scotia. I shol'd not be surprized if my father returned to England, and I assure I sincerely wish myself there, but you know I have a Daughter. since the death of my mother she has lived with my Brothers & Sisters and my sisters being now all married I have been obliged to send for my Daughter, therefore can't with any propriety leave the Country.

Before I left England Col. Fry informed me I could do something here in the way of my Profession, but since my arrival I have found that he knew nothing about the business. All actions here when the sum sued for is not more than twenty pounds are determined in a summary way, and no Declaration being necessary a Lawyer is seldom wanted in such causes, and there being but very few causes except those summary Ones, and this Province being overstocked with starved Lawyers, I do not consider my Profession worth a farthing, and am as much at a loss what to do with myself here, as I was when in England, having no other means of support for myself and Daughter than my small allowance and the Charity of my friends.

On the twenty-fifth of July last I obtained permission from the Commissioners for my Father and myself to receive our allowance by our agents during our absence from Great Britain for One year, and was then directed to make application for a renewal of those permissions at the expiration of that period, otherwise our allowances would cease, and as we expect to go to Annapolis in a short time, and its not probable we shall have another opportunity of forwarding a Letter to London before the year Expires, we now forward to our friend Rogers memorials to the Commissioners for a renewal of those Permissions &c. and my dear Sir after making such alterations as you may think proper we request you will present them. I suppose it will be a very proper time to do it immediately after the Quarterly payment in July next.

I flatter myself something will be done for the Professional men this Session of Parliament, and if it shou'd be necessary to do any thing for me on that Account by way of memorial or otherwise I desire you will consider yourself as my Agent, and do every thing for me that you wou'd wish to have done for yourself. Please to direct your Letters for me to the care of Jonathan Sterne, Esqr. Halifax Nova Scotia.

I am dear Sir Your sincere friend and obliged humble servant,

RUFUS CHANDLER.

Samuel Porter Esq. Halifax 1st of May 1787.

[Addressed] Samuel Porter Esqr.

To the care of Samuel Rogers Esqr No. 23

Charlotte Street, Portland Place

H. the Hope London.

[Endorsed in Mr. Porter's hand]

Mr. Rus. Chandler's of May first 1787.

[WILLIAM JACKSON.]

London, Dec'br 3, 1788.

MR. PORTER,

Sr. My last to you was by Capt. Furber in which I acquainted you that in consequence of my calling on Mr. Cotton and the answer he gave me that he did not know that you had leave of absence, obliged me to apply to the Commissioners, who order'd me to make oath that to the best of my knowledge and belief you held no office or place of profit except the Pension you Received from Government. On the Receipt of yours by Capt. Callahan with one enclosed to Mr. Cotton I waited on him again, and on my producing my Power he has paid me two Quarters amo't'g £50.—up to 10th Octr. At same time told me he should not pay any more except you sent a proper Certificate of your being alive. I suppose it must be attested before a Justice of peace or a minister & Church Wardens of the Church professing the Episcopal Establishment and the[n] attested by a notary publick that they are such.

This Day I was at the Commissioners Office in Lincoln's Inn feilds to examine the list of restitutions granted for Losses. On the list I saw your name, but as I have not a proper Power to Receive the same it must rest until your return, or if you think proper to execute the Enclosed which they gave me I can receive for you what they have granted you, they are now delivering out warrants for payment at the Treasury to be paid next April or May bearing interest till paid.

I understand your Income of the £100 pr annum ceases next Jan'y, as there is a new regulation to take place, and as a proffessional man after that period, you will be paid £50—pr annum for life, the above is all the information I have to write to you respecting your affairs.

By your letter by Capt. Callahan, who had but 25 days passage I was happy to hear you was well, but the account you give me of the Executive and Legislative powers are horrid, and are such that must at present forbid any ones attempting to return or go to America until such are better established that one may not put themselves to the expence and loose their time & labour for nothing but until the[y] do something better or establish their creditt they must appear but little in the Eyes of all Europe. I acquainted you before I left England I thought the next summer I should go again, but as things are I may as well remain here for the present and wait until your new form of Goverment takes place, but it seems long about, and I believe will be a work of time as many jealousies arise among the separate States with parting with their *Freedom* and putting such power into the persons appointed that they may be worse of than ever they were. You know the cry of *Liberty*.

In my last I acquainted you of the King's Indisposition. It has turned to insanity. He is remov'd from Windsor to Kew and attended by severall Physicians. The Parliment met according to prorogation this fall and was prorogued untill next Thursday when no doubt their will be a regency appointed, but I am affraid their will be some warm Debates wether it should be solely in the prince or Prince & Queen. The Lord Chancellor has join'd Mr. Fox's party, and is for the first. Mr. Pitt & party is for the latter which is all the news I have to acquaint you with.

You'l excuse my putting you to expence of this by Packet as it may be of consequence to you & no Boston ship will leave this until March next. You will let me hear from you soon.

Mrs. Jackson joins with me in Respects from Sr yours &c.

WILLIAM JACKSON.

[Addressed]

Samuel Porter Esqr.

To the care of Jacob Ashton Esqr.

Salem

Pr Packet State of Massachusetts.

— Page 240 (*concluded from page* 158 *in* REGISTER). —

		&	[Stephen] ye of Nathaneel Hutchinſon, & of Sarai [his wife.	Hutchinſon.
		&	[William] ye eldeſt ſon of Will: Everton, & of [his wife.	Everton.
Sh:	8.	14.	[Rebekah] ye daughter of Nathaneel Cutler & [Eliſabeth his wife.	Cutler.
Sh:	8	21.	[Rebekah] ye daughter of Jno Knight & of Mary his [wife.	Knight.
Sh:	8.	28.	[Lydia] ye daughter of mr Samuel Hale, & of Lydia [his wife.	Hale.
Sh:	9.	11.	[Joſeph] ye ſon of Nathaneel Frothingham, & of [Mary his wife.	Frothing- [ham.
Sh:	9.	18.	[Katharine] ye daughter of mr Thomas Tuck & of [Eliſabt. his w:	Tuck.
		&	[Mary] ye daughter of Nathaneel Rand, & of Mary [his wife.	Rand.
		&	[Sarai] ye daughter of Zechariah Johnſon, & of [Eliſabeth his wife:	Johnſon:
Sh:	10	2:	[Sarai] ye daughter of John Larkin, & of Johanna [his wife.	Larkin.
Sh:	10.	9.	[Abigail] ye daughter of John Baxter & of Hannah [his wife.	Baxter.
		&	[Mary] ye daughter of Samuel Leman, & of Mary [his wife.	Leman.

	yeer & month	day	The Baptized. — Page 241 —	
	1677.			
Sh:	10.	9.	[Nathaneel] ye ſon of Samuel Leman, & of Mary [his wife.	Leman.
			— — — — — — — — — — —	
			Here ends ye acct, or catalogue of ye Baptized by my wer [?] Hd & bleſsed Father, Faithfull teacher of xts pretious flock: he dying; 22. 10th. 1677.	
			I ws separated unto ye work of ye ministry, & ordained Pastor of this ch.*5. 3d. 1680. Paſce oves[1] & Baptized	*3 mo. 5 day
			— — — — — — — — — — —	[*modern interlining.]
16	80		— — — — — — — — — — —	
Sh	3	9	[William] ye ſon of Timothy Cutler, & of Eliſabeth [his wife.	Cutler.
		&	[Sarai] ye daughter of Samuel Bickner, & Hannah [his wife.	Bickner.
		&	[Mary] ye daughter of Nathaneel Davis, & Mary [his wife.	Davis.
	3	16	[Sarai] ye daughter of Nathan Hayman & of [Eliſabeth his wife.	Hayman.
		&	Samuel] ye ſon of Edwd Wilſon & of Mary his wife.	Wilſon.
		&	Abigail] ye daughter of Nathaniel Rand & Abigail [his wife.	Rand
		&	Samuel] ye ſon of Samuel Dowſe & Faith his wife.	Dowſe
		&	Benjamin] ye ſon of Nathaniel Frothingham & of [Mary his wife.	Frothing- [ham.
		&	Zechariah] ye ſon of Peter Fowl & of Mary his wife	Fowl
		&	Hannah] ye daughter of Samuel Frothingham & [Ruth his wife	Frothing- [ham.
		&	Elenor] ye daughter of James Miller & of Hannah [his wife.	Miller

[1] A few Greek words, blotted and illegible, follow and complete this line.

— Page 241 (*concluded.*) —

3	23	William] ye ſon of Iſaac Johnson & of Mary his wife.	Johnſon
	&	Abigail] ye daughter of Joſeph Frost & of Hannah [his wife.	Frost.
3	30	Nathaneel] ye ſon of Samuel Lord & of Eliſabeth [his wife.	Lord.
4	6.	Eliſabeth] } ye daughters of Andrew Belcher & Sarai	
	&	Mary] } his wife: he a member of ye ch in Cambr: not in full comunion, but had owned ye covent & ws recomended by ye ch to ye ch in Hartford, & had ye privilidge granted him there::	
	&	Abigail] ye daughter of John Foſket & of Eliſabeth [his wife	Foſket
	&	mercy] ye daughtr of Christopher Goodwin & Mercy [his wife	Goodwin.
	&	Deborah] Joanna his wife	
	&	Lydia] ye daughter of John Walker & of Anna his [wife.	Walker.
4.	27	James] ye son of Richard Asting & of Abigail his [wife.	Asting.
	&	Pelatiah] ye son of John Whittamore, & of Mary [his wife.	Whittamore
5	4	Sarai] ye daughter of Edward Wire & of Eliſabeth [his wife.	Wire.
	&	Eliſabeth] ye daughter of Aaron Way, & of Mary [his wife.	Way
5	11	Anderſon] ye son of John Phillips & of Katharine [his wife.	Phillips
	&	Elisabeth] } ye daughters of Nathaniel Cary &	Cary.
	&	Martha] } Elisabeth his wife.	

NOTE.—The upper portion of page 241 is blotted in several places. The writing on pages 241-9, inclusive, is by Thos. Shepard, Jr., in a small, and not very legible hand.

		day	The Baptized. — Page 242 —	
Sh	5	11	Elisabeth] ye daughtr of Jacob Green Junr & Mary [his wife	Green.
		&	Beniamin] ye ſon of William Everton & Sarai his wife	Everton.
	5	18	John] ye ſon of John Cutler Junr & Martha his wife	Cutler.
		&	Hannah] ye daughter of Zechariah Ferris	Ferris.
	5	25	Katharine] ye daughtr of John Jones and Rebeckah [his wife.	Jones.
	6	1	Rebeckah] ye daughter of John Gooſe, & of Sarai [his wife.	Gooſe.
	6	22	John] }	
		&	Lydia] } ye children of Samuel Ballard &	Ballard.
		&	Elisabeth] }	
		&	John] ye son of John Eades, & Mary his wife.	Eades.
		&	Sarah] } ye children of Thomas Chapman, &	Chapman.
		&	Elisabeth] } Sarah his wife.	
		&	Ebenezer] ye ſon of John Kent, & of Hannah his wife	Kent.
		&	Mary] ye daughtr of John Roy, & Elisabeth his wife	Roy.
	6	29	Abigail] ye daughtr of Abel Benjamin, & Amethia [his wife	Benjamin
	7	5	Zechariah] ye son of Zechariah Johnſon, & of [Eliſabeth his wife	Johnſon.
	7	12	Nathaneel] ye son of Nathaniel Cary & Elifabeth [his wife	Cary.
		&	Isaac] } ye children of John Baxter & of Hannah	Baxter
		&	Rebeckah] } his wife: twinns, born at one birth.	

— Page 242 (*concluded.*) —

	&	John] ye fon of John Knell & Elifabeth his wife.	Knell.
7	19	Mercy] ye daughter of Thomas Hitt, & Dorothe his [wife	Hitt.
8	3	William] ye son of Edward Wire & of Elisabeth [his wife	Wire.
8	10	Mary] ye daughter of ye Worshipll James Ruffell, [& Mary his wife	Ruffell.
8	31	Hannah] ye daughtr of Jno. Wilder of Lancastr & [Hannah his wife	Wilder.
9	21	Joanna] ye daughter of Samuel Leman, & of Mary [his wife.	Leman.
10	19	Marget] ye daughter of Jno Cutler Junr & Martha [his wife:	Cutler.
11	30	Katharine] Brackenbury ye daughtr of mrs Lynd [ye wife	Bracken-bury.
	&	Thomas] | & Samuel] | & Elifabeth] | & Mary] | & Sarai] | & Abigail] & Susanna] | ye children of Thomas Addams, & Allice his wife	Addams.[1]
12	6	William] ye son of Jofeph Kettle & Hannah his wife.	Kettle
12	13	John] ye son of John Melvyn & Hannah his wife.	Melvyn.
12	20	Rebeckah.] ye daughter of mr John Blaney & of [Sarai his wife.	Blaney.
12	27	Elisabeth] ye daugtr of or bro: Solomon Phips & of [Mary his wife.	Phips.
16	81		

year & moneth	day	The Baptifed. — Page 243 —	
16 81			
Sh. 1	13	Mercy] ye daughter of mr Samuel Hunting & of Hannah his wife of ye ch of xt in Dedham—	Hunting.
	&	Susanna] ye daughter of mr Nicholas Meade, & Elisabeth his wife	Meade:
1	20	Sarai] ye wife of mr Matthew Soley. — — —	Soley.
	&	John] } ye children of mr Soley, & Sarai his wife.	
	&	Matthew] }	
1	27	Mercy] ye daughter of John Fowl & of Anna his wife	Fowl.
	&	Susanna] ye daughter of Mary Green widdow.	Greene.
2	3	Mary] ye daughter of mr John Long & Mary his wife.	Long.·.
2	10	Anna] ye daughtr of G. Jacob Hurd & Anna his wife	Hurd,
2	17	Benjamin] ye son of G. Benjamin Phillips &	Phillips.
	&	Mercy] ye daughtr of Jno Goodwin, & of Martha [his wife.	Goodwin
2	24	Jacob] ye son of mr Jacob Green Junr. & of Mary [his wife.	Green.
	&	Mary] ye wife of Indego Potter.	Potter
	&	Susanna] ye wife of Robert Wallis.	Wallis.
	&	Hannah Laurence, ye daughtr of or sistr ye	Laurence.
	&	Abigail] widdow Tarbol, formerly Laurence.	
	&	Mary] ye daughtr of G. Indego Pottr, & mary his wife.	Potter.
	&	Rebeckah] Patefield.	Patefield.
	&	Sarai Laurence] ye daughtr of widdow Tarbol.	Lawrence.
	&	John] } ye sons } of G. Indego Potter & mary his wife	
	&	Richard] }	Potter.
	&	Indego] }	
	&	Margaret] ye daughtr	
	&	Susanna] ye daughter of Robert & Susanna wallis	Wallis.

[1] This entry of "Addams" occupies seven lines in the Record.

— Page 243 (*concluded*). —

3	1	John] ye youngest son of or sistr Tarbol, his name [Laurence,	Laurence.
	&	Hannah] ye daughtr of John Knell, & Elisebeth his [wife.	Knell.
3	15	Anne] ye daughtr of Thomas Carter, & of Esther [his wife.	Carter.
3	22	mercy] ye daughtr of Thomas Chapman & of Sarai [his wife.	Chapman.
4	12	James] ye son of Enoch More, & Rebekah his wife	More.
4	19	William] ye son of Will: Vine, & of Elisabeth his [wife.	Vine
4	26	John] Brackenbury, ye son of mrs Lynd	Bracken- [bury
	&	John] | & Joſeph] | & [Andrew | & [Mary[1] | Newell ye children of Joſeph Newell & Hannah [his wife.	Newell.
	&	Hannah] ye daughtr of Jno. Poor, & Elisabeth his [wife (wo ws formrly Dean)	Poor.
5	3	Stephen] } Walters, ye children of Stephen Walters, & Sarai his wife	Walters
	&	Samuel] }	
	&	John] }	

yeare & moneth	day	The Baptized. — Page 244 —	
1681			
5	3	Samuel] ye ſon of Samuel Blunt & Annah his wife	Blunt.
5	10	Dorothy] ye daughter of Capt Johnath: Wade & [of Deborah his wife	Wade.
5	17	Joseph] ye son of G. Joseph Dowſe & Mary his wife	Dowſe
6	7	Hale] ye son of bro. Edwd Wilſon & mary his wife.	Wilson.
	&	Benjamin] ye son of John Walker, & of Anna his [wife.	Walker.
6	14	Elisabeth] ye daughtr of Nich: Meade, & Elisabeth [his wife.	Meade.
	&	Elisabeth] ye daughtr of James Keby, & Sarah his [wiſe.	Keby.
6	21	Hannah] ye daughtr of John Melvyn, & Hannah [his wife.	Melvyn.
7	4	Mary] ye daughtr of Thomas Aſhby, & mary his wife.	Aſhby.
7	11	Eliphalet] ye ſon of bro: Nath: Frothingham & of [mary his wife	Frothing- [ham.
	&	Moſes] ye son of Paul mavrick &	maverick.
	&	Hannah Blanchard, ye daughter of G. George [Blanchard	Blanchard
7	25	Thomas] } ye sons of bro: Samuel Blanchard &	Blanchard
		John] }	
		Samuel] }	
8	2	Hannah } ye daughtr of bro: Samll: Blanchard &	
	&	Amos] ye son of John whittamore, & mary his wife	Whittamore
	&	Rebeckah] ye daughtr of Aaron Way & mary his wife.	Way.
8	9	Edward] ye son of John Eades, & mary his wife.	Eades.
	&	Chriſtopher] ye son of or bro: christopher Goodwyn [& Joanna his wife	Goodwyn.
8	16	Elisabeth] } twins & ye daughtrs of Isaac Johnſon & of mary his wife. — — — — —	Johnſon.
	&	Hannah] }	
	&	Sarai] ye wife of bro: Wm Jimiſon. — — —	Jimiſon
	&	Ruth Bradſhaw. — — — — — — —	Bradſhaw

[1] Four lines in record.

— Page 244 (*concluded.*) —

	&	Sarai Candifh. — — — — — — —	Candifh.
	&	margart ye daughter of our brothr wm & Sarah [Jemifon—	Jim̄ifon.
9	13	John] ye fon of or Bro: Samll Dowfe & Faith his wife.	Dowfe.
10	4	Henry] ye son of mr Jno Phillips & Katharine his wife	Phillips
		James] ye orphan of Joh. Haiden & both deceafed.	Haiden.
10		] ye son of or bro: Richard Austin &	Austin
10	25		Parrick.
		Jonathan] ye fon of Stephen Walters, & Sarai his wife.	Walters
		Barnabas] ye fon of Nathaneel Davis & Mary his [wife:	Davis
11	8	Anna] ye daughter of Timothy Cutler & of Elifabeth [his wife.	Cutler

yeare & moneth	day	The Baptized — Page 245 —	
16|81			
11	29	Jofhuah] } Blanchard ye children of or bro: Blanchard	Blanchard
	&	Jonathan] }	
	&	Mary] }	
	&	Abigail] }	
	&	Robert] } Barret: ye children of of or sistr Barret widdow.	Barret
	&	Christopher] }	
	&	Sarai] }	
	&	Ruth Walley] — — — — — — — — —	Walley
12	5	Jofeph] ye son of bro. Nath: Rand &	Rand.
	&	James] ye fon of bro: James Miller & of Hannah [his wife	Miller.
	&	Thomas] ye son of bro Tho: Rand Junr. &	Rand.
	&	Margaret] ye daughtr of John Ireland & Grace his [wife	Ireland.
12	12	ye son of Thomas Smith & Sarai his wife	Smith
12	19	Rebekah] ye daughtr of mrs Rebeckah Lynd widdow.	Lynd.

16|82 mon|eth	day		
1	12	] of Peter Fowl & of mary his wife	Fowl.
2	2	] of mr matthew soley & Sarai his wife	Soley:
3	14	} ye children of or brother Jonathan Cary & his wife	Cary.
		} ye children of o chamberlain & of Deborah his wife	Camb lain.
	&	] ye son of william wilfon & of his wife	Wilfon.
3	21	Samuel] ye son of mr Samuel Phips & Katharine [his wife	Phips.
3	28	Isaac] ye son of John Fowl & of Anna his wife.	Fowl
4	16	mary] ye daughtr of mr Nathan Hayman & of [Elisabth his wife	Hayman
	&	Hannah] ye daughtr of Edward Loyd & of Hannah [his wife	Loyd.
5	2	Dorcas] ye daughtr of John Brackenbury & of [Dorcas his wife	Bracken- [bury
		Mary] ye daughtr of Peter Frothingham & of	Frothing- [ham
		Isaac] ye son of Thomas Shepperd & of Hannah [his wife	Shepperd

[To be continued.]

EDWARD OXNARD'S JOURNAL.

Concluded from page 121.

[1776.]
[Nov.] 29.. Mr Blowers called on me at one & we went as far as Kensington. The news of the victory at Kings bridge & its being taken looses credit. Spent the evening at Col. Murray^s^. Messrs. Phipps & Saltonstall met with the club. Lost 2*s*.

4.. Dec. Went to Westminster Hall & heard a cause argued before Lord Mansfield. Col. Vassal, Phipps, Mr Ingersoll & Mr Hallowoll spent the evening with us.

12.. called on Mr Bliss, at 12, & as he was not at home on Mr. Quincey, & was told that he had gained forty guineas by insurance in the lottery. Invited by Judge Sewall to dine & accepted the invitation. We had boiled Turkey & oyster sauce,—a saucy dish in this country. Spent the evening at Treasurer Gray^s^.

13.. This day is set apart by government as a day of fasting & prayer for the sins of the people, & that it would please Heaven to prosper his majesty^s^ arms against his subjects in America. The day has been kept more sacredly than I have ever known the observance of Sunday. Dined at Col. Vassal^s^, Berners S^t^., & spent the evening there.

25.. Little did I expect to see a return of this day in England. Christmas is kept here universally by all sects, except the Quakers, and they open their shops & do the ordinary business of every day. Dined with Mr Laurence & there met Mr & Mrs. Curling.

1777

30.. Jan. This being the anniversary on which King Charles suffered martyrdom, went to Westminster Abbey to hear the Bishop of Bangor preach before the house of Lords, or rather the Chancellor & five or six Bishops, who were present. He made a very ingenious discourse, well adapted to the day. He reprobated the act, but seemed to think that Charles aimed at despotism, but that he was born & educated at a time when the rights of the Crown had not been fully determined & settled. Rev. Dr Chandler of New Jersey dined with us.

8 Feb. Went into the City & there heard that Dr. Dodd had been committed for forging a bond on Lord Chesterfield.

Dined with Gov. Hutchinson, in company with Judge Oliver, Commissioner Robinson (who is a queer fish) Mr Gridley & Mr Chipman. A genteel dinner of two courses.

11.. spent the day at home. An extract said to be from a New York paper has much alarmed the people. It is as follows "Wednesday morning last, one of the Hessian brigades, stationed at Trenton, was surprised by a large body of rebels, and after an engagement which lasted for a little time, between three and four hundred made good their retreat. The whole loss is computed to be about nine hundred men.

19.. This morning went to the Treasury, & saw Mr Millw'^d^ Rowe. He informed me, that their Lordships had granted me a hundred pounds a year, while I remained here, to commence from Lady Day. Went with Judge Sewall to the Navy & Pay Offices.

24.. In accordance with the invitation of Mr Lane went to dine with him,

& received a friendly welcome. Our company consisted of Mr Danforth, Chipman, Chandler, Woodbury & Langdon of Portsmouth N. H. We drank Maderia, till we were all jolly.

March 4.. This morning went to the Treasury & called on Mr. Rowe & in consequence of my representation he went with me to see Mr Robinson, who gave orders that I should be paid £50. He accordingly gave me an order on the cashier of the Bank of England. It is necessary that a man should be possessed of some self assurance in order to accomplish his purposes at all public offices here or else he may be neglected all his life time.

10.. It is said that Dr. Bancroft has been taken up as accessory to John the Painter in setting fire to Portsmouth Dock Yard. called on Mr Wiswall, who has just arrived from Halifax, called on Bliss & Taylor at Gray^s Inn & spent the evening.

17.. Heard to day that Mr Tunnieris had arrived in Ireland from America. S^t. Patricks' day, multitudes of Irishmen in the streets with green in their hats. Went into the city & called at the NE Coffee house, where I heard that the states had elected Genl. Washington, *Lord protector*. It being Mrs. Barry^s benefit night, went to Covent Garden Theatre to see Shakespeare^s 12.. night. Mrs. Barry in the character of Viola, which she supported with tolerable ease.

Last week died Sir Joshua Van Neck, said to be worth 500.000 lbs. sterling. He was one of the largest holders of stocks in the kingdom. Having the care of all the Dutch money in the Funds, he could at pleasure make £10.000 of a morning, only by ordering his broker to sell out, which would so alarm other holders, that they would in many cases also sell as fast as possible. When they had fallen one or two per cent., he would purchase back again.

22^d. Mr Chipman set out with me at 11 o'clk to purchase in Monmouth S^t. some articles of clothing. When we arrived at our destination, we were shown into a room with only one window in it, through which so very small a portion of light was admitted, that it was almost impossible to discover the color of the Cloth, much less its fineness. we tried on several suits & at length I bought

coat & waiscoat	£3. 13. 6
2 waits coats	2. 2. 0
2 pair breeches	1. 16. 0
	£7. 11. 6 the asking price.

He took for them £5. 5 making an abatement of £2. 6. 6

The extent of business transacted by this man is almost incredible. He has fourteen or fifteen other shops, the value of each of which is not less than five or six thousand pounds. The owners of shops in this sort of business are great rogues & take every method to deceive. Dined with Judge Sewall & spent the evening. Present Col. Saltonstall, Lewis & H. Gray. The ladies went to Christ Hospital to see the boys sup, & returned not very well pleased.

19.. Col. Vassall & Peter Johonnot started to day for France. Mr Thomas Brinley was seized with a violent fever. As it was rainy spent the forenoon at home.

Messrs. Murray, the Grays, & Blowers called in for a couple of hours & chatted about American affairs, a subject that principally engrosses our time & attention. Received advices that a vessel from Carolina loaded with

Rice & Indigo had been brought into the Clyde, the crew who were mostly British having risen on the Americans, & seized the ship & brought her safe into port.

1st. May. This being May day, the milk men & maids walked their usual rounds, collecting of their customers, what they think proper to give. Went to Westminster & visited the several courts. During my stay at the King's Bench, the master of the Rolls was proclaimed, on which the Judges rose & paid their compliments.

Took a turn in St. James Park, & there heard that Genl Washington was actually dead, & that Mifflin had succeeded him. After visiting our friends in the Row, at 7 P. M., took leave of Mrs. Jesse where I have lived for eight months past, leaving in her charge a trunk containing wearing apparel, a gold seal, crest & cypher, a gold emerald ring & two mourning rings, and went to the Crown & Bell, Holburn, for convenience in starting in the Stage for Buckingham, which leaves early in the morning.

11 — at half past 10 went to St. Marys Church Oxford to hear a university sermon, which is preached every Sunday morning and afternoon by one of the heads of the Colleges.

The Vice Chancellor comes attended by the heads of the colleges in their scarlet gowns, the procters & the beadles with their maces. The person who preached was one that is called a Hack, that is he takes the place of some one else, for which he receives compensation. I must needs say, that in my life, I never heard such an odd discourse. He conveyed to me the idea of Dean Swift, as I have imagined him. His sermon instead of exciting ideas of a serious nature seemed only designed to promote laughter.

Took places in the stage for Bath. Fare 21*s*.

At 12 arrived at Arencester, an old town near which is the seat of Lord Bathurst, the present Lord Chancellor. The colors were displayed for Bromley Chester, who has succeeded in the election, which it is said has cost the parties £50,000 each. Elections now a days may be compared to cases in courts, where one client has gained the cause, but appears in rags, while his opponent, who has lost it, is quite naked. Mr Chester has been elected, but is in all probability ruined.

23d. Having ordered a chaise over night to be at the door at 9, at the time appointed, set out for Bath, the most noted place in the kingdom for dissipation. It is handsomely built of white stone so soft that it can, when first quarried, be sawed like wood, but when exposed to the air for some length of time, it becomes hard & very durable. The circus & crescent are magnificent Buildings with two noble rooms for public assemblies. The Ball room is one hundred feet long & highly finished. The card rooms are very handsome, and when the weather will not allow exercise out of doors are generally used by ladies & gentlemen to walk in.

29 — aroused this morning by the chiming of the bells at the Cathedral & the church of St. Mary Radcliffe & upon inquiry found it to be the anniversary of the restoration of King Charles the Second. I am very confident that most of the inhabitants of this place had rather see a Cromwell rule. While Messrs. Waldo, Barnes, Bliss & Porter were standing with me to see the Mayor & Corporation with a few trading companies going in procession to the Cathedral church to hear prayers & a sermon, who should appear but Mr Wiswell, who had come from Plymouth to make Mrs. Coulson a visit. We drank tea there & afterwards went to hear the famous Sir Harry Trelawney preach. This gentleman has an income of £2000 per year, the greatest part of which he distributes to support the methodistical scheme.

He exhorted the people in a most vehement style to repentance, but there was very little good sense in what he said.

Speaking of Sir H. Trelawney, Mrs. Garnett observed that he was one of the handsomest men she had ever seen. I have noticed that in general, when the women speak of these itinerant preachers they always remark upon their figures & person. It is said that Sir Harry is particularly fond of the sisterhood.

3^d^. June. This has been the most delightful day, that I have experienced for a long time. At 12 o'clock went with Mr Danforth & Dukenfield to the Wells. First to the billiard room & from thence to the Pump room, where we drank a glass of the water. I was much grieved to see so large a number of Invalids, particularly young ladies. In some cases the use of these waters may prove beneficial, but I am inclined to think that this is rarely the case: if they receive any advantage, it is from the air, which is very pure & also from the mode of spending the time, which relieves the mind & disposes it to cheerfulness. Just as we were coming out, who should enter but Mr Dowse, dressed in his black suit, rosette, cane & jack boots. I must needs say that he cut a very ridiculous figure. It is not uncommon to come to the pump room booted, & sometimes to a public breakfast: some even go so far as to dance cotillions in their boots.

A house was pointed out, which was very elegant with fine grounds surrounding, of the owner of which a singular circumstance was related. He had occasion to go to the Bank, & while there an old miserly looking man wanted one of the tellers to exchange a guinea, which he said he had received of him, & was of light weight, but he refused notwithstanding his importunity. This gentleman finding the old man in so much trouble on account of so small a sum, gave him a good guinea in place of that which was short of weight & thereupon the old man was so much pleased, that he cultivated his acquaintance, & at his death left him £10,000. No bad interest on his investment.

21st. Obliged to borrow an umbrella to shelter myself from the rain. It is an article much used here for that purpose by ladies and gentlemen. At Bath they are contrived in connection with a walking stick so as to be very handy.

Passing over Brandon Hill, a gentleman told me that Queen Elizabeth when here, thought the ladies of Bristol so very homely, that to encourage matrimony, she ordained that every man who married a Bristol woman should be free of the City. Dined home alone except Mrs Allard. She desired me not to forget the Mayor of Monmouth' toast, which was "God bless us all." Being at a public feast, he was called upon to give a toast, & this, which he gave, was so outre, that it was much remarked upon.

6~th~. In the morning to Church—one recently built & in elegant style. Here we were shown a place, but by no means the uppermost seat in the synagogue. What with the size of the church, & the weakness of the Speaker' voice, we might as well have been at home, for not the least word could we hear. I dare say many satisfied themselves by the command to assemble themselves together—for they could not have received any edification by the hearing ear. In the afternoon to meeting, & heard a Mr Harrington, a sensible man, but possessed of rather a fanciful imagination. After giving out his text, he merely referred to his notes, a method much in vogue with dissenting parsons.

The people of this town, who are dissenters are universally opposed to the measures of government & I believe it holds good with persons of this sort, throughout the kingdom. There still remains the old leaven of Oliver[s] time.

30 ∴ This day I complete my thirtieth year of age. May Heaven grant me the happy sight of my native land before the return of another birth day. Driven by the unhappy situation of my country to seek that peace in a foreign clime which was denied me in my own—my anxiety, since I left it, words cannot express. Oh God! whatever afflictions thou shalt see fit to lay upon me—grant me the resolution & fortitude to support them manfully.

Aug 22. reached London at 5 oclk having been absent nearly four months. After all there is no place so well calculated for men of leisure as the metropolis. Go into the largest city out of London & you are immediately known & your connections & business. The same spirit and inclination for gossip prevails as in America, the landlords of the Inns being able to give the genealogy of every man in the town & the most minute occurrences of his life.

Sep[r]. 16th. rose at 8 & dressed—& at 11 called upon Mr Rowe & received my quarterly payment by an order on the Bank of England, which was no sooner presented than paid; from thence went to the N. E. Coffee house. Great dearth of news. It is not a little funny to observe the various squibs in the newspapers upon the two brothers Howes & their secret expeditions.

25 ∴ spent the morning at home in writing to my brother. At ½ past 3 went to Mr. Sands to dine. Mess[rs]. Brown, Letchmere, Brinley, Johonnot, Quincey, Danforth, Rowe, H. Gray, Waterhouse & Sargent present. An exceedingly good dinner of fish. Madeira in abundance. As his wife was not at home, we made a late afternoon of it.

Oct 18. dined at Shorter[s] & in the evening called on Judge Brown whose son has been very ill of a slow fever. attended by Dr Perkins who has saved the lives of many by his skill & I look upon it as a great blessing that he came over. He has been likewise at great pecuniary expense in aiding, generally refusing to receive compensation.

I am told that several Gentlemen of the faculty belonging to this country have declined to receive fees from my countrymen. Looked into the N. E. Coffee house but could hear nothing new. Every body is grumbling for news from America & finding fault with men and things.

Nov 19. Dismissed my frissieur, sent for another, but did not agree with him as he asked 42*s*. per quarter. We have rec[d] various accounts from America in different ways, that Gen[l]. Howe has defeated Mr Washington, but no official information as yet. Went to Lewisham, in passing through which somewhat late in the morning, & finding the people in general were in bed King James 1st. inquired the name of the town, and when told said " Long, lazey, lousey, lubberly Lewisham."

20 ∴ Having breakfasted Col. Pickman, Mr Sargent & myself went to the house of Commons to hear the debates upon the king[s] Speech. After waiting some time, we made shift by paying 3*s* to obtain a seat. We got in about 1, & it was 3 o'clk before the usher of the Black rod came to acquaint the House, that his Majesty waited for them. The Speaker preceeded by theMace bearer & followed by a number of the members attended, & after being gone about twenty minutes returned, and having commanded silence, read to the House the King Speech, which being finished, a short pause succeeded.

Lord Hyde then rose & after a short speech moved the address, which was Seconded by Sir Gilbert Elliot. They represented the necessity of prosecuting the war & that the nation had nothing to fear from the other powers of Europe; that the manufacturers were fully employed, & that Commerce had been but little injured, so that the people were abundantly able and could well afford to carry it on. On the part of the opposition, Lord Granby rose and after shewing the inexpediency of continuing the war & observing how little had been accomplished by the most able commanders in the service during the course of three campaigns, moved an amendment to the usual address, praying his majesty to order an immediate cessation of hostilities to be continued until some plan for a perpetual union between the mother country & its colonies could be definitely arranged.

His motion was seconded by Geo. Johnson. Mr Butler & Hon[ble] Charles Fox joined in the discussion. The former a very rapid speaker, deals too much in tropes and figures; the latter is by far the most formidable. He is strong & nervous in his language, but too apt to be scurrilous.

Lord North was the last speaker, & convinced me that he was a good statesman & an able minister. Lord Germaine is clear & distinct in his expressions, but is far from being the eloquent speaker I have heard him described.

Dec 2[d]. Last evening Lord Germaine received a letter from Sir Guy Carleton, acquainting him that two deserters from the Provincial Camp had come in with the report that Gen. Burgoyne with all his army had capitulated. The consternation of the people is very great. A general gloom hangs upon the countenances of every one. The town of Manchester has agreed to raise one thousand men & clothe them. It is almost incredible that people can be found so foolish, as to imagine that tenants can be had for the innumerable dwellings that are going up. The rage for building in England at this time is somewhat similar to the tulip mania in Holland.

1778

15. Jan. rainy. dined in Cram S[t]. Spent the evening at Judge Sewall[s]. Mr Copely & lady, Mess[rs]. Clark, Pelham, Scott, & Quincey were also there. Strong talks prevalent about a French war.

13. March. at 1 went to the Wilton carpet ware house Haymarket & purchased a carpet 3½ yds by 3 yds. for which I paid four guineas. at 2 to see the procession of the Lord Mayor, aldermen & common council going to S[t]. James Palace with a petition praying his Majesty to remove from his presence those evil counsellors, who have brought the nation to the brink of destruction by carrying on a most ruinous & destructive war with America. The rumor of a war with France is every moment gaining ground. Stocks which are the great barometer as indicating the feeling of the nation have been falling for the past fortnight. Yesterday they went down to 59, which is two per cent lower, than they were known to drop during the whole of the last war.

NOTE.—Mr. Oxnard remained in England until the 30th of April, 1785, when he took passage at London for Halifax, arriving there on the 8th of June.

During his stay in England his diary, principally of personal incidents, with occasional allusions to public matters, was with few intermissions regularly kept.

He remained in Halifax until Jan. 1786, when he returned to the United States.

EARLY HISTORY OF GEORGIA, AND SIR ALEXANDER CUMING'S EMBASSY TO THE CHEROKEES.

A paper read in substance before the *New-England Historic, Genealogical Society,* February, 1872, by SAMUEL G. DRAKE, A.M.

BEFORE proceeding to give an account of the labors of Sir Alexander Cuming, it is proposed to notice briefly the country since known as Georgia. Of the tribes of Indians scattered over it, the Cherokees were, at the time it was taken possession of by the English, the principal. In the year 1733, when Gen. Oglethorp brought his colony there, he was received by the Lower Creeks, then consisting of eight tribes or clans, delegates from all of which were in attendance on the landing of the first colonists. These welcomed the English, and gave them all the land in their country except what they themselves used. This was the usual custom of the Indians everywhere, north as well as south, and establishes the fact, that before Europeans taught the aborigines the value of land, they placed no such importance upon it as we do; for they used it only while it afforded them game and a few other natural means of living. When these failed they abandoned it, and it was free for others to possess. Hence it will be perceived that the limits assigned to a tribe or nation of Indians were very uncertain. Territory was often, if not generally, acquired by one tribe dispossessing another. Rivers, mountains, &c., became boundaries, because they were natural defences as well.

We are informed by one of the most elaborate writers on the Cherokees and their country, Mr. James Adair, who had lived among the Cherokees forty years, namely, from 1735 to 1775, that "their country was in latitude 34 deg. north, 340 miles north-west of 'Charlestown;' 140 miles W. S. W. from the Katahba nation, and almost 200 to the north of the Muskohge or Creek country. They were settled on nearly an east and west course, about 140 miles in length from the lower towns where fort Prince George stands, to the late unfortunate Fort Loudon [on the southerly bank of the Tennessee, opposite Tellico]. They were a very numerous and potent nation forty years ago; had sixty-four towns and villages. And according to the most intelligent old traders of that time, they amounted to 6000 fighting men." This author having taken it into his head that these Indians were one of the "lost ten tribes of Israel," finds, or fancies he finds a Hebrew root in almost every word of their language; while we doubt not that with quite as much plausibility it might be made to appear that the Sandwich Islanders, New-Zealanders, or any of the nations of Polynesia are descended from the Cherokees.

The Cherokees were divided into upper, middle, and lower towns. The upper and middle towns were almost constantly at war with the northern Indians, while the lower towns were at war with other tribes on their borders, as the Muskogees, Catawbas, &c. Thus they were continually wasted away, insomuch that at the close of the French war in 1760, they numbered but about 2300, which is Major Rogers's estimate. As late as 1795, they occupied 43 towns, and the number of warriors is put down at 2500. When Mr. Imlay collected his valuable materials on the south-west, he placed the country of the Cherokees "between the Great Bend of Tenasee, and the ridge of hills called the Allegany mountains, the western limits of Georgia, and the eastern branches of the Mobile," and estimated them the same as Major Rogers had done.

The Cherokee country was one of the finest in the world. When Dr. Morse visited it in 1822, by order of the United States government, he remarked,—"Although large tracks have been purchased by our government of this tribe, at different times, their territory is now supposed to comprise 10,000,000 acres, sufficient to fill a space 150 miles by 100 wide; which is larger than the three states of Massachusetts, Rhode Island and Connecticut united." And such was the country upon which the eye of cupidity rested, nor could it ever be diverted, by Christian or other considerations, until its owners were driven from it at the point of the bayonet a few years later; when they had not only been taught by us the value of their land, how to use it by becoming cultivators of its soil, and thus depend on it for support!

In this connection one can hardly forbear making a few remarks respecting the materials for a history of Georgia; as we find almost nothing respecting that territory prior to the arrival of General Oglethorp with his company of emigrants, collected mainly from the debtors' prisons of the metropolis of the British empire. We have indeed histories of Georgia, and historical collections concerning that State. Into these one naturally looks for the earliest notice of the territory; but he looks only to be disappointed.

Whatever of history there was of Georgia before the setting out of Oglethorp would very properly be narrated in a history of South Carolina. But from Montgomery to Simms we have nothing new throwing light on the ante-Oglethorp times. The former author published in 1717, and the latter in 1859. As an apology for Montgomery it may be mentioned that his work does not pretend to be a regular history: yet its title may lead the reader to expect more than its author intended; reminding us of the old author who, in the preface to his work, cautioned the reader not to expect too much, lest it should prove to be like a mean structure with lofty and elegant portals.

To commence the history of Georgia with the colony under Oglethorp, would be extremely like beginning the history of New-England, jumping over all the early voyages and other transactions which led to its settlement. The general himself refers to previous transactions of a deeply interesting character. In his address immediately after his arrival (in 1733) he says,—"There was a time, when every day brought fresh advices of murders, ravages, and burnings." The historian of Georgia is expected, at least, to refer to these matters.

The principal object of this paper is to detail an early embassy to the country of the Cherokee Indians; the chief authority for which is a MS. written by Sir Alexander Cuming, Bart., in the year 1755, the ambassador himself. This MS. came into the writer's hands by purchase from a London bookseller. Accompanying it was a paper, stating that it once belonged to the great Shaksperian scholar, Isaac Read, Esq., from whom it passed into the keeping of George Chalmers, Esq., best known in this country by his great work,—"*The Political Annals of the United Colonies,*" *&c.*, a stout quarto, London, 1780.

Sir Alexander Cuming, Bart., was a son of a gentleman of the same name and title, and was probably born at the paternal seat of the Cumings, of Culter, in Aberdeenshire, Scotland, about the year 1692. His father was created a baronet, Feb. 28, 1695, and was succeeded in the baronetcy by this son. He was designed for the profession of law, and spent some time in its practice in his native Scotland. How he came connected with the affairs of Georgia, does not fully appear; possibly through the agency of Sir Robert Montgomery his countryman. Certain it is, however, that up to the year 1732, the tract of country since Georgia was a wilderness waste, with the Spaniards on its southerly and the French on its westerly borders. These were using every effort to monopolize the Indian trade, and had been very successful. Notwithstanding the treaty of peace signed at Seville, Oct. 28, 1729, between the English, French and Spaniards, it scarcely amounted to a truce. However it was thought a favorable time to establish a trade among the Cherokees, and to secure them to the English interest. To effect this very important object, Sir Alexander Cuming was sent over as an ambassador in 1730; and from certain passages in his MS. it would seem that the affair was kept secret until his return, as no account is found of his preparation or departure upon the service, although arrangements had probably been made for it as early as 1728. It would seem also from the same source, that the stupendous financial projects of John Law had caused a great panic in England, inasmuch as those projects were for the advancement of the French nation in its strides towards universal empire; so much feared and dreaded for a considerable period by a large class in England. As an offset to this gigantic scheme of Law, the great South Sea Company was set on foot. In this Sir Alexander became interested, but to what extent he does not state; but his connection with it, judging from what he does say, did not improve his fortune. He tells us, that in the year 1719, he was "unvoluntarily called from his business of the law of Scotland in order to examine the nature of those principles which were formed by John Law to aggrandize the power of France, and to set her up above that of all other nations upon the face of the globe. The principles then recommended by him had so intoxicating an effect as to create an epidemical distemper which seemed to turn the heads of all Europe, and occasioned the budding forth of several lesser schemes which proved the ruin of many thousands here in England." Among the "lesser schemes" was that already mentioned, usually known as the South Sea Bubble. Although Sir Alexander does not acknowledge himself one of the victims of that great swindle, it is pretty evident that he was; and although he writes like an honest man, it is pretty clear that he was somewhat visionary; asserting at one time that by proper management, the Cherokee country would pay the national debt of England in twenty years. But before he broached this scheme he seems to have had another, which may be best understood by presenting it in his own words; premising that for six years he appears to have been floundering in the John Law scheme and the South Sea Bubble, which bring his history to midsummer 1725. "And then," he says, "it became requisite to pursue the notions I had acquired, and to extend my views to remedy the inconveniencies which Law's schemes had promoted, and procured. The settlement of a college in Bermudas seemed to me the most rational way to stem the torrent of that stream which was then issuing forth from France to overflow all our settlements on the continent of America." Sir Alexander's argument for this college was, that by it "the native Indians being instructed and taught a veneration for the customs, manners and laws of our country, they would be the properest instruments to secure their countrymen to our interest against the French, our most powerful enemies." The question may very likely have occurred to some of the well informed of that day, where Sir Alexander would obtain his

Indian students, for there were no Indians in Bermuda, and we are told by the early voyagers to the Island, that there never were any on the island, or none when discovered. Hence it doubtless seemed preposterous to go into the wilderness of America to procure scholars to be educated some hundreds of miles off in the ocean. Yet, however preposterous this scheme was, it seems to have been a favorite one with others as well as with Sir Alexander; for it appears that an expedition actually sailed for that object, under the leadership of Dean Berkely, in September, 1728; but it soon returned, not able to overcome the obstacles it encountered. The Dean was more successful the following year, when he came to Rhode Island. Although it does not appear that Sir Alexander's college "notion" met with much if any favor, yet his friends were inclined to do something for him; and accordingly he was recommended to the Ministry as a suitable gentleman for governor of Bermudas. This recommendation was by the Rt. Hon. the Earl of Islay, his Grace the Duke of Argyll and Greenwich, "backed in a very emphatical manner by the Rt. Hon. Sir Paul Metheuin, the most distinguished Knight of the Round Table upon the revival of the order of the Knights of the Bath." [Sir Paul was treasurer of the king's household.]

Notwithstanding this high recommendation Sir Alexander did not secure the place, and how he was employed for the next two years does not appear, but upon the accession of George II. (1727) to the throne he appealed directly to him, reminding him that his [Sir Alexander's] father had on a certain time saved the life of his majesty. The king, in acknowledgment of the circumstance, ordered the secretary at war to notify him when any vacancy happened that was suitable for this applicant. This was about two years before the embassy to the Cherokees was undertaken, and hence the conclusion is arrived at, that Sir Alexander's appointment was in consequence of the circumstance just alluded to.

We do not find in our examination of documents any notice of the departure of Sir Alexander and his party; but of his arrival in the Cherokee country and subsequent transactions, there is a minute account, which it is now proposed to sketch. That no record is found of the sailing of the embassy may be accounted for upon the hypothesis that it was secretly undertaken for apparent reasons then existing. News had reached England, that about the middle of March, 1729, an army of Carolinians, consisting of 100 white men and 100 Indians, had killed thirty-two Yomassee Indians and a fryar, burnt their town, and driven others into the castle at St. Augustine; that an alliance was formed between the Creeks and Cherokees against the English, and that in this aspect of affairs the English traders did not dare to resume their business among them. This was the state of things when Sir Alexander Cuming arrived in "Charles Town." Nothing daunted, however, he left that place for the interior, on the 13th of March, 1730, and in ten days arrived at Keeakwee, 300 miles from Charleston. By the way he learned that the Cherokees were governed by seven Mother Towns:—These were Tannassie, Kettooah, Ustenary, Telliquo, Estootowie, Keyowee, and Noyohee. These towns had each their king, but at this time the kings of but three of the towns were alive, namely, those of Tannasee in the upper settlements; of Kettooah in the middle; and of Ustenary in the lower. Besides a king, or head man, each town had a head warrior.

On the 3d of April, Sir Alexander was at Telliquo with his company, which consisted of Eleazar Wiggan, Ludovick Grant, Samuel Brown, William Cooper, Agnus Macpherson, Martin Kane, David Dowie, George Hunter, George Chicken, Lacklain Mackbain, Francis Baver, and Joseph

Cooper, all British subjects. Here, at this time and place, Moytoy (of Telliquo) was chosen emperor over the whole Cherokee nation, and unlimited power was conferred upon him.

When Sir Alexander had arrived at a point about 100 miles from Charleston, he was informed by a Capt. Russel, that for two years the French had been endeavoring to seduce the Lower Cherokees to their interests; that one Whitehead, a native of Paris, was the French agent. But here our documents take us a step back, in the detail of Sir Alexander's journey in the Indian country. It was about five o'clock in the afternoon that he set out from Mr. James Kinloch's plantation at New Gilmorton, being 23 miles from Charles Town. He was attended by Mr. George Chicken, besides Alexander Muckele, Aaron Cheesbrook, and Powel, pack-horse men; but the pack-horse men having got drunk, and overturned the baggage, these were left behind, and Sir Alexander proceeded with only Mr. Chicken and Mr. George Hunter, and lay that night at Mr. Alexander Kinlock's house at Wampee, 14 miles from his brother James's. On the 14th the party reached Mr. Neilson's, about 20 miles from their last named place. During this day's march Sir Alexander employed much of it in searching for springs, ponds and minerals. The 15th they made 35 miles, and stopped at the house of Mr. Coxe. Here Sir Alexander met Mr. William Cooper, a bold man well skilled in the Cherokee language, who engaged to meet him on the next day, and attend him to the Cherokee mountains. March 16, they reached Capt. Russel's before mentioned, but 10 miles from their stopping place; having spent much time in search of curiosities. Among those discovered was a cave. They went into it. Mr. Hunter, Mr. Chicken and Mr. Coxe made marks to show that they had been there; and Sir Alexander cut upon a stone on the left hand of it "KING GEORGE II., of Great Britain, wrote by S. A. C." He also discovered some iron stone, which was one great end of his going in person to the mountains, not being able to depend upon the truth of any report he had heard in Carolina. Here his drunken pack-horse men came up. Two of those he discharged, and hired James Anderson in place of them. The 17th, more iron ore was discovered. On examining it Mr. Hunter found it yielded one third iron. Here Joseph Fairclough told Sir Alexander, privately, of a discovery he had made of copper, about 450 miles from the Catarba nation, and offered to conduct him to it, but Sir Alexander said his intent in going to the Cherokee mountains was more than answered by the discoveries already made, besides the getting roots for the bites of snakes: so he proceeded to Beaver Creek, and encamped under a tree some 18 miles from Capt. Russel's.

March 18. After procuring several roots for the cure of the bites of snakes the party went on to the Congarees, where they again encamped under a tree, distance about 20 miles. Here happened something remarkable: Capt. How, a chief of the Cartaba nation, by his manner towards Sir Alexander, whom Sir A. had made his friend, ordered his men to salute him with feathers, said they would dance round him all night, and would make him a present of all their skins; but understanding that the dancing would disturb, instead of gratifying Sir Alexander, he ordered his men to desist, and withdrew and shot a turkey for his supper.

March 19. William Cooper returned according to promise, but Sir Alexander was plagued because Mr. Chicken had taken away his guide to catch a runaway horse, by which a great part of the morning was lost: so he left Mr. Chicken and Mr. Hunter and the pack-horse men behind at the 18 mile Branch, and proceeded with William Cooper only to Hollow Creek branch, being 30 or 35 miles from Congerees. The following day they went to Ninety-six Mile Swamp, where William Cooper's horse was found lame. It rained heavily all night, while they had only trees for shelter; the wolves making the most hideous howls all about them. Thus ended the 20th of March, on which they had journeyed 38 or 40 miles. On the 21st they reached Long Cane (now in Abbeville county, S. C.), 30 or 35 miles. This day William Cooper killed a buffalo, a viper, a fox squirrel, and wounded three wolves. These attacked their great dog, and were not beaten off till they had nearly killed him, tearing out part of his entrails. On the way Sir Alexander found some small stones which shined like gold, and passed Marrowbone Creek, where a Cherokee the last year killed the Cheekipaw by Mr. Weekly's side. [Who Mr. Weekly was, does not appear.]

March 22. They reached Boggy Gully, 36 or 40 miles from Long Cane, and encamped in the woods; having as usual examined the country for minerals and other curiosities by the way. From this point they went to Keeowee, which they reckoned 20 miles [in the present county of Pendleton]. Here Sir Alexander learned more particulars respecting the hostile disposition of the Cherokees; especially the Lower Towns; that the Lower Creeks were in the French interest, and were exerting themselves to seduce the Cherokees to join them; that but a month before those emissaries had gone to receive presents from the French, and upon their return it was expected that the Cherokees would join them against the English. A great number of the Indians were assembled in their Council-House here at this time. Among these Sir Alexander was resolved to make a bold push. So at night he entered their Council-House, where were above three hundred of them. Surprised at the audacity of the stranger, who demanded their acknowledgment of the king of England's authority over them and their country, they at once submitted, and said they would obey him in everything: Sir Alexander called them to make this submission on their knees, protesting that if they violated this promise they would become no people: a submission they never made before either to God or man. Sir Alexander, upon this great event, ordered expresses to be sent through the whole Cherokee nation, directing that three head men should meet him at Nequassee on the 3d of April, where he proposed to be on his return from the mountains: That these head men should bring full power from the three settlements that what had been promised should be performed. The Indian traders at Nequassee who were eye-witnesses, and Joseph Cooper the interpreter, having declared that what they heard and saw done that night, was so incredible, that they would not have believed it possible had they not seen it themselves; that nobody in Carolina would believe their report to be true, for that he (the interpreter) declared that if he had known what Sir Alexander was going to do, he would not have dared to enter the council-house that night, nor would the traders have ventured to witness the proceedings; believing that none of them could have got out alive; but the Indians being taken by surprise, and amazed at the manner of Sir Alexander, at once submitted to whatever he demanded. He stood up in the midst of them and made his speech through the interpreter; and though armed with three cases of pistols, a gun and a sword under his great coat, it is not reported that he flourished any of these to awe the savages.

As there was a possibility that he might not live to return to England, to report his successes, Sir Alexander drew up a declaration of the whole proceedings, to be sent to his majesty in case any accident might happen to him. This declaration was witnessed by himself, Joseph Cooper, interpreter;

Ludovick Grant, Joseph Barker, Gregory Haines, David Jenkinson, Thomas Goodale, William Cooper, guide; William Hutton, and John Biles. Dated May 23, 1729–30, at Keeowee.

On March 24, Sir Alexander went on 12 miles to Occounny. [Oconee is a town on the river of the same name, the north main branch of the Alatamaha.] Here he slept at Mr. Dawie's, an Indian trader; and observed that a solemnity was acting in the council-house, about creating a new king. On the 25th he proceeded through Keeowee, Chattoogah, Tucharreehee, the Clay-pits, and lay at old Estatoway. Here he made a friend of the head warrior. His discoveries this day quite surprised him [but he does not record what they were]. From Estoway [*sic*] he proceeded on the 26th of March, to Nooulfkah, where he made a friend of Hercules [an Indian powow or medicine man]; got the secret of his several roots for distempers; met on the way the conjuror Toogabow, and made a friend of him; then went by Echvey to Neguassee, where he met Telloquoluftokay, and made a friend of him; thence to Joree, where he passed the night. [Jore is one of the Cherokee mountains.] Here he met Cæsar's brother, who discovered the Indian's plot to massacre the English [in 1715? See Mills's S. C., 487–8]; with him he had some talk. At this place Sir Alexander discovered a transparent stone.

March 27, the party left Joree, passed through Tamauchly, and thence to Tassetchee, being 40 miles. This day's journey was over the steep mountains of Joree: here Sir Alexander made the two head warriors and the conjuror his friends, and spoke about their accompanying him to England. The night following happened the most terrible thunder, lightning and rain; insomuch that the like never happened before in the memory of any of them: here their great conjuror told Sir Alexander that he knew he was come among them to rule, and that their whole nation must do whatever he bid them. [It is elsewhere intimated that this fearful tempest was very opportune, and was turned to good account by Sir Alexander, with the aid of the conjuror.] On the 28th of March he was within 3 miles of Beaverdams, where he spent the night; Ludovick Grant, and his guide, William Cooper, being with him. This day he discovered some iron stone at two different places.

March 29, they proceeded over the mountains, drank some of the water on the top of the high Ooneekaway mountain, near which was a large tree called the poisoned pear. From the top of this mountain to Telliquo is a descent of about 12 miles. They reached Telliquo in the afternoon; saw the petrifying cave; a great many enemy's scalps brought in and put upon poles at the warrior's doors; made a friend of the great Moytoy, and Jacob the conjuror. Moytoy told Sir Alexander, that it was talked among the several towns last year, that they intended to make him emperor over the whole; but now it must be whatever Sir Alexander pleased.

March 30, leaving William Cooper at Great Telliquo, to take care of his lame horse, Sir Alexander took with him only Ludovick Grant to go to Great Tannassy, a town pleasantly situated on a branch of the Mississippi, 16 miles from Great Talliquo. [It is not easy to see by any of the maps to which we have access, how there could be any water course where Sir Alexander now was with Mississippi.] The path was said to be lined with enemies, yet they met with no accident. Here Sir Alexander met with Mr. Wiggan, the complete linguist; saw fifteen enemies' scalps brought in by the Tannassy warriors; made a friend of the king of Tannassy, and made him do homage to George II. on his knee. The same night returned to

Great Telliquo; was particularly distinguished by Moytoy in the Council-house; the Indians singing and dancing about him, and stroked his head and body over with eagles' tails. After this Moytoy and Jacob the conjuror decided to present Sir Alexander with the crown of Tannassy.

From Telliquo he proceeded on March 31, with Moytoy, Jacob the conjuror, the bearer of eagles' tails, and a throng of other Indians, and lay in the woods at night between 20 and 30 miles distant. April 1, they reached Tassetchee, above 30 miles from their last encampment. Here the Indians of the place agreed to what had been done in relation to the crown of Tannassy, declaring that it was an emblem of universal sovereignty over the Cherokee nation. The next day, April 2, they proceeded to Joree, with increased numbers, particularly by the warriors and conjuror of Tassetchee. The journey lay over several steep mountains, near 40 miles. When about a mile from Joree, Sir Alexander was met by Mr. George Chicken, Mr. Hunter, and several English traders on horseback, who conducted him to the town. Here the head warrior of Joree had procured him a specimen of iron ore which he had obtained from a steep craggy mountain, six miles from there. This the warrior had promised when Sir Alexander passed through the place previously, but nobody expected he would perform it; but the warrior said he would, though his death should follow thereupon. [There was no doubt a superstition prevailing among the Indians that no one could ascend that mountain and return alive.]

April 3. This morning they went to Nequassee, being 5 miles from Joree, with an increased retinue. Here the Indians gathered from all parts, agreeably to notice to do so, expressed from Keeowee. This was a day of the greatest solemnity ever seen in the country: There was singing, dancing, feasting, speeches, the creation of Moytoy emperor; a declaration of their resigning their crown, eagles' tails, scalps, as emblems of their owning King George's sovereignty, at the desire of Sir Alexander Cuming, in whom absolute power was placed, without which he could not be answerable to his majesty for their conduct. This submission he caused them to make on their knees. Then Sir Alexander caused a paper to be drawn up detailing the event, which was witnessed by himself, Eleazar Whiggam, Ludovick Grant, Samuel Brown, William Cooper, Agnus Mackferson, David Dowie, Francis Beaver, Lachban Macbain, George Hunter, George Chicken, and Joseph Cooper, interpreter, besides the Indians [whose names are not given].

The next day, April 5, Sir Alexander went to Nooulfkah, attended only by William Cooper and George Hunter, leaving George Chicken to follow. Here he received roots of all kinds, which had ever been held as the greatest secrets by the Indians. He then went to Chattoogay and lay at the house of Joseph Cooper's mother: on the 6th, they went to Ookunny [since Oconee], where Sir Alexander found a house ready built to receive him. The king or head man here was called the mankiller, being the same made king at Ookunny (the same with the king of Keeowkee), and the prince of Tomassy. They came to Sir Alexander and presented him with two eagles tails, and on their knees paid homage to King George II. The same night they got to Keeowee, having looked for mines and minerals on the way. This is the last town of the lower settlements of the Cherokee nation. Six chiefs whom Sir Alexander had chosen accompanied him; selected with Moytoy's consent as evidences of what had taken place; Mr. Hunter, Mr. Chicken, and the pack-horse men, made up the rest of the company. This town (Keowee) is about 200 miles from Great Tannassy, and about 300 from Charles Town; but by reason of the mountains Tannassy is recorded as far distant as Charles Town. This night they all lay at Twenty-three Mile-Creek.

April 8, Sir Alexander left the Indians and baggages to proceed to Charles Town at leisure, and lay at Mulberry Creek, with Mr. George Chicken, and William Cooper, the guide, being about 40 miles from their last encampment. The following night they lay at Salloodee river, 48 miles from Mulberry Creek. April 10, they lay at Congerees, 38 or 40 miles from Mulberry Creek. The 11th, they lay at Capt. Russel's, commonly said to be 35 miles, but is rather 40 from Congerees. The 12th, they reached Arisque's, distant from Capt. Russel's 60 miles.

April 13, went to breakfast with Mr. Chicken at his mother's house; thence to Mr. Kinloch's, a gentleman of the council; dined with Mr. Middleton, president, acting as governor; drank tea at Mrs. Johnson's, called in at Mr. Gadsden's, and lay that night at Charles Town.

The chiefs which Sir Alexander had chosen to accompany him to England he left on the road in the care of Mr. Hunter, who reached Mr. Kinloch's with them the 19th, 23 miles from Charles Town. It was hereabouts they met with the warrior Ounakannowie, a friend of theirs who had just come from the Kettarba nation. He desired to accompany them, and Sir Alexander consented, but several others who were with Ounakannowie he declined to admit into the company. The names of the six chiefs were, Oukah Ulah (that is the king that is to be), the head warrior of Tassetchee, a man of great power and interest, who has a right to be a king; Skallelockee, or Kettagustah (or prince), Tathtowie, the third warrior, and Collannah, a fourth warrior; and from Tannassie, the remotest town of the country, he took Clogoittah and Oukanach, warriors, because the people in Carolina believed it was not possible to travel the length of Tannassie and back again in less than three months, whereas the time that Sir Alexander had limited himself to do it in, was from March 13 to April 20; the distance being 500 miles.

The six chiefs above named, with Sir Alexander, went on board the Fox man of war, on the 4th of May. Moytoy would have accompanied them, but owing to the sickness of his wife was prevented. The Fox, Capt. Arnold, sailed in company with the Garland, Capt. Anson [afterwards Lord Anson?], on the day appointed, and arrived at Dover, June 5, after the remarkable short passage of one month and one day. The same night Sir Alexander arrived by post at London. The Indians were brought up in the ship.

In the mean time Sir Alexander communicated with the secretary of state, and the latter with the king, who ordered that Sir Alexander and the Indians should be present at an installation which had been appointed to take place on the 18th of June, ensuing, which was accordingly arranged, and on the 22d, Sir Alexander was introduced to his majesty, and upon his knee, in presence of the Court, declared the full power he had received; the Indian chiefs all kneeling at the same time: Sir Alexander laying the crown of the Cherokee nation at his majesty's feet, with the five eagles' tails as an emblem of his majesty's sovereignty, and four scalps of Indian enemies; all which his majesty was graciously pleased to accept of.

As the speech of the Indian orator on the occasion, and the treaty made at the time are in print, they do not require to be produced in this article. Before their introduction to the king, they had been conducted on the usual rounds of the city,—to the tower, where they saw the crown-jewels, the coronation-robes, and other curiosities. To these the chief alluded in his speech to the king. How they passed their time for nearly another month, particulars are scanty. The treaty was concluded on the 7th of September, in Whitehall, and they returned to Dover in the beginning of October, and immediately sailed for their own country in the same ship which had brought them over.

There were not wanting at the time those scribblers for the public prints who were prepared to make the most of any odd affairs to gratify their natural propensity for ridicule. One denominated the chief of the Indians: "High and mighty Sagamore of the Cherokees, whose dress was an officer's blue coat with white metal buttons, and this with a laced hat and other martial accoutrements, made him look as soldierly as the late King of Sweden, having as many scarifications on his swarthy face as there are bars in a gridiron; wrought first with a sharp instrument, then inlaid with gunpowder, to add terribility to his awful visage."

"They had severally the honour to kiss the hands of his Majesty, the Prince of Wales, and the Duke. The Indian King had on a scarlet jacket, but all the rest were naked, except an apron about their middles, and a horse's tail hung down behind. Their faces, shoulders, &c. were painted and spotted with red, blue & green. They had bows in their hands & painted feathers in their heads."

In another paragraph is found a severe cut at the sycophantic manner in which people cringe about and fawn upon royalty:—"Our citizens were not a little pleased to see so great a potentate as his Indian majesty is said to be, appear more like a heathen philosopher than a pagan Prince, as if he affected to show the world a true copy of a primitive king, surrounded by no fawning courtiers, to secrete aims from the public; no cringing sycophants to tickle his ears with flattery whilst they picked his pockets; no guards for the security of his person; looking as fearless and unconcerned as if he had nothing to protect him but the Love and Loyalty of his subjects. Nor was his presence, tho' distinguished by no costly badges or embellishments, inconsistent with his royal dignity. He had much sagacity in his looks and majesty in his deportment tho' his shirt and skin happened to be much of a color."

We hear nothing of Sir Alexander in connection with the Indian delegation after the introduction to the king. When they learned that he was not to return with them to Carolina they expressed much disappointment; indicating that he may have made them a promise to do so. And whether he ever returned to America is not known, although from some circumstances and intimations it seems probable that he did; for in a schedule of his effects drawn up in 1755, he mentions property in South Carolina, as houses, an "uninhabited island" which he bought of one Mr. Hill, a merchant there, and which island he named Hilkiah, for which he paid £100 sterling: observing that he named it Hilkiah, from the appearance of two eagles at the time of purchase. [Whether this island was afterward called "Cumming's Point," and had a fortification on it in 1780, near Charleston, is not known.]

In this connection we will narrate all we have been able to learn concerning Sir Alexander Cuming, not before given. And as already remarked, we hear nothing of him after the embarkation of the Cherokees, until by his MS. before us, he reports himself a prisoner in the Poultry Compter, and says he was removed to the Compter from the Fleet. How long he was a prisoner in the latter he makes no mention, nor is there anything by which we can determine how or when he gained his liberty, if at all; but we know that in 1755 he had been confined nearly two years, during which time he was prevented taking the benefit of the act of insolvency, from the want of his papers; yet from a schedule drawn up from his memory, he seems to have had interests in numerous properties in various places, and affirms that his means are sufficient to pay all his honest debts, were he allowed his liberty. And at this point we must close our notice of him with the remark, that there probably is not a monument of any name or nature, in South Carolina or Georgia, that there ever lived such a man as Sir Alexander Cuming, Bart., unless the Point before mentioned be an exception. And it may be further remarked, that in the *Gazetteer* of Georgia we find the counties in that state are named for the distinguished men connected with its history, generally; yet in one or two instances counties appear to be named for persons who, it may be, never had heard of the State of Georgia. To this *Gazetteer* (printed in 1829) are appended brief biographies of Georgians considered the most eminent by the compiler. How it happened that a post-village has, within a few years, been called "Cumming," is unknown to the writer. It is in Forsyth co., 109 miles N. W. from Milledgeville. There is also a railroad station named Cumming, in the same state, 57 miles from Augusta. It is not thought that these places were thus named with any reference to Sir Alexander Cuming. In the map accompanying the *Gazetteer*, such is the scarcity of Indian names upon it, that a stranger might be led to suppose that the country was never occupied by the Indians. Were Indian names looked upon as a blemish? or were they discarded that they should not remind the present lords of the soil how they came by it?

Like all aborigines, the Cherokees were cruel in war, and had been in frequent collisions with the Carolinians, but how often would it be found that the Indians were the first transgressors? We know from the history of our own times, that in a majority of cases in which blood has been shed, the white neighbors of the Indians were the aggressors. And yet they (the Indians) have always been ready to fight our battles. No less than five hundred Cherokee warriors fought on the side of independence in the war of the revolution. In the late southern rebellion, the expatriated Cherokees beyond the Mississippi were entirely surrounded by their rebellious neighbors, and it was next to impossible for them to remain neutral, yet a good number of them continued loyal to the end.

I have already alluded to the manner in which the Cherokees were driven from their country, and it is not proposed to expatiate on that painful subject at this time. Yet there will always be associated with their name a reflection, and a feeling in every humane breast, that their expatriation was a crime as nefarious as ever any one people committed against another. It was a crime precisely like one which any state might commit against another, because that state had strength to overpower the other. The Cherokees were advancing in civilization; they had become farmers, mechanics, and proficients in many useful arts as well as their neighbors; but these acquisitions, it would seem, only made those neighbors more avaricious, and more determined on their ruin. They were even becoming, I may say they had become, literary: they prepared and printed school books, published newspapers in their own language, and with an alphabet of the invention of one of their own people; which alphabet was, and still is, an invention challenging the admiration of the learned world.

The wrong to which allusion has been made, was a crime which will never be forgotten or forgiven, and its perpetrators have gone, many of them, and the rest will go, down to their graves in infamy; and the believer in retributive justice may point to the "MARCH TO THE SEA" as a warning or foreshadowing of one of more terrible desolation, when that colossus, armed with iron hands and leaden feet, shall fully vindicate the law of justice, and the equal rights of man.

NOTES ON SHIP-BUILDING IN MASSACHUSETTS.

Communicated by Capt. GEO. HENRY PREBLE, U. S. N.

Concluded from page 29.

Vessels of War built in, and about Boston, Mass., from 1776 *to* 1872, *inclusive; also, Vessels purchased in Boston, for the U. S. Navy Department, from* 1861 *to* 1871, *inclusive.*

BUILT IN BOSTON.

1776.—HANCOCK 32 guns. Captured by the Rainbow 40, and brig Victor, 1777.

1776.—BOSTON (2d) 24. Captured at Charleston, S. C., 1780.

1797.—CONSTITUTION 44. Commonly called "Old Ironsides," 1576 tons old measurement, 1335 tons new measurement; displacement 2,200. Launched Oct. 21, 1797. Original cost $302,917. Often repaired and rebuilt on the original model, and was in service for many years, and until 1871 at the Naval Academy, Annapolis, as quarters for midshipmen. In 1871, she was towed to Philadelphia, where she is now (1872) "LAID UP."

1798.—WARREN 20, 385 tons, original cost $34,702. Sold in Boston, in 1801, for $19,747.

1798.—HERALD 18, 279 tons, original cost $47,780. Sold in Boston, in 1801, for $17,848.

1798.—PICKERING 14, 187 tons, brig, original cost $32,116. Lost at sea in 1800, with all on board, while in command of Lieut. B. Hillar, having sailed in August for the Guadaloupe station. Had previously performed a cruise, commanded by Lieut. Edward Preble, attached to the squadron of Commodore Barry. In the *History of Newburyport*, she is said to have been built in that place, by Orlando B. Merrill, though the official records say she was built in Boston.

1799.—BOSTON (3d) 28, 700 tons, original cost $137,969. She was burnt at Washington, in 1814, by order of the secretary of the navy, to prevent her falling into the hands of the enemy. She carried our minister to France in 1801. Was reported unworthy repair in 1812.

The Boston was built for the government by subscription. The *Columbian Centinel* of June 17, 1798, contains the following:

"*Notice.*—A subscription will be opened this day for the raising of a fund to purchase or build one or more ships of war, to be loaned to this Government for the service of the United States. Those who wish to join in this testimonial of public spirit, are requested to meet in the chamber over Taylor's insurance office at 1 o'clock precisely to affix their signatures and make necessary arrangements."

The same paper of June 30th, has the following announcement:

"*The Nerve.*—In compliance with the advertisement in the *last* '*Centinel,*' a number of citizens of this metropolis met at Taylor's Insurance Office for the purpose of opening a patriotic voluntary subscription in aid of Government. Last evening, the amount subscribed amounted to $115,250; and as the subscription still continues open, we have not the least doubt that Boston will outdo every city in the Union in Federal patriotism. We will not omit mentioning that the Hon. William Phillips added $10,000 to this free will offering. God bless him for it!"

The papers of Aug. 22, 1798, less than two months from the date of the above notice, say: "The keel of a 36 gun Frigate is now *laying* at Mr. Hart's Navy Yard." A list of the subscribers can be found in the *Boston Evening Gazette* about 1858 or '59, and in the *Army and Navy Journal,* January, 1866. The whole amount of the subscription was $136,600.

June 9, 1799, the *Centinel* says, "the Boston Frigate is almost completely rigged." June 12th, "The Boston frigate yesterday hauled off into the stream." July 24th, "she sailed on a cruise commanded by Capt. Geo. Little," and the *Centinel* declares her one of the handsomest modelled vessels in the world.

1803.—Argus 16, 298 tons, original cost $37,420. Captured in 1813, by H. B. M. brig Pelican 21, after an action of forty-five minutes, in which she lost her commander, Lieut. Wm. H. Allen, and had ten killed and thirteen wounded. She had previously captured *twenty-two* of the enemy's vessels on *his own* coast. She also did good service in the war with Tripoli, 1803–6. The Argus was built under the superintendence of Commodore Edward Preble. Her dimensions were: length of keel, 77 feet; breadth of beam, 27 feet; depth of hold, 12½ feet. Her armament, 14 32-pound carronades and 2 long 18 pounders.

1805.—Spitfire 3, bomb ketch, afterwards increased to 7 guns, 102 tons, ketch-rigged. Original cost $7,000. Broken up at Norfolk, 1820. Built under the superintendence of Commodore Edward Preble.

1805.—Vengeance 3, bomb ketch, 92 tons, purchased by Commodore Edward Preble, original cost $18,445. Broken up at New-York, 1818.

1813.—Frolic 18, 509 tons, original cost $72,095. Captured April 20, 1814, by H. B. M. frigate Orpheus 36, and schooner Shelbourne 12, after a chase of sixty miles, during which the Frolic threw overboard her lee guns.

1814.—Independence 74, 2257 tons old measurement, original cost $421,810. Razeed to a frigate, and at the present time (1872) on the navy list as a second rate 40 guns; tonnage under the new act 1891. She is stationed at Mare Island, California, as a receiving ship for recruits. Her displacement, according to the navy register for 1872, is 3270 tons.

The Independence was the only ship of the line that was got afloat during the war of 1812–14 with Great Britain, and the first ship of the line of the U. S. Navy, if we except the America 74, which before launching was given to the French. Her first and only foreign cruise, as a ship of the line, was to the Mediterranean, wearing the broad pennant of Commodore Wm. Bainbridge, and was the first vessel of that class to display our stars and stripes abroad. It was found, though otherwise a good model, that she carried her lower deck guns too low, and in 1836 she was razeed at Boston, and converted into a fine double-banked 60 gun frigate, and has since performed good service. She was considered a very fine ship of her class in her time, and was, on her first cruise as a razee, much admired by naval critics at Portsmouth, England, and was visited at Cronstadt by the Emperor Nicholas *incog.*

1818.—VERMONT 74, 2633 tons old measurement, 2600 new; displacement 4150; original cost $849,327. Launched in 1848, after having been thirty years on the stocks. Still in service as a third rate 16 guns, and used as a receiving ship for recruits at New-York. In 1853, she was rigged and equipped for sea, intended as the flag ship of Commodore M. C. Perry on the Japan Expedition, but it was found she could not be commissioned without exceeding the number of seamen allowed by law, and she was accordingly dismantled and placed in ordinary. She has never made a foreign cruise.

It is said the Vermont when first put upon the stocks was called the Virginia, and the Virginia, which is yet (1872) on the stocks, was called the Vermont, and that the names were shifted by a southern born commandant of the Boston navy yard, who thought the present Virginia the best model.

1818.—VIRGINIA 74, 2633 tons. Still on the stocks at the navy yard (1872), in an unfinished condition, under one of the ship-houses. Will probably never be launched, unless to be used as a receiving ship. Though considered a fine model when her keel was laid, fifty-two years ago, she is now as unsuited to the purposes of modern warfare as Noah's ark would be.

1821.—ALLIGATOR 3, 108 tons, original cost $26,909. Lost on Carysfort Reef, coast of Florida, in 1823. The shoal spot on which she was lost now bears her name.

1825.—BOSTON (4th) 18, 700 tons, original cost $109,156. Lost on Eletheura, W. Indies, Nov. 15, 1846, during a squall in the night—crew saved. She made six cruises, viz.: to Brazil, 1826–29; Mediterranean, 1830–32; West Indies, 1836–39; East Indies, 1841–43; Brazil, 1843–46.

1825.—CUMBERLAND 44, 1726 tons, original cost $357,475. Launched in 1843. Afterwards razeed, and mounted a battery of 22 heavy guns. Was sunk by the rebel ram Merrimac, in the memorable conflict, Hampton Roads.

1825–6.—WARREN (3d) 20, 697 tons, original cost $104,369. Condemned and sold out of service in 1861, and now (1872) used as a station-hulk, at Panama, by the Pacific Mail Steamship Co.

1826–7.—FALMOUTH 18, 703 tons, original cost $112,535. Her repairs, to 1850, cost $305,092. She was condemned and sold out of the service at Aspinwall, where she had been used as a store and guard ship, in 1861, and foundered at sea on her first return passage from New-York to Aspinwall the same year.

1831.—BOXER (2d) 10, 194 tons, original cost $30,697. She was sold in 1848. She cruized in the Brazils, 1832–3; West Indies, 1834; Pacific, 1835–7, and also 1838–40; Home Squadron, 1842–44; African Squadron, 1846–48.

1836.—CONSORT 6, 230 tons. Built for Wilkes's Exploring Expedition. Original cost $51,724. Was sold at Philadelphia in 1844.

1836.—PORPOISE (2d) 10, 224 tons, brig, original cost $45,000. Lost at sea, in the East Indies, while attached to the Pacific Exploring Expedition, with all on board, 1854.

1837.—CYANE 20, 792 tons old measurement, 695 by the new; displacement 950. She was named after the British ship captured by the Constitution, Feb. 20, 1815. Original cost $143,469. Her repairs to 1850 cost $59,089, and she has been several times repaired since. In 1867 she was fitted out at Mare Island Navy Yard, Cal., as a store ship, and remained in Panama in that capacity until July, 1869, when she returned to Mare Island and was sent to Sitka, as a depot ship for coal and stores, and as a protection to the newly-acquired territory of Alaska. In November, 1870, she was sent to the Isthmus again to assist the expedition, engaged in surveying routes for a ship canal.

1838–9.—MARION 16, 566 tons by the old measurement, 320 by the new; displacement 1840, original cost $124,566. Her repairs to 1850 cost $72,712. In service in 1872 as a school ship for midshipmen, at the naval academy. Is now being rebuilt, as a screw steamer, at Portsmouth, N. H.

1842.—BAINBRIDGE 10, brig, 259 tons, original cost $40,790. Foundered at sea, on our coast, during our civil war,—only one or two lives saved.

1842.—ERIE 4, ship, 611 tons, original cost $84,603. A sloop-of-war of the same name, built in 1813 and rebuilt in 1820, at a cost of $56,174, was broken up at Boston in 1841, and this store ship constructed. The cost of repairs upon the old and new ship amounted to $319,191. She was sold in 1850 for $13,000.

1843.—PLYMOUTH 22, 989 tons, original cost $168,212. She was burnt in Norfolk, by the rebels, in 1861.

1845.—MASSACHUSETTS 2, 765 tons, a screw steamer purchased of R. B. Forbes, Esq., for $80,000. Was re-named the "Farralones" during the war of 1860–64, and had her engines taken out. After the war, she was taken to San Francisco and sold, and is still plying from that port as a merchantman. The Massachusetts sailed from Boston for Liverpool, Sept. 1, 1848. She was the first American propeller packet ship that went to England, and was the first steamer under the United States flag designed for passengers to that country since the Savannah, the pioneer steamer, crossed the Atlantic. Her machinery was designed by Ericcson.

1846.—SUPPLY 4, store ship, 547 tons, purchased when new for $60,000. In 1868, she brought to Boston the remains of Rear Admiral H. H. Bell, and Lt.-Commanders Mackenzie and Read. In 1871, she carried a portion of the charitable contributions of the citizens of New-York to France. Is now (1872) in commission to carry supplies to the South Atlantic vessels. She has been constantly employed, and has proved one of the most useful vessels in our navy.

1846.—FREDONIA 4, store ship, 800 tons, purchased for $63,300. In service in 1867 as a stationary store ship at Callao, Peru, and was, in consequence of the prevalence of the yellow fever at that place, removed thence to Arica, where she was torn from her anchors, during the great earthquake of August, 1869, and lost with all on board.

1846.—ETNA 1, bomb brig, 182 tons, purchased for $17,000. Was sold at Norfolk in 1848 for $3,010.

1846.—STROMBOLI 1, bomb brig, 182 tons, purchased for $17,000. Was sold at Norfolk in 1848 for $3,010.

1847.—EDITH 2, screw steamer, 400 tons, purchased of R. B. Forbes, Esq. Lost on the coast of California in 1848. The Edith, under command of

Capt. George W. Lewis, left New-York for Bombay and China, Jan. 18, 1845, and was the first American steamer that went to British India, and the first square-rigged propeller that went to China under "our flag." Her machinery was designed by Ericcson.

1848.—JOHN HANCOCK, screw steamer, 230 tons, original cost $31,261. Built for the triple purpose of a water boat, anchor hoy and yard tug. Soon after her launch, some negro riots occurring in New-Bedford, the "Hancock" was sent there with an extemporized crew to aid in suppressing them, and her performance at sea being satisfactory she was thought too good to be devoted to the purposes for which she was built, and, in 1851, was sent to Cuba to look after the fillibusters of the Lopez expedition. That duty accomplished, she returned to Boston yard and was placed in ordinary.

1851.—PRINCETON (2d), screw steamer, 990 tons. Built to contain the engines of Princeton (1st), *the first screw steamer in our navy*, and the *first man-of-war screw steamer in the world*,—then broken up. The engines were planned and built under the superintendence of Ericcson. Original cost $104,405, exclusive of engines. Sold at Philadelphia, 1867.

1853.—JOHN HANCOCK (2d), screw steamer, 382 tons, original cost $76,521. This was the same vessel as the "J. H." of 1848, lengthened and rebuilt. When the Behring's Straits, or North Pacific Exploring Expedition was being organized, under Commodore Ringold, in 1853, a small sized steamer was thought essential. The "John Hancock" being the only available vessel of that description in the navy, she was hauled up on ways at the Boston navy yard, and lengthened both at the bow and stern,—the old ends being sawed off, moved away, and new ones substituted,—by which means her tonnage was increased one hundred and fifty-two tons. She was equipped for sea under the superintendence of the present Rear-Admiral, John Rogers, then a lieutenant, who took her to the East Indies, where she continued under his command until he went on board the flag ship Vincennes, and assumed command of the squadron. During the remainder of the cruise she was commanded by passed Midshipman Brooke, the inventor of the deep sea sounding apparatus. Mr. Brooke resigned, and took part with the south in the recent rebellion. When the Pacific exploring expedition was disbanded, the "John Hancock" was laid up at Mare Island navy yard, and continued on that coast, performing such duty as was required of her, until sold out of the service, Aug. 17, 1865.

She was never considered a beauty by nautical critics either in or out of the service, as may be known from the "Heathen Chinee's" remark when he saw her at anchor in Hong Kong: "That sheep number one, ally same as a Chinese junk." However, handsome is that handsome does: she proved a good and faithful servant to our government.

She was sold to the California Steam Navigation Co. In 1868 her boilers and machinery were taken out, and she was purchased by Messrs. McPherson & Weatherbee, who converted her into a barquentine, to be used in the lumber business. Upon overhauling her, the timbers and frame were found in every respect solid; and with trifling repairs, she was made a good and substantial craft. It was thought she was capable of transporting 300,000 feet of lumber.

1855.—MERRIMAC 40, screw frigate, 3200 tons, original cost $879,126. Seized by the rebels at Norfolk, Va., 1861, when nearly ready for sea, and converted into an iron-clad ram. She became notorious for her conflict with the Cumberland and Congress at Hampton Roads, and from her subsequent defeat by the untried little Monitor.

She was set on fire and blown up by the rebels, near Craney Island, to prevent her recapture.

The "Merrimac" sailed from Boston, on a week's trial trip, Feb. 25, 1856. Returned, and sailing thence again, arrived at Annapolis on the 19th of April following. She was the first screw steam frigate launched in our navy, and while at Annapolis was visited and admired by great numbers, including nearly all of the members of both Houses of Congress, then assembled in Washington. On the 6th of May she sailed for Havana, and returned to Boston on the 7th of July following. Sailed thence for England, Sept. 9th, of the same year, and returned to Norfolk via St. Thomas, W. I., March 15, 1857. Leaving Norfolk, she arrived at Boston during the same month, was immediately equipped for sea, and sailed on the 17th of October, 1857, for the Pacific, bearing the broad pennant of Commodore John Collins Long. Returning from the Pacific, she arrived at Norfolk on the 6th of Feb., 1860. This was her last service under our flag. In April, 1861, she was lying in ordinary at Norfolk, waiting her battery and the repairs on her engine to enable her to proceed to sea; she had been got ready, and but for the prevalence of treasonable councils would have been taken out of Norfolk before the destruction of the navy yard, on the 21st of April, 1861. Her conversion by the rebels into an iron-clad, her attack upon the ships in Hampton Roads, her defeat by the Monitor, March 8, 1862, and her destruction by the rebels, May 11, 1862, have became matters of history.

1858.—Hartford 14, screw steamer, 1920 tons old measurement, 1366 tons by the new; increased in 1870, by the addition of a spar-deck, to 2000 tons by the new measurement; displacement 2900. During the war, she carried 22 guns. She was the flag-ship of Farragut at New-Orleans, Mobile, &c., and gained an historic name in our navy, second only to the "Constitution." Her first cruise, 1859–61, was to the East Indies, as the flag-ship of Commodore Stribling. After the war, she was again sent to the East Indies, as the flag-ship of Rear Admiral H. H. Bell, who was Farragut's fleet captain and chief of staff in New-Orleans, and who was drowned at Hiogo, Japan, while she was carrying his flag. On her return to New-York she was placed in ordinary, and has since had a deck added and undergone extensive repairs and alterations, which are about completed. It is worthy of remark that this ship was the next successor launched from the ways which had been occupied by the "Merrimac."

1859.—Narragansett 3, screw steamer, 900 tons old measurement, 566 tons by the new; displacement 1235. Cruised in the Pacific, 1859–'65. Has since performed some service in the West Indies, and sailed from New-York, March, 1871, for the Pacific, where she is now (1872) in commission.

1861.—Wachusett 9, screw steamer, third class, 1032 tons old measurement, 695 by the new; displacement 1575. She was launched at the navy yard, October, 1861. Engines built at the Morgan Iron Works. Total cost $314,362.85. Has made a cruise to the East Indies since the war; was, on her return, repaired at New-York, and is now (1872) in commission and attached to the European fleet.

1861.—MARITANZA 6, wooden, side wheel, double-ender. Launched at the navy yard, Charlestown, November, 1861. Engines built by Harrison Loring & Co., South Boston. Total cost $187,128.19. Sold at Portsmouth, N. H., Aug. 26, 1868.

1861.—HURON 6, fourth rate, screw steamer, 507 tons by the old measurement, 327 by the new. Built by Paul Curtis, South Boston, November, 1861. Engines built by Harrison Loring. Total cost $101,421. Sold at New-York, June 4, 1869.

1861.—CHOCURA 7, fourth rate, screw steamer, 507 tons by the old measurement, 327 by the new. Launched by Curtis & Tilden, in East Boston, November, 1861. Engines built by Harrison Loring. Total cost $99,912.01; amount expended for repairs $8,221.32. Sold July 13, 1867, for $10,000.

1861.—MARBLEHEAD 7, fourth rate, screw steamer, 507 tons by the old measurement. Launched November, 1861. Built by Geo. Jackman, in Newburyport. Engines built at the Highland Iron Works, Newburg, N. Y. She was brought around to the navy yard, Charlestown, and there completed and equipped for sea. Total cost $97,736.75. Sold at auction in New-York, Sept. 30, 1868.

NOTE.—The "Katahdin," "Kineo" and "Penobscot," three vessels of the same class, and built in the State of Maine, were brought around to the navy yard, Charlestown, in November, 1861, and there fitted and equipped for sea, under the superintendence of Capt. R. B. Forbes.

1861.—SAGAMORE 7, fourth rate, screw steamer, 507 tons old measurement, 327 by the new. Built by A. & G. T. Sampson, and launched November, 1861. Engines built at the Atlantic Works. Total cost $101,682.52; amount expended for repairs $14. Sold, June 13, 1866, for $12,300.

1862.—CANANDAIGUA 7, second class, screw steamer, 1395 tons by the old measurement, 955 by the new; displacement 2130. Launched at the navy yard, March, 1862. Engines built at the Atlantic Works, Boston. Total cost $388,541.34. Has been attached to the European Squadron since the war. Was repaired at New-York, 1871, and is now (1872) in commission and attached to the North Atlantic Squadron.

1862.—GENESEE 7, wooden, side-wheeled double-ender, 803 tons. Launched at the navy yard, Charlestown, April, 1862. Engines built at the Neptune Works. Total cost $190,423.63; expended for repairs $8,695.45. Sold at auction, Oct. 3, 1867, for $14,400.

1862.—TIOGA 10, wooden, side-wheeled double-ender, 819 tons. Launched at the navy yard, Charlestown, April, 1862. Engines built at the Morgan Iron Works, New-York. Total cost $199,852.14; expended for repairs $3,533.80. Sold at auction, Oct. 15, 1867, for $15,000.

1863.—MASSASOIT 10, wooden, side-wheeled double-ender, 974 tons. Built by Curtis & Tilden. Launched March, 1863. Engines built at the Globe Works, Boston. Total cost $160,574.41; amount expended on repairs $76,571.58. Sold Oct. 15, 1867, for $15,000.

1863.—OSCEOLA 10, wooden, side-wheeled double-ender, 974 tons. Built by Curtis & Tilden. Launched June, 1863. Engines built at the Globe Works, Boston. Total cost $160,574.41; amount expended on repairs $30,281.58. Sold Oct. 1, 1867, for $16,000, when her engines were taken out by her new owners, and she was converted into a sailing barque.

1863.—MATTABASSETT 10, wooden, side-wheeled double-ender, 974 tons. Built by A. & G. Sampson. Launched June, 1863. Engines built at the Allaire Works, New-York. Total cost $163,595.17; amount expended on repairs $3,723.70. Sold Oct. 15, 1867, for $15,000.

1863.—CHICOPEE 10, wooden, side-wheeled double-ender, 974 tons. Built by Paul Curtis in East Boston. Launched March, 1863. Engines built at the Neptune Works, New-York. Total cost $163,239.35; amount expended for repairs $706.08. Sold Oct. 8, 1867, without the machinery, for $4,000.

1863.—TALLAPOOSA 10, wooden, side-wheeled double-ender, 974 tons old measurement, 650 by the new; displacement 1270. Launched at the navy yard, Charlestown, February, 1863. Engines built at the Neptune Company's Works, New-York. Total cost $241,856.98. Has been fitted up as a despatch vessel between the several navy yards, and used to convey the president of the United States, and other dignitaries, both civil and naval, along the coast. Conveyed Admiral Farragut from New-York to Portsmouth in his last illness. In commission on special service, 1871. Repairing, 1872, at Washington, D. C.

1863.—WINOOSKI 10, wooden, side-wheeled double-ender, 974 tons old measurement, 650 by the new. Launched at the Charlestown navy yard, July, 1863. Engines built at the Providence Steam Company's Works, Providence, R. I. Total cost $239,617.47. Sold at Portsmouth, N. H., Aug. 26, 1868.

1863.—PEQUOT 10, fourth rate, screw steamer, 593 tons old measurement, 410 by the new; displacement 900. Launched at the navy yard, Charlestown, Mass., June, 1863. Engines built by Woodruff & Beach, Hartford, Conn. Total cost $249,231.99. Sold at New-York, May 6, 1869.

1863.—SACO 10, fourth rate, screw steamer, 593 tons old measurement, 410 by the new; displacement 900. Launched at the navy yard, Charlestown, August, 1863. Engines built by the Corliss Steam Engine Company, New-York. Total cost $274,845.14. In commission, 1871, in the European, and in 1872, in the Asiatic Fleet, having passed through the Suez Canal to join it.

1864.—MONADNOCK 4, double-turreted iron-clad, 1564 tons by the old measurement, 1094 by the new. Launched at the Charlestown navy yard, March 23, 1864. Turrets made at the Atlantic Works, Boston; engines by Morris, Towne & Co., Philadelphia. Total cost $981,439.45. She was the first monitor iron-clad to go from the Atlantic to the Pacific Ocean, in 1866. On her passage from Philadelphia to San Francisco, she ran by log 15,385 knots, the greatest distance logged in twenty-four hours being 195.6 knots; the least, 19 knots; her average speed 6.32 knots per hour. For a particular account of her performance, see the Secretary of the Navy's Report, December, 1866.

She is now (1872) in ordinary at Mare Island Navy Yard, Cal., and requires extensive repairs.

1864.—WINNEPEC 10, iron, side-wheeled double-ender, 1030 tons. Built by Donald McKay, East Boston. Engines built by Harrison Loring. Total cost $298,132.94. Sold at Norfolk, Va., July 17, 1869.

1864.—AMMONOOSUC 15 (name changed in 1869 to "IOWA"), first rate, screw steam ship, 3213 tons by the old measurement, 2019 by the new;

displacement 4000. Launched at the navy yard, Charlestown, 1864. Was towed around to New-York to receive her engines. Returned to Boston, under steam, to receive her rigging. Has never been to sea. In ordinary, at the navy yard, Charlestown, 1872.

1865.—ASHUELOT 10, iron, side-wheeled double-ender, 1030 tons by the old measurement, 786 by the new; displacement 1370. Built by Donald McKay at East Boston, July, 1865. Total cost $297,415.92. In commission, and attached to the Asiatic Squadron, 1872.

1865.—SPEEDWELL 2, iron, fourth rate, screw tug, 350 tons by the old measurement, 306 by the new; displacement 420. Built at East Boston by James Felton, on contract. Total cost $146,600. In commission, at Portsmouth, N. H., 1872, as a despatch boat.

1865.—FORTUNE 2, iron, fourth rate, screw tug, 350 tons by the old measurement, 306 by the new. Built at East Boston by James Felton, September, 1865, on contract. Cost $149,600. In ordinary at Washington, 1871.

1865.—GUERRIERE 21, first rate, screw steam ship, 3177 tons by the old measurement, 2516 by the new; displacement 4000. Launched at the navy yard, Charlestown, September, 1865. Engines built at the Globe Works, Boston. Total cost $1,154,325.10. Performed a cruise on the Brazil Station, as the flag-ship of Rear-Admiral Charles H. Davis, and in 1871, took Admiral Farragut's remains from Portsmouth to New-York. Subsequently went to the Mediterranean, from whence she has recently returned, bringing the remains of Major-General Robert Anderson (the hero of Fort Sumter) from Nice to Fortress Munroe. Is now in ordinary in New-York, and will probably never make another cruise.

1866.—LEYDEN 2, fourth rate, iron screw tug, 350 tons by the old measurement, 306 by the new; displacement 420. Built at East Boston by James Felton. Total cost by contracts $128,000. In commission at the Boston yard, 1871.

1866.—PALOS 2, fourth rate, iron screw tug, 350 tons by the old measurement, 306 by the new; displacement 420. Built at East Boston, July, 1866, by James Felton. Contracts cost $128,000. Is now (1871) in commission, and attached to the Asiatic Squadron as a tender. The "Palos" was the first U. S. vessel of war to pass through the Suez Canal. She made the passage from Boston to Singapore in seventy-three sailing days. The history of her voyage and her passage through the Canal, can be found in the appendix to the Secretary of the Navy's Report, December, 1870. She was one of the vessels which participated in the attack upon, and capture of the Corean Forts, 1871.

1866.—STANDISH 2, fourth rate, iron screw tug, 350 tons by the old measurement, 306 by the new; displacement 420. Built at East Boston, January, 1866, by James Felton. Contract cost $106,240. In ordinary at Norfolk, 1871.

1866.—MAYFLOWER 2, fourth rate, iron screw tug, 350 tons by the old measurement, 306 by the new; displacement 420. Built at East Boston, February, 1866. Contract cost $106,240. In commission at Norfolk, Va., 1871; repairing at Washington, 1872.

1866.—MANITOU 13 (name changed in 1869 to "WORCESTER"), second rate, screw steam ship, 2348 tons by the old measurement, 1468 by the new, as launched. Has since had another deck added, and now 2000 tons by the new measurement; displacement 3050. Launched at the navy yard, Charlestown, August, 1866. Engines made at the Globe Works. Remained in ordinary until February, 1871, when she was commissioned as a store-ship, and sailed with the charitable contributions of provisions by the citizens of Boston for the relief of the French people. The "Worcester" is now (1872) in commission as the flag-ship of the North Atlantic Fleet.

1867.—NANTASKET 7, third rate, screw steamer, 900 tons by the old measurement, 523 by the new; displacement 1165. Launched at the navy yard, Charlestown, July, 1867. Engines built by the U. S. government at Portsmouth, N. H., where she was towed to receive them. Is now (1872) in commission, and attached to the North Atlantic Fleet.

1868.—ALASKA 10, second rate, screw steamer, 1740 tons by the old measurement, 1122 by the new; displacement 2400. Launched at the navy yard, Charlestown, Oct. 31, 1868. Engines made at the navy yard, under the direction of Chief Engineer Alexander Henderson, U. S. N., from designs furnished from Washington. Her dimensions are: length, 250 feet; beam, 38 feet; depth of hold, 19 feet. She was put in commission, Dec. 7, 1869, and is now (1872) attached to the Asiatic Squadron.

SINGLE-TURRETED IRON-CLADS.

1863.—NANTUCKET 2, 844 tons by the old measurement, 496 by the new. Built by the Atlantic Works, March, 1863. Total cost $408,091.37. Laid up at League Island, 1871.

1863.—NAHANT 2, 844 tons by the old measurement, 496 by the new. Built by Harrison Loring, January, 1864. Total cost $413,575.14. Laid up at League Island, 1871.

1864.—CANONICUS 2, 1034 tons by the old measurement, 554 by the new. Built by Harrison Loring, Boston, February, 1864. Total cost $622,966.22. Laid up at League Island, 1871. Was commissioned in 1872, and is now (April) at Norfolk, waiting orders.

1864.—CASCO 1 (renamed "HERO" in 1869), 614 tons by the old measurement, 483 by the new. Built by the Atlantic Works. Total cost $529,996.19. Laid up at Washington, D. C., 1871.

1864.—CHIMO 1 (renamed "PISCATAQUA"), 614 tons by the old measurement, 483 by the new. Built by Aquila Adams. Cost $620,445.52. Laid up at Washington, 1871.

1864.—SHAWNEE 2, 614 tons by the old measurement, 438 by the new. Built by Curtis & Tilden. Cost $581,818.50. Repairing at Boston, 1871.

1865.—NAUSETT 2, 614 tons by the old measurement, 438 by the new. Built by Donald McKay, East Boston. Cost $578,100.98. Laid up at League Island, 1871.

1865.—SQUANDO 2 (renamed "ALGOMA"), 614 tons by the old measurement, 438 tons by the new. Built April, 1865, by McKay & Aldus. Cost $589,535.70. Laid up at League Island, 1871.

1865.—SUNCOOK 2, 614 tons by the old measurement, 438 by the new. Built at the Globe Works, South Boston, June, 1865. Cost $593,574.30. Laid up at League Island, 1871.

ON THE STOCKS AT THE NAVY YARD.

AMMONOSUC 17, first class, screw steamship (renamed, in 1869, "CONNECTICUT"), 3713 tons by the old measurement, 2869 by the new; displacement, navy register, 1872, 4450.

KEWAYDIN 23, first rate, screw steamship (renamed, in 1869, "PENNSYLVANIA"), 3177 tons by the old measurement, 2490 by the new; displacement 4000.

QUINSIGAMOND 4, first rate, monitor, double-turreted iron-clad (renamed, in 1869, "OREGON"), 3200 tons by the old measurement, 2127 by the new. Machinery and boilers on board.

PANDALIA, screw steamer; keel laid 1872, to replace sailing sloop of same name, broken up.

Torpedo boat; keel laid 1872.

VESSELS PURCHASED IN BOSTON, FOR U. S. NAVY DEPARTMENT.

1.—ARIS, 820 tons, screw steamer; purchased of Boston Prize Court, June 4, 1863, for $100,000; sold at Boston Aug. 1, 1865, to Sprague, Soule & Co., for $56,500.

2.—ATLANTA, 1,006 tons; screw steamer, ironclad; captured from the rebels, and purchased of Boston Prize Court, Feb. 6, 1864, for $350,829.26; laid up at League Island. She was sold May 4, 1869. Started for the West Indies, and probably foundered at sea, with all on board,—never heard from.

3.—AZALIA, 176 tons; screw tug; purchased Feb. 6, 1864, for $47,000; sold at Philadelphia, Aug. 10, 1865, for $11,100.

4.—BAT, 530 tons; screw steamer; purchased of Boston Prize Court, Nov., 1864, for $150,000; sold at New-York, Oct. 25, 1865, to Russell Sturgis, for $29,500.

5.—BELLE, 52 tons; purchased June 3, 1864, for $20,000; sold at New-York, July 12, 1865, to Cozzen & Co., for $8,000.

6.—BRITANNIA, 495 tons; screw steamer; purchased of Boston Prize Court, Sept. 22, 1863, for $52,000; sold at Philadelphia, Aug. 10, 1865, for $15,000.

7.—CAMBRIDGE, 858 tons; screw steamer; purchased July 30, 1861, for $76,000; sold at Philadelphia, June 20, 1865, for $17,000.

8.—CHEROKEE, 606 tons; screw steamer; purchased June 13, 1864, for $75,000; sold at Boston, Aug. 1, 1865, to Harrison Loring, for $44,500.

9.—CORNUBIA, 800 tons; screw steamer; purchased of Boston Prize Court, November, 1863, for $63,000; sold at New-York, Oct. 25, 1865, to Merrick & Sons, for $19,000.

10.—DON, 390 tons; screw steamer; purchased of Boston Prize Court, April, 1863, for $66,666. In service in the north Atlantic squadron, after the war, and sold at New-York Aug. 29, 1868.

11.—ELLA AND ANNIE, 627 tons; screw steamer; purchased of Boston Prize Court; name changed to MALVERN; sold at New-York, Oct. 25, 1865, to S. G. Bogart, for $113,500.

12.—ETHAN ALLEN, 566 tons; sailing bark; purchased Aug. 30, 1861, for $27,500; sold at Portsmouth, July 20, 1865, to E. Snow, for $20,000.

13.—FEARNOT, 1,012 tons; sailing ship; purchased July 20, 1861, for $40,000; sold at Boston, Oct. 3, 1866, to W. F. Weld & Co., for $19,500.

14.—F. W. LINCOLN, 317 tons; screw tug; name changed to PHLOX; purchased Aug. 1, 1864, for $76,000. In use at U. S. Naval Academy, Annapolis, in 1871, and repairing at Washington, 1872.

15.—GEMSBOK, 622 tons; sailing bark; purchased Sept. 7, 1861, for $29,000; sold at New-York, July 12, 1865, to Smith & Co., for $20,000.

16.—GLIDE, 80 tons; tug, name changed to GLANCE; purchased June 3, 1864, for $20,000. In ordinary at League Island, 1871; in use at Philadelphia Navy Yard, 1872.

17.—HARVEST MOON, 546 tons; side wheel steamer; purchased Nov. 12, 1863, for 99,300; sunk by a torpedo, near Georgetown, S. C., May 1, 1865.

18.—HOUQUAH, 397 tons; purchased June 9, 1863, for $49,000; sold at Philadelphia, Aug. 10, 1865, for $15,900.

19.—INO, 985 tons; sailing ship; purchased Aug. 30, 1861, for $40,000; sold at Boston, March 19, 1867, to Mr. Reed, for $12,500.

20.—IRON AGE, 424 tons; steamer; purchased April 25, 1863, for $60,000; grounded and destroyed at Lockwood, Folly's Inlet, Jan. 10, 1864.

21.—KENSINGTON, 1,052 tons; screw steamer; purchased Jan. 27, 1862, for $99,000; sold at New-York, July 12, 1865, to Brown & Co., for $81,500.

22.—LITTLE ADA, 196 tons; steamer; purchased of Boston Prize Court, Aug. 18, 1864, for $35,000; sold at Washington, to War Department, Aug. 12, 1865, for $21,000.

23.—MASSACHUSETTS, 1,155 tons; purchased May 3, 1861, for $172,500; sold at New York, Oct. 1, 1867, to W. F. Weld & Co., for $50,000.

24.—NIPHON, 475 tons; screw steamer; purchased May 6, 1863, for $75,000; sold at Boston, April 17, 1865, to Atlantic Works, for $18,250.

25.—ONWARD, 874 tons old, 704 tons by new measurement; sailing bark; purchased Sept. 9, 1861, for $27,000; in service (1871) as storeship to the South Pacific squadron, and in 1872 stationed at Callao, Peru.

26.—PHILIPPI, 311 tons; steamer; purchased of Boston Prize Court, Feb. 23, 1864, for $30,000; abandoned and destroyed at Mobile Bay, Aug. 5, 1864.

27.—P. SPRAGUE, 963 tons; screw steamer, name changed to FLAG; purchased April 26, 1861, for $90,000; sold at New-York, July 12, 1865, to M. O. Roberts, for $50,000.

28.—R. B. FORBES, 330 tons; screw steamer; purchased Sept. 4, 1861, for $52,500; wrecked on the coast of North Carolina, Feb. 25, 1862.

29.—R. E. LEE, 900 tons; screw steamer, name changed to FORT DONELSON; purchased of Boston Prize Court, January, 1864, for $73,000; sold at New-York, Oct. 25, 1865, to Brown Bros. for $24,500.

30.—R. T. RENSHAW, 80 tons; name changed to RENSHAW; purchased of Boston Prize Court, Oct. 28, 1863, for $850; sold at Norfolk, Sept. 6, 1865, to J. & B. Baker & Co., for $713.21.

31.—SOUTH CAROLINA, 1,165 tons; iron screw steamer; purchased May 3, 1861, for $172,500; sold at New-York, Oct. 5, 1865, for $71,000.

32.—SUNFLOWER, 294 tons; screw tug; purchased May 2, 1863, for $35,000; sold at Philadelphia, Aug. 10, 1865, for $11,000.

33.—THISTLE, 636 tons; screw, name changed to DUNBARTON; purchased of Boston Prize Court, July, 1864, for $164,000; sold at New-York, Oct. 25, 1867, to Mr. Marvin for $17,000.

34.—TREPOIL, 370 tons; screw tug; purchased Feb. 2, 1865, for $118,070; sold at Boston May 27, 1865, to L. Litchfield, for $11,500.

35.—TRISTAM SHANDY, 444 tons; screw; purchased of Boston Prize Court, May, 1864, for $58,000; name changed to BOXER; in ordinary at League Island, after the war, and sold at Philadelphia, Sept. 1, 1868.

36.—UNION, 500 tons; name changed to UNIT; purchased June 3, 1864, for $60,000; sold at New-York, July 12, 1865, to C. & E. T. Peters, for $6,750.

37.—VICKSBURG, 300 tons; screw steamer; name changed to ACACIA; purchased Oct. 28, 1863, for $——; sold at New-York, June 20, 1865, for $14,000.

38.—VICTORY, 630 tons; screw; name changed to QUEEN; purchased of Boston Prize Court, July 31, 1863, for $65,000; sold at New-York, Oct. 17, 1865, to Smith & Dunning, for $51,300.

39.—WANDO, 645 tons; screw; purchased of Boston Prize Court, Nov., 1864, for $131,000; sold at New-York, Nov. 30, 1865, to H. Allen, for $30,200.

40.—W. G. ANDERSON, 142 tons; sailing bark; purchased April 30, 1861, for $27,000; sold at New-York, Aug. 29, 1866, to A. & A. Low & Brothers, for $12,600.

41.—YOUNG AMERICA, 173 tons; purchased of Boston Prize Court, for $13,500; sold at New-York, July 12, 1865, to Camden & Amboy R. R. Co. for $7,800.

42.—YOUNG ROVER, 418 tons; sailing bark; purchased July 27, 1861, for $27,500; sold at Boston, June 22, 1865, to Mr. Curtis, for $19,250.

43.—YUCCA, 373 tons; screw; purchased Feb. 23, 1865, for $119,134.75; in ordinary at Portsmouth, after the war, and sold there Aug. 26, 1868.

NOTE.—The CONSTITUTION, commonly called "Old Ironsides," noticed on page 271, was modelled by Joshua Humphries, and was built by George Claghorne and Mr. Hartley of Boston. Length 175 feet, beam 43.6 feet, depth of hold 14.3 feet. Stowed six months' provisions and 48,000 gallons of water. Her log-book of 1809 shows a speed of 13½ knots per hour, going free under top-gallant sails. For particulars of her career, see Emmons's *Statistical History of the U. S. Navy*, and Cooper's biography of "*Old Ironsides.*" Of late years she has been attached to the Naval Academy at Newport, R. I., and Annapolis, Md., and used as quarters for midshipmen. LAID UP 1871, at Philadelphia.

The following is a list of the engagements, captures and prizes of the CONSTITUTION, during her eventful career:

ENGAGEMENTS.

Nine batteries, mounting 115 guns, July 25, 1804, Tripoli.

CAPTURES.

Name.	*Class.*	*Guns.*	*Date.*	*Where.*
Sandwich, L. M.	Ship	6	May 10, 1800	St. Domingo.
L. Esther	——	3	May 10, 1800	St. Domingo.
Guerriere	Ship	49	Aug. 19, 1812	Atlantic Ocean.
Java	Ship	38	Dec. 29, 1812	Atlantic Ocean.
Lovely Ann	Ship	10	Feb. 14, 1814	———
Pictou	Sch'r	14	Feb. 15, 1814	West Indies.
Cyane	Ship	20	Feb. 20, 1815	Off Maderia.
Levant	Ship	18	Feb. 20, 1815	Off Maderia.

UNARMED PRIZES.

Brigs "Lady Warren," "Adeona," "Dolphin," "Adeline," "South Carolina," "Catherine," "Lord Nelson;" schooner "Phœnix," ship "Susannah," and sloop "Sally."

LOCAL LAW IN MASSACHUSETTS, HISTORICALLY CONSIDERED.

Communicated by William Chauncey Fowler, LL.D., of Durham, Conn.

Concluded from page 60.

The State Convention for adopting the new Federal Constitution.

The state convention of Massachusetts, for adopting the new federal constitution, assembled January 9, 1788, and continued in session until February 7, 1788. The constitution encountered great opposition, chiefly on the ground that it was supposed to interfere with state and personal rights. Massachusetts had contended too long and too earnestly for these rights, to give them to the federal government. This opposition would have prevailed, had not certain amendments been proposed, which would, if adopted into that instrument, secure their liberties. These amendments proposed by the convention of Massachusetts were nine in number, and as it was confidently expected that they would be adopted by the states, the convention, by the small majority of nineteen, ratified the constitution, one hundred and eighty-seven voting for it, and one hundred and sixty-eight against it.

Amendments proposed by Massachusetts.

First. That it be explicitly declared, that all powers not expressly delegated by the aforesaid constitution are reserved to the several states, to be by them exercised.

Secondly. That there shall be one representative to every thirty thousand persons, according to the census mentioned in the constitution, until the whole number of representatives amounts to two hundred.

Thirdly. That congress do not exercise the powers vested in them by the 4th section of the 1st article, but in cases where a state shall neglect or refuse to make the regulations therein mentioned, or shall make regulations subversive of the rights of the people to a free and equal representation in congress, agreeably to the constitution.

Fourthly. That congress do not lay direct taxes, but when the moneys arising from the impost and excise are insufficient for the public exigencies, nor then, until congress shall have first made a requisition upon the states, to assess, levy, and pay their respective proportion of such requisitions, agreeably to the census fixed in the said constitution, in such way and manner as the legislatures of the states shall think best; and, in such case, if any state shall neglect or refuse to pay its proportion, pursuant to such requisition, then congress may assess and levy such state's proportion, together with interest thereon, at the rate of six per cent. per annum, from the time of payment prescribed in such requisitions.

Fifthly. That congress erect no company with exclusive advantages of commerce.

Sixthly. That no person shall be tried for crime, by which he may incur an infamous punishment, or loss of life, until he be first indicted by a grand jury, except in such cases as may arise in the government and regulation of the land and naval forces.

Seventhly. The supreme judicial federal court shall have no jurisdiction of causes between citizens of different states, unless the matter in dispute, whether it concern the realty or personalty, be of the value of three thousand dollars at the least; nor shall the federal judicial powers extend to any action between citizens of different states, where the matter in dispute, whether it concern the realty or personalty, is not of the value of fifteen hundred dollars at least.

Eighthly. In civil actions between citizens of different states, every issue of fact arising in actions at common law, shall be tried by a jury, if the parties, or either of them, request it.

Ninthly. Congress shall at no time consent that any person holding an office of trust or profit, under the United States, shall accept of a title of nobility, or any other title or office, from any king, prince, or foreign state.

Character of the Amendments Proposed.

These nine amendments proposed by Massachusetts contain a strong assertion of the doctrine of state rights, intended as they were to limit the powers of the federal government. Read the debates in the Massachusetts convention, read these amendments proposed, and you will be convinced that she was as jealous of any encroachments on state rights as she had ever been of encroachments on colony rights. The end aimed at, in these nine amendments, is declared to be, "*more effectually to guard against an undue administration of the federal government.*" The ratification is called "*an explicit and solemn compact.*" The convention evidently well understood that it was prepared *by* the states; that it was "done in the convention by the unanimous consent of the states present;" that it was formed *for* the states as states; that "the ratification of nine states was sufficient for the constitution *between* the states so ratifying the same;" that it could be amended by the states, and abolished by the states; that the states created the constitution and could destroy it.

The first amendment proposed distinctly shows what was the opinion of the Massachusetts convention on the subject of state rights. First. That it be explicitly declared, that all powers not expressly delegated by the aforesaid constitution are reserved to the several states, to be by them exercised." The reserved powers were not to be dormant, but to be asserted and "exercised by the states." It is evident that without the recommendation of these nine amendments, and the expectation that they would substantially be incorporated into the new federal constitution, Massachusetts would have rejected it.

Bradford declares that "the great object of these amendments was to secure the rights of individuals charged on suspicion with treasonable acts against the United States, or with violations of the laws of congress; and to preserve to the respective state governments all the authority and power not clearly vested in the general government by the *federal compact.*"

LEGISLATION AFTER THE ADOPTION OF THE FEDERAL CONSTITUTION.

The Massachusetts convention adopted the federal constitution February 7, 1788. The legislature of Massachusetts, in aid of that provision of the constitution intended to secure the restoration of fugitive slaves to their masters, passed a law by which negroes were prohibited, under the penalty of confinement, "hard labor" in the house of correction, and whipping not exceeding "ten stripes," from taking up their residence in the state.

Thus Massachusetts asserted her own state rights, and recognized the rights of the slaveholding states, and her own obligations to deliver up fugitive slaves to their masters.

THE POSITION OF MASSACHUSETTS IN THE FEDERAL UNION.

From the foregoing statements, we can understand the historical position of Massachusetts in the federal union.

In the year 1787, Massachusetts as a "free, sovereign and independent state," sent delegates to the federal convention which framed the federal constitution, by which the present union of the American states was subsequently consummated. In this convention the voting was *by states*, and not by the numerical majority of the delegates.

In the year 1788, Massachusetts, acting for herself and by herself, and binding herself, and not Rhode Island, adopted the federal constitution. Massachusetts bound herself, and not Rhode Island, as this latter state did not accede to the union until 1790, when she, as a sovereign state, bound herself by her own act, as a party to the compact.

Thus Massachusetts became, in the language of Washington, "a member of the union," one of the states united by the new federal constitution. Thus the states, as states, formed the union, and not the people of America as a mass. The union is a union of states, and not a union of the mass of the people of the several states. Massachusetts,—a "nation," in the language of Montesquieu, who spoke of the colonies as "becoming so many great nations;" Kent, vol. i. p. 274; a "republic," in the language of Lord Clarendon, who spoke of the colonies as "hardened into republics,"—entered into a compact with the other nations, twelve of them, into a compact with the other republics, twelve of them, to form, so far as foreign nations were concerned, one nation. Thus, externally, the United States of America became, in the language of Kossuth, a "republic composed of republics."

That New-Hampshire, Massachusetts, Rhode Island, Connecticut, and the other states of the old thirteen, by entering into the constitutional compact, formed a *confederated* and not a consolidated republic, there is evidence that cannot be gainsaid. In the first congress which assembled under the present federal constitution, President Washington having been inaugurated, the senate made an address to him in which they say:

"We beg you to be assured that the senate will at all times cheerfully cöoperate in any measure that may strengthen the union and conduce to the happiness and perpetuate the liberties of this great *confederated* republic." (See vol. i. Benton's *Debates*, p. 13.)

The President (Washington) in reply, says: "I am happy to learn that the senate will at all times coöperate in every measure which may tend to promote the welfare of this *confederated* republic." Vol. i. Benton, p. 15.

In 1836, John Quincy Adams, of Massachusetts, in the debate in congress on the admission of Arkansas as a state (see 13 Benton's *Debates*, p. 33), speaks of congress as the "representative of that *federation* compounded partly of slaveholding, and partly of entirely free states."

Contemporary Opinion of Massachusetts Statesmen.

Theophilus Parsons, in the convention of Massachusetts that adopted the present federal constitution, remarks: "Congress has only a concurrent right with each state in levying direct taxes, not an exclusive right; and the right of each state to direct taxation is equally *extensive and perfect as the right of congress;* any law, therefore, of the United States for securing to congress *more than concurrent right with each state is usurpation and is void.*" What would he have said to the usurpations which have since been committed by the federal government?

In another speech in the same convention, Chief Justice Parsons said: "An act of usurpation [by the federal government] is not obligatory, it is not law; and any man is justified in his resistance. Let him be considered as a criminal by the general government, yet only his fellow-citizens can convict him; they are his jury, and if they pronounce him innocent, not all the powers of congress can hurt him; and innocent they certainly will pronounce him, if the supposed law he resisted was an act of usurpation."

Samuel Adams, always distinguished for his devotedness to colony rights and state rights, said of the first proposed amendment to the constitution already quoted, in favor of it, that it was "consonant with the second article in the present confederation that each state retains its sovereignty, freedom, and independence, and every power, jurisdiction, and right which is not by this confederation expressly delegated to the United States in congress assembled." When appointed lieutenant-governor of Massachusetts, John Hancock being governor, he said: "I shall be called upon to make a declaration, and I shall do it it cheerfully, that the commonwealth of Massachusetts is, and of right ought to be, a free, sovereign, and independent state. I shall be called upon to make another declaration with the same solemnity *to support the constitution of the United States.* I see no inconsistency in this, for it must be intended that these constitutions should mutually aid and support each other."

James Sullivan, in 1791, speaking of the federal constitution says: "Here they represent the really one *separate* and *sovereign power*, forming no civil relation to each other than what might result from a voluntary and uncompulsory *compact.*" Here this very eminent man, attorney-general of the state, and afterward judge of the supreme court, and governor of the state, speaks of the federal constitution as a "*compact* between the states." He also adds: "Nevertheless, if each state does not retain its sovereignty in some things, there is no union of several existing states but an entire government." So again he says, p. 28: "Treason is a violation of the duties of allegiance to an established government, holding the exercise of sovereign power; and there can be no such crime unless committed against such authority." But the federal constitution recognizes treason against a state, and thus recognizes the sovereignty of the several states.

Bradford, in his *History*, p. 12, remarks that there might have been two thirds of the states in favor of the constitution, without there being two thirds of the whole population of all the states." And again, "the federal features prevail and give the character to the *compact*."

Thus Massachusetts understood that the constitution was a *compact* between the states, just as Gouverneur Morris, who wrote it, understood it; that this compact formed a *confederacy* of states, just as Judge Marshall understood it, and that each state is sovereign and entitled to the allegiance of its citizens. Thus Judge Marshall, in his *Life of Washington*, vol. v., page 133, says: "North Carolina and Rhode Island did not at first accept of the constitution, and New-York was dragged into it by a repugnance to being excluded from the *confederacy*."

Suability of States.

In 1793, the governor (John Hancock) and the attorney-general (James Sullivan), were summoned by the United States marshal to appear in court and answer to a suit of an individual belonging to another state. This summons the governor refused to obey. He then summoned a meeting of the legislature. In his opening speech he said: "I cannot conceive that the people of this commonwealth, who, by their representatives in convention adopted the *federal compact*, expected a state would be held liable to answer a compulsory civil process to an individual of another state or a foreign kingdom." And in the same speech he expressed an opinon in favor of state rights and of the sovereignty of the states in all cases not expressly or plainly prohibited by the federal constitution. He also said that a "consolidation of the states into one government would endanger the nation as a republic, and eventually *divide the states now united, or eradicate* the principles for which we have contended." These "principles" were the principles of the revolution. In view of these facts, the legislature, on the twenty-seventh of September, 1793, passed the following: "*Resolved*, That a power claimed of compelling the state to become a defendant in the court of the United States, at the suit of an individual or individuals, is unnecessary and inexpedient, and in its exercise dangerous to the power, safety, and independence of the several states, and *repugnant to the first principles of a confederate government*."

Accordingly, the legislature of Massachusetts proposed the amendment to the federal constitution, which was adopted, and is known as the eleventh article of the amendments. Besides John Hancock and James Sullivan, other leading men took an active part in favor of states rights and the amendment to the constitution. Among them should be mentioned Samuel Adams, Dr. Jarvis, and Nathan Dane. Samuel Adams was always a consistent advocate or defender of state rights, just as he had been of colony rights. He had taken the leading part, unless Otis or Hancock were entitled to that honor, in obtaining the independence of Massachusetts, and he wished to preserve that independence under the new confederation formed by the new federal constitution.

A Parallel between Colony Rights and State Rights.

These two classes of rights, existing at different periods, are equivalents of each other. Colony rights, under the British government, bore the same relation to charters conferred by the king, which state rights under the federal government bear to the federal constitution. The colonists of Massachusetts, from 1620 to 1776, contended earnestly for their colony rights. The citizens of Massachusetts, from 1776 to the present time, have contended earnestly for state rights. The reasons in each case were substantially the same. These reasons lie in the great fact that the liberties of each individual depended on maintaining colony rights in the one case, and state rights in the other. Accordingly, the friends of liberty have been the friends, and the enemies of liberty have been the enemies, of colony rights and of state rights.

It should, however, be borne in mind that colony rights were "granted" rights—that is, rights granted by the king, in the specific charter, or by former kings as in *Magna Charta* and embodied in the British constitution. But state rights are *reserved* rights—that is, rights reserved by the states, when they granted several powers to the federal government. The colonies, therefore, had to take upon themselves the burden of showing or proving what rights were granted to them in the charter under which they severally acted, or by the British constitution. If the British government encroached upon the granted rights, it was guilty of tyranny which ought to be resisted. But the states are obliged to take upon themselves no such burden, for it rests upon the federal government to prove what powers are granted to it, and if it goes beyond the granted powers and encroaches upon the reserved powers, it is guilty of tyranny which ought to be resisted.

It is a little remarkable that the advocates of colony rights in Massachusetts regarded the charter as a solemn compact between the king and the colony, binding both parties, while the British government and the advocates of the royal prerogative regarded it like the charter of a petty corporation in England, repealable at pleasure, or to be disregarded when the necessities or the convenience of the crown should require it to be disregarded. In like manner the advocates of state rights in Massachusetts have regarded the federal constitution as a solemn compact between the states, binding the parties, namely, the states, and limiting the federal government to *the use only of delegated powers;* while the opposers of state rights attribute to the federal government such large undefined powers under the federal constitution as to deprive the states of their sovereignty, and reduce them very much to the condition of petty corporations. Thus the federal government, according to this last view of it, is the political equivalent, in the present system, of the British government in the colonial system, but with larger powers and a more despotic use of them.

The Purchase of Louisiana.

The purchase of Louisiana took place in 1803, its admission into the federal union in 1812. The statesmen and people of Massachusetts justly regarded this measure, by which the relative importance of the state of Massachusetts would be abridged, as not sanctioned by the constitution, and therefore exonerating the state from its *obligation to remain in the federal union thus violated and broken.*

So thoroughly convinced was Alexander Hamilton that there was a plan in progress for the separation of the union, that on June 11, 1804, on the Saturday previous to his death, he said to Col. John Trumbull, "with a look of deep meaning," "You are going to Boston. You will see the principal men there. Tell them from *me*, as *my* request, for God's sake to cease their conversation and threatenings about the separation of the union. It must hang together as long as it can be made to." Hamilton's *History of the Republic*, vol. vii. p. 822.

The Embargo.

The embargo was laid by congress on the 22d of December, 1807. In

1808, there were strong demonstrations of opposition to it. We have the authority of John Quincy Adams for saying that "the people were constantly instigated to forcible resistance against it, and juries often acquitted the violators of it upon the ground that it was unconstitutional, assumed in the face of a solemn decision of the district court of the United States." A separation of the union was stimulated in the public prints, and a convention of delegates from the New-England states to meet in New-Haven, was intended and proposed.

Mr. John Quincy Adams, in his letter to Mr. Giles, urged that "a continuance of the embargo much longer would certainly be met by forcible resistance, supported by the legislature [of Massachusetts], and probably by the judiciary of the state." . . . "That the object of the leaders had been, for several years, the *dissolution of the union*, and the establishment of a separate confederation, he knew from unequivocal evidence, although not provable in a court of law." Niles's *Register*, vol. xxxv. p. 138. In consequence of this opposition to it the embargo was repealed, March 1, 1809, just before the retirement of Mr. Jefferson from the presidential office.

The War of 1812.

On the 18th day of June, 1812, war was declared by the United States against Great Britain. When, soon after, a requisition was made upon Massachusetts for forty-one companies of artillery and infantry, Governor Caleb Strong refused compliance with the order issued by General Dearborn, notwithstanding the secretary of war wrote to him urging his compliance. In a message to the legislature, in allusion to this refusal to furnish troops to the general government, he said, "I was fully disposed to comply with the requirements of the constitution of the United States, and the laws made in pursuance thereof, and sincerely regret that a request should be made by an officer of the national government with which I could not constitutionally comply. But it appeared to me that the requisition was of this character, and I was under the *same obligation to maintain the rights of the states*, as to support the constitution of the United States." The course pursued by the governor was in accordance with the declared opinion of the judges of the supreme court on the constitutionality of the requisition, and was approved by the legislature and the people of Massachusetts. (See *Massachusetts Reports*, vol. viii. p. 548.)

The Hartford Convention.

In consequence of applications, from many of the towns, the legislature of Massachusetts appointed delegates to a convention in Hartford, held December 15, 1814. This convention, having its origin in Massachusetts, was attended by delegates from that state, Connecticut, Rhode Island, New-Hampshire, and Vermont, who were twenty-six in number. For intelligence and moral worth, for patriotism and dignified deportment, they would compare favorably with any body of men that ever assembled in this country.

After a session of three weeks they made a report, which was approved by the legislature of Massachusetts by a strong vote. The committee of the legislature, in their report on the doings of the convention, say: "The committee entertain a high sense of the wisdom and ability with which this convention have discharged their arduous trust; and while they maintain the principle of state sovereignty, and of the duties which citizens owe to their respective state governments, they give the most satisfactory proofs of attachment to the constitution of the United States and to the national union." This report was adopted by the house, by a vote of one hundred and fifty-nine to forty-eight. "The governor was empowered to appoint three commissioners to proceed immediately to the seat of the national government, requesting the consent of the federal congress to the measures recommended by the convention." The commissioners thus appointed were Thomas H. Perkins, Harrison Gray Otis, and William Sullivan.

Of the seven amendments to the constitution proposed by the convention, and approved by the legislature of Massachusetts, all but one, or possibly two, are intended to limit the power of the federal government, and thus to increase the power of the several states. See Dwight's *History of the Hartford Convention.*

Opinions of the Nature of the Federal Union.

It should be borne in mind that Governor Strong was one of the delegates to the convention in Philadelphia, which framed the constitution, and could hardly have failed to understand what were the provisions of that instrument. It is believed that every member of the Hartford convention was born before the declaration of independence, that several were personally active in procuring the adoption of the federal constitution, and that all were devotedly attached to the union, created by that compact.

A careful study of the history of Massachusetts for above thirty years from the adoption of the federal constitution will show that her leading men, generally, were as devotedly attached to the rights reserved to the states as they were to the powers delegated to the federal government. They regarded the state as competent to take care of its *internal* institutions, and they regarded any encroachment upon *the right of the state to manage its internal concerns as a usurpation.* They had asserted that right from the first settlement of the commonwealth, under the constitution of 1643, under the old confederation, and under the new confederation, formed by the present federal constitution.

"The *allegiance* they owe to this commonwealth as a sovereign, independent state." *Answer of the house of representatives to the governor, October,* 1810.

"This commonwealth forms an important member of the national *confederacy.*"—*Answer of the house to the governor*, 1810.

"If an extensive confederate republic is to be maintained, and we fervently pray that it may, it can only be by a free communication of the grievances felt, and the evils apprehended by any of the members, and by prompt and liberal remedies." *Remonstrance by the legislature of Massachusetts to the hon. senate and house of representatives in congress assembled,* June 14, 1813.

February, 1814, the legislature passed an act by which no prisoners of war were allowed to be placed in the jails of Massachusetts except by *judicial* authority, and all prisoners of war were required to be discharged from said jails in thirty days, unless sooner discharged by the authority of the United States.

On the right inherent in the individual of discussing public measures, and the duty of the state to protect each individual thus doing, the senate in answer to the governor, 1814, made the following declaration: "And may it please your excellency, in the apprehension of this senate, this duty is as incumbent and imperious in a state of war as in a state of peace; union among the people is essential to the success of the government, being necessarily subordinate to the *fundamental doctrine* that in every state of things, in a free country, the right of discussing public measures is essential to the liberties of the people."

Extracts from the State Constitution.

"The people of this commonwealth have the sole and exclusive right of governing themselves as a free, sovereign and independent state; and do, and forever hereafter shall exercise and enjoy every power, jurisdiction and right which is not or may not hereafter be by them expressly delegated to the United States of America in congress assembled."

Oath of office. "I, A. B., solemnly swear that I will bear true and faithful allegiance to the commonwealth of Massachusetts, and will support the constitution thereof; and that I will faithfully and impartially perform all the duties incumbent on me according to the best of my abilities and understanding agreeably to the constitution and laws of this commonwealth. So help me God."

What are state rights? What is a state? 1. "A state, in the most enlarged sense, means the people composing a particular nation or community. In this sense, the state means the whole people united in one body politic, and the state and the people of a state are equivalent expressions." Judge Wilson, in his law lectures, says: "In free states, the people form an artificial person or body politic, the highest that can be known." Each of the United States thus existing became sovereign at the revolution, and by the treaty of peace with Great Britain. In this sense the state of Massachusetts, that is the people of Massachusetts, adopted her own constitution, and the federal constitution. 2. A state means the legislature which means the people, as when we say the state of Massachusetts passed the Maine liquor law. 3. A state means the territory included in physical boundaries. State rights of Massachusetts under the federal constitution, then, are all the rights and powers of a sovereign, free and independent republic or nation, excepting those which she has distinctly and clearly delegated to the federal government.

Dr. Noah Webster, when a citizen of Massachusetts, in his oration before the Washington Benevolent Society, has the following passage: "How can the states, *the parties to the federal compact*, understanding its conditions, and bound in duty to guard their rights, answer to the people and posterity for suffering such a palpable act of arbitrary power [the embargo] to pass into a precedent?" This statement is in harmony with his definition of the word "compact" in his large dictionary.

Timothy Dwight, a native of Massachusetts, and representative in the general court and afterwards president of Yale College, in writing from Greenfield Hill, 1793, says: "A war with Great Britain, we in New-England will not enter into. Sooner would ninety-nine in a hundred of our inhabitants separate from the union than plunge themselves into such an abyss of misery."

"*Would a division of the union be beneficial?*" was one of the mooted questions in Yale College under President Dwight. On this question, Dr. Dwight in one of his decisions says: "By fostering jealousies, creating local feeling in opposition to each other, and indulging violent denunciations, the union of the states may, perhaps, be dissolved; but it will not be suddenly effected. It will be the result of deliberation. Our New-Englanders are deliberate in determining, but when they once begin to act they are resolute. If they ever divide the union, it will be because they are forced to do it; and they will not leave their work unfinished." He was opposed to disunion, but does not question the right.

The several Spheres of Local Law.

I. The local law of the homestead, founded on the relations of parent and child, and sanctioned by the word of God. It has been through many generations the law of kindness on the lips and in the life of the parents, calling into exercise all the sweet charities of the family circle.

II. The local law of the school district.

III. The local law of the church. According to which in its early history it established its own covenant, its own confession of faith, its own discipline, its own rules of holy living.

IV. The laws of the town as distinguished from the laws of the colony or state.

V. The laws of the colony as distinguished from the laws of Great Britain.

VI. The laws of the state as distinguished from those of the United States.

What a noble model in these several circles of power, Massachusetts has furnished to the world! The men of Massachusetts in all the generations would permit no encroachments on these laws by others outside of themselves. What Goldsmith said in complimentary terms of his countrymen, can be said of the men of Massachusetts of past generations:—

> Pride in their port, defiance in their eye,
> I see the lords of human kind pass by;
> Fierce in their native hardiness of soul,
> True to imagined right, above control.

The love of local law has been in vigorous exercise ever since the settlement of the two colonies, during the sixty-three years of the continuance of the first charter of Massachusetts; in the reigns of James I., Charles I., Oliver Cromwell, Charles II., and James II. It showed increasing power under the provincial charter, in the reigns of William and Mary, Queen Anne, George I., George II., and George III., when it produced the American revolution. The same love of local law was shown by Massachusetts, as a member of the New-England confederacy formed in 1643, as a member of the old confederation formed in the revolutionary war, and as a member of the new or present confederation formed in 1788. It has grown with the growth, and strengthened with the strength of the colony and state. Massachusetts would bear no foreign interference with her local laws.

That they were all judicious and proper in aim and spirit, the most dutiful and affectionate of her sons would not pretend. Society is made up of individuals, and therefore is liable to the same errors to which individuals are subject.

In this inherited love of local law, continued through so many generations, may be seen the personal identity of Massachusetts, through the long period of her existence, as distinctly as the personal identity of an individual who has lived through a long life. In this respect we may say of her, *semper eadem*.

In her whole history, wherever the minions of power went on her soil, they found that the spirit of independence was the *genius loci*. That spirit is symbolized in the device and motto on her armorial bearings. The love of local law is but another expression for the love of liberty.

On those bearings, the unsheathed sword uplifted in the strong hand, is a threat to tyrants who interfere with her local laws. The quiet of peace is grateful to her heart, but it must be a quiet under liberty.

Ense petit placidam, sub libertate quietem.

PEDIGREE OF BALDWIN.

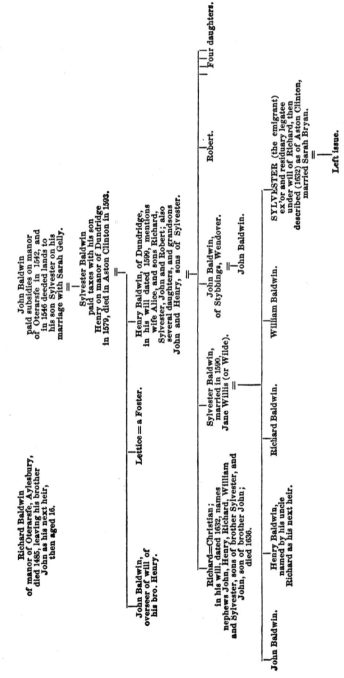

Richard Baldwin
of manor of Oterarsfe, Aylesbury, died 1485, leaving his brother John as his next heir, then aged 16.

John Baldwin
paid subsidies on manor of Oterarsfe in 1542, and in 1546 deeded lands to his son Sylvester on his marriage with Sarah Gelly.
=

Sylvester Baldwin
paid taxes with his son Henry on manor of Dundridge in 1579, died in Aston Clinton in 1593.
=

- **John Baldwin,** overseer of will of his bro. Henry.
- **Lettice = a Foster.**
- **Henry Baldwin, of Dundridge,** in his will dated 1599, mentions wife Alice, and sons Richard, Sylvester, John and Robert; also several daughters, and grandsons John and Henry, sons of Sylvester.
=
  - **Richard = Christian;** in his will, dated 1632, names nephews John, Henry, Richard, William and Sylvester, sons of brother Sylvester, and John, son of brother John; died 1636.
  - **Sylvester Baldwin,** married in 1590, Jane Willis (or Wilde).
  =
    - **John Baldwin.**
    - **Henry Baldwin,** named by his uncle Richard as his next heir.
    - **Richard Baldwin.**
    - **William Baldwin.**
    - **SYLVESTER** (the emigrant) ex'or and residuary legatee under will of Richard, then described (1632) as of Aston Clinton, married Sarah Bryan.
    =
      - **Left issue.**
  - **John Baldwin,** of Stybbings, Wendover.
  =
    - **John Baldwin.**
  - **Robert.**
  - **Four daughters.**

NOTES ON THE ANCESTRY OF SYLVESTER BALDWIN.

Communicated by CHARLES C. BALDWIN, A.M., of Cleveland, Ohio.

SYLVESTER BALDWIN, of Aston Clinton, co. Bucks, from whom most of the Baldwins whose ancestors are found upon the early records of Connecticut claim descent or kinship, took passage with his family for New-England on the ship "Martin," in 1638. He died at sea, and devised by his nuncupative will certain estates in England to his wife Sarah. One of these estates she subsequently conveyed by deed to Edward Baldwin, of Guilford, co. Surrey, Eng., describing it as having been "indentured" to Richard Baldwin, of St. Leonard's, in the parish of Aston Clinton, for 1000 years, and by the said Richard bequeathed to Sylvester, and by him to her. An examination of the will of the Richard Baldwin referred to in this deed, and other investigations made by the writer in England, establishes, by a chain of testimony which seems to be entirely conclusive, the pedigree on the opposite page.

The will of Richard (uncle of Sylvester, the emigrant) has never appeared in print, and as it is the key to the foregoing pedigree, and may have an independent interest to your readers from the numerous references to collateral branches of the family, it is appended in full. It is hoped that the publication of this will, with the accompanying annotations of the writer, may stimulate others of the name to make further investigations.

WILL OF RICHARD BALDWIN OF ST. LEONARDS, CO. BUCKS.

Extracted from the principal Registry of Her Majesty's Court of Probate: — In the Prerogative Court of Canterbury.

In the name of God Amen. The eighteenth daie of February in the eight yeare of the raigne of our Soveraigne Lord Charles by the Grace of God of England Scotland France & Ireland Kinge, Defender of the Faith &c.— anno dni 1632 I Richard Baldwin of Dun-Dridge in the Parishe of Aston Clinton in the Countie of Bucks Yeoman beinge sicke in bodie but of good & perfect remembrance prayse God therefore doe make and declare this my last Will and Testament in manner as followeth. First I comitt my soule unto allmightie God my Maker and Redeemer beleeveinge the forgiveness of all my sinies through the death and passion of Jesus Christe my lord, my onely, and alone Saviour my bodie I comitt to the earth to be buried in decent and christian sort by my Executor touchinge my temporall estate I give and bequeath unto Mr Hall now the minister of S^t. Leonards V^li. to be paide within three moneths after my decease—Itm, I give and bequeath unto Henry Baldwin sonne of my brother Silvester and my next heire all that close of free land called Brayes Bushe with appurtenance lyinge in the Parishes of greate Chesham and Wendover to him and to his heires for ever yeilding and payinge unto the poore people of S^t. Leonards XX^li a yeare every yeare for the tearme of one hundred yeares to be distributed on S^t. Thomas daie by the minister of S^t. Leonards and my heires. Itm I give and bequeath unto the saide Henry Baldwin XX^li of money to be paide unto him within six moneths after my decease uppon condition that he the saide Henry shall suffer all those men wch have bought wood and timber of me quietly and peaceably to fell cut downe and carry away the same and the mony that is behinde to be paide unto my Executor for the discharge of my legacies in this will given. Itm I give and bequeath unto the saide Henry Baldwin one coffer with evidences concerninge this Mannor of Dundridge and also the evidences concerninge the chappell lande and also one mault mill and one coslet and furniture and furniture for one horse for service of the musters, and the tables and frames in the hall with the formes cubbord wainscott, benches and the armor in the said hall. Itm, I give unto the saide Henry the best bedsteede in the new Chamber. Itm I give will and bequeath unto Christian my well beloved wife all the Goods and householde stuffe that is or formerly hath used to be in my bed chamber except the best peice of plate. Itm I give and bequeath unto Christian my wife aforesaide halfe all my bedsteeds not bequeathed and halfe all my bed cloaths halfe all my linnen cloaths halfe all my pewter and brasse and halfe all the moveable goods in the dwellinge house whatsoever unbequeathed to be equally devided betweene the said Christian and my Executor. Itm I give and bequeath unto the saide Christian twoe of my best bease xx sheepe three hoggs, all my poultry one quarter of wheate one quarter of malt and all my wearinge apparell to be delivered unto her within tenn daies next after my decease further more my will and minde is that the saide Christian my wife xx^{lie} pounds a yeare paide unto her yearely every yeare duringe her naturall life by my next heire for & in consideration of her estate and interest in my Mannor of Dundridge and also that she shall have sufficient howse room and firewood. Itm I give and bequeath unto John Baldwin my Brother xx^{li}. and to John Baldwin his sonne xx^{li} all to be paide within one yeare after my decease and the rest of my mony in theire hande's shall be paide to my Executor. Itm I give & bequeath unto Mary Salter my sister x^{li}. Itm I give & bequeath unto John Salter and unto David Salter and unto Mary Salter and unto Sarah Salter all beinge the children of Mary Salter my Sister aforesaide to every one of them x^{li} all which severall legacies of x^{li} a peece bequeathed unto my Sister Mary and her children I will shall be paide unto them within twoe yeares next after my decease. Itm I give and bequeathe unto Henry Bonus xx^{li} and unto James Bonus x^{li} and unto Christian Bonus xxx^{li} all wch legacies bequeathed unto my Sister Bonusses Children I will shall be paide unto them within one yeare after my decease. Itm I give and bequeath unto Mary Bonus daughter of my Sister Jane Bonus one hundred pounds to be paide unto her within one yeare after my decease in full payment of her grand mothers gifte as also of her mothers goods. Itm I give and bequeath unto Jane Bonus Daughter of my Sister Jane Fiftie pounds to be paide unto her within twoe yeares after my decease in full payment of her grandmothers gifte and also of her mothers goods. Itm I give and bequeath unto Anne Bryant Daughter of Robert Baldwin my Brother and unto Richard Bryant her sonne all that tenement with the appurtenances beinge freeholde lying and beinge in Wendover towne to the saide Anne and her sonne Richard and their heires for ever and fortie eight pounds vj^{l} eight pence in mony to be paide within three moneths after my decease. Itm I give and bequeath unto Henry Stonhill sonne of Annie Stonhill my Sister xxx^{li} to be paide unto him when he shall come to the age of xxj^{l} yeares and twentie acres of free land more or lesse in the parishe of Drayton Bechampe to him the saide Henry and his heires for ever. Itm I give and bequeath to Anne Stonhill daughter of Anne Stonhill my Sister x^{li} to be paide within twoe years after my decease. Itm I give and bequeath unto Richard Baldwin sonne of Silvester Baldwin my Brother x^{li} to be paide within one yeare after my decease. Itm I give and bequeath unto Willyam Baldwin sonne of my brother Silvester x^{li} to be paide within one yeare after my decease. Itm I give and bequeath unto Richard Baldwin Sonne of Silvester Baldwin of Aston Clinton x^{li} to be paide within one yeare after my decease. Itm I give and bequeath every one of my Brothers and Sisters Chilldren that shall be liveing at my decease I saie unto every one of them fortie shillings to be paide unto every one of them within one yeare after my decease. Itm I give and bequeath unto Joane Chaffe my wifes sister fortie shillings to be paide within one yeare after my decease. Itm I give and bequeath unto Willyam Darley one whole yeares rent of that messuage wherein he now dwelleth that is to saie the next yeare after my decease he shall paie no rent. Itm I give & bequeath unto Joyce Bernard widowe xx^s and to Silvester Tomkins of St. Leonards xx^s and to John Tompkins of the same parish xx^s. and unto George Baldwin of the same parishe xx^s and unto Richard Gravener of Buckland xx^s and unto widowe Wilkins of the same parishe xx^s and widowe Gourney of the same parishe xx^s and Edward Springall of the same parishe xx^s and to Richard Arnoll of the Parishe of Chesham xx^s and to his sister Mary Garratt xx^s and to Jonas Nuton of Cholesbury xx^s and to widowe Childe of Harridge xx^s and to Robert Wilkins of Buckland xx^s and to Shem Ginger of St. Leonards xx^s. Itm I give and bequeath unto the poore people of Aston Clinton xx^s and to the poore people of St. Leonards xx^s and to the poore people of Cholesbury xx^s all wch bequests by me bequeathed of xx^s a peece I will shall be paide within three months after my decease. Itm I give and bequeath unto every one of my Servants that shall be in my service at the time of my death x^s to be paide within one moneth after my decease. Itm I give and bequeath unto widowe Cocke of St. Leonards xx^s provided alwaies and my will and minde is that all those legacies shall be paide in good and lawfull money of England at the severall times appointed by my Executor and if any of those Children shall be under age then I will that theire legacies shall be paide unto the fathers of the said children at the time appointed theire fathers giving theire owne bonds unto my Executor for the true payment thereof to theire saide children at theire severall ages of xx^6 yeares by the shewinge of the saide bonds together with sufficient letters of attorney made by my saide Executor unto the saide children for the saveinge of the said bonds and to them delivered shall be a sufficient discharge in lawe for my said Executor against Every of the saide children for his or theire legacie or legacies aforesaide respectively. Itm All the rest and residue of all my goods and cattell and chattels not before bequeathed my debts and legacies being paide my funerall orderly performed and discharged and this my will well and truly fullfilled I give unto Silvester Baldwin of Aston Clinton sonne of Silvester Baldwin my Brother whome I make and ordaine my whole and sole Executor of this my last will and testament. In Witness whereof I the saide Richard Baldwin have hereunto put my hande and seale the daie and yeare first above written — — - Sealed subscribed published and declared in the the presence of Willyam Grange — — Henry Stonhill. (Signed)

RICHARD BALDWIN.

Richard Baldwin, whose will is above printed, was buried in the parish of Aston Clinton, co. Bucks, Oct. 14, 1636; proof of the will was made Nov. 29, 1636, and the execution thereof committed to Silvester Baldwin the executor named therein. This will is referred to in several early records in this country, and by Mr. Savage under the name of Silvester Baldwin, whom he styles son of Richard. The mistake arose, no doubt, from an erroneous transcript of a dim record of conveyance in vol. i. p. 3 of records of New Haven county court. The record of the will itself was in Oxford, England, until about two years since; with the other records it was then removed to Doctor's Commons, London. The line of Silvester, the emigrant, plainly appears. He was son of Silvester, deceased, and nephew, and not son, of Richard, of Dundridge. Silvester, the emigrant, married Sarah Bryan, probably sister or other near relative of Alexander Bryan,* the first, of Milford, whose wife Ann is mentioned in the will. Silvester and Sarah Baldwin had children baptized in Aston Clinton as follows: Sarah, April 22, 1621; Richard, Aug. 25, 1622; Mary, Feb. 28, 1623; Mary again, Feb. 19, 1625; Martha, April 20, 1628; Samuel, Jan. 1, 1632, buried next 4th of June; Elizabeth, Jan. 25, 1633, buried Jan. 31, 1633. They also had children John and Ruth, no doubt younger; all the living children seem to have come hither and settled in Milford, Conn. John was afterward of Stonington, and was probably born in 1634 or 1635.

A few words may be said in reference to other mistakes in Savage's account of the Baldwins. He records John of Milford 1639, calling him son of Sylvester, and says he had a son John who died unmarried about 1677, on a voyage. Later on he says John of Milford, eldest son of John the first, married 1663, Hannah Bruen. Here is of course a contradiction and various errors. We will begin first by giving the facts. It is clear that John[1] of Milford was not the son of Sylvester,[1] but that Sylvester's son was John[2] Baldwin, of Stonington, 1671, and New-London, 1672, who came from Milford, a widower, with a son John, and who married in New-London, July 24, 1672, Rebecca Cheeseborough, widow, and had by her five children, the only son being Sylvester,[3] born March 4, 1677. This is proved by the following extract from the New-Haven county court records, vol. ii. p. 89:

"At a court of Probate's held in New-Haven Octob^{r}. ye 10th. day 1702

	Present Majo^{r} Mosses Mansfield	
Silvester Baldwin of Stonington in ye county of New-London appearing & making application to this court for power of	Esquire Judge William Maltbie Jeremiah Osborne John Alling	Esq^{rs}. Jus^{c} Quorum

administracōn upon a certaine Legacy bequeathed to his Brother John Baldwin in and by the Last Will and Testament of M^{rs}. Sarah Astwood which s^{d} John Baldwin by report of Mr Plumb of Milford went to England about twenty five yeares since, and is supposed to be deceased. Upon wch ye court allows administracon of s^{d} Legacy to the said Silvest^{r}. Baldwin he having Given sufficient Bond for his faithfull administration of the same according to Law and refund the Estate if any other heir appeare."

Here Sylvester,[3] grand-son of Mrs. Sarah Astwood (she was the widow of Sylvester, Sr., and married Capt. John Astwood), is the representative of his brother John.[3] They must both be the children of John,[2] because Richard had no son Sylvester, and that identifies the New-London man, who did have a son of that name, as the son of Sylvester,[1] Sr.

Richard[2] Baldwin, the other son of Sylvester,[1] Sr., styled by Mrs. Astwood, in New-Haven Prob. Rec., vol. i. p. 317, her eldest son, Aug. 20, 1657, is said by Savage to have had a son John, and this child is also said

* Alexander Bryan was son of Thomas Bryan, of Aylesbury, co. Bucks, England, and was baptized there Sept. 29, 1602. Was not Henry Stonehill, who was one of the first settlers at Milford, and who returned in 1646 to London, the nephew of testator?

by him to have gone to England "25 years before 1702," evidently referring to the above administration record. This is undoubtedly wrong, because there is no record of any such child of Richard. Richard was town clerk of Milford, but there is no John recorded as his son, and though he left no will, the property was recorded when divided, and no John had any share thereof. We must therefore consider it proved that Savage was in error, and that Richard Baldwin had no son John.* It is evident that having a note of the administration record of the grandson John, Savage tried to place him in the record, and fastened him both on Richard, the true son of Sylvester, and the supposed son, John of Milford; when in reality he belonged to the true son, John of Stonington and New-London.

Sylvester Baldwin, Sr., died at sea. His widow married Capt. John Astwood, of Milford, and died in November, 1669. Her will mentions several of Richard's descendants (he had died July 23, 1665), also her son John and grandson John Baldwin, but not a name occurs that can refer to the children of John Baldwin, of Milford. This confirms our view that the son John was the New-London man, if any proof were needed. John[2] of New-London, whom we accept as Sylvester's son, was probably the man mentioned in a law-suit as living in Milford in 1658, at which time his wife had lately died, leaving him with a young child (*New-Haven Records*, Hoadley's ed. vol. ii. p. 264). This child was doubtless the John who went to England. The name of this first wife is not known; it has been thought that she was his step-sister, a daughter of Capt. Astwood, because that on the Milford records Baldwin is called Astwood's "son-in-law." It is more likely that the term was used by a common mistake for "step-son," in which relation Baldwin certainly stood to Astwood.

Although the two sons of Sylvester are the only persons of the name yet connected with the English stock, there are others probably related to it. John Baldwin, of Guildford, 1653, and Norwich, ancestor of a line recorded by Miss Caulkins (*Hist. Norwich*, p. 161–3), to which belonged Judge Simeon Baldwin and his son Gov. Roger S. Baldwin, *may* have been a relative of Sylvester. Hon. John D. Baldwin, of Worcester, a descendant of Sylvester through John, of Stonington, says that in a family bible which he has seen, though now destroyed, it was stated that John of Stonington and John of Norwich were cousins. In the Norwich family it was a tradition that their ancestor came over with relatives, not his parents.

There were also at Milford, Nathaniel, 1639, and Timothy, 1639, who were brothers; Joseph, 1639,† and John, 1639, all contemporary with Sylvester's son, and living in the same town with his family. It is hardly possible to doubt that they came from the same stock, and that a further search among the brothers and cousins of Sylvester in England, would supply the needed link.

The John who came with Sylvester may have been John of Milford, or even John of Norwich; it could not be his son John, whatever his age at the time, because as a witness he would have been unable to take any

* Savage also gives him a daughter Mary, baptized 1643. This is an error; she was the daughter of Timothy.

† I judge that Joseph was also a brother of Nathaniel and Timothy. In the Milford records it appears that in 1649, Joseph had four acres of land in New Meadow Plain, bounded with Timothy Baldwin west. It seems he "laid down this land again, and April 24, 1654, he hath liberty granted him for to exchange and lay down one piece of land, and take up another for it in the New Meadow Plain (next his brother's land), that he formerly laid down to the town again." This record is rather obscure, but if the punctuation here made, be right, the case would be clear and the relationship fairly established.

interest under the will. As we are correcting Savage's errors, we may state that Hon. John D. Baldwin, of Worcester, writes that after a careful search of the records at Milford, Conn., and Newark, N. J., he is satisfied that John, Sr., of Milford, married for his second wife, Marie, *sister* of Obadiah Bruen, and *never went to Newark;* that his son John married Hannah, *niece, not sister* of his step-mother, and that he and John, son of Nathaniel Baldwin, were the two settlers at Newark.

English Ancestry of Sylvester Baldwin.

From Domesday Book it appears that the name of Baldwin, in the vicinity of Dundridge, dates before the conquest. Baldwin, son of Herluin, had several vassals in the northern part of Bucks, as well as in Gloucestershire, all of whom he lost as vassals under the conqueror. In "Ellesberie" Hundred (in which is Dundridge), Baldwin, a vassal of Archbishop Stigand's, held under Edward the Confessor, the manor of Haddenam, now Hampden. In "Lamva" Hundred under the conqueror, Baldwin held to farm of William, son of Ansculf, land which he had held as fully his own in King Edward's time, and the same was true of a manor towards the north of Bucks. The estate of John Hampden was in "Ellesberie" Hundred, in fact quite near Dundridge. Nugent's Memorials and Macaulay's Review thereof, state on the authority of documents in his house that part of his estates were bestowed by Edward the Confessor on his ancestor Baldwin de Hampden, whom Macaulay presumes to have been one of the Norman favorites of the last Saxon king. Whether the Baldwins who afterward abounded in this vicinity were also descended from him is not known.

John Baldwin, Sr., and John, Jr., were two out of three founders of the fraternity or brotherhood of the town of Aylesbury. John Baldwin appears in Aylesbury in 1429, and also appears in 1433, in the return of gentry of Bucks. The first ancestor of Richard Baldwin, who can be at present identified, however, is named in an inquisition taken in 1486, in Beaconfield, a transcript of which lies before me. The witnesses state that Richard Baldwin died Sept. 21, 1485, seized of the manor of Otterarsfee, in soccage of the king, by the service of finding litter for the king's bed, viz. "in summer grass or herbs & two gray geese & in winter straw & three eels thrice in the year if the king should come thrice in the year to Aylesbury. So that 6 wild geese or 9 eels may be in the year if he should come thither thrice." Richard also had a messuage called "the Crown" in Aylesbury, and also another held of Thomas, Lord Ormond. It was further certified that the next heir of Richard was John his brother, then aged 16 or more. This John, described as "frater & hæres Ricardi Baldwin," paid a relief to the king upon this manor in 1492, as appears by the latin record thereof in *Madox Bar. Angl.* 247, and is the same John named in a note to the first volume of Hume's *History of England*, where he is erroneously assigned to the time of King Henry II. The latin record printed in Madox further recites that upon examination of the rolls "compertum est in memorandis de anno xviii Domini E nuper Regis Angliæ primi, quod Willielmus, filius Willielmi hæres Ricardi de Aylesbury," paid a similar fine. When the estate passed from the de Aylesburys to the Baldwins, or whether the families are identical, we are unable to determine. It was originally granted by Henry II. to "Roger the Kings Minstrel" upon the same singular tenure as is recited in a "confirmation" of the manor to Richard son of Robert de Aylesbury, in I. Richard II. (1377) *Cal. Rot. Pat.* 199. The manor had then been in the continuous possession of the Aylesbury family since the original grant, but we are unable to trace its later history until John Baldwin, brother and heir of Richard, becomes its recognized owner.

In 1542, subsidies were paid upon this manor by John Baldwin, supposed to be the same, but more probably a son of the former John; and in 1546 the last John of this manor deeded to his son Sylvester, on the occasion of his marriage with Sarah Gelley,* some fields in Aston Clinton he had purchased of one George Hale.

Sir John Baldwin, knight and chief justice of the common pleas, from 1536 to 1546, was of the Bucks family and of this vicinity. In 1540, he had a grant of the house and site of Gray Friars, in Aylesbury, at which time there was a John the younger there,—no doubt the father of Sylvester. Sir John was son of William by Agnes, third daughter of Wm. Dormer, Esq., of West Wycombe, Bucks. He had one son, William, who died before him childless, and himself died in 1546, leaving daughters and grandchildren. On the dissolution of the monasteries, he received numerous gifts of lands from the king, Henry VIII. He also, in 1544, received from the king in fee simple the "manor of Dunriche alias During" (being the Dun Dridge of the foregoing will), with the woods or coppices called Braies (also mentioned in the foregoing will) and other lands belonging to the same manor in Aston Clinton, Chesham and Wendover. This manor came to the crown on the attainder of Margaret Countess of Salisbury, and Lipscomb, in his history of Bucks, says it afterward belonged to Silvester Baldwin, descended to others of the name until 1748, when it was conveyed out of the family. This Silvester seems to have been the one who married Sarah Gelly. He paid taxes, with his son Henry, on Dundridge in 1579, and was buried in Aston Clinton, July 3, 1593. His son Henry succeeded him at Dundridge, and he had other children living in 1599; at least John and Lettice, who m. a Foster. The will of Henry, of Dundridge, is dated Jan. 2, 1599. After remembering the poor of Aston Clinton, Chalesbury, Wendover and Great Winchenden, and sundry persons, he devises to his son John four "crofts or closes of ground" in Wendover and £10. To his son Robert all his messuages, &c., in Flaunden and Hempstead or elsewhere in Hertfordshire, and £40. To daughter Agnes, £100, to be paid her on the day of her marriage or within two years after death of testator. To James Bonus (son-in-law, having married daughter Jane), £40. To son Richard, personals in the "Hall" and others, including "the great Brewery Cawderne;" mentions his wife Allice; to son Silvester the advances made him and £10. To John and Henry, sons of Silvester, five and eight pence each. Same to Henry Bonus, son of James. After remembering other persons, to his "son-in-law Richard Salter" (married daughter Mary, Jan. 30, 1598), he mentions the farm property upon Dundridge, but does not devise the soil which apparently went by descent to Richard, who was executor. Alice, the widow of Henry, was buried at Aston Clinton, Nov. 25, 1626. The family of John, of Wendover (near Aston Clinton and Aylesbury), is not easily traced, from the imperfection of records there. In 1660, John, of this parish, was M.P. with Richard Hampden, son of John the patriot.

Sylvester, last mentioned, was married Sept. 30, 1590, at Cholesbury, close by St. Leonard, to Jane Willis or Wilde. His son Harry was buried there Nov. 21, 1594. He was living in 1599, and not in 1632, and then had surviving children, at least Henry, Richard, William and Silvester, the last being the emigrant, in 1632 described of Aston Clinton.

* What relation to John Gelley, cousin to Sir John Baldwin, and remembered in his will?

The writer, in 1870, visited many of the localities before mentioned. Aston Clinton is a quiet little place, about 4 miles from Aylesbury. Nearly as much further is St. Leonard's, now a parish, though not so in 1636. Before the dissolution of the Abbeys it seems to have been supplied from Missenden Abbey (a few miles distant), and had a "chapel." The civil war left only walls, which were rebuilt upon. It is quite a small church, in the old English country style, with a pleasant rectory in the same enclosure, situated along the edge of the Chiltern Hills. Directly opposite is the "chapel Farm," fine and rolling, with no relic of antiquity. There are no Baldwins near, but in the rear of the farm are Baldwin's Woods. The chapel, after the dissolution of the Abbey, was disregarded until Queen Elizabeth granted its site, in 1586, to Edward Wymarke, "it being then in the tenure of Silvester Baldwin, who also had other lands in the same parish which the queen had granted to Sir Edward Stanley kn't;" but in 1587, she further granted to Will Zipper et al "the decayed Free Chapel of St. Leonard, a tenement also called Chapel Farm and all lands thereunto belonging in Aston Clinton and Wendover in the occupation of Silvester Baldwin." It will be noticed that in the foregoing will is bequeathed one coffer containing evidences concerning the chapel lands. Dundridge is a large farm or manor near by. The dwelling is of brick, large for farm purposes, and bordering a long, narrow common extending from the highway. Forty years since there was an ancient building there, of which I learned only that it was of good size and somewhat Elizabethan in style. Toward the common was a deep ditch freshly kept open and called the moat. There were traces of its former continuation extending in front and on the side next the highway. In the rear the ditch, had there been one, would have been filled by the litter of the barn-yard, and on the remaining side I could detect no trace of it. About four miles from Aylesbury and three from St. Leonard's lies Wendover, which recovered two members of parliament through John Hampden, and was five times represented by him. A little beyond from St. Leonard's lies Great Hampden, the paternal home of Hampden, with its grand old avenue of beeches,—so long, that one imagines the 4000 yeomen who are said to have ridden to London with the patriot, congregated about it. Hampden was buried here, in 1643. In his will he remembers John Baldwin.*

The Baldwin arms† of this vicinity are said to be (Lipscomb's *Hist. of Bucks*) three oak leaves slipped acorned proper. They thus appear in the Middle Temple, in London, as arms of Richard Baldwin (though they appear *unacorned)*, and in 1760, in the chapel of St. Leonard, upon the tomb stone of Samuel Baldwin, "formerly of the parish of Aston Clinton," and are stated elsewhere to be a chevron ermine between the oak leaves. Such differences are not uncommon in old arms. The crest is a squirrel sejant or.

There appears in the foregoing will, Richard, brother of Silvester the emigrant, no doubt the one who had the following named children in Aston Clinton: Rebecca, baptized Jan. 23, 1611; Alice, Aug. 22, 1613; John,

* It has been said that at one time in the spring of 1638, John Hampden and Cromwell (his cousin) were about to emigrate to New-England, but were prevented by order of the king. There is yet no sufficient evidence in regard to either. It seems that in the spring or early summer of 1638 numbers from the immediate vicinity of Hampden did emigrate, among whom Silvester, in ship Martin, died June 21.

† Loammi Baldwin, in a letter dated Oct. 23, 1827, says that when, twenty years before, he was in London, he found at Heralds' College only two arms of Baldwins, "neither of them the one which I had seen represented here as ours." *Query*—What arms was his family, to quote again, "said to have borne?"

Feb. 15, 1614; Henry, "son of Richard and Phillipa his wife," Feb. 8, 1623; a daughter, baptized —— 20, 1627. It has been surmised that he might be Richard, who with daughter Jane is known to have been in Braintree in 1637, and that one of the Johns here, and Henry, of Woburn, might be his children. If so, he probably returned to England himself, as his "wife" Phillipa was buried in Aston Clinton, July 30, 1641. The name of Baldwin occurs with so little frequency in this and adjoining parishes, after 1638, as to lead to the conclusion that there were many of the name who left this vicinity, and, I am satisfied, partly to New-England and partly to London.

THE SEAVER FAMILY.*

Communicated by WILLIAM B. TRASK, of Boston.

ROBERT SEAVER was born about the year 1608. The place of his nativity has not been ascertained, but the conjecture is, that it was in England. On the 24th of March, 1633-4, at the age of about 25, he took the oaths of supremacy and allegiance to pass for New-England, in the ship "Mary and John," of London, Robert Sayres, master. (See "*Founders of New-*

* The annexed is the coat of arms of the Seaver family of Heath Hall, co. Armagh, Ireland. This is the only Seaver coat of arms that we have ever seen or heard of, after a due examination of all the heraldic works that have come under our notice. No connection, however, has been established between the Heath Hall family and the one that settled in Roxbury. The coincidence, surely, is singular, that the Seaver and Heath families of Roxbury have been, in one or more of its branches, related to each other.

It gives us much pleasure to be able to furnish here, an extract of a communication from the Rev. Charles Seaver, incumbent of St. John's church, Belfast, Ireland, to a gentleman of the same name in this city, in reply to inquiries on this subject. The letter is dated, 16 Botanic Avenue, Belfast, Aug. 25, 1871. "The only information I have or can procure," he writes, "is that an ancestor of mine was settled in the Townland of Trea, near Armagh, which he held under the Primate of that See. He married a Miss Symonds, granddaughter of Sir Marmaduke Whitchurch, to whom a grant was made of the abbey lands of Killeary, in the 7th of James I., about 1610. This was about 1650, at which date, they, i.e. the Seavers, were settled at Trea. According to tradition, the ancestor came in Cromwell's army to Ireland; if so, this must have been him; his name was Charles. I searched the Registers at Armagh, but they were not kept before 1750, when the burial of Jonathan Seaver of Trea is noted. What part of England they came from, I have never heard. A branch of the family professing the Roman Catholic religion is settled near Dublin, but they have no better information. The change in their religion was effected, I have heard, by a Roman Catholic nurse. I have searched all the available books on genealogical matters to which I had access, but found nothing further. I enclose the Coat of Arms, Crest and Motto, which we have used at least for a century, but I believe they were then chosen by my grandfather, and that the original Coat of Arms, if any, were lost. I think Burke contains almost all the particulars of which I am informed, and your friend seems to have the books."

The coat of arms herewith presented is substantially the same as the one above alluded to, with the crest and motto, and is thus described in Burke's *Heraldic Illustrations*, accompanied, also, with an engraving:—

Arms.—Argent a chevron gules between three doves pecking sheaves of wheat, proper.

Crest.—A hand and arm, holding a sword erect, encircled by a laurel wreath, all proper.

Motto.—Sume superbiam quæsitam meritis. [Assume the pride acquired by merit.]

England," by Samuel G. Drake, page 70.) He reached Roxbury, Massachusetts, it is probable, previous to June, 1634. On the 10th of December of that year, he married Elizabeth Ballard. In the list of those who had taken the requisite oath, March 26th, to pass for New-England, in the above named vessel, we find the name of William Ballard, who it is presumed was a fellow passenger with Mr. Seaver, and a relative, not unlikely, of Elizabeth. The Roxbury Town Records, in giving the marriage, has the name "Allard;" but the Church Records, in the early list of admissions, has the following explicit paragraph. "Elizabeth Ballard, a maide servant,—she came in the year 1633, and soone after joyned to the church,—she was afterwards married to Robert Sever of this church, where she led a godly conversation." Mr. Seaver was made freeman, April 18, 1637. The name is variously written on the Records, Seaver, Sever, Seavers, Civer. Robert, the ancestor, wrote his name "*Seaver*," as will be seen by the facsimile, here given, of his signature to a petition to the General Court, dated May 31, 1647, signed by sixty-four freemen and soldiers of Roxbury, praying the confirmation by the Court of Hugh Pritchard as captain of a military company in that town, he being chosen by these persons to act as their commanding officer. This request was complied with, as appears by the entry on the Colony Records of the May session of the same year. "Mr. Prichard, being chosen capt. of y^e traine band in Roxberry, is confirmed by ord^r of this Co^{r}te."

In 1635, the General Court agreed that "noe dwelling howse shalbe built above halfe a myle from the meeteing howse, in any newe plantacōn," "without leaue from the Court (except myll howses & Ferme howses of such as have their dwelling howses in some towne)." This was confirmed the next year, with an addition to the order, that it should extend to all towns within their jurisdiction. The above statement will explain the following grant of the Court to Robert Seaver and others, May 23, 1639.

"Jasper Gun, Robert Seaver, Abraham Howe, John Tatman and Ralph Sary, vpon their petition, had leave granted them to continue in the houses wch they have built, and do dwell in, though they bee above halfe a mile from their meeting house." This "halfe a myle law" was repealed in 1640.

Robert Seaver was chosen one of the selectmen of Roxbury, Jan. 15, 1665. Elizabeth, his wife, died June 6, 1657. The Church Record says:—"1657. Buryed, mo. 4, day 9, Sister Seaver, ye wife of Robert Seaver." Also, "1669, mo. 10, day 18, wife to Robert Seaver buryed." He must have had a third wife, for in his will, made Jan. 16, 1681, proved July 5, 1683, he provides for his wife (christian name not given) and four children. The names of the latter were, Shubael, Caleb, Joshua, and son Samuel Crafts, who married his daughter Elizabeth. The latter was, probably, dead at the date of the will.

Robert^1 Seaver, according to the Roxbury *Town* Records, died May 13, 1683, aged about 75. The Roxbury *Church* Records say:—"1683, mo. 4, day 6, Robert Seaver an aged Christian buryed." How these dates are to be reconciled we are unable to decide.

Robert and Elizabeth (Ballard) Seaver had:—

2. i. SHUBAEL, born January 31, 1639; died Jan. 18, 1729–30.
3. ii. CALEB, b. Aug. 30, 1641; d. March 6, 1713.
4. iii. JOSHUA (twin brother of Caleb), b. Aug. 30, 1641; died before Aug. 25, 1730, when an inventory of his estate was taken.
iv. ELIZABETH, b. Nov. 19, 1643; m. Samuel Crafts, of Roxbury, Oct. 1661.

(See Savage's *Dictionary* for the births of their nine children, viz.: Hannah, Samuel, Elizabeth, Samuel, Joseph, Mary, Abigail, Nathaniel and Benjamin.) Mr. Crafts died Dec. 9, 1709.

5\. v. NATHANIEL, bap. Jan. 8, 1645. He was slain at Sudbury, Mass., by the Indians, April 21, 1676.

vi. HANNAH, b. Feb. 14, 1647; d. June 3, 1647.

vii. HANNAH, b. Oct. 13, 1650; buried March 3, 1653.

2\. SHUBAEL[2] (*Robert*[1]), b. Jan. 31, 1639; m. Hannah Wilson, dau. of Nathaniel Wilson, Feb. 7, 1668. She died Feb. 13, 1721–22, aged 75. He died Jan. 18, 1729–30. They had:—

i. Robert, b. June 7, 1670.

6\. ii. Joseph, b. June 1, 1672; m. in Sudbury, Mary Reed, Dec. 10, 1701; died in 1754.

iii. Hannah, b. Sept. 1, 1674.

iv. Abigail, b. July 23, 1677; m. Edmund Cole, March 29, 1705.

7\. v. Shubael, b. Oct. 10, 1679. Will proved Jan. 14, 1757.

vi. Thankful, b. April 6, 1684; m. March 29, 1705, Richard Mowear. In the Collections of the Essex Institute, vi. 222, this marriage, with the date given as above, from Roxbury Town Records, is entered as of Lynn. It says, farther:—"Thankfull, their daughter, born January 27, 1705–6."

3\. CALEB[2] (*Robert*[1]), b. Aug. 30, 1641; d. March 6, 1713. He m. Dec. 15, 1671, Sarah Inglesby or Ingoldsbury, who died Jan. 31, 1708. They had:—

8\. i. Caleb, b. March 31, 1673; will proved Jan. 12, 1753.

ii. Elizabeth, b. Jan. 20, 1675 (which should read, doubtless, 1674–5, as the baptism on the church book stands "24.11.1674"), m. Daniel Holbrooke, May 29, 1696.

iii. Nathaniel, b. Oct. 6, 1677; buried March 8, 1688.

9\. iv. Nicholas, b. April 15, 1680; died April 7, 1764.

10\. v. Thomas, b. March 20, 1681; will proved Dec. 21, 1764.

vi. Sarah, b. Aug. 1, 1686; m. Josiah Winchester, March 25, 1707.

4\. JOSHUA[2] (*Robert*[1]), b. Aug. 30, 1641; m. Feb. 28, 1677, Mary, widow of Joseph Pepper; made freeman March 22, 1689–90; will proved 1730. They had:—

11\. i. Joshua, b. Feb. 18, 1678; died intestate. Estate administered upon, Dec. 4, 1739, by his widow Mercy, and Joshua Seaver, weaver.

ii. Mary, b. March 29, 1683; died May 22, 1683.

iii. Mary, b. Aug. 15, 1684; m. May 30, 1728, Samuel Paine; removed to Pomfret, Conn.

12\. iv. Ebenezer, b. Aug. 1, 1687. Will proved Sept. 3, 1773.

v. John, bap. Aug. 7, 1687; probably a twin brother of Ebenezer.

vi. Sarah.

vii. Jemima, m. John Woods, Dec. 3, 1713.

viii. Robert, b. Dec. 30, 1697.

13\. ix. Robert, b. Dec. 30, 1698; will proved Jan. 25, 1771.

14\. x. Jonathan, b. Nov. 8, 1700.

5\. NATHANIEL[2] (*Robert*[1]), bap. Jan. 8, 1645; slain at Sudbury, by the Indians, April 21, 1676; wife Sarah. They had:—

15\. i. John, b. Aug. 18, 1671.

ii. Sarah, died April 18, 1674.

6\. JOSEPH[3] (*Robert*,[1] *Shubael*[2]) b. in Roxbury, June 1, 1672; married in Sudbury, Dec. 10, 1701, Mary Read; d. 1754; his will was proved Aug. 26, of that year. They had:—

16\. i. Robert, m. Eunice Raymond, of Boston, Sept. 2, 1726; had five children; died in 1752.

ii. Mary, b. Oct. 5, 1706; m. Christopher Nixon.

17. iii. Nathaniel, b. April 1, 1709; m. Rebecca Willis, in Sudbury, Feb. 23, 1737–8; had seven children.
iv. Hannah, b. 1712; m. Jonathan Belcher; d. in Framingham, in 1796.
v. Elizabeth, b. Jan. 31, 1714; m. Samuel How, Jan. 25, 1738–9.
vi. Abigail, m. Azariah Walker.

7. SHUBAEL[3] (*Shubael,[2] Robert[1]*), b. Oct. 10, 1679; m. Abigail Twelves, June 12, 1704; will proved Jan. 14, 1757. They had:—

18. i. Shubael, b. April 25, 1705; m. Mary Rogers, of Boston, July 4, 1734.
ii. Joseph, b. Jan. 29, 1706.
19. iii. Peter, b. April 15, 1709; m. Hannah Seaver, dau. of Ebenezer[3] (9), Nov. 23, 1732; died before July 25, 1755.
iv. David, b. Oct. 19, 1711; d. before July 25, 1755.
v. Abigail, b. Oct. 19, 1711; m. George Hews, of Boston, Nov. 14, 1728.
vi. Sarah, b. June 26, 1715; m. Ebenezer Payson, of Roxbury, Aug. 20, 1734.
vii. Ebenezer, b. Aug. 1, 1720; d. Feb. 14, 1736–7.

8. CALEB[3] (*Caleb,[2] Robert[1]*), b. March 31, 1673; m. Hannah Gamblin, May 31, 1704; m. Sarah Polley, Nov. 26, 1723. He died before Jan. 12, 1753. Children by wife Hannah:—

20. i. Benjamin, b. May 24, 1706; m. Deborah Lyon, Oct. 4, 1739. He died before his father; estate administered upon, Jan. 29, 1750.
ii. Sarah, b. Oct. 2, 1709; d. Oct. 6, 1714.
iii. Sarah, b. Oct. 2, 1716.

9. NICHOLAS[3] (*Caleb,[2] Robert[1]*), b. April 15, 1680; grad. H. C. 1701; ord. Dover, N. H., over the First church, April 11, 1711, and resigned his charge there in the spring of 1715, on account of an impediment in his speech.

Previous to this, in the fall of 1708, the church in Haverhill, Mass., was in want of a pastor. Mr. Sever* was engaged and preached regularly to the people, for a specified time. The inhabitants of the town formally thanked him for his pains and labor in the work among them; desired his continuance and settlement; and chose a committee to confer with him about the matter. March 1st, another meeting was called, at which it was voted to pay Mr. Sever annually twenty pounds in money, and forty pounds in corn, as money, if he would settle in the town. Two weeks afterwards, they voted to add one hundred pounds in money to their former offer, "to be improved by him in settling himself with a house," and allow him the use of all the parsonage land. This was indeed a very liberal offer, and the fact that but four persons dissented from it shows that Mr. Sever was highly esteemed by the people of the town.

June 14th, another meeting was held to see about settling Mr. Sever, at which, the town voted to give him four contributions annually, and twenty cords of wood, in addition to what they had previously offered him. They then adjourned to the 21st, when Mr. Sever's proposals were received, read, and declined. The records do not inform us what his proposals were.

Mr. Sever did not continue to preach in town after his proposals were declined. He was succeeded by Rev. Richard Brown, who preached there twenty-four sabbaths. After this, a call was extended to the Rev. Joshua

* The autograph of Robert[1] Seaver, the ancestor, appears on the Roxbury Town Records several times, where it is uniformly written *Seaver*, or what is equivalent, *Seauer*, as in the fac-simile on a previous page of the genealogy. Caleb,[2] the son, and twin-brother of Joshua,[2] wrote his name *Sever*, as did also his son Nicholas.[3] The same manner of spelling has been retained in this branch of the family, while the descendants of the other three brothers, Shubael,[2] Joshua,[2] and Nathaniel,[2] as far as our knowledge of them extends, follow the first Robert.

Gardner, who was ordained Jan. 10, 1711. The salary paid to Mr. Gardner seems to have been satisfactory to him, although it was not so large as the one offered by the town to Mr. Sever. Mr. G. died March 21, 1715. (See Chase's *History of Haverhill*, page 231.)

The interim of two years was spent, probably, by Mr. Sever, in preaching in those places where there chanced to be calls for his professional services. In the spring of 1711, as has been before stated, he was ordained in Dover, where he remained four years, and then resigned.

Mr. Sever was Tutor at Harvard College from 1716 to 1728, and Fellow from 1725 to 1728. Some time in the course of the latter year he resigned his office at Cambridge and removed to Kingston, Mass. On the 21st of November, following, he married at K., Sarah (Warren) Little, daughter of James Warren, who was a grandson of Richard Warren of the Mayflower. Her first husband was Charles Little. She died Aug. 25, 1756.

Mr. Sever was Judge of the Court of Common Pleas for the County of Plymouth from 1731 to 1762. On the 13th of October, 1757, he married Susannah Winslow.

While connected with Harvard College, as one of the officials, Mr. S. took a prominent part in the discussions which took place as to the relative rights, powers and duties of the Corporation and Overseers under the charter; for some of the particulars of which, see Quincy's *History of Harvard University*. There is a petition, also, extant, on this subject, signed by Nicholas Sever and Wm. Welsteed, addressed to the General Court, Cambridge, June 27, 1727. A copy of this may be found in a MSS. volume entitled "Ewer Papers," in the library of the N. E. Historic, Genealogical Society.

He died at Kingston, April 7, 1764, aged about 84. The children of Nicholas and Sarah were:—

21. i. William, b. Oct. 12, 1729; died June 15, 1809.
ii. John, b. Feb. 22, 1730; grad. H. C. 1749; m. Judith Cooper, of Boston, Dec. 13, 1753; was a physician in Kingston; d. Dec. 26, 1760. The Kingston records say:—"Aug. 1, 1761, Wm. Rand, Jr., was published to Mrs. Judith Sever, widow of Dr. John Sever;" one daughter, Judith.
iii. James, b. Jan. 29, 1733; died Sept. 21, 1745.

10. THOMAS[3] (*Caleb,[2] Robert[1]*), b. March 20, 1681; m. Elizabeth Grely, March 26, 1713; will proved Dec. 21, 1764. They had:—

i. Caleb, b. Jan. 18, 1713; d. July 4, 1729, of small pox.
ii. Thomas, b. March 30, 1716; living Feb. 26, 1768.
iii. Elizabeth, b. March 1, 1718; d. Feb. 6, 1739–40.
iv. Nicholas, b. May 4, 1720; m. in Dudley, April 3, 1759, Mary Putney, of D.; had Mary, bap. Oct. 17, 1762.
v. Nathaniel, b. Nov. 5, 1721; m. Elizabeth Craft, Aug. 11, 1743.
22. vi. Daniel, b. Oct. 30, 1723; m. Abiel Woodward, Oct, 15, 1747.
vii. Elisha, b. Nov. 28, 1725; estate administered upon, Oct. 2, 1778.
viii. Elijah, b. Aug. 26, 1728; d. in Roxbury, Feb. 1, 1810.

11. JOSHUA[3] (*Joshua[2], Robert[1]*), b. Feb. 18, 1678; m. Mercy Cooke, Feb. 27, 1706–7; d. Sept. 24, 1739. She died June 5, 1759. They had:—

i. Mary, b. in Dorchester, Feb. 26, 1708–9; d. Oct. 7, 1726.
23. ii. Joshua, m. Abigail Foster, June 21, 1733.
iii. Mercy, b. in D., Feb. 18, 1712–13.
24. iv. Samuel b. in D., Dec. 13, 1715; m. Hannah Faxon, of Braintree, April 29, 1739; d. Sept. 28, 1756, "being killed instantly, by the bursting of one of ye Cannon, at Castle William, where he resided;" had three children.

v. Elizabeth, b. in D., Oct. 19, 1718; m. Oct. 4, 1739, Jerijah Wales, Jr.
25. vi. William, b. in D., Sept. 2, 1721; d. March 4, 1783.

12. EBENEZER[3] (*Joshua,*[2] *Robert*[1]), b. Aug. 1, 1687; m. Margaret Heath, Dec. 2, 1714; d. May 8, 1773. She died Nov. 30, 1765. They had:—

i. Hannah, b. April 24, 1716; m. Peter Seaver, son of Shubael[3] (7), Nov. 23, 1732.
ii. Sarah, b. Aug. 13, 1718; m. John Newell, of Brookline, Oct. 15, 1741.
26. iii. Ebenezer, b. April 26, 1721; m. Mary Weld, Nov. 5, 1755; will proved April 12, 1785.
iv. Mary, b. Feb. 11, 1725. Estate administered upon, by her brother Ebenezer, May 26, 1769.
v. Joshua, b. Sept. 11, 1728; d. Sept. 4, 1773.
vi. Susanna, b. Aug. 28, 1730. Will proved Oct. 6, 1769.

13. ROBERT[3] (*Joshua,*[2] *Robert*[1]), b. Dec. 30, 1698; m. Ruth Bird, June 10, 1731; will proved Jan. 25, 1771.

14. JONATHAN[3] (*Joshua*[2], *Robert*[1]), b. Nov. 8, 1700; m. Anna Heath, Dec. 12, 1732; d. in 1754.

15. JOHN[3] (*Nathaniel,*[2] *Robert*[1]), b. Aug. 18, 1671; wife Sarah. They had:—

i. Sarah, b. Feb. 4, 1696; m. Amariah Winchester, Dec. 15, 1714.
27. ii. Nathaniel, b. Dec. 22, 1697; m. Hannah White it is believed, and afterwards, Oct. 23, 1746, Sarah Stevens. He died in Brookline, Oct. 2, 1768.
iii. John, b. Oct. 6, 1699; d. in Brookline, Oct. 21, 1767.
iv. Anna, b. in 1701; m. Thomas Stedman, Jr., April 9, 1724.
v. Lucy, b. Nov. 24, 1703; m. John Goddard, of Brookline, in 1725. She died without children, and Mr. G. m. Sept. 4, 1729, widow Hannah (Jennison) Stone. See Bond's *Watertown*, p. 241.
28. vi. Andrew, b. in 1705; wife Elizabeth. She died May 14, 1763, aged 45. (Brookline Records.)
vii. Mary, b. in 1707.
viii. Richard, b. in 1710; m. Hannah Everett, of Roxbury, Nov. 30, 1748.
ix. Esther, b. Nov. 13, 1712; m. Edward Sheaf, Cambridge, Dec. 1, 1756.
x. Elizabeth, b. Sept. 12, 1715.

16. ROBERT[4] (*Robert,*[1] *Shubael,*[2] *Joseph*[3]), m. Eunice Raymond, Boston, Sept. 2, 1726. They had:—

i. Joseph, b. June 10, 1727. (Sudbury Records.)
ii. Benjamin, b. Oct. 8, 1728. (Framingham Records.)
iii. Thankful, b. Oct. Oct. 6, 1731.
iv. Samuel, b. April 8, 1747. (Sudbury Records.)
v. Hannah.

17. NATHANIEL[4] (*Robert,*[1] *Shubael,*[2] *Joseph*[3]), b. April 1, 1709; m. Rebecca Willis, in Sudbury, Feb. 23, 1737–8. They had:—

i. Elijah, b. June 16, 1739; m. Bethiah Hosley, Westminster, Mass., Jan. 1, 1767.
ii. Anna, b. Jan. 3, 1740; d. probably before Jan. 5, 1759.
iii. Josiah Willis, b. July 18, 1742; probably lived in Sterling. (Framingham Records.)
iv. Rebecca, b. Feb. 3, 1743.
v. Joseph, b. Jan. 26, 1746.
vi. Mary, b. Jan. 26, 1746.
vii. Catharine, bap. Aug. 28, 1748; m. 1st, Dyer; 2d, Thomas Mellins; lived in Petersham. (Barry's *Framingham.*)

Nathaniel,[4] father of the above children, m. (2d w.) Judith Treadway, of Framingham, July 17, 1754, and had Luther, Calvin, Fanny, Robert, Betty,

Richard Crafts, and John Reed. He is said to have had eight children by his first wife. [Ibid. p. 389.]

Mr. Barry says Nathaniel[4] lived, 1749, near Moses Cutting's, Framingham, and was of Westminster, July 17, 1754, when he married Judith Treadway, as above stated. He died of small pox in Petersham, 1777. Mr. Slafter (*Slafter Memorial*, p. 48) says he resided (besides the other three places) perhaps in Sterling.

viii. Nathaniel.

18. SHUBAEL[4] (*Shubael,[3] Shubael,[2] Robert[1]*), b. April 25, 1705; m. Mary Rogers, July 4, 1734. They had:—

i. Abigail, b. May 17, 1735.
ii. Mary, b. Aug. 17, 1736.
iii. Shubael, b. Aug. 11, 1740; m. Deliverance, dau. of Lieut. Noah Hyde, 1764, and had 1, *Deliverance*,[6] Feb. 7, 1767; 2, *Mary*,[6] Nov. 8, 1764. (Jackson's *Newton*, p. 405.)
iv. Sarah, bap. Sept. 8, 1754.

19. PETER[4] (*Shubael,[3] Shubael,[2] Robert[1]*), b. April 15, 1709; m. Hannah, dau. of Ebenezer[3] (12) and Margaret (Heath) Seaver, Nov. 23, 1732. They had:—

i. William, b. Oct. 1, 1733; d. April 12, 1818.
ii. Peter, b. Feb. 5, 1734.
29. iii. Ebenezer, b. Oct. 21, 1737; m. Sarah Johonnot (b. 1743), March 31, 1763; d. in Boston, April 14, 1812.
iv. Mary, b. March 4, 1739.
v. Margaret, b. Sept. 10, 1744.

20. BENJAMIN[4] (*Caleb,[3] Caleb,[2] Robert[1]*), b. May 24, 1706; m. Deborah Lyon, Oct. 4, 1739. They had:—

i. Sarah, b. Feb. 6, 1740.
ii. Hannah, b. Aug. 7, 1742.

21. WILLIAM[4] (*Nicholas,[3] Caleb,[2] Robert[1]*), b. in Kingston, Mass., Oct. 12, 1729; grad. H. C. 1745; m. Dec. 2, 1755, Sarah Warren (b. May 13, 1730), of Plymouth, dau. of James and Penelope (Winslow) Warren, both lineal descendants of Edward Winslow and Richard Warren of the Mayflower. She died March 15, 1797. He m. June 19, 1798, Mrs. Mercy Russell, who died Feb. 9, 1840. Mr. Sever died June 15, 1809. He was for fifteen years in succession in political life, at the most important period of our history, as representative, member of the provincial congress, at one time president of the council, and delivered the Message, Nov. 10, 1779; was also state senator. (See Bradford's *Biographical Notices of Distinguished Men in New-England*, printed in 1842.)

The children of William and Sarah (Warren) Sever were:—

30. i. Sarah, b. Oct. 3, 1757; d. Nov. 24, 1787.
31. ii. William, b. June 23, 1759; d. Oct. 26, 1798.
32. iii. James, b. Nov. 2, 1761; d. Dec. 16, 1845.
iv. Ann Warren, b. Sept. 25, 1763; d. Jan. 19, 1788, unmarried.
33. v. John, b. May 7, 1766; d. Nov. 7, 1803.

22. DANIEL[4] (*Thomas,[3] Caleb,[2] Robert[1]*), b. Oct. 30, 1723; m. Abiel Woodward, Oct. 15, 1747. They had:—

i. Abigail, b. June 2, 1748. Was she the Abigail who died at Cambridge, aged 90, May 16, 1839?
ii. Thomas, b. Nov. 10, 1750.
iii. Lydia, b. March 14, 1756.
iv. Ichabod, b. Feb. 27, 1759.

v. Elisha, b. July 27, 1761.
vi. William, b Oct. 19, 1765.
vii. Caleb, bap. Sept. 4, 1768.
viii. Susanna, b. Jan. 25, 1770.

23. JOSHUA[4] (*Joshua,*[3] *Joshua,*[2] *Robert*[1]), m. Abigail Foster, both of Dorchester, June 21, 1733. They had:—

i. Mary, b. April 19, 1734.
ii. Comfort, b. May 18, 1736.
iii. Mercy, b. Oct. 11, 1738.

Abigail, wife of Joshua, d. Aug. 29, 1761. He m. Elizabeth Bradley, of Dorchester, March 29, 1764.

34. iv. Jonathan, b. Aug. 27, 1741; m. Priscilla, dau. of Isaiah and Rebecca Leeds. She d. Oct. 10, 1787, in the 33d year of her age.
v. Abigail, b. Jan. 4, 1743–4.
vi. Elizabeth, b. April 13, 1752; m. John Horton, of Dorchester, June 27, 1756.

24. SAMUEL[4] (*Joshua,*[3] *Joshua,*[2] *Robert*[1]), b. Dec. 13, 1715; m. Hannah Faxon, of Braintree, April 29, 1739; d. Sept. 28, 1756, "being killed, instantly, by the bursting of one of y[e] Cannon at Castle William, where he resided." They had:—

i. Samuel, b. Sept. 22, 1739; d. Jan. 13, 1739–40.
ii. Joseph, b. March 13, 1750.
iii. Hannah, b. Jan. 5, 1753.

25. WILLIAM[4] (*Joshua,*[3] *Joshua,*[2] *Robert*[1]), b. Sept. 2, 1721; m. Patience Trescott, both of Dorchester, Feb. 1, 1742. She was born March 20, 1723; d. March 15, 1799. He died March 4, 1782 or 83. They had:—

35. i. William, b. May 8, 1743; d. July 28, 1815.
36. ii. Ebenezer, b. Feb. 26, 1744–5; d. April 19, 1775.
iii. Sarah, b. Feb. 3, 1746.
iv. Rebecca, b. May 14, 1749.
v. Ruth, b. Aug. 27, 1751; m. Jonathan Clark, Nov. 10, 1772.
vi. Jonathan, b. Dec. 20, 1753.
vii. Elizabeth, b. March 29, 1756.
viii. Patience, b. Sept. 16, 1758.
37. ix. Waitstill, b. Aug. 27, 1761.
x. Mary, b. April 10, 1764; d. July 30, 1764.
xi. Robert, b. July 19, 1766; d. Aug. 21, 1766.

26. EBENEZER[4] (*Ebenezer,*[3] *Joshua,*[2] *Robert*[1]), b. April 26, 1721; m. Mary Weld, Nov. 5, 1755, who d. May 8, 1766. He m. afterwards, Tabitha Davenport (b. Aug. 9, 1737), dau. of Ebenezer and Submit Davenport, of Dorchester, who died March 1, 1804, in her 67th year. Children by his wife Mary:—

i. Mary, b. Sept. 1, 1756; d. Nov. 19, 1763.
ii. Hannah, b. Oct. 30, 1758; m. James Lewis, of Roxbury, May 24, 1786; d. in 1839; another account says, March, 1840.
iii. Jonathan, b. May 19, 1761; d. March 6, 1763.
38. iv. Ebenezer, b. July 5, 1763; d. March 1, 1844.

Children by his wife Tabitha:—

v. Margaret, b. April 18, 1772; d. Feb. 20, 1776.
vi. Joshua, b. Sept. 30, 1774; d. Oct. 11, 1774.
vii. Margaret, b. Oct. 24, 1775; m. Rufus Kelton, Dec. 11, 1804; d. Feb. 25, 1816.
39. viii. Joshua, b. Jan. 15, 1779; d. Sept. 11, 1833.

27. Nathaniel⁴ *(John,³ Nathaniel,² Robert¹)*, b. Dec. 22, 1697; m. Hannah White, d. in Brookline Feb. 20, 1742. He m. Sarah Stevens, Oct. 23, 1746. Mr. Seaver died in Brookline, Oct. 2, 1768, aged 70. Children by his wife Hannah:—

i. Benjamin, b. Sept. 11, 1729; d. before Sept. 17, 1768.
ii. Hannah, b. Nov. 13, 1730.
iii. Lucy, b. Nov. 24, 1731.
iv. Sarah, b. April 12, 1733; m. Mr. Gardner.
v. Hannah, b. July 16, 1735; m. John Goddard, of Brookline (his second wife). She died May 31, 1821; had 12 sons and 4 daughters. See Bond's *Watertown*, p. 242; "*Goddard Genealogy*," p. 16.
40. vi. Abijah, b. Aug. 31, 1737.
vii. Lucy, b. Feb. 17, 1739–40; m. Nathaniel Miriam, April 29, 1767.
viii. Mary.
ix. Elizabeth, m. Mr. Warner.
x. Susanna, unmarried.
xi. Nathaniel, m. ——; had three children, viz.:—Nathaniel; Frank; Elizabeth, who m. Moses Grant.

28. Andrew⁴ *(John,³ Nathaniel,² Robert¹)*, b. in 1705; wife Elizabeth. Children born in Cambridge:—

i. Andrew, b. March 28, 1736.
ii. Elizabeth, b. March 25, 1738; m. Ephraim Burridge, Cambridge, June 16, 1768.
iii. Ebenezer, b. April 17, 1740.

Children born in Dorchester:—

iv. Jerusha, b. June 10, 1744; m. Edward Park.
v. Sarah, b. Dec. 14, 1746. Was not this the Sarah Seaver who m. Joseph Hewes, March 19, 1767, afterwards Whitney?
vi. John, b. in Cambridge, Aug. 11, 1749.
vii. Abigail, b. in Cambridge, April 9, 1752.
viii. Mary, b. in Cambridge, Jan. 19, 1755.
ix. Richard, b. in Cambridge, June 30, 1757.
x. Anna, b. in Cambridge, Aug. 9, 1759.
xi. Hannah, b. in Cambridge, May 1, 1763; m. Mr. Adams.

29. Ebenezer⁵ *(Peter,⁴ Shubael,³ Shubael,² Robert¹)*, b. Oct 21, 1737; m. March 31, 1763, Sarah, dau. of Zachariah and Elizabeth (Quincy) Johonnot. Zachariah was the eldest son of Daniel Johonnot, one of the French Huguenots. (See N. E. Hist. & Gen. Reg., vii., 141, 142). Mr. Seaver was a distiller, and for several years Treasurer of the County of Suffolk. He died in Boston, April 14, 1812. They had:—

i. Ebenezer, b. June 7, 1763; d. Sept. 19, 1827.
ii. Sarah, b. Sept. 8, 1765.
iii. Zachariah, b. Feb. 4, 1767; d. Jan. 5, 1809.
iv. Elizabeth, b. April 1, 1768.
v. Peter Johonnot, b. Oct. 18, 1770; d. at Savannah, Sept. 1804.

30. Sarah⁵ *(William,⁴ Nicholas,³ Caleb,² Robert¹)*, b. Oct. 3, 1757; m. Aug. 12, 1784, Hon. Thomas Russell, an eminent merchant of Boston. She died in Boston, Nov. 24, 1787. They had:—

41. i. Sarah Russell, b. Dec. 1, 1786; d. June 8, 1831.

31. William⁵ *(William,⁴ Nicholas,³ Caleb,² Robert¹)*, b. June 23, 1759; m. Oct. 30, 1785, Mary Chandler, dau. of John Chandler of Worcester, and died Oct. 26, 1798. They had:—

42. i. Penelope Winslow, b. July 21, 1786; d. April 2, 1872.
43. ii. Anne Warren, b. Oct. 24, 1789; d. Jan. 30, 1843.

iii. William James, b. Aug. 16, 1793; m. Adeline Trask, of Gloucester, Nov. 19, 1819; d. in Nachitoches, La., Sept. 15, 1835. He entered the United States Army during the war with England; served to the close, when the army was reduced.

32. JAMES[5] (*William,[4] Nicholas,[3] Caleb,[2] Robert[1]*), b. Nov. 2, 1761; m. Jane Russell, of Plymouth, Feb. 22, 1796. He grad. H. C. 1781, and immediately joined the army of the revolution. He continued in this service to the end of the war. In 1798, he was appointed one of the first six Post Captains in the U. S. Navy, by President Adams. He superintended the building of the Frigate "Congress," at Portsmouth, N. H., and was afterwards her Commander. He retired from the Navy in 1801, and settled at Kingston, where he died Dec. 16, 1845. They had:—

44. i. James Warren, b. July 1, 1797; d. Jan. 16, 1871.
ii. Thomas Russell, b. Oct. 28, 1798; d. at sea, off the Cape of Good Hope, Sept. 15, 1836.
iii. Jane Russell, b. Jan. 13, 1802.
iv. Elizabeth Parsons, b. June 5, 1803.
v. Sarah Ann Warren, b. July 20, 1805.

33. JOHN[5] (*William,[4] Nicholas,[3] Caleb,[2] Robert[1]*), b. May 7, 1766; grad. H. C. 1787; m. May 24, 1790, Nancy Russell; d. Nov. 7, 1803. She died May 14, 1848. She was sister of Jane Russell who married his brother Captain James, and daughter of the second wife of Wm. Sever. They had:—

i. William R., b. May 30, 1791; H. C. 1811; lawyer, for many years County Treasurer of the County of Plymouth.
45. ii. John, b. Nov. 4, 1792; first President of the Old Colony Rail Road; d. at Kingston, Feb. 1, 1855.
46. iii. James Nicholas, b. in Kingston, Dec. 13, 1793; d. April 9, 1869.
47. iv. Charles, b. April 9, 1795; d. in Plymouth, Oct. 17, 1834.
v. Winslow Warren, b. Oct. 16, 1796; grad. H. C. 1818; d. Jan. 19, 1832, at Dorchester. He married Charlotte Freeman, of Sandwich; commanded the company of "Boston Sea Fencibles."
48. vi. Sarah Winslow, b. Sept. 3, 1798.

34. JONATHAN[5] (*Joshua,[4] Joshua,[3] Joshua,[2] Robert[1]*), b. Aug. 27, 1741; m. Priscilla, dau. of Isaiah and Rebecca Leeds, who died Oct. 10, 1787, in the 33d year of her age. They had:—

i. Joseph, b. July 6, 1774.
ii. Jonathan, b. Aug. 3, 1778.
iii. William, b. Nov. 4, 1780.
iv. Samuel, b. Sept. 15, 1782; d. Oct. 7, 1782.
v. Beckee Bradley, b. Jan. 16, 1784; d. April 7, 1784.

35. WILLIAM[5] (*William,[4] Joshua,[3] Joshua,[2] Robert[1]*), b. in Dorchester, May 8, 1743; removed to Taunton about the year 1770, and located near the Taunton River, on what is now called Ingell street. His homestead is still standing. He was generally known throughout Bristol county as Major Seaver, having been brigade major for many years. He was connected with the state service from 1775 until 1808. He married, first, Mary Foster, of Dorchester, Oct. 15, 1767. She died July 9, 1768, in the 26th year of her age. They had one child, Molly Foster Seaver, who married Samuel Caswell, of Taunton, the father of Prof. Alexis Caswell, of Brown University. She d. July 9, 1768. He married for his second wife, Mrs. Thankful Stetson, of Braintree, Feb. 20, 1771. She died in Taunton. William died in Taunton, July 28, 1815. They had:—

49\. i. John, b. March 4, 1771 ; d. Feb. 14, 1853.
50\. ii. Nathaniel, b. Feb. 7, 1773 ; d. Oct. 27, 1827.
iii. Hannah, b. March 19, 1775 ; d. 1830 ; m. Barney.
51\. iv. Benjamin, b. April 28, 1777 ; lost at sea.
52\. v. William, b. March 28, 1779 ; d. Feb. 8, 1869.
vi. Samuel, b. Aug. 6, 1781 ; d. July 27, 1806.

36\. EBENEZER[5] (*William,[4] Joshua,[3] Joshua,[2] Robert[1]*), b. in Dorchester, Feb. 26, 1744–5 ; removed to Taunton about the same time that his brother William did, in 1770 ; lived on what was called the Pound Farm. He was married twice ; first, to Ruth Field, of Milton, in 1766 ; his second wife was named Beebe, of Newport. He died April 19, 1775. Their children were:—

i. Ruth.
ii. Sarah.
iii. Mary.
iv. Hannah.
v. Horace, a Baptist minister, removed to New-York, where his descendants now live.
53\. vi. Nathan.

37\. WAITSTILL[5] (*William,[4] Joshua,[3] Joshua,[2] Robert[1]*), b. Aug. 27, 1761 ; m. John Green (b. July 10, 1753). They had:—

i. Elizabeth Green, b. June 17, 1784.
ii. Betsey Green, b. Oct. 16, 1787.
iii. Amasa Green, b. Sept. 27, 1790.
iv. Harriet Green, b. Aug. 4, 1793.
v. Oliver Green, b. Dec. 3, 1795.
vi. Caleb Green, b. Nov. 2, 1798.
vii. Nancy, b. Nov. 12, 1800.

38\. EBENEZER[5] (*Ebenezer,[4] Ebenezer,[3] Joshua,[2] Robert[1]*), b. July 5, 1763 ; m. Elizabeth Clap (b. Jan. 10, 1767), dau. of Noah Clap, of Dorchester, Dec. 22, 1788. She died Feb. 22, 1838. He died March 1, 1844.

The notice that follows was furnished by Ebenezer Clapp, Esq., of Dorchester.

"Hon. Ebenezer Seaver was educated at Harvard College, from which institution he graduated in 1784.

Instead of studying a profession, as was the case with a large portion of the graduates of that day, he chose the calling of a farmer. The fine rich acres of his ancestors had descended to him, and he enjoyed their cultivation. His table was abundantly supplied with the best the market afforded, as the writer hereof can testify, and gave one the idea of a substantial country gentleman.

He was chosen a member of congress in Norfolk district from 1803 to 1813, a period of ten years. He was a member of the State Constitutional Convention of 1820. He was well versed in the history of his country, and true to what he held to be its highest interests. He belonged to the republican in distinction from the federal party of that day. He was in favor of the embargo, and advocated the declaration of war with Great Britain in 1812. He had much influence with the administration during his several terms in congress ; was a great admirer of Jefferson, who was his model of a gentleman, a statesman and politician. Party spirit at that time was exceedingly high ; and numerous were the insults offered him by his opponents, but he bore them with patience and great forbearance. He was, however, more intimately known to his townsmen by his long continued services as selectman, representative of the general court from 1794 to 1802, and moderator of their town meetings. Here he came in contact with his fellow citizens; he knew their history, and the history of their progenitors back to the first settlement of Roxbury. For many years he held the first named office, was generally chairman of the board, and administered their affairs with scrupulous integrity, wisdom and economy. Swindlers and impostors fared hard under his administration, and it was the prevalent opinion that he was more careful and attentive to the affairs of the town, than to his own. No person was so wealthy, or so high, but he would denounce him if he was dishonest. In 1832, the town of Roxbury passed him a vote of thanks 'for his long, faithful and unremitted services for nearly forty years past.'

Notwithstanding his peculiar views in relation to religious opinions and customs, holding sentiments which would now perhaps be termed of the free religious type, his friends, associates and the public had the most unbounded confidence in his integrity and honor. While he was not obstrusive in urging or parading his own views, he was candid, and tolerant of the opinions of others. With all these traits were combined many of the old puritan character. He was tender-hearted as a child; he felt deeply for the sufferings and woes of humanity, yet was firm in every post of honor or of duty, and inflexible against all encroachments prejudicial to the public weal, by whomsoever made.

In his death the town lost an honest man, his neighbors a counsellor and friend."

Ebenezer and Elizabeth (Clap) Seaver had:—

i. Elizabeth, b. Sept. 20, 1789; d. July 19, 1793.
ii. Ebenezer, b. May 12, 1791; d. July 31, 1865; m. Clarissa Weld, Jan. 19, 1817; had *Ebenezer*,[7] *Jacob Weld*,[7] and *George*.[7]
iii. Jonathan, b. June 9, 1793; m. Mary Plumer. He died Jan. 13, 1865.
iv. Elizabeth, b. July 9, 1795; m. Benjamin Baker Davis, of Brookline, Jan. 24, 1839. She was his second wife.
54. v. Sarah, b. April 8, 1797; m. July 27, 1820, Thomas Parker.
vi. Susannah, b. July 13, 1799; d. Sept. 2, 1801.
vii. Joshua, b. May 6, 1801; lost at sea in December, 1832.
viii. Susannah, b. April 26, 1803; d. March 7, 1870.
ix. Lucy, b. Feb. 19, 1805; d. Oct. 16, 1822.
x. Nathaniel, b. March 11, 1807; d. July 16, 1832.

39. JOSHUA[5] (*Ebenezer*,[4] *Ebenezer*,[3] *Joshua*,[2] *Robert*[1]), b. Jan. 15, 1779; m. Nancy Sumner, April 6, 1803. He died Sept. 11 (record says Aug. 11), 1833. She died Oct. 23, 1837, aged 57 years, 6 months. They had:—

i. Joshua, d. Nov. 15, 1863.
ii. Rufus Kelton, b. Oct. 19, 1804; d. Oct. 5, 1805.
iii. Ann Tabitha, b. Jan. 31, 1806.
55. iv. Nathaniel, b. Dec. 14, 1807; m. Ann Jane Codman, March 3, 1833.
v. John Prince, b. Sept. 11, 1809; d. Dec. 1864.
vi. Robert, b. Feb. 23, 1812.
vii. Seth Sumner, b. July 10, 1816; d. Feb. 21, 1817.
viii. William, b. March 17, 1818.
ix. Joseph, b. Dec. 22, 1819; d. March 8, 1821.
x. Joseph, b. Sept. 7, 1822.

40. ABIJAH[5] (*Nathaniel*,[4] *John*,[3] *Nathaniel*,[2] *Robert*[1]), b. Aug. 31, 1737; m. Anne Winchester, of Brookline, March 29, 1764. They had:—

i. William, b. May 6, 1765; m. Lucy Heath, dau. of Peleg Heath, Dec. 1, 1796. She died Feb. 9, 1807, aged 37. They had three children:— 1. *Elizabeth*[7] *Curtis*, b. Oct. 2, 1797. 2. *William*,[7] b. Dec. 31, 1799; d. in Nelson, N. H. 3. *Abijah*,[7] b. Oct. 4, 1800. 4. *Lucy Heath*,[7] b. in 1805.

56. ii. Benjamin, b. Sept. 28, 1766; m. Debby Loud, dau. of Francis and Joanna (Dyer) Loud, May 25, 1794; had five children. He died June 29, 1815.
57. iii. Joseph, bap. Jan. 20, 1771.
iv. Nathaniel, bap. May 16, 1773; m. Lydia Wilson, Nov. 1, 1798; had three children, viz.: 1. *Mary*,^{7} b. Aug. 26, 1799. 2. *Ann Winchester*,^{7} b. June 26, 1805. 3. *Martha*.^{7} A Nathaniel Seaver d. July 4, 1806.
v. Polly, m. Levi Pratt; had one child, *Mary Ann*,^{7} m. George Archibald. They had *Mary Ann*,^{8} who m. Charles V. Gerry.

41. Sarah Russell,^{6} only child of Hon. Thomas Russell (*Sarah*^{5} *Sever*, *William*,^{4} *Nicholas*,^{3} *Caleb*,^{2} *Robert*^{1}), b. Dec. 1, 1786; m. Richard Sullivan, May 22, 1804; d. June 8, 1831. They had:—

i. Elizabeth Lowell Sullivan, b. Aug. 22, 1805; d. April, 1833.
ii. Sarah Sever Sullivan, b. March 30, 1808; m. Steven Higginson Perkins, Nov. 22, 1831. Children:—1. *Francis William*^{8} *Perkins*, b. Dec. 26, 1832; m. Frances Ann McDonald, Jan. 13, 1863. They had:—*Sarah Sullivan*^{9} *Perkins*, b. Feb. 7, 1864; *Caroline Elizabeth*^{9} *Perkins*, b. Dec. 22, 1868. 2. *Stephen George*^{8} *Perkins*, b. Sept. 18, 1835; killed at Cedar Mountain battle, Aug. 9, 1862. 3. *Richard Sullivan*^{8} *Perkins*, b. Nov. 12, 1837; m. Susan K. Adams (b. Feb. 21, 1836) Dec. 25, 1863.
iii. Anna Cabot Lowell Sullivan, b. Dec. 7, 1810; m. Rev. Francis Cunningham, Oct. 8, 1834; d. Sept. 6, 1840; no children.
iv. Richard Sullivan, b. March 2, 1814; d. May 31, 1815.
v. Mary Russell Sullivan, b. Jan. 28, 1816; d. April 27, 1828.
vi. Richard Sullivan, b. March 19, 1820; married Henrietta Gardiner, Sept. 10, 1864; no children.
vii. Francis William Sullivan, b. Nov. 4, 1821; d. Dec. 2, 1824.
viii. James Sullivan, b. June 27, 1829; d. March 28, 1866.

42. Penelope Winslow^6 Sever (*William*,^{5} *William*,^{4} *Nicholas*,^{3} *Caleb*,^{2} *Robert*^{1}), b. July 21, 1786; m. Levi Lincoln, of Worcester, Sept. 6, 1807 (b. Worcester, Oct. 25, 1782, H. C. 1802, d. there May 29, 1868). She d. April 2, 1872. They had:—

i. Sarah Warren Lincoln, b. May, 1808; lived eleven days.
ii. Levi Lincoln, b. Aug. 23, 1810; served several years in the United States Navy; d. Sept. 1, 1845.
iii. William Sever Lincoln, b. Nov. 22, 1811; m. Elizabeth Trumbull, of Worcester, Oct. 22, 1835; served as Lt. Col. 34th Regiment Mass. Infantry, about three years during the rebellion; Oct. 14, 1864, colonel commanding—discharged by expiration of service; Jan. 6, 1865, appointed colonel et brevet brigadier general of U. S. Volunteers; severely wounded in battle, which disabled the right arm. Their children were:—1. *William*,^{8} b. Sept. 15, 1839; d. Aug. 13, 1869. *Levi*,^{8} b. April 27, 1844; m. Mary S. Maynard, of Worcester, Oct. 31, 1867. 3. *George Trumbull*,^{8} b. Feb. 5, 1847; d. Feb. 7, 1869, unmarried. 4. *Winslow*,^{8} b. Oct. 3, 1848.

William,^{8} above, who died in 1869, served in the United States Worcester Light Infantry, which was attached to the famous 6th Massachusetts Regiment, from April, 1861, until discharged by expiration of service in August, 1861.

Levi,^{8} born in 1844, the second son of William Sever Lincoln, served in the 34th Massachusetts Infantry as 2d 1st lieut. and adjutant; discharged in 1864, by reason of disability from a disease contracted in the service. He has a son, *William Sever Lincoln*,^{9} b. April 11, 1870.

iv. Daniel Waldo Lincoln, b. Jan. 16, 1813; H. C. 1831; m. Nov. 30, 1841, Frances Fiske Merrick, of Worcester. Children:—1. *Frances Merrick*,^{8} b. July 1, 1843. 2. *Mary Waldo*,^{8} b. Sept. 15, 1845. 3. *Anne Warren*,^{8} b. Feb. 6, 1848; d. July 31, 1849. 4. *Daniel Waldo*,^{8} b. Dec. 31, 1849.
v. Penelope Sever Lincoln, b. July 1, 1815; m. Mahlon Dickinson Canfield, of New-Jersey, May 24, 1843; had one child, *Penelope Winslow Sever*,^{8} b. Dec. 30, 1845.

vi. George Lincoln, b. Oct. 19, 1816; m. Nancy Hoard, of Ogdensburg, N. Y., May 24, 1839: killed at the battle of Buena Vista, Mexico; had a daughter, *Georgiana De Villars*,[8] b. May 10, 1840, m. Francis Blake Rice, of Worcester, Jan. 8, 1861, and d. in child-bed, Dec. 28, 1861.

vii. Anne Warren Lincoln, b. Aug. 28, 1818; d. July 24, 1846.

viii. John Waldo, — name changed to Edward Winslow Lincoln in 1846, —b. Dec. 2, 1820; m. March 29, 1848, Sarah Rhodes Arnold (b. Mar. 29, 1827, d. July 1, 1856). Children:—1. *Eliza Paddleford*,[8] b. Aug. 31, 1850, d. May 7, 1851. 2. *John Waldo*,[8] b. Oct. 30, 1852. 3. *Arnold*,[8] b. Oct. 27, 1853, d. July 27, 1854. 4. *Charles Frederick*,[8] b. June 16, 1856, d. June 17, 1856. He married second, Aug. 4, 1858, Kate Von Weber Wanton. Children:—5. *Annie Marston*,[8] b. Oct. 25, 1859. 6. *Marian Vinal*,[8] b. May 27, 1862. 7. *Marston*,[8] b. June 23, 1864. 8. *Adeline Sever*,[8] b. June 17, 1867. 9. *Helen*,[8] b. April 8, 1870.

43. ANNE WARREN[6] SEVER (*William*,[5] *William*,[4] *Nicholas*,[3] *Caleb*,[2] *Robert*[1]) b. Oct. 24, 1789; m. Rev. John Brazer, D.D., of Worcester (H. C. 1813, minister at Salem), April 19, 1821; d. in South Carolina, Jan. 30, 1843. They had:—

i. Mary Chandler Brazer, b. July 13, 1823; m. John Wait Draper, of Dorchester, Sept. 30, 1851; have one child, *John Brazer*[8] *Draper*, b. Nov. 28, 1853.

ii. John Allen Brazer, b. Sept. 9, 1826; d. March 25, 1861. } twins.
iii. William Brazer, b. " " d. July 17, 1849. }

iv. Anne Warren Brazer, b. June 10, 1829; m. Henry P. Ellis, of Boston, Oct. 2, 1854. Children: 1. *Katherine*[8] *Ellis*, b. April 7, 1857. 2. *William Brazer*[8] *Ellis*, b. Oct. 25, 1858. 3. *Mary Brazer*[8] *Ellis*, b. June 11, 1862.

v. Edward Winslow Brazer, b. Nov. 17, 1831; d. in Dorchester, June 8, 1854, unmarried.

44. JAMES WARREN[6] (*James*,[5] *William*,[4] *Nicholas*,[3] *Caleb*,[2] *Robert*[1]), b. July 1, 1797. The following sketch of his life was read before the New-England Historic, Genealogical Society, April 5, 1871, by Charles W. Tuttle, Esq., assistant historiographer:—

"He entered Dummer Academy in 1811, and there fitted for college. Two years later he entered Harvard College, and graduated in 1817, being the fourth graduate in his line of descent, his father, grandfather and great-grandfather having graduated at this college. Among his classmates, afterward distinguished, were, Caleb Cushing, George Bancroft, and President Woods of Bowdoin College. While in college he gave much attention to military studies and exercise, and was member and commander of the Harvard Washington Company, a military organization composed of students of the senior and junior classes. On the occasion of the visit of President Munroe to Cambridge in 1817, this company performed escort duty under the command of young Sever. The president was so much pleased with his military bearing and capacity that he urged him to go to West Point, and qualify himself for a command in the army. The next year, having graduated, he was appointed a cadet in the Academy; but his mother prevailed on him not to accept the appointment, she being averse to such a calling, much against his own inclination. He immediately entered the law-office of Gov. Levi Lincoln in Worcester, and there pursued his studies two years. While yet a law student he delivered the 4th of July oration at Leicester, in 1820, his subject being, "The Era of Good Feeling." In October of this year he quit Worcester, and entered the merchant marine service, in the employ of the house of Thomas H. Perkins, of Boston. This he did at the suggestion and urgency of James Perkins of that house. His first voyage was to the North West Coast of America. He continued in the service of this house till 1835, having been part of the time in command of an East Indiaman. He commanded the "Alert," the first ship that ever entered the Canton River without issuing the usual rations of ardent spirits to officers and men.

On quitting the sea he settled in Boston, where he was member of the common council in 1850 and 1851. His refusal to pledge himself to a particular policy in reference to the fire department of the city, prevented his election to the office of alderman, by a few votes, in 1852. In 1853, and again in 1856, he was member of the house of representatives, and chairman of the committee of finance on both occasions. His reports on the financial condition of the commonwealth were regarded able state papers, and gave him the reputation of being master of finance.

His early fondness for military life never left him. He connected himself with the Independent Corps of Cadets, and was adjutant of the same in 1844. He devoted much time to the discipline of this company, "in order," to use his own words "that by its example as a body guard to the governor of the commonwealth, it might stimulate the waning military spirit of the state militia." In 1849, having filled all the intermediate grades of office, he was elected lieutenant colonel of the Cadets, which office he held two years. On the occasion of the presentation of a standard to the Cadets in 1862, Col. Sever made a public address at the State House in the presence of the governor and other state officials, which was much commended for its aptness and for its ability.

For many years Col. Sever was recording secretary of the Society of the Cincinnati, and was elected president of the same in 1866. In 1869, he was chosen vice president of the General Society of the Cincinnati, at the annual meeting held at Trenton, New York. He felt great interest in the objects and purposes of this society; and he always found it a pleasant duty to discharge the various offices which he held in that organization.

In 1868, Col. Sever established a scholarship in Harvard College, giving $2,500 for that purpose. He directed the income to be given to meritorious under-graduates, preference being given to those from his native town, Kingston, or from Plymouth, the birth-place of his mother. He requested the selection of the beneficiary to be made without special reference to academic rank, and that "no sectional or denominational test" be required. He took a deep interest in this foundation, and it occupied his thoughts till the close of his days.

Late in life, as usual, he became inspired with a deep interest in the history of his ancestors. He secured the services of one of our most esteemed members, and proceeded to investigate and prepare for publication the history of the descendants of Robert Seaver, the emigrant, his great ancestor, from whom he was descended in the sixth degree.

His domestic life covered a period of thirty-five years, and was marked with few incidents. He married Dec. 7, 1836, Elizabeth Parsons, daughter of James Carter, of Boston, who survives him. They had no children.

In the spring of 1870, his health began to decline; this was followed by a prolonged illness, which ended in his death January 16, 1871.

Col. Sever was a gentleman of marked traits of character, moral and intellectual. In his religious and political views he was eminently conservative. His integrity, firmness and intelligence qualified him for public employment. He had that true elevation of mind which commanded respect, and caused him to be esteemed by a select circle of acquaintances. He was chosen a resident member of this Society in May, 1869."

45. John[6] (*John,[5] William,[4] Nicholas,[3] Caleb,[2] Robert[1]*), b. Nov. 4, 1792; m. Oct. 10, 1825, Anna, daughter of Hon. Samuel Dana, of Groton. She was b. Aug. 28, 1800; d. Feb. 10, 1864. The maiden name of her mother was Rebecca Barrett. Mr. Sever died at Kingston, Feb. 1, 1855. They had:—

i. John, b. July 4, 1826; d. April 19, 1827.
ii. Anna Dana, b. April 23, 1828.
iii. Herbert, b. Aug., 1829; d. in October, 1830.
iv. Charles William, died in infancy.
v. Mary, b. Sept. 5, 1832.
vi. Emily, b. Jan. 2, 1834.
vii. Ellen, b. June 14, 1835; m. June 3, 1857, Rev. Theodore Tebbets, of Rochester, N. H., then pastor of the Unitarian Church in Medford, who died in the city of New York, Jan. 29, 1863, aged 31. Their only son, *John Tebbets*,[8] b. July 4, 1858, in Medford, Mass. She married Nov. 24, 1868, George Silsbee Hale, born in Keene, N. H., lawyer in Boston; one son, *Robert Sever Hale*,[8] b. Oct. 3, 1869.
viii. Martha, b. March 4, 1839; d. Nov. 3, 1864; in the service of the Sanitary Commission.

46. James Nicholas[6] (*John,[5] William,[4] Nicholas,[3] Caleb,[2] Robert[1]*), b. in Kingston, Dec. 13, 1793; m. Mercy Russell, Nov. 14, 1819, who died, and he m. Jane R. Nichols, Sept. 15, 1845. Mr. Sever died April 9, 1869. Children by his wife Mercy:—

i. George Russsell, b. May 9, 1822; d. July 6, 1823.
ii. James Russell, b. Feb. 27, 1823; d. Nov. 18, 1825.
iii. James Nicholas, b. Jan. 20, 1828; died at sea, Oct. 21, 1846.
iv. Sarah, b. June 30, 1829; d. April 15, 1831.
v. Winslow Warren, b. Jan. 31, 1832; Protestant Episcopal clergyman; of St. Luke's Hospital, in the city of New-York.
vi. Charlotte Freeman, b. Dec. 17, 1833.
vii. Mary Russell, b. Nov. 28, 1835; m. June 22, 1869, Rev. Henry L. Chase, of Dyersville, Iowa, b. in Milford, Vt., Sept. 9, 1832.

47. Charles[6] (*John,[5] William,[4] Nicholas,[3] Caleb,[2] Robert[1]*), b. April 9, 1795; m. Jan. 15, 1827, Jane A. Elliot, b. in Waynesborough, Georgia, July 30, 1805, granddaughter of Dr. James Thacher, of Plymouth, where he settled; d. in Plymouth, Oct. 17, 1834. She died in Boston, March 10, 1871, aged 65. They had:—

i. Kate Elliot, b. Nov. 10, 1827.
ii. John Elliot, b. Aug. 21, 1829.
iii. Jennie Elliot, b. Nov. 7, 1831; m. Oct. 25, 1858, Alexander Madera Harrison, of Philadelphia, b. in New-Haven, Conn., May 27, 1829; of the U. S. Coast Survey. Children:—1. *William Sever*[8] *Harrison*, b. Dec. 27, 1859. *Jennie Seaton*[8] *Harrison*, b. Jan. 28, 1865.
iv. Charles William, b. July 1, 1834; m. Mary C. Webber, granddaughter of Wendell Webber, Oct. 29, 1862, head of the house of Sever, Francis & Co., booksellers and publishers at Cambridge, where he settled. Children:—1. *Martha*,[8] b. Feb. 17, 1865. 2. *George F.*,[8] b. July 30, 1866. 3. *Frank W.*,[8] b. Nov. 9, 1868.

48. Sarah Winslow[6] Sever (*John,[5] William,[4] Nicholas,[3] Caleb,[2] Robert[1]*), b. Sept. 3, 1798, in Kingston; m. Nov. 29, 1816, William Thomas, of Plymouth, born in Plymouth, March 15, 1789, son of Joshua Thomas. They had one child:—

i. Ann Thomas, b. in Boston, July 29, 1817; d. in Plymouth, Nov. 26, 1855. She m. Nov. 25, 1846, Wm. Henry Whitman, b. in Pembroke, Mass., Jan. 26, 1817. They had three children born in Plymouth:—1. *Isabella Thomas*[8] *Whitman*, b. Oct. 19, 1848. 2. *Elizabeth Winslow*[8] *Whitman*, b. Nov. 8, 1850. 3. *William Thomas*[8] *Whitman*, b. June 30, 1853.

49. JOHN[6] (*William,[5] William,[4] Joshua,[3] Joshua,[2] Robert[1]*), b. March 4, 1771; m. Lydia Porter, of Taunton. He lived near the Taunton River, was a farmer, and for many years town clerk; died Feb. 14, 1853. They had:—

i. John, died unmarried.
ii. Mary, m. Howard.
iii. Benjamin, m. Susan Hull, of Raynham, They had: *Susan*,[8] d. unmarried. *Julia*.[8] *Martha*,[8] m. Dr. Ira Sampson.
iv. Sally, m. Christopher A. Hack, of Taunton.

50. NATHANIEL[6] (*William,[5] William,[4] Joshua,[3] Joshua,[2] Robert[1]*), b. Feb. 7, 1773; m. Hannah Loco. He resided in Boston, and was engaged in the shipping business for many years. He died Oct. 27, 1827. They had:—

i. James, died unmarried.
ii. Sophia.
iii. Horace, unmarried, now living in Boston.
iv. William, now living in Boston, has no children.
v. Henry, died unmarried. vi. Amasa.

51. BENJAMIN[6] (*William,[5] William,[4] Joshua,[3] Joshua,[2] Robert[1]*), b. April 28, 1777; m. Porter, of Taunton; was lost at sea. They had:—

i. Margaret, m. Edward Mitchell, of Bridgewater.
ii. Mary, m. Bela Mitchell, " "
iii. James, died unmarried.

52. WILLIAM[6] (*William,[5] William,[4] Joshua,[3] Joshua,[2] Robert[1]*), b. March 28. 1779; was a farmer, resided near the Taunton River, for many years selectman of the town, and county commissioner. He married Lydia Presbrey, of Taunton. Lydia died 1849. He died Feb. 8, 1869. They had:—

i. Lydia P., b. June 9, 1799; m. Allen Danforth. She died in 1859.
ii. Hannah B., b. Jan. 25, 1802; m. David Standish.
58. iii. William, b. 1804; d. 1859.
iv. Hertilla, b. 1806; d. 1833; m. John Wade.
59. v. Samuel, b. 1808.

53. NATHAN[6] (*Ebenezer,[5] William,[4] Joshua,[3] Joshua,[2] Robert[1]*), m. Rebecca Leonard, of Taunton. They had:—

i. Rebecca, died unmarried.
60. ii. Ebenezer, b. in 1801.
iii. Mary, m. Benjamin Spinney, of Lynn.
iv. Caroline, m. Smith.
v. Nathaniel Leonard, m. Carver, of Taunton; removed to Carverdale, Ill.
vi. Angeline, m. Samuel D. Godfrey, of Taunton.
vii. Nathan B., now residing in Taunton; m. Caroline Williams. Their children: 1. *Frank*.[8] 2. *Mark H*.[8] 3. *Emily*.[8] 4. *Henry W*.[8] 5. *Horace*.[8]

54. SARAH[6] (*Ebenezer,[5] Ebenezer,[4] Ebenezer,[3] Joshua,[2] Robert[1]*), b. April 8, 1797; m. Thomas Parker, July 27, 1820. They had:—

61. i. Thomas Henderson, b. May 24, 1821.
ii. Lucy Elizabeth, b. March 11, 1823; d. April 20, 1862.
iii. George Jackson, b. Dec. 31, 1825; d. Jan. 13, 1860.
62. iv. Augustus, b. Aug. 30, 1827; m. Mary Elizabeth Baker.
v. Sarah, b. Dec. 21, 1828.

55. NATHANIEL[6] (*Joshua,[5] Ebenezer,[4] Ebenezer,[3] Joshua,[2] Robert[1]*), b. Dec. 14, 1807; m. Ann Jane Codman, March 3, 1833. They had:—

i. Ann Maria, b. in Jamaica Plain, Roxbury, 1834.

ii. Nathaniel, b. in Boston, 1836; m. Marietta Mills White, daughter of William H. White, of Littleton, Mass., Nov. 21, 1865; have two children.
iii. Harriet Augusta, b. in Boston, 1838; m. Ichabod Sampson, of Duxbury, Aug. 4, 1862.

56. Benjamin^{6} (*Abijah,^{5} Nathaniel,^{4} John,^{3} Nathaniel,^{2} Robert^{1}*) b. Sept. 28, 1766; m. Debby Loud, daughter of Francis and Joanna (Dyer) Loud, May 25, 1794. He died June 29, 1815. They had:—

63. i. Benjamin, b. April 12, 1795; d. Feb. 14, 1856.
64. ii. Charles, b. Jan. 19, 1797.
65. iii. George, b. Dec. 13, 1798.
iv. Francis, d. June 20, 1803.
66. v. Ann Frances, b. April 4, 1804; m. Hugh R. Kendall, Jr., May 17, 1826.

57. Joseph^{6} (*Abijah,^{5} Nathaniel,^{4} John,^{3} Nathaniel,^{2} Robert^{1}*), bap. Jan. 20, 1771; m. Abigail, daughter of Elisha Whitney, Nov. 17, 1799. They had:—

67. i. Joseph, b. June 17, 1804.
ii. Elizabeth Whitney, m. George Seaver (Par. 65), June 29, 1823.
68. iii. William Whitney, b. April 6, 1806.
iv. Nathaniel, b. Sept. 24, 1808; d. unmarried.
v. Abigail Dana, b. Sept. 16, 1810; d. unmarried.

58. William^{7} (*William,^{6} William,^{5} William,^{4} Joshua,^{3} Joshua,^{2} Robert^{1}*), b. in 1804; removed to Providence; m. first, Louisa Olney; second, Elizabeth Ricketson. He died in 1859. They had:—

i. William H., died in 1863, of disease contracted while in the U. S. service, 1861–2.
ii. James A., now living in Providence; served during the war from 1861 to 1863, as lieutenant in the Rhode Island Artillery.
iii. Mary, m. William Kenyon.
iv. Elizabeth, m. John Easterbrook.

59. Samuel^{7} (*William,^{6} William,^{5} William,^{4} Joshua,^{3} Joshua,^{2} Robert^{1}*), b. in 1808; now residing in Taunton, on homestead of (William^{1}); m. Lepha M. Hodges, of Norton. They had:—

i. Samuel L., now residing in Bridgewater; m. Lucy Byram; had one son, Charlie L.
ii. George F., now living in Taunton; served during the war 1861–3, as lieutenant in Rhode Island Artillery; m. Jennie Montgomery, of Lakeville; had two children, one named Emma.
iii. James E., now living in Taunton; served during the war 1861–63, as lieutenant of the 7th Mass. Vol.; m. Fannie E. Monagle.

60. Ebenezer^{7} (*Nathan,^{6} Ebenezer,^{5} William,^{4} Joshua,^{3} Joshua,^{2} Robert^{1}*), b. in 1801; m. Susan H. Harris. They had:—

i. S. C., b. 1825; d. 1858.
ii. Ebenezer, b. 1828; now living at Gallop's Island, Boston harbor.
iii. Mark H., b. 1830; d. 1837.
iv. Joseph, b. 1832; d. 1837.
v. Ann E., b. 1835; d. 1839.
vi. Mary E., b. 1840; d. 1843.

61. Thomas Henderson Parker^{7} (*Sarah,^{6} Ebenezer,^{5} Ebenezer,^{4} Ebenezer,^{3} Joshua,^{2} Robert^{1}*), b. in Dorchester, May 24, 1821; m. Oct. 4, 1849, Mary Joanna Cheever, born in Providence, R. I., Nov. 4, 1831. They had:—

i. Howard Judson, b. in Cincinnati, Ohio, Dec. 21, 1850.
ii. George Henderson, b. " " Sept. 17, 1852.
iii. Edward Wayland, b. near Hillsboro', " Nov. 3, 1855.
iv. William Henry, b. " " " Feb. 12, 1858.

v. Abbott Arnold, b. near Hillsboro', Ohio, Mar. 21, 1859.
vi. Seaver, b. " " " July 15, 1860.
vii. Omar Noble, b. " " " July 17, 1864.
viii. Stella, b. " " " Oct. 19, 1869; d. Aug. 12, 1870.

62. AUGUSTUS PARKER[7] (*Sarah,*[6] *Ebenezer,*[5] *Ebenezer,*[4] *Ebenezer,*[3] *Joshua,*[2] *Robert*[1]), b. Aug. 30, 1827; m. Mary Elizabeth Baker, Nov. 16, 1854. They had:—

i. William Prentiss, b. Dec. 11, 1857.
ii. Lizzie Seaver, b. Oct. 5, 1861; d. Sept. 5, 1863.
iii. Lucy, b. Sept. 7, 1863.
iv. Mary Scollay, b. Aug. 3, 1869.

63. BENJAMIN[7] (*Benjamin,*[6] *Abijah,*[5] *Nathaniel,*[4] *John,*[3] *Nathaniel,*[2] *Robert*[1]), b. April 12, 1795; m. Sarah Johnson; died Feb. 14, 1856. She was born June 17, 1796, and died Nov. 7, 1865.

The following notice of Mr. Seaver was furnished by Hon. George S. Hillard, of this city.

"Benjamin Seaver was born in Roxbury, April 12, 1795. In 1812 he entered the auction and commission store of Whitwell & Bond, as an apprentice. In 1816, when he had reached his majority, he was admitted as a partner, and the name of the firm was changed to Whitwell, Bond & Co. For a long period this house occupied a prominent position among the leading business firms of New-England, and none enjoyed more fully the confidence of the community. At the close of the year 1837, Mr. Whitwell and Mr. Seaver, in conjunction with Mr. Benjamin F. White, a special partner, formed a copartnership under the firm of Whitwell & Seaver. This firm was successful in business, and some years before his death Mr. Seaver was able to retire with a moderate competence.

In 1845, he was elected a member of the common council from ward five, and was re-elected in 1846 and 1847. The next year he changed his residence to ward four, but was retained in the council from his new constituency in 1848 and 1849. From July, 1847, he was president of the council, to the close of his term of service, two and a half years. He served in the house of representatives in 1846, 1847, and 1848. In 1850, he was elected to the senate, and was sent again the next year. In 1852 and 1853, he was mayor of the city of Boston. In all these public trusts Mr. Seaver was a diligent and conscientious public servant. He discharged the duties of all of them with exemplary punctuality and fidelity. He was uniformly courteous in manner, but firm in maintaining his own views. During his term of service as chief magistrate of the city, he was called upon to act on several questions on which the community was strongly divided. Mr. Seaver was always firm in adherence to his convictions, and though often bitterly assailed he never swerved from the line he had marked out for himself. During his term of office the Normal School for Girls and the Public Library were established, and various improvements were introduced into the public schools.

While yet a young man Mr. Seaver became much interested in the various societies and organizations in Boston for the relief of poverty and the removal of ignorance. He was an active member and officer of more than one of them. He made a public profession of his religious faith by becoming a member of the Twelfth Congregational Church in Boston, and long before his participation in political matters he held the office of deacon in the church under the pastoral care of the Rev. Samuel Barrett, D.D., and died in the office. Between him and his pastor there was an intimate and long continued friendship.

Mr. Seaver was eminently a public-spirited man. His thoughts, his time, his purse were ever at the service of every public cause which he espoused. According to his means, he was a generous benefactor to the poor.

In all the relations of private and domestic life Mr. Seaver was most estimable and amiable. No man had warmer friends, and no man better deserved to have warm friends. He had a sound understanding and a large amount of practical sense, which, in addition to his perfect integrity and strong sense of justice, caused him to be often appealed to for the settlement of business questions. His manners were simple, cordial, and attractive; and both in matters of substance and matters of form he was a gentleman. He had a nice tact and a delicate perception of what was due to all men.

After leaving the office of mayor Mr. Seaver visited Europe, and also travelled in the western states.

Though never a man of robust frame, he had always enjoyed good health, and from his active temperament and methodical habits he was able to do a great deal of work. But for some months before his death it was evident that his health was affected, though no serious apprehensions were entertained. His disease proved to be a scirrhous or cancerous affection of the intestines, from which he must have suffered much. But his death, which occurred Feb. 14, 1856, was without pain. The frame of mind in which he died was happily expressed in a remark he made the day before his decease: "I am willing to go, though perhaps not ready." His funeral, which took place on Saturday, Feb. 16, at Rev. Dr. Putnam's Church in Roxbury, was largely attended. Dr. Putnam and Dr. Barrett officiated. On Sunday morning, Feb. 24, 1856, Dr. Barrett preached an excellent sermon, giving a very discriminating sketch of Mr. Seaver's character, which was listened to by a large congregation."

Benjamin and Sarah (Johnson) Seaver had:—

i. Benjamin Francis, b. Aug. 14, 1820; m. Lucy Barrett Jewett, and died at Orange, N. J., Jan. 19, 1866; had four children: *Henry Gardner*,[9] *Lucy Jewett*,[9] *Grace Milton*,[9] *Benjamin Frank*.[9]

ii. Henry Gardner, b. Nov. 7, 1822; drowned while bathing in Charles River, June 23, 1838.

iii. Mary Elizabeth, b. Sept. 8, 1825; m. William Blanchard; had children: —*Sarah Lowell*,[9] b. June 17, 1848, d. May 9, 1851; *Francis Kendall*,[9] b. March 29, 1852; *Benjamin Seaver*,[9] b. Sept. 22, 1856; *Mary Lambert*,[9] b. June 20, 1860.

iv. Charles Milton, b. March 18, 1829.

64. CHARLES[7] (*Benjamin*,[6] *Abijah*,[5] *Nathaniel*,[4] *John*,[3] *Nathaniel*,[2] *Robert*[1]), b. Jan. 19, 1797; m. first, Catharine Vose; second, Charlotte Webster. He had by his wife Catharine:—

i. Catharine Frances, m. Rev. Jacob R. Scott. They had:—*Charles S.*[9] *Frank R.*,[9] *Annie L.*[9] By his wife Charlotte:—had one daughter, *Martha*,[9] who m. Walter H. Cowing. They have a daughter Grace.

ii. Mary Ann Pratt, m. Emerson Leland; had:—*Edward E.*,[9] *Arthur Stevens*,[9] *Herbert M.*[9]

65. GEORGE[7] (*Benjamin*,[6] *Abijah*,[5] *Nathaniel*,[4] *John*,[3] *Nathaniel*,[2] *Robert*[1]), b. Dec. 13, 1798; m. Elizabeth Whitney Seaver, daughter of Joseph[6] and Abigail. They had:—

i. George, d. Aug. 10, 1825, aged 15 months.

ii. George W., m. Betsey Baker, April 5, 1853; had *George*,[9] *Joseph*,[9] *Frances A.*,[9] *Mary F.*[9]

iii. Abigail Frances.

iv. Joseph Augustus.

v. Elizabeth Augusta.

vi. Ellen Maria.

66. ANN FRANCES^{7} (*Benjamin,^{6} Abijah,^{5} Nathaniel,^{4} John,^{3} Nathaniel,^{2} Robert^{1}*), b. April 4, 1804; m. Hugh R. Kendall, Jr., May 17, 1826. They had:—

i. Benjamin Frank, m. first, Charlotte Fessenden. Children:—*Frances Kendall,^{9} Hugh Fessenden,^{9} Charles Fessenden.^{9}* He m. second, Elizabeth A. Sargeant, and had one child.
ii. Ann Frances, m. George E. Stone, and had *Frances S.,^{9} George C.^{9}*
iii. Mary Louisa, m. Giovanni Sconcia. They had *Elizabeth Barnes.^{9}*

67. JOSEPH^{7} (*Joseph,^{6} Abijah,^{5} Nathaniel,^{4} John,^{3} Nathaniel,^{2} Robert^{1}*), b. June 17, 1804; m. Phebe S. Elmes. They had:—

i. Joseph H.
ii. Emma.
iii. Thomas Elmes.
iv. Maria E.
v. William Archer.
vi. Frank.
vii. Charles.
viii. Mary.
ix. James R. S.

68. WILLIAM WHITNEY^{7} (*Joseph,^{6} Abijah,^{5} Nathaniel,^{4} John,^{3} Nathaniel,^{2} Robert^{1}*), b. April 6, 1806; m. Hannah Hunneman. They had:—

i. George A.
ii. William A., m. Helen Smith.
iii. Joseph N., m. Mary Hamlenbach:—had *Blanche,^{9} Bessie,^{9}* and one other child.
iv. Hannah N.
v. Alexander H., m. Abby Badger. They had *Charles,^{9} Cara,^{9} Daniel Badger.^{9}*
vi. Abby A., m. first, Warren White; second, Joseph Milner.
vii. Frances A., m. Josiah Quincy; have no child.

EXTRACTS FROM THE PRESBYTERIAN CHURCH RECORDS OF WESTERLY, R. I.

Communicated by BENJAMIN PARKE, LL.D., of Parkvale, Penn.

THE Records of a "Presbyterian or rather Congregational" church or society in Westerly, R. I., from 1750 to about 1769, having been temporarily placed in my hands, I have copied the principal parts thereof for publication in the REGISTER.

As all the proceedings were carefully recorded, they most fully illustrate the usages of that day in regard to church affairs. Family covenants made and renewed, written out and signed; written confessions of candidates for membership, and the form of their reception to full communion with the society; petitions for dismission and letters to other churches, are in all cases fully recorded. They are thought to be unique; certainly very curious and interesting,—worthy of being preserved and handed down, if not studied, as evidences of the character and tone of piety among our New-England ancestry.

I shall omit such parts of the record as merely refer to the examination of the trifling difficulties with each other, and the discipline of members; each of whom, by the terms of their covenant, were placed under the watch and guardianship of all the rest.

The original record is written on sheets of foolscap paper, stitched together without binding or cover. Several of the leaves are mutilated and some entirely gone, especially at the commencement and ending. As their pastor lived, died and was buried there, it is presumed that nearly ten years of the latter part of the record is gone.[1]

Some notes on the history of this church and its pastor were published in the *Narraganset Weekly* in 1862. In these notes there is no reference to these records, as they had been taken away by the last surviving son of the pastor, who removed to Searsport, in Maine, in 1788, and their existence was not known outside of his family until 1865. Some extracts from these records formed the basis of an article on "Ancient confessions of faith and family covenants" in the *Congregational Quarterly* for October, 1869.

The Rev. Joseph Park, the pastor of this church and society, was the great-grandson of Richard Park, one of the "founders of New-England." He was born in Newton, Mass., March 12, 1705; graduated at Harvard College in 1724; married Abigail Green 1732, and was sent as a missionary to Rhode Island in 1733.

In the notes on "Westerly Settlers, No. 9," it is said:

"About a hundred years after the settlement of the Plymouth Colony, the Commissioners at Boston, who were appointed by that government to send out and support missionaries among the Indians (*they* were the heathen then), sent Mr. Joseph Park, a Congregational minister, to Westerly, for the purpose of organizing a church of that persuasion, or, if that was not advisable, to preach God's word in its simplicity to the Narragansett tribe of Indians. This occurred in 1733, five years before the division of the town of Westerly. Mr. Park took up his residence near the centre of the town (now in Charlestown, near the boundary line), as being the best location near the tribe for whose benefit he was sent. His house was situated upon a commanding elevation near the road (on the north side), and the meeting-house in which he officiated was not far distant.

"At the time of Mr. Park's arrival, the white inhabitants of the town attended at the Sabbatarian church, but probably that house of worship accommodated but a part of the population; yet, in his account of the religious standing of the people, he must have been grievously mistaken. He says, 'At my arrival, I found a comfortable appearance of humanity and courtesy among the people, but a spirit of profaneness and irreligion awfully prevailed. There was not (as far as I learnt) one house of prayer in two large towns, that contained some hundreds of families, nor any that professed the faith of God's own operations, or the true doctrines of grace."[2]

"But the Indians of the Narragansett tribe were not so easily influenced for good as the Plymouth settlers imagined. Their ancient chieftain, Ninigret, had forbidden Christians dealing with, or preaching to, his people, until the effect of their doctrines was visible on the white people, and his will was so strictly followed, that after a residence of *nine years*, not a solitary Narragansett was a member of Mr. Park's church. Yet at that time he had a respectable congregation of English and natives.

"But after having labored nine years, in the year 1742, 'a great revival sprung up among the English,' and fourteen members were immediately added to his church. This was succeeded by a great inquiry among the

[1] On a tomb-stone, near where the meeting-house stood, is the following inscription, still legible: "In memory of the Rev. Joseph Park, who died March 1st, 1777, in the 72d year of his age, & forty-fifth year of his ministry.—He was a faithful minister of the gospel, a great patriot, a kind husband, a tender parent, a great friend to the widow & fatherless, and an excellent neighbour."

[2] In 1713, Dr. Cotton Mather described Rhode Island as filled with "Antinomians, Familists, Anabaptists, Anti-Sabbatarians, Arminians, Socinians, Quakers, Ranters * * * * so that if a man had lost his Religion, he might find it at this general muster of opinionists."

Indians, many of whom joined his church, and more than a hundred of them, it is said, composed a part of his congregation.

"Now, in those days the magistracy was considered to be an 'awful power,' and it was expected that all men should bow down to its behests without complaint. But Mr. Park, in his stern integrity, supposed the law of God to be superior to that of man, and in one instance in particular, cast himself upon that 'higher law,' when the laws of man were administered in opposition to it—*in his opinion.* A sermon of his is before me, printed in 1761, preceded by a narrative of the cause which led to its publication."

"He says:

"'Some time in the winter of the year 1759, it pleased God to visit the town of Westerly with his sore judgment, the small-pox; brought from New York by some boatmen. The authority pressed the widow Deborah Lambert one to nurse the sick; she was by birth an English woman, had lived several years in the town, and been employed by some of the principal inhabitants, as a school mistress for their children, to good acceptance; and by her industry had something considerable. The persons with whom she assisted to nurse, died; immediately she was ordered by the authority to be cleansed and sent home; which was accordingly done.'

"A maid in the house where she was boarding caught the disease, and a woman who was pressed to take care of her, Ann Chroncher by name, carried it to another family. She being complained of, had nearly perished for want of a place to live — not belonging to the town — but was finally received at Deacon Gavitt's. A terrible clamor was raised against her, and when she appeared in court, no one undertook her defence, until Mr. Park kindly attempted to assist her. During the examination, he was sharply rebuked by the justices for his interference. He took the woman home to his house, until he could succeed in mitigating the sentence passed upon her by the justice. His efforts were of no avail, and he then refused compliance with their judgment as contrary to law."

"In his narrative, he says:

"'As I did privately testify against such things, that they would bring down the heavy judgments of God; I thought it my duty also to give public warning; and accordingly, the next Lord's day, preached the following sermon, Jeremiah, 5 chap., 9 verse—'Shall I not visit for these things? saith the Lord: and shall not my soul be avenged on such a nation as this?'"

"In the sermon he says:

"'I have told you, and it is the truth of God, that nothing short of sincere repentance, faith unfeigned, and new obedience, will help to prevent our ruin; I am sure, if we go on in the course we now generally do, destruction and misery are in our way; I know not a law of God, or a word of his grace, but is broken, despised, and trampled under foot, by one or another; and will God bear long with such things? Surely, no! or, if he does, has he not done it already? and will he always bear with it?'"[1]

From the mutilated leaves at the commencement of the record, it would seem that about 1751, difficulties arose in the church, from what cause cannot be ascertained, but that the feeling was such as to cause one of the deacons and nine others to ask a dismission from their special covenant relation to the church. With this I shall commence the transcript from the record.

[1] In the narrative, dated Sept. 30, 1760, it is said, "This sermon was preached in the Presbyterian Meeting house in Westerly R. I. upon the 24th day of February 1760 by Joseph Park M.A. Minister of the Word of God."

Extracts from Westerly Church Records.

June ye 2, 1751—being Lords day &c after public worship was ended, a number of the brethren of the church offered the following memorial and petition to the church.

May ye 29, 1751 Westerly & Charlestown

To ye Revd Pastor & brethren of y^e
church of Christ in Westerly

Revd Sir & dear brethren

We whose names are hereunto affixed having entered into solemn covenant bonds with you to watch over each other, & by no means to suffer sin upon one another, have had a great sense of ye vows of God upon us, & seeing many of our brethren & some of ye principal of ye flock, neglecting of ye work of God, & (as we apprehend) unmindful of their covenant vows, have from a sincere regard to ye glory of God & the edification of His saints, dealt faithfully with them from time to time. But we have been misunderstood & misrepresented by them all along to our inexpressible grief & discouragement, & there is such darkness between us as gives no hopes of its being ever otherwise, which makes our covenant bonds intolerable. And we not daring to make a schism in ye body of Christ, but desiring to keep ye faith & order of ye gospel, do earnestly desire a peaceable & regular dismission from our Special covenant relation to you, & to be recommended to ye grace of God & to the communion of ye Churches of Christ in Special ordinances, wherever God in His Providence shall call us, or cast our lot, or to be a distinct church, if the Lord should open a door for it.

D^{ea}. Ezekiel Gavitt
Christopher Sugar
Amie Gavitt
Ruth Sugar
Anna York
Hopestill York
Stanton York
Abigail Parke
Jemima York
Lois Ross
Hannah Stanton York

Which petition was read & voted by the church
Test. Joseph Parke clerk

The dismission & recommendation of D^n. Ezekiel Gavit, Stanton York, Christopher Sugar, Abigail Parke, Jemima York, Amie Gavit, Ruth Sugar, Lois Ross, Anna York, Hopestill York & Hannah Stanton York from the Church of Christ in Westerly.

Whereas you & each of you have jointly & severally represented to this Church of Christ, your inexpressible grief and discouragement arising from ye misunderstanding & misrepresentation which there has been of what ye have said & done as you apprehend in a sincere regard to ye glory of God & ye Edification of His saints in ye faithful discharge of your covenant duty towards such as have been unmindful of their covenant vows, & the darkness being so great between you & your brethren as leaves no room for you to hope it will ever be otherwise, which makes your covenant bonds insupportable, and not daring to make a Schism in ye body of Christ, but desiring to keep ye faith & order of ye gospel have desired a peaceable & regular dismission from your special covenant relation to this Church & to be recommended to the grace of God & ye communion of ye Churches of Christ in Special ordinances wherever God in His Providence shall call ye or cast your lot, or to be a distinct Church if the Lord should open a door for it.

I do therefore in the name of the Lord Jesus Christ, the glorious head of the Church, declare you & each of you jointly & severally, to be dismissed from your special covenant relation to this Church, heartily commending of you to the grace of God & our Lord Jesus Christ y[e] great Shepherd of the sheep to watch over & keep you, and likewise recommend you to the special communion of the Churches of Christ where or whenever God in His providence shall give you opportunity, or to have a right as a distinct Church to have the Special ordinances of the Gospel administered to you if God in His Providence should open a door. Amen.

Westerly June y[e] 9th. 1751

Joseph Parke Pastor
of the Church of Christ
in Westerly.

Being dismissed from the Church of Christ in Westerly & the Rev. Mr. Parke being providentially called away to Southold on Long Island, & there being no public worship of God in this place, Mr. Parke gave us his advice to assemble together at his house on Lord's days for y[e] social worship of God, which we did & joined in prayer to God & reading His word & books of piety & singing His praises & contributed for pious uses as God had prospered us. But thinking it to be our duty, considering the devil's incessant endeavours to divide & Scatter y[e] faithful followers of Jesus Christ to come under more particular & explicit bonds to each other. We therefore unitedly come unto the y[e] following declaration & renewal of covenant.

" Westerly & Charlestown July y[e] 14th 1751

" We the Subscribers being dismissed from our Special covenant relation to the Presbyterian or rather Congregational Church of Christ in Westerly and recommended to the grace of God and the communion of the churches of Christ in special ordinances or to be a distinct church if the Lord should open a door for it, do still firmly adhere to the covenant entered into by them at their embodying into church fellowship and as renewed Nov[r] the 24th, 1745, as a clear gospel covenant excepting the last clause relating to the Indians which we judge not particularly binding to us.

"We likewise highly approve of and heartily subscribe to the two articles annexed to that covenant, Jan[y] the 6th, 1751. And we do this day solemnly promise before God, angels and one another to keep these covenant vows so far as our present circumstances will admit, carefully and tenderly watching over one another, not forsaking the assembling of ourselves together as the manner of some is (but avoiding the communion of such as make light of or break their covenant vows), diligently improving what means of grace we can have and so continue waiting upon God to establish complete gospel ordinances to us if it be his holy pleasure. This we promise only in the strength of the Lord Jesus Christ, our alone righteousness and strength. Amen.

"N.B. That the Rev. Mr. Parke having given us liberty and an invitation to meet at his house to accommodate his family, we agree to meet at his house every Lord's Day to worship God, except when we have an opportunity to hear the word preached in the house of God.

"D[n]. Ezekiel Gavit, Stanton York, Christopher Sugar, Abigail Park, Amie Gavit, Jemima York, Ruth Sugar, Anna York, Hopestill York, Hannah Stanton York.

(To be continued.)

THE GREAT SEAL OF THE COMMONWEALTH OF VIRGINIA.

We are indebted to the Hon. Thomas H. Wynne, of Richmond, Va., for a copy of the following valuable and very interesting article, which under the above title was contributed by Sherwin McRae, Esq., to the December number (1871) of the *Old Dominion Magazine*, and for the author's permission to reprint the article. In the April number of the Register (page 102), we stated that a bill had passed the legislature of Virginia re-establishing the ancient seal, in place of the mongrel seal which was put in use in 1866. In this we were in error. The bill passed one branch of the legislature, but was not reached in the other before the assembly adjourned. [Editor.]

The Great Seal of the Commonwealth of Virginia is interesting not only in its historical, but also in its legal aspect. As the emblem of sovereignty and the evidence of high political functions, it is an important instrument of state.

Thus its character and authenticity are matters of the gravest import. That its character should be worthy of the state which it represents, the convention of 1776 entrusted to a committee of its most distinguished members the work of preparing a proper device for this important instrument. In pursuance of this direction, the illustrious George Mason, on the 5th day of July, 1776, reported the following device, which was immediately adopted and directed to be engraved on the great seal of the Commonwealth: Virtus, the Genius of the Commonwealth, dressed like an Amazon, resting on a spear with one hand, and holding a sword in the other, and treading on Tyranny, represented by a Man prostrate, a Crown fallen from his head, a broken Chain in his left hand, and a Scourge in his right.

In the exergon the word *Virginia* over the head of *Virtus*, and underneath the words *Sic Semper Tyrannis.* On the reverse a group, Libertas with her wand and pileus. On one side of her, Ceres with the cornucopia in one hand, and an ear of wheat in the other. On the other side Æternitas, with the globe and phœnix. In the exergon these words: *Deus nobis hæc otia fecit.*

George Wythe and John Page, Esquires, were requested to superintend the engraving of the said seal, and *take care* that the same be properly executed.

At a session of the General Assembly, which commenced on the 4th day of October, 1779, the Governor was required to provide a great seal for the Commonwealth, and to procure the same to be *engraved* either in America or Europe, with the same device as was directed by the resolution of the convention in the year 1776, save only that the motto on the reverse be changed to the word *Perseverando.* The General Assembly further enacted that the seal which had already been provided by virtue of the said resolution of the convention be henceforth called the lesser seal of the Commonwealth. This lesser seal is similar to the obverse side of the great seal, save that its dimensions are smaller. The great seal is the instrument of attestation, impressed on official papers to be used beyond the limits of the State, the lesser seal in cases purely domestic. During the gubernatorial service of Governor Pierpoint, new seals were introduced, and are used at the present time, and are similar to the old, except that the words "Liberty and Union" are added to the new seals.

On the 28th day of February, 1866, the General Assembly enacted "that the great seal and the lesser seal now under the care of the Secretary of the Commonwealth, as the keeper of the seals, are and shall continue to be the seals of the Commonwealth." At the time of this enactment the old or original seals were not only in existence, but also in the executive care. No direction or authority is given to destroy them, nor is there on them any mark indicating their *disuse* and repudiation. Nor is there any description of the new seals so as to identify them as the seals in use on the 28th day of February, 1866. The identity and authenticity of the great seal should be placed beyond the pale of doubt and question.

The convention of 1776 described the original great seal, and prescribed its devices and mottoes with absolute exactness. The slightest departure from this description denotes the counterfeit. Any change in the seal should be marked by the same exactness which distinguished the originals. Two seals of State cannot exist at the same time as rivals. Nor can a seal once established be destroyed by implication. The evidence of its destruction, whether physical or constructive, must be unequivocal. The history of the great seal of England illustrates the truth of the foregoing propositions.

When Charles I. was besieged in Oxford with the great seal in his possession, Cromwell's Parliament ordered one to be made resembling it in every particular. Charles denounced this new seal as a counterfeit, and its use as treason; and the Parliament prohibited the use of the seal which was in the possession of Charles under heavy penalties. Thus there was no authoritative seal which could be *safely* used in England until the 11th day of August, 1646, when the great seal was captured at Oxford, and formally brought into Parliament, and in the presence of both houses, broken with great solemnity. The Parliament seal was now supreme, but it bore on its face the effigy of King Charles, which was regarded as a perpetual reproach to the new Commonwealth. Whereupon, on the 9th of January, 1649, this memorable body ordered a new seal to be made, having on "one side the map of England, Ireland, Jersey, and Guernsey, and on the other side a representation of the House of Commons sitting, the speaker in the chair, with the inscription: the first year of freedom, 1648;" and on the 7th day of February, 1649, the old great seal was brought into parliament (House of Commons), and broken by a smith, and the fragments and purse given to the Commissioners, and an ordinance passed legalizing the use of the new seal, and making it treason to counterfeit it. These ceremonies are suggestive not only of the dignity and representative character of a great seal, but also of the *necessity* of preserving its authenticity free from question.

The great seal of a Commonwealth is not only the symbol of sovereignty, and amongst the most valuable and enduring of the treasures of history, but should be a faithful reflex of some grand idea, action or quality, and an expositor of the science, literature, and art of its period. It is the multum in parvo, making the heaviest exaction on *learning* and *wisdom*, and in great emergencies, he only can supply the demand who has at his command the fulness of their treasures. The great seal of the Commonwealth of Virginia is not the least of the monuments on which the fame of George Mason rests.[1] The conception and adoption of its device and mot-

[1] In the ascription of the honor of preparing the Great Seal of Virginia to Geo. Mason, I have supposed myself justified by the journal of the Convention of 1776, and have had neither design nor wish to deprive Mr. Wythe or any other member of the committee of

toes attest the grandeur of his intellect, the fertility and extent of his literary resources, and his wonderful skill in their use. The rules which control devices and mottoes are plain. The difficulty exists in their application. The chief of these rules is, that there shall be harmony among all the members of the device, and between the entire device and the motto. Next that the motto shall be expressed in a *fixed* language with the utmost brevity consistent with appropriateness, or in every case in a single language. The practice of this art is one of the highest achievements of the great man and scholar. The eagle with his clutched bundle of arrows, his olive branch, his scroll, and his scintillating stars (a device so significant and suggestive), is accompanied by the brief motto: *E Pluribus Unum.*

The genius of the Commonwealth, resting on a spear with one hand and holding a sword in the other, and treading on a prostrate tyrant, a crown fallen from his head, a broken chain in his left hand, and a scourge in his right, is a grand conception and volume of thought, yet the motto consists of but three words: *Sic Semper Tyrannis.*

A single *additional* word would impair. The best English word in the vocabulary, by its incongruity, would spoil. The thirteen stars, the thirteen arrows, the escutcheon on the breast of the eagle, and the scroll in his mouth, with the impartial motto *E Pluribus Unum*, inscribed on the seal of the United States, represent our relation to the Union and our estimate of its value. A commingling of the devices and mottoes of the two seals would be as incongruous as blending the constitutions of the two governments.

Between the seal of the United States and the seal of Virginia[1] there is a distinct line of separation, and yet a beautiful harmony. No one has been bold enough to propose any alteration of the former. Wisdom suggested equal forbearance as to the latter.

The unanimous verdict of enlightened criticism pronounces the devices and mottoes of the Great Seal reported by George Mason as an achievement, combining grandeur of conception, appropriateness of device and motto, and the beauties of literature and art, equalling if not surpassing any similar work extant. The justness of this verdict is vindicated in the fact that each of the changes made in the device and mottoes ordered by the convention of 1776, violate some of the principles and rules heretofore stated. The word *Perseverando*, substituted in 1779 for the words *Deus Nobis hæc Otia fecit*, is not in harmony with the device which it illustrates, while the latter words are so felicitous as to show that the person who used them added the largest learning to the most discriminating judgment. The least that can be said is that the word *Perseverando* is less appropriate than the words displaced. The words Liberty and Union recently introduced are in violation of all the cardinal rules which apply to the subject of devices and mottoes. There is not only a want of correspondence between the device on either side of the seal and these words, but they are used on both sides of the seal, commingling a living and changing language with a *dead* and *fixed* one, and presenting the patent incongruity of applying the same motto to dissimilar devices. They also make an unsuccessful effort to express a sentiment, beautifully and appropriately expressed, in the seal of the United States—a seal which will bear no rival in its appropriate sphere,

their proper share of that honor. Nor do I consider that the mind of Mason was less imbued with the grand conceptions which the occasions demanded, nor his learning and judgment less utilized because the design was not his own. In the application of the design to the purposes of the seal, the mind passes through the same processes as in its conception. The seal is none the less interesting if ascribed to Mr. Wythe, or Mason and Wythe jointly, or even the entire committee.

and to the creation of which Virginia contributed as much if not more than any of her sister states.

The obverse of this noble seal is inscribed all over with the sentiment of Liberty and Union. The paleway, the star, and arrow of Virginia are her special instrumentalities in the expression of this sentiment. Its repetition in an improper place is obnoxious to just criticism. The great seal of Virginia is one of the historic facts which will contribute much to fix her place in the scale of civilization. Its *excellence*, therefore, is a matter of public concern.

Should legislation on this subject be deemed necessary, no more fit opportunity can occur for the adoption of the seal ordered by the Convention of 1776—in a word, the devices and mottoes reported by George Mason. In view of the existence of two great seals and lesser seals in the Executive Department of the Government, the law should describe the size, devices and mottoes of the adopted seal, with the *utmost particularity*, and cause the destruction or disuse of the rival seal in such a manner as to obviate the possibility of its future use.

NOTES AND QUERIES.

Reyner.—Baylies's *New Plymouth* says (vol. ii. p. 65), that Capt. Southworth married "his cousin Elizabeth Reyner, daughter of Rev. John Reyner." Plymouth Colony Records give the date, viz., Sept. 1, 1641, but do *not* give her parentage. Mr. Whitmore, in his invaluable notes, Register, vol. xi. etc., evidently considers the "cousin"-ship imaginary.

What is the proof that this Elizabeth Reyner was the daughter of Rev. John? Is it anything more than an inference from the fact that Rev. John was then pastor there?

On the other hand,—Rev. John Reyner graduated at Emanuel in 1625. If he had a daughter marriageable in 1641, she must have been born before he left college, which is hardly probable.

Further, she must have been a daughter by his first wife, for he married his second wife in Boston, and necessarily after 1635. He made his will April 19, 1669 (dying, Hull says, April 20, not 19th as repeatedly printed). In his will he makes two groups of children. First group,—Jachin, and "Hannah Lane, wife of Job Lane; who we know were children by his first wife, by whom he had the use of some property in England, and to whom the will alludes as "their mother." Second group,—John, and "my daughters Elizabeth, Dorothy, Abigail, and Judith." These five he classes together, alludes to his confidence in his then wife's "care of, and motherly affection to her children," puts most of his estate in this wife's hands, but makes the five equal legatees eventually. With this grouping, Mr. Whitmore's papers agree.

Rev. John had, therefore, a daughter Elizabeth living in 1669, to whom he gives no married name. Further, in his will he says: "if any of my four children yet unmarried shall, by God's providence, be so disposed as to enter upon marriage," etc. (I think this "four" should read "five," as the same error occurs in another part, where he mentions *five* names, and it is an error for want of proof-reading.) Evidently none of those daughters were married at the date of the will. Further, he implies that some of them, at least, were under age; giving them power to dispose of rights when of age.

It is barely possible that Rev. John had a daughter born early enough to marry in 1641. If he had, and if she died soon after marriage, there was time enough to have another Elizabeth. But, if so, she was born before he left college; she married nineteen years before either her brother or sister by the same mother; and she left a child living when Rev. John made his will, to whom he makes no allusion whatever.

I think we must look elsewhere for the parentage of Elizabeth Reyner who married Thomas Southworth. In the Register, vol. xi. p. 238, it is said that "Judith no doubt married Rev. Jabez Fox, of Woburn, and, 2d, Col. Jona. Tyng, and d. 5 June, 1736, aged 98." If this age is correct, she was born in 1638. If so, she should have been, probably, one of the first wife's children, instead of the last named of the second wife's, and under age in 1669. She would have been forty years old when her first child was born, and fifty-two at the birth of her last. Savage makes her to be a daughter of the second Rev. John Reyner; but as he was born in 1643, it is hardly probable that he had a daughter marriageable in 1671, whose mother was born in 1655, and who (the daughter) was born in 1636! It is more likely that the age "98" is purely imaginary. Besides, the second John had no children.

Can anybody unravel these several entanglements?

The following facts seem to be settled. Rev. John Reyner was born at Gildersome, parish of Batley, co. York (when?); graduated at Emanuel in 1625; married (1), —— Boys, and (2), before 1642, Frances Clarke, of Boston, Mass.; came to this country about 1635, and settled as pastor in Plymouth in 1636, where he remained until November, 1654; spent the following winter in Boston; was settled as pastor over the church in Dover, N. H., in 1655, and died there, still in pastoral office, April 20, 1669.

He had children: by first wife,—Jachin, of Rowley; and Hannah, m. Job Lane. By second wife,—(Rev.) John, born 1643; Elizabeth; Dorothy; Abigail; and Judith. All these were living in 1669. He had also, by second wife, Joseph, born Aug. 15, 1650, died Nov. 23, 1652; and one of the above daughters (name lost) was born Dec. 26, 1647.

Of these children:

Jachin married, Nov. 12, 1662, Elizabeth Denison, who died July 8, 1708, having had: Edward, born July 6, 1671; Jachin, born Jan. 31, 1673–4; Anna, born July 22, 1678; and Jachin, born Jan. 20, 1681–2. (I believe these statements are correct, though they differ from Savage.)

Hannah married, September, 1660, Job Lane, of Billerica, for whom see REGISTER, vols. xi. and xii.

John, H. C. 1663, is said to have been in feeble health. He was assistant to his father, at Dover, for some years before the decease of the latter. Soon after his father's death, he was invited, July 22, 1669, to officiate for one year. He did so, and evidently continued, but was not ordained until July 12, 1671. Fitch says "he possessed a double portion of his father's spirit." He died in office, Dec. 21, 1676. Some say he died at Braintree (where he married); Hull (a connection) says: "Mr. John Rayner, minister of Dover, died of a cold and fever that he took in the field among the soldiers." The time was that of the expedition of Capts. Syll and Hathorne, with soldiers from Major Waldron's command, eastward from Dover. Evidently he accompanied the Dover soldiers. Whether in his sickness he went to Braintree, I cannot find satisfactory authority. His wife was Judith, daughter of the second Edmund Quincy, of Braintree. She was born 25 4 mo., 1655. Her tomb-stone in Quincy says: "Judith Reyner, Daughter to Edmund and Joanna Quincy, Relic of the Reverend John Reyner, late Minister of Dover, aged 23 years." His mother administered upon his estate.

Whether the four daughters of the first Rev. John ever married, is still left to investigation, saving what is said of Judith. A. H. QUINT.

New-Bedford, May, 1872.

LOTHROP—LAYTHROPE.—Were Mark Lothrop (sometimes spelled Marke Laythrope) of Salem in 1636, and afterward of Duxbury and Bridgewater, Rev. John of Scituate, and Thomas of Beverly, connected by blood relationship? From what places in England did Mark and Thomas come, and in what vessels? Were the remains of Capt. Thomas, killed by the Indians in Deerfield, recognized and buried either there or in Beverly? D. W. LOTHROP.

ATKINSON ACADEMY—ENOCH HALE.—(REGISTER, *ante*, p. 125). In Mr. Todd's article on Atkinson Academy, Enoch Hale, a principal of that academy, is said to have been "not a college graduate." This is an error. Mr. Hale was a native of Alstead, a brother of the late David Hale of Newport, and of the late Salma Hale of Keene. He graduated at the University of Vermont in 1826,—taught in New-London, Alstead and Atkinson, and died in the latter place Nov. 16, 1830. He took orders in the Episcopal church shortly before his death.

This correction is the more desirable as Mr. Hale appears in Mr. Todd's article as the only principal of the Academy, during its long existence, not having a full collegiate education. ROBERT S. HALE.

Elizabethtown, N. Y.

CONN. TROOPS IN 1775.—List of names appearing on the pay-roll of the 9th company in the 8th regiment of Connecticut troops, Abraham Tyler Capt., for the service of 1775:—

Capt. Abraham Tyler, Lieut. Timothy Percivil, Lieut. Solomon Orcut, Ensign Aaron Hale, Serg't Cornelius Higgins, Serg't Elias Lay, Serg't Henry Walbridge, Serg't Joseph Markham, Clerk William Smith, Corporal Aaron Thomas, Corporal John Johnson, Corporal Elisha Benton, Corporal Samuel Hurlbut, Drummer George Bush, Drummer Joseph Daley, Fifer Nathaniel Montgomery, Fifer Ebenezer Rowley, Stephen Ackley, Jehial Arnold, John Arnold, John Attwood, William Bevin, Thomas Brown, Aaron Brainerd, Aseph Brainerd (died Dec. 3d, 1775), Jacob Bailey, Gideon Bailey, Robert Bailey, John Bailey, Joel Burbank, Jeptha Brainerd, Joseph Crook, Joseph Caswell, Nathaniel Cook, Robert Clark, Abel Crandel, Elisha Culver, Josiah Coben, Thomas Daniels, Jabez Dilano, Jonathan Dilano, Abijah Fuller, Gideon Goff, Hezekiah Goff, Nathaniel Garnsey, Epephas Gear.

ENGLISH EXPEDITIONS, 1739–59.—The following table is found in the volume containing Daniel Lane's Journal (*ante*, pp. 236–43), and is in his handwriting

EXPEDITIONS taken in hand, against our Enemies & their Success

Year when.	Who commanded.	Against what place.	What success.
1739	S^{r}. John Norris	Expedition against Ferrol	Miscarried
40	Adm^{l}. Anson	d^{o}. To the South Seas	do.
41	Genl. Wentworth	d^{o}. Agst. Carthagena (Loss of ye Genl)	do.
46	Genl. Sinclair	d^{o}. against Canada	do.
ibid	Adm^{l}. Lestock	do. against Port L'Orient	do.
47	Adm^{l}. Boscawen	do. to the East Indies	do.
1755	Genl. Braddock	do. agst. Fort du Quesne	do.
56	d^{o}.	do. to the Relief of Oswego	do.
1757	Genl. Mordaunt & Adm^{l}. Knowles	Against Rochfort	Miscarried
1758	Genl. Amherst & Adm^{l}. Boscawen	do. Louisbourg	Succeeded
ibid	Comm^{de}. Marsh & Major Mason	do. Senegal	Ditto
ibid	Col: Bradstreet	do. Fort Frontenac	do.
ibid	Genl. Forbes	do. Fort du Quesne	do.
ibid	Comm^{de}. Kepple	do. Island of Goree	do.
ibid	G^{l}: Abercrombie	do. Ticonderoga	Miscarried
1759	Wolf	do. Quebec	Succeeded
	Amherst	do. Montreal	do.
		do. Bellisle	do.
	Kepple & L^{d}. Albemarle	do. Havannah	do.
	Monckton	do. Martinico	do.
		Do. Niagara, Crown Point &c	do.
		Newfoundland regained	do.
	Elliot	Thurot destroy'd & himself Killed	do.

CARVER.—John Carver, the first governor of Plymouth colony, and Robert Carver of Duxbury, who lived 1594–1680, were brothers, if we accept a tradition resting upon direct and credible testimony. Miss Marcia A. Thomas, the scrupulous and cautious antiquary of Marshfield, had it from Joshua Carver, 1732–1826, son of William Carver, 1659–1760, who lived 21 years with his grandfather Robert, 1594–1680: so that Miss Thomas's information was but one move from the lips of Robert himself. They all lived on the old homestead from 1649 to date. This is well worthy of note in a search for the lineage of Governor Carver. J. W. THORNTON.

BELL TAVERN,—DANVERS, MASS. (N. and Q. *ante*, p. 84).—A portion of the Bell Tavern is now standing, about a mile from its original site.

In Hanson's *History of Danvers*, pp. 167 to 171, inclusive, is an article in reference to this house, and on p. 170 is a wood-cut showing its appearance before it was moved; p. 206 also affords some information as to the same house, which then stood at the corner of Main and Washington streets, South Danvers, now Peabody.

Peabody, Mass., 1872. J. WARREN UPTON.

WIN-NI-PE-SOC-EE.—A word upon the orthography of our title.

It is said there are forty and one ways to spell the name of the lake which forms so important and beautiful a feature in the scenery of New-Hampshire.

Mr. Farmer, in his edition of Belknap's *History of New-Hampshire*, gives eighteen of the different forms which came under his observation and which probably exhibit the most important variations.

They are as follows:

Seven Syllables.—Winnepisseockegee.

Six Syllables.—Wenapesioche; Winnepasiake; Winnapissiaukee; Winnepissiaukee; Winnepiseaukee; Winnapuseakit; Winnipisioke; Wennepisseoka; Winnipisseoca; Winnipisiakit; Winnipisiackit; Winnepessioke.

Five Syllables.—Winnopisseag; Winnepissocay; Winnipesocket; Winnipeshoky; Winnipisinket.

Of these, it will be seen that one has seven syllables, twelve have six, and five have five syllables. Among them all, there is not the form that, for two generations, has afflicted the world, to wit: Winnipisseogee. And what could have induced the adoption of that form, it is now difficult to conceive.

But common usage in the vicinity of the lake has long since irrevocably decided that the name consists of five, instead of six or seven syllables, and it has been an improvement to adopt the form which has of late partially prevailed, to wit: Winnipesaukay, but this has an ungainly look and sound, ill adapted to the beautiful object to which it is attached, as well as an un-Indian appearance. The authority for its correctness is also questionable, it being derived from Hutchinson, an early historian of Massachusetts, and from Trumbull, the historian of Connecticut. They are the 4th, 5th and 6th above given.

The 16th is on the authority of one who was a captive to the Indians, who would be as likely to be correct as any other; but the prevailing forms have a vowel termination, and, by changing the *t* into *e* in the final syllable of the 16th, and dropping the *k* in the penult, as surplusage, we have: Winnipesocee, which has the ring of the true Indian sound and the virtue of compliance with common usage as well as good authority for its adoption.—*Suncook Valley* [N. H.] *Times*, Oct. 15, 1868.

REV. DANIEL WILKINS, of Amherst, N. H.—Strolling in the old burying-ground, in Amherst, N. H., I copied the following inscription on a massive slate stone erected over the grave of the first minister, and as it contains some facts relative to the early history of the town, I send it for your use:

ECCE ADDISCE VIVERE.

Erected by the town of Amherst, To the memory of the Reverend Daniel Wilkins who departed this life Feby ye 11th 1783 in the 73d year of his age: & 42d of his ministry.

He was a gentleman of good natural & aquired Abilities. He received the honors of ye University at Cambridge in 1736. & was separated to ye work of ye Ministry in 1741; at which time his church consisted of only five male members & his charge of fourteen families.

As a minister he was laborious, his public discources were liberal & sentimental, pathetic solemn & persuasive. He was endowed with a Venerable presence, a commanding Voice, & an emphatical delivery. He had a tender feeling for his charge & was a partner with them in all their joys & sorrows: his conversation among them was enlightening edifying & comforting. He was an example of patience & Meekness and always endeavored to promote peace.

His natural temper was remarkably sweet & pleasant. He had a high relish for ye refined pleasure of friendship. his behaviour was not cerimonious but grave yet sprightly & agreeable. In a word he was a faithful Minister a devout Christian a good companion a tender husband & an indulgent parent.

"The sweet remembrance of the just
Shall flourish when he sleeps in dust."

Mr. Wilkins was a native of Middleton, Essex county, Mass., and some of his descendants still reside here. In this cemetery under a large mountain repose the remains of the following named well-known and revered citizens: Robert Means, died 1823, aged eighty years; Joshua Atherton, aged seventy-six; Charles H. Atherton, died 1853, aged seventy-nine years; Matthias Spaulding, M.D., died 1862, aged eighty-four years.—Cor. of *Transcript*, Aug. 22, 1871.

LONGEVITY, REMARKABLE INSTANCES OF, IN MENDON, MASS.—The following most remarkable instance of longevity occurred in a family of eleven children, the last and youngest of whom (the father of your correspondent) died at Peterboro', N. H., Feb. 10, 1871. They were the children of William and Sarah (Locke) Clark, of Townsend, Mass. Their father, Wm. C., was the son of William and Eunice (Taylor) Clark, of Concord and Townsend, who was the son of Samuel and Rachel (Nichols?) Clark, who were of Concord about 1680. Tradition says this Samuel C. came from England, when about 12 years old, with his father Joseph. Where Joseph settled we have been unable to ascertain. Samuel, of Concord, died at an advanced age, Jan. 30, 1729-30; his wife having died Oct. 19, 1722.

Children of Wm. and Sarah Clark:—

			yrs.	mos.	days.
Sarah,	died	aged	74	0	28
Mary,	"	"	78	2	2
William,	"	"	91	10	15
Elizabeth,	"	"	87	3	5
Martha,	"	"	89	3	20
Rebecca,	"	"	102	1	23
Abigail,	"	"	93	0	19
Lydia,	"	"	96	4	18
Samuel,	"	"	88	6	2
James,	"	"	77	5	23
Jonas,	"	"	95	8	7
Total ages			973	11	12
Average age			88	6	14+
Total ages of the six eldest			568	5	12
Average age " " "			94	8	27

If any one can show an instance of greater length of years, in a single family, I should be glad to have it put on record.

I have collected a large amount of material for a history of the descendants of Samuel and Rachel Clark, which I shall be happy to publish whenever sufficient encouragement to do so is offered. G. F. CLARK.

Mendon, August, 1871.

MARSHALL (N. and Q. *ante*, pp. 74, 83 and 200).—Thomas Marshall, of Boston, with others in 1637, was disarmed for his opinions.—*Mass. Colony Records.*

Nov. 16. 1637. He was by the general Court disfranchised for signing a petition, etc.—*Mass. Colony Records.*

Thomas Marshall was settled at Linn Village, afterwards Reading; and was selectman there 1647-'52, '54.

Case of Brown vs. Laughton, 1681. Bound Scrap books of *Court Records*, Salem, Mass.

Thomas Marshall makes affidavit, aged 66 etc. 1681. Hence born 1615. I think this case was of Reading (part now Wakefield), or of Lynnfield.

"12 : 3 : 1663." Joan Marshall having spoken some offensive words against sister Bancroft—(Elizabeth (Metcalf) Bancroft)—and they dealing to give them satisfaction. She staying at ye Lord's Supper two of the brethren rising up and attested that she had not attended to give satisfaction, she was required to forbear communion with us at that time, she gave some offensive words before she went out, but God helped her to come upp to ye rule & to make acknowledgement before the church and was again received into our hearts."—*Reading Church Records*, now in possession of Rev. Mr. Bliss, of Wakefield, Mass. (same church).

Reading Town Records are in Reading, W. J. Wightman, representative and town clerk. JOHN M. BANCROFT.

New-York, P. O. Box 382.

AVERY (N. and Q. *ante*, p. 197).—The 2d Ebenezer Avery there mentioned, married, June 11, 1761, Phebe Denison, dau. of Daniel Denison. She was b. June 22, 1741. She subsequently m. Jona. Fish, and d. Dec. 22, 1818.

Mary E. Avery, a grand-daughter of the same Ebenezer, m. Nathan F. Denison, Dec. 25, 1823. LEDYARD BILL.

INSCRIPTIONS FROM THE OLD GRAVE-YARD IN BRADFORD, MASS.—[First minister of the Congregational Church, as follows:]

"Conditum hic corpus viri vere reverendi, *D. Zachariæ Symmes*, Collegii Harudini quondam socii, Evangelii ministri, patre avoque præclaris evangelii ministris nati, omnigena eruditione ornati, pietate vitæque sanctitate maxime conspicui, ecclesiæ Christi quæ est Bradfordiæ per XL annos pastoris vigilantissimi, qui commutavit vitam mortalem cum immortali, die XXII Martii anno Domini MDCCVII ætate suæ LXXI."

[Third minister, as follows:]

"Rev. Joseph Parsons A.M., son of Rev. Joseph of Salisbury; graduated 1720, ordained 1726. He preached the Artillery Election sermon, 1744, and the Governor's Election sermon 1759. Died May 1, 1765, in the 63d year of his age, and the 39th of his ministry."

"Hon. Nathaniel Thurston died at Lansingburg, N. Y. Oct. 21, 1811, æ 56.

"For many years he was a member of the Legislature, was distinguished for his benevolence and greatly lamented by his friends."

[His seventh wife survived him as his widow,—a fact well known in Bradford,—and his six former wives are buried at the left of his grave, with inscriptions, as follow:]

(1.) "Memento mori.

"Here lies interred the remains of Mrs. Betsey Thurston, the Consort of Capt. Nathaniel Thurston, who departed this life the 25th of November A.D. 1790, æ 34."

(2.) "Mrs. Martha Thurston, consort of Nathaniel Thurston Esq.; died May 12, 1799, æ 32."

(3.) "Mrs. Huldah Thurston, consort of Nathaniel Thurston Esq., died Sept. 8, 1801, æ 24."

(4.) "Mrs. Clarissa Thurston consort of Nathaniel Thurston Esq. died Nov. 14, 1803 æ 36."

(5.) "Mrs. Martha B. Thurston consort of Nathaniel Thurston Esq; died July 27, 1804, æ 25."

(6.) "Mrs. Mary Thurston, consort of Hon. Nathaniel Thurston, died Mar. 3, 1808, æ 27."

I certify to the *verbatim et literatim* correctness of all the above inscriptions.

Sanbornton, N. H. MOSES T. RUNNELS.

CHURCH AND STATE.—In a Thursday lecture on Rev. xiii. 2, in the winter of 1639–40, Mr. Cotton said: "It was a matter in question here not long agoe, whether the court should not take a course to punish such persons as stood Excommunicate, out of the Church, if they should stand long Excommunicate, but it was a good providence of God, that such thing was prevented: Let not any court *Ipso facto*, take things from the church: If such a Law were made (the Fathers live not forever;) and if such a Law were once Established, that a church-member standing so long Excommunicated, the commonwealth should then proceed against him; were this Established, it would make a Beast of the church * * * * But I say it is a great liberty to be freed from this great beast, that he hath no finger amongst us, we are out of his paw, and out of his smell, here in New-England." What was the instance "in question here not long agoe," to which Mr. Cotton referred? J. W. THORNTON.

PERHAM—PERRUM—PERRIN.—In Savage's *Genealogical Dictionary* the names of John and Abraham "Perham" or "Perrum" and John and Abraham "Perrin" are given as belonging to early residents of Rehoboth. I am satisfied that here is a confusion of names, and that only one set of the above named persons ever lived in that ancient town. Misled by Savage, I recently employed the clerk of Rehoboth to copy for me from the town records, everything relating to the Perham or Perrum family. In response I received the genealogy of Abraham and John *Perrin*. On further communication with the clerk, he informed me that "Perrin" was sometimes called Parum in the old records, and that the families referred to in Savage's *Dictionary* are identical and that the name is now spelled Perrin. If this be so, it becomes evident that John Perham of Chelmsford, 1665, is the common ancestor of all the Perhams in America. If my conclusions are wrong, I should be very glad to be corrected.

Augusta, Me., March, 1872. W. B. LAPHAM.

MARTHA COREY, OF SALEM VILLAGE.—The following extracts from the journal of the Massachusetts house of representatives, will be found to add to our knowledge of the personal history of one of the victims of the witchcraft delusion. It appears that Martha Corey, of whose life previous to 1692 but little is known, was a widow when she married Giles Corey. Obadiah Rich, of Salem, who married Bethia Williams, July 6, 1662, may have been of the family of her husband.

June 27, 1723. "A Petition of *Thomas Rich* of *Salem*, only Surviving Child of *Martha Corey*, alias *Martha Rich* late of *Salem* deceased, praying the Compassionate Consideration and Commisseration of this Court for the great Losses the Petitioner met with in the Year 1692, for the Reasons in said Petition at large Enumerated, &c. Read, and Committed to the Committee for Petitions

And *Ordered*, That Capt. *Epes* be added to the Committee for the Consideration of this Petition."

June 29, 1723. "On the Petition of *Thomas Rich*, The Committee Reported, That in Consideration of the Loss the Petitioner might sustain by being deprived of the Goods mentioned in the Petition together with the many Illegal Actions of the Sheriff and his Officers respecting the Persons charged as Witches, They are humbly of Opinion That the Sum of £50 be allowed and paid out of the Publick Treasury to the Petitioner *Thomas Rich*, in full Recompence of what Damage might accrue to him thereby.

Read and Accepted. And accordingly, *Resolved*, That the sum of *Fifty Pounds* be allowed and paid out of the Publick Treasury to the Petitioner *Thomas Rich*, in full satisfaction for the Losses he may have sustained as at large set forth in the Petition.

Sent up for Concurrence."

Malden, Mass. D. P. COREY.

MILES.—Elder John Miles was settled over a Baptist church in Rehoboth, in 1663. He went to England, and on his return to America in 1665, he was accompanied by a colony. Can any of the readers of the REGISTER give any information in regard to those who came over with Elder John Miles in 1665? H. J. MARTIN.

Washington, D. C., May, 1872.

NEW-ENGLAND HISTORIC, GENEALOGICAL SOCIETY.

NECROLOGY.

Prepared by Rev. DORUS CLARKE, D.D., Historiographer.

HON. OLIVER BLISS MORRIS. Oliver Bliss Morris, of Springfield, Mass., who was elected a corresponding member of the Society January, 1846, was born in South Wilbraham, Mass., Sept. 22, 1782, and died in Springfield, April 9, 1871, at the age of 88 years. At the time of his death, Judge Morris was the oldest inhabitant of Springfield, and the oldest alumnus of Williams College. His father was Edward Morris, of South Wilbraham, a soldier in the revolutionary war, and his mother was the daughter of John Bliss, of Wilbraham, who was an officer in the Massachusetts militia, which served at White Plains, and after the war was a county judge and a representative to the general court. Judge Morris prepared for college with his pastor, the Rev. Moses Warren, of the Orthodox Congregational Church in South Wilbraham, and at the early age of fifteen he entered Williams College, where he was graduated with distinction in 1801. Upon his graduation, he commenced the study of the law at Springfield, in the office of the Hon. George Bliss, at that time and for many years afterward one of the leading lawyers in Western Massachusetts. During his studies he boarded in the family of Mr. Bliss, and in 1813, nine years after he entered upon the practice of the law in Springfield, he married his daughter, Miss Caroline Bliss. In 1813 also, and very soon after the division of the old county of Hampshire, into the three counties of Hampshire, Franklin and Hampden, he was appointed register of probate for the county of Hampden, the Hon. John Hooker being the judge of probate for that county. Mr. Morris held that office until 1829, when, upon the demise of Judge Hooker, he was appointed the judge of that court, and he continued to hold that office till the court itself was reconstructed into its present form in 1858. From 1820 to 1832, he also held the office of prosecuting attorney for the county. During the years 1809, 1810, 1811 and 1813, Judge Morris represented the town of Springfield in the legislature, and he was also a member of the state convention which in 1820 revised the constitution of the commonwealth.

For more than half a century, Judge Morris bore a very prominent share in the public life of Springfield, and the offices he held so long were such as were bestowed upon ability and merit, rather than upon mere partisanship. His long continuance in various public offices, and his repeated re-election to the legislature, were not only proofs of his general ability, but also his continued and growing power in the community.

Judge Morris was a man of deep and positive convictions. Originally, he was a federalist in politics, afterward a whig, and finally he became a republican, though he was never fully reconciled to the destruction of the whig party. In the great political gatherings in Hampshire county, he was an influential leader, and few speakers were welcomed and carried greater weight than he. In the town meetings, too, Judge Morris took a prominent part, and on the important questions of appropriation of moneys, of schools, of bridge-building and road-making, and of the numerous *et ceteras* of the large and flourishing town and city of his residence; and few questions were passed upon, till the citizens had listened to his earnest advocacy or his emphatic remonstrance. He was always in earnest, and that is an element of great power. His earnestness was enforced by a good voice and commanding presence, and a full vocabulary. At the bar, and every where else as well, his addresses were *re-enforced* by the conviction that he was a conscientious and christian man, and that what he said he believed to be the simple, unvarnished truth.

No man in Springfield, of the present generation, was so well acquainted with the local history of that place, as Judge Morris. It was a rich treat to meet him in the street, or at the "old corner bookstore" in Springfield, as the writer has often done, and by starting some historical inquiry, to listen to his immense outpouring of anecdote, respecting the original settlers and the principal inhabitants of that town and its vicinity. He was a *thesaurus* of the most valuable information upon all historical matters in that county, and, indeed, in the whole western section of the commonwealth.

For many years, Judge Morris has been a leading member of the First Congregational Church in Springfield. He was not only a successful lawyer, an upright, a public spirited citizen, and an accurate historical scholar, but he was an intelligent and devoted christian.

In the last five or six months of his life, the decay of his mental and physical powers confined him to his house and grounds, and at his dinner table he was suddenly stricken with paralysis, of which he died the next morning.

His wife died many years ago. His brothers, Edward, Richard D. and John B.—the latter remaining at the old home at Wilbraham, the others following their elder brother to Springfield,—have all preceded him to the grave; and of his immediate family, a sister, his niece, who has been for a long time his housekeeper, and his two children, Judge Henry Morris, and George B. Morris, clerk of the courts of Hampden county, only survive him. To them, and to a wide circle of old friends, and to the town, of whose history he was a prominent part, there remain grateful memories of a long and useful and honorable life.

Elmer Townsend, Esq. Elmer Townsend was born in Reading, county of Windsor, Vermont, on the 3d of March, 1807, and died at his residence in Boston, April 13, 1871. His parents were William and Susannah (Smith) Townsend. William Townsend was a son of Joseph Townsend, who fought in the French and Indian war, and in the first portion of the war of the revolution. Daniel Townsend, a brother of Joseph Townsend, was killed at the battle of Lexington.

William Townsend married again after the decease of his wife, which occurred when Elmer was quite young. He followed the vocation of farming, and lived to a good old age, being between 80 and 90 when he died, some years since. Elmer Townsend had four own brothers, and two own sisters; of the former only one survives, but both of the latter are living, one a widow, the other the wife of the Rev. Horace Herrick, of Wolcott, Vermont.

He received a good education, having been instructed for a time by the Hon. Salmon P. Chase, and at the age of 20, in the year 1827, arrived in Boston, having in his possession moderate means. He went into a counting-house, and afterwards became a partner in the house of J. W. Forbush & Co., then a pioneer house in the wholesale manufacture and sale of boots and shoes. After this he carried on the same business alone; and later became a partner with T. P. Rich, with whom he remained till he retired from that business some seven years ago.

During his business career he became interested in a number of letters patent relating to the manufacture of boots and shoes, and it is owing to his indomitable perseverance that manufacturers possess the numerous labor-saving contrivances, which have proved of so much benefit to the manufacturing interests of the country.

He was distinguished for his generosity, and though very unostentatious, few men gave more to the needy poor than he. His love of country was intense, as was his hatred of slavery. He desired that every man should have his rights, no matter what his birth or color. His politics were strongly republican. He was a thoroughly upright man, and tenaciously honest. In his own family he was idolized; he was one of the kindest of fathers.

In 1834, he married Weltha Ann, daughter of the late Benjamin Beecher, of New-Haven, Conn., by whom he had five children, three daughters and two sons; one daughter, Helen Cordelia, and two sons, Henry Elmer and Benjamin Beecher, both graduates of Harvard University, survive him.

Elmer Townsend attended divine service at the Church of the Advent. He was a member of the Boston board of trade, and was admitted a resident member of this Society, Oct. 26, 1868.

Henry Oxnard Preble. Henry Oxnard Preble, the youngest member of this society, except one, was born in Portland, Me., Jan. 4, 1847, and died suddenly, of diphtheria, in Charlestown, Mass., May 24, 1871, at the age of 24 years. He was the eldest son of our highly esteemed associate, Capt. George Henry Preble, U. S. N., and of Susan Zabiah (Cox) Preble, daughter of John Cox, of Portland, Me., who was, in his day, a distinguished merchant in the African trade. His early education was largely conducted under the paternal roof, by his faithful and intelligent parents. He also attended the best schools in Portland, Charlestown and Cambridge. The Sunday School also was an efficient means of forming his intellectual, as well as his moral character. At the early age of thirteen years, he was appointed librarian of the Sunday School of the Rev. Dr. Newell's society in Cambridge. In the war of the rebellion, he was clerk to his father while commanding the United States man-of-war St. Louis, from April, 1863, to Dec. 1864. His journal of the cruise of the St. Louis is a fine specimen of his habits of order and close observation. On his return to the peaceful pursuits of life, he resumed his position as librarian of the sunday school, and continued to fill it with acceptance until his removal from Cambridge, 1866. When the Massachusetts Institute of Technology was opened in 1865, he entered it, as a general student; but the next year, his taste for chemistry became so decidedly developed, that he entered that department, intending to adopt it as a profession. His attainments in that branch of science soon attracted the attention of Prof. Storer, and he appointed him an assistant in that department of the Institute. In 1870, he was chosen superintendent of the Kidder chemical works in Charlestown. He was also elected superintendent of the sunday school connected with the ministry at large of the Harvard Church in Charlestown,—an office which he filled acceptably till his death. In 1868, he became a member of the Naval Library and Institute; in 1869, he was chosen a member of the Union Navy Association; and was elected a resident member of the New-England Historic, Genealogical Society in September, 1870. A few months before his death he delivered a lecture before the "People's Course," in Charlestown, upon the results of his observations in his visits to the Azores.

But his work was unexpectedly approaching its termination. His singularly fine and matured abilities, his high promise of future usefulness, and all the sanguine hopes and expectations of a large circle of warmly attached and admiring friends, could not ward off the shaft of the fell destroyer. In the midst of all these conditions of promise and expectation, he was suddenly arrested in his earthly career by a disease, which seems to have become acclimated among us, and which yet baffles the most eminent medical skill.

His funeral was attended at his father's residence in Charlestown, when his remains were removed to Portland, Me., where, after other appropriate solemnities at the First Parish Church, they were interred in the Evergreen Cemetery at Deering.

A beautiful pamphlet, elegantly printed for circulation among his friends, has made its appearance, containing several handsome tributes to his memory, both in prose and in verse, which his sorrowing relatives and associates have laid as a garland upon his tomb.

REV. JOSEPH RICHARDSON. The Rev. Joseph Richardson, of Hingham, Mass., was born in Billerica, Mass., Feb. 1, 1778, and died in Hingham, Sept. 25, 1871, at the age of 93 years, 7 months and 24 days. His parents were Joseph and Patty (Chapman) Richardson, of Billerica. During his boyhood he worked upon a farm, and had but limited opportunities for acquiring an education. He fitted for college, partly in his native town and partly in Tewksbury, entered the freshman class in Dartmouth College, in 1789, and was graduated in 1802. Among his classmates were Dr. Amos Twitchell, of Keene, N. H., and the Rev. Brown Emerson, D.D., of Salem, Mass.

Mr. Richardson, upon his graduation, commenced the study of theology, with the Rev. Henry Cumings, D.D., of Billerica, and was licensed to preach in 1803. For two years thereafter he was principally occupied with teaching in the grammar schools of Billerica and Charlestown. In August, 1805, he was invited to supply the pulpit of the First Parish in Hingham, then recently vacated by the resignation of Rev. Dr. Henry Ware, on his acceptance of his appointment to the Hollis Professorship of Divinity in Harvard College. He accepted the invitation, and was ordained as pastor of that church and minister of that parish, July 2, 1806. The Rev. Dr. Bentley, of Salem, preached the sermon at his ordination.

For several years, in his earlier ministry, Mr. Richardson received into his family a large number of young men, for education and instruction, several of whom he fitted for college. He was chosen one of the delegates from the town of Hingham to the convention which met in 1820 to revise the constitution of Massachusetts. It is said that some important propositions which he then advocated, without success, have since been incorporated into that instrument, and that others which he unsuccessfully opposed were rejected by the people. In May, 1821, Mr. Richardson was elected as one of three representatives from Hingham in the general court, and the next year he was the sole representative of the town. In 1823, 1824 and 1826, he was a member of the senate for the county of Plymouth. In 1826, he was elected a member of congress, and was re-elected in 1828. He was succeeded, in 1830, by the Hon. John Quincy Adams. Upon his retirement from political life, he resumed his parochial labors, which were continued, with only occasional interruptions, till 1855, when the Rev. Calvin Lincoln, a native of the town, and who had been for thirty years the minister of the First Parish in Fitchburg, Mass., was settled with him as associate pastor. At the induction of Mr. Lincoln into office, sermons were preached by both the associated pastors. In 1856, Mr. Richardson delivered a discourse, in two parts, on the fiftieth anniversary of his settlement, which was published; and he prepared, for his eighty-fifth birth-day, an appropriate sermon, from Joshua 14, 10: "And now, lo I am this day four score and five years old," which was read to the people by Mr. Lincoln. It is a striking coincidence that his predecessor, the Rev. Dr. Gay, preached his celebrated discourse, entitled "*The Old Man's Calendar*," from the same text, in the same pulpit, and at the same age.

Mr. Richardson published "The American Reader" in 1813, and the "Young Ladies' Selection" in 1816. His "Letters to Congress," in 1822, attracted at the time considerable attention.

Born before the American Union was established, and before the constitutions of his native state and of the United States were adopted, he lived to see the great principles of freedom asserted in those immortal instruments, in successful operation, in both this state and the nation.

He was of a sanguine temperament, frank and decided in the expression of his opinions, and generous even beyond the extent of his ability.

Mr. Richardson was married in Billerica, May 23, 1807, to Anne, daughter of Benjamin Bowers, of that town. They had no children, and she survives him. He was admitted a resident member of the New-England Historic, Genealogical Society, June 9, 1857.

Prepared by CHARLES W. TUTTLE, Esq., Assistant Historiographer.

HON. NATHANIEL GOOKIN UPHAM, LL.D., was a lineal descendant in the seventh generation of John Upham, who was born in England, came to this country in 1635, and settled in Weymouth. His father, Nathaniel, was the eldest son of the Rev. Timothy Upham (H. C. 1768), who was settled in the ministry in Deerfield, N. H., from 1772 to 1811. Nathaniel Upham was bred a merchant, and carried on business for several years in Deerfield. About 1802 he removed to Portsmouth, and, almost immediately, to Rochester, where he resided till his death. While living in Deerfield he married Judith, only daughter of the Hon. Thomas Cogswell, of Gilmanton, and had issue seven sons and four daughters. All the sons became distinguished in public employments, the eldest of whom was Thomas Cogswell Upham, late professor of moral philosophy in Bowdoin College.

Nathaniel Gookin Upham was born in Deerfield, January 8, 1801. He early manifested so decided an inclination for books and reading that it was decided to give him a liberal education. He was fitted for college at the Exeter Academy, and entered the freshman class of Dartmouth College in 1816. After a very successful college career, during which he maintained a high rank for general scholarship, he graduated in 1820, in a class since distinguished by the public eminence of several of its members.

On leaving college he entered the law-office of his brother-in-law, the Hon. David Barker, Jr., of Rochester. On finishing his law studies and being admitted to the bar, he settled in the practice of his profession, in Bristol, N. H. He continued in practice here till 1829, when he removed to Concord, and entered a wider field of professional life. His integrity, legal ability, and general attainments were such, that in 1833, when only thirty-two years of age, he was selected to fill a vacancy on the bench of the superior court, the highest judicial tribunal in the state. With but one exception he was the youngest person that had ever been elected to this position. This office he held ten years, with a constantly increasing reputation for judicial ability, and for large and comprehensive views of public affairs.

The introduction of railroads into New-Hampshire was the occasion of much public interest, and met with much opposition. Many perplexing difficulties surrounded the Concord railroad, the first that penetrated the centre of the state. Judge Upham's interest in the success of this undertaking, and his admitted fitness to control and direct its affairs, led to his appointment, in 1843, to the office of superintendent of the road. He was soon after chosen president of the corporation, and held the office till 1866. During his connection with the road it was eminently successful, and he showed himself to have a large share of executive ability.

A still more public recognition of his capacity occurred in 1853, when he was appointed by President Pierce a commissioner on the claims in controversy between the United States and Great Britain. Judge Upham and the English commissioner met in London in the autumn of 1853, and examined and allowed or rejected all the numerous matters, of a pecuniary nature, which had arisen between the two governments since the treaty of Ghent in 1814. This commission was entirely successful, and both commissioners were highly praised for their labors by our ministers, Everett and Buchanan.

A further public recognition of his ability to deal with questions of a high public character occurred in 1862, when he was chosen umpire of a commission appointed by the United States and New-Grenada to adjust claims and counter claims between these two governments. This duty he discharged to the entire satisfaction of both governments.

Judge Upham meddled but little with active politics, although he was cognizant of what was going on in that stormy field. In 1850 he was a member of the constitutional convention. He was in the house of representatives in 1865 and 1866, and was chairman of the committee for remodelling the State-House. He was for many years president of the New-Hampshire Colonization Society, in the purposes of which he was much interested.

He had a decided taste for literary pursuits and investigations, and was well acquainted with the whole range of English literature. During his leisure time he made a selection of the best thoughts of authors, both ancient and modern, and classified them according to subjects ready for publication. They would make several volumes, if printed. On a few occasions he publicly showed his interest in these pursuits. In 1835, at the request of the legislature, he delivered a eulogy on Lafayette, which was commended for its many excellencies. He also delivered an address before the New-Hampshire Historical Society, his subject being one involving the political history of the state. He was for several years president of that Society, having become a member in 1833. Dartmouth College conferred on him the honorary degree of doctor of laws in 1862.

Judge Upham was a man of great and persevering industry. His application to a subject was continuous till it was finished. The versatility of his mind enabled him to turn with ease from one subject to another. In the multiplicity of affairs in which he was concerned he always maintained a high character. "He was," says Prof. Noyes, "a man of uprightness and strict integrity, a man who was true to his engagements, faithful to every contract, expressed or implied, doing what he regarded as right in the sight of God and man. This is the judgment which the entire community, with one consent, has expressed." His pastor says of him, "It is much to his praise that it can be justly said of him, that he has completed a long life of business with all classes of men, and gone down to his grave without a spot upon him."

He was twice married. Betsey Watts, daughter of Nathaniel Lord, of Kennebunk, was his first wife. She died Aug. 17, 1833, leaving two children, Elizabeth L., wife of Joseph B. Walker, of Concord, and the Rev. Nathaniel L. Upham, who survive their father. His second wife, who survives him, was Eliza W., daughter of the Rev. Abraham Burnham, D.D., of Pembroke. They had two children, viz.: an infant, and Francis A. Upham. Judge Upham died Dec. 11, 1869. He was chosen a member of the New-England Historic, Genealogical Society in 1855.

Proceedings.

Boston, Massachusetts, Wednesday, April 3, 1872. A quarterly meeting was held at the Society's House, No. 18 Somerset Street, this afternoon, at three o'clock, the president, Hon. Marshall P. Wilder, in the chair.

Samuel H. Wentworth, Esq., the recording secretary, read the record of the proceedings at the March meeting, which was approved.

John Ward Dean, the librarian, reported that during the month of March 33 volumes, 289 pamphlets, 3 years files of newspapers, 6 maps, 2 manuscripts, 1 broadside and 10 rare coins had been presented to the Society. Of the volumes 2 were bound volumes of newspapers.

Rev. Edmund F. Slafter, the corresponding secretary, reported the correspondence since the last meeting.

Rev. Dorus Clarke, D.D., the historiographer, read biographical sketches of two deceased members, namely, Gen. Guy Mannering Fessenden, of Warren, R. I., and Henry Theodore Tuckerman, of New-York city.

The president read a letter from Hon. Silas N. Martin, mayor of Wilmington, N. C., presenting to the society two bound volumes of the *Wilmington Journal*, a weekly newspaper, from January, 1862, to January, 1865. Complete files of newspapers like this printed at the south during the late civil war are very rare, and are quite valuable as historical materials.

The board of directors nominated five candidates for membership, who were balloted for and elected.

Col. Albert H. Hoyt read a brief history of the stamp acts of Virginia, prepared by Hon. Thomas H. Wynne, of Richmond, Va., and presented in his behalf samples of the stamps then issued.

Charles W. Tuttle then read a paper on *Capt. John Mason, the Founder of New-Hampshire*, containing many facts not heretofore known to historians concerning Capt. Mason and the settlement of New-Hampshire. He has for some time been engaged on a life of Capt. Mason, which will be put to press next autumn. Mr. Tuttle acknowledged his indebtedness to Col. Chester, of London, Eng., for valuable aid in his researches.

Boston, May 1.—A meeting was held this afternoon, president Wilder in the chair.

The secretary read the record of the previous meeting, which was approved.

The librarian reported as donations during the month of April, 103 volumes, 416 pamphlets, files of newspapers for 44 years, 4 manuscripts, 2 broadsides, 1 photograph, 2 maps and 1 lock of hair; the last taken from the remains of Lady Alice Fenwick, after a burial of over 200 years. These donations include a valuable series of newspapers presented by John Wells Parker, making a continuous file for 97 years. They commence with the *Essex Gazette*, published at Salem from Jan. 4, 1774, to May 2, 1775, then removed to Cambridge and published under the title of the *New-England Chronicle*, and after the evacuation of Boston removed there. Passing through various changes it finally became merged in the *Daily Advertiser*, and is still published as the *Semi-Weekly Advertiser*.

The historiographer read biographical sketches of Hon. Lilley Eaton, of Wakefield, Mass., and Henry Benjamin Humphrey, of Newport, R. I., deceased members of the society.

The president presented the original MS. of a petition of Stephen Minot, of Boston, to the Court of General Sessions and the selectmen of Boston, in the year 1737, for a license "to sell Rum."

The board of directors nominated 2 candidates for membership, who were both elected.

Rev. Increase N. Tarbox, D.D., then read an elaborate paper paper on *Ruling Elders in the Early New-England Churches;* after which some remarks on the same subject were made by Rev. Dorus Clarke, D.D., of Boston.

Boston, June 5. A monthly meeting was held this afternoon, president Wilder in the chair.

The secretary read the record of the last meeting, which was approved.

The librarian reported as donations during the previous month, 62 volumes, 381 pamphlets, 15 maps, 7 ancient parchment documents, 19 manuscript volumes and documents, 11 files of military orders, 4 files of old manuscripts and 1 photograph.

Charles W. Tuttle, the assistant historiographer, read a biographical sketch of William Frederick Goodwin, of Concord, N. H., a member of the society lately deceased.

The directors nominated 3 candidates for resident and 1 for corresponding membership, who were balloted for and elected.

Hon. Thomas C. Amory, of Boston, then read an interesting and instructive paper on *Our English Ancestors.*

BOOK-NOTICES.

The Gilman Family traced in the line of Hon. John Gilman of Exeter, N. H., with an Account of many other Gilmans in England and America. Albany, N. Y.: Joel Munsell. 1869. Sm. 4to. pp. 324.

In 1863, the author of this book published a brief genealogy of the Gilmans, which was noticed at the time in the Register (xvii. 375). The family was then traced only to Edward Gilman, the emigrant ancestor, who came from Hingham, in Norfolk, in 1638, and settled at Hingham in New-England, but afterwards removed to other places and finally settled in Exeter, N. H., where he died. Since then, researches in England have traced the ancestry of Edward Gilman, of Exeter, to his grandfather Edward, of Caston in Norfolk, who married Rose Rysse in 1550. The author has been able to collect many interesting details concerning his English ancestors.

The main object of the present volume, which we have delayed too long to notice, is to preserve the genealogy of the descendants of Hon. John Gilman, of Exeter, N. H., the second son of the emigrant. This is given very fully, and the biographical sketches are minute and particular as to dates and facts. Many of the sketches are illustrated by superior steel portraits. Concerning the descendants of the other sons of the emigrant, though no attempt is made to prepare a complete genealogy, considerable matter has been obtained.

The book is got up in the elegant style for which Mr. Munsell's press is so famous, and, like most of his publications, the indices are all that can be desired. J. W. D.

The Corwin Genealogy (Curwin, Curwen, Corwine), in the United States. By Edward Tanjore Corwin, Millstone, N. J. New-York: S. W. Green, Printer. 1872. 8vo. pp. 284.

We regret to state that this neatly printed volume will obtain for its author but a small part of the credit due to his labor. By a faulty system of arrangement he has so obscured the merits of his work that few will recognize the value of his collections. The plan is simply the worst we have ever seen. There being four or five distinct families of the name, the book is prepared by putting all of the descendants in the alphabetical sequence of their christian names, and referring back by a complicated system, to their ancestry. Thus all the Georges, Ellens, Marthas, Marys, &c., are found together. Of course the family arrangement is lost, and the peculiar value of a family history,—its explanation of existing relationships,—is entirely wanting. The book is not a genealogy, but a classified index to one. It is strange that authors will not consent to be instructed by the experience of the past twenty years, and to recognize the fact that the best plan for a genealogy is the one used in the Register.

When we proceed to the more general matters in the book, we find the author too lax in his examination of authorities. There are two main families of the name, that descended from George Corwin, of Salem, and that from Matthias Corwin, of Ipswich, and Southold, L. I., with possibly some lines from other emigrants of the name. The author evidently inclines to the truth of a tradition which makes Matthew a Hungarian; and he wastes a number of pages on persons who have borne the name Corvinus. Such speculations are useless and are liable to lead to error; we always regret to see them occupying the pages of a family history meant for general circulation.

As to George Curwen, of Salem, our author says that he was descended from the family in Workington (p. xxvi.), and on pp. 247–50 prints the pedigree. This is an unfounded assumption. It is probable that George Curwen was of gentle birth, but nothing certain is known about his ancestry. (See the *Heraldic Journal*, vol. i. pp. 145–49, for a statement of the facts known.) It is a mistake, calling for censure, to repeat these assumptions of a pedigree where no proofs have been found.

The one item of news given on this point, is in a letter on p. viii., showing that Rev. George C., who died in 1717, grandson of the emigrant George, regarded Matthias and Thomas as brothers of this emigrant, and sons of a John Curwin. This document is of value as an early testimony to the relationship, but it needs substantiating by English records.

We recognize Mr. Corwin's diligence and zeal in collecting materials for this history, but it is impossible to avoid the conclusion that he has been unwise in his selection of a plan, and doubly so in stating surmises as facts in that part which treats of the origin of either emigrant. W. H. W.

Narrative of the Settlement of George Christian Anthon in America, and of the Removal of the Family from Detroit and its Establishment in New-York City. By CHARLES EDWARD ANTHON, one of his grand-children. New-York: A small number of copies printed for the Family by the Bradstreet Press. 1872. 8vo. pp. 22.

If it were only as the ancestor of a family so distinguished in the literature of our country as the Anthons of New-York, the subject of this pamphlet would have an interest to us. But independent of this, the narrative will have an attraction as the record of a somewhat eventful life. Mr. Anthon was born in Salzungen, in the Duchy of Saxe-Meiningen, Aug. 25, 1734, studied medicine and in 1750 passed an examination before the medical authorities at Eisenach. In 1754, he quitted Germany, never to return. He repaired to Amsterdam, and became the surgeon to a Dutch vessel engaged in the West India trade. In 1757 he was captured by a British privateer and carried into New-York. He acted as assistant surgeon in the military hospital at Albany, and in 1758, when the hospital was broken up, was appointed assistant surgeon to the 16th regiment of Royal Americans. In 1760, he was of the party which under Major Rogers took possession of Detroit, Nov. 29. Here he remained till 1764, when he returned to New-York. In 1767, he again went to Detroit, where he continued till 1786, when he resigned his position in the British army, and removed from Detroit to New-York and engaged in the practice of his profession. Here he died Dec. 22, 1815, aged 81, respected and beloved by the community.

An appendix contains the family record of Mr. Anthon, three of whose sons graduated at Columbia College, and became eminent in different professions. A brief genealogy of the Macomb family is also given. J. W. D.

List of Members of the Massachusetts Society of the Cincinnati; including a Complete Roll of the Original Members, with Brief Biographies compiled from the Records of the Society and other Original Sources. By FRANCIS S. DRAKE. Boston: Printed for the Society. 1872. 8vo. pp. 75.

The title-page gives a sufficient idea of the contents of this pamphlet. It is preliminary to a memorial volume which the Society intends to to have compiled and printed, and which will contain a history of the Society and full memoirs of the members as far as it is practicable to obtain them. Mr. Drake, the compiler of this pamphlet, is the author of the *Dictionary of American Biography* noticed in the last number (*ante*, p. 209). He left this country on a European tour on the 28th of May last, intending to be absent about six months. On his return he will begin work upon the Memorial Volume. Those who have materials that will assist him, can leave them with the librarian of the New-England Historic, Genealogical Society, 18 Somerset street, who will deliver them to Mr. Drake on his return. J. W. D.

A Red Rose from the Olden Time: A Ramble through the Annals of the Rose Inn, on the Barony of Nazareth, in the Days of the Province; based on "The Old Inns at Nazareth." A Paper read at the Centenary of the "Nazareth Inn," June 9, 1871. By MAURICE C. JONES, of Bethlehem, Penn. Philadelphia: King & Baird, Printers. 1872. Sm. 4to. pp. 50.

Much of the local history of Nazareth township and the biography of some of its prominent settlers is embodied in the handsome pamphlet before us. "The Rose," as the earliest of the two inns at Nazareth here commemorated was called, was established in 1752. It was so called from the device on its sign, a full-blown scarlet rose, which was intended to keep in remembrance the rent paid by Letitia Aubrey to her half-brothers, John, Thomas and Richard Penn, for the release of five thousand acres of land in Pennsylvania from the estate of their father, William Penn, the founder of that colony. The second inn, known as "The Old Inn at Nazareth," was opened in 1772, a century ago, about the same time that "The Rose" ceased to be used as an inn. It was to mark the one hundredth anniversary of the last inn, which is still used as such, that a commemorative dinner was held in it last summer, at which the paper here printed was read. J. W. D.

An Historical Address delivered before the Massachusetts Agricultural Society on the occasion of graduating its First Class, July 19, 1871. By MARSHALL P. WILDER. Boston: Wright & Potter. 1871. 8vo. pp. 37.

Ninth Annual Report of the Trustees of the Massachusetts Agricultural College, January, 1872. Boston: Wright & Potter. 1871. 8vo. pp. 108.

In the memoirs of Elkanah Watson (*ante*, xviii. 97-105), and Marshall P. Wilder (xxi. 97-100), some facts in relation to the origin and history of agricultural societies in this country were presented to our readers. From the labors of these societies, now become very numerous, have grown our agricultural colleges. In the pamphlet whose title is first given, other particulars concerning the history of both will be found.

The first movement towards establishing an agricultural college in this state was in the year 1850, when Mr. Wilder, president of the Massachusetts senate, introduced a bill providing for the establishment of such an institution. The bill passed that body but was defeated in the house. Had it become a law, our state would have had the honor of establishing the first Agricultural College in America.

The present college was incorporated in the year 1863; but four years elapsed before its doors were opened to students, and it was only last year that its first class was graduated. Col. William S. Clark, now at the head of the college, has held this position from the opening, except a few of the first months, when Hon. P. A. Chadbourne, whom ill health compelled to resign, had charge of the institution. Col. Clark has proved himself eminently fitted for the duties of his office, and it is to his services, in a great degree, that the prosperity of the college is owing.

Mr. Wilder, in his address, after glancing at the struggles for agricultural education which have been crowned with such signal success, and acknowledging the goodness of Providence in prolonging the lives of so many of the early friends of the cause and permitting them to see the fruit of their labor, thus proceeds:

"It is not often that the projectors of like enterprises are permitted to reap the harvest of their sowing. Soon, all those who twenty years ago were banded together for the promotion of agricultural education in this state will have gone to their reward; but I esteem it as among the choicest reminiscences of my life, that I have enjoyed the friendship of those wise and good men. I have climbed the summit of the hill of life, and am descending on the other side. Ere long I shall reach the valley below and be buried in the bosom of my mother earth; but while I live, I shall labor with such ability as I possess to promote the welfare of this college, and the good cause which we have so long had at heart. May this institution live on, prospering and to prosper. May it rise higher and higher in the scale of popular favor and usefulness, sharing the good will of the people, the munificence of noble-hearted men, and the fostering care of a generous government."

In the report of the trustees, prepared by President Clark, great credit is given to Mr. Wilder for his services in behalf of the college. He has, to use the words of the report, "been more closely identified with efforts for the promotion of agricultural and horticultural improvement than any other American." We are pleased to learn that the labors of this public benefactor are appreciated in Europe as well as America. In

April last, the *Gardener's Chronicle and Agricultural Gazette*, the leading agricultural paper in Europe, gave a sketch of his life, illustrated by a life-like engraved portrait, which is introduced by the following merited compliment:—

"We are glad to have the opportunity of laying before our readers, the portrait of one of the most distinguished of transatlantic horticulturists, and one who by his zeal, industry and determination has not only conferred lasting benefits on his native country, but has by his careful researches and experiments in hybridization and fruit culture laid the horticulturists of all nations under heavy obligations to him. The name and repute of Marshall P. Wilder are highly esteemed among the elect fraternity in Great Britain as they are in America." J. W. D.

Notices of the Ellises of England, Scotland and Ireland, from the Conquest to the present time, including the families of Alis, Fitz-Elys, Helles, etc. By WILLIAM SMITH ELLIS, ESQ., of the Middle Temple. 1857. [Not Published.] 1866. 4 parts, 8vo. pp. 300. Supplement, 1868, pp. 1–32. Second Supplement, 1872, pp. 33–96.

The title gives a fair indication of the object of this book, which is a collection of numerous families of the name of Ellis, or a similar name, such as would usually be considered hopelessly separated genealogically. The writer however has for a long time maintained that coat armor was in use before the Conquest, contrary to the usual view, and that certain coats were common to certain races or clans of gentry and thus afford proof of relationships otherwise not to be proved.

We cannot follow Mr. Ellis in the widely extended and interesting field opened by his book, but he has evidently been an enthusiastic collector of facts and his book must be of interest to all of the name. Of course there are a number of branches traced out, but there are also a great many brief notes and gleanings, some of which may be of service to the American genealogist. W. H. W.

Memoir of Rev. Samuel Whiting, D.D., and of his wife, Elizabeth St. John; with references to some of their English Ancestors and American Descendants. By WILLIAM WHITING, former President of the N. E. Hist., Geneal. Society. Author of "War Powers under the Constitution of the United States," etc. Fifty copies printed, not published. Boston: printed by Rand, Avery & Co. 1871.

The first 190 pages of this book are given to a memoir of Rev. Samuel Whiting, who was born in Boston, co. Lincoln, Eng., in 1597, was graduated at Emanuel College, Cambridge, and came to New-England in 1636. He was settled as minister at Lynn, Mass., and died there in 1679. He belonged to a family of gentry long resident in Lincolnshire, and his wife had a still more distinguished pedigree, being the sister of Oliver St. John, Lord Chief Justice of England, of the race of the Barons St. John of Bletsoe; she was a cousin of Oliver Cromwell.

This memoir is, as the title indicates, the chief object of interest, and is a comprehensive collection of all that can be found concerning the worthy Puritan minister.

The pedigrees are much less elaborated and would be much improved by some system of numbering. But few branches apparently are traced. In regard to the English part, a number of records of wills and baptisms are given, to aid any future inquirer, but without any attempt to arrange the material so collected.

Notice is also taken of other families of the name, or of a similar one. Thus there are many descendants of Nathaniel Whiting of Dedham, and William Whiting of Hartford, both of whom are thought to have come from Boxford, co. Suffolk, Eng., and of James, Matthew and Thomas Whiton of Hingham, Mass. Considerable space is given to the Virginian family of Whiting, to which belonged Beverly Whiting, a god-father of George Washington's.

The illustrations of the volume are an engraving of the Whiting coat-of-arms, and a large tabular pedigree of the ancestors of Elizabeth (St. John) Whiting.

We rejoice that our honored ex-president has found time, amid the exactions of a profession in which he ranks so high, to prepare this volume. We hope he may hereafter resume the task and extend the genealogical portion to a corresponding volume. W. H. W.

Historical Genealogy of the Kirk Family, as established by Roger Kirk, who settled in Nottingham, Chester County, Province of Pennsylvania, about the year 1714, *containing impartial biographical sketches of his Descendants as far as ascertained; Also a record of two hundred and nine of the Descendants of Alphonsus Kirk, who migrated from Lurgan, North Ireland, and settled in the County of New Castle, Delaware.* By CHARLES STUBBS, M.D., Cor. Mem. of the Maryland Academy of Science, &c. Lancaster, Pa.: Wylie & Griest. 1872. Large 16mo. pp. 252.

The Roger Kirk whose record occupies most of this volume, was a settler as early as 1712. He married Elizabeth Richards and had five children who married. His two sons and his daughter Elizabeth, who married Thomas Woodward, are regarded as equally founders of families, and their descendants are traced with great fulness through many families of various names. The work is well arranged and must be of great value to many persons besides the Kirks. Pp. 217–252 are given to the record of Alphonsus Kirk, of Newcastle, whose father is said to be Roger, and whose oldest son was named Roger. This last name was contemporary with Roger of Nottingham, but the author says, "what relation these two Roger Kirks bore to each other, is a problem we have been unable to solve."

We are glad to record this proof of the continuance of a taste for genealogy outside of New-England. W. H. W.

Historical Notes of the Family of Kip, of Kipsburg and Kip's Bay. New-York. Privately printed. 1871. [Press of J. Munsell, Albany.] 8vo. pp. 49.

In this beautiful volume, Bishop Kip of California has given the pedigree of his kindred, one of the old "Knickerbocker" families of New-York. The pedigree is traced to Ruloffe De Kype, who died in 1569, and whose grandson Hendrick Kype came to this country in 1635. Two grandsons of Hendrick were the co-patentees of the Manor of Kips burg, in 1688. The family also owned land at Kip's Bay, and in the present city of New-York.

In Appendix I., is a notice of the Ingraham family of South Carolina (distinct from the New-England family of the name), whose English pedigree is said to be ascertained. In Appendix II. we find the usual unproved statements about the Lawrence pedigree. Appendix III. contains a short note on the Van Rensselaers.

W. H. W.

A Contribution to the Genealogy of the Bearse or Bearss Family in America: 1618–1871. *Ancestry and Descendants of Dea. John Bearss and his wife Molly (Beardsley) Bearss, of New Fairfield, Ct., and Westmoreland, N. Y.* By JOHN BEARSS NEWCOMB, of Elgin, Ill. Privately printed for the use of the family. Elgin, Ill.: Dec. 7, 1871. 8vo. pp. 16.

The title of this little tract fully describes the book. The author traces one branch from Augustine Bearsse, of Barnstable, Mass., to his gr. gr. grandson John Bearss, who was born in 1763, and married Molly Beardsley in 1714. The descendants of that marriage are then traced very thoroughly in both the male and female branches. W. H. W.

Genealogy of the Family of Winchell in America; embracing the Etymology and History of the Name, and the Outlines of some Collateral Genealogies. By ALEXANDER WINCHELL, LL.D., Professor of Geology, &c. in the Univ. of Michigan. Ann Arbor. 1869. 8vo. pp. 271.

The main part of this book, 218 pages, is given to the descendants of Robert Wincoll or Winchell, of Dorchester, Mass., and Windsor, Conn. Pp. 219–228 give the family of Munson W., of Goshen, a very late immigrant; pp. 229–237 record German families of the name.

The plan is simple and good. Each man who became the head of a family has a serial number *after* his name, as well as his regular number reckoning from the first. The reader must, however, seek this number as a family one. Thus the author is recorded on p. 150, 1749 Alexander **476**. On p. 206, as **1749** Alexander, Family 476. By the statement of the plan, viz.: that the family number was a thick faced numeral, we should have looked for **476** which occurs on p. 116 as **476** Martha, Family 195. This typographical change is a little troublesome at first; the thin numeral should have been kept throughout *before* the name.

The book is a useful and unpretentious one, and we trust the author will be encouraged to proceed with an enlarged edition. W. H. W.

A School History of the United States. By W. H. VENABLE, of the Chickering Classical and Scientific Institute. Wilson, Hinkle & Co., Cincinnati and New-York. 1872. 12mo. pp. 250 and xxx.

June on the Miami, and other Poems. By W. H. VENABLE. Cincinnati: R. W. Carroll & Co., Publishers. 1872. 12mo. pp. 122.

One of the most difficult tasks for the educator, is to find text books in all respects suitable for children; and very few even of those persons who have had long experience as teachers, and only such, are competent to prepare books of that character. The History before us is a very successful attempt by a scholar and teacher of experience to produce a systematic, brief, clear, and authentic history of the United States.

The plan is simple; a strictly chronological order of arrangement is followed; the most important dates are made prominent by a peculiar type; a condensed record of general progress is placed at the end of almost every chapter; and the narrative is kept unincumbered by matters of minor importance. Foot notes, profuse and attractive illustrations, a large number of colored maps showing the progressive settlement of the country, an appendix and index are furnished. The latter is full enough to serve as a capital guide to teachers and committees in the examination of classes.

We have noticed a few blemishes in the text. Some of them are probably typographical errors, but a few are errors of fact, and all can easily be corrected in another edition. The reference to Castile and Leon (p. 9) is not quite exact. The author speaks of *Giovanni* Cabot (p. 16) and of *John* Verazzano (p. 12). Juan Ponce de Leon (*the Conqueror and Governor of Porto Rico*) set out on his first expedition to the mainland in 1513, not in 1512 (See Kohl's *Disc. of Maine*, the best authority), and consequently as he discovered Florida on Easter day, it was not on the 28th (p. 11), but on the 27th of March. Walter Raleigh and Humphrey Gilbert had the same mother but different fathers; they were not *brothers-in-law*, in the modern use of that expression (pp. 26 and 27). The Gov. Haynes mentioned on page 41 is the same person as the Gov. *Haines* referred to on page 43. Ferdinando, not *Fernando* was the christian name of Gorges (pp. 46 and xxv); and Thomas Gorges (p. 46) was not his son, but may have been his nephew. Puritanism (p. 47), Congregationalism and Episcopacy (p. 131) are spoken of as *religions*. "The Articles of Confederation" (p. 134) are not explained, nor their history given. On page 159 Josiah Quincy is distinguished for his *legal* attainments. He is more distinguished for having introduced *disunion resolutions into congress.* The reference to Channing, on page 161, needs further qualification.

Of Mr. Venable's volume of poems, whose title is given above, we can find no fault. Many of the poems are delightful; a few are exquisite in thought, feeling and measure; none are tame or maudlin, or lean of sense. The writer is a poet, and we crave further fruits of his genius.

Notes relating to Rawlins or Rollins, with Notices of Early Settlers of the name in America, and Family Records of Thomas of Boston, Nicholas of Newbury, William of Gloucester. By JOHN R. ROLLINS, A.M., member of the N. E. Hist. Gen. Society. Lawrence, Mass. 1870. 8vo. pp. 84.

This pamphlet is essentially a collection of notes. There is an interesting essay on family names, a number of gleanings about Englishmen of the name, accounts of many settlers in America, and quite extensive records of the three branches named in the title.

The author intends to continue his investigations as to other branches of the family, and eventually, perhaps, to prepare a complete genealogy of all bearing the above surnames, in its different forms. We notice this preliminary publication, now, mainly for the purpose of calling the attention of the family and its connections to it, in order that they may aid Mr. Rollins as much as possible.

Life of Henry Dunster, First President of Harvard College. By Rev. JEREMIAH CHAPLIN, D.D. Boston: James R. Osgood & Co. 1872. 12mo. pp. xx. and 315.

Not only was Dunster the first president of the first established college in America, but he had the chief part in framing its rules and regulations, and in fixing its courses of study. He administered its laws, collected and dispensed its revenues, and exercised his rare gifts and learning as the principal instructor of its students for about fourteen years,—perhaps the most important period of its early history. More than two hundred years have elapsed since he was laid to rest, and now, for the first time, we have his memoir. For it we are perhaps mainly indebted to the fact, that as Dunster was the first prominent anabaptist in New-England, his life and character attract the interest of a large religious denomination. This long silence in regard to him is not so remarkable as it might seem at first thought, if we consider the circumstances under which his connection with the college was suddenly terminated, and the feelings thereby engendered among his contemporaries. Neither they, nor his surviving acquaintances, nor those who inherited their prejudices, found in his life and doctrines a pleasant subject for their pens, or even for meditation.

Dr. Chaplin has collected the chief facts of Dunster's eventful career, and produced a memoir creditable to his reputation for ability and industry. The main interest of the narrative centres about the facts connected with his removal from the presidency of the college,—the most important event in his life. The story is a sad one, and, considered solely in the light of the present day, reflects little credit upon any of the parties involved in the transaction. To his biographer, and those of similar theological views, the narrative presents aspects and points of peculiar interest, and to some extent the memoir is shaped and colored by the writer's prepossessions. Hence it is in part, at least, a defence of Dunster; and where it is defensive it is criticisable mainly for the reason that the writer falls into the common error of applying modern tests and standards to occurrences and institutions of another age. We are accustomed to say that the standard of right and wrong is fixed from eternity to eternity. This is true as to all the moral relations of the individual to his Creator; but in the varied relations of man to man, or of the individual man to society, events occur and questions arise to all aspects of which we cannot apply this moral standard. As to such events and questions, the institutions, customs and circumstances of each age, and of each distinct people or community, fix the standard by which they are to be judged.

Dr. Chaplin regards Dunster as a "martyr" to the cause of religious liberty; and he cites Quincy's application of the term to Dunster. This word "martyr" is usually very loosely applied. It is so in this instance by Quincy, who was an illogical thinker, and conspicuous for his impulsiveness and hasty judgments. In the long roll of so-called martyrs, very few are entitled to the name. If Dunster was a martyr, he was so only by virtue of his own acts.

Let us recall the circumstances. He was called to the presidency of the college by the "elders, ministers, and magistrates." He had the reputation of great learning, of special fitness for the office, and of being sound upon all matters pertaining to the established religious faith and practice of the colony; and during his term of office the standards of faith and practice had been resolved upon and declared in his very presence as it were, if not by his counsel and vote. These declarations were explicit upon the subject of baptism.

Again. He was placed over the only theological school in America, and young men were entrusted to his care to be fitted for the office of teacher of the true faith and practice. Under these circumstances was it consistent with a good conscience that he should remain in office after he had changed his views on this point? Could any reasonable man have expected to be retained there? Would any man, unless he were blinded by too much conceit, or led by self-will, seek to hold his office? The overseers invited Dunster to resign. They could do no less. They did, in this particular, no more than the overseers of any one of the theological schools of our own day would be expected to do, and would justly do, if they removed a professor of "heresy." Dr. Chaplin, himself, must be aware, we think, that the charter of at least one of our New-England Colleges requires its president to profess a particular form of faith, and that this requirement has always been enforced.

Dunster's interruption of the administration of the ordinance of infant baptism was not only in violation of law, but it was a pernicious example to the youth under his charge. He acknowledged as much as this. Of this offence he was convicted by the county court, and admonished. Surely he could not properly complain if his own previous teachings in regard to the duty of the civil power towards the church were put into practice, even upon himself.

The plea of "liberty of conscience," urged by Dunster himself and renewed by his biographer, does not hold good. We have no faith in the plea which translates obdurate self-will into "liberty of conscience." No man has the liberty to seek to force his private notions upon the acceptance of a dissident majority. And what is this liberty of conscience about which so much has been written and said for three hundred years? Is any man certain his conscience is right? Can he be certain of it? If not, then his liberty is only the liberty of doing what he prefers to do. In a community of equals, no man has absolute rights; his "liberties" are relative and limited. Practically what is called liberty of conscience is impossible, except as a condition or concomitant of anarchy or sheer license. Better than all the prating about "liberty of conscience" would it be, if every man who cannot agree with his neighbors would depart and go to his own place.

Dr. Chaplin has placed in the appendix to his book a brief genealogy of the Dunster family, and other matters germane to his subject. The volume as a whole is instructive and interesting, and is a valuable addition to our list of New-England biographies.

History of the Rise and Fall of the Slave Power in America. By HENRY WILSON. Vol. I. Boston: James R. Osgood and Company. 1872. 8vo. pp. xxiv. and 670.

Mr. Wilson has entered upon a great undertaking if we may judge from the volume before us, which he states in the preface is the first of three on the same subject. The clearest and most concise form in which we can state the plan and method of this volume, will be to quote the running titles of a few of the first chapters, which are forty-five in number. They are as follows:—

The Beginning and Growth of Slavery, and the Early Development of the Slave Power; Abolition—Abolition Societies; Slavery in the Territories—Ordinance of 1787; Compromises of the Constitution—Slave-Representation—Slave Trade—Rendition of Fugitive Slaves; Proposed Tax on Slaves—First Slavery Debate in Congress—Petitions for Emancipation—Powers of the Government Defined; The Fugitive Slave Act of 1793—Proposed Amendments; The Slave-Trade—its Prohibition; Domestic and Foreign Slave-Trade—Negotiations with Foreign Powers; Foreign Relations of the Government influenced by Slavery; Indian Policy affected by Slavery—Exiles of Florida; The Missouri Struggle—The Compromises; Admission of Missouri—Attempt to introduce Slavery into Illinois; Early Anti-Slavery Movements—Benjamin Lundy—William Lloyd Garrison; The Virginia Constitutional Convention—Southampton Insurrection—Slavery Debates in the Legislature. The volume ends with the admission of Texas as a State.

It will be seen from this list that the volume embraces a wide survey of the field, and an exhaustive statement of the leading events and incidents of the history of American Slavery.

The author is a man of affairs; unused to philosophical speculations or abstract reasoning. His life, or the main part of it, has been passed in the halls of legislation and other arenas of political action; and practical questions, relating to the general interests of the country, or to the interests of federal and local politics, have engrossed his attention. The habits of his mind, thus determined by the conditions of his public life, are stamped on every page of his book. His thoughts are well defined, and his style is simple and perspicuous, as was becoming in what was intended as a narrative of events. In those parts of the volume in which the author deals with documentary matter, debates in Congress, &c., he shows skill in seizing upon and reproducing their pith and marrow.

In most respects the volume has been well edited; but it would have been improved, as a literary work, had the author pursued a more rigid system of condensation, and had eliminated all redundant words and sentences. The writer has long been identified with the anti-slavery cause; was one of its ablest and most active supporters; mingled in the fiercest warfare which it waged or suffered, and came out of it, saturated, so to speak, with its spirit. So far as he has gained upon his adversaries or his fellows in the long and hot contest, he owes it to the anti-slavery agitation. As a public man, he is one of its chief offspring.

The struggle was long and bitter, and when it ceased it left behind it scars and blisterings wounds. The men engaged in it acquired the habit of sturdy words and incisive forms of expression, and no one was ever at a loss to comprehend their meaning. Among their survivors the habit of plain speaking, thus acquired by long practice, still continues, together with a recollection of their severe warfare. It was natural, therefore, that something of this spirit should be reflected in this book, and so far as it is excessive, in phrase or statement, it is in derogation of the historical value of the treatise. It is difficult, we admit, for men of strong convictions to restrain their feelings when they come to deal with what they regard as moral crimes, but even here we must always concede that other men,—the authors or abettors of these "crimes,"—may have had, and doubtless did have, convictions equally clear, and for them equally authoritative.

The most difficult part of Mr. Wilson's task is yet before him, for he is about to enter upon a chapter in which he was personally concerned. We shall await the appearance of his second volume with no little interest.

This series of volumes will undoubtedly have a large sale, and will be received by a portion of the American people as a fair, complete, and truthful narrative. It can hardly be expected, however, that it will be as readily accepted by those who had no sympathy with the anti-slavery cause, or by that larger class who had no sympathy for the measures by which that "cause" was carried to its final triumph. All intelligent and patriotic men rejoice now or soon will, we believe, in the fact that the curse of slavery is removed, but it is too much to expect that all such men will very soon or very cordially rejoice in the mode of its "taking off."

The Life of Abraham Lincoln, from his Birth to his Inauguration as President. By WARD H. LAMON. With Illustrations. Boston: James R. Osgood & Co. 1872. 8vo. pp. xvi. and 547.

This is the first serious attempt, of which we have any knowledge, to write the life of Mr. Lincoln; and we speak with due caution, we are assured, when we say that the books hitherto put forth on this subject, with the exception, perhaps, of Holland's, are utterly unreliable and therefore worthless. Mr. Lamon, an intimate acquaintance of Mr. Lincoln, has spent many years on his work, using his own materials, and having the coöperation of others, among whom was William H. Herndon, Esq., the partner in business, and the intimate personal associate of Mr. Lincoln for about a quarter of a century. The author had also the use of the materials collected by Mr. Herndon, which he describes as the "richest, rarest, and fullest collection it was possible to conceive * * *. They comprise the recollections of Mr. Lincoln's nearest friends; of the surviving members of his family and his family connections; of the men still living who knew him and his parents in Kentucky; of his schoolfellows, neighbors, and acquaintances in Indiana; of the better part of the population of New-Salem [Ind.]; of his associates and friends in Springfield [Ill.], and of lawyers, judges, politicians and statesmen everywhere, who had anything of interest or moment to relate. They were collected at a vast expense of time, labor and money, involving the employment of many agents, long journeys, tedious examinations, and voluminous correspondence." No adequate estimate can be placed upon the value of such materials, nor upon the amount of labor and research which brought them together.

With such resources, and inspired by motives of friendship for Mr. Lincoln, the author has prepared the first volume of the memoir now before us. He seems to have written with the utmost frankness, as he certainly has with the evident purpose of giving the truth, the whole truth, and nothing but the truth relative to his subject.

Beginning with the emigration of Thomas Lincoln from Virginia to Kentucky, and the birth of his distinguished son, the author traces the latter's history in detail through his eventful and remarkable career down to the point where and when his life-long ambition,—the hope of his boyhood, the aspiration and effort of his mature years,—at last culminated in his election and inauguration as president of the United States.

Considering that Mr. Lincoln sprang from the lowest stratum of society, and that too a frontier society; that his boyhood and early manhood were passed among a people of low tastes and ill regulated habits, and under conditions the most unpropitious which it is possible to imagine; that, above all the disadvantages of his birth and early associations, he rose superior by the force of native powers alone; educated and trained himself to be an acceptable companion of educated and refined men and women; that he became a lawyer of commanding influence, a politician of the highest order of shrewdness and ability, the idol of a great party, and finally the chief executive of a powerful and free people,—this certainly is unexampled in our history, and entitles him to be ranked as the most extraordinary man whom this country has yet produced.

The author's purpose was to present a faithful portrait of Mr. Lincoln in all the stages and in all the relations of his life; hence, unlike most of his predecessors in this field, he has written without special regard to personal or party considerations, the pride of political friends, or the susceptibilities and sensibilities of surviving relatives. The volume is far from being a eulogy, and its chief value lies in the fact that it is made up of facts. The writer disguises nothing, and leaves little or nothing for the imagination to supply. We look in vain, on the one hand, for the ideal character which the inflated and extravagant laudations of political friends, or heated partizans, has created; and on the other, for the monster of duplicity, vulgarity and low cunning conceived of by many of Mr. Lincoln's political opponents.

Mr. Lamon devotes considerable, and perhaps an unreasonable share of his space to Mr. Lincoln's "love affairs;" and in this connection seems to transgress the bounds of strict propriety. This criticism will apply also to the use he has made of private correspondence. It may be that he had full authority for its use in the way and manner it appears here; if so, the question resolves itself into one of good taste. As a rule, however, the sensibilities of the living are as worthy of respect as the honor of the dead.

Much has been said and a great deal written in regard to Mr. Lincoln's religious belief, while his moral character has never been assailed. Upon the first point the evidence is explicit.

His religious opinions when he resided in New-Salem, in Springfield and in Washington, are here stated at great length, and may be briefly summed up in the following language of his biographer (p. 486): "Mr. Lincoln was never a member of any church, nor did he believe in the divinity of Christ, or the inspiration of the Scriptures in the sense understood by evangelical christians. His theological opinions were substantially those expounded by Theodore Parker. Overwhelming testimony out of many mouths, and none stronger than that out of his own, place these facts beyond controversy." The opinions as held by him in 1837, he continued to hold to the last, but for prudential reasons he became more and more reticent in regard to them. His biographer further says: "it is probable that much of Mr. Lincoln's unhappiness, the melancholy that 'dripped from him as he walked,' was due to his want of religious faith. When the black fit was on him [he was three times insane, and once or twice violently so], he suffered as much mental misery as Bunyan or Cowper in the deepest anguish of their conflicts with the evil one. But the unfortunate conviction fastened upon him by his early associations that there was no truth in the Bible made all consolation impossible, and penitence useless. To a man of his temperament, predisposed as it was to depression of spirits, there could be no chance of happiness, if doomed to live without hope and without God in the world. He might force himself to be merry with his chosen comrades; he might 'banish sadness' in mirthful conversation, or find relief in a jest; gratified ambition might elevate his feelings, and give him ease for a time: but solid comfort and permanent peace could come to him only through 'a correspondence fixed with heaven.' The fatal misfortune of his life, looking at it only as it affected him in this world, was the influence at New-Salem and Springfield which enlisted him on the side of unbelief. He paid the bitter penalty in a life of misery."

The reader will find that many of the popular notions of Mr. Lincoln, and not a few of the "incidents" of his life, to which his other biographers have given their sanction, are here exploded. One of the most interesting chapters in the volume is that in which Mr. Lamon shows beyond question, or doubt, that the famous and almost universally credited story about the "Baltimore conspiracy" against Mr. Lincoln's life, in February, 1861, was as base in its origin as it was baseless in fact.

We shall look with impatience for the second volume, which will treat of Mr. Lincoln's career as president. When that volume appears we presume that we shall gain new and important light in regard to the war, its conduct and vicissitudes; upon the action of individuals and parties; and in relation to the vexed political questions which grew out of the war.

This volume is handsomely printed and illustrated with several portraits.

It is destined to create a great sensation, if we mistake not, and will find quite as many readers among his political opponents as among his friends and supporters.

Collections of the Vermont Historical Society. Prepared and Published by the Printing and Publishing Committee in Pursuance of a Vote of the Society. Vol. II. Montpelier: Printed for the Society. 1871. 8vo. pp. xxvii. and 530.

The contents of this volume are as follows:

1. *Vermont Historical Society:* List of its pamphlet publications; officers from Oct. 1870 to Oct. 1872.

2. *Additions and Corrections to Vols. I. and II.* Vol. I. of Vermont Historical Society Vindicated. This Vindication is a reply to the criticisms of H. B. Dawson, Esq., editor and publisher of the Historical Magazine (Morrisania N. Y.). The criticisms are sharp and numerous, but we think that Mr. Dawson's friends will admit that the vindication is substantially, if not in all respects technically, complete.

3. *The Haldimand Papers, with Contemporaneous History.* 4. Opinions of the Haldimand Negotiations. 5. Completeness of the Haldimand Papers in the Negotiation.

The "Haldimand Papers" consist mainly of the correspondence and memoranda connected with the negotiations between Vermont and the Governer of Canada, from January 11, 1779, to March 25, 1783, and are copies of the most important portion of the "Canada Papers" belonging to the Lord Dorchester collection in the Royal Institution, London. They relate to the most interesting event in the history of Vermont, namely; the negotiations carried on by a few of the leading inhabitants with Gen. Haldimand, the commander of the British forces in Canada, ostensibly, and perhaps really, for a truce and exchange of prisoners, secretly, but not seriously, for reconciliation with Great Britain. By means of these negotiations the British were kept out of Vermont, their military operations retarded, and perhaps the independence of the United States secured. At any rate, it is a matter of grave doubt whether the New-England territory could have been saved to the United States, if these negotiations had not taken place. It will be readily seen therefore that the publication of these papers adds valuable material for study in the domain of American history, and the Vermont Historical Society is deserving of great commendation for their publication.

The 6th article in this volume is a brief *History of Vermont as a State, from* 1783 *to* 1791. The 7th article relates to the Early Eastern Boundary of New-York. In this question much is involved relating to the history of New-York, Connecticut, Massachusetts and New-Hampshire. It is an interesting and fruitful subject.

The text is supplied with valuable notes, and the committee of publication have performed their share of the labor with ability and sound discretion.

The most Beautiful City in America.—Essay and Plan for the Improvement of the City of Boston. By ROBERT MORRIS COPELAND. Boston: Lee & Shepard. 1872. 8vo. pp. 46.

Mr. Copeland is a very competent authority upon all subjects relating to his profession. He has written and spoken a good deal upon the subject of landscape gardening, and his views and suggestions are worthy of special attention. He sees that in the new parts of Boston and its suburbs, the amplest opportunities exist for making the city and its present environs healthy, and attractive to the eye. His plans do not contemplate large and immediate outlays of money, to be made a burden to the present and a legacy to coming generations, but that in all future changes of the old and in the development of new territory systematic plans shall be followed, in laying out streets, building houses, and reserving spaces for water, parks, drive ways, trees, &c.

Annexed to this pamphlet is a map showing the plan of improvements and reservations proposed by Mr. Copeland.

Supplement to Coins, Tokens and Medals, of the Dominion of Canada. By ALFRED SANDHAM, Author of "Montreal Past and Present," "Prince of Wales's Medals," &c., Corresponding Member of the Amer. Num. & Arc. Soc. (New-York), Num. & Antiq. Soc. of Philadelphia, and the New-England Historic, Genealogical Soc. [Boston]. From the Second Edition—Copy Right Secured. Montreal: 1872. 8vo. pp. 11.

This pamphlet contains a chart representing various medals not contained in the previous work.

Memoir of Rev. Patrick Copland, Rector elect of the first projected College in the United States. A Chapter of the English Colonization of America. By EDWARD D. NEILL, author of "Terra Mariæ," the "Virginia Company," the "English Colonization of America during the Seventeenth Century," etc. *Ne falsa dicere, nec vera reticere.* New-York: Charles Scribner & Co., 654 Broadway. 1871. 12mo. pp. 96.

The name of Patrick Copland, a clergyman of the Church of England, and a friend of Nicholas Ferrar and Sir George Sandys, will be forever honorably and interestingly associated with the first efforts to Christianize the aborigines of America, and to provide suitable schools for the children of the planters of Virginia. The date and place of his birth are unknown, and the exact date and place of his death have not been definitely ascertained. He entered the service of the East India Company soon after it was organized, and there continued till the summer of 1616, when he returned to England, bringing with him a native convert, one of his pupils, from Bengola, who within a few months afterward was baptized by the Rev. Dr. John Wood, in the church of St. Dennis, London, in the presence of the Lord Mayor of the city, members of the Privy Council, and other distinguished personages. Soon afterward he returned to India with his pupil. In 1621 he was again in England, and there became acquainted with the members of the Virginia Company. He found them actively engaged in their plans for colonizing Virginia, and connected therewith, in the plan of establishing there a university, or college, and other schools. As early as 1618 this enlightened purpose had deeply interested the company, and Copland at once on his arrival entered into the plan with zeal fired by his labors and success in India. Even on his voyage home he had learned of this purpose, and had obtained from his fellow passengers a gift of £70 to that end.

Mr. Copland was chosen a member of the company, and rector of the projected college, but before he was ready to leave England news came of the terrible calamity that befel the colony in 1622, and after that little was done for the educational enterprise.

After the dissolution of the Virginia Company Mr. Copland proceeded to the Bermudas, and there labored for many years. Here as early as 1642 he was an elder in a religious society which held a weekly love-feast, rejected infant baptism, and used a catechism prepared by Oxenstiern, called "Milk for Babes." Subsequently, with his wife and others, he went to an island of the Bahama group, and organized a Puritan church. It is said that he and his companions were aided, while here, by supplies sent from Massachusetts. He returned to the Bermudas, and died there in 1651, it is conjectured.

Mr. Neill has carefully compiled the scattered facts in the life of Copland and produced a very interesting narrative. The book is worth preserving.

Memorial of the Church in Brattle Square. A Discourse preached in the Church in Brattle Square, on the last Sunday of its use for Public Worship, July 30, 1871. By SAMUEL K. LOTHROP, D.D., Pastor of the Society. With an Appendix, an account of laying the Corner-stone of the New Church. Boston: Press of John Wilson & Son. 1871. 8vo. pp. 56.

The title-page of this well-favored pamphlet, sufficiently explains the nature of its contents. The sermon is an eloquent discourse, and contains much interesting and valuable historical matter relating to the religious society of which the Rev. Dr. Lothrop has been the useful and honored pastor for about thirty-eight years.

Boston Illustrated. Boston: James R. Osgood & Co. 1872. 8vo. pp. 122.

This elegant volume is devoted to (1) the history, and (2) the topography of Boston. Under the latter division it treats of the North End, the West End, the Central District, the South End, New Boston, the Harbor, and the suburbs. The letter press is handsomely printed; is concise, full and interesting. The illustrations are 119 in number, consisting of churches, hotels, and other public buildings, and views and scenes in Boston and its suburbs. They are well done, and render the book a pleasant guide to all objects of interest, and a valuable memento of Boston as it is in 1872. The work is sold at the nominal price of fifty cents.

An Account of the Battle of Bunker Hill, Compiled from Authentic Sources. By DAVID PULSIFER, A.M., Member of the New-England Historic, Genealogical Society; Corresponding Member of the New-York Historical Society, the Essex Institute in Salem, and other Historical Societies. With General Burgoyne's Account of the Battle. Boston: A. Williams & Co., 135 Washington Street. 1872. 16mo. pp. 76.

Mr. Pulsifer's account of the Battle of Bunker Hill, as it is commonly styled, accompanied by a map of Boston and Charlestown as they were in 1775, showing the positions occupied by the contending forces, has been prepared with evident care, the best authorities have been consulted, all the important facts are given in sufficient detail, and both sides are represented; that of the British in an account of the battle as described in a letter of Gen. Burgoyne (see *ante*, vol. xi., p. 126). This little tract is handsomely printed and bound, and furnished to the public at fifty cents a copy.

The near approach of the 100th anniversary of the battle will render this pamphlet especially useful.

Memorial of Ebenezer Dale. [Boston: 1872.] 8vo. pp. 26.

A Memorial Sermon on the Death of Theron J. Dale, preached in St. John's Church, Gloucester, Sunday, Sept. 3, 1871. By Rev. JAMES D. REED, Rector. For private distribution. Boston: Printed by Rand, Avery & Co. 1871. 8vo. pp. 16.

Mr. Ebenezer Dale was born in Gloucester, Mass., April 2, 1812, and died in Boston, Dec. 3, 1871. He was an enterprising, upright, and successful merchant and highly esteemed in all business and social relations. This memorial pamphlet was printed probably under the direction of the Brattle Square Church and Society, of which Mr. Dale was a prominent and active member. It contains the memorial sermon preached by the Rev. Dr. Lothrop, the pastor, in the Old South Chapel, Freeman Place, Dec. 10, 1871, where the society formerly worshipping in Brattle Square holds its religious services, pending the construction of their new church edifice on the corner of Commonwealth Avenue and Berkeley Street. The appendix contains the votes and resolves of various organizations and corporations of which Mr. Dale was a member or officer, and an obituary notice printed in the Sunday Courier of Dec. 10, 1871.

A few months preceding the death of Ebenezer Dale, his youngest brother, and partner in business, Mr. Theron J. Dale, died suddenly, at his summer residence in Gloucester. He was a man of sterling worth and virtue, and like his brother above named, was actively devoted to every good work. Prefixed to the memorial sermon by his rector is a tribute from his friend the Rev. Dr. Doane, the bishop of Albany.

The American Church Review (Nos. for January and April, 1872.)

This work is published by M. M. Mallory & Co., Hartford, Conn., at $4 per year. Its dress is equal to that of the best printed English or American quarterlies. As the organ of the highest type of Christian scholarship in the Protestant Episcopal Church, the character of its contents, both in scope and treatment, commend the work to the members of that Church, especially, while many of the articles will challenge the attention of scholarly and thinking minds generally.

The contents of the January No. are: 1. The Church and the Laboring Classes. 2. Scientific Speculation vs. Theological Interpretation. 3. Remarks on the American Church. By the Bishop [Coxe] of Western New-York. 4. Deaconesses. 5. Modern Thought in its Relations to the Person of the Lord Jesus Christ. 6. Munificence in Giving,—a Present Need of the Times. 7. The Changes in England during half a Century. 8. Regeneration in Baptism. 9. The Analysis of the Sunbeam. 10. Book-Notices. Of the April No.: 1. The [Vatican] Council and the State. 2. The Ober-Ammergau Passion-Play. By the Rev. E. A. Washburn, D.D. 3. Unitarianism in New-England. 4. St. Mark and his Critics. 5. Physical Cause of the Death of Our Lord. 6. Ary Scheffer. 7. Christianity and the Old Testament. 8. Ancient Icelandic Literature. 9. Man in Darwinism and in Christianity. 10. Our Romanized Brethren. 11. The First Bishop of New-Hampshire. 12. Book-Notices.

MARRIAGES AND DEATHS.

MARRIAGES.

AVERY=SHIPMAN. In Jewett City, Ct., May 23, by the Rev. Thomas L. Shipman, George W. Avery, M.D., of Hartford, Conn., and Miss Lydia L. Shipman, daughter of the officiating clergyman.

GERRISH=NASON. In North Billerica, Mass., Feb. 15, by the Rev. Elias Nason, Charles Henry Gerrish, of Exeter, N. H., and Miss Emily Georgiana Nason, daughter of the officiating clergyman.

DEATHS.

HALE, Mrs. Lucida (Eddy), widow of Henry Hale, Esq., of Chelsea, Vt., and daughter of Ephraim and Mary (Safford) Eddy, of Woodstock, Vt., died in Chelsea, August 1, 1871, aged 86.

Mrs. Hale was born in Woodstock, May 28, 1785. In the paternal line she was seventh in descent from Samuel Eddy,[1] who came with his brother John in the "Handmaid" to Plymouth in 1630, the line of descent being Obadiah,[2] who married — Bennett; Samuel,[3] who married Meletiah Pratt; Samuel,[4] who married Lydia Alden; Nathan,[5] who married Eunice Sampson; and Ephraim,[6] who married Mary Safford. Through her grandmother Eunice Sampson, she was lineally descended from Capt. Miles Standish and his wife Barbara, as well as from John and Priscilla Alden, through Alexander Standish, eldest son of Miles and Barbara, who married Sarah, daughter of John and Priscilla Alden; their daughter Lydia married Isaac Sampson, son of Abraham; Ephraim, son of Isaac and Lydia (Standish) Sampson, married Abigail Horree; and their daughter Eunice became the wife of Nathan Eddy. Her great grandmother Lydia Alden, was also fourth in descent by another line from John and Priscilla Alden, through Joseph,[2] John,[3] the latter being the father of Lydia. Among her original immigrant ancestors in New-England are reckoned Miles Standish, John Alden, William Mullins and wife, and daughter Priscilla, all of whom came in the Mayflower, 1620; Samuel Eddy, Plymouth, 1630; Moses Simmons, Plymouth, 1621; Thomas White, Weymouth, before 1636; Abraham Sampson, Duxbury, 1629 or 30; Thomas Safford, Ipswich, 1641; John Wheeler, Newbury, 1635; Aquila Chase, Hampton, 1639, Newbury, 1646; and Walter Powers, Malden, 1660.

Her husband, Harry Hale, whose second wife she became, Nov. 14, 1815, was sixth in descent from Thomas Hale, of Newbury, 1635, through Thomas,[2] who married Mary Hutchinson, Thomas,[3] who married Sarah Northend, Moses,[4] who married Elizabeth Wheeler, and Nathan,[5])colonel in the revolutionary army), who married Abigail Grout. Among his original immigrant ancestors in New-England, were Thomas Hale, Newbury 1635; Richard Hutchinson, Salem 1635; Ezekiel Northend, Rowley 1645; Francis Lambert, Rowley before 1640; John Wheeler, Newbury 1635; Humphrey Wise, Ipswich, 1639; John Grant, Watertown 1634; Nicholas Bresby, Watertown 1637; Edward Dix, Boston 1630, and John Barnard, Watertown 1634.

Mrs. Hale became the mother of seven children, all of whom survived her, and all, with three of her four surviving step-children, followed her body to the grave. Her husband died June, 2, 1861, at the age of 81.

Mrs. Hale was a woman of rare mental and moral endowments, intelligent, acute, vigorous, just, conscientious, kind and genial. She retained her physical vigor to her last sickness, and her intellectual strength almost to the day of her death. In all the relations of her long life she bore herself most blamelessly and lovingly, and her children "rise up and call her *blessed*."

WHITMORE, Frederick H., in Farmington, Conn., Sept. 11, 1871, of apoplexy. He was born Dec. 8, 1824, son of Josiah Crooker and Elizabeth Ann (Culver) Whitmore, of New-York, a merchant of that city, for many years engaged in trade with St. Thomas, W.I. The earlier generations of the family are recorded in the REGISTER, x. 295, Isaiah C. being the fourth son of John and Huldah (Crooker) Whitmore, and grandson of Francis and Mary (Hall) Whitmore, who removed from Medford to Bowdoinham.

Mr. Frederick Whitmore was for a long time in business in St. Thomas, but retired from active life some years ago on account of impaired health. He married, Oct. 21, 1848, Mary Emily Curtis, of New-Haven, Conn., by whom he had several children.

John A. Poor

NEW-ENGLAND
HISTORICAL AND GENEALOGICAL REGISTER
AND
ANTIQUARIAN JOURNAL.

VOL. XXVI. OCTOBER, 1872. No. 4.

HON. JOHN ALFRED POOR, OF PORTLAND, ME.

Communicated by CHARLES W. TUTTLE, A.M.

JOHN ALFRED POOR was born in the town of Andover, in the western part of the state of Maine, January 8, 1808. His ancestors were sterling New-England people, and lived, for more than two hundred years, on the southern borders of the Merrimac river in Massachusetts. The names of Poor and Merrill are distinguished in the annals of Essex county. His maternal grandfather, Ezekiel Merrill, of Newbury, was the first white settler in the valley of the Androscoggin, where the new town of Andover was afterward seated. Merrill was soon followed to his home in the wilderness by a number of persons from Andover, Massachusetts, among whom was Dr. Silvanus Poor, the father of the subject of this memoir. For intelligence, character and energy, the first settlers were far above the average in such places. In a dozen years they wrought out, in those wilds, the elements of a town. The new settlement had grown large enough in 1804, to receive municipal privileges; and the residents applied for and received the corporate name of Andover, being the name of the town where the Poor family originated.

Dr. Poor united in his calling the functions of physician and farmer, not an uncommon occurrence in remote towns in New-England. He was a man of considerable mental power, an original and independent thinker, and well versed in the current topics of the day. He was a member of the convention which formed the first constitution of Maine; and he filled several other public positions. His home was the centre of an intelligent circle, and was visited by strangers of education and distinction. The books of the social library were kept at his house, bringing his family in contact with authors as well as readers. His brother, Dr. Ebenezer Poor, an intelligent and much respected physician, was a near neighbor.

In this place, with these surroundings, John Alfred Poor, the second son and third child of Dr. Silvanus Poor and his wife Mary, daughter of Ezekiel Merrill, the pioneer settler, passed the first twelve years of his life. During this period he attended the short terms of the public schools, in summer and winter, the current of his life being much the same as that of all boys living in country towns. Nearly fifty years later, in the presence of a scene that revived recollections of his youthful days, he made this touching allusion to this period of his life: "Reared among the hills of Oxford, where the hoary summits of White-Cap and Bald-Pate rear their lofty heads high above the surrounding mountains, my imagination was stimulated by familiarity with the most beautiful valleys and the grandest mountain scenery of New-England; but my heart panted for a sight of the ocean, whose sublimer aspects and mysterious revels had been pictured to my youthful mind by stories of travellers and descriptions in the impassioned language of poetry; and when, a boy of twelve, I first beheld in the clear sunlight of a winter's morning the outstretching waters of Belfast Bay,—embosomed by its surrounding hills and distant islands,—I experienced all those sublime emotions of delight that Wordsworth has recorded in the finest of all his poems. * * * My desires were then as wild and fathomless as the great deep, and the recollections of a not inactive life have already taught the lesson, that experience alone can teach, that the achievements of a man's life are of trifling account compared with the boundlessness of youthful hope and aspiration. This first visit to the seaside influenced no doubt my whole life,—made me fond of adventure on the ocean, eager for geographical knowledge, and studious of those agencies that stimulate commercial progress. I love the ocean with almost filial devotion, and without a daily sight of it I am never fully satisfied and contented." [1]

His longing for other scenes and other pursuits was soon gratified. In January, 1820, a year memorable in the history of Maine, he was sent to Bangor for the purpose of receiving an academical education preparatory to entering college. He lived there in the family of the Hon. Jacob McGaw, an eminent lawyer, whose wife was a younger sister of Dr. Poor.[2] Bangor was then fast becoming the leading commercial city in eastern Maine. The spirit of industrial enterprise, prevailing there, must have made a deep impression on the mind of the young student, coming from the quiet town of Andover, and possibly quickened in him a fondness for public enterprises. He pursued his studies in the Bangor Academy two years, during which time he made good progress in the classics, and in other branches of learning. It was now ascertained that his father's means were insufficient to defray the expense of a college education, as designed; and he returned immediately to his home in Andover. For a period of five years he labored, with little intermission, on his father's farm. During this time he received private instruction from his brother-in-law, the Rev. Thomas T. Stone, pastor of the Congregational church in Andover. In the winter of 1826, he taught successfully a public school in the town of Bethel. His life was varied by occasional visits to Portland, the theatre of his future active life, on business connected with the farm. This employment failed to satisfy his desires. He longed for a wider field of action, and for more congenial pursuits. He now resolved to study law. A good opportunity offered in the office of his uncle McGaw, who was in full practice at Bangor and president of the Penobscot Bar. On the fifth of September, 1827, he entered this office, as a law

[1] *Remarks at Belfast, Me.*, July 4, 1867, pp. 3, 4.

[2] Mr. McGaw, a graduate of Dartmouth College, was a life-long friend and correspondent of Daniel Webster. His wife, Phebe V. Poor, was often a visitor in the family of Senator Thompson in Salisbury before her marriage, and was well acquainted with Mr. Webster. She is often mentioned in his correspondence. "I am now ready for my departure, and only wait to give myself the pleasure of a ride to the upper part of Maine to accompany thither Miss Poor, who has been a while in Mr. Thompson's family, and whom you have heard mentioned." (Webster to Merrill, May 28, 1804; *Correspondence*, vol. i. p. 172.)

student, and remained four years and four months. During this time he lived with Mr. McGaw's family, a circumstance that contributed much to his advancement and personal comfort. Having finished his law studies he was admitted to the bar on his twenty-fourth birthday. Mr. McGaw immediately proposed to him a law partnership with himself, on equal terms, which Mr. Poor declined, preferring to begin professional life alone and in another place. Two days after his admission, he established himself in the historic village of Oldtown, twelve miles above Bangor. He secured a fair law business; but he soon discovered that this was too small a field for his ambition. The commercial enterprise of Bangor, a town about to receive civic honors, had a magnetic influence over him; and, after eight months residence at Oldtown, he returned to Bangor and formed a law partnership with his uncle McGaw, which continued till the autumn of 1838, when that gentleman retired from practice. Mr. Poor immediately formed a partnership with his younger brother, Henry Varnum Poor, Esq., a graduate of Bowdoin College, who had just completed his law studies in the office of McGaw & Poor. The brothers continued in the practice of law till April, 1846, when Mr. Poor, senior, removed to Portland, to enable him to carry out his great railway enterprises more effectually.

During the fourteen years he was at the bar in Bangor, he earned the reputation of being a sound lawyer and a public spirited citizen. His practice was large, and extended to all branches of the law. Among the notable causes in which he was retained, was the suit of Veazie vs. Wadleigh, involving title to valuable lands, and water power, on the Penobscot. This suit attracted a good deal of public attention at the time, not only on account of the parties interested, and the matter in issue, but of the great eminence of the counsel engaged. Daniel Webster was opposed by Jeremiah Mason, and they were the acknowledged heads of the bar in New-England. Mr. Poor, who was associated with Mr. Webster as junior counsel, prepared the history of the legal title to the disputed territory, with so much completeness, that Mr. Webster personally complimented him for the work. This was in 1835, only three years after his admission to practice.

While residing in Bangor he took an active part in the literary and municipal affairs of that city He was instrumental in establishing the Social Library, afterwards merged in the Mercantile Library Association; and, also, the Bangor Lyceum. For several years he was a member of the city government, and active in promoting the various interests of Bangor. He early predicted the future growth and prosperity of that city. In 1869, he attended the centennial celebration there, and made a characteristic address, which is printed in the proceedings on that occasion. Speaking of his relations with that place, he said: "In Bangor I spent my youth and early manhood. Here I formed my earliest and strongest attachments, and within her enclosures lie the remains of the departed. And while I can look with pride at the growth of Portland as the result of measures to which the best of my days were devoted, I can never look upon Bangor with any other emotions than those of the deepest regard and affection, and under the inspiration of a Centennial Celebration, I may be permitted, while reviewing the history of Bangor for fifty years, to speak with the confidence of a well assured judgment, of the true pathway to still higher achievements in the future."[1]

American politics come to the door of every man. It is almost impossible

[1] *Bangor Centennial Celebration*, p. 89.

for a young man to escape being drawn into political life, especially if he has a talent for public speaking. Mr. Poor became early interested on the whig side of politics, and was active in the support of the measures of that party. For many years he was a member of the state committee; and was eminently serviceable to the whigs in the year 1837 and again in 1840, when they carried the state election. He was among the first, in Portland, to advocate the nomination of Taylor for president. In later years his other, and higher interests, kept him from active politics; and only the graver and more philosophical political questions attracted his attention. He saw, regretfully, the wasting of the best energies in the state, in party strifes; and he lamented that for a period of forty years "struggles for personal success in politics had been paramount ideas, with few intermittent exceptions,"[1] in Maine, while the great natural resources of the state excited no public interest and lay undeveloped. He always contended that if a state policy favorable to railways and to manufactures had been early adopted, Maine would have been, at this time, not inferior to Massachusetts as a manufacturing state.

Many years before moving to Portland he became profoundly interested in the subject, then fresh, of locomotive railways, especially as they were likely to affect the commercial and other interests of Maine. The introduction of railways into New-England was an event that made a deep impression on his mind, and gave direction to his future life. He seems to have comprehended, at once, the full magnitude and importance of this new method of transportation, which he tersely characterized as "The great achievement of man, the most extraordinary instrument for good the world has yet reached."[2] The year 1834 is memorable in the history of locomotive railways in New-England. On the sixteenth of April, of that year, the first locomotive engine, with passenger cars attached, ran over a railway freshly laid between Boston and Newton, and afterwards extended to Worcester and beyond. A large number of persons were present in Boston to witness this novel experiment of travel by railway. Among the spectators who waited with breathless anxiety the first movement of the train, was Mr. Poor, then only twenty-six years of age, who had come from Bangor to witness the introduction of this new wonder of the age. Many years after the event, he described this scene and the impression it made on him. "Placed," he says, "upon the track, its driver, who came with it from England, stepped upon the platform with almost the airs of a juggler or a professor of chemistry, placed his hand upon the lever, and with a slight move of it the engine started at a speed worthy of the companion of the 'Rocket,'[3] amid the shouts and cheers of the multitude. It gave me such a shock that my hair seemed to start from the roots rather than to stand on end; and as I reflected in after years, the locomotive-engine grew into a greatness in my mind that left all other created things far behind it as marvels and wonders."[4] This kindled in him an enthusiasm on the subject of locomotive railways which continued to the end of life. He returned to Maine to meditate and reflect on what he had seen with his own eyes, little dreaming of the fame he was to achieve for himself in railway enterprises, within the next forty years.

[1] *Remarks at Belfast*, 1867, p. 38.
[2] *Ibid*, p. 51.
[3] The name of the first successful locomotive-engine built by the Stephensons in England, in 1829; it won the prize of £500 offered by the directors of the Liverpool and Manchester Railway.
[4] *Remarks at Belfast*, pp. 50, 51.

In 1836 the first locomotive railway was built in Maine, singularly enough, between Bangor and Oldtown. The practical working of this road was under his own observation; and from it he probably learned his first lessons in railway economy. This new mode of travelling soon commended itself to the public. The legislature adopted measures which led to the survey of several routes, for a railroad, between the seaboard in Maine and the St. Lawrence in Canada. That which connected Belfast and Quebec was regarded the shortest and most practicable route. This enterprise died in its birth, and nothing, but the report of the engineer, ever came of it. A railway from the seaboard to the St. Lawrence was more and more desired in Maine, as well as in Canada. In 1839 a survey was made for a railway between Portland and Lake Champlain; but this enterprise also died. It was obvious now that a hand to execute, as well as a head to plan, was needed in such an undertaking; that vast energy, rare executive powers and great persistency were required to carry out so great an enterprise.

While Mr. Poor was busily engaged in his profession in Bangor, he was not unmindful of what had been going on. He was studying the whole subject of future railways in Maine from the highest point of view, and aiming to construct a system. Thoroughly acquainted with its physical geography, the commercial, agricultural and manufacturing capacities of the state, he had a grasp of the entire subject superior to any other person; and, in 1844, he made public his plan for two great railways, both coming from without the state, traversing it nearly its entire length, and converging on Portland. The eastern terminus of one road was Halifax, and the western terminus of the other, Montreal. This stupendous project of connecting two empires by a common interest, besides the inestimable commercial advantages designed for Maine, looked to the shortening of the time of passage between New-York and Liverpool, about two days, and to a direct railway route from Portland to Montreal, thence to the great lakes and prairies in the west. This magnificent scheme, which must have seemed impossible of execution to most persons when he projected it, in the infancy of railways in Maine, he lived to see accomplished, through his own agency and indomitable perseverance, in less than thirty years.

In the autumn of 1844, having matured his plans, he bravely entered upon the execution of his great design to connect Portland and Montreal by an international railway, the first ever projected on this continent. The undertaking then might well seem appalling; more than two hundred and fifty miles of railway, at an estimated cost of $10,000,000! He traversed the valley of the St. Lawrence from Lake Erie downwards, to gain information for his purpose. From Montreal he crossed over his projected route to Portland, part of the way on foot, examining the country and making known his railway project. In Canada, Vermont, New-Hampshire, and in Maine, he caused public meetings to be held, at which he appeared and advocated the building of the road, and asked assistance and cöoperation in the enterprise. He wrote long communications to the Canadian and American press, calling public attention to it, and setting forth the necessity of building it immediately. Early in September he wrote a long letter from his native town, where he happened to be at the time, to the Portland *Advertiser*, giving an account of the various commercial and industrial interests of Canada which centred at Montreal, stating that the Canadian people desired direct communication with the seaboard, especially during the winter months when the St. Lawrence was closed with ice, and that the advantages of opening a trade with Montreal would be very great. He closed with an appeal to the citizens of Portland to take immediate action in favor of a railway between the two cities. His letter created a profound sensation in Portland, which he compared to "an alarm bell in the night, struck by the hand of a stranger."[1] He went to Portland, with a deputation from the country, and urged the citizens to embark in the undertaking. The principal citizens, appreciating the force of his arguments, and seeing the advantages certainly to accrue to the city, immediately came forward, headed by Judge Preble, to assist the Bangor lawyer in his great enterprise. The favorable action of Portland was felt throughout the whole length of the proposed route, and the work of preliminary organization went rapidly forward. A provisional survey of the route was executed before December. He devoted his energies to the organizing of a company, and to the procuring of a charter for the road. Just before the charter was obtained it was discovered that the wealth and the enterprise of Boston were in Canada, urging the Canadians to unite with that city and build the road to Boston. This created great alarm among the friends of Mr. Poor's project. It was a critical moment for Portland and for Maine interests. Canada desired an outlet for her staple products and merchandise, and it mattered but little to her in which of the Atlantic ports she found it. The commercial strength of Boston was immense, and was active. The capitalists and business men of that city joined in a protest to the parliament of Canada and to the merchants of Montreal, against his project. Vermont and New-Hampshire interests were also opposed to it, for it was not designed to stretch athwart these states, but only their northern extremities. Mr. Poor hastened to Canada to prevent the board of trade of Montreal from committing itself to the Boston interests. The circumstances of his journey, and the success of his mission, are memorable incidents in his life. He set out from Portland, at midnight, on the fifth of February, five days before the legislature of Maine granted the charter for his road, in the face of the most terrific snow storm of the winter, and drove through deep snows to Montreal, reaching that city on the morning of the fifth day of his journey, where the thermometer was standing 29° below zero. Speaking of this dreadful journey, and his mission, many years later, he said: "Every fibre of my frame thrills with horror at the recollection of it. I accomplished my task. I met the Montreal Board of Trade at 10 A.M. of that day, and prevented the adoption of a resolution, previously prepared, in favor of going to Boston with their line, instead of Portland, which would have been carried unanimously, but for my sudden appearance and the assurances given by me of the superior advantages of Portland over Boston. I was justly proud of the achievement. In return, I carry in my person the renewals of suffering, which fever and sciatica, following in the train of fatigue and exposure, have entailed upon an otherwise strong physical constitution. I could not go through such another exposure again, if I would, and I would not do it for all the wealth of the world. The terrors of a Canadian winter are too fearful to encounter in this way a second time. But my heart was in the enterprise, and my health, my life, and my future sufferings, were not thought of. All the events of this early history are more fresh in my mind than those of the last session of the legislature, for I trembled at every step with the timidity of a youthful adventurer over the perilous Alps, in view of the vast importance of the enterprise to the State."[2] But for his well directed efforts in Montreal, the road would have been built to Boston instead of Portland. This struggle for the Atlantic

[1] *Remarks at Rutland, Vt.*, 1869, p. 25.
[2] *Argument before Committee of Legislature*, 1865, pp. 17, 18.

terminus of the road was severe and protracted. He fought, single-handed, against every argument which wealth and commercial prestige could devise, before the committee on railways of the Canadian parliament, then in session. The arrival of Judge Preble at Montreal, a week later, with the charter granted by the legislature, assisted him in giving a final blow to the opposition. The work of organizing under the charter, and of procuring subscriptions to build the road, went rapidly forward. Judge Preble was chosen president, and Mr. Poor director, of the Atlantic and St. Lawrence Railroad Company, this being the corporate name of the American part of the line. So important was the undertaking considered, that the fourth of July, 1846, was selected to begin the construction of the Portland end of the line. In the presence of the assembled senators and representatives of Maine, and a vast concourse of citizens and strangers, and with great ceremony and applause, the work of building began on this memorable day, at Fish Point, at the entrance to Portland Harbor. This must have been a proud day for him. The Canadian company having organized and formed a union with the American for the purpose of constructing the entire road, as one line, the work of construction began also at Montreal.

The guage of this road, known as the medium broad guage, was determined on after the fullest consideration. Mr. Poor satisfied himself by extensive enquiries among railway engineers and others that the five foot six inch guage was the best theory or experience had devised for a railway where the highest working capacity was required. This guage was deliberately agreed on for this road by the two companies. In 1851, when the question of guage for the Great Western Railroad of Canada was before the Provincial Parliament, he went to Toronto and before the committee, and urged, with success, the adoption of this guage, which is now the standard for all British North America. The Maine Central, and European and North American roads are built with this guage. It was his purpose to extend the same guage road to Boston and New-York.

Mr. Poor watched over the work with the greatest anxiety, his interest in it never lessening for an instant, during the period of its construction. Its progress was marked by occasional festivals, at which he was always present. The road was completed through to Montreal, and the first train passed over it on the 18th of July, 1853. The consummation of this great work afforded him the highest satisfaction; and he lived to see his native state, and the city of Portland, derive all the great benefit from it which he had anticipated. His official connection with the Atlantic and St. Lawrence road continued till it was leased to the Grand Trunk Railway of Canada, in the summer of 1853. This disposition of the road originated with him and was carried out mainly by his personal exertions. It was a great benefit and relief to the company and to the contractors, who were born down and nearly wearied out with the vast expense of the undertaking.

As soon as he had secured the road to Montreal, and the work of construction was well under way, he turned his attention to this other railway project, connecting Portland, Bangor, St. John, and Halifax or some port east of it, in Nova Scotia. This line he regarded as an appropriate extension of the Montreal road, making but one international line of railway across the states, more than eight hundred miles long. His design was not only to shorten the time of passage between Europe and New-York, but to open the way for commercial and manufacturing enterprise, as well as for settlements, in the unoccupied lands of the state, abounding in rich soils, mineral treasures, great forests of lumber, and immense water power. His plan was to build a single line from Portland east by way of Lewiston, Gardner, Augusta, Waterville and Bangor, using the line of the Montreal road as a common trunk as far as the Danville junction, throwing branch lines, east and west, to other parts of the state. Immediately rival lines between Portland and Bangor were not only proposed, but actually begun, which so delayed and hindered the building of this line, that it was not completed to Bangor till 1855.

Early in the summer of 1850 he petitioned the legislature to authorize a survey to discover the best and most practical route between Bangor and the New-Brunswick line, for this road. In this petition he took occasion to present strong reasons why the state should favor the building of this railway. Very soon after, as chairman of a committee of citizens of Portland, he issued a circular letter addressed to the governor and council and the legislature of Maine, and, also, to railroad companies, and to friends of public improvement, in the United States and in the British provinces, inviting them to attend a convention at Portland to consider the project of reducing the time of passage between London and New-York to five days. This convention met on the last day of July, and continued in session three days, presided over by the governor of Maine. There was a large attendance of distinguished persons from the British Provinces as well as from the United States. Mr. Poor was recognized by the convention as the originator of great railway enterprises, especially the projected one to extend as far east as there was land to build on. The convention appointed a committee, with Mr. Poor as chairman, to open communication with the English and American governments in relation to mail contracts on this route, and also to confer with other great companies concerning the building of this railway. This convention was recognized as the first actual reunion of the people of the provinces and the states since the revolution. It produced favorable effects, both commercially and politically, on the relations between these two countries. His favorite maxim was that political boundaries should form no restriction on commercial enterprise.

The legislature of Maine immediately granted a charter for his road and appropriated $5000 to survey the route, and instructed the governor to apply to the United States for aid to this enterprise. The Province of New-Brunswick soon granted a charter for the road in that Province. Want of means to build the road through eastern Maine seemed, for a long time, likely to defeat it. The Montreal road had absorbed all the capital that could be spared for great lines of railway; and local railways were in want of building capital. He exerted himself, in every conceivable way, to procure the means. First he applied to Massachusetts for a grant of its public lands lying in Maine in aid of this road, and came near obtaining it. He applied to congress for aid, without any favorable result. In 1853, the company organized under the charter, as the European and North American Railway Company, and he was chosen president of the company, and held the office till 1866. He immediately located the road, and for ten years labored to get funds to build it. Meantime the road in New-Brunswick and Nova Scotia, to connect with it, was got under way and partly built. In 1861 he presented to the Maine legislature a long memorial, which was printed by order of the senate, in behalf of the European and North American Railway Company. It contains an elaborate statistical review of the various resources and industries of Maine, with his views and plans of developing and improving the same. The primary design of this memorial was to procure state aid for building the road, as well as to show the pressing need of adopting a state policy encouraging manufactures as well as settlements on the public lands of the state. In 1864 the state yielded to his solicitations, and granted eight hundred thousand acres of the public lands, subject to a claim of Massachusetts on the same for a certain amount, and all the timber in ten townships, to aid the building of the road. The state, at the same time, passed over to the company all its claim against the general government accruing prior to 1860, and, by a resolve, invited the co-operation of Massachusetts in aid of this enterprise. On application to that State for aid, it was refused on the ground of a statute of Maine, passed in 1860, forbidding the change of guage on any railroad in Maine, which was regarded as unfriendly legislation. Without the aid of Massachusetts, the grant by Maine to aid the building of the road was not available. Mr. Poor regarded the statute of no advantage to the interests of Maine, but otherwise, and he applied at once to the legislature then sitting, for a repeal of it, and for leave to lay a third rail on the Portland, Saco and Portsmouth Railroad, with a view of extending the broad guage line from Halifax to Boston and New-York. He appeared before the committee on railways on the fourteenth of February, 1865, and made a long argument in favor of repeal, reviewing at length, and with great ability, the railway interests of Maine, and the history of the various roads, which is printed. He claimed that there should be no restriction on railway transit. The legislature, not without much opposition from interested parties, and from those of narrow views in these matters, repealed the act, and then he prevailed on Massachusetts to release its claim on these lands granted by Maine, and also to allow the road the part of her joint claim with Maine against the general government. Upon this being done the work of construction immediately began, and in less than six years was completed. It is now in operation, and fulfils all that he predicted for it.

A considerable part of twenty years of his life was devoted to the consummation of this great enterprise. "His name," says one well acquainted with the history of the road, "will be forever associated with the European and North American Railway, as inseparably as the name of De Witt Clinton with the Erie Canal. With no funds to build the road except a small land grant and an assignment of the claims of Maine and Massachusetts upon the general government; claims which that government had repudiated for more than thirty years, he went to work alone, and by ceaseless industry and by using influences which no one else knew how to wield, by persistent and unanswerable arguments everywhere plied, by both pen and tongue, he enlisted legislators in congress and public men in the states in his favor, secured the confidence of capitalists, overcame all difficulty, bore down all opposition, wearied out delay itself, and achieved a final and complete success."[1]

In 1851 he was chosen president of the York and Cumberland Railroad. He immediately reorganized the company and secured the building of the road from Gorham to the Saco river. Soon after his re-election in 1852, he resigned the presidency in favor of Col. Clapp, who had became chief proprietor, and the name was changed to the Portland and Rochester Railroad. This road is now built, and in full and successful operation.

He lent his aid in carrying out other railway projects, the Maine Central, the Belfast and Moosehead Lake, the Bangor and Piscataquis, and the

[1] *Speech of the Hon. W. H. M'Crillis at a banquet given to the President of the United States and the Gov. General of the Dominion of Canada, in Norembega Hall, at Bangor,* Oct. 18, 1871.

Somerset railroads. He believed in the sufficiency of railroads properly guided to develope the immense resources of Maine, the great object of all his thoughts and actions.

One of his favorite plans for developing the material resources of the state, and adding to the public wealth, was legislative encouragement of settlements on the unoccupied public lands. His grand idea of the capacities of the state and his plans of improvement, looked to an almost indefinite enlargement of the wealth and population of the state in this direction. "The State of Maine," he says, "from the extent of its territory,—its geographical position,—its physical geography, and its geological structure, has all the elements essential to an independent empire. By a development of its resources, it can sustain a population, at a rate per square mile, equal to that of the most densely populated countries in Europe."[1] In several memorials written by him and presented to the legislature, between 1849 and 1862, he fully set forth his views on this subject, and urged the legislature to adopt a state policy favorable to settlements on these lands. As early as June, 1850, he wrote: "We have failed so far to attract to the state the most valuable class of emigrants that seek for a climate and soil similar to that of Germany and Switzerland, which resemble our own. If proper encouragement were held out to them we might expect the emigrants from the north of Europe to prefer the soil and climate of Maine to that of the Mississippi valley."[2]

He aimed at arresting emigration from the state, as well as inviting immigration to it. A comparative view of the population at various epochs showed that emigration from the state was constantly going on. "This," he says, "is a great draw-back to her prosperity. No finer people are born on the face of the globe, and those who leave her distinguish themselves all over the country. Our duty is to keep these men at home, to develope our own state; to rear villages at all the waterfalls; to cultivate the rich soils of the Penobscot, the Kennebec, the Aroostook and St. John Valleys; to own as well as build and sail our own commercial marine."[3] Persuaded that some immediate legislative action favorable to immigration and settlement in the great forests of the state was required, he delivered a public address, in 1864, in the hall of the house of representatives, giving his views on the subject and urging public action in the matter. Gradually the importance of his suggestions began to be appreciated; and, in 1867, his project of inviting emigrants from the north of Europe to settle on the public lands began to be favorably received. In 1870 the legislature of Maine established a board of immigration to carry out this plan of settling a Scandinavian population in the north-eastern part of the state; and in July of this year the first colony from Sweden arrived and settled in the valley of the Aroostook. This colony has since been much increased, and is in a flourishing condition, promising to be as great a public benefit as he anticipated, twenty years before.

Always aiming to achieve great commercial results, and to make great public improvements, regardless of political boundaries and prejudices, he directed the whole force of his energies, early in 1868, to the carrying out of his long meditated plan of making an eastern outlet, for the great staple commodities of the west, superior to any in existence or hitherto projected.

[1] *Memorial of European and North American Railroad Company*, p. 3.
[2] *Petition to the Legislature of Maine for a Survey of the European and North American Railway.*
[3] *Argument before Legislative Committee*, p. 47.

His plan was to connect, by railway, Chicago and other great commercial centres in that direction, with the capacious harbor of Portland, the ocean terminus of his other great railways. But this did not embrace his ultimate design; for he grasped the commercial relations of the whole continent, leaving no room for another railroad projector between the Atlantic and Pacific Ocean in these latitudes. He looked upon this line, designed mainly to afford ready and cheap transportation of bread stuffs to the Atlantic States, and to Europe, as "a chief link in that golden belt which is to span the continent of North America at its widest part, under the name of *The Trans-Continental Railway.*"[1] This stupendous design had for its object the connecting, so far as possible by railway, of the great commercial centres of Europe, North America and Asia.

He began by procuring a charter for a railroad from Portland direct to Rutland, Vermont. Soon after he conceived the idea of advancing the interests of his projected road, by an international commercial convention to be held at Portland, for the purpose of concentrating public attention upon the splendid harbor there, as the cheapest port of exportation of western produce, as well as upon his great plan of a direct railway across the continent from the Atlantic to the Pacific shore. He prepared a call for the convention, in which he set forth, with a masterly hand, his railway plans and designs. The convention met in Portland on the fourth of August, 1868, and was presided over by Gov. Merrill, of Iowa. More than three hundred persons responded, and were present, many of them distinguished in public life, from all parts of the United States and the British Provinces. Mr. Poor was active in the convention and served on its committees. His plans of railway extension were heartily approved.

On the 24th of June, 1869, he delivered before a railroad convention, at Rutland, an address on the subject of his plan for a continental railway, but more especially in favor of building, at once, the road from Portland to Rutland and Oswego. This address fills seventy-five octavo pages, and bears the marks of a mature judgment, profound and various knowledge on the subject of the economy of railroads, and of their relations to the commerce of the country.

In March, 1870, the charter for this road was amended and it took the name of the Portland, Rutland, Oswego and Chicago Railway Company. In December following, the company organized under it with Mr. Poor as president. In January, 1871, he drew up and presented to congress, on behalf of the company, a memorial setting forth the merits of the proposed road as a public enterprise, and asked congress to constitute it a national highway. He also prepared a bill, which was laid before congress by Senator Hamlin, authorizing the postmaster general to contract with this company to carry the mails between Chicago and Portland, and also authorizing government assistance for building the road. As president of the company he prepared the first annual report of the directors, which he presented at the annual meeting on the 26th of July, 1871. His elaborate report shows that he had succeeded in devising a plan for building the road. Six railway companies, along the projected route, had agreed to unite and act as one, and aid in building the road. Owing to the delay of one company the joint agreement could not be carried into effect at that meeting, and it was adjourned to the twenty-ninth day of September. Two weeks before

[1] *Remarks at Rutland*, 1869, p. 3.

the day of the adjourned meeting the great head of the enterprise was no more, having died suddenly on the fifth of September.

Mr. Poor's interest in the development and utilization of the natural powers of his native State is well illustrated in the history of the hydrographic survey of Maine, an undertaking suggested by him, and mainly carried out under his direction. "Maine," he says, "with her extended and deeply indented seacoast, on the line of favoring winds; her mountainous regions that distil in profusion the clear waters that swell its rivers, descending from high elevations, by circuitous courses, in a succession of cascades to the ocean,—and rich forests, and through a productive soil, may in time rival any region of the globe, in the extent of her manufactures and commerce. Its great and distinguishing natural feature is its water power, surpassing that of any section of the globe of equal extent."[1] In a memorial to the legislature, prepared by him for the Agricultural Society of Maine, in 1858, he strongly urged a public survey of the water power of the State. This appeal was renewed, and supported with a great variety of illustrations, in a memorial to the legislature in 1861, prepared by him in behalf of the European and North American Railway Company. The necessity and expediency of such a survey were at length recognized by the legislature; and, in the spring of 1867, it authorized the survey to be made under the direction of three commissioners to be appointed by the governor and council. He was appointed one of the commissioners and chairman of the board. In December, 1867, the commissioners made their report to the governor. This report, filling thirty closely printed octavo pages, was written by Mr. Poor; and it bears all the marks of his vast knowledge and full appreciation of the geographical and physical characteristics of Maine. The result of the survey is, two printed volumes, making over eight hundred pages, containing a full description of the water power of the State, prepared by Walter Wells, Esq., secretary of the commissioners.

Mr. Poor never was an aspirant for public office. His capacity, energy, address, and knowledge of public affairs, admirably fitted him for public employment. In several instances he accepted responsible positions tendered him by the governor of Maine. In 1852 he was appointed by Gov. Hubbard a joint agent, with Hon. Anson P. Morrill, to conduct the negotiation which ultimately led to the purchase, of Massachusetts, by Maine, of the public lands of the former state lying in Maine. In 1861 and 1862, he was joint commissioner, with Hon. Reuel Williams, in behalf of Maine, on the subject of the coast defences of that state, and was active in this service. President Lincoln tendered him the office of commissioner in charge of the public defences of the north-eastern coast, a position of great responsibility, which he declined. He also declined an honorable position tendered to him in the treasury department in Washington. In 1861, the office of consul general to Canada was open to him, but he did not desire it.

In 1868 the commissioner of the general land office in Washington applied to Gov. Chamberlain for an account of the progress, in population, manufactures, agriculture and commerce, in Maine, since the last national census. The governor immediately requested Mr. Poor to furnish this important information, recognizing in him the best qualified person in the state for this undertaking. He accepted the commission, and executed it with his usual ability and to the entire satisfaction of the government.

[1] *Memorial of European and North American Railway Company*, p. 20.

His elaborate statistical report fills fourteen closely printed pages of the published documents of Maine.

Mr. Poor's historical investigations, which form no inconsiderable part of his title to public consideration and remembrance, occupied much of his attention during the best years of his life. However widely different this interest may seem from the leading pursuit of his life, it is embraced in his early design to place his native state, in all respects, where the motto on its official seal assigns her. "If there is anything," he says "which I desire above all things else, it is to do what in me lies for the honor, the welfare, and the glory and renown of Maine. It is my native State, and I inherit, perhaps to a fault of weakness, a love for her, as my native land and home. I have seen something of other states and other lands, and until I had gone abroad, I never knew the true beauty, the inherent greatness, the wonderful resources of Maine; so rich in its natural scenery, so full of all the elements of wealth and power, and so capable of the highest results of the most refined civilization."[1] All the acts of his life were in harmony with this declaration. His steady devotion to the public interests of Maine, and his firm loyalty to that state, have few if any parallels in its history.

His interest in local history must have begun early; for he furnished Williamson, for the history of Maine, a sketch of his native town, while a student of law. Some acquaintance with the provincial and ante-provincial history of Maine he must have made while tracing the title to lands in the Veazie suit. His interest in the history of Maine was much stimulated by his experience in Canada, in 1845, when the commercial position of Maine was matched with Massachusetts in the contest for the Atlantic terminus of his projected railway. His opponents did not spare his native state, nor forget how recently she was substantially a province of Massachusetts. Neither commercially, politically, nor historically was she allowed the standing he claimed for her, by those opposed to Portland as the terminus of the railway. His indignation was thoroughly aroused, and he resolved to examine more thoroughly, not only the merits of his own state, but the foundation of the pretences of her assailants.

The next year, 1846, he was chosen a member of the Maine Historical Society, and was a most useful and active member to the end of his days. It was at this time that Gorges's *Briefe Narration* appeared in the second volume of the Collections of the Maine Historical Society, and fixed his attention upon this great author whom he never after ceased to praise and to honor. He devoted his leisure time to the study of the early history of New-England, seeking for the facts in documents and publications of that period, rather than in later writers. His interest in the subject grew stronger as he advanced; and, when he traced English navigators and English settlers, to the shores of Maine prior to 1620, the assumed beginning of New-England history, the subject became a passion with him, and never abated while he lived.

Among the memorable historical occurrences, connected with early English colonization in America, those which transpired within the limits of Maine prior to any consecrated in our popular history, made a deep impression on his mind. Not less impressive was the fact, that, prominent among the noble men concerned in that great achievement which secured for England a portion of the vast domain of the New World, was Sir Ferdinando Gorges, the illustrious founder of Maine. As soon as he had mastered the

[1] *Argument before the Committee of Legislation*, 1865, p. 65.

history of English colonization on this continent, he resolved to give Maine, and to her great founder, their true historic position in New-England history.

The first fruit of his historical studies and investigation, was an elaborate paper on *English Colonization in America*, which he read before the Maine Historical Society, in June, 1859, and also before the New-York Historical Society, in October following, receiving the thanks of both societies. In this paper, which attracted a good deal of attention among historical students, he declared his intention to be "to trace the earliest practical efforts to plant the English race in America, and to vindicate the claims of Sir Ferdinando Gorges, the proprietor of my native State, to the proud title of FATHER OF ENGLISH COLONIZATION IN AMERICA."[1]

The title by which England held possessions in North America, and the services of those actively concerned in securing this title, and maintaining it by acts of jurisdiction and possession, to the exclusion of other European nations, were the points which he aimed to make conspicuous, and to invite public attention. He fixed upon the royal charter granted by King James of England to a company of his subjects, April 10, 1606, authorizing the "planting of colonies or plantations in North America," between the thirty-fourth and forty-fifth degrees of latitude, as the initial step in the establishment of English title to New-England. The taking of formal possession, under this charter, at the mouth of the Sagadahoc, now Kennebec, river, Aug. 19, 1607, by a company of English Colonists, he regarded as the consummation of the English title, and as the great event in American history.

Of those concerned in this great undertaking, and in the events which led to it, and followed it, he claimed the leadership for Sir Ferdinando Gorges and his associates. After reviewing the efforts of Gorges, and his associates, to plant English Colonies in New-England, and also the movements of the Puritans at home and abroad, he concludes, that "The history of the times disproves the popular theory, that 'religious impulse accomplished the early settlement of New-England;' by which is meant the settlement therein of the Puritans. But the plan of colonizing America did not originate with them, nor were they in any sense the leaders of the movement. They resorted hither from necessity, and while they profited by the labors and enterprise of others, achieved nothing beyond those in a subordinate position. The settlement of New-England was the work of many years, and was achieved by the same influences as those still at work to extend the Saxo-Norman race. It was the legitimate result of commercial ideas and adventurous spirit of the times."[2] This position, sustained by all the facts of history, he fearlessly maintained. In his zeal to defend it, and to make prominent the merits of Gorges and his associates, he was led to speak of some of the Plymouth colonists with rather too much severity, which occasioned some resentment. Puritan intolerance was shocking to him, made him feel indignant towards those who practised it, and he never let an occasion pass to speak of its persecutions, as he thought.

To the enterprising Sir Ferdinando Gorges, whom he so much resembled in energy of character, persistency, and public spirit, he awards the merit of saving the territory of New-England from the grasp of the French, and of introducing and settling it with English colonists. "But for Gorges," he

[1] *English Colonization in America*, p. 6.

[2] *Ibid*, p. 53.

says, "the western continent must have fallen under the dominion of Roman Catholic France, and Celtic civilization would have changed its destiny; for all New-England was in possession of the French prior to 1606."[1]

He expresses his indignation in strong terms, at the treatment which Gorges, and his associates, received at the hands of their puritan contemporaries, and of our historians, on account of their religious and political attachments in that age, and rejoices that the time has come when a more liberal spirit prevails, and when the merits of these men can be recognized. "But Gorges's fame," he adds, "shall yet eclipse that of any other name in our American annals. My native state has been remiss in the discharge of this duty, and supinely allowed the history of New-England to cluster around the Rock of Plymouth instead of standing clearly out in the earlier deeds of the great minds that saved New-England and the continent from the grasp of the French."[2]

Designing to procure some honorable recognition in Maine for the name of Gorges, he drew up, in 1860, a petition addressed to the secretary of war, and procured signers to it, asking that the new fort in Portland harbor may be named Fort Gorges, and it was ordered to take this name. He had a design to form an association for the purpose of erecting a monument to the memory of Gorges, within the limits of the ancient "Province of Mayne."

The position he had taken with regard to the historical and political significance of the royal charter of 1606, and the settlement at Sagadahoc the following year, awakened a new interest, especially in Maine, in the subject of English colonization in New-England. The transfer of the point of the initial movement of English colonization from the shores of Massachusetts to the shores of Maine, and the placing of Gorges at the head of it, created a new era in historical investigation.

Believing the settlement at Sagadahoc to have all the significance which he claimed for it, he aimed to direct public attention to the event, and to revive the memory of the actors in the great enterprise. In the autumn of 1861, he persuaded Mr. Williams, his associate commissioner on the coast defences of Maine, to join with him in an application to the secretary of war, requesting that the new fort about to be erected at the mouth of the Kennebec river, on the site of the first settlement, may be named Fort Popham, in honor of the venerable George Popham who led the first British colony into New-England in 1607. This name was approved by the national government, and the work of construction begun.

His associates of the Maine Historical Society, approving his design of attaching these historic names of Popham and Gorges to great national works of defence within the state, joined readily with him in a design to place a memorial stone, with appropriate inscriptions, in the walls of fort Popham. Leave to do this being obtained of the government, it was agreed by all interested to make the act of placing the stone in position, one of solemn commemoration; and August 29, 1862, being the anniversary of the settlement, was selected for the commemoration service. A large executive committee, of which Mr. Poor was one, consisting of leading citizens in all parts of the state, carried out the design on a scale commensurate with the magnitude and importance of the occasion. He was selected to deliver the historical address, while several of his distinguished associates

[1] *English Colonization in America*, p. 84.
[2] *Ibid*, p. 90.

of the Historical Society performed conspicuous parts in the commemoration services. He delivered the address at Fort Popham on the two hundred and fifty-fifth anniversary of the event, in the presence of the principal officers of state, and of many distinguished persons from other New-England States. It is estimated that six thousand persons were present on the occasion. It was a day never forgotten by him; for this act and this ceremonial was the result of his own efforts to secure for Maine her true place in history. His address was appropriate, full of historical research, and contained a complete narrative of English colonization on these shores. He enforced his views of the importance of the event with vigorous reasoning and with full historical illustration. This address, and the one on English Colonization, with many historical papers procured by him from European archives, are printed in the Memorial volume of the Popham Celebration.

About this time he drew up a memorial asking for an appropriation to defray the expense of procuring copies of documents bearing on the early history of Maine, from the British State Paper office, and was joined, in this, by the Rev. Dr. Woods and the Rev. Dr. Ballard, both eminent historical scholars, and deeply interested in Mr. Poor's historical investigations. This memorial was presented to the legislature and an appropriation made.

Commemorative services have been held annually ever since at Fort Popham. On nearly every occasion he has been present and taken part in the proceedings. In 1868 he prepared and read there an elaborate address, in which he restated his position on the "Popham question," as it is called, added some freshly discovered evidence in support of his views, chiefly from De Carayon, and reviewed the various attacks made on the position he had taken with regard to the historical and political importance of the settlement under Popham. He was present there, for the last time, on the two hundred and sixty-second anniversary of the event, and made a brief speech.

At the field meeting of the historical society held in the ancient town of York on the twenty-ninth of August, 1870, he was present and read a carefully prepared paper, reviewing the events leading to colonization on these shores, and introducing important documentary evidence, recently obtained from European archives through the agency of the Rev. Dr. Woods, bearing on the title which England asserted to the territory of New-England in 1613, when Argall destroyed the French settlement at Mt. Desert. It appears that the English government justified the act of Argall on the ground that the French were then within the limits of territory granted to English subjects, in 1606, who were in possession of the same, and that France acquiesced in the claim. A few days later, at a joint meeting of the Maine and New-Hampshire Historical Societies, held at Portsmouth, he was present and made a brief characteristic speech, reviewing the early history of the two States, which closed his public historical addresses.

It is quite impossible to give an adequate idea, in this brief sketch, of Mr. Poor's historical labors, covering a period of more than fifteen years. The results are known and appreciated by historical students. Besides awakening a general interest in our early history, he gave an immense impulse to the work of the Maine Historical Society, resulting in sending the Rev. Dr. Woods to Europe to make historical researches, bearing on the early discovery and settlement of Maine, and in the publication of a valuable volume on discovery, soon to be followed by others on colonization. It was always his design to go to Europe and there study the history of the period of discovery and colonization of New-England, in the light of original records preserved in the archives of the maritime nations. Long before his death he had no superior in knowledge, and in appreciation of our early history He was member of the New-England Historic, Genealogical Soeiety, and corresponding member of the historical societies of New-Hampshire, Vermont, New-York and Pennsylvania.

In 1848 he, and his brother, purchased the American Railway Journal, and it was edited by his brother till 1861, when they sold their interest in it. He was occasionally a contributor to its columns; and always on the subject of railways, to the public press in the United States and Canada.

Finding that he was unable to reach the public mind and to give full exposition of his plans of railway extension through the medium of a press guided and controlled by others, he resolved on finding means to give his views to the public, and to advocate his measures, in his own way. To this end he projected and established a newspaper in Portland, and was the editor from the time of its first issue in 1853, to 1859, when it became merged in the *Daily Advertiser*, a paper in which he had purchased an interest. It was called *The State of Maine*, a name purposely and felicitously chosen, since it was specially devoted to the advocacy of the development of the great interests of the state, and was issued daily, tri-weekly and weekly. His foremost purpose in this enterprise was that of educating the public to a full comprehension of the importance, to the interests of Maine, of building the European and North American Railway, and to secure for it favorable legislative action. To the carrying out of this great railway enterprise, projected by him many years before, he labored with his pen without ceasing. He made the columns of his paper a vehicle to carry far and near every argument which could be devised favorable to the execution of this great undertaking.

While steadily devoted to the various purposes for which it was originally established, it was a medium for making public his views on the few political questions in which he took an active interest. Originally a whig, he was found, when that party melted away, acting with the republicans; but he reserved for himself a freedom of political action and opinion. He took the lead in opposition to the prohibitory liquor law to which the republican party committed itself in 1855, and devoted the strength of the columns of his paper to defeat that measure. At his suggestion, the Hon. Hannibal Hamlin, an avowed opponent of prohibition, was brought forward as candidate for governor in 1856, and elected by a large majority. He was strongly opposed to the repeal of the Missouri compromise, and he directed the whole force of his paper against that measure. In the arena of politics he was much the same, as in other things, bold, fearless and uncompromising. Seeking no political preferment himself, he could act independently and with greater effect.

Mr. Poor always felt the greatest interest in whatever related to the welfare and prosperity of Portland, his residence for the last twenty-five years of his life. His name is memorably associated with its great commercial and industrial interests. By the effect of enterprises of his own device and execution, he lived to see it advance in wealth and population far beyond the limits set for it by the most hopeful. Soon after removing there he formed a law-partnership with John M. Adams, Esq., which continued several years, the firm being chiefly engaged in railway causes. After the dissolution of the partnership Mr. Poor soon abandoned the practice of law, other matters absorbing his whole attention.

With a true perception of its maritime position and fitness for a great commercial metropolis, he made it the Atlantic terminus of his first great railway enterprise. While other seaports, in the gulf of Maine, were bidding for the ocean terminus of the Atlantic and St. Lawrence Railroad, he fought stoutly and bravely for Portland, and won, placing that city in the very front rank of marine ports. Soon after he came to Portland he organized a company, and procured for it a charter, for the manufacture of locomotives and cars. This was an entirely successful enterprise, and a great public benefit to the city as well as to the state. It was known as the "Portland Locomotive Works," and the leading manufactory in the state. For many years he was president of the company. In 1857 he proposed the building of a new city hall on a scale commensurate with his anticipated growth and importance of the city, on the site of the court house and jail. His design was to fill the entire square from Chestnut to Myrtle street with the new edifice. The proposition met with much opposition at first. He zealously advocated the scheme, in his paper and otherwise, until his plan was substantially adopted. The hall was built, and was the most beautiful and elaborate public structure in Maine. It was partly destroyed by the memorable fire of July 4, 1866; but has since been rebuilt.

He is identified with the successful establishment of the Gas Light Company in Portland. He organized the company and was president till the sale to the city of half its stock, a step which put it on a good financial basis.

He is conspicuous in the history of another great city improvement, projected by him prior to 1852. This was the opening of Commercial street, making direct communication across the city from the station of the Atlantic and St. Lawrence road to the station of the Portland and Portsmouth road. While this was recognized as a desirable public improvement, still the difficulties and the expense attending it were looked upon as formidable. The measure met with great opposition, and by this means awakened the attention of all classes of citizens. He advocated, with all his force, the opening of this street, and persisted in keeping his arguments before the public till the measure was adopted, and the road opened. The benefit which resulted to the city from opening this street was immense; and he was always justly proud of being the originator of the enterprise.

At the time of the great fire in Portland he was in Washington, and active in the efforts there made to collect subscriptions for the sufferers. The mayor of that city publicly expressed his obligation to Mr. Poor for the plan which led to so generous a subscription in that city.

No other person accomplished so much for the commercial interests of Portland as Mr. Poor did while he lived there. Never, for a moment, did his zeal for its advancement abate; and never did his efforts to make it the leading commercial metropolis of New-England lessen. He was fond of contrasting its comparative magnitude, at various epochs within his memory, and of forming estimates of its future greatness. "I am proud," he said a few years ago, "of Portland; I rejoice at her prosperity. I cannot walk the streets of that beautiful city, without a feeling of conscious pride. I have watched its prosperity, step by step. I have seen it grow up from the 'deserted village' of 1843, to the commercial metropolis of 1865."[1]

Mr. Poor was a ready and efficient writer, and his pen was never long idle. His industry is attested by more than fifty printed pamphlets, written by him, on various subjects; while his contributions to the public press, at

[1] *Argument before Legislative Committee*, Feb. 14, 1865, p. 18.

home and abroad, are without number. He always wrote for a purpose, and all his writings are characterized for clearness and force. His principal writings were his historical memoirs, addresses at railway conventions, memorials to Legislatures, and a memoir of the Hon. Reuel Williams, prepared and read before the historical society at the request of that body. The character and eminent ability of Mr. Williams procured for him the title of the "first citizen of Maine." He was always a firm friend to Mr. Poor, and had great respect for his ability as a railway projector, statistician, and historical investigator.

Having already much exceeded the limits assigned for this memoir, I must here pause, and leave to others the labor of delineating more completely the character and the deeds of this remarkable man. His achievements attest his great powers, his unwearied industry, and the biases of his mind. His name and memory are interwoven with the history of his native state during the period of his activity. Mr. Poor was distinguished for the courteousness of his manners, liberal views, and social feelings. He was bred in the Congregational church, and in that religious faith he lived and died. In domestic life he was delightful, free, easy, and contented. He died suddenly, at his residence in Portland, on Tuesday morning, September 5, 1871. The day before, he was busy and active in the matters of his projected railway to Chicago. Late in that day he wrote an article on railways, which appeared in the *Argus* newspaper the morning he died. His death made a profound sensation; for he had been publicly and widely known for a quarter of a century. The city government and the Board of Trade, of Portland, met and passed resolutions, expressing their sense of his merits and of the public loss. In the Superior Court appropriate notice of his decease was taken by the bar, and Judge Goddard adjourned the court, after a somewhat extended review of his life and public services. The Maine Historical Society held a special meeting and passed a series of resolutions, expressing a sense of deep obligation to Mr. Poor for his great services in the department of history, as well as in behalf of the material interests of the state, and declaring that he is entitled to be regarded as a public benefactor and to be held in grateful remembrance by his fellow citizens.

Mr. Poor married July 8, 1833, Elizabeth Adams, daughter of the Hon. Thomas Adams Hill, a lawyer, and at one time the anti-masonic candidate for governor, of Bangor, She died January 14, 1837, having had children, viz.: Laura Elizabeth, Thomas Barker and Mary Frances Appleton, the eldest of whom alone survived her and her father. His second wife was Elizabeth, eldest daughter of the Hon. Benjamin Orr, an eminent lawyer, and sometime member of congress, of Brunswick. She died at Bangor, June 2, 1844, having had one son, Thomas, who died before her. He married, July 19, 1860, his third wife, Mrs. Margaret Robinson Gwynne, daughter of the late William Barr, of Cincinnati, who survives him.[1]

[1] The Maine Historical Society invited Mr. Tuttle to prepare and read before the society, a memoir of Mr. Poor, but being previously engaged to write one for the REGISTER, he was obliged to decline, for want of time. The society then requested him to read this memoir, and, with leave of the editor, it was read by Mr. Tuttle, before the society in Wiscasset, Me., on Thursday evening, Sept. 12, 1872.

A RECORD OF BIRTHS, MARRIAGES AND DEATHS IN PORTSMOUTH, N. H., FROM 1706 TO 1742.

Communicated by Col. JOSHUA W. PEIRCE, of Portsmouth.

Continued from vol. xxv. page 122.

Ruth Lebby Daughter of Isaac Lebby and Mary his wife was born Sep^{t} ye 5th 1730.

Jane Lebby Daughter of Isaac Lebby and Mary his wife was born Sep^{t} ye 11th 1733.

Ruben Lebby son of Isaac and Mary Lebby his wife was born Augt ye 11th 1734.

Mary Sevey Daughter of Ithamar Sevey and Mary his wife was born Decr ye 23 1734.

Henry Sevey son of Sam^{ll} Sevey and Abigail his wife was born ye 23^{d} of Apr^{l} 1719.

Meribah Lock Daughter of James Lock and Sarah his wife was born Octr ye 13th 1733.

Robert Moulton son of Jon^{a}. Moulton and Elizth his wife was born ye 20th of May 1733.

Eliz^{a}. Elkins Daughter of Henry Elkins and Catharine his wife was born March ye 11th 1733.

Mary Elkins Daughter of Henry Elkins and Catharine his wife was born Novr 12th 1734.

Mary Elkins ye Daughter of Henry Elkins and Catharine his wife was born ye 16th of feb^{y} 1731.

Mary Elkins Daughter of Henry Elkins and Catharine his wife was born ye 4th of Jany 1733.

Sarah Sevey Daught^{r} of Sam^{ll} Sevey and Abigail his wife was born Novr ye 20th 1716.

Joshua Rand son of Josh and Ruth Rand was born 23^{d} of Augt 1735.

Eliz^{a} Rand Daughter of Nathl and Eliz^{a} Rand was born ye 2^{d} of Augt 1716.

Mathew Nelson and Deliverance Lang Both of Portsm^{o} wr marry^{d} ye 30th of March 1736.

Henry Benson of Portsm^{o} and Mary Quint of Newington w^{r} marry^{d} ye 4th of Apr^{l} 1736.

Richard ye son of Rich^{d} and Love Cut was born 31st of Octr 1720.

Anna ye Daughter of Rich^{d} and Love Cut was born ye 29th of March 1723.

Wm Simpson of Portsm^{o} and Sarah Frost of N-Castle w^{r} marry^{d} 22^{d} Apr^{l} 1736.

Thomas Main of Portsm^{o} and Mercy Cromwell of Dover w^{r} marry^{d} ye 27th of Apr^{l} 1736.

Joseph Welch son of Joseph and Sarah Welch was born ye 27th of Sep^{t} 1735.

George Warren and Martha Noble both of Portsm^{o} w^{r} marry^{d} ye 24th of June 1736.

George Taylor of Saint Mary's Parish in Limerick in ye Kingdom of Ireland and Sarah Phicket of Portsm^{o} w^{r} marry^{d} 23^{d} of June 1736.

Stacye Dalling and Sarah Pevey both of Portsm^o were marry^d ye 1st of July 1736.

Hugh Mory of Tarkum in Devonshire in Great Brittain and Grace Lee wid^o of Portsm^o w^r marry^d 22^d Augt 1736.

John Sherburn and Eliz^a Sherburn both of Portsm^o were marry^d ye 12th of Sep^t 1736.

Thomas Roe and Eliz^a Samson both of Portsm^o w^r marry^d ye 28th of Octr 1736.

Benjamin Welch born at Ipswitch and Hannah Furnill of Kittery w^r marry^d ye 9th of Novr 1736.

Samuel Miller born in ye county of Derry in Ireland and Margaret Calwell w^r marry^d ye 25th of Novr 1736.

John Sherburn tert^s and Sarah Manson both of Portsm^o w^r marry^d ye 25th of Novr 1736.

James Wason of ye Parish of Bellemanus in ye County of Antrim in Ireland and Hannah Calwell of ye same place w^r marry^d ye 30th of Novr 1736.

Samuel Marshal and Elonor Sherburn Wid^o both of Portsm^o w^r marry^d ye 2 of Decr 1736.

Anthony Row and Easter Dennet both of Portsm^o were marry^d ye 12th of Decr 1736.

John Larey of Portsm^o and Rachel White of Stratham w^r marry^d 19th Decr 1736.

Freeman Jarvis of Great Brittain and Mehitable Hatch of Charlestown w^r marry^d ye 23^d of Decr 1736.

Saml Jackson of New Castle and Amye Dennet of Portsm^o w^r marry^d ye 28th of Decr 1736.

Isaac Toby of Portsm^o and Eliz^a Page of Hampton w^r marry^d 13th of Jany 1736–7.

Nicholas Dennet and Eliz^a Miller both of Portsm^o w^r marry^d ye 25th of Jany 1736–7.

Richard ye son of Tobias and Sarah Langdon was Born ye 4th of Jany 1736–7.

George Meservey and Eliz^a Ham both of Portsm^o were marry^d ye 17th of feb^y 1736–7.

Daniel Grant of ——— and Catharine McBride—w^r marry^d the 14th of March 1736.

Peter Shores and Susannah Ball both of Portsm^o w^r marry^d 31 March 1737.

Peter Massuerre [?] Giron and Sarah Loud both of Portsm^o w^r marry^d 31st of March 1737.

Joseph Thresher born at Salem in N.-Engl^d and Hannah Blashfield of Portsm^o w^r marry^d ye 14th July 1737.

Joseph Gray of York in ye Pro^c of Main and Grace Lang of Portsm^o w^r marry^d ye 8th Sep^t 1737.

Thomas Loud and Lucy Abbit both of Portsm^o were marry^d ye 20th of Sep^t 1737.

John Barratt of Hamps^r in the Parish of —— in Great Brittain and Ann Broton of Portsm^o w^r marry^d ye 19th of Sept. 1737.

Abraham Crusey of New Castle and Margaret Mardin of Portsm^o w^r marry^d ye 25th Sep^t 1737.

Richard Whitehorn of —— and Mary Dockum of Portsm^o w^r marry^d ye 29th of Sep^t 1737.

Noah Sevey born at New Castle and Mary Green born at Kittery w^r marry^d ye 13th of Octr 1737.

Joseph Peirce Junr of Portsm^o and Elizabeth Parker of Kittery w^r marry^d 17th of Octr 1737.

Robert Hart and Eliz^a Sargent both of Portsm^o were marry^d ye 24th of Octr 1737.

John Tomson and Mary Sloper both of Portsm^o were marry^d ye 31st of Octr 1737.

Nathaniel Shannon of Portsm^o and Alice Frost of Newcastle w^r marry^d Novr ye 10th 1737.

Thomas Lang of Portsm^o and Mary Downs of Gosper w^r marry^d ye 17th of Novr 1737.

Joseph Sevey and Rebecka Reed both of Portsm^o w^r marry^d ye 27th of Novr 1737.

Benjn Green of Boston and Margr^{tt} Peirce of Portsm^o w^r marry^d 24th of Novr 1737.

Charles Gorwood of ye Parish of Brigg in Lincolnshire in Great Brittain and Joanna Alcock of Portsm^o w^r marry^d ye 29th Novr 1737.

Eliz^a ye 2^d Daughter of Mathew and Mary Livermore was born ye 18th of Octr 1736 and Dyed ye 4th day of feb^y ye same year.

Mary ye 3^d Daughter of Mathew and Mary Livermore was born ye 24th of Novr 1737.

Joseph Berry Junr and Anne Miller both of Portsm^o w^r marry^d ye 7th of Decr 1737.

David Mendum of Kittery and Eliz^a Jackson of Portsm^o w^r marry^d ye 8th of Decr 1737.

Willm Fling of ye Parish of Killrich in the County of Waterford and Jean Cook of ye county of Tipperary both in Ireland w^r marry^d ye 18th of Decr 1737.

Christopher Skinner of Miley in ye County of Cornwall in Great Britain and Sarah Grindle of Portsm^o were marry^d ye 20th of Decr 1737.

Joshua Goss and Anna Abbit both of Portsm^o w^r marry^d ye 25th of Decr 1737.

Benj Acreman Junr and Eliz^a Meed both of Portsm^o w^r marry^d ye 29th of Decr 1737.

Arthur Waterhouse aud Hannah Bickford both of Portsm^o w^r marry^d Jany 15th 1737–8.

Sarah the Daughter of Joseph and Sarah Welch was born Sep^t 18th 1737.

George Peirce Junr of Portsm^o and Jerush Furbur of Newington w^r marry^d ye 25 March 1738.

Nahum ye Son of Benjamin and Mary Akerman was born ye 21st day of Jany 1736–7.

John Pendexter and Allice Miller both of Portsm^o w^r marry^d ye 7th of May 1738.

Giles Seward of Portsm^o and Mary Hodgden born at Boston w^r marry^d 4th of June 1738.

Elihu Gunnison Junr of Kittery and Dorothy Emerson of Portsm^o w^r marry^d ye 8th of June 1738.

Capt William Hayton of ye county of Kent in ye town of Sandwitch in ye Par^s of St Peters in Great Brittain and Mrs Ann Harvey of Portsm^o w^r marry^d the 15th of feb^y 1537-8.

Mathias Hilton of ye Parish of Monkwaymouth in ye county of Durham in Great Brittain and Margarett King of Portsm^o w^r marry^d the 13th of Augt 1738.

Joseph Chatbun of Berwick and Sarah Phipps were marryd Sept ye 14th 1738.

Joseph Cotton of Portsmo and Susanah Newmarch of Marblehead wr marryd 23d of Octr 1738.

Richard Tebbets and Mary Pendexter both of Portsmo wr marryd ye 3d of Novr 1738.

George Janverin and Eliza Mendum both of Portsmo wr marryd Novr 10th 1738.

James Shores and Mary Snow both of Portsmo wr marryd Novr ye 12th 1738.

Jonathan Sprague of Cambridge In ye Prove of ye Massa Bay and Hannah Phipps of Portsmo wr marryd ye 16th of Novr 1738.

Joshua Rand of Rye and Mary Moses of Portsmo were marryd Novr ye 23d 1738.

Charles Drew of ye Parish of Snt Sover In ye Island of Jersey in Great Brittain and Mary Mongomery of —— wr marryd 27th of Novr 1738.

Stephen Noble and Sarah Partridge both of Portsmo wr marryd ye 10th of Decr 1738.

John Wilson and Lydia Sherburn both of Portsmo wr marryd March ye 8th 1738-9.

Abraham Center Junr and Sarah Jones both of Portsmo wr marryd 8th of March 1738-9.

Elliott Vaughan of Portsmo and Anna Gerrish of Kittery were marryd 14th of March 1738-9.

Mary ye Daughter of Joseph and Joanna fuller was born Augt ye 1st 1736.

Saml ye son of Jonathan and Ann Palmer was born Jany 28th 1736-7.

James ye Son of James and Eliza Philbrick was born Augt ye 30th 1737.

Hannah ye Daughter of Wm and Eliza Lock was born Feby ye 18th 1737-8.

Saml ye Son of Jacob and Sarah Lebby was Born Feby ye 9th 1720.

Sarah ye Daughter of Jacob and Sarah Lebby was Born Feby ye 2d 1724-5.

Job ye Son of Jacob and Sarah Lebby was Born Jany 15th 1734-5.

Joseph and Benjn ye Sons of Jacob and Sarah Lebby were Born Feby 25th 1737-8.

Joanna ye Daughter of Jacob and Sarah Lebby was Born Octr ye 10th 1737.

Nathan ye Son of James and Judith Marden was Born Novr ye 15th 1721.

John ye Son of James and Judith Marden was Born Feby ye 29th 1725-6.

Mary ye Daughter of James and Judith Marden was Born Sept ye 20th 1727.

James ye Son of James and Judith Marden was Born Sept ye 26th 1729.

Abigail ye Daughter of James and Judith Marden was Born March ye 21st 1731-2.

Willm ye Son of James and Judith Marden was Born Octr ye 13th 1733.

Hannah ye Daughter of James and Judith Marden was Born May ye 14th 1736.

Temperance ye Daughter of Joshua and Ruth Rand was Born June ye 13th 1738.

Joseph ye Son of Joseph and Joanna Fuller was Born Novr ye 4th 1738.

William ye Son of John and Hannah Turner was Born March ye 28th 1706.

Job ye Son of John and Hannah Jennes was Born Octr ye 15th 1708.

Mark ye Son of John and Hannah Jennes was Born Octr ye 12th 1710.

Hannah ye Daughter of John and Hannah Jennes was Born Novr ye 1st 1712.

Richard ye Son of John and Hannah Jennes was Born Septr ye 25th 1714.

Francis ye Son of John and Mary Jennes was Born June ye 7th 1721.

Thomas ye Son of John and Mary Jennes was Born Decr ye 10th 1722.

Nathaniel ye Son of John and Mary Jennes was Born Augt ye 22^{d} 1725.

Mary ye Daughter of Hezekiah and Ann Jennes was Born Jany 25th 1718.

Hezekiah ye Son of Job and Mary Jennes was Born Augt ye 26th 1736.

Jonathan ye Son of Nickles and Sarah Doleby was Born Apr^{l} ye 17th 1720.

Daniel ye Son of Nicholas and Sarah Doleby was Born March ye 17th 1724.

Mary ye Daughter of Nicholas and Sarah Doleby was Born Apr^{l} ye 10th 1726.

Anne ye Daughter of Amos and Esther Rand was Born Augt ye 23^{d} 1727.

Philbrick ye Son of Amos and Esther Rand was Born Decr ye 11th 1729.

Esther ye Daughter of Amos and Esther Rand was Born May ye 13th 1732.

Joseph ye Son of Amos and Esther Rand was Born March ye 1st 1734.

Eliz^{a} ye Daughter of Amos and Esther Rand was Born April ye 12th 1736.

Sarah ye Daughter of Amos and Esther Rand was Born Feby ye 12th 1736.

Adam Templeton of ye County of Antrim and Parish of Bellawille and Margaret Lendsey in ye County of Derry both in ye Kingdom of Ireland was marry^{d} 12th of April 1739.

Daniel Wentworth and Eliz^{a} Frost both of Portsm^{o} were sometime since Joyn^{d} in marriage 21st Sep^{t} 1736.

Jonathan Crockett of Portsm^{o} and Elizabeth Rice of Kittery w^{r} marry^{d} April ye 26th 1739.

David Bluntt of Andover in ye Pro^{c} of ye Mass^{a} Bay and Mary Peirce of Portsm^{o} in N-Hamp^{r} w^{r} marry^{d} Novr 17th 1739.

Joel Wittemore of Kittery and Abishag Hoit of Newington w^{r} marry^{d} ye 14th of June 1739.

Thomas Noble and Lydia Berry both of Portsm^{o} were marry^{d} June ye 20th 1739.

Josiah ye Son of Benjn and Mary Akerman was Born ye 1st of May 1737.

Anne ye Daughter of Gershom and Mary Griffith was Born ye 4th of May 1739.

Nathl Bartlet of Exeter and Eliz^{a} Dennet of Portsm^{o} w^{r} marry^{d} 23^{d} of Octr 1739.

Benjn Welch and Eliz^{a} Studly both of Portsm^{o} w^{r} marry^{d} Octr ye 11th 1739.

Joseph Dynnine and Gennit Simson were marry^{d} Octr ye 14th 1739.

Philip Jewel of ye Parish of Yanton in ye County of Biddeford in Great Brittain and Elizabeth Wilkinson of Portsm^{o} w^{r} marry^{d} Novr 8th 1739.

John Frost and Elizabeth Whidden both of Portsm^{o} were marry^{d} ye 11th of Novr 1739.

John Fernald of Portsm^{o} and Catherine Staple of Kittery w^{r} marry^{d} Novr 18th 1739.

Robert Beard of Nottingham Born in Colerain in ye Kingdom of Ireland and Grissoll Beverland of the same kingdom w^{r} marry^{d} 27th of Novr 1739.

Mathew Nealy of Nottingham Born at Bellycarry in ye County of Derry in ye Kingdom of Ireland and Margret Beverland of ye same kingdom were marry^{d} ye 27th of Novr 1739.

Caleb Beck and Allice Dunn both of Portsm^{o} were marry^{d} Decr ye 2^{d} 1739.

(To be continued.)

GORGES AND HARDING.

Communicated by JOHN WARD DEAN, A.M.

THE following genealogical statement prepared by Rev. Frederick Brown, of Nailsea, near Bristol, England, is printed from the original found among the papers presented to the New-England Historic, Genealogical Society by the sons of the late Rev. Abner Morse (*ante*, xix. 371). It was received by them subsequent to the death of their father. Mr. Brown, in a letter accompanying the manuscript dated June 26, 1865, and addressed to W. M. Harding of New-York city, writes: "The whole of the account of Sir Robert Gorges, I can verify from registers, wills and authentic documents. I am quite sure of my ground as to the Gorges family." He also states that he had been collecting materials concerning that family for fifteen years.

In 1861, Mr. Drake printed in the REGISTER (xv. 17–20) some pedigrees of the Gorges family from Heralds' Visitations, with memoranda from other sources. The present paper gives some new facts concerning the relatives of Sir Ferdinando Gorges, the proprietor of the province of Maine. Mr. Drake's article showed that Sir Ferdinando was a cousin-nephew of Edward, Lord Gorges. This paper shows that he was also a brother-in-law. We would suggest whether Thomas Gorges, whom Sir Ferdinando called his "trusty and well-beloved cousin," when he placed him at the head of the government of the province of Maine in 1640, may not have been the Thomas Gorges, below, born in 1613, who married Margaret Pointz. This Thomas was his second cousin by blood and his nephew by marriage.[1]

The first wife of Sir Ferdinando Gorges, and the mother of all his children, was, it appears, Ann Bell. His second wife was Elizabeth, widow of Sir Hugh Smith, and daughter of Sir Thomas Gorges. Her mother, Eleanor, dowager Marchioness of Northampton, was, we presume, the third wife of William Parr, Marquess of Northampton, brother of Catharine Parr, queen of Henry VIII.

PEDIGREE.

SIR THOMAS GORGES = Marchioness of Northampton.

b. 1636, d. 1610; 5th son of Sir Edw. Gorges, of Wraxall, Somerset. | Both buried in Salisbury Cathedral, under a superb monument.

Edw. Lord Gorges.	Sir Theobald Gorges, of Ashley Wilts, m. Ann Poole.	Sir Robert Gorges, of Redlynch, m. Mary Harding.	Elizabeth, m. Sir Hugh Smyth. m. 2nd, Sir Ferdinando Gorges.	Frances, m. Sir T. Tyringham (Bucks).	Bridget, m. Sir R. Philips, of Montacute.

Sir Robert Gorges, 3d son.

In Records of Oxford.—"The King (James 1st) came to Oxford & was entertained at Magdalene College with speeches & Philosophical Disputations. Mr. W. Seymour, 2d son of Edwd. Lord Beauchamp and grandson of the Earl of Hertford, Respondent. Opposed by Charles sixth son of Earl of Worcester, Edwd Seymour eldest son of Lord Beauchamp, Mr. Robert Gorges son of Sir Thos. Gorges by March. of Northampton &c., all of whom gave his Highness so much satisfaction by the readiness of their wits that he gave them his hands to kiss."

He was knighted by James I., June 30, 1616.—Nichols's *Progresses of James I.*, vol. iii. p. 176.

He is described as of *Redlynch, Somerset.* He m. Mary, dau. of Will.

[1] It was this fact which led us in the July number (*ante*, p. 348) to say that Thomas Gorges, who came to New-England, was possibly a nephew of Sir Ferdinando.—ED.

Harding.—*History of Surrey.* Manor of Cleygate, Surrey, was conveyed in 1567 to William Harding, of Wanborough (near Guildford, Surrey), who married Catharine, dau. of Sir John White, Alderman and afterwards Lord Mayor of London, 1563.

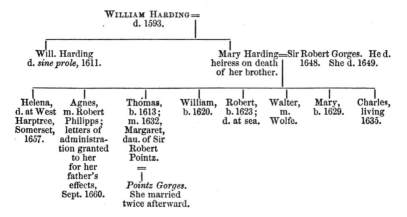

WILLIAM HARDING =
d. 1593.

Will. Harding
d. *sine prole*, 1611.

Mary Harding = Sir Robert Gorges. He d. 1648. She d. 1649.
heiress on death of her brother.

Helena,	Agnes,	Thomas,	William,	Robert,	Walter,	Mary,	Charles,
d. at West Harptree, Somerset, 1657.	m. Robert Philipps; letters of administration granted to her for her father's effects, Sept. 1660.	b. 1613; m. 1632, Margaret, dau. of Sir Robert Pointz. = *Pointz Gorges.* She married twice afterward.	b. 1620.	b. 1623; d. at sea.	m. Wolfe.	b. 1629.	living 1635.

Sir Robert Gorges of Redlynch was present at the consecration of the Church of Wich Champflower [Huish Champflower], by Bishop Lake, July 18, 1624.—Collinson's *History of Somerset.*

He purchased the Manor of Olney, Bucks, of Sir John Rumsay and endowed the Vicarage, & 1642 conveyed the Advowson & Titles to Will: Johnson.—*History of Bucks.*

He was M.P. for Taunton 1625 } Browne Willis
ditto Ilchester, Somerset, 1628 } Notitia Parl:

He is frequently mentioned in the wills of his father and mother. Of the latter he was sole executor.

He settled the Manor of Redlynch on the wife of his eldest son.

At his death his affairs were much involved.

In the Registry of Wills, Doctors Commons, London, Letters of Adm. granted Feb. 1659 to Will Johnson, the principal Creditor to Sir Robert Gorges of Redlynch, Somerset, deceased.

2nd Letters of Adm: granted, Sept. 1660, to *Agnes Philipps*, natural & legitimate *daughter* of Sir Robert Gorges of Redlynch, deceased.

A very interesting, nuncupative will of Helena Gorges of West Harptree, Somerset, made June 11, 1657, daughter, unmarried, of Sir Robert Gorges.

1651. Administration granted to Elizabeth Buckland, wife of John Buckland of West Harptree, niece by the natural & legitimate sister of Lady Maria Gorges, widow, lately of West Harptree, deceased.

She was the widow of Sir Robert Gorges.

N.B. It is evident from the above entry that Mary Harding who married Sir Robert Gorges, had another sister, Elizabeth, who married John Buckland.

The Bucklands were a very ancient family of West Harptree. There are many entries of their names in the West Harptree Registers.

There are no monuments in Redlynch Church, nor is any burial ground attached. The present church was erected as late as 1740.

N. B. The Robert Gorges, who came to N. England, Sept. 1623, to begin a Plantation, was the son of Sir *Ferdinando Gorges* by *Ann Bell.* (Sir F. Gorges had no children by his second wife, Lady Elis. Smyth, who was the sister of Sir Robert Gorges.) On Robert Gorges's death, the patents he had obtained from the Council of Plymouth descended to his brother John.

EXTRACTS FROM THE PRESBYTERIAN CHURCH RECORDS OF WESTERLY, R. I.

Communicated by BENJAMIN PARKE, LL.D., of Parkvale, Penn.

Continued from page 327.

August ye 4 [1751]. The Rev Mr Park returned from Long Island & tarried upon the Main more than three weeks. We had opportunity & attended his preaching ye Word of God three Lord's days, one of which, being 18 August, was communion day. Mr Park administered the Sacrament of the Lords Supper to his Church we desired ye privilege of occasional communion with them at ye Lord's table which was granted.

After these things, we judged it expedient for ye glory of God and the credit of Religion that there should be a record made & kept of our conducting ourselves as a religious Society; and to choose one of our number, whose particular office it should be to record what was transacted of importance by us.[1] Accordingly, upon September ye 1st 1751, we unanimously chose our brother, Christopher Sugar, to ye office of Clerk, to keep a record from the time of our petitioning for dismission from ye Church in Westerly until we know what God will do for us. Test. Christopher Sugar.

September ye 22 1751. Having thought it to be our duty to use all proper means to have Gospel ordinances settled among us, & our hearts being fixed upon the Rev^d^ Mr Joseph Park, knowing no man, like minded, who would naturally care for our good, he being the only person who has carried on the Work of God in this place, that has stood faithfully & resisted ye powers of darkness against manifold errors & enormities which Satan has troubled ye Church with in Westerly and elsewhere. And he being by ye providence of God called to be absent preaching for a Season at Long Island, & being solicited by them to settle there, we thought it our duty to endeavour to secure ye blessing of his ministry for ourselves & our ofspring, stedfastly relying upon God to enable us to support him, believing that God will do it; accordingly we sent a letter to him, bearing date September ye 17th 1751, signed by Deacon Ezekiel Gavit, Stanton York & Christopher Sugar, containing an earnest call to him to come & take the pastoral charge of us, if God in His providence should dismiss him from the Church in Westerly. Christopher Sugar, Clerk.

[1] This would seem to indicate that no record had been kept by the church from which they had been dismissed. None has ever been found or heard of. And as those who separated, afterwards absorbed the church and had possession of the meeting house and preserved their own record, it may be presumed they would have had or noticed the earlier record if any existed.

Sabbath day, the 6th October, 1751. We appointed thursday the 17th day of October to be observed for a public day of thanksgiving to God, and being destitute of the preached word we sent our desire to the Rev Mr Eells in writing to come & give us a sermon at the house of ye Rev Joseph Park where is our appointed place of worship at one oclock afternoon, or to procure the assistance of some other regular Minister of Christ for us.

Christopher Sugar, Clerk.

October ye 13 1751.

We have heard by Mr Marvin that Rev Mr Eells received our request & manifested his willingness to come if he had been able, but not being able, proposed our defering our thanksgiving a fortnight longer and he would endeavour to come then. But we thought it not our duty to alter our appointment, but sent Mr Eells word, in writing, that we would be glad to attend a lecture at that time, but thought it not duty to defer our thanksgiving. Christopher Sugar, Clerk.

According to the appointment of this society, Oct ye 17, 1751, was observed by us as a day of public thanksgiving to God for all His goodness to us, public & private, both of spiritual & temporal nature, particularly for manifesting Himself graciously present with us in our religiously assembling ourselves together, & appearing for us in a time of sickness & distress; and we assembled together at our stated place of public worship & jointly worshipped God. Christ. Sugar, Clerk.

October ye 27, 1751, being Lords day, ye Rev Mr Park being upon a visit to us from Long Island, preached at ye meeting house, & we attended.

Lords day November ye 3, ye Rev Mr Park, being dismissed from ye Church in Westerly[1] at our desire preached a Sermon & administered the sacrament of the Lords supper to us at his own house.

November ye 3, 1751—baptized Zebadiah Shaw and Simeon Forster—by me Joseph Park. Christopher Sugar, Clerk.

Lords day, November ye 10th, 1751.

The Revd Mr Park, being detained from going to Long Island, preached us a sermon from 1st of Sam. 30 & last clause of 6 verse.

Christopher Sugar, Clerk.

Lords day, January ye 5, 1752.

We thought it expedient considering the severity of the season & our present circumstances, both on temporal and spiritual accounts, & the threatening of Gods providence upon us, to appoint a day of fasting & prayer, to implore Gods mercy for us & our children, that we perish not. Accordingly, we appointed Wednesday, the 8th of January 1752, to be observed by us as a day of humiliation.

January ye 8, 1752.

According to our appointment, we kept the day in fasting & prayer to God, when Jonathan Green Park, ye son of ye Rev Mr. Park, our former pastor, came in remembrance before God, who had been absent at sea some

[1] It does not appear from any record or tradition that this church ever again had a settled pastor. Those who had separated, with others who joined them, after having entered into a covenant, transacted business, received and dismissed members and discharged other church functions, having occasionally the aid of Mr. Park and other neighboring ministers. In March, 1756, Mr. Park removed from Long Island to his house in Charlestown, and statedly preached to them, receiving such support as they were able to give. He was afterwards installed as their pastor, and as such remained till his death, March 1, 1777.

years, & no tidings of him, earnestly praying to God that He would let in light upon that affair, & bring us to a hearty acquiescence in His will. The Lord hear and answer for Jesus Christ's Sake, Amen.

Christopher Sugar, Clerk.

January ye 19 1752.

This society having before agreed to have explicit family covenants, according to their several & various circumstances & dispositions, judging it may greatly advance the glory of God & the edification of our own Souls, have this day passed a vote to have the several copies recorded in this book.

December 6th, 1750.

We whose names are underwritten do this day covenant with God and one another, depending upon God alone to work it in us both to will and to do of his own good pleasure to put away all filthiness both of flesh and spirit and perfect holiness in the fear of God. We promise particularly to avoid all evil communication which corrupts good manners, especially all filthy unclean conversation which is an awful sign of a filthy and rotten heart. We promise likewise to testify against it in others wherever we shall hear it and resolve by the grace of God to have no fellowship with the unfruitful works of Darkness but rather reprove them, and that neither the fear of man or our own guilt or any other impediment shall hinder the faithful discharge of our duty.

And farther we promise to attend all the duties of religion, particularly we will reverendly attend the worship of God both in public and private, especially will we sanctify God's Sabbath and reverence his sanctuary, we will read a portion of the Holy Scriptures daily and sing the praises of God and pray to him and teach and learn the Assembly's Catechism and in all things behave as the disciples of Jesus Christ, begging his presence and help, depending upon him alone for strength to perform these promises. Amen.

Abigail Park. Thomas Park.
Joseph Park, Jr. John Park.
Benjamin Park. Anna Park.
Hopestill York.

N. B. The reason of Hopestill Yorks setting her name to this covenant is because she was resident here.

February ye 9, 1752.

Wrote a letter to ye Rev^d Mr Park, in Southold upon Long Island, desiring or rather intreating him, not to remove his family upon uncertainties and expressing our firm expectation of God revisiting this place with His salvation, & that we still desired him & no other for our Pastor.

Christopher Sugar, Clerk.

February ye 9, 1752. Wrote a letter to Rev Mr Joseph Fish which is as follows:

Charlestown Feby 9, 1752.

Rev. Sir —

With great patience we have waited in expectation of your fulfilling the promise Revd Sir, if you remember, at ye council at Capt Thompsons, when you advised us to dismiss our Rev^d & well beloved Pastor. We asked what we should do for we did not expect ever to have another minister in this place. You answered that you would take turns to come & preach to us. Now Revd Sir, our Pastor is dismissed, & we are left destitute, and we according to the encouragement you gave us, have sent a letter to Rev. Mr

Eells first to come & preach for us at our thanksgiving last November. He sent word, by Maj. Marvin, that he did not feel well enough; but, if we should defer our feast some time longer, he would try to come. But we wrote to him that we dare not alter our appointment, but would be glad to attend a lecture at any time, & be heartily thankful. But ye Revd Mr Eells is not come yet. Since that Sir we have had some encouragement by Mr Park from you, but we thought the coldness of the winter might hinder. Now Revd Sir we unanimously send praying you to come & see us, & give us a lecture at ye Rev Mr Parks house, & we should be glad if you could send word when. And, Rev Sir, if you & the rest of the Rev^d fathers should fail us, if ever we should have another minister we shall, I hope, not part with him upon such encouragement. From Rev Sir, your poor suffering & neglected servants & brethren.—N. B. We were no wise consenting to the dismission of the Revd Mr Park, but had obtained our dismission from the Church in Westerly in hope to secure ye blessing of his Ministry for us & our children in Gods own time.

Ezekiel Gavit, Stanton York, Christopher Sugar.

We received an answer from ye Rev Mr Fish, in a letter as follows:—

Gent— Stonington Feby ye 13, 1752.

Yours of ye Feby 9th came to hand & can assure y^u I'^m affected with y^r disconsolate state, & ye poor people about you. Would just observe that (as I remember) I was suitably cautious about my promise, as to the time of a lecture, but really intend one. The severity of ye winter & many pressures upon me, have hitherto hindered my giving any lecture (except one or two) to my own people, though frequently desired; so y^t I^m deeply in arrears at home. However with leave of Providence & my family's health, which is now in a low state, & ye season favorable, I will endeavour to attend a lecture at Mr Park's house on Wednesday next, ye 19th inst., one oclock, & advise y^t general notice may be given to y^e. neighbours & inhabitants, y^t no exceptions may be taken.

I^m Gent^le men, with hearty service, to y^r. selves & M^m Park, y^r. assured friend & unworthy servant Joseph Fish.

P. S. I having no horse fit
to ride, should be thankful
if I might have one in readiness
for me at Dea^n Gavet's— Christopher Sugar, Clerk.

MARRIAGES IN HAMILTON, MASS., BY REV. SAMUEL WIGGLESWORTH, 1714–1733.

Copied for the Register by Rev. S. J. Spalding, D.D., of Newburyport, Mass.

The Third Parish in Ipswich, Mass., known as the Hamlet Parish and incorporated as a separate town in 1793, was organized Oct. 14, 1713. The meeting-house was completed in November of the same year. Rev. Samuel Wigglesworth, son of Rev. Michael Wigglesworth, of Malden (*ante*, xvii. p. 129), was ordained its first pastor, Oct. 27, 1714. A sketch of his life may be found in Felt's *History of Ipswich*, pp. 279–283.

The following is a list of marriages found in his old account-book, which came into the possession of Dea. John P. Pearson, of Newburyport, and by him has been presented to the N. E. Hist. Gen. Society.

Mr. Wigglesworth died Sept. 3, 1768, in his eightieth year, and the fifty-fourth of his ministry. The following list is therefore imperfect and embraces only the earlier years. In the account book there is a statement of the terms of his settlement, and of subscriptions to his salary year by year. It also contains the terms of the contract for the building of his dwelling-house and out buildings. In the same book are also his charges as a physician during the short time he practised medicine before entering the ministry.

Dec. 23, 1714. Jh°. Davis & Elizabeth Gilbert.
Dec. 23, 1714. Timothy Bragg & Martha Killom.
June 7, 1715. John Whipple & Hannah Whipple.
May 20, 1716. Edward Fuller of Salem & Sarah Quarles of Ipswich.
Aug. 9, 1716. Benjamin Gilbert of Ipswich & Ester Perkins of Wenham.
Sept. 18, 1716. Arthur Abbot & Mercy Smith both of Ipswich.
Jany. 23, 1716-17. Danl. Connet of Beverly & Lucy Dodge of Ipswich.
Jany. 29, 1716-17. Nathl. Pike & Mary Thompson both of Ipswich.
Feb. 7, 1716-17. Josiah Bishop & Sarah Adams.
March, 1716-17. Nathl. Dane & Anna Loe.
April 4, 1717. Coomes Humfreys of Marblehead & Bethiah Porland of [Ipswich.
June 22, 1717. James Patch & Mary Thompson of Ipswich.
July 31, 1717. John Poole of Capan [Cape Ann] & Deborah Dodge of [Ipswich.
Oct. 23, 1717. Jonath. Cogswell & Hannah Wiggins.
Nov. 28, 1717. Jacob Annable & Jemima Thorn.
Jan. 1, 1717-18. Robert Fitts & Hannah Dike.
Jan. 8, 1717-18. Benj. Edwards of Wenham & Abigail Lamson of Ipswich.
March 26, 1718. Pitman Howard & Lydia Davison.
March 27, 1718. Benj. Patch & Lydia Walker.
11, 1718. Jno. Parland & Abial Davis.
Nov. 11, 1718. Saml. Parland Senr. & Widow Sarah Dodge.
Nov. 13, 1718. Jacob Smith & Lydia Wells.
Nov. 25, 1718. Jabez Dodge & Margery Knolton.
April, 1719. John Whipple & Elizabeth Annable.
Aug. 10, 1719. George Holmes & Margerett Davison.
Sept. 17, 1719. Abraham Hobbs & Susanna Abbett.
Jany. 8, 1719-20. Joseph Knolton & Abigail Porland.
Feb. 1, 1719-20. Joseph Bowles & Phebe Smith both of Ipswich.
Sept. 1, 1720. Hugh Galloway & Esther Perkins of Ipswich.
—— 23, 1720. John Patch & Abigail Bowles.
—— 19, 1720-21. Daniel Buckman & Elizabeth Edwards.
Jan. 24, 1720-21. Benj. Connant of Beverly & Martha Davison of Ipswich.
March 17, 1720-21. John Roberts & Mary Abbit.
Oct. 18, 1721. John Patch & Mercy Potter.
April 17, 1722. Thomas Adams & Deborah Knolton.
—— 8, 1722. Nicolaus Woodbury & Elizabeth Thorn.
Jan. 12, 1722-23. Benj. Woodbury & Lydia Adams.
—— 3, 1722-23. Nathl. Potter & Sarah Graves.
—— 21, 1722-23. Nehemiah Herrick of Beverly & Hannah Loverill of [Ipswich.
—— 20, 1723. John Johnson & Sarah Pain of Ipswich.
—— —, 1723. Richard Marshall & Susanna Hobs.
March 8, 1725. James Kemball of Wenham & Mary Loverill of Ipswich
March 22, 1725. Jno. Sackwell & Phebe Brown of Ipswich.
March 28, 1726. Nehemiah Wood of Ipswich & Deborah Leech of Wenham.

May 26, 1726. Benj. Hadley of Amesbury & Susannah Smith of Ipswich.
July 26, 1726. Gabriel Pouchi & Sarah Williams.
Aug. 2, 1726. Dan[l]. Griffin & Anne Buffam both of Ipswich.
Nov. 8, 1726. Ephraim Dow of —— & Elizabeth Clark of Rowley.
Nov. 11, 1726. Benj. Hoyt of Hamton & Katherine Baker of Ipswich.
Nov. 16, 1726. Nath[l]. Jones & Sarah Annable of Ipswich.
Feb. 1, 1726. Jacob Thomson & Lois Quarles.
May 11, ——. Francis Whipple & Abigail Lamson of Ipswich.
Oct. 12, 1727. Henry Bennet & Mary Giddings of Ipswich.
Nov. —, 1727. Joseph Goodhue & Widdow Elisabeth Gilbert. [Ipswich.
Feb. 9, 1727-8. Joseph Sanderson of Roxbury & Judith Le-Grove of
Feb. 12, ——. Noah Gilbert & Sarah Allen.
Feb. 20, ——. Dan[l]. Greenough & Mary Allen.
Feb. 26, ——. Daniel Choate & Mary Adams.
April 2, 1728. Andrew Darby & Elizabeth Patch.
April 16, 1728. George Frizel & Katharine Garland.
April 18, 1728. Peter Lamson & Elizabeth Adams.
May —, 1728. Jno. Lindsey of Marblehead & Mercy Brown of Chebacco.
Oct. 16, 1728. Joshua Claflin & Mary Davison.
Jan. 1, 1728-9. Peter Shaw & Jemima Woodbury.
Jan. 9, 1728-8. James Whipple & Sarah Adams.
ditto Oliver Appleton & Bethiah Whipple.
March 26, 1729. Jason Wait of Sutton & Mercy Thomson of Ipswich.
Nov. 21, 1729. Anthony Dike & Ruth Bowles.
Feb. 10, 1729-30. John Bowles & Lydia Howard.
Feb. 18, ——, David Roberts & Elizabeth Brown.
May 21, 1730. Samuel Dodge & Widdow Margaret Holms.
Sept. 27, 1731. Thomas Vittory & Sarah Merrifield of Ipswich.
Oct. 2, 1731. Benj. Fayrfield of Wenham & Lydia Lamson of Ipswich.
Sept. 21, 1732. Thomas Brown & Mary Lampson of Ipswich.
Dec. 23, 1732. Nath[l]. Dane & Esther Kembal of Wenham.
June 27, 1733. Abner How of —— & Mary Adams of Ipswich.

HAM FAMILY IN DOVER, N. H.

Communicated by JOHN R. HAM, M.D., of Dover.

WILLIAM HAM, an English emigrant, was settled in Exeter, N. H., in 1646, and removed to Portsmouth, N. H., in 1652. He had a grant of 50 acres of land from the town of Portsmouth in this year, at what is now called Freeman's Point, just above Portsmouth bridge. He had at least two children, viz., Matthew, who had one grant of land from the town in 1654 and another in 1660, and Elizabeth who married —— Cotton.

William Ham died in 1672, and his will is recorded in Exeter, N. H. His son Matthew was dead, as he bequeathed his property to his daughter Elizabeth (Cotton), and to his grandsons William, Thomas, and John. It seems that he had a grandson Matthew whom he did not mention in his will.

The descendants of this family are numerous in Portsmouth and vicinity.

1. JOHN[1] HAM, of Dover, N. H., the subject of this sketch, was born in 1649, and first appears on the Tax List at Cochecho (Dover) in 1665. Whether son, grandson or nephew of William Ham of Portsmouth, does not yet appear.

He married Mary (dau. John) Heard, of Dover, in 1668; his first homestead was at "Tolend," near the second falls of the Cochecho, in Dover—later he moved to another farm below Garrison Hill, Dover; was juryman in 1688; acquired the title of lieutenant; was town clerk in 1694; wife died 1706; he d. 1727; will is recorded at Exeter, N. H., and the following children are named in it, viz.:—

i. MARY, b. Oct. 2, 1668; m. John Waldron.
2. ii. JOHN, b. 1671.
3. iii. SAMUEL.
4. iv. JOSEPH, b. June 3, 1678.
v. ELIZABETH, b. Jan. 29, 1681; m. Jeremiah Rollins. Children: 1. *Elizabeth.* 2. *Sarah.* 3. *Mary.* 4. *Lydia.* 5. *Deborah.* 6. *Ichabod.*
vi. TRIPHENA, m. John Tucker. He was captured by the Indians in 1696, but soon found his way back to Dover. He had a grant of land from that town at "Scatterwit."
vii. SARAH, m. Thomas Downs. Ch.: 1. *Mary.* 2. *Sarah*, m. Daniel Ham. 3. *Elizabeth.* 4. *Anna*, m. Benjamin Heard. 5. *Mercy*, m. Thomas Downs. 6. *Patience.* 7. *Abigail.*
viii. MERCY, m. Richard Nason.
5. ix. BENJAMIN, b. 1693.

2. JOHN[2] HAM (*John*[1]), b. 1671; w. Elizabeth; lived on the first homestead near the second falls of the Cochecho; like his father, he also acquired the title of lieutenant; had one full share of the common lands which were divided among the freeholders of Dover in 1732; was assessor and lot layer in 1735; wife d. in 1739; he d. Jan. 11, 1754; his grave, by the side of his wife and daughter Elizabeth (Roberts), may be seen near the Cushing Monument, on "Pine Hill," Dover; his will is on record at Exeter, N. H. His children were:—

6. i. JOHN, b. 1699.
7. ii. EPHRAIM, b. 1701.
iii. ELIZABETH, b. 1703; m. "Ensign" Joseph Roberts; d. 1742. Ch: 1. *Ephraim.* 2. *Joseph.* 3. *Elizabeth*, m. Mr. Evans. 4. *Mary.* 5. *Abigail.* 6. *Lydia.*
iv. MARY, b. 1706; bap. Aug. 9, 1730; m. Benjamin Hanson. Ch.: 1. *Anthony.* 2. *Sarah.* 3. *Abigail.* 4. *Elizabeth.*
8. v. SAMUEL, b. 1708.
9. vi. NATHANIEL, b. 1711.
vii. JOANNA, b. 1713; m. —— Jones. Ch.: 1. *Ebenezer.* 2. *Dodavah.* 3. *Lydia.* 4. *Susanna.*
viii. DODAVAH, b. 1715; d. single, 1742.
ix. PATIENCE, b. 1718; m. —— Shackford.

3. SAMUEL[2] HAM (*John*[1]), left Dover and all trace of him was lost; five pounds sterling were given him by his father in his will, in 1727, "if he be in the land of the living, and do come and demand it." He left one son:—

10. i. ELEAZER, b. 1700.

4. JOSEPH[2] HAM (*John*[1]), b. June 3, 1678; m. Tamson Meserve, 1704; was killed by the Indians, 1723, and two of his children captured.

The mother went to Canada and redeemed them. His *estate* had one full share of the common lands in 1732.

i. ELIZABETH, b. Feb. 22, 1705; m. Benj. Libbey. Ch.: *James*, b. July 27, 1739.
ii. MARY, b. Dec. 28, 1706; m. Shadrach Hodgdon. Ch.: 1. *Mary*. 2. *Shadrach*. 3. *Abigail*. 4. *Susanna*. 5. *Daniel*.
iii. TAMSON, b. July 19, 1708; bap. Aug. 20, 1830; m. —— Spinney.
iv. ABIGAIL, b. March 15, 1710; m. Clement Meserve.
v. ANNA, b. Dec. 12, 1712; m. —— Young.
11. vi. DANIEL, b. July 24, 1714.
12. vii. JOSEPH, b. April 25, 1716.
13. viii. CLEMENT, b. Dec. 16, 1718.
14. ix. JONATHAN, b. June 8, 1720.
x. JANE, b. June 26, 1722; bap. Oct. 14, 1722, with her mother.

5. BENJAMIN[2] HAM (*John*[1]), b. 1693; m. Patience (dau. Nicholas), Hartford, in 1720; was heir to the farm of his father which lay near Garrison Hill and where the last days of John[1] were spent; was constable in 1731; had one full share of the common lands in 1732; his wife joined "First Church," in 1737; was surveyor of highways in 1738; voted in 1757 with twelve others against building a new meeting-house at "Pine Hill," Dover,—26 for the measure and 13 against it; d. 1781.

His farm was purchased by John[1] (his father) of Peter Coffin, in 1690; the deed and part of the land are now in possession of John T. W. Ham. His children were:—

15. i. WILLIAM, b. Nov. 25, 1722.
ii. MARY, b. Oct. 8, 1723; bap. Oct. 23, 1737; m. —— Young.
16. iii. JOHN, b. 1736.
iv. PATIENCE, b. 1737; bap. March 25, 1739.
v. ELIZABETH, b. 1739; bap. Dec. 10, 1749; m. —— Jenness.

6. JOHN[3] HAM (*John*,[2] *John*[1]), b. 1699; w. Abigail; lived near Bellamy River, Dover; had two thirds of one full share of the common lands in 1732; was surveyor of high ways in 1728, 1730, 1731, 1734, 1741, and 1742; was tythingman in 1731; constable in 1732; assessor in 1742, 1743 and 1744; was baptized "on a sick bed" in 1743; was executor of his father's will in 1754; d. 1763; estate was inventoried at 38,789 pounds.

i. MARY, m. Joseph Ham[3] (son Joseph[2]).
ii. ELIZABETH, b. Sept., 1725; bap. June 16, 1728; m. Jonathan Ham.[3]
iii. ABIGAIL, bap. June 16, 1728.
iv. JOHN, bap. July 22, 1733.
v. EBENEZER, bap. Aug. 8, 1736. vi. ISRAEL, bap. July 2, 1738.
vii. PAUL, bap. Sept. 21, 1740. viii. ANNA, bap. Oct. 16, 1748.
ix. PATIENCE, bap. Jan. 6, 1753, while "sick with throat distemper."

7. EPHRAIM[3] HAM (*John*,[2] *John*[1]), b. 1701; bap. Nov. 9, 1735; w. Anna; had two thirds of one full share of the common lands in 1732; was tythingman in 1734 and 1746; collector in 1737; assessor in 1740; surveyor, 1741; lot layer in 1745; commissioner for schools and poor in 1741, 1742 and 1743; selectman in 1744, 1745, 1747, 1749 and in 1750; lived on his grandfather's farm at the second falls of the Cocheco; d. 1752. The inventory of his estate at his death was 11,744 pounds.

i. JOSHUA, b. 1729; m. Martha Kimball, d. *s. p.* 1770.
17. ii. EPHRAIM, b. 1731.
iii. MOSES, b. July 19, 1733; m. 1756, Anna Grafton. Ch.: 1. *Ephraim*.

2. *Samuel.* 3. *Ichabod.* 4. *Jotham.* 5. *Lois.* 6. *Nancy.* 7. *Moses.* 8. *Samuel.* 9. *Thomas.* 10. *Robert.* 11. *Sarah.* 12. *Mary.*

iv. Aaron, b. 1735; m. Lucy Watson; d. 1817. Ch.: 1. *Lucy.* 2. *Joanna.* 3. *Lydia.* 4. *Sarah.*

v. Anna, b. 1737; bap. 1737; died an infant.

vi. Ichabod, bap. April 15, 1739; killed in battle with the Indians.

vii. Anna, bap. April 15, 1744; d. single, 1835.

viii. Susan, bap. April 25, 1746; d. in childhood.

ix. Eliza, bap. Sept. 27, 1747; m. James Hayes, May 6, 1779.

x. Joanna, bap. Oct. 26, 1749; died in childhood.

8. Samuel[3] Ham (*John,*[2] *John*[1]), b. 1708; bap. "on a sick bed," Aug. 26, 1739; w. Lydia; had one third of one full share of the common lands in 1732; d. 1739.

i. Samuel, bap. Aug. 26, 1739; m. first, Sarah Wingate, second, Sarah Morse. Ch.: 1. *Sarah*, m. John Titcomb. 2. *Lydia*, m. Amos Peaslee. 3. *Samuel.* 4. *Jeremy W.* 5. *George J.* 6. *William.* 7. *Mehitable*, m. Mr. Crummett. 8. *Ebenezer.*

ii. Stephen, bap. Aug. 26, 1739; d. 1790. Ch.: 1. *Nathaniel.* 2. *Samuel.* 3. *Stephen.* 4. *Benjamin.* 5. *Paul.* 6. *Ephraim.* 7. *James.*

iii. Lydia, bap. Aug. 26, 1739; m. Ephraim Ham.[4]

9. Nathaniel[3] Ham (*John,*[2] *John*[1]), b. 1711; had one third of a full share of the common lands in 1732; w. Deborah; lived on Silver street, Dover; d. 1753. Inventory of his estate at death, was 11,483 pounds.

i. Elizabeth, b. 1739; joined First Church, 1777; d. single, 1809.

ii. Dodavah, b. 1743; m. Lydia Plummer; d. 1812. Ch.: 1. *Nathaniel.* 2. *John.* 3. *Deborah*, m. William Palmer. 4. *Rebecca*, m. Eben Buzzell.

iii. Nathaniel, b. 1749; m. Bathsheba Hanson and Hannah Watson; died 1803. Ch.: 1. *Elizabeth.* 2. *Nathaniel.* 3. *Dudley.* 4. *Samuel.*

10. Eleazer[3] Ham (*Samuel,*[2] *John*[1]), b. 1700; was brought up in the family of his grandfather and uncle Benjamin; moved to Rochester, N. H.; m. Elizabeth Carr; d. 1760.

i. ——, a daughter; m. —— Fogg.

ii. Ephraim, b. 1736; resided in Rochester, N. H.; m. Eleanor Place, 1760; d. 1826. Ch.: 1. *Eleazer.* 2. *Susan*, m. Daniel Ham. 3. *Elizabeth*, m. Moses Hodgdon. 4. *James.*

iii. William, m. Abigail Hodgdon; removed to Vermont.

iv. John, m. Elizabeth Roberts; d. 1809. Ch.: 1. *Elizabeth*, m. Ephraim Ham. 2. *Francis*, d. in Savannah, Ga. 3. *Sarah*, m. John Hardy. 4. *Mary*, m. Mr. Hill. 5. *George W.* 6. *Hannah.* 7. *Susan*, m. Daniel Tripe.

11. Daniel[3] Ham (*Joseph,*[2] *John*[1]), b. July 24, 1714; joined "First Church," Dover, Dec. 13, 1742; was made deacon in 1758; constable in 1740; tythingman in 1742; surveyor of highways in 1753, 1754, 1755 and 1756; first wife was Sarah (dau. Thomas) Downs; second wife was Mary ——; he d. 1803.

i. Daniel (twin), bap. March 21, 1740; w. Elizabeth; removed to Barrington, N. H.; d. 1791. Ch.: 1. *Joseph.* 2. *Shadrach.* 3. *Daniel.* 4. *Paul.* 5. *Thomas.* 6. *Sarah*, m. John Randall.

ii. Shadrach (twin), bap. March 21, 1740; ship-carpenter; removed to Portsmouth, N. H.; supposed to be lost at sea.

iii. Joseph, b. Dec. 13, 1741; m. Elizabeth Jennings; removed to Barrington, N. H. Ch.: 1. *Joseph.* 2. *Daniel.* 3. *Paul.*

iv. and v. Clement and Jonathan, twins, bap. Jan. 3, 1742; Clement d. an infant.

vi. Thomas, bap. 1743; d. in infancy.

vii. CLEMENT, bap. July 20, 1746; m. Margaret Roberts and Elizabeth Horne; removed to Barrington, N. H.; d. 1827. Ch.: 1. *Daniel.* 2. *Mary*, m. Jonathan Hayes. 3. *Lydia*, m. Thomas Babb. 4. *Margaret*, m. David Foss. 5. *Samuel.* 6. *Elizabeth*, m. Joseph Hussey. 7. *Abigail*, m. Samuel Downs.
viii. THOMAS, bap. March 5, 1749; m. Jemima; removed to Durham, N. H.; d. 1796. Ch.: 1. *Patience*, m. Mr. Bennett. 2. *Jemima*, m. Mr. Chesley. 3. *Abigail.* 4. *Hannah.* 5. *Mary.* 6. *Jacob T.* 7. *Thomas.* 8. *Samuel.* 9. *Joseph.* 10. *John.*
ix. SARAH, bap. Oct. 22, 1750; d. an infant.
x. JANE, bap. Nov. 25, 1753.
xi. DAVID, bap. 1756; a soldier in the revolution: m. Hannah Runnels; d. 1811. Ch.: 1. *Joseph.* 2. *Hannah*, m. John Young. 3. *Elizabeth*, m. Jonathan Gage. 4. *Daniel.* 5. *Lydia*, m. Samuel Pinkham. 6. *David.* 7. *Robert.* 8. *Sarah.* 9. *Mary*, m. Nicholas Tripe.
xii. MARY, bap. Oct. 8, 1758; m. John Garland, 1781.
xiii. PAUL, bap. Nov. 11, 1759.
xiv. SARAH, bap. Oct. 3, 1762.

12. JOSEPH[3] HAM (*Joseph,*[2] *John*[1]), b. April 25, 1716; corporal in the expedition against Forts Du Quesne and Crown Point in 1755; moved to Barrington, N. H.; m. Mary Ham[4] (dau. John[3]); he died before his wife; she died 1803.

i. EBENEZER, b. 1746; m. Sarah Field, settled in Lewiston, Me.; d. 1790. Ch.: 1. *Israel.* 2. *James.* 3. *Anna*, m. William Brooks.
ii. TAMSON, b. 1748; m. —— Runnells.
iii. ANNA, b. 1750; m. —— Runnells.
iv. JOHN, b. 1752; killed by the Indians in youth.
v. DEBORAH, b. 1754; m. Joseph Hicks.
vi. JONATHAN, b. 1756; w. Mary; settled at Barrington, N. H.; d. before 1801. Ch.: 1. *Mary*, m. Mr. Horne. 2. *John.* 3. *Isaac.* 4. *Enoch.* 5. *Jacob.*
vii. HANNAH, b. 1758; m. —— Garland.
viii. PATIENCE, b. 1760; m. —— Pinkham.
ix. ABIGAIL, b. 1763; d, in infancy.
x. ABIGAIL, b. 1764; m. —— Whitehouse.
xi. JAMES, b. 1765; m. Esther Copp; settled at Barrington, N. H. Ch.: 1. *Jonathan.* 2. *Asa.* 3. *Joseph.*
xii. DODAVAH, b. 1771; m. Nancy Tufts; settled at Rochester, N. H.; d. 1806. Ch.: 1. *John.* 2. *Martha*, m. John Garland. 3. *Anna.* 4. *Hannah*, m. Eliphalet Hill.

13. CLEMENT HAM[3] (*Joseph,*[2] *John*[1]), b. Dec. 16, 1718; joined "First Church," Dover, N. H., in 1742; m. Patience ——; moved to Barrington, N. H.; d. 1748.

i. SARAH, bap. Sept. 9, 1744.

14. JONATHAN HAM[3] (*Joseph,*[2] *John*[1]), b. June 8, 1720; joined "First Church," Dover, in 1742; m. Elizabeth Ham (dau. John[3]) in 1742; was captain of militia; moved to Rochester, N. H.; d. 1793.

i. JANE, bap. Sept. 16, 1744; died in infancy.
ii. CLEMENT, bap. May 18, 1746; died in childhood.
iii. ABIGAIL, bap. June 12, 1748; m. Capt. John Flagg.
iv. ELIZABETH, m. Howard Henderson, Oct. 20, 1771.
v. SARAH, m. Simon Torr, of Rochester.
vi. SUSANNA, m. Beard Plummer, of Milton.
vii. ISRAEL, b. Feb. 14, 1759; m. Mehitable Hayes; settled in Rochester, N. H.; d. June 25, 1801. Ch.: 1. *Elizabeth*, m. Joseph Chesley. 2. *Sarah.* 3. *Jonathan.* 4. *Abigail*, m. Charles Dennett. 5. *Israel.* 6. *Susanna*, m. Eben. C. Locke.

15. WILLIAM[3] HAM (*Benjamin,*[2] *John*[1]), b. Nov. 25, 1722; joined First

Church, Dover, N. H., Jan. 3, 1742; removed to Rochester, N. H.; d. 1800. His children were:—

i. Charity, m. Job Allard.
ii. Benjamin, b. 1753; m. Mary Waldron; removed to Farmington, N. H.; d. 1846. Ch.: 1. *John W.* 2. *Jonathan W.* 3. *Moses W.* 4. *Patience*, m. Mr. Brock. 5. *Mary*, m. Mr. Scruton. 6. *Charlotte*, m. Mr. Berry. 7. *Nancy*, m. Benjamin Waterhouse.
iii. William, b. May 8, 1757; a soldier of the revolution; removed to Gilmanton, N. H.; m. Anna Meader; d. 1843. Ch.: 1. *Miriam*, m. Francis Elliott. 2. *Sarah*, m. Ezekiel Hayes. 3. *Eli.* 4. *Ezra.*
iv. Francis, b. May 3, 1763; m. Experience Knowles; removed to Albany, N. H.; d. Sept. 20, 1831. Ch.: 1. *Elizabeth*, m. Samuel Kinerson. 2. *Nicholas C.* 3. *James K.* 4. *Mary*, m. Oliver Roberts. 5. *Francis.*
v. Ephraim, d. single.
vi. Eleanor, m. Samuel Twombly.

16. John[3] Ham (*Benjamin,[2] John*[1]), b. 1736; bap. Oct. 23, 1737; m. first ———, second Elizabeth Seavey; lived in Dover, N. H.; d. 1824. Children:—

i. Elizabeth, b. 1765; d. unmarried, 1843.
ii. Charlotte, m. Mr. Paul.
iii. James, b. 1767; lived in Dover; m. Hannah Davis; d. 1801. Ch.: 1. *Ivory.* 2. *Elizabeth*, m. John Crockett. 3. *Caroline*, m. Jeremiah Goodwin.
iv. George, b. 1770; lived in Dover; m. Hannah Tripe; d. 1848. Ch.: 1. *Seth.* 2. *Hamilton.* 3. *Lydia*, m. Thomas Pickering. 4. *Esther*, m. Gershom Lord. 5. *Thomas.* 6. *Hosea S.*
v. John, b. 1779; lived in Dover; m. first Mary Wentworth, second Martha Wentworth; d. 1860. Ch.: 1. *Hall.* 2. *Charlotte*, m. Nathaniel Clarke. 3. *Ruth*, m. Hiram P. Roberts. 4. *Joseph.* 5. *Edward.* 6. *Elizabeth*, m. Joseph Kay. 7. *Sarah*, m. Edward S. Wentworth. 8. *Martha*, m. first D. Varney, second J. F. McDuffee. 9. *John T. W.*
vi. Benjamin, left a daughter Mary.

17. Ephraim[4] Ham (*Ephraim,[3] John,[2] John*[1]), b. 1731; bap. Nov. 9, 1735; m. Lydia[4] Ham (8, iii.); was selectman of Dover, 1767, 1777 and 1778; a soldier in the revolutionary war 1779; his wife joined the "First Church" in 1793. He d. 1806. His children were:—

i. Susanna, m. William Waldron, April 16, 1779; d. June 10, 1804.
ii. Elizabeth, m. George Guppy.
18. iii. Ephraim, b. 1760.
iv. Joshua, b. 1781; lived in Dover, N. H.; m. Mehitable Horne and Susanna Horne; d. 1834. His ch. were: 1. *Susanna*, b. 1805; m. Daniel H. Watson. 2. *Sarah B.*, b. 1808, living unm. 1871. 3. *Walter*, b. 1809. 4. *Ephraim*, b. 1812, living unm. in 1871. 5. *Lucy*, b. Aug. 15, 1814; m. Elisha Watson. 6. *Olive*, b. 1819; m. Joseph Delaney. 7. *Joshua*, b. 1824; d. unmarried.

18. Ephraim[5] Ham (*Ephraim,[4] Ephraim,[3] John,[2] John*[1]), b. 1760; lived on the homestead of John,[1] at the second falls of the Cochecho, Dover, N. H.; m. Hannah Kelley in 1785; was a soldier in the revolution; was selectman of Dover, 1791–2, 1806–7 and 8; d. 1847. His children were:—

i. Abigail, b. 1785; d. unmarried, 1854.
ii. Samuel, b. 1787; resided in Dover; m. Lydia Waldron, 1812; d. 1814. Ch.: 1. *Samuel.* 2. *Eliza*, m. Oliver K. Hayes.
iii. John Kelly, b. 1789; d. unmarried, 1857.
iv. Lydia, b. 1792; m. John Kelly; living in 1871.
v. Eliza, b. 1794; d. 1813.

vi. STEPHEN, b. 1797; lost at sea.
19. vii. CHARLES, b. 1800.
viii. SARAH F., b. 1803; m. Timothy Hussey.
ix. EPHRAIM, b. 1806; d. unmarried, 1833.
x. HANNAH, b. 1807; m. Daniel K. Webster.
xi. JANE, b. 1808; d. unmarried, 1840.

19. CHARLES[6] HAM (*Ephraim,*[5] *Ephraim,*[4] *Ephraim,*[3] *John,*[2] *John*[1]), b. May, 1800; m. Abigail Dana Bartlett in 1826; was captain of militia; was member of N. H. legislature in 1837 and 1844; resides in Dover, N. H. His children were:—

i. CHARLES-CARROLL, b. 1827; m. Caroline H. Colbath; d. 1859.
ii. MARTHA-ANSTRESS, b. 1829.
iii. JULIA-AMANDA, b. 1832; d. unmarried, 1859.
iv. EPHRAIM, b. 1836; resides in Dover, N. H.
v. SARAH-ELMA, b. 1838.
vi. JOHN-RANDOLPH [compiler of this genealogy], b. Oct. 23, 1842; grad. Bowdoin Med. Coll. 1866; surgeon of 115th regt. U. S. Colored Infantry, in the war of the rebellion; now a physician in Dover, N. H.; m. Emily-Caroline Hersey, of Wolfsboro', N. H., 1871.
vii. EDWARD-BARTLETT, b. Aug., 1844; physician of Stafford, N. H.; m. Aramantha E., dau. of Jonathan-Plummer Ham.
viii. HELEN-JANE, b. Dec. 30, 1846.
ix. CHARLOTTE-ABIGAIL, b. June 30, 1849.

☞ A number of families in the 6th and 7th generations, and fuller details concerning the families in the 5th generation whose names only are given in this article, will be found in Dr. Ham's manuscript deposited in the library of the N. E. Historic, Genealogical Society.

FAMILY OF THOMAS FOSTER.

Communicated by the Rev. LUCIUS R. PAIGE, D.D., of Cambridgeport.

1. SEVERAL persons bearing the name of Foster, but apparently of different families, are found among the early inhabitants of New-England. One of those persons was THOMAS FOSTER, who resided in Weymouth as early as 1640. There seems to be good reason to suppose, with Farmer and Savage, that he subsequently resided in Braintree and in Billerica; and in what follows I assume that this supposition is true. It is not unlikely that he was brother to Hopestill Foster, of Dorchester, and son of another "Hopestill Foster, whose wife Patience came in the Elizabeth, 1635;" for he gave this unusual name to one of his sons, and other names were common to both families. He was a blacksmith, and the progenitor of a long line of blacksmiths. According to the fashion which then prevailed, the scrivener was careful to describe him as "sargeant" in a deed dated 1679. In his old age, he was repeatedly called before the Middlesex county court and punished for worshipping the God of his fathers after the way which his judges called heresy. To the first accusation he offered a satisfactory defence, but afterwards he was condemned. Thus it is recorded:—Oct. 4, 1671, "Thomas Foster appearing before the Court, to answer the presentment of the grand-jury, for absenting himself from the public ordinances of Christ on the Lord's-days, pleaded that the reason of his absence was the providence of God necessitating him thereto, was discharged, paying costs."

— June 18, 1672. "George Farley, Thomas Foster, and William Hamlet, being presented for breach of the Ecclesiastical Laws, they all confess the presentment, were admonished, and ordered to pay costs, 4s. 6d. a piece." — June 15, 1675. "Thomas Foster appearing before the Court to answer the presentment of the grand-jury for not attending the public worship of God on sabbath days and days of humiliation and thanksgiving, and by his own confession in open Court being convicted of constant and ordinary frequenting the meetings of the Anabaptists on Lord's-days &c., is sentenced to pay a fine of five pounds, and costs eight shillings six pence." If Mr. Foster was a heretic, his posterity made ample amends by service to the Orthodox church in the office of deacon. No record is found of his marriage; but in March, 1648, and in November, 1679, he had a wife Elizabeth, probably the same who is provided for by his will, dated April 18, 1682, and probably also the mother of all his children. He died April 20, 1682. His children were:—

2. i. THOMAS, b. in Weymouth, Aug. 18, 1640; d. Sept. or Oct., 1679.
3. ii. JOHN, b. " " Oct. 7, 1642; d. June 13, 1732.
iii. INCREASE, b. " " No trace is found of his history; the name is inserted on authority of Mr. Savage.
iv. ELIZABETH, b. in ——; m. Jan. 22, 1666–7, Deac. James Frost, of Billerica.
4. v. HOPESTILL, b. in Braintree, March 26, 1648; d. May 26, 1679.
5. vi. JOSEPH, b. " " March 28, 1650; d. Dec. 12, 1721.

2. THOMAS[2] FOSTER (*Thomas*[1]), born at Weymouth, Aug. 18, 1640, resided in Roxbury as many as ten years before 1672, about which time he removed to Cambridge, where he died, Sept. 16, 1679, according to the town record, or Oct. 28, 1679, as inscribed on his headstone, "aged 39 years." On the court files, 1678, he is styled "Physician." He married, Oct. 15, 1662, Sarah, dau. of Robert Parker, of Cambridge, who survived him, and was mentioned in her father's will, 1684. Their children were:—

i. THOMAS, b. in Roxbury, Aug. 1, 1663; d. Aug. 14, 1663.
6. ii. THOMAS, bap. " " June 4, 1665.
iii. SARAH, b. " " June 3, 1667; probably m. Sept. 22, 1686, Thomas Williams, of Stow.
iv. HANNAH, b. in Roxbury, July 23, 1669.
v. JONATHAN, b. " " April 21, 1671.
vi. ELIZABETH, b. in Cambridge, Sept. 26, 1677.

3. JOHN[2] FOSTER (*Thomas*[1]), born in Weymouth, Oct. 7, 1642; was a blacksmith, and early became a permanent resident in Marshfield. He served his townsmen as selectman 1690, but declined to be their representative in the general court when they elected him to that office. He was elected, April 6, 1700, deacon of the first church in Marshfield; and it is recorded that "John Foster was ordained Deacon in this Church July 20, 1701." About 1663, he married Mary, dau. of Thomas Chillingsworth,* of Marshfield; she died Sept. 25, 1702, and he married Dec. 30, 1702, Sarah Thomas, who died May 26, 1731. His own death is recorded in Marshfield thus:—

* This was probably the only male bearing this name in New-England in the seventeenth century. After a short residence in Lynn and Sandwich, he settled in Marshfield, and was representative in 1648 and 1652. Administration on his estate was granted, March, 1652–3, to his widow Joanna, who m. May 17, 1654, Thomas Doggett, and was buried in Marshfield, Sept. 4, 1684. Mr. Chillingsworth had four daughters, but no son:—*Elizabeth*, d. unm. Sept. 28, 1655; *Mehitabel*, m. May 2, 1661, Justus Eames, of Marshfield; *Mary*, m. Deac. John Foster; *Sarah*, m. Samuel Sprague, the last secretary of Plymouth colony.

"Deacon John Foster deceased June the 13 day 1732, in the 91 year of his age, and left 7 living children, and 45 grandchildren, and 83 great-grandchildren, and had 26 grandchildren die before himself." The age here mentioned exceeds by one year that which is indicated by the record of his birth in Weymouth; but such a variation is not extraordinary. His children, all by his first wife, were:—

i. ELIZABETH, b. Oct. 12, 1666; m. Jan. 18, 1682-3, William Carver, of Marshfield, who d. Oct. 1, 1760, aged 102; she d. June, 1715.
7. ii. JOHN, b. Oct 12, 1666; d. Dec. 24, 1741.
8. iii. JOSIAH, b. June 7, 1669; d. about 1757.
iv. MARY, b. Sept. 13, 1671; m. Dec. 30, 1696, John Hatch, of Marshfield, and d. April 3, 1750.
9. v. JOSEPH, b. about 1674; d. April, 1750.
vi. SARAH, b. about 1677; d. unm. April 7, 1702.
10. vii. CHILLINGSWORTH, b. June 11, 1680; d. Dec. 22, 1764.
viii. JAMES, b. May 22, 1683; d. July 21, 1683.
11. ix. THOMAS, b. about 1685; d. Feb. 6, 1758.
x. DEBORAH, b. about 1691; d. unm. Nov. 4, 1732, aged 41.

4. HOPESTILL[2] FOSTER (*Thomas*[1]), born in Braintree, March 26, 1648, was also a blacksmith, and became a resident in Woburn about the time of his marriage, Oct. 15, 1670, to Elizabeth, widow of Thomas Whittemore, and dau. of Thomas Peirce, all of Woburn. He seems to have sympathized and suffered with his father for conscience' sake. Thus it is recorded, Dec. 19, 1675:—"Hopestill Foster and John Peirce of Oburne, appearing before the Court to answer to the presentment of the grand-jury for turning their backs on the holy ordinance of baptism, confessed the presentment, and being the first time, the Court sentenced them to be admonished, which was accordingly performed in open Court, and paying fees of Court were discharged." He died, while his father was yet living, May 26, 1679. His children were:—

i. THOMAS, b. April 17, 1672; d. May 1, 1672.
ii. ABIGAIL, b. March 12, 1673-4; m. Timothy Farley, of Billerica.
iii. JOHN, b. Feb. 14, 1676-7.
iv. MARY, b. Feb. 26, 1677-8.

5. JOSEPH[2] FOSTER (*Thomas*[1]), born in Braintree, March 28, 1650, was also a blacksmith, and resided in Billerica. If he did not cultivate the soil, he owned many acres of it. He was one of the proprietors of the township of Rutland, and sold his share ($\frac{1}{32}$ part, containing about 2700 acres) to Jonathan Waldo, of Boston, Jan. 12, 1715-16, for £25. He was deacon of the first church in Billerica, and for many years his associate in office was his brother-in-law, deacon James Frost, son of the famous Elder Frost, of Cambridge. He married, Dec. 11, 1672, Alice Gorton, of Roxbury, who was the mother of all his children; she died and he married Margaret ——, who was living Jan. 12, 1715-16; she died and he married Rebecca ——, who survived him. In his will, dated July 26, 1721, he names his wife, son Thomas, dau. Elizabeth Wilson and her children Joseph and Joanna. Dea. Foster died Dec. 12, 1721. His children were:—

i. ELIZABETH, b. Oct. 7, 1673; m. Oct. 27, 1694, John Wilson, jr.
ii. JOSEPH, b. July 15, 1678.
12. iii. THOMAS, b. Feb. 11, 1680-1.
iv. SARAH, b. Aug. 23, 1683.
v. JOHN, b. May 12, 1685.

6. THOMAS[3] FOSTER (*Thomas,[2] Thomas[1]*), bap. in Roxbury, June 4, 1665; married, Nov. 30, 1686, Experience Parker in Cambridge, and settled in Stow, where he was living as late as Oct. 28, 1715. They had:—

i. THOMAS, b. in Stow, Sept. 18, 1687; and perhaps others.

7. JOHN[3] FOSTER (*John,[2] Thomas[1]*), born in Marshfield, Oct. 12, 1666; early settled in Plymouth, and represented that town in the general court nine years. Like his father, he was a blacksmith and a deacon in the church. He married, 1692, Hannah Stetson, of Scituate, dau. of Thomas, and grand-daughter of Cornet Robert Stetson. He died Dec. 24, 1741; and in his will, dated Jan. 9, 1739–40, his wife Hannah and all the children named below, except John, Ichabod and Gershom, are recognized as then living. His children were:—

i. HANNAH, b. July 25, 1694; m. William Bradford, of Plymouth; he d. and she m. George Partridge, of Duxbury; she d. Dec. 17, 1778.
ii. SARAH, b. April 16, 1696; m. William Bartlett, of Plymouth; he d. and she m. Nathan Thomas, of Marshfield; he d. Nov. 3, 1741, and she m. Oct. 24, 1743, Jedediah Bourn, of Marshfield; she d. Feb. 7, 1778.
iii. MERCY, m. Capt. Ebenezer Morton.
iv. JOHN, b. Nov. 7, 1699; probably d. young.
v. SAMUEL, m. Margaret Tilden.
vi. THOMAS, b. March 19, 1705; m. Lois Fuller. Like his ancestors he was a blacksmith and deacon. He represented Plymouth in the general court many years, commencing in 1741; was justice of the peace and of the quorum, and judge of the court of common pleas. He adhered to the king and retired to Halifax, N. S., when the British troops evacuated Boston. His son Thomas grad. H. C. 1745, and taught school in Plymouth.
vii. ICHABOD, b. Feb. 7, 1706–7; d. Aug. 8, 1707.
viii. GERSHOM, b. March 2, 1708–9; probably d. young.
ix. NATHANIEL, b. June 6, 1711.
x. SETH, b. Sept. 16, 1713.

8. JOSIAH[3] FOSTER (*John,[2] Thomas[1]*), born in Marshfield, June 7, 1669, early settled in Pembroke, and appears to have been a farmer. He probably lived nearly ninety years, as administration on his estate was granted to Isaac Foster as late as April 4, 1757. I have not been able to obtain a record of his family; but the Plymouth county records furnish proof that he married Sarah, dau. of Samuel Sherman, of Marshfield, and indicate that he had sons Isaac, Josiah and Benjamin. His wife appears to have deceased before the division of her father's estate, July 2, 1718, and probably two years earlier; for Josiah Foster, of Pembroke, and Ursula Rand, of Scituate, were married May 2, 1717.

9. JOSEPH[3] FOSTER (*John,[2] Thomas[1]*), born in Marshfield about 1674, resided in Barnstable, Sept. 8, 1696, when he married Rachel Bassett, of Sandwich. Soon afterwards he removed to Sandwich, where he died, April, 1750. The following account of his children is found in Freeman's *Hist. of Cape Cod*, vol. ii. p. 111:—

i. MARY, b. Sept. 1, 1697; m. Dec. 24, 1719, Moses Swift.
ii. JOSEPH, b. Sept. 19, 1698.
iii. BENJAMIN, b. Nov. 16, 1699; m. Dec. 31, 1724, Maria Tobey.
iv. WILLIAM, b. March 31, 1702.
v. THANKFUL, b. Nov. 3, 1703; m. Sept. 25, 1725, Nathan Tobey.
vi. JOHN, b. April 12, 1705.
vii. NATHAN, b. Jan. 3, 1707–8.

viii. ABIGAIL, b. Feb. 27, 1708–9; m. May 15, 1735, Zaccheus Swift.
ix. DEBORAH, b. Jan. 18, 1710–11; m. Nov. 22, 1733, Isaac Freeman.
x. EBENEZER, b. May 10, 1713.
xi. SOLOMON, b. Sept. 4, 1714; town clerk and much engaged in public affairs; m. July 15, 1739, Rebecca Nye.
xii. RACHEL, b. Oct. 30, 1716.
xiii. HANNAH, b. June 17, 1718; m. Dec. 10, 1743, Jonathan Churchill, of Plymouth.
xiv. SARAH, b. Sept. 23, 1721; m. Nov. 11, 1742, Nathaniel Nye.

10. CHILLINGSWORTH[3] FOSTER *(John,[2] Thomas[1])*, born in Marshfield, June 11, 1680; early settled in that part of Harwich which is now Brewster. Like his father and grandfather, he was a blacksmith, and instructed some of his sons in the mysteries of the same craft. Like his father, also, he served the church many years as deacon, to which office he was elected, July 4, 1731. He was also selectman, nine years; treasurer, twenty-five years; town clerk, twenty-eight years; and representative, eight years. About 1705, he married Mercy, dau. of John Freeman,* of Harwich, now Brewster; she died July 7, 1720, aged 33, and he married Susanna, widow of Nathaniel Sears, and dau. of John Gray, of Harwich; she died Dec. 7, 1730, and he married, Dec. 7, 1731, Ruth, widow of Samuel Sears, and dau. of William Merrick, of Harwich, who survived him and died Feb. 13, 1766, aged 82. At the time of his third marriage, Deac. Foster had six children surviving of his first wife, and three of his second wife; and in his family also was a daughter of his second wife by her former husband;—ten in all, of whom only two were more than twenty years old. His third wife was the mother of nine children, the eldest of whom was only twenty years old. It is a family tradition, communicated to me by one of his granddaughters, who often visited him, that nearly all these children were gathered together under one roof, and constituted a very harmonious family. Deacon Foster closed his useful life on earth Dec. 22, 1764. His children, nine of whom are mentioned in his will, dated Sept. 30, 1763, were:—

i. JAMES, b. Jan. 6, 1705–6, early settled in Rochester. Like his father and grandfather, he was a blacksmith and deacon of the church, to which office he was elected Aug. 5, 1748. He was also selectman, town clerk and treasurer. He m. July 10, 1729, Lydia, dau. of Maj. Edward Winslow, of Rochester (*ante*, p. 72); she d. Jan. 7, 1770, and he m. May 13, 1771, Phebe Axtell, of Berkley. In 1774 he removed to Athol, where he d. in 1778. [His dau. Mary, b. April 11, 1732, m. Oct. 24, 1754, Col. Timothy Paige, of Hardwick, and d. at New Braintree, July 21, 1825, aged 93 years and 3 months. His son James Foster, b. April 12, 1737, resided in Rochester, and was the fourth in a direct line who was both blacksmith and deacon. Late in life he removed to Montpelier, Vt., where he d. Nov. 1829, aged 92 years and 7 months.]

ii. CHILLINGSWORTH, b. Dec. 25, 1707, was a blacksmith, and resided generally in Harwich, now Brewster, but seems to have been in Barnstable a few years, where two of his children were born in 1735 and 1737. He was selectman of Harwich, two years; representative, ten years; justice of the peace, and special justice of the Court of Common Pleas.

* John Freeman (b. Dec. 1651; d. July 27, 1721), father of Mrs. Mercy Foster, was son of Maj. John Freeman, of Eastham (d. Oct. 28, 1719, aged 97), by his wife Mercy (d. Sept. 28, 1711, aged 80), dau. of Gov. Thomas Prence (d. March 29, 1673, aged 73), by his wife Patience (d. 1634), dau. of Elder William Brewster, of blessed memory. Maj. John Freeman, of Eastham, was son of Mr. Edmund Freeman, of Sandwich, who d. 1682, aged 92. See REGISTER, xx. 59, 353; Freeman's *Hist. Cape Cod*, ii. 385, 765.

He m. Oct. 10, 1730, Mercy, dau. of Maj. Edward Winslow, of Rochester (*ante*, p. 72); she d. Jan. 25, 1757, and he m. July 7, 1757, Sarah Freeman, of Harwich. His will, dated Dec. 28, 1776, was proved June 9, 1779.

iii. MARY, b. Jan. 5, 1709–10; m. Oct. 12, 1727, David Paddock, of Yarmouth.
iv. THOMAS, b. March 15, 1711–12; m. July 11, 1734, Mary Hopkins, of Harwich.
v. NATHAN, b. June 10, 1715; m. June 14, 1739, Sarah Lincoln, of Harwich.
vi. ISAAC, b. June 17, 1718; a blacksmith, resided on the homestead; m. Nov. 2, 1738, Hannah Sears, dau. of his stepmother, and d. Sept. 10, 1777.
vii. MERCY, b. March 30, 1720; d. Aug. 28, 1720.
viii. MERCY, b. July 29, 1722; m. Oct. 7, 1742, Isaac Crosby, of Harwich.
ix. NATHANIEL, b. April 17, 1725.
x. JERUSHA, b. Dec. 9, 1727.

11. THOMAS[3] FOSTER (*John,[2] Thomas[1]*), born about 1685, was a farmer, inherited the homestead, and resided in Marshfield. He was town clerk, and deacon of the church. Miss Thomas says, "he m. Faith (Oakman), widow of Benjamin White." He d. Feb. 6, 1758, aged 72; she d. Dec. 26, 1758, aged 62. Their children were:—

i. THOMAS, b. May 4, 1735, and m. Mary ——. He was a blacksmith, inherited the homestead, which he sold to Nathan Thomas and removed to Middleborough.
ii. DEBORAH, b. March 10, 1736–7; m. 1760, Anthony Waterman. See *Memorials of Marshfield*, p. 76.

12. THOMAS[3] FOSTER (*Joseph,[2] Thomas[1]*), born Feb. 11, 1680, was a farmer, and resided in Billerica. I have not seen a register of his family, but he seems to have had at least two children. He executed a deed of gift, Jan. 11, 1733, to his dau. Sarah, wife of David Crosby, of Shrewsbury; and, by a similar deed, Jan. 17, 1733, he conveyed to his son John Foster, of Billerica, husbandman, twenty acres of land, described as "being part of my homestead, which my honored father Joseph Foster, late of Billerica aforesaid, gave to me." His subsequent history I have not ascertained.

WHO WAS THOMAS PELHAM?

Communicated by WILLIAM H. WHITMORE, A.M.

IN the *Heraldic Journal*, iv. 178–182, I have traced the descendants of Peter Pelham, an artist of very considerable merit, who came here from London between 1722 and 1727. I have shown that he brought with him sons Peter and Charles, who married here and have left a numerous progeny.

There was, however, in Boston, a Thomas Pelham who became the father of a family, concerning whose ancestry more information is needed. The two families were certainly acquainted, and one of the witnesses to the will of Mary Singleton (Copley) Pelham, widow of Peter, was Penelope Pelham, possibly daughter of Thomas Pelham.

Thomas Pelham, of Boston, married in 1757 (pub. March 9), Hannah Gerrish, widow of John G. Her maiden name was Hannah Cooper, and she was published with him Jan. 2, 1752. This is clear by the administration on her estate, in which Armitage Gerrish is mentioned as her son. By Suffolk Deeds, cii. 41, it is evident that she was a relative of Jonathan Armitage and received a legacy in his will of April 16, 1751.

1. Thomas and Hannah (Gerrish) Pelham had:—

i. Elizabeth, b. Aug. 2, 1758; m. Wm. Higgins.
ii. Penelope, b. March 6, 1760.
2. iii. Thomas, b. Jan. 4, 1762.
iv. Mary, b. Nov. 17, 1766; ? m. Joseph Beath, of Boothbay.

Both parents were dead in 1780, when Josiah Waters, jr., was administrator on estate of widow Hannah (Suffolk Wills, 83. p. 363), and the children were: Armitage Gerrish, Elizabeth, Penelope, Thomas and Mary Pelham.

2. Thomas Pelham, jr., baker, married Lydia Robinson[1] (pub. June 8, 1784) and had:—

i. Penelope. ii. Hannah.
3. iii. Thomas.
4. iv. William.
v. Sarah, m. Benj. Yeaton.
vi. Lydia, m. John A. Shaw.

He died March, 1802, aged 39, says the record of Central burying ground, and his widow died Dec. 22, 1820, aged 55.

3. Thomas Pelham, 3d, married Sarah Sworthen, Dec. 13, 1807, and probably had:—

i. Charles, b. 1812; d. Feb. 14, 1822, aged 10 years.

4. William Pelham, tailor.

He must not be confounded with William Pelham, bookseller, whose name occurs in Boston directories, 1796–1809, when William, son of Thomas, jr., was an infant. The bookseller was clearly the son of Peter Pelham, jr., and Ann Creese, for his aunt Sarah Creese, who died unm. April 21, 1809, aged 80, so mentions him. She mentions her nephews John P. of Charlestown, merchant, and William P. of Boston, bookseller, also William Creese Pelham, son of nephew William, and Penelope, wife of nephew William, also niece Mrs. Sarah Blagrove and her son William Blagrove, bookseller. To her nephew William P. she gave the estate, No. 59 Cornhill, which her uncle, Rev. Wm. Price, had given King's Chapel, because as she says, "she knew such a good Churchman as Price would not have left it to the Unitarians." But alas! in 1813 the wardens of King's Chapel sued Pelham and recovered the estate from him. Sarah, wife of John Pelham, died in Charlestown, June, 1808, but I know nothing more of this branch.

Before proceeding to suggest the possible ancestry of Thomas Pelham, I will note the following marriages in Boston:

1721, Sept. 21, Elizabeth Pelham and William Buxsee, pub.
1727, Nov. 1, Frances " " Elias Hanmon, pub.
1731, Oct. 5, Joseph " " Sarah Brown, pub.
1763, April 7, Joseph " " Hannah Grouard.
1768, April 3, Thomas " " Susanna Griffin, of Gloucester.

[1] This marriage is proved by deeds in 1825, when Wm. Pelham, tailor, and Penelope Pelham, single, with others, sell land of their grandfather Robert Robinson in Rainsford's lane.

Also I find in Middlesex court records:

1698–9, March 14, John Pelham, wife and four children were warned at Woburn; 1730, Sept. William Pelham and family at Billerica; 1722, widow Rebecca P. and dau. at Charlestown.

It will be noticed that Thomas Pelham had a daughter Penelope and a grand-daughter Penelope. Now there is a family in which this Christian name has been very often used. Herbert Pelham, one of the early settlers and a magistrate [whose will is printed in the REGISTER, *ante*, xviii. 172–5], had a sister Penelope, who married Gov. Bellingham, a daughter Penelope, who married Gov. Josias Winslow, and his grandson, Edward P., jr., had a daughter Penelope. Herbert's mother was Penelope West, dau. of Lord Delawar.

It is also known that Edward, son of Herbert Pelham, went to Newport, married one if not two daughters of Gov. Benedict Arnold and had children. The records there are very imperfect, but two deeds on Middlesex files (xvi. 412, and lix. 236) prove as follows:—Oct. 24, 1713, Edward Pelham, jr., and Thomas Pelham, of Newport, sons of Capt. Edward Pelham, and Abigail, wife of said Thomas, sell for £1000, land which was the property of Herbert Pelham, father of said Capt. Edward P. In 1761 there was a claim made by Herbert Pelham, of Bures Hamlet, co. Essex, England, that his grandfather Herbert left children: Waldegrave, Edward, Henry and Penelope; that he is the only son of Waldegrave, and that Edward, who died Sept. 20, 1730, had only a life estate in the lands which he claims as heir.

We note that Capt. Edward Pelham (son of Herbert) had:—

i. Edward. ii. Thomas.
iii. Elizabeth, m. John Goodson, June 26, 1711.

I have also a record that Edward, sen., had a daughter.

Edward Pelham, jr., married in Newport, March 14, 1717–18, Arabella Williams, and had:—

i. Hermione, b. Dec. 3, 1718; m. says Jackson, John Banister, of Boston, and had *John*, *Thomas* and *Samuel*.
ii. Elizabeth, b. Oct. 20, 1721.
iii. Penelope, b. May 23, 1724.

He and his wife were living May 17, 1738, when they signed a deed to J. Banister.

Thomas Pelham, son of Capt. Edward, had a wife Abigail in 1713. Is it not possible that he was the father of Thomas Pelham, of Boston?

I have already mentioned that William Pelham, bookseller, son of Peter Pelham, jr., had a wife Penelope. It is probable that she was the daughter of Thomas Pelham, since it was a tradition in the family that she married a cousin of the same surname. It is possible, of course, that Peter and Thomas were relatives, but highly improbable that they were nearly connected, since a letter, printed elsewhere, written by Peter's sister in England, mentions all the known members of Peter's family, but is silent as to Thomas.

I give considerable importance to the persistent use of the name Penelope in the family of Thomas Pelham, and submit that until we can dispose of Thomas Pelham, son of Capt. Edward P. of Newport, this line is the most promising field of search for the ancestry of Thomas P. of Boston.

GLEANINGS.

Continued from vol. xx. p. 36.

60.

"A System of Notation; representing the Sounds of Alphabetical Characters by a new Application of the Accentual Marks in present use: with such additions as were necessary to supply deficiencies. By WILLIAM PELHAM. Boston: Printed for W. Pelham, No. 59 Cornhill. 1808." pp. 301.

Of this book, pp. 52–296 are occupied with Johnson's Rasselas, the pages being printed both in the usual type and with all the marks of Pelham's system,—the two facing each other. It is of course impossible to give an idea of the system without the aid of types, but the main principle seems to be the adoption of certain dots and accents to represent the vowel sounds, and a number of special types to indicate the peculiar sounds of consonants. So far as we can judge the system fully represents the sounds.

The author was the son of Peter Pelham, jr., and grandson of Peter Pelham, the first resident artist in Boston. After the unsuccessful attempt made to retain the Creese property, as elsewhere mentioned in our pages, Mr. William Pelham is said to have removed to Harmony, Ind., where he died.

61.

By the kindness of A. C. Goodell, jr., Esq., I give the following memorandum of the dates of commissions, recorded at the State Paper Office, London.

From Plant. Gen. B.T. Vol. 52.

1727, Oct. 17.	William Dummer commissioned Lt.-Gov. of Mass.	p. 52
1727–8, Feb. 29.	Josiah Willard " Secretary "	53
1730, April 15.	William Tailer " Lt.-Gov. "	56
1732, April 29.	Spencer Phipps " Lt.-Gov. "	59
1733, June 28.	Benjamin Pemberton " Clerk of the Naval Office	60
1734, Sept. 10.	do. license of absence	62
1737, April 5.	Warrant for settling the boundaries between Mass. & New Hampshire	177
1743–4, Feb. 28.	License to Joseph Gulston to fell trees in New England	182

Do. Vol. 51.

1717, Oct. 16.	Horatio Walpole, jr.,—patent for the office of Surveyor and Auditor General of all the Revenues in America	p. 7
1725, Aug. 19.	Francis Fane, patent to be Counsel to the Board of Trade	36
1726–7, Feb. 9.	Bishop of London's Commission to exercise Ecclesiastical jurisdiction in H. M. Plantations in America	39
1727, Dec. 12.	David Dunbar, commission to be Surveyor General of H. M. woods in America	51

1751, Nov. 20. Robert Cholmondeley, patent—Surveyor and Auditor General of all the Revenues in America 187

62.

The Jessop Family.—In the Register, x. 357, 8, I made a few notes on the Puritan family of Jessop, to which I am now able to add somewhat. A pedigree of the family is given in the Visitation of Yorkshire for 1665–6, published by the Surtees society. Various facts are also recorded by Hunter in his "Founders of New Plymouth," pp. 126–8. From these it seems that Richard[1] Jessop, of Bromehall, co. York, living in 1575, married Anne, dau. of Robert Swift, and had:—

i. William,[2] b. about 1562. ii. Richard.[2] iii. Francis.[2]

William[2] had:—

i. Wortley.[3] ii. George,[3] of Brantcliffe, co. York.

Wortley[3] Jessop, of Bromehall, married —— D'Oyle and had Ann,[4] wife of —— Wade, and William[4] who married Jane, dau. of Sir Francis South. By her he had Francis,[5] William,[5] d. *s. p.*, and Anne.[5] This Francis[5] Jessop, who was aged 27 in 1665, married Barbara Eyre and had William,[6] born in 1665, who lived to be a judge and M. P., and died Nov. 15, 1734, aged 70 years. He married Mary, dau. of James Darcy, first Baron Darcy, of Navan in Ireland, and had one son and four daughters. The son James Jessop succeeded his maternal grandfather as Baron Darcy, but died unm. June 15, 1733, aged 26 years. (See *Notes and Queries*, 2nd S., ii. 294.)

So ends the oldest line of the family.

The parish registers of Worksop, which were carefully examined by Col. Joseph L. Chester, supply a number of items.

Of the children of Richard[1] Jessop we find Marie, bap. May 10, 1567, and Francis, bap. Nov. 12, 1568.

Then the marriage of William[2] Jessop to Ann Cotes, Nov. 19, 1587, and baptisms of his children, viz.: Wortley, April 17, 1583, and Margaret, Sept. 24, 1588.

Next the marriage of Francis[2] Jessop and Frances White, Jan. 24, 1604–5.

Wortley[3] Jessop had baptized William, April 8, 1610, Anne, Feb. 23, 1611–12 (she married William Wade, April 13, 1637). Wortley's will was dated 1615, and it is probably his widow, "Mrs. Katherine Jessop," who married Henry Lukin, Dec. 22, 1618. George[3] (brother of Wortley probably) had Mary, bap. May 14, 1627.

Mr. William[4] Jessop had Esther, bap. Feb. 20, 1631–2; Wortley, Aug. 13, 1633; William, Oct., 1634; Hannah, Feb. 4, 1654–5, buried 18th same month; and Elizabeth, bapt. Feb. 28, 1655–6. William Jessop was buried Aug. 25, 1657.

In the same register are some dates connected with another family of the same name, probably the descendants of a brother of Richard[1] Jessop. They begin with the marriage of John[1] Jessop and Alice Holt, Nov. 29, 1575, and Margaret Jessop (presumably his sister) to Thomas Simcox, of Butley, co. Somerset, Sept. 15, 1582.

John[1] Jessop had baptized, Gartrett (Gertrude[2]), Aug. 11, 1577 (who probably had a dau. Isabel, bap. Aug. 20, 1606, and married Wm. Lowson, Sept. 20, 1606); Margaret,[2] Sept. 15, 1579; Lawrence,[2] May 6, 1582.

There was also Anne Jessop, buried Sept. 22, 1587. A John Jessop married Anne Sparrow, July 13, 1595, and a John J. buried June 12, 1614. These may be the same as the first John, or a son of his.

Lawrence[2] Jessop married Elizabeth Teasdell, Nov. 30, 1612, and had baptized: Margaret,[3] Sept. 5, 1613 (buried June 4, 1614); Elizabeth,[3] May 7, 1615 (probably married Richard Clayton, Nov. 13, 1634); John,[3] Feb. 14, 1618–19, died soon; Gertrude,[3] May 6, 1621; John[3] again, Feb. 29, 1623–4; William,[3] July 30, 1626; Anna,[3] July 19, 1629; and Sarah,[3] Aug. 4, 1633 (possibly married John Stacie, July 19, 1655).

There was a Francis Jessop who married Mary Clayton, July 29, 1655. This can hardly be Francis[5] who married Barbara Eyre, as he was only 17 years old then. But Francis[5] was no doubt the one who had a dau. Barbara bap. April 28, 1679. Possibly also he was the father of Sarah who was buried Jan. 23, 1678–9.

It was Mr. Hunter's opinion that Francis[2] Jessop, son of Richard Jessop, of Bromehall, was the Puritan of Amsterdam and of Leyden. In Mass. Hist. Soc. Coll., 1st S., iii. 44, is a letter dated Leyden, Nov. 30, 1625, to Bradford and Brewster, announcing the death of Rev. John Robinson. It is signed by Francis Jessop, Thomas Nash, Thomas Blossom, Roger White and Richard Maisterson.

It is also stated by Hon. Henry C. Murphy, in the third volume of the Historical Magazine, that Roger White was the brother of Robinson's wife, and that another sister, Jane White (maid, of Bebel), married April 11, 1611, Raynulph Tickens. I do not find the precise authority for calling Mrs. Robinson a White, but in Mass. Hist. Soc. Coll., 4th S., i. 155, Roger White's letter on Robinson's death terms him "your and our loving and faithful pastor, and my dear and reverend brother," words warranting a close relation.

There was also at Leyden a William White, who married, Feb., 1612, Anna Fuller, came to New-England with wife and son Resolved, and had Peregrine born on the way. He died two months after landing, and his widow married Edward Winslow. I think she figures as *Agnes* White in 1613 at the marriage at Leyden of Samuel Fuller, presumably her brother. William may or may not be a member of this family of Whites.

We have seen that Francis Jessop married Frances White in 1605, at Worksop, and that Robinson was the minister at Scrooby from 1604 till he removed to Holland; it is not a violent conjecture that he and Jessop married sisters.

This family of Whites is one worth tracing.

We learn nothing of Francis Jessop after 1625, but the name occurs in Connecticut quite early. John Jessop and Edward Jessop were of Stamford about 1642, and the name has since continued. Possibly these were descended from Francis J., of Leyden, or some other branch of the Broomhall stock. The only item we can glean is given in the introduction to the "Wetmore Genealogy," p. 2. It seems that in 1657, Joseph Mead deposed that when "Edward Jessop and his mother the widow Whitmore went from Stamford to live elsewhere they left two mares" in his charge. This was the widow of John Whitmore, of Stamford, but whether she was Edward's mother or mother-in-law cannot be determined. W. H. W.

OUR ENGLISH ANCESTORS.

HAVING occasion for others as well as for myself to recover various broken links of connection between our American and transatlantic progenitors, the difficulties encountered and successfully surmounted suggest a few considerations which may be of service to such as are engaged in similar researches. Whether the pursuit be regarded as idle and frivolous, excusable as gratifying a sentiment deeply rooted in our nature, or even praiseworthy as garnering up for other generations information they may value, there will always be sensible persons whose attention it attracts. Whatever concerns our European origin, those ever multiplying lines as they recede of venerable shades from whom proceeded the sturdy men that planted our infant states, has for all of us an especial charm, not only from what we know, but for what we hope to ascertain. The profound obscurity which settles down on times remote as those they inhabited is at first discouraging, but as we grope our way on and become wonted to the gloom, it is pleasant to find how much yet remains to be learned. For those of British descent the vast accumulation of books and rare manuscripts bearing on family history in England would often prove an embarrassment, were it not that pioneers have opened up the paths, and shed thereon the light of their learning.

That country is for most of us in America the father-land. Language and literature, laws and usages, common origin and history, constitute bonds of affection and fellowship with its people time can neither weaken nor political differences disturb. This has been the frequent theme of orator and historian, and is too obvious to need any additional illustration here. Nor is it intended to dwell on the social and religious condition of England which influenced our ancestors to leave it, or on the inducements which led them to select this for their home. These likewise are sufficiently familiar. But there are other considerations growing naturally out of the fact that our New-England colonies were a swarm from the mother hive, from a peculiar civilization of which the raciness and pungency to this day modify taste and sentiment, habits of life and modes of thought, indeed whatever we possess of distinctive national character, which have a bearing on our subject, and to those we propose to allude.

Noble qualities abound in other races entering largely into the composition of our community, of which those of English origin still form the principal part. German and French, Celt and Italian, are blest with many admirable traits and gifts, in which the Anglo Saxon must be content to confess inferiority. In musical genius, sensibility to art, grace of manner, wit and gaiety of social intercourse, some or all of them have an advantage. But in sound common sense, in honesty and steadfastness of principle and purpose, in fidelity to truth and duty, in courage moral and physical, in warmth and depth and refinement of affection, he equals if he does not easily surpass all other nationalities. When in the seventeenth century our American colonies were planted, these virtues, with their reasonable alloy of what was less estimable, had become firmly fixed as the groundwork of English character. Upon this solid foundation had been raised a superstructure of the adventurous spirit of the Norman, his chivalric sense of honor, dignity and self-reliance, and to them gradually attached the practical wisdom and poetic sensibility of the Scotch, the vivacity and persistency proof against discouragement of the Irish. If these characteristics trickled in the vein from sire to son, or spread infectiously through those hidden influences which shape a people, our British ancestors, tracing back their lineage to Pict and Dane, to the legionaries of Rome or the sea-kings of the Baltic, had gained strength from the fusion in their nature of various and opposing elements, and combined what was best of many races.

This ancestral type, however variously compounded, exerted an all-powerful influence in moulding character, whether individual or national. But there were other circumstances which had also much to do with both. To explain what manner of men peopled New-England, we must allude to certain conditions in their social life at home, which helped to make them what they were. In the tenure of land, in the different grades and ranks of society, in their military and maritime habits and training, religious culture and distribution of political power, there was much that was peculiar to shape their ideas and determine their lot in life, as it had for centuries those of their fathers, whom they left mouldering beneath the sod of their native country.

England was then, as it still is, trammelled by the bondage of earlier days. Not only government in church and state was despotic and arbitrary, but the land, though not to the same extent as now, was in the ownership of few proprietors, constantly tending by intermarriage and the laws of inheritance to become less. The feudal system in its subordination of tenure had existed under Dane and Saxon long before the Normans brought over its later refinements, and the impression that the Conqueror, as he reduced England to subjection, parcelled it out among his followers by metes and bounds then first established, is far from being correct. The first known domesday survey dates back to King Alfred, and in that made twenty years after the battle of Hastings are constant references to the tenure under Edward the Confessor, the several manors and estates bearing the same designations and being subdivided and distributed among the actual tillers of the soil in different ranks and classes, as at that period.

Dispossessing many of the large Saxon proprietors, though sparing such as gave in their allegiance, King William appropriated to his own use twelve hundred and ninety manors in different counties, assigning the rest to his Norman followers. The great mass of cultivators attached to the soil, or villains in gross, were left undisturbed, their services or rent charges being simply transferred to the new lords. The tenants in chief under the king enfeoffed their kinsmen, friends or adherents with such portions of their estates as they did not care to retain in their own possession or demesne, one obligation being the same for all, that of military service. In taking possession by force of England, as previously of Normandy, the feudal system naturally suggested itself to the conquerors as the only method of retaining their hold.

The whole number of tenants in chief mentioned in Domesday, as stated by Sir Henry Ellis, is fourteen hundred, of mesne tenants eight thousand, while of the gross aggregate of persons enumerated, 283,242, twenty-five thousand were slaves, nearly as many socmen and 208,407 villains or farmers. The Saxon far outnumbered the Norman, and as they mingled in course of time in marriage with their conquerors or in other ways assimilated, they infused, as the more numerous, the prevailing tincture of race and trait in the common stock.

Allowing five for each family and for the survey not embracing three of the northern counties then but partially reduced to tranquillity, the approximate population may be estimated at that time as a million and a half, about equal to that now of Massachusetts. Three centuries later it is rated at only two millions and a quarter, while in 1415 it is stated at three, in 1600 at five, in 1800 at nine, and now at twenty-six, all but the first number embracing Wales.

As the survey is in Latin and with abbreviations, and the officers employed in the several counties were of different degrees of scholarship and dependent upon local and imperfect sources of information, its manifold discrepancies require explanation. Both family and christian names as they passed from Saxon or French into the law language, underwent considerable changes. It is often difficult to determine even to which nationality they belonged, whether those mentioned are the same under different forms, or whether distinct personages were intended. Surnames were not by any means of universal use before the thirteenth century, and many names of Saxon places attaching to Norman families who possessed them created still farther complications. Moreover so many changes had already taken place, since the invasion, from death, sale or confiscation, that it is not easy in all instances to connect and identify those who then held, with the knights and leaders mentioned by Wace in his Roman de Rou, or by Vitalis in his chronicles, as taking part in the subjugation. As many of the progenitors of Americans were no doubt not only on the roll of Battle Abbey, but mentioned as proprietors of land in Domesday, this precious record will be studied by them with more interest than ever, as it becomes better understood. Copies of it, thanks to the liberality of the British government, are to be found in most of our large cities, and the rich historical material which such writers as Palsgrave and Freeman have derived from it for the elucidation of their historical works on the period, they have been able generously to repay by their intelligent explanation of much in it that was obscure.

In social development, diffusion of culture, refinement and comforts of life, England, under the Plantagenets, kept pace with the other civilized portions of Europe, and though the climate was harsh, resources limited, and numberless contrivances now indispensable unknown, human nature was the same. Manners were dignified and decorous, and the order of life rational and varied. Food and ale abounded. Garments of cloth or skins, if not as conducive to personal neatness as our present abundance of linen and cotton admits, were warm, and in shape and ornament sufficiently in good taste. Forests overspread the land; they were for the general benefit of lord and peasant, and fuel was cheap and plentiful. Intercourse at inns and manor houses as in the conventual establishments, was hospitable and convivial, and both for security and society all classes were gregarious. Hunting and fishing, archery, wrestling and other sports of the village green, courts and fairs, religious ceremonials, including masques and moralities, dramatic performances in the churches, brought people of all ranks and conditions into closer companionship, quickened their faculties and fostered graces and accomplishments to inspire respect or win affection. The Canterbury tales of Chaucer afford an insight into the picturesque elements composing the social circles of middle life. History tells us of the manners and pleasures of the court, while the lesser barons who dwelt in moated halls possessed influence and power, and found useful and agreeable occupation in the management of their estates, in the performance of judicial functions, or in attending the king with their followers in his wars and crusades.

Under King Stephen it is stated there were eleven hundred castles in England. If not all as stately as Arundel, then already ancient, or Carnarvon erected a century later, their remains show they were spacious and well fitted to withstand assault. What is left of convent and baronial residence, what idea we can form of them from the pleasant sites they occupied, surrounded by park and forest, seated by the sea or on those pretty streams which constitute an especial charm of England, what we know by tradition or record of their inmates, encourage the belief that they were the abode of much domestic happiness, and that time within their walls or in the rural and sylvan pursuits of the period, flowed on with at least the usual average of enjoyment.

Saxon and Norman were equally devout. Churches of architectural elegance, rites varied and interesting, of which music, as on the continent, formed a prominent part, kept alive the religious spirit, which was still further exhibited in numberless abbies and convents, amply endowed and crowded with acolytes. To every principal household was attached its private chapel, and the chaplain possessed of the best culture of the period educated the children and afforded intellectual companionship for the older members of the family. Rectors of parishes, of which the lord had the appointment, regulars from neighboring monasteries planted or endowed by him or his ancestors for the salvation of their souls or as asylums for the infirm or scholarly of their kindred, relieved the monotony of country life, spreading around their own culture. Woman was respected and had her appropriate sphere in the household, but if unmarried or left unprotected in widowhood, found shelter and congenial companionship in the cloister.

The statement that thirty thousand young men were at one time in the schools of Oxford, seems difficult to credit, but education in the humanities, such as it was, appears to have been more generally diffused before the reformation than afterwards. The church ritual, pleadings in court made indispensable for many a knowledge of latin, and this and other learning, were not confined to the scions of nobility, to children of the affluent, or youth in training for religious life, which then absorbed large numbers of the better sort, but the moderate cost of instruction brought it within the reach of very limited means. As printed books cheap enough for general use were not available before the middle of the sixteenth century for educational purposes, it must have been restricted in range and pursued at disadvantage.

College buildings, apart from ecclesiastical institutions, of any pretension, were unknown before 1250, but under the Edwards were greatly multiplied, and castle and convent shared in the growing taste in architecture. Windows of exquisite tracery, in stone elaborately carved, with bible stories in brilliant colors painted on their glass, lead to the belief that private dwellings at the period were not only substantial, but richly adorned. Where means permitted, they were of stone, crenellated, flanked by towers for defence and surrounded by moats, gardens and outbuildings, protected by walls that added to their strength. Some were of timber, filled in with brick and clay, which after exposure for centuries to the weather, still stand in good preservation. Lands descending to the oldest representative, unless in the case there were only daughters, when they shared alike, these abodes continued for generations in the same families. The pedigrees preserved in visitations, court and parish records and county histories, greatly facilitate the labor of American genealogists who thus can trace back their lines of ancestors to the days of the Plantagenets.

Most of those abodes have mouldered and few remain that have preserved their original form, dating earlier than Queen Bess. Even of that period little is left unmodernized but outer walls. If any part remains unaltered it is generally the hall, which formed the gathering place of the family, and on which was lavished the chief decoration. All who have been in England must well remember many such apartments. They are the more impressive to us from their novelty, since they rarely form part of an American mansion, and even in England are passing out of use. From what we know of mediæval days from poet and novelist, it is easy to people them again of summer mornings or winter nights with their wonted groups. The yule log again blazes on the ample hearth, mail traditional from Crecy hangs from the wall, helm and shield battered at Bosworth or Edgehill. Antlers suggest the chase; fishing gear that Lady Bernard or Isaac Walton might have envied, the streams and brooks. Upon the dais sits the baron as the judge or presiding at the banquet. Minstrels sing Chevy Chace to the harp, or hunting glees awaken the echoes. The bridal dance, the funeral solemnity, men in complete steel parting for the war or in Kendal green for a merry day in the forest. Time was too social for books, too busy for studies banished to the cloister, but by open lattice which reveals sunny spread of wood and dale, young men and maidens whisper pleasant truths or interchange the vow to which thousands of happy mortals since have owed the boon of life.

Last summer on the Severn, with a companion who had some special quest there, we visited an ancient mansion with such a hall. The edifice extended fifty yards in front with projecting bows, their vast lattices purpled with painted panes. The hall door stood invitingly open, and there was every indication the place was inhabited, but our knocks, though repeated, failed to summon either dog or wardour. Not disposed, having come so far, to abandon our purpose, we sought another side of the dwelling, and there under an arched portal on a flight of stone steps, stood a lovely maiden in white attire, who when our object was stated expressed her regret that her uncle, the master of the house, was absent, but said that her aunt and mother would be glad to receive us. We found them in such a hall as that referred to, fifty feet square and twenty high, its dark wainscot hung with portraits of many garbs and generations. One side, towards the court-yard of this noble apartment, consisted mainly of one of the projecting bays all aglow with painted panes of gold and ruby, too subdued to dazzle. After the invariable hospitality of tea, anything more substantial being declined, we were carried over the mansion, above and below, and certainly not Bracebridge Hall as Irving so happily describes it, or the abode of Sir Roger de Coverly, had Addison condescended to tell us what it was, possessed more exquisite apartments. Nor could be easily conceived a pleasanter combination of what was picturesque and quaint in the past with modern elegance and comfort. It had been the home of the family for six or seven generations, but constructed centuries before; under its roof had come and passed all their shifting phases of social life, had been brought home to its inmates all their varied political changes and vicissitudes. The hall itself dated back beyond the wars of the Roses, Stuarts and Tudors, five centuries or more, to the reign of Edward the Second, but the whole edifice is ancient. Few survive more venerable than this, but there are numberless interesting dwellings in England that existed before our colonies were planted, and it would be hard for an American inclined to link his existence with that of his English progenitors, if he could not occasionally find one which they called their own.

That our British ancestors were fond of fighting, when provoked, regardless of personal safety or private advantage, cannot be denied. For the five centuries following the conquest, wars at home and abroad succeeded with little cessation. Military duty was incumbent on all who could bear arms. Every landed proprietor, in proportion to his knight fees, furnished hobblers or mounted men, and in the crusades, Scotch or French wars, so brilliantly described by Froissart and Monstrelet, numbers were in the field. Gunpowder, first employed at Crecy, darkened but little the battle grounds of Europe till a much later period, and personal encounters of knight and squire in mail, with lance and battle-axe, the rest in quilted doublets with pike and bow, made men indifferent to danger, induced habits of hardihood and daring. From her insular position, the mariners of England were early afloat on every known sea; trade and free-booting went hand in hand; and whether off Sluys with King Edward the third in 1340, as buccaneers in the Spanish main, or under Raleigh in defeating the armada, English knights and yeomen fought bravely, gaining glory by their prowess.

Continual warfare, not always after Azincourt accompanied by victory the unseemly scramble for the throne, bringing to block or dagger every male Plantagenet, for nearly a century drenched the land with its best blood, making sad havoc alike of the yeomanry of England and its nobility and gentry. Whoever is familiar with Dugdale and the early genealogical writers recognizes the frequent extinction of families or transfer of their estates through females to other names. Expenses attending military preparation, ransom of the unfortunate captured in war, enforced loans and forfeitures for taking the wrong side in rebellion, exhausted their property, and the representatives of the proudest names of Battle Abbey, five centuries later, if not extinct, had sunk into comparative obscurity. New men who had won their spurs in the field, or fortune from court favor or professional success, occupied their places. Very few families of wealth or distinction in England, when the Mayflower crossed the ocean, dated back an uninterrupted prosperity to the days of the crusades. The peerage, which had dwindled after Bosworth to twenty-three, then numbered in all little more than a hundred, and the rank of baronet was created 1611. Under the commonwealth, fortunes both of roundhead and cavalier were laid low, and names till then almost unknown became familiar. Thus though rank and social condition have been at all times in England barriers, well defined and not easily surmounted, there as in other countries families possessing them have undergone vicissitudes, been compelled to succumb to the caprices of fortune.

What essentially weakened the stability of family prosperity was the want of that patriarchal system of clans or septs which prevailed among the Irish and Scotch. Kinship was little regarded. It ensured neither allegiance to the chief nor his aid and protection to younger branches. Younger sons left without inheritance were forced to become architects of their own fortune. Three centuries ago there were fewer chances in army or navy, fewer prizes in civil life. Many when impoverished retired to the cloister, while others thrown on their own energies for subsistence fought out an inheritance on the continent or in Ireland. That unfortunate country, since 1172, had been the coveted prey of her neighbors. Without any efficient central government, she was placed at disadvantage, but the courage of her chiefs and loyalty of her septs for centuries kept at bay the better disciplined and better armed forces sent over to subdue them. Partly through intrigue, partly through marriage, a foothold was eventually gained beyond the pale, and more and more of the territory appropriated. For young Englishmen without other opening, the island was an unfailing resource, and after the catholic wars under Elizabeth and wholesale confiscation under Cromwell, many made it their abode. Americans in search of some clue to their progenitors may often find them settled for a while in Ireland before venturing further west, for which it was a good preparation. Invasion and ruthless war had reduced it nearly to a wilderness, and the red men of the forest were hardly more to be feared than its exasperated people.

In order more thoroughly to effect the work of subjugation, it was thought necessary to divest the proprietors of all interest in the soil, and one mode adopted to accomplish this was religious persecution. Had no other pretext equally plausible been discovered for the purpose and the Irish been less staunch adherents to the faith of their fathers, they might have saved their property from confiscation. But the cruelties of bloody Mary and her bigoted husband, as later of Alva, gave the excuse of retaliating the sanction of public opinion to force and fraud. It was a poor plea for spoliation, but toleration or freedom of conscience were then little understood by either protestant or catholic.

Notwithstanding these occasional inconsistencies, our English progenitors both before and after the reformation were devout and conscientious. The religious sentiment under the druids never degenerated into fetichism, and christianity when accepted rose early to a high type. Vast appropriations of land to pious uses, mouldering remains of fane and cloister, cathedrals and parish churches, the admiration and despair of modern architects, antedating the Plantagenets and still in good preservation, show how little there was at any time of indifference or infidelity, how deep and universal was the sense of dependence, how close the relation between man and his God. Blind subservience to authority found little place among an intelligent people. The slaughter of Becket was an early protest against papal thraldom. The banishment of the Legates, suppression of the Templars, rise of the Lollards, the breaking up under the Tudors of the monastic establishments, religious wars and persecutions if indicating the prevailing intolerance of the age, proved that less superstition existed among them than among their continental neighbors, that they valued liberty of conscience, were unwilling to submit to priestly rule, and before Luther had commenced the reformation. Early translations removing the seals from the sacred volume dispelled error and loosened the hold of Rome, which kept ignorance in bondage. If differences of interpretation engendered controversy, its effect was diffusion of knowledge which quickened faith, finding expression in religious observance, obedience to precept and moral life. It was especially fortunate for our fathers embarking in their perilous enterprise of founding a new world amidst many discouragements, that they should have had the support of a religion they could understand, inculcating self-sacrifice and trust. Had they ventured without its aid across the deep, hardships and uncertainties would have speedily disheartened mere love of adventure or pursuit of gain. Relying on divine guidance they persevered, and whatever defects of character may justly be imputed to pilgrim or puritan, the deep sense of religious obligation which sustained them in their sore trials and arduous toil long continued unabated and to this day has left its mark upon their descendants.

Not only in religious culture but in many manly virtues, in fidelity to principle and dignity of character was the Englishman fitted for colonization. The best criterion of what he in reality was three centuries ago, both as regards his merits and defects, is to be found in the dramatists of the period, in Shakespeare and Jonson. If fairly described in their day by Fielding and Smollet, he had then degenerated, and the extremes of wealth and poverty, of intelligence and dulness, of arrogance and servility, painfully portrayed by Thackeray and Dickens, have grown out of the combined influences later of primogeniture, of the spirit of trade and redundant population. For the mediæval period with which our own transatlantic ancestors were connected we owe much to Scott and Lytton, James and Ainsworth, whose descriptions were derived from a careful study of their materials. These materials are constantly becoming enriched by later discoveries among heaps of manuscript in strange language and chirography not easy to decipher, now first made accessible. What Lytton and Tennyson have accomplished for the days of King Arthur by bringing to bear what is known to explain what is obscure, modern historians are doing for the first four centuries after the conquest. With that period, its wars and legislation, its personages and modes of life, we are becoming as well acquainted as with those described by Macaulay, Stanhope or Alison. The publishers of Palsgrave, Freeman and Froude, find a large sale for their works in our country, showing how deep an interest is taken by Americans in the land of their fathers.

The enlightenment accompanying the reformation was not confined to the affluent, learned or powerful, but extended through all classes, and we may well feel proud that our fathers emanated from a people of whom Shakespeare, Spenser and Jonson, Bacon, Sydney and Raleigh, were but representative types. Knowing what material prosperity existed, what opportunities for growth of intelligence and principle and how generally they were improved, among its independent yeomanry, merchants, manufacturers and mechanics we may well be contented to find progenitors. Rank is but the guinea's stamp, and the manly and social virtues that constitute worth are not confined to any condition. It should be no discouragement to a right thinking man in retracing the vestiges of his ancestors to discover that they shared the common lot, contributing by industry or ingenuity to the general welfare. However pleasant to be above the necessity of work, it cannot be denied that it is the best stimulus in developing faculty and character. No one is happy idle, or happier than he who has his daily tasks. We may covet wealth as commanding what we wish to possess, but it is dearly bought at the cost of strength and ability acquired in employments, which in supplying the wants of other men provide for our own. All honor to him, who with no obligation to labor, devotes his gratuitous service to the public. But if fortune compels a useless existence, better poverty with occupation than princely revenues without. Happily the greater part of mankind must depend upon their own exertions, and in every family and of every name there will be some poor as well as rich. If we trace back the progenitors of those now most conspicuous in social, political or professional life, we shall find them three centuries back among those who toiled, and probably among the descendants of historic personages this day are many engaged in humble walks. Names as proud as deck the pages of Burke may be seen on the workshops of English cities. When a late duke of Norfolk proposed to gather all the Howards descended from Dickon, "be not too bold," two thousand were found in every social position.

But whether derived from peer or peasant, the American who claims

England for his fatherland cannot but glory in his birth-right. No other nation boasts a nobler history. Struggles ever since Runymede for civil and religious freedom, wisdom in the cabinet and courage in the field, giving ascendancy over nations superior in territory, wealth and numbers, proudest achievements in literature and science, justice well administered, professions well sustained, crowds of men of genius not England's but the world's. And this natal soil of our ancestors, not surpassed in luxuriance of growth, in the treasures beneath its surface or beauties above by the fabled Hesperides, its remains of other days encrusted with associations sacred or historic, its present wealth of art and utility, well may be called the island of the blest. In its tempered clime, joust and chase have yielded to other pursuits as manly, and to their influence may be ascribed that energy and indomitable courage which have asserted British supremacy till its morning drum-beat circles the earth.

Such a home our fathers left no doubt with heavy hearts. Recent experience in our own day and generation in the migration to the west of the courageous and enterprising from our towns and villages, gives us some idea how the chosen seed was sifted from the old England to plant the new. Prosperous men engaged in lucrative employments or raised above the need of them by ample inheritance, staid for the most part at home. Now and then one of the more adventurous took stock in the companies and sent over colonists. But it was chiefly those without occupation and with scanty means for whom no cover was laid among their own kinsfolk and acquaintance, who were instigated by love of independence to brave the discomforts and perils of the ocean and wilderness to provide for themselves and families here. To break away from the familiar scenes of childhood, with little prospect of again beholding father, brother or friend, demanded a resolute spirit, such as animated the brave hearts and vigorous frames ready to cope with the difficulties and hardships awaiting them in this waste of wood and water, till then unfrequented but by beast and savage.

The hurry of departure, engrossing cares attending preparation, the connection still unsevered with correspondents at home, prevented their realizing in how few generations would be lost all trace, even of their places of birth, of those ties of consanguinity which, growing weaker as they became more remote, would eventually pass out of mind. The frequent instances this has chanced in the history of American families, even where the original patriarchs were possessed of means and culture, is of common observation. To reunite these lost links, and ascertain from whom our patriarchs descended, is one of the problems this society was organized to solve. If at one time usual to ridicule this curiosity to know who our ancestors were, it is so no longer. It is now generally acknowledged that the inquiry is fraught with instruction in fixing in the memory historical epochs and events, in affording us an insight into the habits of life and social ways of periods long past. So long as it tends neither to foster pride nor vanity, to produce neither mortification nor envy, sense of humiliation that our ancestors were not famous or undue respect for those whose ancestors were, it deserves indulgence if not encouragement.

Our early planters were from all classes and conditions. With lawyers but few, clergymen in greater number, men of estate who had enjoyed the advantages of Oxford and Cambridge, came off-shoots from families still in affluence or become reduced, yeomen such as constituted the strength and glory of England, merchants from her marts and sailors from her marine. Among the four thousand names in Savage, borne by the forty thousand individuals supposed by Palfrey to have come over before 1700, are many well known in her annals, constantly recurring in her county histories and ancient records. Many are now extinct. But of those mentioned in 1685 by Bishop Kennett in his history of a few places in Oxfordshire, a large number are borne by persons we know. It cannot be justly disputed that the settlers in America were a fair representation of the six millions they left at home. Fortunes like those of the Marquis of Winchester, who lost with Basing House during the civil war half a million sterling, were the exception there, and those brought over must be compared with what were usual at the time, not with modern standards. But not only in birth and breeding, but in less intrinsic claims to consideration, the planters were by no means the dregs of society, but well up in the social scale. Many we know to have been connected with families of great prosperity and influence. The frequent escutcheons, plate transmitted as heirlooms from generation to generation, wills that mention relatives at home of position, go to prove that in the accidents of birth and social condition they were equal to the best. And this is no disparagement to those not so distinguished. For by our American standards and ideas, fortunately, no man is estimated more or less for the rank or condition of his ancestors. We do not of course mean to profess that a long line of honored ancestry is not to republicans or monarchists an agreeable subject of contemplation, but in America a true value is attached to it, and bringing in its train neither rank nor fortune, it enters little into the estimate of social position or individual consequence. Wealth, political influence, literary celebrity, personal qualities, affect the degree of respect entertained for our neighbors, but little importance is attached to birth, which is oftener a hindrance than a help.

Not even among savage tribes do we find perfect social equality. Differences of constitution, mental and physical opportunity, accidents of birth and connection, affect the promise of the start, influence progress, control results. This is manifestly part of the providential scheme for developing faculty and character, and glittering generalities insisting on social levels are utopian and delusive. Equality before the law is recognized in both countries as a right, inherent and universal, and with us at the polls, though there is a growing conviction that the franchise should be so regulated as to be exercised with honesty and intelligence and without prejudice to liberty. An American citizen acknowledges no superior in rank, but there exist here, as everywhere else, differences of education, means and usefulness, of endowment and acquirement; circumstances intrinsic or adventitious which govern the relations of each of us to his neighbors, and which it would be absurd to ignore.

These social distinctions have been more marked in England in consequence of the legal sanctions to rank growing out of a government under which political power vests in an aristocratic class. If the system be artificial and repugnant to the common sense of nations more advanced in enlightenment, it is deeply rooted in the whole social fabric. The people have become not only accustomed but attached to it, and it is beyond the reach of radical reform unless by revolution. Its hereditary law-givers, its various orders of nobility and gentry, the law of primogeniture and consequent consolidation of wealth and power in a privileged few, give it a stability which must yield slowly to any pressure brought to disturb it from the growing sense of its injustice or impolicy. The geographical position of Great Britain towards the continent of Europe, the peril to social order were ignorance and want to dictate legislation, lessons of experience from past times and present, discourage changes which instead of bettering the general condition might bring in their train calamities unnumbered and unforeseen. It is the boast of the national constitution that it yields to pressure. If the social load line is badly adjusted, this must be retrimmed till again safe. If an aristocracy, from wealth, alliances and privilege the most imposing the world has ever known, becomes a menace or offence to the masses who have the numerical superiority, primogeniture, rank, political supremacy must in turn be surrendered till it has accommodated itself to the spirit of the age. Such has been the course heretofore and the like good sense will long preserve it from violence and overthrow. It would be idle to resist social development. If arrogance offends or power crowds, something must give way, and whatever blocks the steady advance towards political or social equality, so far as it is based on what is reasonable and just, must be trampled down. Power which in 1688 passed from the throne to the landholders will soon by recent changes of legislation be transferred to the people, who it is hoped will be wise enough to effect every needed reform without revolution.

If the English race at home have long clung with tenacity to an organization working for the benefit of a few to the disadvantage of the many, they deserve credit for adopting when circumstances favored one founded on liberty and equality. Our fathers in separating from the mother country rejected the hereditary principle in government as well as rank in society, all titles and special privileges, and abolished primogeniture which had existed in a mild form in some of the colonies, together with entails, as prejudicial to equal rights. They constructed their new system upon the basis of general education, diffusion of knowledge, good manners, good principles and entire freedom of conscience, and these have been constantly tending not to bring down, but to elevate up all to a social level. If distinctions exist they are recognized without jealousy. Deference is paid to worth, other usual claims to consideration respected, and individuals left to their own preferences and opportunities in selecting their associates. But there is little arrogance to offend or over-sensitive pride to be wounded, and only the frivolous are inclined to claim, and no one who is honest and courteous is compelled to brook superiority.

Should it be asked what direct bearing this has on our subject, the importance attached to ideas of better or worse, higher or lower, rank and consequence, enter so largely into genealogical inquiry that it seems worth while, now and then, to re-examine the grounds on which they rest. An American, believing in his birthright to equality with the best, is sensitive about seeking amid the pride and circumstance of English social life for progenitors in a position of inferiority, not always reflecting, as he should, that if our scale of comparison as to respectability among the living be perverted by adventitious considerations of wealth or rank, the memory of the dead depends for its halo on character and worth. Such fallacies should not be permitted to chill our interest in our progenitors beyond the sea, nor in their native land. The tender associations that cluster around England, the romantic incidents and heroic achievements in its annals, its natural beauties and noble monuments, even the picturesque varieties of its social structure, are an inheritance too precious to be lost or undervalued. This we share with its present inhabitants, rich and poor, gentle and simple, and most of those who occupy the heights of its social pre-eminence would find, should they count over their ancestors three or four centuries ago, the same variety of condition as ourselves.

What is intrinsically respectable is confined to no class, but graces alike the poor man's house and the rich man's palace. Among the monarchs of England there has been little for praise or pride. Neither son of the conqueror inherited his capacity in field or council. The second Henry, like the third and sixth, was feeble and dull. Richard the lion-hearted was a brave crusader but sorry king. Edward the great Plantagenet and his grandson were wise and vigorous rulers, and the fifth Henry gallant in war. But not all the talent and learning of Froude can make the eighth Henry much better than a brute, or his daughter Elizabeth other than a woman in whom every feminine trait was turned to acidity. The Stewarts evinced a marvellous unfitness for the throne, and the merciless pen of Thackeray has described the Georges. In the ranks of nobility there have been few instances of extraordinary genius or power, though many advantages favor their development. Now and then Stanleys and Howards, Russells or Stanhopes have been well endowed by nature and justly distinguished. But in arts and arms, in the cabinet, senate and professional careers, the great minds that have done good service and made their names remembered have been from the middle walks of social life and often from the lowest. As one price for intellectual superiority, not only it rarely descends, but the race itself, exhausted by its extraordinary yield, tends to extinction. Lineal descendants disappear after a few generations. Chaucer, Shakespeare, Milton, Bacon and Newton, and the most brilliant stars that stud the firmament of English genius, live only in their works.

Ten generations ago, if there have been no intermarriages, a case hardly supposable, one thousand individuals bearing as many different names stood in the like degree of ancestry to the present; twenty back, over a million. In this multitudinous array by the doctrine of chances we should probably all of us be equally fortunate in discovering persons of worth and usefulness, of eminent ability and social consequence, of health and wealth, and all other blessings that we value ourselves, or should be glad to find they possessed. But if the larger part of them were the rude forefathers of England's hamlets, such as Gray describes in his immortal elegy, it would be still a satisfaction to learn their names and occupations, and from what little can be ascertained or conjectured, form some notion of those homely joys, the destiny obscure that constituted their short and simple annals. If by chance are found in our diverging lines persons of more note and wider culture, to reconstruct their career from what we know of them and the times they lived in, to become familiar with their traits of character, peculiarities of temper and disposition, the incidents of their lives, trials and enjoyments, reveals a new world of hidden treasures, abounding in objects of affection and attachment around which is encrusted all we know that they knew, all that they experienced of events of historical importance, of far more absorbing interest to us than the stately inanities of kings and courtiers, of Tudors or Stewarts, extending our horizon of thought, adding a new zest to existence.

Such knowledge has other uses. As the child is father of the man, so descend ancestral traits. Through the mysterious germ that links us with the past, come not only similarity of gait and voice, of form and function, susceptibility to disease, proclivities to evil, but aptitudes and capacity for work. Who has not recognized as heirlooms in his blood, skill or taste not of his own acquiring, and guiding the helm or rein, wielding the sword or pen, been conscious that some ancestral salt or jehu, knight or scribe has done the like before. Who has not met about the world namesakes, the common ancestor in centuries remote, whose manner, tone and lineaments recalled his nearest kinsfolk, and not in mere marks external only, but in trains of thought, likes and dislikes, common to both, found proof of common stock. If this view be just, unconscious cerebration, puzzling with memories undefined of mental states or combination of events inexplicably recurring, instead of wraiths of dreams forgotten, as Miss Cobbe suggests, may be actual experiences of foregoing generations.

Old England has ever been a prolific mother of colonies, "fons gentium;" so also the new. Whilst the parents mind the sterile farm, or croon in winter over the iron substitute for the once ample hearth, the children carry over the land the four great institutions of New-England, church and school, town meeting and training field. When prospered they freshen up the homestead, and gather hundreds or thousands of the name and blood from all parts of the continent, to renew their associations with the ancestral abode. From old Tristram Coffin, patriarch of Nantucket, thousands of descendants are spread broadcast throughout the union. In their old home at Newbury, erected more than two centuries ago and ever since dwelt in by their name, more than a score of college graduates have been born to be of good service to society. At Alwington in Devon also there has been a long succession of their race from the Conquest, in every generation honored and respected. This instance is but one of many where the posterity of our immigrant fathers would derive a special pleasure from learning the details of their family history in England. Sordid motives sometimes mingle with and debase the sentiment. Expectation of inheritance has often collected crowds of aspirants to some old estate left without heirs to claim it; but as great hopes are chilled by frequent disappointments, this weakness has grown less.

Genealogical inquiry has been pursued with so much ardor of late in New-England that individuals at a loss to trace back to the earliest immigrant ancestor are the exception. The Genealogical Dictionary of Mr. Savage, a monument of patient industry in which he gives some account of those who came over prior to 1692, and two succeeding generations, family bibles, town and family histories and probate records, ancient correspondence and the vast accumulation of family lore in our REGISTER, render it comparatively easy to construct pedigrees from all of our American progenitors. Realizing as we must the danger of procrastination, how much precious information has already been lost forever out of mind by neglecting so simple a precaution, we cannot too forcibly impress upon whoever have not yet availed themselves of its pages, the wisdom of transplanting their family trees to an enclosure where they are sure to be preserved.

When, however, we seek to gather up the broken thread beyond the sea and ascertain the early abodes of those who came over, and their ancestral lines, we find the task less easy. Some families go back for many generations, even to the Conquest. Others, and often among the most distinguished in our colonial annals, are lost in an impenetrable cloud after a step or two, in the host of the same patronymic then existing, or perhaps in the utter extinction there of the race; whilst others again only know their ancestors were English from their names. It is hardly a misfortune, should not certainly be regarded as any humiliation, to be ignorant; in some instances ignorance may be preferable to learning what is disagreeable. Still the truth, pleasant or otherwise, may be of use in chastening pride or correcting false views of life and its obligations. If the inquiry involves waste of time or means needed for other duties, it is not worth pursuing; but where researches can be made at little cost, and with fair promise of success, there is generally some one in every family group with leisure and taste to collect names and dates and whatever else can be known.

No country is better provided with facilities for genealogical inquiry than Great Britain. Her record offices are now kept in good order and made reasonably accessible. Documents from suppressed ecclesiastical establishments and family muniment rooms, state papers and private correspondence, visitations, pedigrees and collections of genealogies are constantly drifting towards the national archives, British Museum, and similar repositories. In the Birmingham Tower at Dublin are an immensity of papers in card boxes assorted and calendared under the supervision of Sir Bernard Burke, and in the Bodleian Library, at Oxford, there are rooms lined with ponderous volumes of manuscript full of material for the elucidation of family history. Conveyances are not recorded as with us, but probate archives, court files, parish registers, if some of them are difficult to decipher, contain for experts special treasures. The registers beginning with the Reformation are not easy to read, the hands being often cramped and the ink faded, but when gathered up and systematized as they will be some day, and births, deaths and marriages of names not too extensively multiplied up to the period of emigration brought together and indexed, a larger proportion of the ancestry of American settlers will be ascertained.

But if unrivalled in her manuscript treasures, the printed books on family history in England largely exceed in number, variety and interest anything to be found elsewhere in the world. One of the earliest is Dugdale's Baronage, of which we have a copy in our public library. But the peerages and similar works of Collins, Burke, Bankes, Sharpe, Lodge and Betham, the Beauties of England, Camden's Magna Britannia and Lysons's, county histories and family annals, biographies and biographical dictionaries, the Archaeologia, and that admirable work while it recorded what concerned families, the *Gentleman's Magazine*, by Sylvanus Urban, now unfortunately perverted from its original character, embrace an immense extent of information about old times and those that lived in them. While with us no life is considered so valueless as not to be entitled to remembrance and record, in England such a privilege is reserved for wealth and rank. Of the from one to two hundred millions forming the twenty-six generations since the Conquest, the greater number have melted into oblivion and left no sign. Whole names and families have utterly perished. Publications on the subject of family history date for the most part since the landing of the Pilgrims at Plymouth, and illustrate families still flourishing, not those once in prosperity which have become reduced. This is true, also, of documents, records and brasses, which have been suffered to perish where no one remained with any special interest or influence to have them preserved. History has been written, historical incidents distorted to flatter the pride or prejudice of the powerful at the expense of many with a better title to consideration but without advocates to defend it. Humble worth has never stood, in the mother country, much chance of memorial or monument, and, unless for some vague tradition among descendants, or brief entry in the parish books of baptism, marriage or burial, has been ever speedily forgotten and passed out of mind.

The very superabundance of material is an embarrassment to the American inquirer. The public offices are accessible for any useful purpose only to experts, and dependence must be mainly placed upon professed genealogists well enough acquainted with all the sources of information to economize effort. There are now many who make it a profession, and so general is the desire of our people to know whatever is to be known of their family history, that an adept is sure of lucrative employment. There are, also, accomplished devotees to the work, such as Mr. Savage, Col. Chester and Mr. Somerby once were, and others, who, from taste for such researches and a generous wish to be useful to others, devote their time and means without stint or recompense, where the occasion is fit. We are still on the threshold of our subject, but our limits admonish us to defer or leave for those better informed, what should be known to genealogists about the Heralds' College and coats of arms, the public and prerogative record offices and their several departments, the Birmingham Tower, College Libraries, and British Museum, with their genealogical treasures. We had also intended to give some account of the principal works likely to be useful to whoever makes such inquiries an occupation or is interested in their results; but this, too, must be postponed for the present. T. C. A.

BOSTON MINISTERS.

Communicated by John Ward Dean, A.M.

In the Register for April, 1859 (vol. xiii. pp. 131–3), we gave our readers the second of these two famous poems, which though not printed at the time, were evidently very popular and have often been quoted.

The whole of the first poem has not hitherto been preserved in print, though James S. Loring, in 1852, printed in his *Hundred Boston Orators* (p. 11), the greater portion of it, collected from the recollection of old persons then living. The date when the poem was written cannot be precisely ascertained; but it must have been composed between Sept. 25, 1771, and May 12, 1772, as it characterizes Rev. Messrs. Hunt and Bacon, who were settled at the former date, and Rev. Mr. Bowen, who was dismissed at the latter.

We had supposed that the first poem, except what has been preserved by Mr. Loring, was hopelessly lost, till recently, when we saw in the possession of J. Wingate Thornton, Esq., a manuscript by Mrs. Hannah Mather Crocker, author of *Observations on the Rights of Women*, which contained copies of both poems. The manuscript is entitled: "*Interesting Memoirs and Original Anecdotes, giving an account of the Original Proprietors of the town of Boston, the manners and customs of our Venerable Ancestors as handed down by tradition and recollections of an original Inhabitant, from generation to generation the fifth. By Nature's Antiquarian, H. M. Crocker.*" By Mr. Thornton's permission we copy the first poem for our readers. The second poem having already been printed from what we consider a more reliable copy,[1] we shall not repeat it here.

The poems are in the stanza made familiar to the people of New-England by Wigglesworth's *Day of Doom*. The first poem is said by Mrs. Crocker to have been "laid to Dr. Benjamin Church," and the second to Trumbull[2]

[1] Mrs. Crocker omits two stanzas (13 and 14) "Now what the deuce . . . . . his preaching eke;" and has many verbal variations which do not seem to us to be improvements.

[2] There are two copies of Mrs. Crocker's MS. Both assign the first poem to Dr. Church, but in regard to the second poem, there is a variation, the first copy naming Trumbull only as the author.

or Dexter of Dedham. Mr. Loring, who gives portions of both ballads, without being aware that there was more than one poem, states that the verses he prints had been ascribed to John Fenno, the keeper of the "Granery," and also to Joseph Green, the poet and wit. The copy of the second poem, in the handwriting of Thomas M. Jones, which was printed in the REGISTER for April, 1859, states that it was "written in 1774," which is probably correct. Mrs. Crocker states that both poems were "handed about in manuscript" in that year. As the author of *M'Fingal* studied law in Boston from November, 1773, to September, 1774,* it is possible that he may have written the latter poem.

We have added a few foot-notes explaining the allusions in the poem and noting the variations of this copy from that printed in the *Hundred Boston Orators*.

FIRST POEM.

Old Mathr's race will not disgrace[1]
  Their noble[2] pedigree;
And Charles Old Brick,[3] both[4] well and sick,
  Will plead[5] for liberty.
There's puffing Pem,[6] who does condemn
  All Freedom's noble sons,
And Andrew Sly,[7] who oft draws nigh
  To Thomy Skin and Bones.[8]

In Brattle Street, we seldom meet
  With Silver Tonguèd Sam,[9]
Who smoothly glides between both sides
  And so[10] escapes a jam.

There's[11] Pennel Puff[12] is hearty enough,
  And so is Simeon Howard,[13]
And Long Lane Teague[14] will join the League,
  And never prove a coward.[15]

There's[16] little Hopper[17] if you think proper[18]
  In Liberty's cause so[19] bold;
And John Old North,[20] tho' little worth
  Wont sacrifice for gold.[21]
There's puny John,[22] from Northampton,
  A meek mouthed moderate man,
And colleague stout,[23] who, without doubt,
  Is linked in Tory Clan.[24]

* J. Hammond Trumbull, LL.D., in *Historical Magazine*, 2d series, vol. iii. p. 1.

1 Loring's version reads, "The Mather race will ne'er disgrace." The "Mather race" here referred to we take to be the Rev. Samuel Mather, D.D., Rev. Mather Byles, D.D. and Rev. Mather Byles, Jr. The first had been pastor of the Old North Church from 1732 to 1741, and was now pastor of a seceding church in Hanover Street; the second was pastor of the Hollis Street Church from 1733 to 1776; and the last was rector of Christ Church from 1768 to 1775.

2 "ancient."—*Loring.*

3 Rev. Charles Chauncy, D.D., pastor of the First or Old Brick Church from 1727 to 1787.

4 "if."—*Loring.* 5 "cry."—*Loring.*

6 Rev. Ebenezer Pemberton, D.D., pastor of the New Brick Church from 1745 to 1747.

7 Rev. Andrew Eliot, D.D., pastor of the New North Church from 1742 to 1778.

8 Gov. Thomas Hutchinson, author of the *History of Massachusetts Bay.*

9 Rev. Samuel Cooper, pastor of Brattle Street Church from 1745 to 1783.

10 "thus."—*Loring.* 11 "There's" omitted by Loring.

12 Rev. Penuel Bowen, pastor of the New South from 1766 to 1772.

13 Rev. Simeon Howard, D.D., pastor of the West Church from 1767 to 1804.

14 Rev. John Moorhead, a native of Belfast, Ireland, pastor of the Presbyterian Church in Long Lane, now Federal Street, from 1730 to 1773.

15 "He never was a coward."—*Loring.*

16 "There's" omitted by Loring.

17 Rev. Samuel Stillman, D.D., pastor of the First Baptist Church from 1765 to 1807. He was a small and active man.

18 "when he thinks proper."—*Loring.*

19 "is."—*Loring.*

20 Rev. John Lathrop, D.D., pastor of the Old North Church from 1768 to 1816.

21 This quartrain "Little Hopper . . . . for gold" is placed before the preceding by Loring, making lines 13 to 16.

22 Rev. John Hunt, a native of Northampton, Mass., pastor of the Old South Church from 1771 to 1775.

23 Rev. John Bacon, pastor of the Old South Church from 1771 to 1775.

24 The last four lines are omitted by Loring, instead of which he prints twelve lines from the later poem, namely stanza 12, lines 5 to 8 (slightly varied, thus:

"Trout's Sunday aim is to reclaim
  Those that in sin are sunk;
When Monday comes, he stills them rum
  And gets them woful drunk.")

And the whole of stanza 4, "There's punning Byles provokes . . . . . he meets."

MEMOIR OF JOHN EVANS, DEPUTY GOVERNOR OF PENNSYLVANIA.

Communicated by the Rev. EDWARD D. NEILL, of St. Anthony's Falls, Minn.

JOHN EVANS was of Welsh extraction, the son of Thomas Evans, of London, who had been a seafaring man, an old friend of William Penn "who loved him not a little."

He was about twenty-six years of age when he was commissioned as lieutenant governor of Pennsylvania. The proprietor, in a letter to the secretary of the province, in 1703, alludes to his appointment in these words:—

"He shows not much, but has a good deal to show, and will gain upon the esteem of the better sort. He has travelled and seen armies, but never been in them. Book learning as to men and government he inclines to; carries over some good books, and expects among mine and thine to help himself with more. Give him as soon as he comes a hint of persons and things and guide his reading."

He did not profess to be a member of the society of Friends, and Richard Hill, a Quaker, described him as "an Episcopal man, young and solid."

Accompanied by William Penn, Jr., the surviving son of the first wife of the proprietor, he reached Philadelphia on 11th day 12th month, 1703–4. Isaac Norris wrote to a friend: "The Governor and William Penn, Jr. caught us napping, arrived late last night."

Norris had come to Philadelphia from Jamaica, stood high in the society of Friends, and was a solid and intelligent merchant. From respect to the proprietor, and a love of hospitality, he was willing to receive young Penn into his family, although his wife had the care of "six children small and tender."

Evans lodged at first with a Mr. Paxton, and then at Sheriff Finney's, but the habits of both of the young gentlemen were such that respectable housewives soon felt that their absence was more agreeable than their presence.

James Logan, the virtuous and scholarly secretary of the province, always anxious to serve the proprietor and to preserve the dignity of the province, at length rented for a government house the great brick, double front mansion of lawyer William Clarke. It was considered the most splendid residence in the city, and stood in capacious grounds at the corner of Third and Chestnut streets, facing the latter and also Dock creek. Here were gathered as fellow-boarders—Penn, Evans, and Mompesson; the latter had been a member of parliament and recorder of Southampton, now a judge of the province, subsequently chief-justice of New-York. Logan gave them the best rooms, and, to use his own language, "turned up into the garret," preferring, no doubt, the retirement of an humble attic with his classical books to the bacchanalian orgies of the lower floors.

Not many weeks elapsed, before the three inmates of Clarke Hall became the town talk. At a late hour one night, there was a riot in a tavern, kept by one Enoch Story, in which young Penn and Gov. Evans were participants. It is said that Penn called for pistols, and that the lights being blown out, a city alderman "availed himself of the darkness to give

Evans a severe drubbing."[1] Evans, on the other hand, about this time is alleged to have called into a tavern and there flogged a constable named Solomon Cresson.[2]

Penn was indignant at being arraigned before the mayor's court, and was afterward more intemperate. About this time Lord Cornbury, son of the Earl of Clarendon, visited Philadelphia and with his wife was handsomely entertained by young Penn at Pennsbury, the country seat of the proprietor. After this, Penn determined to return to England by way of New-York, Byerly, collector of the customs there, agreeing to loan him money.

Norris, writing to a friend, says: "William Penn, Jr., is quite gone off from Friends. He being in company with some extravagants that beat the watch at Enoch Story's was presented with them. * * * * He talks of going home in the Jersey man-of-war next month. I wish things had been better, or he had never come."

The following letter to his friend Evans was written before he sailed.

[Wm. Penn, Jr., to Lt. Gov. Evans.]

N. York 8br 18th, 1704.

Dr Sr,

The Hurry I have been in, in preparing for my voyage has been ye only occasion of my not writing sooner, but I could not omitt this opportunity wth ou^t^ assuring yow How much I (wth ou^t^ a Compliment) your Humble servant. I hope if I can serve you, you will not scruple to command me, nobody shall be a more faithful friend. God Prosper you in all your undertakings and make ye People ——— and Happy.

Your very Hum^ble^ friend,
Wm. Penn, Jr.[3]

What is amiss,
Pray impute to our
way of living Here—

There was no improvement upon the part of the governor after his friend's departure. He was self-important and "had more of the rake in his character than of any thing else."[4]

On one occasion he met a countryman coming to town with a heavily loaded wagon. He ordered the man to halt and allow him to pass by. The teamster being slow in his movements, with a louder voice he repeated the demand with threats. The countryman now roused, in not very nice

[1] Watson's *Annals*, ed. of 1830, p. 104.

[2] Hazard's *Register*, vol. iv. p. 112.

[3] William Penn, Jr., was the surviving son of Penn's first wife, Gulielma Springett. Before he came to America he had married Mary Jones. Logan wrote to his father: "'Tis a pity his wife came not with him, for her presence would have confined him within bounds he was not too regular in observing." To pay his debts and return to England he was obliged to sell his manor, now the site of Norristown. Penn wrote to Evans in 1705 of his son: "He is like to be somebody here in a while I think." But the father's hopes were never realized. His intemperate habits increased. Leaving his family in England he went to France and died there in 1720, from the result of dissipation, two years after his father's decease.

His widow was a foolish, extravagant woman, and Hannah, the second wife of the proprietor, once wrote that she wished "she had brought more money since she had brought so little wisdom to help the family."

The children of William Penn, Jr., were: Gulielma Maria, Springett and William. The grandfather, in his letters of 1703, speaks of "my grandson Springett a mere Saracen, his sister a beauty." In another he calls the infant William, "the little Billy, the spark of them all." This William died in 1746. He married first, Miss Forbes, then after her death, Ann Vaux. His daughter married Mr. Gaskill, whose descendants are living in Pennsylvania.

[4] Extract from Smith MSS. *New-Jersey Historical Society Proceedings*, vol. viii. p. 131.

language, asked "Who he was, that being *on foot*, wanted a cart with a heavy load to turn out for him?" He answered, "I am the governor." The countryman rejoined by saying "he lied, for the governor was more of a gentleman, and had more consideration," and began to ply his whip upon the person that he felt was an impostor. At length the wagoner discovered that every governor was not a gentleman, and that he had assaulted Governor Evans, and with humble apologies escaped from the awkward dilemma into which he had been forced by the churlishness of Penn's representative.

The Quakers were opposed to even defensive war. They believed that if they never used, they would never need the sword. The encroachments of the French, and the growing hostility of the Indians, clearly demanded a militia organization, and Evans, soon after his arrival, began to form military companies.

As the Quakers were slow to respond to his plans, he resorted to a "boyish trick" to frighten them into his measures. By his instigation, a letter came to the sheriff of New-Castle with the forged name of Seymour, governor of Maryland subscribed, stating that a French fleet was approaching, and requesting that Governor Evans be immediately informed. The unsuspecting sheriff instantly despatched a messenger to Philadelphia, and the letter reached Evans while dining on the banks of the Schuylkill, at the residence of a Mr. Roche, "a generous liver," lately from Antigua. Hurrying to town, the governor convened the council, and read the letter to them with the solemn face of one who believed that every statement was as true as Holy Writ. The result was the issuing of a proclamation requiring all persons to furnish themselves with arms and ammunition, and for two nights the militia were on duty. During the excitement he rode about town with drawn sword, urging people to bear arms. Many of the unsuspecting citizens, fearing the approach of the French, fled from town, others hid their valuables in wells or buried them in their cellars.

The next step of the governor was still more impolitic, well stigmatized by Penn as "an extreme false step." He insisted that all vessels passing the fort at New-Castle, should pay a duty of one half pound of powder for each ton of burden. The merchants of Philadelphia resisted the exaction and complained to the proprietor, who considered the free and undisturbed passage of ships up and down the Delaware river a fundamental right of the charter of the province.

In the year 1708, without the knowledge of Secretary Logan, he gave Michel,[1] a Swiss adventurer, a permit to mine toward the sources of the Potomac, and made the proprietor believe that there were great prospects. William Penn, deep in debt, harassed by creditors, neglected by those whom he had befriended, was excited by the thought that he might through a silver mine replenish his fortune, and he clung to the expectation as a drowning man clings to a straw. In a letter to Logan, dated from London, 29 day 7 mo. 1708, he says: "Pray go to the bottom with Colonel Evans about the mines, and what has become of Michel? Who are let into the secret? Where are they? Who have worked them? It is a test upon J. Evans's honour and regard to me. I take his story (if he stays) to be a proof he believes it and stays to benefit himself."

Logan in reply said: "There is yet nothing certainly discovered about the mines. Col. Evans has been very free with me upon that head. There has been none opened, and I heartily wish I may be able to tell thee more

[1] Michelle, or Mitchell, afterwards settled, with other Swiss, in New Berne, North Carolina.

of the matter hereafter, for I fear Michel has tricked us all. He has gone over to England with an intention we believe of putting his countrymen, the Swiss, upon purchasing a tract beyond the Potomac."[1]

The private life of Evans was as censurable as his public conduct. Shunning the company of the correct and judicious Logan,[2] the secretary of the province, he for a time lived in an obscure house near the northern suburbs of the city. He had a liaison with one Susan Harwood, whose mother had escaped out of a debtors' prison, to which Penn alludes in deep sorrow in one of the appended letters. When he was removed from office he was a good deal surprised, and "broke his intended match with J. Moore's beautiful daughter,"[3] and the continuing of improvements upon a plantation he had obtained near New-Castle on the Brandywine, but it was ultimately renewed, and on the 28th 8 mo., 1709, he married the "fair Reb. Moore," the daughter of the advocate of the admiralty court, and until he left America kept house in the then fine Fairman mansion, near the treaty tree.

His successor, as deputy-governor, was Charles Gookin, about 48 years of age, whose grandfather, Sir Vincent Gookin, was nearly related to Daniel Gookin, who as early as 1620 sent cattle from Ireland to Virginia, and came himself in 1621, settled at Newport News, and whose son Daniel became the friend of the Indian missionary Eliot, died in 1687, and was buried in Cambridge, Mass.[4]

Penn had known the Gookin family in Ireland for forty years, and Charles, who had served in the army and had a soldier's religion,"[5] had been highly recommended as a successor to Evans by the Ingoldsby family and Generals Earle and Cadogan. Although not a free-liver he was eccentric, failed as an executive officer, and bore himself like a martinet.

Watson states that he sent for one of the judges and kicked him because he would not grant his wish. This and other strange conduct created the impression that he was partially deranged.

Evans, after surrendering his office to Gookin, remained for a time in Philadelphia, but at length retired to Denbigh, Wales. In November, 1716, he purchased of his former companion, young William Penn, 2000 acres of the manor of Steyning on Brandywine creek, and the following March gave John Moore, his father-in-law, power to sell the same;[6] but in 1731, as John Evans, of Pentry Manor, co. Denbigh, he declares before a master in chancery that he never authorized Moore to sell any land.[7]

[1] *The Friend*, vol. xix. p. 122.

[2] Logan thus complains about Evans not paying his board, in a letter to the proprietor: "After Master William had been here a few months lodging at Isaac Norris' we became so troublesome to his numerous family that we were obliged to remove and take a house. The lieutenant-governor first took lodgings at A. Paxton's, when his [Paxton's] wife's health rendering his stay improper, he removed to John Finney's, whence in a little time he was obliged to look out again, but finding no place, and I considering that we were already at the charge of housekeeping, and that wherever he went till money were otherwise raised, I must answer it on thy account, concluded therefore to invite him to the same house, as it was in general thought most proper.

Upon which to give way to him I turned up into the garret. Thy son departing in a few months after, we were left to keep house by ourselves. When we first entered on it I told Master William I could bear no other part than to pay as a boarder, that at Isaac Norris' I paid £30 per annum, and at another's £20 for a servant, and that here I would allow £60 per annum but would no more."—*Friend*, vol. xviii.

[3] Logan correspondence, in *Friend*, 1846.

[4] For genealogical information relative to the Gookin family, see REGISTER, vol. i. pp. 345–52; vol. ii. pp. 167–74; vol. iv. pp. 79–82 and 185–8.

[5] Penn to Logan.

[6] Deed-Books, Philadelphia.

[7] Catalogue of Benjamin Coleman, London, July, 1870.

His daughter Mary married a Dr. Barry, and her great-grandchild, an Irish maiden lady, gave the writer the originals of two of the following letters, and allowed him to copy the others that follow.

[WILLIAM PENN TO LT.-GOV. EVANS.]

COLL. EVANS London 5th of ye 7m (Mar.) 1704.

Esteem'd ffr'd

It is now neer six months Since you sayl'd from Spithead, and not ye least intimation yet arriv'd as of your getting well to your Journey's end, which makes all uneasy. We understood by ye master of one of yr fleet yt was carried into Martineco by a French Privateer & was deliver'd by one of our ships takeing ye Privateer in his way to France, that you were all well, ye ffleet I mean, ye 2 of Xbr being four days after our unexampled storme yt has more than taxt ye nation 4ss in ye pound by ye divastations it has occasioned.

My tax is 30lb where I live but I have sustained about fifty, & am come off more than equall with ye best. But you will have the Prints to tell you all. It seems America the Continent at least had a mighty Tempest on ye 7th of 8br, while you were upon yr voyage, but the winds of neither side made themselves knowne, that to this, or this to yt side of the world.

I hope thyn & my son's arrivall have contributed to ye quelling that which has so long agitated the people of my Governm't—I shall say nothing of their unfairness to make the want of things a reason of Complaint & then hinder supplying that want by secretly discourageing the means used to answer it, as wt my Depty Goverr did about Capitall Cases, trying men for life by oath, and the Militia, which one Bantifeux harrangu'd so clamorously about & reggistring of vessels upon oath only since thy arrivall & approbation will putt an end to all those things.

Positively stand to ye letter of ye pow'rs of my Patent, whatever orders come from hence yt I know nothing of, or thos fractious Spirits do, or say there. Without resolution as well as meekness & Patience there is no Good; wherefore keeping within the Compass of the Laws of ye Province & powrs of my Grant fear nothing, while I am here & able to follow my own business; I hope by this opertunity to send you a letter, or at least to get one sent, or a coppy thereof from ye Lords Comrs for Trd & Plants in reproof C. Quarry's Insolence to address, wth his vestry Lord Cornberry a Guest in our own town & Goverm't, Civilly invited and treated, to write to the Queen to take our Goverm't away from us, an Imprudence yt is without precedent, & for wch he deserves ye severest rebukes & discountenance.

I must tell thee, I am much more like to keep my Goverm't than to sell or loose it, & therefore am not upon those uncertain and precarious Circumstances they hope yt are my enimys & our fr'ds may fear; ffor our great men plainly see ye motives of these folks to vex us & more resolve to support us in our just rights, and to less vallue the clamour ag'st us. But pray take care of Trade & Queen's Revenue and then feed ym wth good hard meal yt with softer treatment will be Insolent or disorderly to Goverm't.

Thy mother sent to-day to see me & I have dispatcht one to her business, C. Puckler being gone to-day & I going out of Town at 3 this afternoon. C. L.[1] thinks to write to thee and my son, now, or by way of N. York: intending then my resentm't to yt Lord, of Quarry's business.

John, lett honour, conscience, and old friendship prevaile to acquit thyselfe to me & my family and the Country according to our Laws and Constitution, not yet repeal'd, till they are so, in a legal manner wch as yet is farr off. My son and daughter salute ye & so does with good wishes

Thy true ffriend,

WM. PENN.

P. S. I can say no more till I heare from thee of the state of things. Be just and then wise. Salute me to ye Councill and Magestrates—Farewell. W. P.

Thy Mother's business was only to hear of thy wellfare.

[1] Charlewood Lawton, Penn's lawyer.

[From the Same to the Same.]

Bristoll 6 9bre 1704.

Esteemed Friend

I cannot let this Bearer goe without a salutation (for it is by another hand in ye same ship that I have writ to thee already but 'tis about 6 weeks if not two months agoe.

ffirst thy relatives were lately well to whom I took care to deliver thy letters; thy uncle is now or lately was on his circuit & in Cornhill. I have given thy salutes to L'd Clarendon &c. and the character I have had of thy conduct, and with them, has done thee service.

I can make no Judgem't of our affaires, only that the adverse Interests struggle mightily and 'tis thought this session of Parliament will issue it one way or t'other.

Our affaires in Germany in a secure condition, not so in Portugall & yet worse in Savoy, but ye other successes more than Ballance yt & some think that yt war is but begun. Vast preparations on both sides.

I have both thine, as in a former I intimated, I only desire thee steer legally by Just interest, and w't room there is for favour to be on ye side of my affaires; for If I keep my Gov'rm't, thou keepest my Lieftenantcy and If I resigne, one article will be to continue thee there, for it will be hardly done, but by consent.

As I would have thee just to all, so discreet to our enemys, but kinde to ye ffriends of ye Country, & of my honest interest. I have hinted at large to ye Secretary, my minde about ye division of ye up'er and lower countys, and let James Coutts know whatever they can desire of thee as my Dept I shall acquiesce in what thou does upon thy best consideration, and those of ye Province that one of ye worthiest mindes, and further confirme the same notwithstanding the ungratefull and unworthy behaviour of Rob't ffrench & John Hill.

Lett W. Clarke[1] know pray that I have his, per last opertunity, and have his former, and writ an answeare. Tell him I shall complain to ye Comrs of Trade & Plantations about ye Marylanders, and consider of ye rest he writt of.

I need not bid thee respect my Son & yet I would not carry yt too farr, and I hope there will be no need of it. Thy ff'ds remain such. I wish I could say the same. If it lays in thy way to help ye bearer pray do, he is a poor kinsman of my wife's, who salutes thee, as does with a true regard

Thy Sincere &
affect. ffriend
Wm. Penn.

My salutes
to ye Council & Magistrate
& ye well inclined at large.

[From the Same to the Same.]

Coll. Evans &
Esteemed Frd.

London 30th 7, 1705.

Thy last was of the 5th month last, in haste, So Short, chiefly intimating the hasty coming over of Coll. Quary. I hope he has no Com'issions from our ungrateful crew on that Side the water, the unwearied troubler of our poor Israel, and here are our Pennsilvania Company and *Lumby*[2] that wait upon him, and I fancy next Coll. Nicholson and perhaps—Ld. Corn. affaires, those Law Suits may go a good way to engage him upon this Voyage. However I hope the man that knows him to ye Bottom will tread hard upon his heeles, or close at least, if you there apprehend any mischief.

I have in mine by Burnam and in my last by Guy, or that Ship at least been Cargo to Several of thine, and therefore Shall only tell thee that thine of 7th 1*mo.* 1703-4, 29*th* 3*mo.* 1704, 30*th* 3*mo.* 1704, 27*th* 5*mo.* 1704, 25*th* 6*mo.* 1704, 4*th* 8*mo.* 1704 *and* 6*th* 2*mo.* 1704, 30*th* 3*mo* 1705 came alsoe to hand which saving that I have mentioned, I have answered. I lament the Separation of the Province and Counties; and I affirm I never intended So, but upon Condition I lost my Governm't and then that ye Countyes—as well as Province Should have the Same freedome.

[1] Had been a lawyer in Lewes, Delaware.

[2] Quarry, as judge of the admiralty court in 1699, had condemned the ship Providence of Stockwith, Capt. Lumby, because it had not been registered.

After the sale of the cargo, one-third of the proceeds was offered to Penn as proprietor, which he declined to use, and notified the owners of the vessel that it was at their disposal. Quarry and the advocate Moore were considered to have acted dishonorably in the case.

But the Lower Countyes were soo much the Occasion of all this Confusion, I fear by adhearing to ye Enemys of the Province, Quary, Moor, those villanous vipers. And it pleases me not a little, to find thee So apprehensive of their practises, and that thou hast made So great a part of the best of the Church People Sensible of their Base—and unreasonable designes. Not but that D. L. (one of ye worst of men) envying Moor, as folks of a Trade use to do, as well as Moor—leading him they may by begrudging —— Loyd his large practice among our Fr^ds hath contributed to our Confusion. I have not yet *presented the Queen any of the Addresses Sent me*, because signd by a person *So obnoxious as D. L.*[1] and I am discouraged from it on that Acct. As for the Laws if the Fleet stays but 14 days longer, what are allowed Shall be Sent and *a letter from the Lords Comissioners for Trade and Plantations that will not disgust thee.* No Surrender yet, but when done (if done) depend upon it, I shall make it my Care for myself as well as thee, to Secure ye Govern^rs place for thee. The old Keeper is out, and William Cooper will be declared to morrow, and changes after that manner else where are expected which I hint for thy Aime. *Coll. Quary with his Protector Perry* have been with me, professes all fairness and friendlyness, and though thou didst not take his advice in proceeding ag^t the Vessell in an Admiralty way, yet he will only ask ye opinion of the Comissioners of y^e *Customs for information and not complaint.* I know the Lords of Trade will drop it, and that of the Wool if not press, for they were pleased ye New-Englanders came at the Wool of Road Island[2] so ingenuously as they did 2 years ago by sheering of them on Connetticutt Side. *But complaint came to me from Philadelphia against ye increase of publick*, and the high rates *of* 8 *per c. Licence yearly which at* 50 *of them* Comes to 400£ per Ann. And they say it is more than twice the value of what they have or give here for them. I called to-day at thy mother's, but she was not at home, is well. So thy Friends Salute thee, *much is said of the Lewdnes of Pennsylvania. I beg of thee to have regard to my Character*, and give not that advantage against me either with God or good or bad men whose ill use of it I most fear, on a publick acct. I have just now Rec'd thine of 5th 5mo. (July) and am very Sorry that wicked man D. L. could blow up any of his Mermidons to such a pitch of brutishness as thy Acct. of William Biles[3] relates that is a meer vox et praeterea nihil, a Coxcomb, and a Prag-matick in graine. That fellow's plantation is a Robbery upon Pennsbury, and, if there be a grant, was not a purchase from me, nor any Towed Land writs, for it was surveyed long before and done in my absence, formerly, and Judge Mompresson[4] can tell if I may not be deceived, in my Grant as well as the Crown, be it King or Queen,—Since, if confirmed, it was upon Surprize, and rattle an Inquisition about his eares, if not a prosecution. And know that when the time is expired of Session he may be taken to task, Since the Service he may pretend he was to attend is over. And first complain to the Friends, and if they wont or cant bow him to make Satisfaction, take it by Law thy Selfe. Pray mind what I say, be Secret, which is discreet, and fall on him or any other such unruly People at once, and make Some one Example to terrifie the rest. Thou hast not only my leave, but liking and encouragement whether called Quakers or others.

I hope yet to weather my difficulties here and there, and I hope what I Sent pr J. Guy 3 or 4ms. ago to testifie my case about the Laws, and in case of a Surrender, of their Priviledges, every way will deeply affect the honest hearted to be thankful and grateful. I have told thee of Coll. Q's discourse and professions before Merch^t Perry and Some of our Friends and Shall watch his Steps I pretty well ken and

[1] David Lloyd was born in 1656 in Manoron, co. Montgomery, Wales. Is said to have studied under Judge Jeffries. Arrived in Pennsylvania, in 1686, in ship Amity. A Quaker from policy and not principle it is thought, occasioned by his marriage in the province of Grace Growden, a superior woman. The last twenty years of his life he resided in Chester. He was chief-justice of Pennsylvania, and died at the age of 78, in 1731.

[2] The wool act of England punished with imprisonment and the loss of the left hand the sending of live sheep out of the kingdom, and no encouragement was given to the dressing of skins, or to manufactures in the colonies.

[3] William Biles was a prominent member of the council. He had come to Pennsylvania before Penn, and had settled on the Delaware river under a grant from Governor Andros. His plantation is marked on a map of 1679-80. He had a contempt for Evans and had used these expressions concerning him: "He is but a boy." "He is not fit to govern us." "We will kick him out." He and his wife were preachers.

[4] Roger Mompesson is thus described by Penn in a letter to Logan: "He is a moderate churchman, knows the world here, has been in two several parliaments and recorder of Southampton, only steps abroad to ease his fortune of some of his father's debts." Was a favorite of Earl of Clarendon and proved worthless.

Shall watch him. Do you that are my good Friends there, your part to compose and maintain my just cause there, and I hope with God's assistance to prevent our Enemies here. I long since told J. Logan I wanted a Duplicate of the Laws, those Sent under ye great Seal, being presented to the Lords, and so out of my power, but as I occasionally borrow them. Howbeit almost ½ of them are demur'd to, as I have—already observ'd Perhaps by this opportunity I may say more about them, I could have those that are approv'd to Send presently but all ye Laws being under one Seale they Scruple having them presented by parcells and they cant present the body but the rest will receive the Queen's Negative, and then they cease and you will be thereby difficient in Governm't; So that I am at a Stand, whether it may not be best to let them rest as they are, till those excepted ag^t^ *are amended*, wording them more properly being the greatest reason for the Attorney Genl and Lords Exceptions. Wherefore if the approved by the Lords go no farther, it is to Save the rest till they come in fuller Termes to be approved also. My Toyle and expensive daily Attendance with a boy to wait on me and a Scribe to Assist me at above 40 pr Ann. besides lodgings and food &c. are well known here even to great Streightness. How I can do more and Serve them better I dont know. The Lord uphold my life to my poor Family under all my troubles. Among many that ask for thee *Sr. Roger Mosson* [Mompesson] *is one*, 'twas yesterday and remember to thee, and was not displeased at the Acc^t^. I gave him.

Our heats here are great, and the mightiest party making that has been known, So that it Seems the Crisis of affaires and what way they take now is like to be lasting for the future. I beseech God to prevent farther breaches. Ch. Lawton is and all is well. Sr Jos. Fredenham dined there this week and myself. He has writ he tells me and will by this opportunity. For *my Son he has now writ to thee*, and other persons more largely than he did to me when there. He is like to be Somebody here in a while I think. Is glad,—with my Selfe, that there Seems a returne to me and my abused Interest, indeed to Justice, and Self preservation, among our Friends there, through the Example of those y^t^ were always reasonable in their thoughts and inclinations, pray cherrish and Smile upon Such and frequent and be easy and friendly with them totally to recover and establish them. *Birely is Arriv'd* mightily requested by *Ld. Cla. and Ld. Rochester*, not to appear against Ld. Corn. if that will do.

There's no certain news of ye taking of Barcelona, but there is certainly a Great revolt in Catalonia in favour of Ch. 3^d^. but thou'lt have this and much more from ye com'n prints, to wch I refer thee. I shall be glad to hear of the good effects of ye opening of Trade with ye Spaniards and of your unanimity this Assembly for the publick good. Give my love to all our Sincere hearted Friends, whether Magistrates or others and let 'em know I have delay'd my Surrender on purpose, till the Laws that concern their Security are confirmed tho' reduc'd to great difficulties for want of Consideration I may justly expect thence. When thou hast occasion to write to the Ld of Trade or Com'issioners of the Customes inclose thy Letters to me that I may Second them.

I think I shall hardly Say much more at present But that I am with real affection

Thy faithful Fr^d^.

WM. PENN.

[FROM THE SAME TO THE SAME.]

London 7th 12 mo. 1705.

Honoured Friend,

I did in my last inform thee, of what Letters I Rec'd. from thee; Since which came that of the 22^d^ Augt. the last before being of 5th of July as thy dates express. I am truly glad thy state of health returns thy great usefuleness to me engages me to desire and hope it and my Friendship not less, and as it is pleasing news to all thy Friends.

I sent thy Mother and friend Lawton theirs, who are with the rest of thy Friends well and salute thee. Mine are also I bless God, with the addition of another boy, now five in all, and with their Mother at their Grandfathers at Bristoll. Our laws are before the Queen, and what cannot be done at onse must be done at twise; for I will take the confirmation as I can get it. J. Logans last was of 9th 9^br^ that by the Nonsuch is not yet come to hand nor L^d^. Cornberrys 2 days ago, the lesson Letters are come to hand, which I admire at. So can send no answer.

Things go smooth with the Queen, as to home and foreign business and in Spain by Ld. Peterboroughs letter to me (who succeeds so far that most of Valentia and

Arrogan have declared for the new King Charles the 3rd) who has made him Generallissimo of all his Armies every where, I have a letter from him of 2d, 9mo last, too days after the Secretarys and if the Recruits sent him, get time enough that King will in all probability, be in possession of Spain in a years time. For my surrender I govern myself by the dealings I find among you towards me. If I may believe Coll. Quary he goes highly Desposed to favour our affaires, words and his had, before divers, have pledged performances and I cannot perceive here otherwise, he sees how it is with me and that it will not hurt his interests to befriend mine, and a little time after his arrival if thou &c. think it for my advantage that he comes into the Counsil, he is willing, and I should be so too and that he be first or Second thereof to show he is reconsiled.

I wait ye Conclusion of the last Assembly, finally to take my own measures, and I hope to have it by the Pacquet not yet come to hand. I cannot at this distance Judge, but must depend upon thy Judgmt and my best friends and time, and again ye people would not have me to do so, if not done, pray agree what I have to do and send it me pr. first I will loose no opportunity the inclosed is the Original of wt I sent of 7m and 8m last, by our last opportunity, fear not my regards to thee. I hear by Coll. Quarys Pacquet that is arrived pr. Nonsuch that the lower Countys have granted 1d pr pound. I hope ye Province will in no wise come behind them the continuation whereof would make our wheels go the faster, and you then get fresh heart. I know thy natural abilitys, and acquired address, and hope to feel the good effects thereof. I send thee a new Com'ission wt that Bullbegger left out of reservation to me or my Heirs in Legislation lodging that in thy brest of Integrity, which I rely upon, for that was made a mighty thing of. I hope thou keeps a good Correspondence wth Coll. Seymour and next neighbour because of Marylanders claim that I hope is more vexatious than hurtfull. I shall press the runing of the line, as I have done, and so no fault of mine it has not been before, but I know not what James Logan means by securing against ye Crowns pretentions as to the Boundaries. I have writ him of my private affairs and I hope his Zeal honesty and good Service, will keep him firme, and his own prudence in a due temper to give them acceptance with the concerned. In all occasions Show an utmost care not to offend on the side of the Queens Revenue, and the Just bounds of Admiralty authority. Coll. Quary has promised great moderation, and prays thou wilt take him with thee in those things, that so all occasions of misunderstanding may be prevented. I have writ also largely to our Frds. that writ so copiously to me, and they and their Interest prevails in this last Election and Assembly.

My Sister, Cous. Pools, Cousin John from Dantzik, my own son and Self dined at my Son and Daughter Aubreys to day all well and salute thee Coll Quary going early to-morrow. I must close, leave much to him to discourse and advise, upon honour, for the Ships lye in the Downs, but not without the honest love and regards wishing thee the best Success, for thy own honr and interest as well as mine and am,

Thy faithful and affect. friend,

Wm. Penn.

Give my Salutes to all
our friends in Governmt.
& profession as if named.
Vale.

[From the Same to the Same.]

London, 27th 3 mo. 1708.

Esteemed Fr'd

Since my last to thee 15th 3 moth by Capt Hamilton, I have not till 2 days agoe of ye 28th 7 br 1707 r'cved one title from thee, tho' so necessary to both our affairs, as well to my Enemies contrivances agst my Property, as ye seditions agst ye Goverm't by yt lett'r thou wilt perceive ye objections to thy conduct. Since wch by other folks lettrs I have heard of an extreme false step abt a law made at N. Castle to ye prejudice of the fundamentall right and claime of ye Province; viz't free and undisturbed passage to and from ye Province, in my Patent, most pathetically worded, wch seemes to have united ye sevll Partys agst thee, and me, in consequence upon a common interest wch indeed looks like a finishing stroke to thy unhappyness. However that is not all, for ye charge of a lewed deportmt at Conostogoe is mightily aggravated, wth thy journey incognito to bring ye mother and daughter on their voyage, or at least journey to ye ship after soe much freedom with the latter, at least knowing of ye former's escapeing out of prison to ye loss of her creditors. Two such capitall breaches of God's commandm'ts, and yt of ye debtoress directly in ye very eye of ye governm't, yt all I have been able to prevent some of our fr'ds from goeing to Queen and Councill, with ye complaints from ye Assembly there, and rather quietly to lay thee aside after soe many years being in, wch is customary wth ye Queen or Councill to doe as in ye case of ye Duke of Ormond, Ld Cornberry &c. than by an obstinate dispute to have such things exposed, as must have disabled thee from other services or Employmts yt yet thou mayst stand fairly for. This I thought the best way and so some of thy truest and kindest frds to prevent ye mallice of some ill Spirits. So yt thou must give such a Proof of thy discretion as may bespeake thy Preferm't in some Station not Less beneficial.

Esqr Lawton, Parson Evans,[1] Netervill thy uncle & motr have been acquainted wth ye reason of this, for no Longer agoe than ye begining of this month 3 Persons who had rec'd ye last as well as former Assembly's Invectives agst thee Came wth a sort of Impeachment from them there agst thee to ye Queen, and made me their last Complaint, and if rejected to proceed to Queen and Councill; so yt wt we have done was ye best yt offered for thy advantage, some things being to likely to be proved, and by some upon ye Spott, yt are of a very reprovable nature, and Injustice to my own character there and here, I could not any longer reject their request, to Change hands, and therefore I Petitioned ye Queen in these Termes, and yt was all ye reason I gave for praying her approbation of my Choice and Commission.

Now know that I take thy care of my interst in Minerall mattrs. very kindly, and shall certainly hold myself obliged if Mitchell[2] be made true, and yt ye vallue rises as I have heard by J. Logan, &c. who I perceive by thine seems to guess rather than know. His on yt subject was dated this moth a year or near it. Such an affair Judiciously, and as honestly Performed will quickly end my misfortunes, and enable me to doe wondrs for yt poor Country after all ye ingratitude as well as Injustice of some Perverse tempers in it, whome God forgive. I hope ye tenor of this Lettr will not be able to provoke thee to either, but after wt has been said, and reasons for it, rather quicken thee to recommend thyself to ye Services, I and mine here away may be able to rendr thee in a future regard, and for ye New Castle people they may happen to find themselves mistaken at Last, I mean the Lower Countys busy folks yt have not used me wth Justice or gratitude or Common Civility, but I committ my Cause to God agst all my unworthy Enemy's of whome R. Hallwell I have heard is ye Greatest, time fails me, ye bearer is sent for to Liverpool where ye Ship lyes he has taken a passage in, and sets out to-morrow early upon his Journey of wch I had no notice till to-day by himself, Lord Lovelace sailes in a month, and I think by him to write wt I omitt now, and therefore conclude, wth ye good wishes of me, mine, and all thy best frd's wt I am and desire to be. Thy assured fr'd to serve thee when I may.

29. 4m. 1708.

I have yesterday thine of the 12 of 11mo. (Jan.) 1707-8, and I shall improve it the best I can with those warm'd ag'st thee, but it comes 2 months to late; a publick war or a change of hands must be, and accordingly, Coll. Charles Gooking will succeed thee who will I hope give at least some content. He has commanded men, is about 48 years of age, and intends to Sow all he has in ye Country & become a planter & will waite on Lord Lovelace yt goes in 3 weeks they say. I hope for a word about the ——— thy last mentioned. Thy unckle brought thine yesterday, as well to thy Mother. Thy ff'ds wish thee well, but nobody more than

Thy reall ffriend

WM. PENN.

T. Grey is wth me & gives thee
his best respects. Endeavours me for
thy service here, by thy ff'ds.

[1] Rev. Evan Evans came to Philadelphia in 1700, and was the preacher at Christ (the Episcopal) Church. After the first meeting of a presbytery in Philadelphia, he went to London in 1707, and urged the appointment of a bishop or suffragan for America. In his memorial he alludes to the recently formed presbytery in these words: "Wheresoever presbytery is established, there they have the face and appearance of an ecclesiastical jurisdiction and authority after their way, to resort to upon all occasions. But our clergy in America are left destitute of any advantages of this kind."

His connection with Christ Church terminated in 1719. Although a Welshman he was not a relative of the governor.

[2] See foot-note [1] on p. 423.

SALEM LOYALISTS.—MRS. MEHITABLE HIGGINSON.

Communicated by JOHN J. LATTING, Esq., of New-York city.

MRS. MEHITABLE HIGGINSON was the daughter of Dr. Thomas Robie, of Salem, born in 1724, and married Dec. 29th, 1755, John Higginson, of Salem (his third wife), descendant in the sixth generation from the Rev. Francis. He died on 23 Sept. 1774, leaving her a widow with one child, a daughter, Mehitable, born in Salem, March 26th, 1764. At the beginning of the war she, with this daughter and her father's family and friends, who were on the side of the Loyalists, fled to Halifax, where they continued till the restoration of peace, when they returned to Salem. Here she and her daughter took up their abode in a small house on Essex, near the corner of Monroe street, where for many years they kept a school for the small children of the neighborhood. The daughter was universally known as 'Miss Hitty,' and was noted for her aptitude in teaching spelling, in which all her pupils invariably became proficient.

A lady of Salem, recently deceased, and who was an attendant at her school, was accustomed to relate that she had her scholars arranged in a semicircle and kept at her side a long cane-rod, with which she could reach each scholar and thus inflict summary punishment, without leaving her seat. She used also to pin delinquent pupils to her dress, a mode of punishment common in Salem schools of that day, and which, it is said, more than any other, was dreaded by her scholars.

"Madam Higginson," writes another lady of Salem, "was a woman of great intelligence, piety, wisdom and energy,—very dignified in demeanor and very aristocratic in feeling. In our Revolutionary war, she unfortunately favored the wrong side,—saying on one occasion, 'It would be a joy to ride through American blood to the hubs of my chariot wheels.' Of course, it was neither pleasant or prudent for her to remain here; and with her father's family, she removed to Nova Scotia; but returned at the close of the war, and opened a school for young ladies, which became quite celebrated. Some of her pupils were day-boarders; our old neighbor, Mrs. Dodge, was one of them. I can call to mind only one of the stories she used to tell us children, of her school life. A rule, never to be broken, was, that everything put on the plate at dinner, must be eaten. One poor child had a great dislike for carrot; so, one day, when she was helped to some, she thought she would eat it at once, that she might enjoy the rest of her dinner. This did not escape the notice of Madam Higginson, who said, as she laid another large one on her plate, 'I perceive you are extravagantly fond of carrot!'

Their servant was an old black woman, named *Violet;* who was often sent into the closet for her wrong doings. She seemed to think little of the disgrace, saying, 'she didn't care; while she was there, they had all the work to do.' * * *

Miss Hetty continued to teach as long as she was able. How well I remember her tall, erect form, as she stood at her door, to watch the little ones, till they had safely crossed the street. In looks, dress, words and deeds, she was a peculiar person. * * * * She was always popular as a teacher of young children, taking a motherly interest in all that interested them. Some of the best men and women in Salem were taught by her lessons of truthfulness and benevolence that influenced them through life. When once asked what she taught her children, she replied 'Ethics.' She certainly inculcated the very essence of generosity, when she gave a child who had been very good in school, a strawberry: telling her to 'slice it, and share it with her brothers and sisters.' * * * * * *

You say you 'remember her little damsel.'[1] I can see her now, as she walked to church on Sunday; so staid, so clean. Strange as it may seem, she who had before her eyes so bright an example of single blessedness, listened to the voice that has lured so many from its peaceful paths. She married a widower, and the last I heard from her, she was the affectionate wife of a loving husband.

So, one after another, they passed away. Matron, maiden, and little damsel. All gone. And our farm wagon rattles four times a day over the very spot where the school room stood, and where both teachers saw 'the last of earth.'"

Mrs. Higginson the mother lived to be 94 years of age, and died in Salem in Jan. 1818. The daughter continued the school, and died in Salem July 19th, 1846. Her virtues were commemorated in an obituary notice by the late Hon. Daniel Appleton White, published in the Salem Gazette of July 21st, 1846. In his diary of July 20th, 1846, Judge White pays the following tribute to her:

"Passed forenoon mostly in completing my obituary notice of Miss Higginson, whose worth and excellence as a teacher I endeavored to set forth as an example to others as well as to make them better known and appreciated, having ever regarded her as one of the choicest blessings Salem ever had." He then speaks of her *great service* in the moral training of the children under her charge, and adds, "I feel her loss and am grateful for her lessons and efforts for my own children. Her whole history as well as ancestry is interesting."

LETTER FROM THE REV. JACOB CROWINSHIELD TO THE REV. DR. BENTLEY.

From the Collection of Miss Mary R. Crowninshield.

Washington, 3d Dec'r, 1803.
Saturday.

Dear Sir.

At 10 O. C. last night the all important constitutional amendment passed the Senate of the U. S. by the necessary majority of two thirds, twenty-two senators being in favour and ten against it, *Mr. Stone* voting on the right side, having been secured by an amendment providing for an event which I believe never will happen.

If the election is ever bro't into the house of representatives (which of itself is very improbable now the discriminating principle is adopted) and no President is chosen by *the 4th of March*, the Vice President is to be the Presid't, and the number out of whom a choice is to be made, is reduced to 3 instead of 5, in case the Presid't shall not have been elected by the Electors in the first instance.

The 9 federal senators from New Hampshire, Massachusetts, Connecticut, Delaware & New Jersey (1. Mr. Dayton) with Gen'l Butler of South Carolina, calling

[1] Her waiting maid; well known in the neighborhood as "Miss Hetty's little damsel."

himself republican, voted in the negative, and those in the affirmative were of Vermont, Rhode Isld, New York (1. Bailey) New Jersey (1. Condit) Pennsylvania, Maryland, Virginia, North Carolina, Georgia, Kentucky, Tennessee & Ohio, in all 22 Senators; the other New York Senator Genl Armstrong, republican, & the South Carolina Senator Genl Sumpter, a genuine republican being absent.

I beg leave to congratulate you on this occasion as I have no doubt you will consider it as of the highest importance. Federalism may now hang its head and weep over the misfortunes which it has bro't upon itself, for had the party not opposed the will of the people, when the election was bro't into the House of representatives in 1800, it is probable this amendment would not have been now bro't forward. The subject will be introduced into our branch on Monday or Tuesday at furthest & there cannot be a doubt of its obtaining the proper majority. In the course of the debate in the Senate, which I attended the whole evening to its close, many severe things were said on both sides. A *friend* of yours from Massachusetts, in the course of his arguments against the amendment took occasion to quote poetry; he said people differed in their religious as well as political opinions & then alluding to the President, in a manner not to be mistaken, he added the following memorable words from the Poet.

> " Some think on Calvin, Heaven's own spirit fell;
> While others think he was the instrument of Hell."

I do not know that I quote him right, & the Gentleman, himself, said he was not sure that he did, but you know the lines in Pope & can easily correct the mistake. This is between ourselves & you will see the propriety of keeping my name out of sight, but you may relate the fact, for it was said in full Senate. The debates however were all taken down & you will, I dare say, see it in the gentlemans speech. I am happy, also to inform you that we have peace with Morocco. The Secret'y of the Navy has assured me that everything is settled to our entire satisfaction. The old treaty is revived, no tribute to be paid and the Gov[r] of Tangiers mulct. $40,000 for having issued the orders to capture our vessels without being authorized, as is alleged. Previous to this settlement which took place on the 10th Oct'r our little fleet was drawn up before Tangiers, which they threatened to bombard and destroy & no doubt the Emperor was frightened into peace. After the proper acknowledgments on his part, and after every point had been arranged, Com[r] Preble & Mr. Lear came forward & presented the Emperor, his captured ship & crew, & even added a Tripolitan prize, of no use to us, upon the condition that she should not be restored to Tripoli until an adjustment of our differences with that power, and then it was that the Emperor said the Americans were his good friends and *the President of the United States, the best Christian he had ever known.*—As hostilities have now ceased with Morocco, the bill authorizing reprisals on their vessels goods & effects, which was on its passage through the House will be stopped. It is expected that we shall soon have peace with the Bey of Tripoli, as the Emperor of M. promises his influence, the Bey having married his niece, but we depend more on our Squadron which has gone directly up to Tripoli, and where the ships will soon be bro't into actual employment, if the Bey still proves obstinately bent on continuing the war.

All quiet at N. O. on the 5th Nov. We shall have later news tomorrow & you may rest assured no opposition will be offered. I would not say so if it was not the unanimous opinion of every republican in this city.—Excuse this hasty letter, and permit me to add, I am very sincerely Your friend,

Rev[d] W[m] Bentley, JACOB CROWNINSHIELD.
Salem, Mass.

NEWMARCH.—The following inscription was recently copied from the headstone standing over the grave of Rev. John Newmarch in Kittery, Maine, who was one of the earliest settled ministers in York County:

" Rev. John Newmarch the first pastor of the first Congregational church in Kittery, died January 15, 1754, aged 81 years.

He graduated at Harvard, 1690, commenced his ministry in Kittery as early as April, 1695, was ordained pastor of the church Nov. 4, 1714, and continued until 1751." N. J. HERRICK.

Alfred, Me.

NOTES AND QUERIES.

Toppan Lane, Newburyport, Mass.—Toppan Lane, or street, as it is now called, well deserves the name, as during most of the time since its first settlement, it has been occupied by the Toppan family. The old spelling of the name was Topham. A large part of the names of the original settlers have been much changed in their descendants. As an illustration, the name of *Kimball* is a corruption of the English *Kemble;* Cilley has been improved from Silly.

The first of the Newbury Toppans, Abraham, sailed from Yarmouth, Eng., with his wife and two children, May 10, 1637, and in the same year was *licensed* to live in Newbury, for at that time new comers were closely scrutinized. They had seven children, of whom the fourth, Jacob, married Hannah Sewall, a sister of Chief Justice Sewall, Aug. 2d, 1670, and built and occupied the same year, according to Rev. Benjamin Hale, D.D., one of his descendants, the old Toppan house. The land was conveyed to him by his father, who received it from Mr. Sewall, by a deed still preserved in the old house. It will thus be seen that this house is more than two hundred years old, and, if not the oldest, is certainly one of the oldest houses in what is now Newburyport. It has always been in the hands of Jacob Toppan's descendants, and is now occupied by Mrs. Moses Toppan. For more than a hundred years it was the only house in Toppan Lane, when, in 1785, Stephen Toppan, a great grandson of Jacob, built the house now No. 6, occupied for so many years by his two daughters, and in which one of them, Mrs. Green, recently died in the same house where she was born eighty-two years before.

The third house was built in 1787, on the corner of Toppan and High streets, by Jonathan Harris, who married Anna Toppan, a great-granddaughter of Jacob. She died in 1860, wanting only three months of a hundred years of age, and there her daughter, who married Daniel T. Colman, still resides. Mr. and Mrs. Colman celebrated their golden wedding three years ago, and with one exception are the only couple surviving, who lived on High street at the time of their marriage.

The fourth house was erected in 1820, by Edward Toppan, another descendant of Jacob Toppan, and there his widow now resides. These were the only houses on the street till a dozen years ago, and up to that time none but a descendant of Jacob Toppan had ever lived on the street. Since then four houses have been erected, three of them by families strangers to the Toppan blood.

The descendants of Jacob Toppan of Toppan Lane are very numerous and respectable, embracing the Hales and Littles of Belleville, the Atkinsons, Coffins, Doles, and other well known families. In 1846, an interesting gathering of these descendants, to the number of a hundred and fifty, was held in the old Toppan house, of which Joshua Coffin, himself one, published an account.

We have spoken only of the descendants of Jacob Toppan, the fourth child of Abraham. The descendants of the other children are very numerous, especially of Peter, the oldest, who came with his father from England. We will not attempt a list of the honorable names, tracing their ancestry back to their parent stock, but there is certainly no richer blood in New-England, which statement will not be doubted when it is known that Nathaniel Thayer, of Boston, is a direct descendant of Abraham Toppan through his son Peter.

Though the town of Newbury was the cradle of the Toppans, the name has existed there for nearly a century in only one family, and that is now reduced to two members.

W. C. Todd.

Genealogy.—Mrs. de Salis née Bainbridge, who continues her professional labors as Genealogist and Herald at her Literary Agency, Gower Street, Euston Square, under her maiden name, has discovered the birth place of John Eliot the Indian Apostle, his mother's baptism and his grandfather's decease. He comes of the old Essex family of Eliots, who originally settled there at a very early period from Devonshire. Mrs. de Salis expects to have the pedigree quite perfect after October.

She has many notes relating to Fitch (a genealogy of which she is preparing for the English Fitches), Grappenried, Perkins, Page, Bolton, Seymour, Warren, Waters, and Webster.

William Tyler.

Auburndale, Mass.

LONGEVITY.—The names and ages of the family of Col. James Davis, of Oyster River,—formerly a parish of Dover, now Durham, N. H.,—are given by Jeremy Belknap, in his "History of New Hampshire." He says of this family that it was "remarkable for longevity as well as superior stature." Col. Davis served in the French and Indian wars, being a Lieutenant in King William's war, beginning in 1688, a Captain in Queen Anne's war in 1704, and afterward Colonel. He was also, for many years, a prominent and useful member of the General Assembly of New-Hampshire.[1]

The names and ages are as follows:—

The father died in 1749, aged		88
His children	James,	93
	Thomas,	88
	Samuel, 1788,	99
	Daniel,	65
	Sarah,	91
	Hannah,	77
	Elizabeth,	79
	Ephraim, 1791,	87
	Phebe æt. 85, and the widow of Samuel æt. 102, are yet living.	
This table was printed in 1792. Including Phebe's age as then given,		85
And the total would be,		852 years,

an average of 85 1-5 years each. The average age of the six oldest children is 91 years. It will be difficult to find, in the families of to-day, instances of such longevity, as the above, and that of the Clarks, as given in the "Notes and Queries" of the July number. E. H. Goss.

Melrose, Mass.

LOTHROP.—The following will answer one of the questions concerning this name, in the July "Notes and Queries." On a stone-slab imbedded in the side-walk of the main street in South Deerfield, Mass., near where Bloody Brook crosses, is this inscription, which I have often seen: "Grave of Captain Lathrop and men slain by the Indians." A few rods to the north stands the monument erected to their memory, at the laying of the corner-stone of which, in 1835, Edward Everett delivered one of his most pleasing and eloquent orations, commemorative of the event which took place Sept. 18, 1675, "that most fatal Day, the Saddest that ever befel New-England," says Hubbard. E. H. Goss.

Melrose, July, 1872.

[1] Among the documents printed in the "Provincial Papers," relating to the Province of New-Hampshire, is one by Col. Davis as follows:—

"A claim of the several persons under named for their snow-shoes and mogasans which were imprest for her Maj'tys service by Capt. James Davis, by order of Collo. Hilton. (Then follows a list of eighteen names.) Tweve pare of snow-shoes and mogasins was Improved under Coll. Hilton to the asteward to Picwacket and Marigewock, and non of them Returned. The Reast of them Improved in the winter scout above the heds of the province under Capt. James Davis."

Indorsed — "Capt. Davis acctt of snow-shoes. Dec. 6, 1709." Allowed nine pounds pr the Committee & Assembly.

This claim grew out of an "Act for the better enabling the Inhabitants to pursue the Enemy in the Winter season," passed Aug. 23, 1704, whereby "every Householder within the several Towns of this Province" was to provide, under penalty, "one good pair of snow-shoes and mogasheens," "and if at any time the said shoes shall be improved in proceeding after the enemy, and wore out, or damaged such shoes and mogasheens shall be repaired and made good at the province charge, and to be delivered to the owners, who is hereby injoyned to keep them continually in good repaire during the present Warr with the French & Indian enemy."

We find also that, in 1722, the Province of N. Hamp^{r}. was indebted to Col. Davis "For service done in surveying The road to Winnipishoky, 5 days, £2. 10. 0;" and a few months afterwards "for taking the whole care and management of the affairs in Cutting ye way to Winnipishoky pond, 8 days at 10s. £4." EDITOR.

The "Stars and Stripes,"—the First Display on Board Ship.—Mrs. Harriet Prescott Spofford, in her *New-England Legends*, published by J. R. Osgood & Co., 1871, under the heading *Newburyport*, p. 26, says: "Here was built the first ship that ever displayed our flag upon the Thames, a broom at her peak that day, after Van Tromp's fashion, to tell the story of how she had swept the seas." That honor has been claimed for the Comte de Grasse, Nicholas Johnson master, a Newburyport ship, but it is clearly proved by the Custom House records, English newspapers, parliamentary speeches, and other evidence (See *Hist. of Origin and Progress of the Flag of the U. S.*), that the ship Bedford, of Nantucket, Wm. Mooers master, entered at the Custom House, Feb. 3, 1783, and was beyond doubt the first American vessel to wear our stars and stripes on the Thames. Van Tromp carried his broom at the masthead, not at the peak. Mrs. Spofford also says (p. 40), under the heading Portsmouth, that the America 74, built at Portsmouth, and presented to the French King, was captured by the English "who admired her structure and ornament so much, that they added to her carvings the crest of the Prince of Wales, and considered her peerless in their fine navy," and that during the last war with England she did service against her builders and is still afloat, a fifty gun ship of the Queen's, "an honor," says Mr. Brewster in his Rambles, "to Piscataqua shipwrights and to our coast oak."

The fact is (see Register, vol. xxii. 1868, pp. 397, 398) the America, 74, launched at Portsmouth, 1782, was constructed of unseasoned wood, and twelve years after her launch, in Lord Howe's action of the 1st of June, 1794, another ship of the same name and of different dimensions, her successor in the French navy, was captured by the English, and placed upon their navy list as the Impetueux.

The Frigate *America*, 50, now on the royal navy list, as a hulk, is an entirely different vessel. Geo. Henry Preble.

Ward, Hawley, Nichols, Hill.—Ebenezer Hawley, son of Joseph of Stratford, m. 1678, Esther, *widow* and only heir of William Ward, and d. 1681. His widow m. 3d, 1682, Ephraim, son of Isaac Nichols, of Stratford. Ephraim Nichols d. about 1690, and his widow Esther m. 4th, Eliphalet Hill.

The above is according to Savage.

According to the Fairfield records, Eliphalet Hill m. November, 1691, "Esther Nichols, who was the *daughter* of William Ward."

Again, "Ephraim Nichols, of Stratford, married with Esther Hawley, of Fairfield, on ye 7th day of October, 1682."

At Fairfield is also recorded, under date of April 19, 1678, a marriage covenant between Ebenezer Hawley, son of Joseph, of Stratford, and "Hester Ward, daughter unto Mrs. Deborah Ward Tappin, of South Hampton." It begins: "Whereas there is a marriage intended," and refers to "the house and all the lands that the said Hester is now possessed of within the county of Fairfield."

It appears from this that William Ward's widow was Deborah instead of Esther, and that she married, before 1678, a Tappin of South Hampton, L. I. Savage places a Jonathan Tappin there in 1673. William Ward's inventory bears date, March 4, 1675-6. It is also evident that Esther or Hester Ward, who m. Hawley, Nichols, and Hill, was the daughter of William and Deborah Ward.

John D. Champlin, Jr.

New-York, Sept. 1872.

Life of Admiral Richard Deane.—The Rev. J. Bathurst Deane, M.A., F.S.A., of Bath, England, the author of the above work noticed in the Register, vol. xxv. p. 299, has prepared two tabular pedigrees to be inserted opposite pages 690 and 691 of his book. One table gives the descendants of Joseph Deane, brother of the Admiral, and the other, the descendants of his sister Jane, who married 1st, Dru Sparrow, secretary to Admirals Blake and Deane, and 2d, Stephen Monteage, a London merchant. "They are remarkable as showing how many of the great Whig families of England and Ireland share the blood of the General-at-Sea, who, up to this time, has been chiefly known as 'The Regicide,' and the companion of Blake." A grandson of Joseph, his brother, was Joseph Deane, Privy Councillor, Baron of the Exchequer, Lord Chief Justice, who died 1715 and was buried in the Earl of Cork's vault, St. Patrick's Cathedral, Dublin. The two pedigrees show alliances with the families of the Duke of Devonshire, the Marquises of Exeter and Townsend and the Earls of Cork, Mayo, Spencer, Carlisle, Granville, Westmoreland, Lucan and Bessborough. J. W. D.

CLARK—KILBY.—Since the publication of the memoir of Christopher Kilby (*ante*, p. 43), some interesting facts relative to his father-in-law, Clark, have come to my knowledge: The Hon. William Clark (never written by him or his sons with a final *e*) lived in the largest, most elaborately finished, and furnished, house, in Boston. It was a brick structure, standing on Clark's Square, so called, next to the mansion house afterwards occupied by Gov. Hutchinson, at the North End. It was subsequently owned and occupied by Sir Henry Frankland, and is celebrated in one of Cooper's Novels. Mr. Rowland Ellis, of Boston, who lived in it many years, has a fine exterior view of this famous house, and, also, several elaborate paintings taken from its walls; he also has the centre part of a wooden mosaic floor of the house, having the arms of Clark wrought therein. Mr. Peter Wainwright, of this city, has, among his collection of family portraits, one of Hon. William Clark, full size, painted in 1732. The following facts respecting Mr. Clark's family, are gleaned mostly from public records.

William[3] Clark died in 1742 (*ante*, p. 43), leaving widow Sarah, whose maiden name is wanted. Their ch. were: I. Sarah,[4] m. Christopher Kilby, had three ch. and died (*ante*, p. 46); II. Robert,[4] appears never to have married; III. Benjamin,[4] m. Miriam, daughter of Christopher and Sarah Kilby. Miriam was probably cousin to her brother-in-law, Christopher Kilby; IV. Rebecca,[4] m. Samuel Winslow; V. Martha,[4] m. Dea. Thomas Greenough. Benjamin[4] Clark d. 1747, having had ch.: I. Benjamin[5] (H. C. 1750); II. Christopher[5]; III. Miriam,[5] m. Jonathan Mason, and had son Jonathan, who was U. S. Senator from Mass.; IV. Sarah,[5] m. ——— Barkers?; V. Mary,[5] m. John Cutler and had a numerous progeny. Benjamin[5] and Christopher[5] lived to old age, and never married, the family name dying out with them.

Christopher Kilby's only surviving daughter Sarah (*ante*, pp. 46, 47) died in Ayrshire, Scotland, July 15, 1779. Her second dau., Susanna Cunningham, married, for her second husband, John Henry Mills, of Scotland, and had son John and dau. Mary, who came to Boston, where Mary m. Col. Abraham Moore (H. C. 1806) and had Susanna Varnum; and Mary Frances, who m. the Hon. John Cochran Park (H. C. 1824). C. W. T.

VIRGINIA.—STATE STAMP ACTS.—In the act imposing taxes for the support of government which was passed by the Legislature of Virginia on the 20th of February, 1813, it was enacted, that from and after the first day of May next, there shall be levied and collected for every piece of vellum, parchment or paper, upon which shall be written or printed, any note or bill made payable at or negotiable, or which may be paid or negotiated at, either of the public Banks of Virginia or at the branches thereof, the following rates, to wit: for each note or bill above $20.00 and not exceeding $100.00, 10 cents; above $100.00 and not exceeding $500.00, 25 cents; and so on up, including stamps of .50, .75, $1.00, $1.25, and for $5,000.00, 1.50 cents: and for every $1,000.00 above 5,000.00, 25 cents additional. Provided that if any such note or bill shall be payable at or within sixty days the same shall be subject only to the following rates: above $20 and not exceeding $100, 4 cents; not exceeding $500, 10 cents; not exceeding $1,000, 20 cents; and for every $1,000 above $1,000, 25 cents additional.

And on the 22d of February, 1813, it was enacted that to the end that the stamp duties may be duly collected, there shall be appointed by the Governor with the advice of the privy council, a stamp master whose duty it shall be to provide and distribute paper, parchment and vellum properly stamped, to the cashiers of banks or to any person or persons who may apply for them and to attend to the collection of the stamp duties. He was required to give security in the amount of $25,000.00, and to receive for his services 5 per centum on the whole amount collected.

In the act imposing taxes, passed February 10th, 1814, the value of stamps to be used was reduced, and all notes or bills without regard to length of time they had to run were to be stamped as follows: $100.00, 4 cents; $200.00, 6 cents: $500.00, 12 cents; $1000.00, 25 cents; $1,500.00, 37 cents; $2,000.00, 50 cents; $3,000.00, 75 cents; $4,000.00, $1.00; $5,000.00, $1.25; $7,000.00, $1.75; $8,000.00, $2.00; and for every $20,000.00 above $8,000.00, 25 cents additional.

In the act imposing taxes, December 21st, 1814, the act of February the 10th was re-enacted *verbatim*, except in the last item which read, and for every *one thousand dollars* above $8,000.00, 25 cents additional, which would seem to imply that there had been an error committed either by the engrossing clerk or the printer in publishing the laws of the previous session.

On the 7th of January, 1815, all acts relating to stamps were omitted in the tax bill then adopted, and they were repealed by implication, and on the 15th of January,

1817, the Legislature passed an act for refunding the money paid for stamps, and required the auditor of public accounts to redeem all stamps which had been purchased from the stamp master, provided the same were presented for redemption on or before the 1st day of May, 1817. See acts of the Assembly of Virginia, 1812, pp. 6, 11; do. 1813, p. 6; do. 1815, p. 8; do. 1817, pp. 29, 30. T. H. WYNNE.

Richmond, Va.

SMYTH (*ante*, p. 190). In the account of "the family of Ralph Smyth, of Hingham, Mass.," in the REGISTER for April last, I stated, "There can be but little doubt that Thomas, of Eastham, who in 1690, June 24, took at Barnstable 'ye oath of a freeman,' was also a son of Ralph; but having made very careful examination, and finding no documentary proof of the same, we omit a record of his family."

The following, a copy from the original document, which will explain itself, and which has come into my possession within a very few days, settles the question beyond a doubt. THOMAS SMYTH.

Boston, September, 1872.

Whereas, Thomas Smith, has made complaint that the bounds of his lands lying on the southeasterly side of the Town Cove, upon "Pocha," that was formerly his father's, Ralph Smith, are gone to decay, and some of them lost, we whose names are hereunto subscribed, being appointed by the Town, to settle the bounds of lands that may be in controversy, having viewed sd lands, do settle the bounds thereof as follows, viz: Beginning at the N. E. corner, at a rock near the bank, marked T. S., from there ranging about 40 poles southerly, up into the woods, to another rock marked T. S., from there ranging about 48 poles westerly, to a stone set in the ground, marked T. S., from there ranging to the bank by the Cove side, to a pine tree, marked, and so along by the bank easterly, to the first bound mark."

March 22d, 1694. JONATHAN SPARROW,
SAMUEL FREEMAN,
THOMAS PAINE, JR.

The above is a true copy from the ancient records of the Town of Eastham, now in the office of the Town Clerk of Orleans, Book No. 13, page 199.

Orleans, Sept. 9, 1872. Attest: FREEMAN MAYO, Town Clerk of Orleans.

PENACOOK IN 1741.—"April 24, we hear from Penny-Cook that there lately came in there several Indians from toward Canada, who were in a pining condition and almost starved begging for sustinence, which was readily granted them, and for which they were exceedingly thankful. They give a sad account of the deplorible circumstances of the Indians the winter past by reason of the excessive cold and vast snows (in some places near 20 feet high) which has prevented their hunting, so that great numbers of them perished from extreame hunger and cold. And that by last accounts they had from Canada the French are in a distressed condition for want of provisions and by a sickness that has prov'd very mortal among them."—*Boston Gazette*, 1741.

CALEF.—The undersigned has nearly ready for publication, a Genealogy of the Calef Family, embracing all of the name in the United States and British Provinces. He desires information of James Calef (b. in Boston, Nov. 7, 1714, son of Robert, the author) of Bath Town[1], in Bath County, in the Province of North Carolina, merchant. July 18, 1752, he appoints John Scollay, of Boston, brazier, his attorney, to sell land and houses in Boston, formerly his father Robert Calef's. Did he leave descendants?

Who were the parents of John Calef, styled Captain and Esquire, honorary member of the Mass. Humane Society, 1789, and one of its Benefactors, then living at St. Christopher, West Indies? Did he leave descendants?

Robert Calef commanded, 1768, 1769, 1770, the London Packet, which sailed between Boston and London. Was he the Capt. Robert Calef who died in Weston, Mass., Jan. 1814, æ. 83? Was he born in Nantucket? Can any further information be given of him? MATTHEW A. STICKNEY.

No. 119 *Boston Street, Salem, Mass.*

* [Bath is situated on the Tar River in the present Beaufort county, and was formerly a place of some importance. It is now nearly deserted, the business and many of the inhabitants having long ago removed to Washington on the same river.—F. K.]

AN ENGLISH FRIGATE THREE DAYS IN BOSTON, AUG. 1785.—The following notes of a correspondence between Capt. Edwin Stanhope, R. N., Commanding H. B. M. S. Mercury, and Governor Bowdoin, of Massachusetts, relating to alleged insults offered to the former by the inhabitants of Boston, in 1785, I found in the 2d volume of Schomberg's *Naval Chronology*.[1] Never having seen any account of the occurrences elsewhere, I place the matter at your disposal, for the Notes department of the REGISTER. GEO. HENRY PREBLE.

Charlestown, Mass.

[From Schomberg's Naval Chronology.]

In August, 1785, the Mercury frigate, commanded by Captain Edwin Stanhope, was sent to Boston in North America, by Commodore Sawyer, to convoy some small vessels which were to take on board live stock, hay, &c., for Shelbourne and some other of the new settlements. Upon Captain Stanhope's arrival, he waited on the governor, as a matter of ceremony, but on his return to his boat he was insulted by a mob, which had collected for the purpose, and himself and people extremely ill treated: this, with various other insults which he experienced at Boston, induced Captain Stanhope to write a complaint, and remonstrate with the governor on the impropriety of these proceedings. The following are the letters which passed on this occasion.

"Mercury, Boston Harbour, August 1, 1785.

"SIR,

"I am sorry to be obliged to represent to your excellency, the continued insults and disgraceful indignities offered by hundreds in this town to me and my officers, which hitherto we have taken no notice of, nor of the illiberal and indecent language with which the newspapers have been filled; nor should I have troubled you now, had I not been pursued, and my life as well as that of one of my officers, been endangered by the violent rage of a mob yesterday evening, without provocation of any sort.

"I trust it is needless to recommend to your excellency, to adopt such measures as may discover the ring-leaders, and bring them to public justice, as well as to protect us from further insult.

"I have the honour to be
"Your excellency's most obedient
"humble servant,
"E. H. STANHOPE.

"To His Excellency
"Governor Bowdoin."

"*Commonwealth of Massachusetts.*

"Boston, Aug. 1, 1785.

"Sir,

"Your letter of this date is now before me. It is a great misfortune that the subjects or citizens of different countries, which have been at enmity, cannot easily recover that degree of good humour which would induce them to treat each other with proper decorum, when the governments to which they respectively belong have entered into a treaty of amity, and sheathed the sword. But you must have observed, that disturbances arising from this source, too frequently happen, especially in populous seaport towns.

If you have been insulted, and your life has been endangered, in the manner as you have represented to me, I must inform you, that our laws afford you ample satisfaction. Foreigners are entitled to the protection of the laws as well as amenable to it, equally with any citizen of the United States, while they continue within the jurisdiction of this Commonwealth. Any learned practitioner in the law, if applied to, will direct you to the mode of legal process in the obtaining a redress of injury, if you have been injured; and the judiciary court will cause due inquiry to be made touching riotous and unlawful assemblies and their misdemeanors, and inflict legal punishment on such as by verdict of a jury may be found guilty.

"I have the honour to be, &c.

"To Captain Stanhope."

[1] *Naval Chronology, or an Historical Summary of Naval and Maritime Events, from the times of the Romans to the treaty of Peace,* 1802. *With an Appendix.* In five volumes. By ISAAC SCHOMBERG, Esq., Captain in the Royal Navy. London: Printed for S. Egerton, at the Military, Whitehall; Bickerstaff, 210 Strand; and Richardson, Royal Exchange, by C. Roworth, Hudson Court, Strand. 1802.

"Mercury, Boston Harbour, Aug. 1785.

"SIR,

"When I had the honour of applying to your Excellency to discountenance the disgraceful attacks made upon me and the officers of his Britannic Majesty's ship Mercury, under my command, and to afford us your protection, it was on your positive assurance to that effect, in their presence, I rested my hope. How much your conduct contradicts both that and my expectations is too obvious either to satisfy me, or even to do credit to yourself; for your Excellency must excuse me, when I remark that I never received a letter so insulting to my senses, as your answer to my requisition of yesterday.

"I am however happy in finding a much better disposition in the first class of inhabitants, whose assistance I am glad to acknowledge is more acceptable, after your apparent evasion from the substance of my letter; and however well informed your Excellency may believe yourself upon the laws and customs of nations, in similar cases, allow me to assure you, there is not one, no not even "the Ally of the states," that would not most severely reprobate, either the want of energy in government, or of disinclination of the governor, to correct such notorious insults to public characters, in which light only we can desire to be received.

"I have the honour to be, &c.

"To his Excellency, Governor Bowdoin."

"CAPTAIN STANHOPE.

"Your letter's being dated the 2d instant, was delivered to me by your lieutenant Mr. Nash, at four o'clock this morning.

"I hereby let you know, that as the letter is conceived in terms of insolence and abuse, altogether unprovoked, I shall take such measures concerning it, as the dignity of my station, and a just regard to the honor of this commonwealth, connected with the honour of the United States in general shall require.

"Boston, Aug. 3, 1785, six o'clock P.M."

"Mercury, Nantasket Road, Aug. 4th, 1785, half past 12, A.M.

"SIR,

"I am to acknowledge the honour of your Excellency's letter, this moment received, and have to assure you, I shall most cheerfully submit to the worst consequences that can arrive from our correspondence, which I do not conceive on my part to have been couched in terms of either "insolence or abuse," which is more than I could venture to say of yours; and however exalted your Excellency's station is, I know not of any more respectable than that I have the honor to fill.

"I have the honour to be, &c."

"To his Excellency, Governor Bowdoin."

TUCKER—MAGILL, *Errata and Additions* (REGISTER, Jan. No. p. 30, Art. "Early History of Printing in Virginia").

DEAR SIR:—On page 33, of the above entitled article, Dr. Magill's name should be Alfred T.

Although in my first letter, furnishing the material from which, in part, you compiled your notes, I omitted one of Judge Henry St. George Tucker's sons, I think I supplied the omission in a subsequent letter, written probably in the month of May. His name, Dr. Alfred Magill Tucker, with the particulars given, should have come in on the same page (33), after the paragraph relating to St. George who married a daughter of the late Gov. Gilmer.

Page 34. The name of Dr. Emmet was John P.

Page 35. In the paragraph relating to Drury Bolling, you have mistaken Judge Nathaniel Beverley Tucker, one of the sons of Judge St. George Tucker, and who married Lucy Ann Smith, for my brother-in-law of the same name, who was a son of Judge *Henry* St. George Tucker.

The additional material relating to the Tuckers, alluded to in my last letter, I condense as follows:

Three brothers, Daniel, Henry and George Tucker, of English stock, settled in Bermuda. Daniel was the first governor of the island, in 1616. From him descended *John*, of Devonshire, in Bermuda, Chief Justice, who married a daughter of Henry, above named; and from them descended:—

1. *Daniel*, who was the immediate ancestor of Professor George Tucker, of the University of Virginia;

2. *Elizabeth*, who married John Tucker (son of Henry, who was the son of John, above named), and he was the immediate ancestor of Henry Tucker, of Henderson, Kentucky, who married Mary Friend, of Charlotte County, Virginia;

3. *Henry*, who married Frances Tucker (daughter of Henry, third in descent from George, above named), lived at Somerset Bridge, and was the father of John, who was the father of Mary Byrd Tucker, who married Professor John P. Emmet, of the University of Virginia, who was the father of Dr. Thomas Addis Emmet, of New-York city (who married Catherine R. Duncan, of Montgomery, Alabama), and of Jane L. Emmet (who married John N. A. Griswold, of Rhode Island).

From George descended:—

George, who settled in Port Royal, Bermuda; from him:—

George, baptized May 25, 1651; from him:—

Henry, who married Anne Butterfield, and was the father of:—

1. *Henry*, Lieutenant and Acting Governor of Bermuda, who died in the year 1808, and was the father of the late Hon. Henry St. George Tucker, of London, head of the East India Company; also, of Thomas Tudor, a captain in the Royal Navy, and of five others, all officers in the British Army;
2. *Frances*, who married Henry Tucker, son of John, as above stated;
3. *Thomas Tudor*, some time Treasurer of the United States;
4. *Elizabeth;*
5. *Nathaniel*, of Hull, in England, author of "The Bermudian;"
6. *St. George*, of whom a sufficiently full account is given in the article above referred to.

Appreciating your services in rescuing from oblivion many a name justly entitled to honor, I am, dear Sir,

Very respectfully,

Your obedient servant,

THOMAS H. ELLIS.

ALBERT H. HOYT, ESQ., Editor, &c.
No. 18 Somerset Street, Boston, Mass.

HINMAN'S FIRST PURITAN SETTLERS OF CONNECTICUT.—The first edition of this work, which was issued in numbers about a quarter of a century ago, has for a long time been very scarce, and has been much sought for, since it contains the whole letters of the alphabet, while the second edition only reaches the letter C. Last Spring Joel Munsell, of Albany, completed about 20 copies of the work by reprinting two numbers. He has added to it a thorough index, making 51 pages and containing every name in the book. We presume most of the copies have been sold before this time. Mr. Munsell's price is ten dollars a copy, which will only return the cash outlay for printing and binding, giving no pay for making the index. J. W. D.

NEW-ENGLAND HISTORIC, GENEALOGICAL SOCIETY.

NECROLOGY.

Prepared by Rev. DORUS CLARKE, D.D., Historiographer.

ELI FRENCH, a corresponding member, was born at Dummerston, Vt., Sept. 8, 1800, and died at Dover, N. H., July 21, 1868, in his 68th year. He was a son of Samuel and Sally (Gates) French, of Dummerston. He was prepared for college by Rev. Hosea Beckley, author of a History of Vermont. He entered Dartmouth College in 1824, but left at the beginning of his Junior year, and taught school in Dover, N. H., until 1828, in which year he received his degree upon examination. Afterward he was engaged in the bookselling business in Dover until February, 1832, when he removed to Philadelphia, Pa., where he carried on that business until September, 1833. He was subsequently engaged in bookselling in New-York city until his decease.

He married May 26, 1835, Miss Hannah Rogers Draper, of Dover. They had five children, four of whom survived him, namely three sons, William Rogers, Samuel Gates, and George Rogers, of New-York city, and one daughter, Hannah Draper, wife of Dr. James H. Wheeler, of Dover.

He was admitted a member of this Society August 4, 1857.

Samuel Holden Parsons, Esq., of Middletown, Ct. Samuel Holden Parsons, Esq., a life member, was born at Middletown, Ct., August 11, 1800, and died in that city February 23, 1871, aged 70. He was a descendant in the 6th generation from Benjamin[1] Parsons, an early settler of Springfield, Mass., his descent being through Ebenezer,[2] Jonathan,[3] Gen. Samuel Holden,[4] and Enoch.[5] His father, Enoch Parsons, of Middletown, was president of the Connecticut branch of the Bank of the United States, located first at Middletown, and afterward at Hartford. His mother was Mary Wyman Sullivan, of Philadelphia, daughter of John Sullivan, of London, England. (See Register, vol. i. pp. 159 and 273.)

He graduated at Yale College in 1819, studied law, and having in April, 1822, been admitted to the bar, commenced practice in his native town. In 1824, having been appointed attorney to the Hartford Branch of the United States Bank, and U. S. pension agent for Connecticut, he removed to Hartford and resided there until the expiration of the charter of the parent bank and the winding up of its affairs in 1847. For the remainder of his life, his home was at Middletown. In 1851, he was made the first president of the Farmers' and Mechanics' Savings Bank, and held that office for many years.

He made large collections for a genealogy of the Parsons family, and some of his materials were published in the Historical and Genealogical Register for July, 1847. After his retirement from active life, he devoted much time to the study of New-England history, in some branches of which he was remarkably well informed.

He died of congestion of the lungs after an illness of only two or three days. He was unmarried, and the large property left by him fell by inheritance to his half-brother, Henry E. Parsons, Esq., of Ashtabula, O., the only surviving child of his father.

He was elected a corresponding member in 1845, and became a life member August 29, 1865.

Gen. Guy Mannering Fessenden. Gen. Guy M. Fessenden, of Warren, R. I., a corresponding member of this society, was born in Warren, March 30, 1804, and died there Nov. 1, 1871, aged 67. He was a son of John and Abigail Miller (Child) Fessenden, and a descendant in the 5th generation from Nicholas Fessenden, of Cambridge. On his mother's side he was descended from Gov. William Bradford, of Plymouth Colony, his maternal grandmother being Priscilla Bradford, a descendant in the 6th generation from the governor.

He was educated chiefly by his father, who was a graduate of Brown University in the class of 1798, and afterward a successful teacher, at one time being the principal of Warren Academy. At the age of fifteen he went to sea, but after four years' trial was obliged to give up the sailor's life on account of his health.

In 1821, he sailed with his uncle, Capt. S. P. Child, for Java, where he was prostrated with a disease incidental to the climate, from the effects of which he never entirely recovered. During the voyage to Amsterdam, he became so feeble, that it was considered inadvisable for him to continue the voyage. He remained in Amsterdam, attending school and acquiring the Dutch language, until 1822, when he returned to Warren and remained an invalid in his uncle's family for six months. Finally, a tour among the Green Mountains partially restored his health, and he made Brattleboro', Vermont, his residence for a few years, where he became a member of the Congregational church. In 1830 he returned to Warren and engaged in business with Capt. S. P. Child, in which he continued until his death.

The chief business in which his uncle and himself were engaged was the whale fishery.

In 1849, he married the youngest daughter of the late Capt. Samuel Barton, of Warren.

He was admitted a member of this society Oct. 24, 1846. He was also a member of the R. I. Historical Society, to which he contributed valuable papers on the Northmen Theory, Indian History, Roger Williams, and other subjects. During the Dorr rebellion he was in command of the Warren militia. At the time of his death he was president of the Philanthropic Society of Warren, a director of the Warren Bank, and one of the School Committee. His benevolence was ever active in aid of objects either religious or secular, and the liberality of his religious views led him to attend the Baptist and afterward the Episcopal churches.

He was at one time town treasurer of Warren, and held at different times other town offices. He was commissioned by the Rhode Island Legislature a brigadier general.

In 1840, he published in the Warren newspaper a series of five articles, entitled

"Travels in the West." In 1845, he published a "*History of Warren, R. I.;*" and in 1850, in the REGISTER, a "*Genealogy of the Bradford Family,*" which was reprinted as a separate work.

Gen. Fessenden's last years were spent amid the refinements of his retired home, where his books were his constant companions.

HENRY THEODORE TUCKERMAN, A.M. Henry T. Tuckerman was born in Boston, Mass., April 20, 1813, and died in the city of New-York, December 17, 1871, at the age of 58 years. He was a son of Henry H. Tuckerman, a merchant of this city. On his father's side, he was of English origin; on his mother's, he was of Irish descent. The Rev. Joseph Tuckerman, of the "Ministry at Large," in this city, was his uncle. He was educated at the best schools in Boston, entered Harvard College, and would have graduated, had not ill health driven him to a milder climate. Though he did not graduate, Harvard conferred on him the degree of Master of Arts in 1850. In early life he made two visits to Italy, and resided there long enough to form and develope a decided taste for literature and art. He was there during that receptive and impressible period of life, which generally gives character to all the subsequent career. On his return to this country, he devoted some seven years to mental cultivation in Boston, when incipient pulmonary difficulties induced him to remove to New-York, which afterwards was his place of residence. In 1835, his first work, entitled "*The Italian Sketch Book,*" was published; and two years afterward he published a book on Sicily. From the time he established himself in New-York, his pen seems to have been almost incessantly active till it fell from his hand in death. He published a dozen or fifteen volumes upon art, travels, literature, criticism, biography and history, one volume of poetry, and a very large number of articles in the reviews and magazines of the day. Mr. Tuckerman was never married, and this fact, together with a partial deafness, made him seclude himself somewhat from general society, though he enjoyed society, and imparted to it great piquancy and interest. He would sometimes convulse a social circle by his felicitous anecdotes and repartees. He was early affianced to literature and art, and to them, and to cognate studies, he devoted himself with the most assiduous attention. Though he was a great reader, he could not be called a profound scholar. To the dead languages and to science he made little pretension. His genius lay rather in the direction of taste and æsthetics. The beautiful, the ornate, with a spice of the sentimental, constituted the region in which he loved to roam, and from which he gathered the choicest productions. He was eminently at home in English and American literature, and in Italian letters and art. As a literary artist he very much excels the popular yet superficial Parton, and is much below the diversified learning and the brilliant analytical disquisitions of Taine. Though Mr. Tuckerman wrote upon a great variety of subjects, there is still a remarkable evenness of plane running through all his productions. He never rises above himself. If he had little genius, he had remarkable industry. Always good, yes, always excellent, but never pre-eminently excellent. He had none of the genuine wit of Sydney Smith which imparted such flavor and zest to his articles, and *therefore* he never gave occasion for the sharp retorts to which the great English satirist was so often exposed. To matters of literary criticism, in the technical sense of that term, he paid little attention, because, for them, he had little taste. He chose the broader field of letters, and was more at home in the general character and equable dignity of the *North American Review*, than in the trenchant criticisms which gave such popularity to the early career of the *Edinburgh Review*.

Mr. Tuckerman was a gentleman. He was never unmindful of the proprieties of life. He had none of that crusty, assuming, consequential spirit, which makes some men so uncomfortable and distasteful to others. He was self-forgetful, sunny, genial, popular. American scholarship has so few such ornaments, that when one of them disappears, every scholar feels that the republic of letters has not only sustained a serious injury, but that he himself, too, has met with a personal loss. Though Mr. Tuckerman has left behind him no work which will exert a controlling influence upon the opinions of this remarkable age, he will long be remembered for his indomitable industry, his extensive reading, his multifarious writings, his refined taste, and his genial spirit. He was admitted a corresponding member, January 12, 1858.

AND EMERSON, Esq., a resident member, was born in Pepperell, Mass., Feb. 3, 1823, and died in Boston, Mass., May 3, 1871, aged 68 years 3 months. He was a son of Joseph and Phebe Emerson, and a grandson of Rev. Joseph Emerson, the first pastor of the First Church in Pepperell. His education was obtained at the common schools. He first learned the trade of a cooper; but at the age of twenty engaged in mercantile business in his native town. He also held the office of postmaster there for many years. He was engaged in the manufacture of paper, and we are informed that it was at his mill and under his superintendence that the rolls for the finishing of paper, now used in every manufactory, were invented. For the last twenty years he resided in Boston, where he was a dealer in paper stock and cotton waste.

Mr. Emerson left considerable property, accumulated in his later years. His charities during his life and in his will were large. We have understood that having, at some period, failed in business, he paid in full, before his death, his former obligations, startling his old creditors who supposed their debts were hopelessly lost.

He was married May 8, 1860, by Rev. C. D. Bradlee, to Miss Kate P. Thayer, a native of Boston. He left no children. His death occurred after a painful illness of about two years, which he bore with great patience. His disease was coloid cancer of the stomach. He was buried in Forest Hills Cemetery, May 8, 1871, on the 11th anniversary of his marriage. His funeral services were performed at the house, by Rev. Dr. Webb, of the Shawmut Congregational Church, and Rev. C. D. Bradlee, of the Church of the Redeemer, and at the grave by Mr. Bradlee.

William Saxton Morton, Esq., was a son Joseph Morton and a nephew of Hon. Perez Morton, formerly Attorney General of Massachusetts. He was born in Roxbury, Mass., Sept. 22, 1809, and died in Quincy, Mass., Sept. 21, 1871, at the age of 62 years, wanting one day. He was fitted for college at the Phillips Academy, in Exeter, N. H., and graduated at Harvard University in 1831. He was warm and genial in his impulses, but had no ambition for literary distinction. Soon after his graduation he went abroad, to avail himself of the advantages of foreign travel. Upon his return, he began the study of the law in the office of Sidney Bartlett, Esq., continued his studies at Hopkinton, N. H., and commenced practice at Amherst, N. H., in the office of the Hon. Perley Dodge. Soon afterwards he removed to Quincy, Mass., and continued to reside there from 1840 to the time of his decease. While engaged in his profession, he performed the duties of a magistrate, a commissioner of insolvency and trial justice, and was connected with many local business organizations. He was a member of the Constitutional Convention in 1853, and two or three times served the town of Quincy as their representative in the general court. As a member of school committees, as presiding officer at public meetings, as a trustee of Milton Academy, and in other public trusts, he was an active and useful citizen. But his deepest public interest, perhaps, centered in the improvement of the public schools. The education of children and youth was with him a matter of paramount importance. He had a decided literary taste. His love of poetry amounted almost to a passion, so much so that he not only became well versed in the modern works of romance and fiction, but cultivated a personal acquaintance with the muses. He left behind him a large collection of fugitive pieces of poetry, which appeared in various public journals. At the commencement of the war, he earnestly espoused the side of liberty and union, and gave two sons to the cause, one of whom was a cavalry officer, who, after able service in the field, died in consequence of his exposure and sufferings. Mr. Morton had little taste for public life. It was in the domestic circle that he shone the brightest and enjoyed the most. He was admitted a resident member of this society March 24, 1855, and made himself a life member in 1871.

Mr. Morton was married Oct. 3, 1839, to Mary Jane Woodbury Grimes, of Francestown, N. H., a niece of the Hon. Levi Woodbury. They had six children, namely:—

1. *Joseph William*, born July 22, 1840, and died Dec. 17, 1865. He was taken prisoner at the battle of Gainesville, Aug. 17, 1864, was marched to Macon, thence to Augusta, thence to Andersonville, thence to Charleston, and last to Columbus, where he escaped and joined the cavalry on Sherman's "march to the sea." 2. *George Woodbury*, b. May 2, 1842, and served in the navy in the last war. 3. *Mary*, b. June 17, 1844. 4. *Arthur Austerfield*, b. Jan. 11, 1847, d. March 24, 1854. 5. *Martha Woodbury*, b. Dec. 25, 1849, d. April 26, 1870. 6. *Arthur Austerfield*, b July 22, 1855. 7. *Sarah Josephine*, b. Aug. 12, 1858.

The earliest American ancestor of Mr. Morton, was George Morton, who, with his wife, Julian, daughter of Alexander Carpenter and sister of Gov. Bradford's second wife, arrived at Plymouth in the ship Ann, Capt. William Pearce, master, in July, 1623. They were married at Leyden, July 23, 1612. They brought with them four children, viz.: Nathaniel, who was afterward secretary of the Plymouth Colony, and author of *New-England's Memorial*, and a brief *Ecclesiastical History;* John, who afterward removed to Middleboro'; Patience, who married John Faunce, and was the mother of Elder Faunce; and Ephraim, who was born on the passage. The descent of Mr. Morton, kindly furnished by the family, is subjoined :—

EPHRAIM[2] MORTON, youngest son of George,[1] died Oct. 7, 1693, aged 70. He had ch. George, *Ephraim*, Nathaniel, Josiah, Eleazer, Thomas.

EPHRAIM[3] had Ephraim, John, *Joseph*, Hannah, Ebenezer.

JOSEPH,[4] b. March 25, 1683, d. Feb. 24, 1754, had *Joseph*, Ezekiel, Hannah.

JOSEPH,[5] b. Oct. 25, 1712, d. July 26, 1792, had Perez, d. young, Diman, Hon. Perez, *Joseph*, Ephraim, Abigail.

JOSEPH,[6] b. Aug. 6, 1764, d. Oct. 13, 1843, had Mary Hersey, mar. George Thompson; Joseph Ephraim, deceased; William Saxton, deceased; *William Saxton*, the subject of this sketch; Sarah Bradford, Caroline Stimson, deceased; Abigail, deceased.

REV. JAMES THURSTON was born at Newmarket, N.H., Dec. 11, 1806. His father, James Thurston, was the son of James Thurston and Mary Jones; his mother, Elizabeth Peabody, was the daughter of Thomas Peabody and Elizabeth Shaw. He fitted for college at Phillips Academy, Exeter, under Dr. Abbot; graduated at Harvard College in 1829; was employed as a teacher in the English High School, Boston, three years; graduated at the Divinity School, Cambridge, 1835. After leaving the school, he went to the West for one year. He was ordained over the Unitarian society in Windsor, Vt., in 1838. After leaving that post, he preached in several places; and at length, in 1844, took charge of the First Congregational Society in Billerica, where he continued six years. He then supplied the pulpit in South Natick two years, when, in 1853, he was installed as pastor of the Allen-street Church, in Cambridge. He resigned that charge the following year, on account of severe illness; and in 1855, entered on an engagement to supply the pulpit in Lunenburgh, where he remained till 1859. He afterward preached two years at Leicester. The state of his health having unfitted him for ministerial duties, he became agent for the Massachusetts Temperance Society. After the war, he was sent by the Memorial Society to Wilmington, North Carolina, where for some months he took charge of a school for Freedmen.

For the last eight years of his life, his home was at West Newton, where he died Jan. 13, 1872.

He was married in Charlestown, Mass., Sept. 11, 1844, to Elizabeth, daughter of Hon. William Austin.

He left five children :—1. *James Peabody*, born March 8, 1847; 2. *William Austin*, born July 9, 1848; 3. *Elizabeth Peabody*, born Jan. 10, 1850; 4. *Charles Abbot*, born June 25, 1851; and 5. *Charlotte Williams*, born Feb. 7, 1854.

His funeral ceremonies took place at the Unitarian Church on the Tuesday following his death. Eight of his college classmates walked in front of the coffin as it was taken to the church, among them Rev. Samuel F. Smith, Rev. James Freeman Clarke and Samuel May, Jr. Rev. Mr. Clarke took the lead in the services. "It may be said that the entire population of the village were sincere mourners at the grave of the departed, who had endeared himself to all by his upright life, steadfast friendship, unselfish devotion to the best good of those about him, and by his amiable disposition."

WILLIAM THOMAS, Esq. William Thomas, Esq., a life member and benefactor of the society, was born in Worcester, Mass., April 11, 1808, and died in Boston, after a long illness, June 19, 1872, aged 64 years. He was the eighth of eleven children of Isaiah and Mary (Weld) Thomas, of Worcester, and a grandson of Hon. Isaiah Thomas who is recognized as the "Father of American Printing." His boyhood was devoted to the acquisition of such an education as the schools of Worcester afforded, and he also enjoyed the privilege of attending the academy in Wakefield, N. H.; and subsequently, he was placed under the tuition of Rev. Joseph Allen, D.D., of Northboro', Mass., for whom he sustained through life the most affectionate regard.

At fourteen years of age, he entered a store in Worcester, and after four years of faithful service, during which he acquired a taste for mercantile pursuits and those habits of industry which qualified him for a wider field of action, at the age of eighteen he came to Boston, and obtained a situation in the store of those well known and successful merchants, George and Jabez C. Howe. In their employment, he strengthened his early business habits and enlarged his capacity for mercantile pursuits, which became so serviceable to him at later periods of life. He entered upon his chosen branch of mercantile business, with a determination, by constant devotion to it, to succeed. He associated at various times with different partners. These connections were dissolved by death and other causes, until at last, Mr. Thomas was left alone to conduct his own affairs, which he did with eminent ability and success. He acquired a reputation for fairness and a high sense of honor in all his business negotiations. These qualities, with unwearied industry, thorough knowledge of the principles of trade, gave him a high degree of credit, and secured to him the entire confidence of all who knew him. After a period of twenty-five years of active employment, and the acquisition of property sufficient to satisfy a moderate ambition, he sought relief from the pressure of a laborious calling, and retired from active business, and in the year 1852, with his brother (Hon. Benjamin F. Thomas), made a very pleasant visit to Europe. Being a member of the city government in that year, and a member of the committee on finance, he was entrusted with authority to negotiate a loan to the city, in London, which he obtained on terms which were regarded as highly satisfactory. The distinguished banker, Mr. George Peabody, remarked to the writer of this notice that Mr. Thomas accomplished, in obtaining the loan, what had seemed to Mr. Peabody an impossibility. He spoke of the services of Mr. Thomas in the language of high commendation.

On his return from Europe, Mr. Thomas soon discovered that some active employment was necessary for his health and happiness. In 1853, he applied to the legislature for an act to establish the Webster Bank, which was obtained, and he had not the slightest difficulty in securing subscriptions for its stock to twice the amount of the capital which the legislature was willing to grant. At the organization of the bank, he was chosen president, and continued in that office until January 12, 1869, when he retired from the position, feeling that his health required relaxation from the pressure of duties which accumulated with increasing years. How faithfully he devoted himself to the discharge of those duties, was warmly expressed by the stockholders, upon his retirement; and by their order an elegant testimonial was procured and presented to him by a committee, at a meeting of the directors and friends of the bank, in a manner as agreeable as it was honorable to both parties. Mr. Thomas remained in the board of directors until his death.

During the whole period of Mr. Thomas's active life, he found time to devote much attention to various interests and institutions which he regarded as of importance to the city of Boston, and to the community at large. He gave much time to the promotion of many enterprises of internal improvements, which although not always promising great results, at the time of their inception, yet terminated in a manner as creditable to his foresight as they were agreeable to his feelings. He had the satisfaction of realizing liberal rewards for his perseverance and courage under difficulties, and he achieved success by deserving it.

Mr. Thomas was a liberal man in the true sense. His attachment to his friends was warm and sincere. His sympathies were always active. He opened his heart and his hand to relieve distress and to alleviate the burdens which bore heavily upon others, whether within or without the circle of his acquaintance. He did not forget the friends of his youth, and sought opportunities to minister to them in acts of kindness with a delicacy which touched many a heart.

During the later years of his life, he connected himself with various charitable institutions, entering into their management with great zeal, and frequently bestowing upon them liberal donations to supply their wants. And by his will, he marked his sense of the value of several of them by handsome bequests.

We may allude in this connection to the Home for Aged Men—the Children's Mission—the Sailor's Snug Harbor—the Children's Hospital and the Industrial School for Girls. Nor did he overlook a large number of distant relatives, and friends of his early and later days, in making bequests in obedience to those generous feelings which prompted him through life to benevolent deeds.

Several public corporations, of which he was a director, paid most respectful tributes of respect to his memory by votes of their directors, expressive of their deep sense of the value of his services and their regret at the decease of one who had done so much to promote their highest interests.

Mr. Thomas had no ambition for political office. His honors were those of the citizen and the man. His beloved pastor well said of him, in the beautiful tribute to his memory which he paid in a discourse on the next Sabbath after his decease:

"His was a true and kind heart, and the sunshine of a loving spirit shone through him, as through very few whom I have ever known. Its pure flame was not extinguished by the gusts of business life, while so many shut themselves up from the sympathies and humanities of life, but burned steadily there and made him a cheery and benign presence in State street and his bank parlor, as well as in his home. The friends of his boyhood he kept unchanged to the threshold of age, because the heart kept its freshness, and loved them with the same love.

"Dr. Freeman was the minister of his boyhood, Dr. Greenwood of his youth, Dr. Peabody of his manhood, and their names were on his lips as the names of beloved and honored friends."

It may be remarked, that Mr. Thomas manifested "more than kindness" in his treatment of their successor, Rev. Mr. Foote. He was senior warden of King's Chapel for nine years, and at the hour of his death was still its treasurer.

Mr. Thomas was twice married—first in 1831, to Miss Catharine Crombie, daughter of Calvin and Naomi Crombie, of Plymouth, who was the mother of his children. Mrs. Thomas died June 10, 1838. His second wife was Miss Cornelia J. Bangs, daughter of the late Benjamin Bangs, Esq., a well known merchant of Boston. She survives her husband.

The children of Mr. Thomas are Helen, wife of Charles M. Ellis, Esq., counsellor at law, of Boston; Mary T. Guild, widow of George D. Guild, Esq., deceased, a member of the Suffolk Bar; and Catharine C. Thomas. S. L.

Lucius Manlius Sargent, A.M., a resident member, died in West Roxbury, Mass., June 2, 1867, aged 63. For memoir see Register, vol. xxv. pp. 209–20.

Hon. David Lowry Swain, LL.D., a corresponding member, died in Chapel Hill, N. C., Sept. 3, 1868, a. 67. For memoir see Register, vol. xxiv. pp. 349–53.

Thomas Sherwin, A.M., a resident member, d. in Dedham, Mass., July 23, 1870, a. 70. For memoir see Register, vol. xxiv. pp. 249–53.

Rev. Joseph Barlow Felt, LL.D., an honorary member, d. in Salem, Mass., Sept. 9, 1869, a. 79. For memoir see Register, vol. xxiv. pp. 1–5.

Benjamin Parker Richardson, Esq., a resident member, d. in Boston, Mass., Nov. 17, 1870, a. 68. For memoir see Register, vol. xxvi. pp. 1–3.

Col. James Warren Sever, A.M., a resident member, d. in Boston, Mass., Jan. 16, 1871, a. 73. For memoir see Register, vol. xxvi. pp. 316–17.

Hon. John Alfred Poor, A.M., a resident member, d. in Portland, Me., Sept. 6, 1872, a. 63. For memoir see Register, vol. xxvi. pp. 357–75.

Proceedings.

Boston, Massachusetts, Wednesday, September 4, 1872. The first stated meeting, after the summer vacation, was held this afternoon, at three o'clock, at the Society's House, No. 18 Somerset street, the president, the Hon. Marshall P. Wilder, in the chair.

Samuel H. Wentworth, A.M., the recording secretary, read the record of the proceedings at the June meeting, which was approved.

John Ward Dean, A.M., the librarian, reported that during the months of June, July and August, there had been received as donations 557 printed volumes, 10 manuscript volumes, 1245 pamphlets, 7 files of manuscripts, 12 manuscripts, 15 maps and charts, 2 broadsides, 1 Indian hatchet, 1 Revolutionary powder horn, and 1 cane from the famous apple tree planted by Peregrine White, the first white child born in New-England. The cane and powder horn were exhibited. The cane and a large number of books, manuscripts and pamphlets were presented to the society by Miss Shattuck, daughter of the late Lemuel Shattuck, one of the founders and the first vice-president of this Society. Mr. Dean also presented, in behalf of Capt. George H. Preble, U. S. N., a cane made from the wood of the Frigate Constitution, presented to his father, Capt. Enoch Preble, of Portland, Me., by Com. William Bainbridge.

Rev. Dorus Clarke, D.D., the historiographer, read biographical sketches of two deceased members, namely: Samuel Holden Parsons, Esq., of Middletown, Ct., and Hon. Noah Amherst Phelps, of Simsbury, Ct. Rev. Dr. Clarke also exhibited a copy of the Holy Bible, printed in 1563, which has long been in possession of the family of George G. Brewster, of Portsmouth, N. H., recently deceased.

A letter from Harry H. Edes, Esq., of Charlestown, was read, presenting in behalf of Miss Caroline Dorr, of Dorchester, for deposit, two portraits of Ephraim Turner, one of them marked "J. G. pinxt 1749;" a portrait of Thomas Turner, son of the preceding, and a certificate of membership of the Society of the Cincinnati for the latter, signed by Gens. Washington and Knox.

Six candidates for resident membership, nominated by the board of directors, were balloted for and elected.

Rev. George D. Johnson, rector of St. Paul's Church, Newburyport, read a paper on Rev. Samuel Johnson, D.D., of Stratford, Ct., afterward the first president of King's College, New-York, now Columbia. It was chiefly prepared from family papers in the possession of Rev. Mr. Johnson, which contain much new material concerning the early history of Episcopacy in New-England. We hope to be favored with this paper for the pages of the REGISTER.

BOOK-NOTICES.

Transactions of the Historical Society. Edited by the Rev. CHARLES ROGERS, LL.D., F.S.A. Scot., Historiographer to the Society. Vol. I. London: Printed for the Historical Society. 1872. pp. 550.

The Historical Society of Great Britain was established in 1869. Its object is to deal with such historical subjects as have not hitherto fallen within the scope of other institutions, especially subjects of a biographical or chronological character. Like most other historical societies, it proposes by associated effort to do that in rendering the researches of individuals available, which could not otherwise be accomplished. It will therefore reproduce and illustrate rare tracts, and bring to light the material which has either been neglected or has escaped the attention of the historical student.

The volume before us is the first fruits of the Society's labors, and is a most valuable contribution to English history. It is divided into two parts, and treats of nineteen distinct subjects. Most of them are general in their character, while some of them are local and of a more limited interest. We cannot better exhibit the character of the volume, in the brief space to which this notice must be confined, than by giving the titles of the several subjects treated, which are as follows:

1. The Study of History, by Professor De Vericour.
2. The Personal Expenses of Charles II. in the city of Worcester, by Richard Woof, Esq., F.S.A., F.R.S.L.
3. The Mounds at Dunblane and the Roman Station of Alauna, by W. T. Black, Esq.
4. Notes on the Perkin Warbeck Insurrection, by J. E. Cussans, Esq.
5. The Christian Era, by John J. Bond, Esq.
6. Latin Aphorisms and Proverbs, by Sir John Bowring, LL.D., F.R.S.
7. Memoir and Poems of Sir Robert Aytoun, by the Rev. Charles Rogers, LL.D., F.S.A. Scot.
8. Notes in the History of Sir Jerome Alexander, by the Rev. Charles Rogers, LL.D., F.S.A. Scot.
9. The Early Bristol Charters and their chief object, by J. F. Nicholls, Esq.
10. The Life of Fra Salimbene, 1221–1290, by T. L. Kington Oliphant, Esq., F.S.A.
11. On some Tudor prices in Kent (1577 chiefly), by J. M. Cowper, Esq.
12. The Jacquerie, by Professor De Vericour.
13. The Free Grammar School of Bristol, and the Thorns, its founders, by J. F. Nicholls, Esq.
14. Notes from the Records of Faversham, 1560–1600, by J. M. Cowper.
15. An Official Inaccuracy respecting the death and burial of the Princess Mary, daughter of King James I., by Col. Joseph Lemuel Chester.
16. Was the Old English Aristocracy destroyed by the Wars of the Roses? by T. L. Kington Oliphant, Esq., F.S.A.
17. Observations on the Scottish Branch of the Norman House of Roger, by the Rev. Charles Rogers, LL.D., F.S.A. Scot.

18. The Staggering State of Scottish Statesmen from 1550 to 1650, by Sir John Scot, of Scotstarvet; with a Memoir of the author, and Historical Illustrations, by the Rev. Charles Rogers, LL.D., F.S.A. Scot.

19. A list of the Great Officers of State of Scotland from 1057 to the year 1660.

The volume is edited by the Rev. Charles Rogers, LL.D., and appears to be done with great painstaking and thoroughness. It is rich in annotations, an important feature in a work of this kind, as it enables the writer to convey much exact and valuable information germain to the subject, but which is often omitted in the text, or could not well be incorporated into it. We regret to add that the volume contains no index, and if none is to be furnished in the future publications of the Society, it will be a defect of the gravest character. E. F. S.

Proceedings of the Massachusetts Historical Society for May, June, July and August, 1871. [Boston, 1871.] pp. 76.

Letter of Sir John Stanhope to Secretary Davison concerning Elder Brewster. Read before the Massachusetts Historical Society, May, 1871. By CHARLES DEANE. [Boston, 1871.] 8vo. pp. 8.

The number of the Proceedings of the Massachusetts Historical Society before us, which is the second of the current volume, is rich in historical materials. It contains some writings of Rev. Michael Wigglesworth, formerly in the possession of Charles Ewer, Esq., which were presented by his sisters to Rev. Lemuel Willis, by him to Rev. Thomas J. Greenwood, and by the latter to the Massachusetts Historical Society; a letter of Sir John Stanhope; extracts from the Hutchinson Papers; a letter from Rev. Dr. Dexter, then at Bawtry, Yorkshire, giving an account of his researches into the history of the Pilgrims; and other interesting matters.

Among the Wigglesworth manuscripts is the poem for which inquiry was made in the REGISTER, vol. xxiii. p. 102, entitled *God's Controversy with New-England.* The letter of Sir John Stanhope has been reprinted from the *Proceedings* in a pamphlet, the title of which is given above. It shows that Elder William Brewster was the successor as postmaster at Scrooby of his father, also named William, who died in the summer of 1690, and that the son claimed to have held the office a year and a half previous to his father's death. This fixes the period when Elder Brewster received the appointment, namely, the beginning of the year 1689, or five years before Mr. Hunter's earliest date. Other important facts are brought out in the letter and Mr. Deane's notes. J. W. D.

History of Ancient Woodbury, Connecticut, from the First Indian Deed in 1659 *to* 1872, *including the present towns of Washington, Southbury, Bethlehem, Roxbury, and a part of Oxford and Middlebury.* By WILLIAM COTHREN. Vol. II. Woodbury, Conn.: Published by William Cothren. 1872. 8vo. pp. 790.

The first volume of this work was published in 1854, and was noticed in high terms by Mr. Drake, in the REGISTER for April of that year (viii. 193). The second volume, now before us, continues the history of Ancient Woodbury to the present time. It contains full accounts of the Bi-Centennial Celebration in 1859; the Masonic Centennial Celebration in 1865; the Bi-Centennial Celebration of the First Congregational Church, and the Dedication of the Fathers' Monument in 1870; the Centennial Celebration of St. Paul's Church in 1871; and the Dedication of the Soldiers' Monument the same year. Copious extracts from the speeches on the several occasions are given. An important feature of the work is a particular and minute history of the aid furnished by the several towns in the ancient territory and of their inhabitants in the late war for the preservation of the Union.

The two volumes contain genealogies of more than a hundred of the early Woodbury families, and biographical sketches of about two hundred individuals connected with that locality, not a few of whom have a national reputation.

The book bears evidence of great labor and research. The author states that the careful labors, at leisure hours, of a quarter of a century have been bestowed upon it. The work is profusely illustrated.

A small edition of the first volume has been reprinted; but we understood that, some months ago, there were only twenty-five copies remaining on hand. Those who wish to obtain it, must therefore make an early application. The price of the second volume is $4, and of the complete work $6.50. J. W. D.

History of the Town of Whately, Mass., including a Narrative of Leading Events from the First Planting of Hatfield: 1660–1871. By J. H. TEMPLE, Fourth Pastor of the Congregational Church. With Family Genealogies. Printed for the Town by T. R. Marvin & Son, 131 Congress Street, Boston. 1872. 8vo. pp. 332.

The town of Whately was incorporated in the year 1771, and was named in honor of Thomas Whately, Esq., of London, a friend of Hutchinson the historian, who was governor when the act of incorporation was passed. The author prints the act in full from the engrossed parchment roll in the archives of the state. This document shows that the bill when sent to the governor for his signature had the name of the town left blank ; for the name *Whately* is not in the handwriting of the engrossing clerk, but in that of Gov. Hutchinson himself. It is said that this was a custom under the Provincial government. Will some one who has the opportunity and leisure examine the engrossed bills at the State House, and ascertain when this complementary custom began and ended?

Previous to its incorporation, Whately formed the northern portion of Hatfield. In 1659, Gov. Bradstreet and his brother-in-law, Major Gen. Denison, had farms of 500 acres each granted them by the General Court, which they chose here; but three quarters of a century elapsed before this part of Hatfield was settled. Rev. Mr. Temple gives a succinct account of the settlement of Hatfield, and the principal events that transpired there previous to 1771.

Besides an excellent history of Whately, there is a very full genealogy of the inhabitants of that town to the present time. This is an enlargement of a genealogy of the "Original Settlers of Whately," embracing two generations, which was prepared by the author in 1849, and appended to his *Ecclesiastical History of Whately*. There is also a report of the proceedings at the Centennial Celebration of the town July 4, 1871, with the addresses and poems on that occasion.

The book is well printed and bound, and has a good index of names. J. W. D.

Collections of the New-Jersey Historical Society. Vol. VII. Newark, N. J.: Published for the Society by Martin R. Dennis & Co. 1872. 8vo. pp. 495.

Proceedings of the New-Jersey Historical Society. Second Series, Vol. III. No. 1. 1872. 8vo. pp. 46.

The New-Jersey Historical Society was organized in the year 1845; and, during the twenty-seven years of its existence, it has published seven octavo volumes of *Collections*, printed twelve complete volumes of *Proceedings*, and issued the first number of a thirteenth volume. The volume of their *Collections* now before us is the production of the Hon. Lucius Q. C. Elmer, LL.D., formerly of the Supreme Court of New-Jersey. Its title is : *The Constitution and Government of the Province and State of New-Jersey, with Biographical Sketches of the Governors from* 1776 *to* 1845 ; *and Reminiscences of the Bench and Bar, during more than half a century.* It is intended as a sequel to the able work by Hon. Richard S. Field, which forms the third volume of these *Collections*, and which bears this title : *The Provincial Courts of New-Jersey, with Sketches of the Bench and Bar.* The two volumes contain a mass of material illustrating the history and biography of the native state of their authors, much of which would have perished had it not been thus timely preserved. It is high praise for an historical work to say that it is deserving of a place beside the previous volumes of the *New-Jersey Historical Collections;* but this may be said of Judge Elmer's book.

The number of the *Proceedings* before us is devoted to the doings of the society at its meeting, May 16, 1872, including a valuable paper read then by Hon. Joel Parker, governor of New-Jersey, entitled *Monmouth County during the Provincial Era.* J. W. D.

The Peirce Family Record. 8vo. pp. 5.

This tract was compiled by Edward W. West, Esq., of New-York city, and was issued in October, 1864. In 1869, Mr. West issued a supplement of 7 pages, consisting of additions and corrections. The two tracts are devoted to the descendants of Isaac Peirce, of Boston, born about 1683, who was married in 1708, by Rev. Cotton Mather, to Grace Tucker. The author has prepared a very interesting record of his branch of the Peirce family. We understand that he has now in preparation a genealogy of the West family. J. W. D.

The Life and Public Services of Hon. Henry Wilson. By Hon. THOMAS RUSSELL, Collector of the Port of Boston; and Rev. ELIAS NASON, for many years Pastor of Mr. Wilson. Boston: Published by B. B. Russell, 55 Cornhill. 1872. 12 mo. pp. 419.

It is several years since we heard that the Rev. Mr. Nason was engaged in preparing a life of Mr. Wilson; and, we believe that, before the nomination of that gentleman for the second office in the gift of the people of the United States, he had a large portion of such a work written. For more than twenty years he has been Mr. Wilson's intimate friend, and for six years he was his pastor and near neighbor. He, therefore, has had excellent opportunities to learn the history and become familiar with the character of the Republican candidate for vice-president, and his admiration of the man has led him to improve his opportunities.

The lives of self-made men, of whom Mr. Wilson is an eminent example, are always instructive and interesting. One loves to follow the steps of their progress, to mark how obstacles are met and overcome by that persistent energy, which is always a characteristic of such people, and which is conspicuous in Mr. Wilson. Few have had more difficulties to overcome in their efforts for distinction, and few have succeeded as well as he in attaining the object of their ambition.

Mr. Wilson's position as a statesman is well known to our readers. It is nearly a third of a century since he entered political life, and he has lived to see the almost hopeless cause which won the sympathy and support of his early manhood, and which he has adhered to through its varying fortunes, at length triumphant. From 1855, when he was elected to the United States Senate, he has had a national reputation, and for a dozen years at least he has been one of the most influential members of Congress. He has probably carried through that body more bills of importance than any other member.

The volume before us is a model biography, written in a clear and animated style, abounding in graphic descriptions and evincing a scrupulous desire for accuracy in the details. It does great credit to Mr. Nason, from whose pen nearly or quite the whole of it has emanated.

J. W. D.

A Centennial History of Alfred, York County, Maine. By the late Dr. USHER PARSONS. With a Supplement by SAMUEL M. CAME, Esq. Published by Sanford, Everts & Co. Philadelphia: Collins, Printer, 705 Jayne Street. 1872. 18mo. pp. 36.

This is the first history that has been published of the town of Alfred, which was incorporated in the year 1808. It was previously a part of Sanford. The author of this pamphlet is Usher Parsons, M.D., vice-president of this society and a valued contributor to the REGISTER, of whom sketches will be found *ante* xvii. 20, and xxiii. 359. He has compressed into the 24 pages which he occupies a great amount of historic details concerning his native town. Mr. Came has continued the work, which was composed some years ago, to the present time, and the publishers have prefixed to it an account of Dr. Parsons compiled from the memoir by his son, Charles W. Parsons, M.D., of Providence, R. I.

J. W. D.

The Institution of the Society of the Cincinnati, together with the Roll of the Original, Hereditary and Honorary Members of the Order in the State of New-Jersey, from 1783 *to* 1866. Albany, N. Y.: Printed for the Society by J. Munsell. 1866. 8vo. pp. 79.

The parent Society of the Cincinnati was instituted in May, 1783, at the cantonment of the American Army on the banks of the Hudson, by the officers of that army then about to retire to peaceful pursuits, and had for its object the founding of an association which should perpetuate the attachments formed during a long period of hardship and privation. Gen. Washington was the first president, and Gen. Knox the first secretary of the parent or "General Society."

Besides the General Society, subordinate societies were formed, in the thirteen original states, seven of which have become extinct or dormant. In the REGISTER for July last (p. 344), a pamphlet by the Massachusetts Society giving a biographical list of its members was noticed. The present pamphlet gives a similar list of the members of the New-Jersey Society of the Cincinnati. But it contains, in addition, a record of the procedings at the institution of the General Society, with a list of its officers to the present time, and other matter of interest connected with the subject. The pamphlet was prepared, we believe, by Clifford Stanley Sims, Esq., at present the United States Consul at Prescott, Canada, and reflects great credit upon the research of the writer. J. W. D.

The Report of the Commissioners on the Boundary Line between the State of Virginia and the States of Maryland, North Carolina and Tennessee, read in the Senate, Jan. 17, 1872. 8vo. pp. 22.

In the year 1870, the legislature of Virginia authorized and the governor appointed commissioners to ascertain, and in conjunction with commissioners on the part of Maryland, to establish the boundary line between said states. One of the commissioners was sent to England to procure evidence. The report contains the official correspondence of the commissioners and the governor of Virginia on this subject, and the report of the special agent sent to England, excepting the papers therein referred to by the agent. These may be published hereafter.

It is probable that the long vexed question of the true boundary lines of Virginia will shortly be settled, and then a complete history of the controversy may be expected. Such a work will be an interesting and valuable addition to American history.

An Historical Discourse delivered at the Celebration of the Two Hundredth Anniversary of the Formation of the North Church, Portsmouth, N. H., July 19, 1871. By [the] Rev. George M. Adams, Pastor of the Church. Portsmouth: Frank W. Robinson. 1871. 8vo. pp. 72.

The history of this ancient religious society forms an interesting and important chapter in the annals of New-Hampshire, and the seventy-two pages of this superbly printed pamphlet contain the substance of that history in a condensed form. We feel sure that all its statements of fact, names, dates, &c., can be safely taken as true, because they have, as we know, been carefully verified by the Hon. Marcellus Bufford, one of the committee by whose management the celebration was successfully carried through to its end.

We are glad to see that towns, cities, churches and societies are paying more and more attention to their histories, and that they are publishing in permanent form, and in a greatly improved style, the proceedings of their anniversary celebrations. It is as true in this matter as in most others, that what is worth doing at all is worth doing well. The cost, whether it be a few hundred dollars more or less, is of little account. A poorly printed and lean town history is a perpetual monument of somebody's meanness, or bad taste, or both, which any number of dismal wood-cut portraits and pictures of houses will not atone for.

Who now will undertake to give us the history of Portsmouth? The work would require two octavo volumes of 700 or 800 pages each. Such a work, well prepared, well printed, and supplied with maps, would be an honor to the town, and meet with a ready sale.

We understand that the city of Dover proposes to give the Rev. Dr. Quint ample time and ample means to enable him to make his history of that ancient town worthy of the subject. This is encouraging, and should be imitated by other towns and cities.

A Sketch of the Organization, Objects and Membership of the Old Settlers' Association of Minnesota; together with an Account of the Excursion of the Red River of the North, October 25 *and* 26, 1871. *Prepared by order of the Association.* Hæc olim meminisse Juvabit.—Virgil. Saint Paul: Ramaley, Chaney & Co., Printers. 1872. 8vo. pp. 29.

We have received from J. F. Williams, Esq., of St. Paul, a copy of this pamphlet. It contains a copy of the charter of the association, bearing date May 23, 1857; the seal and a list of the members of the association, and their proceedings on the occasion referred to in the title of the pamphlet. Ex-Gov. Sibley mentions a circumstance, showing how the passage of the bill creating a territorial government for Minnesota in 1849 was made to depend not on its own merits, nor on the necessities of the early settlers, but upon the selfish schemes of political factions. We have improved upon all that!

A Lecture on the University of Cincinnati, its Aims, Needs, and Resources, Delivered before the Young Men's Mercantile Library Association, May 9, 1872. By ALONZO TAFT. "Crafty men contemn studies, simple men admire them, and wise men use them."—*Lord Bacon.* Cincinnati. Robert Clarke & Co. 1872.

Mr. Taft has put into a compact form a very full statement of the history of the origin and management of certain funds left in trust for educational purposes in Cincinnati, and he points out with clearness aud force of suggestion how these trusts may be combined and utilized in laying the foundations of a university.

We say foundations, for contrary to the seemingly general impression in America, a university is not the creation of a day, nor can it be begotten by simple testamentary bequests. It does not consist in money, or buildings, or throngs of students, nor necessarily in all combined. It is of slow growth.

In the United States there are an indefinite number of colleges, and not far from twenty-five so-called universities, but no one of them as yet is entitled to rank any higher than the European gymnasia of the better sort. But the university will come in due time. The United States, — with their present resources of population and wealth, and with the present limited appreciation of and demand among us for the highest learning and scholarship, — could easily support one, perhaps two such universities as Oxford or Cambridge, Heidelberg or Bonn; but for some years,—say twenty-five, at least,—we should have to import our chief instructors from Europe. At present we go to Germany for the best scholarship.

These considerations ought not to chill the enthusiasm of those who fancy that they are administering "universities," among us, nor check the liberality of such as are disposed to leave their superfluous wealth behind them at their death, for the founding or endowment of schools. We cannot prevent every Mr. Smith, or White, or Brown, from founding a university at his death, to be called by his name; but we should be glad if we could persuade a majority of such authors of monumental folly to concentrate their wealth upon a single object.

Cincinnati ought to be the seat of a university, where every art, science, trade and philosophy could be studied under the best living masters. She ought to lose no time in laying the first foundations of such an institution.

Addresses and Proceedings at the Centennial Anniversary of the Congregational Church in Sanbornton, N. H., November 12 *and* 13, 1871. *Compiled by order of the Church.* By M. T. RUNNELS, Pastor. Hartford, Conn. Press of Case, Lockwood & Brainard. 1872. 8vo. pp. 82.

We are indebted to the Rev. Mr. Runnels for a copy of this interesting historical pamphlet, and the Congregational Church referred to is probably mainly indebted to him for the successful celebration of the event above described.

The pamphlet contains the sermon of the Rev. Prof. Joseph C. Bodwell, of the Hartford Theological Seminary, the address of the Rev. Frederic T. Perkins, of Hartford, Ct., remarks, brief addresses, toasts, and other proceedings connected with the celebration. As an interesting historical fact it may be worth while to quote from the editor's preface a statement showing some of the changes that have taken place in the town. He says, page 5: "The present situation of the Congregational Parish of Sanbornton, N. H., is peculiar. Fifty years ago the Square, where the church is located, was a large business centre; but now all trade, nearly all branches of mechanical industry have deserted that place and gone to the neighboring villages. The present members of the church and society belong to two different towns [Tilton and Sanbornton], and go to no less than seven different localities for store and post-office accommodations."

The pamphlet is handsomely printed.

School Histories and Some Errors in them. By SAMUEL A. GREEN, M.D. Boston: For Private Distribution. 1872. 8vo. pp. 7.

This is a reprint of an article which originally appeared in "*The Educational Monthly*" for June, 1872, in which the learned author has pointed out a few errors of the most important character in a few books. The authors and publishers of the books referred to will undoubtedly take heed of his criticisms. It would be a good service to teachers and scholars if he would point out the errors of fact in all the school histories in general use.

Proceedings of the American Antiquarian Society, at the Semi-Annual Meeting held in Boston, April 23, 1872. [No. 58.]

Besides the official reports, which show the prosperous condition of this well managed society, this pamphlet contains the report of the council, read by Colonel John D. Washburn, which is mainly devoted to the question, Who was the first discoverer of the bay of San Francisco and the Golden Gate; On the likelihood of an admixture of Japanese Blood on our North-West Coast, by Horace Davis, Esq., of San Francisco; and the Cosmogony of Dante and Columbus, by the Rev. E. E. Hale: all interesting papers.

The Rev. Dr. G. E. Ellis discussed one of the chief topics of the Rev. Dr. Peabody's election sermon (see REGISTER, *ante*, p. 218), viz.: town debts. Too much cannot be said or done in order to call public attention to this subject.

MARRIAGES AND DEATHS.

MARRIAGES.

DE SALIS = BAINBRIDGE. In London, April 11, at St. George's Church, Hanover Square, Mr. William John de Salis of the War Office, a descendant of the cadet branch of the Count de Salis, an ancient family from the Island of Rhodes naturalized in England, and Miss Harriet Anne Bainbridge, daughter of the late Henry Bainbridge, Esq., of the ancient family of Bainbridge of Westmoreland, settled there before the Conquest.

SWEETSER = PENHALLOW. In Berwick, Me., April 19, 1871, by Rev. Mr. Hidden, Mr. Albert Henry Sweetser, of Saugus, Mass., and Miss Annie Penhallow, youngest daughter of Hon. Ichabod G. Jordan, of Berwick.

SPINNEY=PAUL. In Newington, N.H., June 15, 1871, by Rev. Mr. Smith, Ephraim C. Spinney, Esq., of Kittery, Me., and Miss Mary Pickering Paul, of Newington.

TUTTLE = PARK. In Boston, Jan. 31, at the Arlington Street Church, by the Rev. Andrew Preston Peabody, D.D., LL.D., Professor of Christian Morals in Harvard University, Charles Wesley Tuttle, counsellor-at-law, of Boston, and Mary Louisa, only daughter of the Hon. John Cochran Park, of Dedham.

DEATHS.

BACON, Francis, Esq., in Kittery, Maine, April 5, 1871, aged 56 years. He was a son of the late Dr. David Bacon, of Buxton, Maine, and a member of the bar of the county of York, and for several years register of deeds and subsequently register of probate for that county.

BOWMAN, Mrs. Almira, in the city of Cambridge, Aug. 31, widow of the late Hon. Francis Bowman, aged 77 years and 1 month, the youngest daughter of the late William Wellington, of Waltham, Mass. There is an error in the record of her husband's obituary in the April number of the REGISTER. His native place was Lexington, and his age was 79 years 7 months and 29 days. H. W.

BUSHNELL, Miss Annie Eliza, in New-York city, Sept. 6, 1872, in her 18th year, only daughter of Charles I. and Abby J. Bushnell.

CHISHOLM, Alexander F., in Saco, Maine, Nov. 19, 1871, aged 60 years. He was a native of Salem, Mass., and a member of the bar of the county of York, Me.

EMERSON, Capt. Joseph, in Alfred, Maine, Sept. 9, 1871, aged 86 years. He was a son of Joseph Emerson, Esq., of that town, who graduated at Harvard in the class of 1771.

ERRATA.—Page 12, stanza 2, line 8, *for* eternall *read* external; p. 202, l. 19, *for* Brodburg *read* Bradbury; p. 245, l. 15, *for* Palace *read* Place; p. 420, l. 4, *for* Granery *read* Granary; p. 420, col. 1, l. 1, *for* Mathr's *read* Mather's; p. 432, l. 31, *for* Rev. Jacob Crowninshield *read* Hon. Jacob Crowninshield.

The memoir of B. F. Mason, in the July number, being condensed and printed without revision by the author, misprints may be noted as follows: Page 226, line 28, *for* showing *read* staling; p. 227, l. 37, *read* 1834, l. 49 *read* Lamar; p. 228, l. 20, *for* Warren *read* Warner; l. 30, *for* Seaver *read* Starr; same page note 4, *for* Secretary *read* Senator; p. 229, l. 2, *for* Elza *read* Elga; l. 15, *for* even *read* ever. In the closing paragraph only the suggestion of a monument was intended.

INDEX OF NAMES.